PARIS

THE BLUE GUIDES

PARIS

Edited by

STUART ROSSITER
M.A.

With 39 Maps and Plans

1968

LONDON: ERNEST BENN LIMITED
CHICAGO: RAND McNALLY & COMPANY

THIRD EDITION (revised and reset in new format) 1968

Published by Ernest Benn Limited
Bouverie House · Fleet Street · London · EC4

Rand McNally & Company
Chicago · Illinois 60680 · USA

© Ernest Benn Limited 1968

Printed in Great Britain

510−02201−4

PREFACE

The first Blue Guide appeared in 1918. In the fifty years since that date a hundred or so different editions of various guides in the Series have been published. Though every country and city has demanded its own approach, as far as possible the volumes have conformed to a standard pattern to aid ease of reference. Their format, like their content, has undergone a process of gradual change. Different type-faces, binding materials, cover design, have caught the contemporary mood, while the Series preserved a sense of continuity and uniformity.

The present BLUE GUIDE TO PARIS carries the process of change several stages further. The type-face, the page size, the method of printing, the presentation of the town plans, are all new. In addition the arrangement of the routes by which the city is described has been completely revised to accord with the changing social and topographical scene. The result, nevertheless, is unmistakably a Blue Guide. The changes are designed to make it more useful while keeping its price (in the face of ever-increasing production costs) as low as possible. One aspect of its preparation has undergone no change whatever: the thoroughness with which its accuracy has been checked.

The revised order in which the city is described will, it is hoped, meet the needs of the majority of visitors. The routes have been arranged as far as possible in a logical progression and the highlights indicated by bold type. This will assist those visiting Paris briefly or for the first time. But the arrangement is designed as much to aid the seasoned traveller, already knowing Paris well, who wishes to explore the city in greater depth and come to an intelligent understanding of what he sees. A completely new set of sectional plans has been drawn to accord more nearly with the routes described, which are related one to another by means of an outline plan of the whole city.

The section giving practical information of a general nature about the city's amenities has been expanded. A selection of restaurants of established repute has been indicated by areas corresponding with the routes described. A brief sketch of French history has been added to this edition, together with a summary account of the special place of Paris in the story of the nation. It is hoped that these will provide the chronological framework necessary to an understanding of Parisian monuments and institutions.

A word of explanation is necessary about the Louvre. A letter, received from the Director while the book was in proof, intimated that the principal picture galleries are likely to remain closed at least until 1969, with consequent temporary presentation of many important paintings. The account given in this book will inevitably, therefore, conform only partially to the arrangement of the exhibits as found by the reader. Rooms are numbered on our plans to conform with the *plan* (Pl.) references in our text: they bear no relation to any scheme of numbering that may be adopted by the museum authorities to show the continuity of their present or future display (though these are also given in the text where they are relatively permanent). Still less do any of these figures correspond to the room numbering in one sequence to be seen on the walls of the building itself, which is an administrative convenience and bears little relationship to the order in which their contents should be viewed. A sub-index to the contents of the Louvre has been provided to help ease the confusion.

The preparation of this volume has been in great part the work of the editorial staff, who have received much good advice, practical help, hospitality, and kindness from Mlle Jacqueline Léauté of Paris; to her special thanks are due. The Editor acknowledges with gratitude general assistance from the Director and staff of the French Government Tourist Office in London. The great majority of the plans were redrawn by Mr Peter Atwell.

No one is better aware than the Editor of the difficulty of avoiding errors, and suggestions for the correction or improvement of the Guide will be most gratefully welcomed.

Note: On 1 October 1967 **admission charges** to many Paris **Museums** were raised from 1 fr. to 3 fr.

Recent renumbering of the upper floors in the *Musée des Arts Décoratifs* has impaired the accuracy of the lower plan on p. 156.

CONTENTS

		Page
PREFACE		v
HISTORICAL SKETCH OF FRANCE		xi
RULERS OF FRANCE		xvii
PARIS IN HISTORY		xix

PRACTICAL INFORMATION

I	APPROACHES TO PARIS	xxv
II	HOTELS	xxix
III	RESTAURANTS AND CAFÉS	xxx
IV	CONVEYANCES	xxxvi
	Taxis—Motor-buses—Métro—Coaches—River Steamers	
V	POSTAL AND OTHER SERVICES	xxxvii
	Information Bureaux	
VI	AMUSEMENTS	xxxviii
	Theatres—Music-Halls—Cabarets—Cinemas—Art Exhibitions—Music—Sports and Games	
VII	USEFUL ADDRESSES	xlii
	Embassies and Consulates—English Churches—Banks—Clubs—Police—Hospitals	
VIII	GENERAL HINTS	xlvi
	Season—Expenses—Language—French Usages—Holidays—Shops—Markets	
IX	THE SIGHTS OF PARIS	xlvii
X	CALENDAR OF EVENTS	li
XI	BOOKS ABOUT PARIS	lii

I PARIS

Route		Page
1	FROM THE PLACE DE LA CONCORDE TO THE LOUVRE AND ST-GERMAIN-L'AUXERROIS	4
	Tuileries Gardens	
2	THE SEINE	11
	A. From the Louvre to the Pont National 12	
	B. From the Louvre to Auteuil 13	
3	THE CITÉ AND THE ÎLE-ST-LOUIS	17
	Palais de Justice—Sainte Chapelle—Conciergerie—Notre-Dame	
4	THE LATIN QUARTER	26
	Boulevard St-Michel—St-Séverin—St-Julien-le-Pauvre—St-Nicolas-du-Chardonnet — St-Médard — St-Étienne-du-Mont — Panthéon—Sorbonne	

5   THE FAUBOURG ST-GERMAIN   page 37
    A. The Luxembourg and St-Germain-des-Prés   37
        Palais de l'Institut—La Monnaie—Place de l'Odéon—St-Sulpice—
        École des Beaux-Arts
    B. West Part of the Faubourg St-Germain   47
        Quai d'Orsay—Palais Bourbon—Rue de Grenelle

6   THE INVALIDES, CHAMP-DE-MARS, AND EIFFEL TOWER   51
        Unesco—École Militaire

7   QUARTIER CHAILLOT AND PASSY   57
    A. From the Place de la Concorde to the Palais de Chaillot   57
        Quai de la Conférence—Musée National d'Art Moderne
    B. From the Eiffel Tower to the Bois   59
        Palais de Chaillot—La Muette—Musée Marmottan

8   FROM THE PLACE DE LA CONCORDE TO THE ARC DE TRIOMPHE   62
        Champs Élysées—Petit Palais—Grand Palais

9   THE PALAIS-ROYAL AND THE BOURSE   65
        Place Vendôme—St-Roch—Théâtre-Français

10 ST-EUSTACHE AND THE HALLES CENTRALES   71

11 FROM THE PLACE DU CHÂTELET TO THE BASTILLE   75
        Hôtel de Ville—St-Gervais—Grands-Jésuites—Quartier de l'Arsenal

12 THE MARAIS   80
    A. From the Bastille to the Square du Temple   81
        Place des Vosges—Musée Victor Hugo—Rue des Francs-Bourgeois—
        Archives Nationales
    B. The Quartier du Temple   87
        Square du Temple—St-Nicolas-des-Champs—St-Merri

13 THE OPÉRA AND THE GRANDS BOULEVARDS   90
    A. The Western Boulevards: from the Rue Royale to the Porte St-Martin   90
        Madeleine—Musée Cognacq-Jay—Opéra Comique—Porte St-Denis
    B. The Eastern Boulevards: from the Porte St-Martin to the Bastille   94
        Place de la République—Boulevard du Temple—Bastille

14 THE DISTRICTS TO THE NORTH OF THE GRANDS BOULEVARDS   96
    A. Faubourg St-Martin and Faubourg St-Denis   96
        Gare de l'Est—Gare du Nord—St-Vincent-de-Paul—La Trinité
    B. Montmartre   98
        Boulevard de Clichy—Place Pigalle—Sacré-Cœur
    C. Quartier de l'Opéra, Quartier de l'Europe, and Batignolles   102
        Boulevard Haussmann—Gare St-Lazare—Musée Henner

15 THE EASTERN DISTRICTS   104
    A. Belleville and the Buttes-Chaumont   104
        Hôpital St-Louis—Bassin de la Villette
    B. Père Lachaise   106
    C. The Faubourg St-Antoine and Bercy   107
        Place de la Nation—Cimetière de Picpus—Gare de Lyon

16 THE JARDIN DES PLANTES AND FAUBOURG ST-MARCEL   108
        Gare d'Austerlitz—Salpêtrière—Gobelins—Place d'Italie

17 OBSERVATOIRE, MONTPARNASSE, AND THE CITÉ UNIVERSITAIRE   111
        Schola Cantorum—Val-de-Grâce—Catacombs—Parc de Montsouris

18 FAUBOURG ST-HONORÉ AND NEUILLY   117
        British Embassy—Palais de l'Élysée—Parc Monceau—Rond-Point
        de la Défense

19 THE BOIS DE BOULOGNE   120
        Longchamp

II THE LOUVRE AND OTHER
GREAT COLLECTIONS

20 THE COLLECTIONS IN THE LOUVRE   *page* 122
21 THE MUSÉE DE L'ARMÉE   153
22 THE MUSÉE DES ARTS DÉCORATIFS   155
23 THE CONSERVATOIRE DES ARTS ET MÉTIERS   157
24 THE BIBLIOTHÈQUE NATIONALE   160
25 THE MUSÉE CARNAVALET   162
26 THE PALAIS DE CHAILLOT   167
       Musée des Monuments Français   167
       Musée de l'Homme   169
       Musée de la Marine   170
27 THE MUSÉE DE CLUNY   170
28 THE MUSÉE GUIMET   174
29 THE MUSÉE JACQUEMART ANDRÉ   176
30 THE MUSÉE DU JEU DE PAUME   178
31 THE MUSÉE NISSIM DE CAMONDO   180
32 THE MUSÉE RODIN   182

III EXCURSIONS FROM PARIS

33 VERSAILLES   183
       Sèvres—Meudon—St-Cloud
34 VINCENNES   200
35 MALMAISON   202
       St-Germain-en-Laye—Maisons-Laffitte
36 SAINT-DENIS AND CHANTILLY   205
       Écouen—Musée Condé—Senlis
37 FONTAINEBLEAU   214
       Melun—Barbizon

INDEX   224

PLANS

General Plan of Paris   *page* 3
Approaches to Paris   xxvii
Métropolitain   xxxv
Arrondissements   xlv
The Seine   15
Index to Street Plans   223
Street Plans
    Tuileries   7
    Cité   19
    Latin Quarter   27
    Luxembourg   39
    Invalides and Champ-de-Mars   55
    Champs Élysées   63
    Palais Royal   69
    Châtelet to Bastille   75
    The Marais   83
    Montmartre   101
    Jardin des Plantes   109
    Montparnasse   113
Arts Décoratifs, Musée des   156
Arts et Métiers, Conservatoire des   158, 159
Carnavelet, Musée   163, 166
Chantilly, Musée Condé   211
Cluny, Musée de   171, 173
Fontainebleau Palace   218, 219
Guimet, Musée   175
Invalides, Hôtel des   53
Louvre, Historical Plan   9
Louvre, Ground Floor   124, 125, 151
Louvre, First Floor   134, 135
Notre-Dame   25
St-Germain-des-Prés   45
Versailles Palace   189
Versailles Town   197

HISTORICAL SKETCH OF FRANCE

Roman Period. The foundations of modern France may be said to date from the passage of the Alps by the Romans in 121 B.C. and the establishment of the province of Gallia Narbonensis; but the whole of France as we now understand it did not pass under the control of Rome until after Cæsar's decisive defeat of VERCINGETORIX at Alésia in 52. The speech, the culture, and the roads of Rome soon spread over Gaul, and in the 2C the country was christianized. The barbarian mercenaries (Visigoths and Burgundians) came to defend the frontiers of the declining Roman Empire but wearied of their alliance with the degenerate Gallo-Romans, and after the repulse of Attila and his Huns at the Catalaunian Fields (451), they became masters of the land. However, the Salian Franks, under their leader Merovius, attained supremacy, thanks to the support of the Bishop of Gaul who opposed the Burgundians and Visigoths because of their adherence to the Arian heresy.

Merovingian Period. CLOVIS, grandson of Merovius, defeated the Romans at Soissons (486) and the Alemanni at Tolbiac (496), and soon afterwards adopted the religion of the beaten Gauls. The division of the kingdom among Clovis's sons, after 512, resulted in the bloody conflict between Austrasia (Lorraine and the Rhineland) and Neustria (north-west France). Internecine struggles weakened the Merovingian dynasty and the ruling power passed into the hands of the mayors of the palace. Greatest of these was the Austrasian CHARLES MARTEL, who checked the tide of the Arab invasion near Poitiers in 732; his son PEPIN THE SHORT (752–68) deposed the last of the Merovingians and founded a new dynasty.

Carolingian Period. CHARLEMAGNE (768–814), the son of Pepin, in close alliance with the Pope, widely extended his dominions, and in 800, being supreme in France, Germany, and Italy, was crowned Emperor of the West. The system of dividing the central power, which was to bring so much trouble to France, soon disintegrated Charlemagne's empire, and in 843, by the treaty of Verdun, the portion of his territories that was destined to become the realm of France fell to his grandson CHARLES THE BALD (843–77). Further division ensued and France became little more than a collection of feudal states, the situation being worse complicated by the attacks of Northern pirates (from the 850's) who eventually won for themselves the duchy of Normandy (912). In 987 the Carolingian monarchy disappeared when the Duke of France (i.e. Île-de-France), HUGH CAPET (987–96), was elected king.

House of Capet. The next 150 years were occupied in the struggle between the central power and the subordinate feudal lordships, while a new factor arose with the wealth and influence of the great cities. The Capetians made Paris their capital. In 1152 the marriage of the future Henry II of England (1154) to Eleanor of Aquitaine, who brought him about one-third of France as her dowry, began the long struggle between the King of France and his greatest vassal the King of England. PHILIP AUGUSTUS (1180–1223) won back a great part of the lost provinces from John of England; but his energetic reign was followed by a century of intermittent wars and attempted reforms which endured until the extinction of the direct branch of the Capetians in 1328.

House of Valois. The claim of PHILIP OF VALOIS (1328–50) to the throne of France was disputed by Edward III, who invaded France, routed the French army at Crécy (1346), and inflicted another defeat on JOHN II at Poitiers in 1356. The ravages of the French and English soldiery aroused both peasants and burgesses to revolt and, immediately after Poitiers, Étienne Marcel, provost of the merchants, raised the standard of rebellion in Paris, while the land was tormented by the Jacquerie or peasants' rising. Both disturbances were quelled, and in 1360, by the treaty of Brétigny, the King of England abandoned his right to the French throne. However, the war was to continue after 1369, successfully for France, thanks to Du Guesclin's tactics. The prudence of CHARLES V (1364–80) was in a fair way to settle the troubles of his stricken kingdom, but the fatal madness of his son CHARLES VI (1380–1422) resulted in the division of the country between rival regents, which developed into the struggle between the Burgundians and the Armagnacs. Henry V of England, seizing the occasion, invaded France, defeated a French force at Agincourt (1415), and by the treaty of Troyes (1420) received the hand of Catherine, daughter of Charles, together with the right of succession to the French throne. But England in its turn was disturbed by the minority of Henry VI, and a new champion arose to defend the rights of CHARLES VII (1422–61). JOAN OF ARC (d. 1431), born at Domrémy in 1412, raised the standard of France, and, after a brilliant campaign, defeated the English at Orléans in 1429. Captured at Compiègne in 1430 by the Burgundians, she was delivered to the English and burned at the stake in Rouen. But her campaign continued its success, and by 1453, of all the once extensive English possessions in France, Calais alone remained.

With LOUIS XI (1461–83) the change from a medieval social system to the modern state was accelerated. This brilliant and unscrupulous politician, relieved from the English menace, proceeded to crush the great feudal lordships that encroached upon his sovereignty. Greatest of these was the duchy of Burgundy, ruled by CHARLES THE BOLD (1433–77), the scion of a younger branch of the House of Valois and a worthy opponent of Louis. The peace of Péronne (1468) gave Charles a momentary advantage, but Louis managed to alienate Charles's English allies by the treaty of Picquigny (1475), and, after Charles's death before the walls of Nancy, speedily overwhelmed his successor and entered Dijon in triumph. Louis quickly mastered his lesser adversaries, and brought Artois, Franche-Comté, Provence, Anjou, and Maine into direct allegiance to the crown. CHARLES VIII (1483–98), LOUIS XII (1498–1515), and FRANCIS I (1515–47) were occupied largely with the indecisive Italian Wars, which saw the beginning of the rivalry between the Habsburgs and France. The only tangible result of their campaigns was the establishment in France of the literary ideas and artistic conceptions of the Italian Renaissance. Charles and Louis were successive husbands of Anne de Bretagne, whose dowry, the important duchy of Brittany, was formally united to France in 1532, on the death of her daughter, wife of Francis I. The reign of HENRI II (1547–59) saw the acquisition by France of the Three Bishoprics (Metz, Toul, and Verdun), the first step towards expansion to the Rhine, and of Calais, and the conclusion of the Italian wars; but under FRANCIS II (1559–60) began the bitter struggle of the religious wars which darkened the remaining years of the century. The oppression of the Protestant Huguenots culminated under CHARLES IX (1560–74), who was dominated by his mother Catherine de Médicis, with the Massacre of St Bartholomew (23 and 24 Aug 1572), and the reign of HENRI III (1574–89) saw the bitter struggle of the 'three Henries':

the king, the ultra-Catholic Henri de Guise (murdered in 1588), and the Protestant Henri de Navarre.

House of Bourbon. The struggle ended in the assassination of Henri III and the accession of Navarre as HENRI IV (1589–1610), who was obliged to accept conversion to the Church of Rome before he could assume royal power ("Paris is worth a Mass"; 1593). He signalized his success by the promulgation of the Edict of Nantes (1598), awarding liberty to the Protestants. The admirable reforms and economies instituted by Henri and his minister Sully were brought to naught by the extravagant favourites of his successor, LOUIS XIII (1610–43), until the advent of CARDINAL RICHELIEU (1624). The great minister's chief aims were the establishment of absolute royal power, the suppression of Protestant influence in politics, and the supremacy of France abroad. The capture of La Rochelle in 1628 destroyed Protestant power, while the insurrections of the great nobles were repressed with heavy penalties. Richelieu next turned his attention to the house of Habsburg, which under the great Emperor Charles V had enlarged its powers by encroaching on the boundaries of France. The entry of France into the Thirty Years' War, in alliance with Gustavus Adolphus of Sweden, with the ostensible object of aiding the German Protestants, was followed by the capture of Artois, Alsace, and Roussillon. Richelieu died in 1642 and Louis in the following year.

LOUIS XIV (1643–1715) succeeded as a minor. His mother, the Queen-Regent, aided by CARDINAL MAZARIN, continued his predecessor's policy with success signalized by the brilliant campaigns of the Grand Condé and Turenne. Meanwhile, however, the expenses of campaigning were causing trouble at home, and after the treaty of Westphalia (1648), which assured to France the possession of Alsace and the Three Bishoprics, the civil war known as the Fronde broke out in France. Condé, having quarrelled with the court party, allied himself with Spain, who had not subscribed to the Westphalian treaty, but the victory of Turenne, the royal leader, at the battle of the Dunes (1658) forced the Spaniards to sign the treaty of the Pyrenees, ceding Artois and Roussillon to France. At the death of Mazarin, in 1661, Louis announced his intention of governing without a prime minister. Ably seconded by subordinate commanders, notably Colbert, who developed the French Navy and improved trade, and Vauban, who reinforced the army, Louis entered upon a series of campaigns which increased the territory of France, but depleted the national wealth. The War of Devolution of 1667–68 secured the possession of many towns in Flanders, while the Dutch War of 1672–78 ended in the peace of Nimeguen and the absorption of Franche-Comté. The less successful War of the Grand Alliance (1686–97) and the War of the Spanish Succession (1701–13), in which the French forces suffered at the hands of Marlborough and Prince Eugene, though Marshal Villars won a victory at Denain (1712) after the withdrawal of the English from the war, brought Louis's long reign to a disastrous close.

The marriage of LOUIS XV (1715–74) to Maria, daughter of Stanislas Leczinski, the deposed king of Poland, drew France into the War of the Polish Succession (1733). Stanislas was consoled for the loss of his throne by becoming Duke of Lorraine for life; and on his death (1766) the province passed to the French crown. Next followed the War of the Austrian Succession, in which Louis was allied with Frederick the Great of Prussia, in opposition to England and Holland, who supported the cause of Maria Theresa, Empress of Austria. In spite of a brilliant victory under Saxe at Fontenoy (1745), the French gained little from the war, which saw the increase of English maritime power and the expansion of the kingdom of Prussia. The Seven Years' War (1756–63) saw the reversal of French alliances, with Austria now an ally. It brought disaster to the French arms in three continents, with the loss of some of the most flourishing colonies, notably in India, North America, and the West Indies. LOUIS XVI (1774–92) on his succession found the people enraged by his predecessor's extravagance and want of military success, and he was too weak to cope with the situation, more especially as he was handicapped by an unpopular wife and a reactionary court party.

The foreign policy, which gave support to the Americans in their struggle against England, was not only financially disastrous but also did much to spread democratic ideas. The ensuing financial crisis inspired reforms, which, if accepted, would have affected adversely the privileged estates, the clergy, and nobility, who therefore rejected them. As a result, the Estates General was summoned to meet at Versailles in 1789, for the first time since 1614. The first political act of the **Revolution** was the creation of the NATIONAL ASSEMBLY (17–20 June), when the third estate (the representatives of the majority of the nation) swore not to disband until a constitution had been given to the country which would limit royal power and guarantee liberty, equality, and fraternity. The resistance of the privileged classes provoked the Parisians, whose rebellion culminated in the fall of the Bastille (14 July). After failing to flee the country in 1791, Louis was forced to accept the constitution which the Constituent Assembly had been preparing since 1789. Marie Antoinette and her party sought aid from abroad, but the new Legislative Assembly declared war on Austria (April 1793) before help could come. The war went badly and the exasperated people dethroned Louis and power passed to the more advanced republicans. The CONVENTION (the newly elected assembly) met on 20 Sept, the day when victory at Valmy turned the tide of war in France's favour, and established the Republic. Louis was guillotined in 1793; royalist insurrections and general unrest were countered by the institution of a dictatorship by committees (the most powerful being the *Committee of Public Safety*), which continued until 27 July 1794, the date of the fall of Robespierre.

In 1795 the DIRECTORY of five members assumed power, and General Bonaparte first came into prominence as leader of the French campaign against the Austrians in Italy. A series of brilliant victories ended in the peace of Campo-Formio in 1797, and Bonaparte directed his attention to the resistance of England. After an ineffectual attempt in 1799 to destroy the British fleet at the battle of the Nile, he returned to France, and, finding the Directory generally detested, established the CONSULATE by the coup d'état of 9 and 10 Nov 1799, becoming himself First Consul the following year. A new constitution (1802) awarded Bonaparte the consulate for life, and on 18 May 1804 he caused himself to be declared Emperor of the French. The Civil Code, largely retaining the liberal laws of the Revolution, was enacted in 1804.

First Empire. Brought face to face with a new coalition of England, Austria, and Russia, NAPOLEON I crushed the two last at Austerlitz in 1805 and imposed on them the humiliating peace of Pressburg, only to find that his fleet had been destroyed in the same year at Trafalgar. Immediately afterwards Prussia united herself with the Allies, a move which was answered by the crushing defeat of her armies at Jena and Auerstadt (1806). A further campaign against the Russians ended in the agreement of Tilsit between Napoleon and the Czar. Meanwhile the Spaniards by their resistance to Joseph Bonaparte, who had been declared King of Spain by his brother, had induced England to send an army to their assistance. The success of the British forces tempted Austria to renew her struggle, but the battles of Essling and Wagram completed Austria's defeat and the peace of Vienna (1809) marks the apogee of Napoleon's power. A succession of disasters followed. A suicidal expedition into Russia led to the annihilation of the French army by 'Generals January and February' at the crossing of the Beresina (1813), while the British army drove the French foot by foot out of the Peninsula, crushing them finally at Toulouse (1813). In the same year the defeated Prussians made a final effort, won a great success at Leipzig, and in 1814 invaded France. By the treaty of Fontainebleau, Napoleon abdicated and retired to the island of Elba.

House of Bourbon (restored). The treaty of Paris (30 May 1814) cancelled almost all the conquests of the Republic and the Empire. This was the first humiliation of the reign of LOUIS XVIII (1814–24), and another followed when, in 1815, Napoleon escaped from Elba for the 'Hundred Days' (26 March–24 June), which, however, ended after Waterloo (18 June) in his banishment to St Helena. CHARLES X (1824–30) proved that the Bourbons could 'learn nothing and forget nothing', and the reactionary ordinances of St-Cloud, suppressing the liberty of the press, and reducing the electorate to the landed class, led to the 'July Revolution' of 1830 and the loss of the throne.

House of Orléans. LOUIS-PHILIPPE (1830–48), son of 'Philippe-Égalité' d'Orléans of the Revolution, was chosen head of the 'July Monarchy', and the upper middle class, who had striven for power since 1789, now achieved it. Louis-Philippe completed the conquest of Algeria, begun by his predecessor. The conservative policy of Guizot, however, did not suit the temper of the French, among whom socialist ideas were spreading, and the 'February Revolution' of 1848 overthrew the last king of France.

Second Republic and Second Empire. The moderate provisional government which succeeded was soon abolished (June 1848) and Louis Napoleon, nephew of the Emperor, was elected president of the republic; taking advantage of the sentimental prevalence of the 'Napoleonic idea' throughout the country he achieved his celebrated 'coup d'état' in Dec 1851. Next year a plebiscite accepted him almost unanimously as emperor. NAPOLEON III (1851–70) adopted the skilfully misleading motto of 'L'Empire c'est la paix'. In fact his reign was a succession of wars. In the Crimean War he allied himself with England and Turkey against Russia (1854–56). In 1859 he undertook the deliverance of Italy from the Austrian oppressor, and having won Italian friendship by the conquest of Lombardy, threw away his advantage by demanding Savoy and Nice in payment. Lack of allies and an ill-prepared army rendered France in the FRANCO-PRUSSIAN WAR of 1870–71 an easy prey to the extending power of Prussia, and an inglorious campaign ended with the capitulation of Sedan and the eventual loss of Alsace and Lorraine. Attributing their humiliation to the unwisdom of the Emperor, the infuriated French nation deposed him, and on 4 Sept 1870 the Third Republic was established.

Third Republic. The history of the Republic began inauspiciously with the siege and surrender of Paris (Jan 1871). The establishment of order was delayed by the rising of the *Commune* in Paris (18 March–21 May), but the trouble subsided and Adolphe Thiers was declared president. In 1873–93 France suffered economically at home, while expanding her colonial empire. Political crises embittered by the Dreyfus affair coloured the years before the outbreak of the First World War (1914–18). France emerged from the war victorious, though sorely stricken. The treaty of Versailles restored to her the provinces she had lost in 1871.

Between the two World Wars the French lost confidence in the central administration. The government adopted a predominantly defensive attitude towards the outer world, the visible expression of which was the construction of the Maginot Line, a supposedly impregnable defence system along the German frontier. Thus, although France with Britain declared war on Germany in 1939, her forces were in no state to resist the prepared onslaught of the German armour in 1940; and on 22 June of that year an armistice was signed with the triumphant German authorities. For all practical purposes the Third Republic died at Vichy on 10 July 1940, when by a large majority the National Assembly voted that full power should be granted to Marshal Pétain to legislate by decree, and the 'Vichy Government' came into being. Pétain's government, by an agreement of Oct 1940, arranged to collaborate with the German invaders, who had occupied the northern half of France and the whole Atlantic coastal strip. Meanwhile a provisional government under General Charles de Gaulle had been set up in London, while in France itself, the 'Résistance', a powerful 'underground' movement, came into being, thwarting the Vichy and German authorities at every turn, aided by arms from overseas. In 1944 the Vichy Government was swept aside by the Germans before the threat of an allied invasion of France; the landings of British and American troops in Normandy on 6 June and of American and French troops on the S. coast on 15 Aug soon led to the complete liberation of France and to victory over Germany in 1945. General de Gaulle became president of an interim government but failed to win political support as a candidate for the Presidency.

Fourth Republic. The constitution of the Fourth Republic was proclaimed in Oct 1946. Women now had a vote and proportional representation was adopted. Most power was vested in the lower chamber, the National Assembly. Despite many changes of government, by 1958 France was restored to prosperity after the devastation of the war.

Fifth Republic. In 1958 General de Gaulle prepared a new constitution, and this was approved by popular referendum. De Gaulle was elected first President of the Fifth Republic by universal direct suffrage for a period of seven years. The powers of the President were considerably increased; he nominates the prime minister, who, in turn, recommends the members of the government; he can make laws and refer decisions of major importance to popular vote by referendum; in extreme cases he has the power to dismiss the National Assembly. The government is answerable to Parliament composed of the National Assembly and the Senate elected by indirect suffrage. A further referendum in 1965 returned de Gaulle to power with enthusiasm though with a reduced majority.

Administration

For administrative purposes France is divided into ninety-four *Départements* (including those restored by the treaty of Versailles) formed arbitrarily in 1790 out of the old provinces or military governments, and with few exceptions named after some natural feature, generally a river. Each department is administered by a 'préfet', appointed by the President and assisted by a 'conseil général', and its chief town is the seat of the 'préfecture'. Departments are subdivided into *Arrondissements*, each with its 'sous-préfet' and its 'sous-préfecture'. The *Canton*, a subdivision of the arrondissement, is the judicial unit, under a 'juge de paix'. Each canton sends one representative (who is elected by direct suffrage) to the 'conseil général' of the department and another to the 'conseil d'arrondissement', but is not otherwise an administrative division. The canton includes a number of *Communes*, or parishes, each presided over by a 'maire', and the commune is the administrative unit of local government. In large towns, as in England, the mayor is a dignitary of much importance, but in villages he often follows a humble calling. In Paris the chief magistrate is the Préfet de la Seine, though each of the twenty arrondissements into which the city is divided has its local 'maire'.

RULERS OF FRANCE

Merovingians

481–511 CLOVIS, king of the Franks
511–752 KINGS of Paris, Neustria, Austrasia, Burgundy, etc.

Carolingians

752–768 PEPIN THE SHORT
768–814 CHARLEMAGNE
814–840 LOUIS THE PIOUS
843–877 CHARLES THE BALD
877–879 LOUIS II (le Bègue)
879–882 LOUIS III [and CARLOMAN]
882–884 CARLOMAN
884–888 CHARLES THE FAT
[888–898 COUNT ODO (Eudes) of Paris]
898–922 CHARLES THE SIMPLE
936–954 LOUIS D'OUTREMER
954–986 LOTHAIR
986–987 LOUIS V

House of Capet

987–996 HUGH CAPET
996–1031 ROBERT
1031–1060 HENRI I
1060–1108 PHILIP I
1108–1137 LOUIS VI (le Gros)
1137–1180 LOUIS VII (le Jeune)
1180–1223 PHILIP AUGUSTUS
1223–1226 LOUIS VIII
1226–1270 LOUIS IX (St Louis)
1270–1285 PHILIP III (le Hardi)
1285–1314 PHILIP IV (le Bel)
1314–1316 LOUIS X (le Hutin)
1316 JOHN I
1316–1322 PHILIP V (le Long)
1322–1328 CHARLES IV (le Bel)

House of Valois

1328–1350 PHILIP VI
1350–1364 JOHN II (le Bon)
1364–1380 CHARLES V (le Sage)
1380–1422 CHARLES VI
1422–1461 CHARLES VII
1461–1483 LOUIS XI
1483–1498 CHARLES VIII
1498–1515 LOUIS XII
1515–1547 FRANCIS I
1547–1559 HENRI II
1559–1560 FRANCIS II
1560–1574 CHARLES IX
1574–1589 HENRI III

House of Bourbon

1589–1610 HENRI IV
1610–1643 LOUIS XIII
1643–1715 LOUIS XIV
1715–1774 LOUIS XV
1774–1792 LOUIS XVI (d. 1793)

Revolution and First Empire

1792–1804 FIRST REPUBLIC
1804–1814 NAPOLEON I

House of Bourbon

1814–1815 LOUIS XVIII
1815 NAPOLEON I ('the Hundred Days')
1815–1824 LOUIS XVIII
1824–1830 CHARLES X

House of Orléans and Second Republic

1830–1848 LOUIS-PHILIPPE
1848–1852 SECOND REPUBLIC

Second Empire
1852–1870 NAPOLEON III

Third Republic
Presidents:
1871–1873 Adolphe Thiers
1873–1879 Marshal MacMahon
1879–1887 Jules Grévy
1887–1894 Sadi Carnot
1894–1895 J. Casimir-Périer
1895–1899 Félix Faure
1899–1906 Émile Loubet
1906–1913 Armand Fallières

1913–1920 Raymond Poincaré
1920   Paul Deschanel
1920–1924 Alexandre Millerand
1924–1931 Gaston Doumergue
1931–1932 Paul Doumer
1932–1940 Albert Lebrun

Fourth Republic
1947–1954 Vincent Auriol
1954–1958 René Coty

Fifth Republic
1958–   Charles de Gaulle

PARIS IN HISTORY

Paris is first mentioned, under the name of Lutetia, by Julius Cæsar in 53 B.C., when he appointed it as the meeting-place of deputies from conquered Gaul. It was then the fortified capital of the Parisii, an insignificant Gallic tribe, and was confined to an island in the Seine (Île de la Cité). A revolt of the Parisii was crushed by Labienus in 52 B.C. Extant Roman baths (Palais des Thermes) have been dated c. 215 B.C. Christianity was introduced to Paris by St Dionysius or Denis (c. A.D. 250), first Bishop of Paris. The town became in 292 a residence of the emperor Constantius Chlorus, and in 360 of Julian the Apostate, under whom the Nautæ Parisiaci, or merchant boatmen of the Seine, set up an altar to Jupiter. The name Paris, as applied to the town, first occurs in a synodal letter convening a council here in 360.

Merovingian Period. On the advice of St Genevieve Paris opened its gates to the invading Franks in 497, after the conversion of their king CLOVIS, who made Paris his official capital in 508, choosing the Palais de la Cité as the royal residence. After his death (511) Paris remained the political centre of the conflicting Frankish interests. During this period pious foundations were numerous, and the population, grown too large for the island, overflowed to form suburbs around the monasteries on both banks of the Seine.

Carolingian Period. PEPIN THE SHORT, Mayor of the Palace and son of Charles Martel, seized the throne for himself (752). He lived occasionally at Paris, but CHARLEMAGNE transferred the seat of government to Aix-la-Chapelle, and Paris fell a prey to the Norman pirates, who pillaged the suburbs and (885) besieged the city itself from their camp sited on the present Place du Louvre. The heroic defence by Bishop Gozlin and COUNT ODO (Eudes) placed the latter in power, and his nephew Hugh Capet wrested the last remains of sovereignty from the Carolingians.

House of Capet. Under HUGH CAPET (987) the capital of the duchy of France (i.e. the Île de France) definitively became the capital of the kingdom, and the town steadily increased in size and wealth. Under LOUIS VI (d. 1137), or perhaps earlier, the second wall of Paris was built, and the establishment of the Hanse Parisienne, or merchants' league, marks the foundation of the Paris municipality, whose arms, a freighted vessel on a sea argent, with the device 'Fluctuat nec mergitur' (tossed, but not engulfed), probably date from this period. In the reign of LOUIS VII the Romanesque style of architecture began to yield to the Gothic style, and in 1163 the foundation-stone of Notre-Dame was laid. PHILIP AUGUSTUS, the 'second founder of Paris', built for himself the fortress of the Louvre, whose keep was the official centre of feudalism. Under his patronage the schools of Paris were united into one University, to which Pope Innocent III granted its first Statutes in 1208. This famous seat of learning considerably augmented the local population and formed virtually a new town on the Left bank. The Right bank established itself as the centre of commerce, industry and administration. The streets were paved, the two old wooden bridges replaced with stone and the town enclosed in a new line of fortifications.

LOUIS IX (St Louis) reformed the office of Provost, and drew up, with the aid of the great lawgiver Étienne Boileau, those statutes of the commercial and industrial guilds of the city which remained in force until the Revolution. This was the 'golden age' of medieval French architecture and poetry. Louis rebuilt the Palais de la Cité, parts of which—notably the Ste Chapelle—still exist, and founded the Hospice des Quinze-Vingts and the modest theological college of the Sorbonne (1253), which became the dominant influence in the University.

House of Valois. While France lay practically at the mercy of the English after Poitiers (1356), and the misery of the country districts found expression in the revolt of the Jacquerie, the mayor of Paris (prévôt des marchands), Étienne Marcel, sought to take advantage of the unrest and increase the power of the municipality. But he offended public sentiment by an attempt to deliver the city to Charles the Bad of Navarre, and was assassinated in 1358. CHARLES V raised the fortress of the Bastille, continued the fourth wall, begun by Marcel, and embellished the Louvre, but his weak-minded son CHARLES VI, swayed by the greed of his uncles, oppressed the city with odious taxation. A revolt of the 'Maillotins' (maillet = mallet or mace) was bloodily suppressed (1380), and for forty years of tumult the Armagnacs (nobles and merchants) and the Burgundians (the people's party) disputed the city. Henry V of England entered Paris in 1420, and the English ruled until 1436, the Duke of Bedford repelling an assault by Joan of Arc in 1429.

LOUIS XI successfully achieved administrative and territorial unity. A post-office was established and the first French printing-press was set up in the Sorbonne (1469). Under FRANCIS I the artistic movement of the Renaissance made itself felt, with the foundation of the Hôtel de Ville (1533). CHARLES IX plunged Paris into bloodshed by signing the order for the Massacre of St Bartholomew (23 and 24 Aug 1572) at the instigation of Catherine de Médicis, from whom "the taste for murder chiefly sprang". The last years of the Valois were darkened by the religious Wars of the League, and the ultra-Catholic Council of Sixteen held in Paris under a yoke of iron for four years (1587–91). HENRI III, menaced by the partisans of the Duc de Guise, fled from Paris in 1588 but returned to besiege it next year. He was, however, assassinated in the château of St-Cloud; and, after a second siege and a famine, the city surrendered in 1594 to Henry of Navarre (Henri IV), who as a condition abandoned his Protestantism with (it is said) the cynical remark that "Paris vaut bien une messe".

House of Bourbon. HENRI IV enlarged the Louvre and the Tuileries, planned several squares, including the Place Royale, completed the Pont Neuf, and greatly improved the city's paving and sanitation. In 1610 he was assassinated in the Rue de la Ferronnerie. Under LOUIS XIII the archbishopric of Paris was created (1623), and the Imprimerie Royale (1640) and the Académie Française (1635) were established. The fifth wall was erected, and several new quarters arose, e.g. in the Pré-aux-Clercs (Faubourg St-Germain), the Île St-Louis, and the Marais, which became the favourite residence of the nobility. Marie de Médicis, the king's mother, built the Luxembourg, Anne of Austria, his wife, founded the church of Val de Grâce, and Richelieu built for himself the Palais-Cardinal, the later Palais-Royal.

The minority of LOUIS XIV (Le Roi Soleil) was agitated by the trouble of the Fronde (1648–53) when the Parlement and people under the leadership of Condé rose against the Queen-Mother and Cardinal Mazarin. Little that was decisive came of this disturbance save that, until the Revolution, Paris was not again the seat of the court. At the death of Mazarin, Louis assumed absolute power. He ruled without a prime minister and for the rest of his life upheld the conviction that "L'État c'est moi". The nobles were reduced to ineffectual courtiers and the King drew his ministers from the ablest among the 'haut bourgeois'. In 1672 boulevards were laid down on the lines of Étienne Marcel's wall, and the University quarter was incorporated in the city. Paris became the literary centre of Europe, as Corneille, Racine, Molière, La Fontaine, and Pascal made their home in the city. Paris was now a city of about 25,000 houses, with 560,000 inhabitants.

Louis XV and Louis XVI, though the royal residence was at Versailles, continued the works of their predecessors (Panthéon, Palais-Bourbon, Invalides, etc.). The sixth wall of Paris, a simple customs-barrier put up at the demand of the farmers-general of taxes, caused general discontent ("Le mur murant Paris rend Paris murmurant").

Though the **French Revolution** began at Versailles with the transformation of the States-General into a NATIONAL ASSEMBLY (17 June 1789), the centre of the movement was speedily transferred to the capital, where the storming of the Bastille (14 July) was the first act of revolutionary violence. From the beginning of 1790 Louis XVI was virtually a prisoner in the Tuileries, and many of the nobility left the country. The assembly set to work to frame a constitution, and on 19 June all nobility was abolished. In June 1791 the royal family, in an attempt to flee the country, were arrested at Varennes, and brought back to Paris. On 1 October 1791 the new LEGISLATIVE ASSEMBLY was formed. This body was at first swayed by the moderate Girondists, largely under the influence of Mme Roland, but, after insurrections on 20 June and 10 Aug 1792, power was seized by the extreme Jacobins under Danton, the stalwart plebeian, Robespierre, the 'sea-green incorruptible', and the blood-thirsty Marat, and on 1 Oct 1792 the NATIONAL CONVENTION assumed power. On 21 Jan Louis XVI was executed in the Place de la Révolution. The deser-tion to the enemy of the Girondist Gen. Dumouriez cast suspicion on the moderate party, and the Jacobins, seizing the occasion, created the terrible *Committee of Public Safety* (March 1793) and bloodily suppressed all royalist, and even moderate, movements. The assassination of Marat on 13 July further inflamed the minds of the people, and at the end of the year the Dantonists, hitherto the extreme party, found themselves the moderating force opposed to the Hébertists, the party of terror and reckless bloodshed.

A new **Republican Calendar** was instituted on 24 Nov 1793, and Year I was considered to have begun at the autumnal equinox (22 Sept) of 1792, the date of the proclamation of the Republic. The year was divided into 12 months of 30 days each; each month was divided into 3 periods of 10 days; and 5 days ('Sans-culottides') were added at the end of each year (6 in leap years). The months received poetic names devised by Fabre d'Eglantine: VENDÉMIAIRE (the month of the *vendange*, or vintage), BRUMAIRE (*brume*, fog), and FRIMAIRE (*frimas*, hoar-frost) in autumn; NIVÔSE (*neige*, Lat. *nivem*, snow), PLUVIÔSE (*Pluie*, rain), and VENTÔSE (*vent*, wind) in winter; GERMINAL (*germination*, seed-time), PRAIRIAL (*prairie*, meadow), and FLORÉAL (*fleur*, flower) in spring; MESSIDOR (*moisson*, Lat. *messem*, harvest), THERMIDOR (Greek, *thermé*, heat), and FRUCTIDOR (Lat. *fructum*, fruit) in summer. The republican calendar was officially replaced by the Gregorian on 1 Jan 1806.

Robespierre's personal ambition brooked no rivals, and early in 1794 both Hébert and Danton were guillotined; a little later he renewed the ferocity of the Reign of Terror in order to regain the influence which he had lost by the part he played during a festival (8 June 1794) in honour of the Supreme Being, whose worship he sought to substitute for the atheistic cult of Reason in-stituted by the Hébertists. After two months of reckless murder, the reaction came, and on 27 July (9 Thermidor) Robespierre fell a victim to his own guillotine. In 1795 the Girondists, once more in power, established the Constitution of the Year III, and on 5 Oct (19 Vendémiaire) Napoléon Bonaparte, with his 'whiff of grape-shot', crushed a determined effort of the Royalists. On 28 Oct the DIRECTORY assumed power, and quelled every rising of Royalists and Terrorists alike. After four years of successful warfare abroad, Bonaparte returned to find the Directory unpopular, and the five Directors regarded as tyrants. With the help of the Army, and the support of Siéyès, he succeeded, by the coup d'état of 9 and 10 Nov 1799 (18 and 19 Brumaire, Year VIII), in establishing himself, Siéyès, and Roger-Ducos as the leaders of the CONSULATE. In 1800 Napoleon became First Consul, with two new colleagues, and after a new constitution (Year X, 1802) which still further increased his power, he caused himself to be declared Emperor of the French on 18 May 1804, and was crowned in Notre-Dame by Pope Pius VII.

First Empire. The reign of NAPOLEON I saw important changes in the appearance of Paris and many new monuments and bridges were erected. Art treasures and other booty of the Napoleonic campaigns were used to embellish the capital. But ten years of war culminated in the surrender of the city to the Allies (31 March 1814) after a battle on the heights of Montmartre, the abdication of the Emperor at Fontainebleau, and the restoration of the Bourbons.

House of Bourbon (restored). During the Restoration Paris enjoyed a period of prosperity, and French literature and art flourished anew. Hugo, Lamartine, Stendhal and de Vigny spread the new Romantic spirit which had crossed the Channel with Sir Walter Scott, and influenced in turn the painters Géricault and Delacroix and the music of Berlioz. In several of the sciences and notably in oriental studies, Paris held the foremost rank.

House of Orléans. Following the 'July Revolution' (1830) LOUIS PHILIPPE elected to succeed Charles X as King. He devoted himself, with great energy but dubious taste, to the embellishment of Paris, and many more or less handsome buildings date from this reign. In 1840 the body of Napoleon I was transferred with great ceremony from St Helena to Paris. In 1841–45 the city was made a fortress and enclosed by the last enceinte.

Second Republic. The 'February Revolution' of 1848, inspired by the feeble foreign policy and reactionary domestic policy of the King, overthrew Louis Philippe, and the Second Republic was set up by the provisional government. The 'Napoleonic idea', however, found expression in the election as president of Louis Napoleon, who achieved his celebrated 'coup d'état' in Dec 1851. Next year a plebiscite accepted him almost unanimously as emperor.

Second Empire. Under NAPOLEON III many broad modern boulevards (St-Michel, Haussmann, etc.) were laid out in Paris by Baron Haussmann, with the political object of clearing the mass of narrow and tortuous streets that had favoured the erection of barricades in 1830 and 1848; the Bois de Boulogne and Bois de Vincennes were transformed into great public parks; and many public buildings were completed, while the whole area within the fortifications was included in the city (1859). Two great Exhibitions were held in Paris (1855 and 1867). The Franco-Prussian War put an end to the Empire, and Napoleon capitulated to the Germans at Sedan on 1 Sept 1870.

The **Third Republic** was formally proclaimed on 4 Sept 1870, while the Germans were advancing on Paris. The Louvre was turned into an armament workshop, the Gare d'Orléans into a balloon factory, and the Gare de Lyon into a cannon-foundry. The city, invested on 19 Sept, capitulated on 28 Jan 1871, after a siege that had caused great suffering. The Prussians entered Paris on 1 March, and occupied the Louvre and the Champs-Elysées for three days. Establishment of law and order in the capital was delayed by the *Communard Insurrection* (18 March to 29 May 1871), which compelled the removal of the seat of government to Versailles, and ended only after a week of pitched battle in the barricaded streets, during which the Archbishop of Paris was murdered and the Tuileries Palace and other public buildings were destroyed. Government retaliatory measures included the massacre of 20,000 Parisians. In 1879, however, the Legislature returned to Paris, and the city and the country shared in the general material prosperity of the later 19C, proof of which was given by the 'Expositions Universelles' of 1878, 1889, and 1900.

Many new education buildings, the Parc de Montsouris, squares, and the important underground railway were constructed. Sculptures purchased by the city during the international exhibitions were erected in the public parks and gardens, transforming them into open-air museums of contemporary art. Paris became the artistic capital of the world. If the official and ecclesiastical architecture of the time is unfortunately both abundant and tasteless, in compensation the era also left the legacy of the Impressionists; Debussy, Ravel and Fauré; Verlaine, Rimbaud, Mallarmé, and the recorder of the passing age, Proust. The basilica of Sacré-Cœur, which was begun in 1875 as a national votive offering of humiliation and repentance for the 1870–71 war, was completed in 1914.

German troops entered French territory on 2 Aug 1914 and on 3 Aug the two countries were at war. At the battle of the Marne (7 Sept; 'jour des taxis') Gen. Maunoury was dramatically reinforced on the Ourcq by 11,000 men despatched in taxicabs from the 'army of Paris', and during the ensuing days (8–12 Sept) the citizens had the satisfaction of hearing the din of battle gradually recede. Air raids became frequent towards the close of the struggle. On 23 March 1918, two days after the opening of Ludendorff's great offensive, a German long-range gun began firing upon Paris from the neighbourhood of Crépy-en-Laonnais (Forest of St-Gobain), at a range of 82 miles. The bombardment by this and other 'Berthas' was renewed at intervals until 8 Aug 1918. All danger to Paris was removed by Foch's great counter-offensive on 18 July 1918, which drove the enemy back from the Marne for the second time.

The signature of the treaty of Versailles was celebrated by an allied march of Victory through Paris (14 July 1919); and on the second anniversary of the Armistice (11 Nov 1920) the body of an 'unknown soldier' was interred beneath the Arc de Triomphe.

The period between the two World Wars was one of economic crises and political unrest, but for Paris also one of civic expansion. The Thiers fortifications were demolished in 1919–24, affording an opportunity for a new ring of boulevards. The Bois de Boulogne and de Vincennes were annexed to the city and the boundaries widened to include Montmartre, Issy, and other outlying suburbs. Paris kept and augmented its reputation as the literary centre of the avant-garde. The building of museums, begun before the war, continued, and the use of reinforced concrete quickly spread. In 1937 the Palais de Chaillot, completed in time for the exhibition of decorative arts, altered a familiar perspective.

On 14 June 1939, Paris was occupied by the Germans without a shot being fired. Throughout the long years of occupation, the underground Resistance movement worked towards liberation, and on 17 Aug 1944 this culminated in open rebellion. The Allied armies were approaching and 24 Aug witnessed the last battle with the enemy in the capital and the arrival of French forces under General de Gaulle.

The choice of Paris for the permanent headquarters of SHAPE and of NATO (both since moved to Belgium) and of UNESCO and Interpol has been disappointingly unproductive of notable building, the teams of architects involved by international bureaucracy producing designs below their individual best. Systematic cleaning of ancient monuments in the central area has brightened the city and revealed many charming details. The authorities have accepted the protection and restoration of the Marais as an official responsibility. Of the new projects on the outskirts the Rond-Point de la Défense began well with the Centre National des Industries et Techniques, a notable building on a triangular plan with a soaring curved roof. The growing Cité Universitaire was embellished with a second work of Le Corbusier (Maison du Brésil). Elsewhere the usual vast schemes of 'aménagement' and 'rénovation' proceeded on a scale resulting too often in huge windswept spaces between ugly horizontal and vertical boxes (perhaps the worst of which has transformed the skyline of Montparnasse). More conspicuously successful are the efforts of the road engineers, with attractive landscaping of the autoroute to Versailles and the viaducts of the Autoroute du Sud near Orly.

PRACTICAL INFORMATION

I APPROACHES TO PARIS

PARIS is connected by rail with the principal cities of Europe and by air with many cities of the world. From London Paris can be reached in c. 6 hrs by train and boat, either by day (several routes, including 'Golden Arrow') or by the Night Ferry. By train and air ('Silver Arrow') or by coach and air the journey is reduced to c. 4 hours. Direct flights, taking 50–60 min., operate at intervals all day, but the journey from city terminal to city terminal can still not be achieved in much under 4 hours. By car (crossing the Channel by sea or air) the total time taken is likely to be 7–8 hours. There are direct air services to Paris from Birmingham, Manchester, and Glasgow. Some trans-atlantic liner services accept cross-Channel passengers between Southampton (or Plymouth) and Le Havre or Cherbourg.

Intending travellers who wish to be spared the trouble and anxiety con-nected with the planning of a journey abroad will doubtless call on the services of one or other of the numerous **Tourist Agents.** These organizations, for a small fee, obtain travel tickets, make hotel reservations, deal with the problems of foreign currency, and, if desired, arrange tours for individuals or parties. A selection of agents in London is given below; several of them have branches in other towns.

Thomas Cook & Son, 45 Berkeley St, W.1, and many branches; *American Express,* 6 Haymarket, S.W.1, 89 Mount St, W.1; *Dean & Dawson,* 81 Piccadilly, W.1, etc.; *Frames' Tours,* 25 Tavistock Place, W.C.1, 42 Albemarle St, W.1, 80 Southampton Row, W.C.1, etc.; *Global Tours,* 318 High Holborn, W.C.1, 191 Regent St, W.1, etc.; *Poly Travel Ltd,* 311 Regent St, W.1, 73 Oxford St, W.1, etc.

Travellers who enjoy planning their own journey cannot do better than consult the French Government Tourist Office, 178 Piccadilly, W.1, for general information. They can then work out their schedules with the aid of the time-tables listed below and purchase tickets at the relevant addresses given.

TIMETABLES. *Cook's Continental Timetable* (monthly; 10s.) is the leading international timetable. The chief French timetable is the *Indicateur Chaix* published both in 1 vol. (16,50 fr.) for all French railways (and many motor-bus services, etc.) or in smaller parts, one for each region. The large timetable is obtainable in England (40s.) from B.A.S. Overseas Publications, 50a Sheen Lane, London, S.W.14.

The *A.B.C. World Airways Guide* (monthly; 12s. 6d.) is the most comprehensive air travel guide published in England.

Air Services between London (etc.) and Paris are maintained by British European Airways (B.E.A.) and Air France. Full information may be obtained from *B.E.A.,* Dorland Hall, Lower Regent St, S.W.1, and from *Air France,* 158 New Bond St, W.1.

By Rail and Air. SILVER ARROW service (run in co-operation by British United Airways and French Railways) from London (Victoria) to Paris (Gare du Nord), flying between Gatwick and Le Touquet. Information from British United Airways.

By Coach and Air, SKYWAYS services from London (Victoria Coach Stn) viâ Lympne and from Derby (East Midlands Airport) to Beauvais (air) and thence (coach) to Paris (République Coach Stn); for details apply Skyways, 33 Elizabeth St, S.W.1.

By Rail and Sea. The *British Rail Travel Centre,* Rex House, Lower Regent St, London, S.W.1, provides travel tickets, sleeping berth tickets, seat reservations, etc., on Continental (as well as British) transport services.

Car Ferries are operated by British and French Railways from Dover to Calais, Boulogne, and Dunkirk and from Newhaven to Dieppe; also by Townsend Ferries from Dover to Calais; and by Thoresen Ferries from Southampton to Le Havre and Cherbourg. In London full particulars are available from the A.A., R.A.C., or British Rail, all at the *Continental Car Ferry Centre*, 52 Grosvenor Gardens, S.W.1.

Air Ferries for cars are run by *British United Air Ferries* (Portland House, Victoria, London, S.W.1) from Southend, Lydd, or Coventry to Calais or Le Touquet.

Motoring. British motorists and motor-cyclists driving to Paris will save much trouble by joining the *Automobile Association* (Fanum House, Leicester Square, London, W.C.2), the *Royal Automobile Club* (83 Pall Mall, S.W.1), the *Royal Scottish Automobile Club*, or other clubs recognized by the Automobile Club de France (6 Place de la Concorde, Paris, 8e) or the Touring Club de France (65 Av. de la Grande-Armée, Paris, 16e). The only documents now required by British owner-drivers are the vehicle registration book, a valid national driving-licence, and an International Insurance Certificate (the 'Green Card'). A nationality plate (e.g. GB) must be affixed to the rear of the vehicle, where it is illuminated by the tail lamp.

The U.K. motoring organizations are represented at most of the sea and air ports, both at home and on the Continent, to assist their members with Customs formalities.

The RULE OF THE ROAD in France is to drive on the right and to overtake on the left. At forks and cross-roads right of way must be given to traffic on the 'routes nationales'; when there is no 'superior' road, to traffic coming from the right. British tourists would be well advised to study the Continental 'Code de la Route', since the rule at roundabouts is now opposed to that in Britain.

Lighting. It is obligatory for French-registered vehicles to use amber-coloured head-lights. As a matter of courtesy, British motorists will probably wish to follow this practice. This can be done for many cars by fitting special amber shields which by prismatic ribbing also dip the headlights the reverse way. They take ten minutes to fit, and cost (with fitting) approx. 35s. For other models amber-coloured bulbs are fitted and the dipping system mechanically altered.

Petrol is sold in multiples of 5 litres (just over a gallon). The price varies a little from region to region. The cost in Paris of ordinary 'essence' is 0,98 fr. per litre (c. 7s. 4d. per gal.) and of 'super' 1,04 fr. per litre (7s. 10d. per gal.)

Parking is restricted in central Paris between 9 and 6 to 1 hr and regulated by the 'disc' system.

Bicycles may be taken into France without any need to produce a customs document. The machine should be declared to the British Customs before leaving Great Britain to ensure duty-free re-entry. Bicycles must be equipped with adequate brakes, a bell that works, a forward lighting system, and a red rear *lamp* (a reflector is NOT sufficient). The cross-channel charge for a bicycle is 7s.

Passports are necessary for all British, Irish, and American travellers entering France and must bear the photograph of the holder. Every foreign traveller must report to the Police within 48 hrs of arrival in France. The usual procedure is to fill in a form provided by the hotel, but foreigners staying with friends, etc., should not fail to report to the authorities.

British, American, Irish, Canadian, South African, Australian and New Zealand passports do not require visas, but travellers from most other British Dominions must obtain a French consular visa. Any foreigners intending to remain in France for more than three months should apply (at least six weeks in advance) to the nearest French Consulate (in London, 51 Bedford Square, W.C.1), if in France already, to the Préfecture de Police (Service des Étrangers) in Paris, or, in the provinces, to the Préfecture of the department in which they are residing.

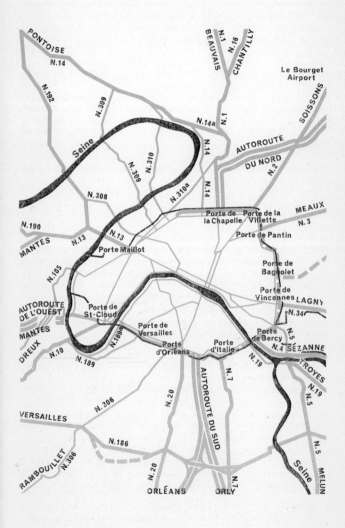

Custom House. Hand luggage is usually examined in France at the port of entry and departure, but on the fast trains to Paris and certain other expresses the customs examination takes place in the train.

Provided that dutiable articles are declared, bonâ-fide travellers will find the French customs authorities courteous and reasonable. Tobacco is dutiable, but 200 cigarettes or $\frac{3}{4}$ lb. of tobacco are usually passed free. The following are admitted without formalities for personal use (and may not be disposed of in France): two pairs of skis, field-glasses, two tennis racquets, camping equipment, two sporting guns with 100 cartridges, two cameras of different types with ten rolls of film each, ciné camera with ten rolls of film, typewriter, musical instrument, gramophone equipped with up to twenty (or four L.P.) records, radio, and tape-recorder with two spools of tape.

Returning travellers may be reminded that all articles purchased abroad are now dutiable or forbidden in Britain, special attention being paid to watches and cameras, but a limited amount of new personal clothing, 200 cigarettes or $\frac{1}{2}$ lb. of tobacco, a bottle of wine and a bottle of spirits, a small bottle of perfume, and souvenirs to the value of £5 are usually passed free, if declared. Foreign reprints of copyright English books may be confiscated.

Souvenirs bought in France may be exported without licence up to any value, but works of art and antiques require a special permit. Personal jewellery (wedding and engagement rings; wrist-watch), a worn fur coat, and personal valuables up to a value of £1000 may be taken out of Britain at the discretion of the customs officers; but valuables beyond this quantity may not be taken out of the country (except by persons not resident in the United Kingdom).

Currency Regulations. The foreign currency allowance permitted by the British Government for pleasure travel per yearly period varies from time to time. At the moment (1967) it is £50 (plus an allowance of £25 if a private car is taken), which may all be in foreign currency; there is no limit to the amount of French currency that can be taken into France. In sterling notes not more than an additional £10 (plus £5 in silver) may be taken out of Great Britain by British or American travellers.

Not more than 1000 fr. in French notes may be taken out of France nor more foreign currency than has been imported.

Money. The unit is the franc, or New Franc (N.F.), subdivided into centimes. Banknotes for 10, 20, 50, 100, 500, 1000, and 5000 fr. are in circulation, and there are also coins of 1, 5, 10, 20 and 50 c. ($\frac{1}{2}$ fr.), 1 fr., and 5 fr. The travellers' cheques issued by the chief British banks, by Messrs Thos. Cook, and by the principal American express companies and the Association of American Banks are the most convenient way of carrying money. These may be changed at most banks and travel agents (passports must be shown); many of the larger hotels display a notice to the effect that they are officially entitled to change such cheques, affording a convenient service outside banking hours. A supply of French change, for gratuities and other incidental expenses of the journey, should be obtained before leaving home. The rate of exchange of the pound sterling is at present (1967) 12 fr., of the dollar 5 fr.

Arrival in Paris. (a) BY TRAIN. Below is an alphabetical list of the chief Paris RAILWAY TERMINI. All of them are connected by underground (Métro) and motor-bus routes and are provided with restaurants (not cheap), post offices, and information offices. The left-luggage office or cloakroom (charge 0,80 fr. per day per package) is known as the 'consigne'. Railway porters are entitled to a fee of 1 fr. per article of luggage and expect a small tip in addition.

Gare d'Austerlitz, for the Région Sud-Ouest of the S.N.C.F. (Tours, Bordeaux, Toulouse, the Pyrenees, Madrid, etc.).

Gare de l'Est, for the Région Est (Reims, Metz, Strasbourg, Germany, etc.).

Gare des Invalides, for some electric trains to Versailles, adjoining the Aérogare (see below).

Gare de Lyon, for the Région Sud-Est (Lyons, Geneva, Provence, the Riviera, Barcelona, etc.).

Gare du Maine (Montparnasse), a terminus of the Région Ouest (lines to Brittany, La Rochelle, etc.).

Gare du Nord, for the Région Nord (Lille, Laon, Brussels, etc.) and for boat-trains to Boulogne, Calais, and Dunkerque.

Gare St-Lazare, another terminus of the Région Ouest (Normandy lines), and for boat-trains to Dieppe, Le Havre, and Cherbourg.

Other termini of minor importance are the *Gare du Luxembourg*, Rue Gay-Lussac, for suburban trains to Sceaux, St-Rémy-lès-Chevreuse, and other S. suburbs; the *Gare de Vincennes* or *de la Bastille*, for trains to Vincennes, Joinville-le-Pont, Boissy-St-Léger, and other E. suburbs.

(b) BY AIR. The airports serving Paris are **Orly**, $11\frac{1}{2}$ m. S., and **Le Bourget**, 10 m. N.E., of the centre of the city. From Orly motor-coaches leave every $\frac{1}{4}$ hr (fare 3,50 fr.) for the *Aérogare* at the Invalides which is equipped with restaurant (excellent), post office, information bureau, and exchange facilities (none at Orly); from Le Bourget every $\frac{1}{4}$ hr for the Aérogare, calling also (8 a.m. to 9 p.m. only) at the *Place Péreire* terminal.

II HOTELS

Hotels of every class and size abound in Paris, but during the tourist season they are often full, and it is prudent to engage rooms in advance, especially if the traveller arrives late in the evening.

The most expensive hotels, the clientèle at which is international (largely American), are mostly situated in the neighbourhood of the Place Vendôme, the Place de la Concorde, and the Champs-Élysées. For the average visitor the most convenient quarters are near the Boulevards, from the Madeleine to the Faubourg Poissonnière and the adjoining regions (2e), the Avenue de l'Opéra, the Rue de Rivoli between the Palais-Royal and the Place de la Concorde (1er), the Faubourg St-Honoré and the Champs-Élysées neighbourhood (8e). Hotels on the Left Bank tend to be slightly cheaper than their counterparts on the Right, and favourite areas are: the Latin Quarter (5e), including the Odéon and the Luxembourg; Motte-Piquet—Av. Duquesne—St-Germain (7e); the Faubourg St-Germain (6e). French Railway hotels are recommended, but otherwise hotels clustered around the main stations should be approached warily.

Before taking possession of his rooms at a hotel the traveller should have a precise understanding as to the charge. Notice of departure should be given before noon. Valuables or money should not be kept in the traveller's room, but deposited with the manager of the hotel, in exchange for a receipt, or at a bank.

Charges vary of course, and there are seasonal increases. The better-known hotels sumptuously equipped with palatial suites of rooms, restaurants, grill-rooms, etc., and priced accordingly, include: *Bristol*, 112 Faubourg St-Honoré (The '*Claridges*' of Paris); *Ritz*, 15 Pl. Vendôme; *George V*, 31 Av. George V; *Hilton*, 18 Av. Suffren; *Meurice*, 228 Rue de Rivoli; *Crillon*, 10 Pl. de la Concorde.

A room with a bath in a luxury hotel in the height of the season may cost anything from 100 fr., whereas a comfortable single room in a less fashionable quarter need not cost more than 11 or 12 fr. Many of the smaller hotels are without restaurants. The tips expected by hotel servants amount to not less than 15 per cent of the bill. In most hotels a percentage is added to the bill for 'service' and, at these, gratuities need not be given. A state tax, varying according to the grade of the hotel, is also added to the bill, and many hotels, when quoting terms (especially 'en pension' terms), give their charges as 'service et taxes compris' (s.t.c.), which includes all these extras.

Further information concerning hotels can be obtained from the French Tourist Office in London, which issues a 'Selected International Tourist Hotels' guide. In Paris, a Welcome Information Office will make free on-the-spot reservations, valid for one and a half hours: failure to check in within this time automatically cancels the booking. The location of Welcome offices can be found below, under section V. The central office also makes Telex reservations to other parts of France, and some other countries.

III   RESTAURANTS

Good **Restaurants** of every class abound in Paris. Prices are high, and except in the less pretentious establishments the convenient table d'hôte at fixed prices ('à prix fixe') is infrequent; but at the same time it should be remembered that good value for money is nearly always obtained. At most restaurants the day's menu, with prices, is affixed outside the establishment. The head-waiter ('maître d'hôtel') should not be addressed as 'garçon', a term reserved for his subordinates.

The famous French cookery reaches its perfection in the sumptuous à la carte restaurants of the highest class, where 45–60 fr. is a conservative estimate for the price of a reasonable dinner. The diner will note that such items as hors d'œuvre, fruit, etc., will swell the bill very considerably, and he should not allow the suggestions of the waiter to add more dishes to the menu than he really wishes. It is, moreover, uneconomical to dine alone at these restaurants, as a 'portion' is often sufficient for two.

Excellent meals at considerably lower charges (12 or 15 fr. upwards) may be enjoyed in other good à la carte restaurants in the Grands Boulevards and other main thoroughfares; and various restaurants, brasseries, and café-restaurants offer meals at fixed prices ranging from c. 9 fr. upwards. Even at the cheaper establishments the standard of cooking will be found remarkably good, though some of the more modest 'prix fixe' meals are unimaginative. In restaurants à la carte there is a liberal choice of wines at relatively high prices. The red, white and 'rosé' table-wines in carafes or 'pichets' (jugs) are usually very fair at any restaurant.

The bill ('l'addition') should be in writing, and the prudent traveller will check the items charged. The correct percentage of gratuity is usually added to the bill, but possible misunderstanding can be avoided by asking, "Est-ce que le service est compris?" (Is service included?).

The 8th and 1st arrondissements are the 'de luxe' quarters and many of the expensive hotels have suitably priced restaurants. The 5th, 6th, and 7th have, in addition to a myriad of restaurants of every price and variety, several of the best in Paris. There are very few in the Marais or near the Palais de

Chaillot (which, however, has its own), and in the outer suburbs they tend to become scarcer and poorer in quality.

Among the better-known restaurants de luxe are: *La Tour d'Argent*, 15 Quai de la Tournelle (5e; closed Mon); *Maxim's*, 3 Rue Royale (8e; closed Sun); *Hotel Ritz*, 15 Pl. Vendôme (8e); *Lassarre*, 17 Av. Franklin-Roosevelt (8e; closed Sun; Aug); *Lucas-Carton*, 9 Pl. Madeleine (8e).

The following list has been divided to accord with the main text, each group of restaurants falling within the areas described by the routes. Where these overlap, the restaurants have been mentioned only once. In each section they are arranged roughly in order of their charges, the cheaper restaurants being named last. Times at which they are closed are indicated in brackets, and many close on public holidays. This list is of course by no means exhaustive and the omission of names does not imply any derogatory judgement.

Route 1. See Routes 9 and 10.

Route 3. *Auberge du Vert Galant*, 42 Quai des Orfèvres; *Quasimodo*, 42 Quai d'Orléans; *Au Gourmet de l'Isle* (closed Mon lunch, Fri; Sept), 42 Rue St-Louis-en-l'Île; *Le Bossu, Franc Pinot*, 27 and 1 Quai de Bourbon (Île St-Louis).

Routes 4 and 5. *Calvet*, 165 Boul. St-Germain; *Méditéranée*, 2 Pl. de l'Odéon; *Cris de Paris* (closed Sun), 10 Rue St-Julien-le Pauvre; *Chez Maître Paul, Le Hoggar* (Algerian), 12 and 67 Rue Monsieur-le-Prince; *Vagenende*, 142 Boul. St-Germain; *Au Feu de Brise* (closed Fri), 66 Rue Mazerine; *L'Oenothèque* (closed Sun), 37 Rue de Lille; *A l'Alsacienne*, 54 Boul. St-Michel; *Brasserie Lipp*, 151 Boul. St-Germain; *Taverne du Palais*, 5 Pl. St-Michel.

Route 6. *La Bourgogne* (closed Sun), 6 Av. Bosquet; *Chez les Anges* (closed Mon), 54 Boul. Latour-Maubourg; *Le Champ de Mars* (closed Mon; Aug), *Auberge Bressane* (closed Sat; Sept), 17 and 18 Av. Motte-Piquet; *Antoine et Antoinette* (closed Sun), 16 Av. Rapp.

Route 7A. *Marius et Janette*, 4 Av. George V; *Chez Francis*, Pl. Alma; *Chez Tante Louise*, 41 Rue Boissy-d'Anglas; *Ramponneau*, 21 Av. Marceau.

Route 7B. *Vivarois* (closed Mon; Aug), 192 Av. Victor-Hugo; *Jamin* (closed Sun; Aug), 32 Rue de Longchamps; *La Rotonde de la Muette* (closed Mon), 12 Chausée de la Muette. (None of the restaurants in 7A or 7B is very cheap.)

Route 8. *Laurent* (closed Sun; Aug), 41 Av. Gabriel; *Fouquet's*, 99 Av. Champs-Élysées; *Auberge de Chamonix* (closed Sun; Aug), 17 Rue Pantieu; *Chiberta*, 3 Rue Arsène-Haussage; *Chez Remo* (closed Sun; Aug), 23 Rue Washington; *Corsair Basque* (closed Sun), 14 Arc de Triomphe.

Route 9. *Grand Vefour*, 17 Rue Beaujolais; *Drouant* (closed 3rd week in Aug), Pl. Gaillon; *La Régence, Hôtel du Louvre*, Pl. du Théâtre Français; *L'Embassy*, 280 Rue St-Honoré; *Chez Dominique*, 3 Rue de l'Echelle; *Au Caveau Montpensier* (closed Sun), 15 Rue Montpensier; *Allience* (closed Sun; July), 18 Rue Vivienne; *Ancien Gauclair* (closed Sun; 25 July–4 Sept), 96 Rue Richelieu; *Chez Nous* (closed Sun), 40 Pl. Marché-St-Honoré.

Route 10. *Grand Comptoir* (closed Sun; July), 24 Rue Pierre-Lescot; *Pharamonde* (closed Sun from Easter to Sept), 24 Rue Grande-Truanderie; *Chez Gabriel* (closed Mon), 123 Rue St-Honoré; *Au Pied de Cochon*, 6 Rue Coquillière; *Lavigne* (closed Sun even.; Mon), 30 Rue Arbre-Sec.

Route 11. *Galan* (closed Sun; 2nd week in Aug), 36 Boul. Henri IV; *Montecatini* (closed Sun), 3 Rue Turenne; *Chez Benoît* (closed Sun; Aug),

20 Rue St-Martin; *Chez Bouysse* (closed Sun from June to Sept), 11bis Rue Jacques-Cœur; *Brasserie Bofinger*, 5 Rue de la Bastille.

Route 12A. *Coconnas* (closed Tues), 2bis Pl. des Vosges; *A l'Enclos de Ninon*, 21 Boul. Beaumarchais.

Route 12B. *Chez l'Ami Louis*, 32 Rue de Vertbois; *Taverne Nicolas Flamel*, 5 Rue Montmorency.

Route 13. *Prunier* (closed Mon; July, Aug), 9 Rue Duphot; *Laverne*, 51 Rue du Faubourg St-Martin; *La Madeleine* (closed Aug), 31 Pl. Madeleine; *Café de la Paix*, 12 Boul. des Capucines; *Aron* (Moroccan), 19 Boul. Montmartre; *La Thermomètre*, 4 Pl. de la République.

Route 14A. *Relais Paris-Est* (closed Sun), Cour d'Honneur (Gare de l'Est: First Floor); *Louis XIV* (closed Tues; June–Sept), 8 Boul. St-Denis; *Au Châteaubriant* (closed Sun; Aug), 23 Rue Chabrol; *Nicolas* (closed Sat; Aug), 12 Rue de la Fidelité; *Brasserie Flo* (closed Sun; Aug), 7 Cours Petites-Écuries.

Route 14B. *A la Mère Catherine*, Pl. du Tertre; *D'Chez Nous à Paris* (closed July), 108 Boul. Rochechouart; *Sanglier Bleu*, 102 Boul. de Clichy; *Merveilles des Mers*, 128 Boul. de Clichy; *Les Bosquets* (closed Fri; Feb), *Relais Normand* (closed Mon), 39 and 32bis Rue Orsel; *La Culbute* (closed Mon; Aug), 41 Rue Lépic.

Route 14C. *Table du Roy* (closed Sun; Aug), 10 Cité d'Antin; *Mayfair* (closed Sun), 5 Rue de la Chaussée d'Antin; *Au Gratin Dauphinoise* (closed Sun), 8 Rue St-Lazare; *Au Petit Riche* (closed Sun; Aug), 25 Rue le Peletier; *Le Helder* (closed Sun), 6 Rue du Helder.

Route 15A. *Cochon d'Or, Dagorno, Bœuf Couronné*, 192, 190 and 188 Av. Jean-Jaurès; *La Biche Egarée* (closed Sun; Aug), 66 Av. Jean-Jaurès.

Route 15B. *Relais des Pyrénées* (closed Sat; Aug), 1 Rue Jourdain; *A Sousceyrac* (closed Sun; Mon from Easter to Whit; Aug), 35 Rue Faideherbe; *Le Relais d'Alsace*, 1 Boul. Voltaire.

Route 15C. *Michel* (closed Tues; Aug), 5 Boul. Soult; *Brasserie Alsacienne, Lyon-Austerlitz*, 5 and 25 Rue de Lyon; *A la Biche au Bois* (closed Tues even), 45 Av. Ledru-Rollin.

Route 16. *Les Marronniers Arago* (closed Sat; 15–31 Aug, 15–28 Feb), 53bis Boul. Arago; *Marty*, 20 Av. Gobelins.

Route 17. *Closerie des Lilas*, 171 Boul. Montparnasse; *Chez Albert* (closed Mon; Aug), 122 Av. Maine; *Clos du Moulin*, 34bis Rue Plantes; *La Coupole*, 102 Boul. Montparnasse; *Chaumière des Gourmets* (closed Sun; Aug), 22 Pl. Denfert-Rochereau; *Commerce* (closed Fri; Aug), 49 Av. Général-Leclerc; *Mon Pays*, 49 Av. Jean-Moulin; *Jean Robic* (closed Sun; Aug), 61 Av. Maine.

Route 18. *Maisonette Russe*, 6 Rue d'Armaillé; *La Truite* (closed Sun; Aug), 30 Faubourg St-Honoré; *Bras. Lorraine*, 2 Pl. des Ternes; *Les Grillades*, 277 Boul. Péreire; *Paris-Bar* (closed Aug), 20 Av. Neuilly; *Au Fin Gourmet*, 46 Rue Sablonville.

Route 19. *Prunier-Traktir* (closed Mon), 16 Av. Victor-Hugo; *Relais du Bois* (closed Mon), 9 Rue Faisanderie.—*La Grande Cascade, Pavillon Royal Pav. d'Armenonville*, these three in the Bois, and not cheap.

Within the last few years many **'Self-Service' Restaurants** have sprung up all over Paris (near the Opéra, the Place du Théâtre-Français, in the Champs-Élysées, in the Boul. St-Michel, etc.); these provide a quick and cheap meal (c. 6 fr.) and the bill is paid at the cashier's desk on leaving. A list of inexpensive eating-places entitled '400 Restaurants in Paris' can be obtained free of charge from the French Tourist Office.—The *Maisons du Café*, at the Place de l'Opéra and elsewhere, are convenient for light refreshment (excellent coffee).

...ne thousand cafés of Paris are distributed all over the city, but are ...erous on the Boulevards, near the railway stations, and in the larger ...Some of them provide music in the afternoon and evening, and in most ...tables and chairs are set out on the pavement in front (the 'terrasse'), ...e the customer may spend a pleasant hour in watching the passers-by. ...e coffee, beer, liqueurs, and other beverages supplied are generally of good ...uality. Café nature or café crème is served both in cups and in glasses. Café filtre served in a glass or cup with a percolator is of better quality, but is now being ousted by the 'espresso'. A mazagran is a glass of iced coffee. The usual order for beer is for a bock or a demi. Customers should not pay the waiter after each drink, but wait until they wish to leave. It is cheaper to stand at the bar, but the price is automatically raised if one subsequently takes a seat. In either case a tip must be left.

In all cafés, 'petit déjeuner' may be obtained in the morning, consisting of coffee or chocolate, rolls or 'croissants', and butter. French tea-making leaves much to be desired, and travellers are advised to limit themselves to the coffee and chocolate, both of which are excellent. Given below are the names of a few of the better-known cafés.

NEAR THE OPÉRA AND GRANDS BOULEVARDS

Café de la Paix, 12 Boul. des Capucines; **Royal Capucines**, 24 Boul. des Capucines; **Viel**, 8 Boul. de la Madeleine; **Queenie, Weber**, Rue Royale; **Cardinal**, 1 Boul. des Italiens; **Napolitain**, 1 Boul. des Capucines.

NEAR THE LOUVRE

Café de l'Univers, La Régence, Place du Théâtre-Français; **Café du Louvre**, Place du Palais-Royal.

NEAR THE CHAMPS-ÉLYSÉES AND ÉTOILE

Le Colisée, 44 Av. des Champs-Élysées; **Le Marignan**, 33 Av. des Champs-Élysées; **Grande Taverne**, 21 Av. des Champs-Élysées; **Le Sélect**, 100 Av. des Champs-Élysées; **Monte Carlo**, 9 Av. de Wagram.

IN MONTPARNASSE

Closerie des Lilas, 171 Boul. du Montparnasse; **Le Dôme**, 108 Boul. du Montparnasse; **Coupole**, 102 Boul. du Montparnasse.

IN MONTMARTRE

Wepler, 14 Place de Clichy; **Les Pierrots**, 18 Boul. de Clichy.

IN THE LATIN QUARTER

Capoulade, 63 Boul. St-Michel; **Café de Flore**, 172 Boul. St-Germain; **Deux Magots**, 170 Boul. St-Germain; **Cluny**, 20 Boul. St-Michel.

NEAR THE GARES DU NORD AND DE L'EST

Taverne des Flandres, 8 Boul. de Denain; **Ducastaing**, 4 Boul. de Denain.

NEAR THE GARE ST-LAZARE

Mollard, 115 Rue St-Lazare; **Garnier**, 111 Rue St-Lazare.

Tea Rooms. Afternoon tea in the English style is highly popular, the usual hour being between 5 and 6. *A la Marquise de Sévigné*, 11 Boul. de la Madeleine and 62 Champs-Élysées; *Colombin*, 4 Rue Cambon; *Ixe Opéra*, 6 Rue Halévy; *Royalty*, 35 Av. des Champs-Élysées (Rue Marignan); *English Tea Room* (over Smith's bookshop), 248 Rue de Rivoli; *Kardomah*, 184 Rue de Rivoli.

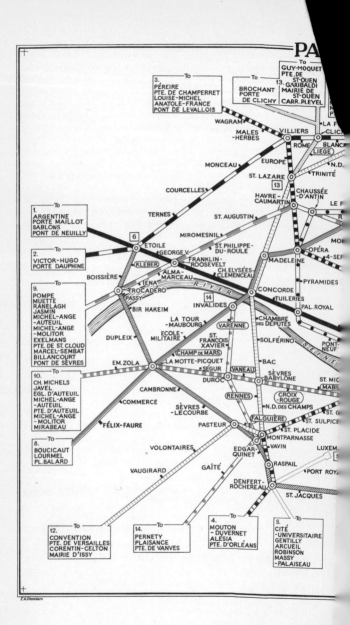

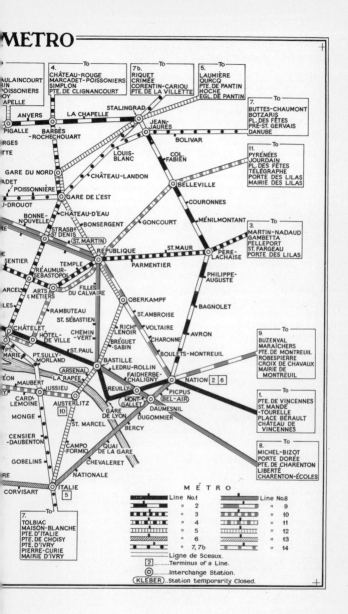

METRO

To 4. CHÂTEAU-ROUGE / MARCADET-POISSONIERS / SIMPLON / PTE. DE CLIGNANCOURT

To 7b. RIQUET / CRIMÉE / CORENTIN-CARIOU / PTE. DE LA VILLETTE

To 5. LAUMIÈRE / OURCQ / PTE. DE PANTIN / HOCHE / ÉGL. DE PANTIN

To 7. BUTTES-CHAUMONT / BOTZARIS / PL. DES FÊTES / PRÉ-ST. GERVAIS / DANUBE

To 11. PYRÉNÉES / JOURDAIN / PL. DES FÊTES / TÉLÉGRAPHE / PORTE DES LILAS / MAIRIE DES LILAS

To 3. MARTIN-NADAUD / GAMBETTA / PELLEPORT / ST. FARGEAU / PORTE DES LILAS

To 9. BUZENVAL / MARAÎCHERS / PTE. DE MONTREUIL / ROBESPIERRE / CROIX DE CHAVAUX / MAIRIE DE MONTREUIL

To 1. PTE. DE VINCENNES / ST. MANDÉ-TOURELLE / PLACE BÉRAULT / CHÂTEAU DE VINCENNES

To 8. MICHEL-BIZOT / PORTE DORÉE / PTE. DE CHARENTON / LIBERTÉ / CHARENTON-ÉCOLES

To 7. TOLBIAC / MAISON-BLANCHE / PTE. D'ITALIE / PTE. DE CHOISY / PTE. D'IVRY / PIERRE-CURIE / MAIRIE D'IVRY

AULAINCOURT / RIN / POISSONIERS / OY / APELLE / ANVERS / LA CHAPELLE / STALINGRAD / PIGALLE / BARBÈS-ROCHECHOUART / JEAN-JAURÈS / BOLIVAR / RGES / TTE / LOUIS-BLANC / COL.FABIEN / GARE DU NORD / ADET / POISSONNIÈRE / CHÂTEAU-LANDON / BELLEVILLE / J-DROUOT / GARE DE L'EST / COURONNES / BONNE-NOUVELLE / CHÂTEAU-D'EAU / BONSERGENT / GONCOURT / MÉNILMONTANT / RE / STRASB.-ST DENIS / (ST. MARTIN) / ST. MAUR / PÈRE-LACHAISE / SENTIER / RÉPUBLIQUE / PARMENTIER / TEMPLE / RÉAUMUR-SÉBASTOPOL / PHILIPPE-AUGUSTE / ARCEL / ARTS & MÉTIERS / FILLES DU CALVAIRE / LES / OBERKAMPF / RAMBUTEAU / ST. AMBROISE / BAGNOLET / ST. SÉBASTIEN / CHÂTELET / HÔTEL-DE-VILLE / CHEMIN-VERT / RICH.-LENOIR / VOLTAIRE / PT. MARIE / ST. PAUL / BRÉGUET-SABIN / CHARONNE / AVRON / PT. SULLY-MORLAND / BOULETS-MONTREUIL / ÉON / MAUBERT / (ARSENAL) / LA RAPÉE / BASTILLE / LEDRU-ROLLIN / FAIDHERBE-CHALIGNY / NATION 2 6 / Y / JUSSIEU / REUILLY / PICPUS / CARD.-LEMOINE / AUSTERLITZ 10 / MONT-GALLET / (BEL-AIR) / MONGE / GARE DE LYON / DAUMESNIL / CENSIER-DAUBENTON / ST. MARCEL / DUGOMMIER / CAMPO-FORMIO / BERCY / GOBELINS / QUAI DE LA GARE / RE / CHEVALERET / NATIONALE / CORVISART / ITALIE 5

MÉTRO

▬▬▬	Line No.1	▬▬▬	Line No.8
▬■▬■	" 2	▬▬▬	" 9
■■■■	" 3	▬■▬■	" 10
▬●▬●	" 4	■■■■	" 11
▥▥▥	" 5	▥▥▥	" 12
▨▨▨	" 6	▤▤▤	" 13
●▬●▬	" 7, 7b	▬●▬●	" 14

Ligne de Sceaux.
2 ....Terminus of a Line.
◎ ....Interchange Station.
(KLÉBER)..Station temporarily Closed.

IV CONVEYANCES

Taxis. Present charge 1,50 fr. on hiring, then 0,58 fr. per km. (day rates) or 0,85 fr. per km. (night rates: 11 p.m.–6.30 a.m.), plus 0,10 fr. for each small suitcase, 0,20 fr. for a large case or trunk. Extra charges for the Bois or to race-courses. Drivers expect a tip of 15–20 per cent.

PRIVATE MOTOR CARS can be hired through any of the larger tourist agencies.

Public Transport. All the motor-buses and the underground railway (Métro) in Paris are controlled by the R.A.T.P., 53ter Quai des Grands-Augustins. From their *Information Office* (open 8–8), Place de la Madeleine, may be obtained an excellent free leaflet ('Paris et sa Banlieue par Autobus/Métro') showing diagrammatically the routes of both services; also a leaflet in English ('Paris by Métro and by Bus') explaining how to use both (buying tickets, bus queue system, etc.). A 7-day 'Billet de Tourisme' (20 fr.), available for unlimited travel on buses and Métro, may be bought at S.N.C.F. offices abroad or at R.A.T.P. headquarters.

MOTOR-BUSES. Stops, which are now all 'request stops' ('arrêt facultatif'), are indicated by green placards showing the numbers and destinations. During the 'rush hours' (8–9 a.m., 12–2 p.m., and 5.30–7.30) it is essential to take a 'numéro d'ordre' (a numbered queue ticket) from the apparatus at the bus-stop, in order to establish one's position in the queue. A notice with the word 'complet' means that a bus is full. The normal service runs between 6 a.m. and 9 p.m. Tickets cost 0,25 fr. each, but it is cheaper to buy a 'carnet' of twenty tickets (3,70 fr.). The number of tickets required from fare-stage to fare-stage is indicated on a little map in the interior of the bus, but passengers should state their destination to the conductor, and in order to avoid any mis-understanding the 'carnet' should be presented to the conductor on each journey. Smoking is forbidden.

The MÉTRO provides a cheap and fairly rapid method of transit. The stations, almost uniformly 500 metres ($\frac{1}{3}$ m.) apart, are reached mainly by long staircases, and access to platforms is controlled by automatic barriers as the trains arrive. Trains run at intervals of 2–8 min. from 5.30 to 1.15 a.m. The halts are very brief and there is frequent overcrowding. The fares (1st cl. 0,85 fr., 2nd cl. 0,55 fr.) are the same for any distance, including all necessary changes. 'Carnets' of ten tickets are on sale at all booking offices (1st cl. 5,60 fr., 2nd cl. 3,70 fr.), and it is cheaper and more convenient to buy a carnet rather than a 'billet simple'.

The various lines of the Métro are called by the names of their terminal stations (e.g. Ligne 1, Vincennes-Neuilly) and the direction of the trains (which keep to the right) is indicated by a placard with the name of the terminus. The connecting passages at ex-change stations are indicated by an orange-lighted sign 'Correspondance', followed by the terminal station of the connecting line (e.g. Correspondance Clignancourt).

Fares on the *Ligne de Sceaux* (connecting with the Métro at Denfert-Rochereau) are not covered by one price, and visitors should state their destination at the ticket office. Smoking is not forbidden on this line, as it is in the Métro.

Motor Coaches. During the season, the *Régie Autonome des Transports Parisiens* (R.A.T.P.) organizes drives (Sun and holidays) to Malmaison, Fontainebleau, Versailles, etc. Full particulars may be obtained from the Bureau des Excursions in the Place de la Madeleine (opp. Nos. 18–20; tel. ANJou 31–18) or at 53bis Quai des Grands-Augustins (tel. DANton 98–50). It is advisable to book seats in advance. Many of the tourist agencies run daily trips to the numerous historic and picturesque spots around Paris, and coach tours to view the floodlighting start nightly in summer c. 9.30 from the Place de l'Opéra, the Madeleine, the Champs-Élysées, etc. Visitors who wish to strike out on their own should take full advantage of the services (from 100 km. to 200 km. outside Paris) run by the following firms:

Transports Citroën (14 Rue de Lubeck): coaches to Mantes, Beauvais, Compiègne, Chantilly, etc.

Cars Renault (149 Rue Oberkampf): coaches to Compiègne, Chantilly, Senlis, Fontainebleau, Orléans, etc.

The principal coach stations are at the Porte Maillot, the Rotonde de la Villette (Pl. Stalingrad), and the Place de la Bastille. Other services start from the Place d'Italie and the Porte de St-Cloud.

River Steamers. The regular passenger services on the Seine have not been revived since the war, but 'Les Bateaux Mouches' run pleasure trips for visitors at frequent intervals during the summer months, once or twice every afternoon in winter. The embarkation point is on the right bank between the Pont de l'Alma (car entrance) and the Pont des Invalides. Full particulars can be obtained from the offices at the Port de la Conférence (Pont de l'Alma).

In addition, motor-launches holding c. 60 passengers make trips on the river hourly or more often in summer starting from the Pont d'Iéna (left bank), and (afternoon only) from the Port de l'Hôtel-de-Ville.

V   POSTAL AND OTHER SERVICES

Postal Information

The postal rates given below are those in force in Aug 1967 and are subject to alteration.

	IN FRANCE	ABROAD
LETTERS	0,30 fr. per 20 gr.	0,60 fr. per 20 gr.
POST CARDS	0,25 fr.	0,40 fr.; 0,25 fr. for 5 words or under
TELEGRAMS	3,24 fr. up to 10 words	4,86 fr. per word for Great Britain
	0,35 fr. for every extra word	

* Letters for Canada, Belgium, Luxembourg, and Italy are subject to the inland rate.

The General Post Office in Paris is the *Hôtel des Postes* at 48–52 Rue du Louvre. Post offices are open on weekdays from 8 a.m. to 7 p.m. (4 on Sat); but are closed on Sundays, except for one office in each arrondissement which remains open until 11 a.m. The offices at the Bourse and at 103 Rue de Grenelle are open permanently (day and night) for telegrams, etc. Correspondence marked 'poste restante' may be addressed to any post office, and is handed to the addressee on proof of identity (passport preferable) and payment of a fee of 0,30 fr. for each letter, 0,15 fr. for each newspaper.

REGISTRATION. Letters may be registered ('recommandé') for a fee of 1 fr. in addition to the postage. Registered letters are not delivered without proof of identity.

AIR MAIL. For most European countries only ordinary postage is needed, exceptions include Austria, Germany, Greece, and Portugal, for which an additional 0,20 fr. is charged. For all letters of more than 20 gr. an additional 0,20 fr. per 20 gr. is charged; to the U.S.A. 0,35 fr. additional to postage per 5 gr.; to other parts of the world various charges in proportion.

LETTER-BOXES, always formerly painted blue, are now appearing in yellow.—Postage stamps are on sale at most tobacconists' shops.

Telegrams. Full information is available at any post office.—PNEUMATIQUES. For messages within Paris and certain suburbs letters and 'cartes télégrammes', transmitted by pneumatic tubes, are much cheaper than telegrams and almost as quick. They should be posted in the special letter-boxes marked 'pneumatiques' (last collection c. 7.30 p.m.).

Telephones. Public call offices are found at nearly all post offices, Métro stations, cafés, and restaurants. A 'jeton' (0,40 fr.; from the Métro booking office, etc.) is inserted in the box instead of coins; should the number be engaged, the jeton may be recovered by replacing the receiver. At post offices the number required is given (preferably in writing) to an employee who will establish the connection. Paris has telephonic communication (including S.T.D.) with all parts of the British Isles and reversed-charge calls ('P.V.C.') are accepted.

Information Bureaux

The *Comité de Tourisme de Paris*, 7 Rue Balzac, 8e (open daily 9 a.m. to midnight), has a 'Welcome' Information Office (Bureau d'Accueil), with a most helpful English-speaking staff, for all general information concerning Paris, including hotel reservations (tel. ÉLYsées 52–78), lecture-tours, etc. Other Welcome Offices, attached to which are the 'hôtesses de Paris', in their blue uniform, are at the Aérogare, the Gare de l'Est (arrival hall), the Gare de Lyon (exit of the Grandes Lignes), Gare du Nord, and Gare St-Lazare (these two on the international arrival platform).

The *Bureau d'Information* of the Commissariat Général au Tourisme, 8 Av. de l'Opéra (9–12, 1.30–6.30; closed on Sun) supplies the fullest and most authoritative answers to visitors' travel problems. A railway booking and information office is in the same hall. There is another office of the French Railways at 16 Boul. des Capucines.

The office of the *Accueil de Paris* at the Hôtel de Ville is open Mon–Fri 9–12, 2.30–6, Sat 9–12.

Tourist Agents. *Wagons-Lits/Cook*, 14 Rue Guichard, 62 Rue du Bac, 14 Boul. des Capucines, 91 Champs-Élysées; *American Express*, 11 Rue Scribe; *Poly-Tours*, 26 Rue de la Pépinière; *Bennett's*, 4 Rue Scribe; *Le Tourisme Français*, 50 Rue de Châteaudun, and 96 Rue de la Victoire; *Cie. Française de Tourisme*, 14 Boul. de la Madeleine.

British Railways, 12 Boul. de la Madeleine; *British Travel Centre*, 6 Place Vendôme.

VI AMUSEMENTS

Useful and topical information about theatres, cinemas, cabarets, restaurants, night clubs, and sport, are given in 'L'Officiel des Spectacles' (0,50 fr.) and 'Allo Paris' and 'Une Semaine de Paris' (these two 0,80 fr.), published every Wednesday, from all book-stalls and most tourist agents.

Theatres. In most of the Paris theatres performances are given nightly, starting about 8.30 to 9 and finishing about 11.45. Except at the height of summer, matinée performances are given on Sundays, and sometimes on Thursdays, starting at 2.30 to 3, and finishing about 5.30. Nearly all the big theatres close for some weeks in the summer and most theatres are closed on one evening every week (usually Mon or Tues). The best seats are the 'fauteuils d'orchestre' or stalls, and next come the 'fauteuils de balcon' (dress circle) and the 'loges de face'. The side seats should be avoided. Seats may be booked in advance either at the theatre box-office (generally open for booking 11–6.30 or 7) or through theatrical agencies (14 Boul. Madeleine; 14 Rue de Castiglione; 16 Rue de la Paix; 52 or 116 Champs-Élysées; etc.). Tickets bought at an agency are more expensive than those bought at the theatre. Official programme sellers and usherettes expect to be tipped. Smoking is forbidden in theatres.

The OPÉRA, the most famous house of entertainment in Paris, stages performances of opera and ballet on Sun, Mon, Wed, Fri, and Sat (matinée on Sun during the season). The box-office is open 11–6.30, Sun 11–12. At the OPÉRA-COMIQUE, Place Boïeldieu, similar performances are given on Sun, Wed, Thurs, Fri, and Sat (matinée on Sun), the distinction between the repertories of the two being quite conventional and arbitrary. Box-office open 11–6.30, Sun 10–1.

In addition to these two national 'lyric' theatres, there are four 'théâtres subventionnés' or state-subsidized theatres in Paris. By far the most famous is the COMÉDIE FRANÇAISE or THÉÂTRE FRANÇAIS, which stages performances nightly (matinées on Thurs and Sun). Both this theatre and the THÉÂTRE DE L'ODÉON or THÉÂTRE DE FRANCE, in the Place de l'Odéon, stage classics and the works of modern playwrights. The THÉÂTRE NATIONAL POPULAIRE, in the Palais de Chaillot, is used for many sorts of performance, including concerts, ballet, and films; and the THÉÂTRE DE L'EST PARISIEN also has a varied repertory of the arts.

The following is an alphabetical list of the other principal theatres:

AMBASSADEURS, 1 Av. Gabriel
AMBIGU, 2ter Boul. St-Martin
ANTOINE, 14 Boul. de Strasbourg
ARTS, 66 Rue Rochechouart
ATELIER, Place Charles Dullin
ATHENÉE, 24 Rue Caumartin
AUJOURD'HUI, 101 Boul. Raspail
BOUFFES-PARISIENS, 4 Rue Monsigny
CAPUCINES, 39 Boul. des Capucines
CHAMPS-ÉLYSÉES, 15 Av. Montaigne
CHARLES DE ROCHEFORT, 64 Rue du Rocher
CHÂTELET, Place du Châtelet
COMÉDIE DES CHAMPS-ÉLYSÉES, 15 Av. Montaigne
DAUNOU, 7 Rue Daunou
GAÎTÉ-MONTPARNASSE, 24 Rue de la Gaîté
GRAMONT, 30 Rue Gramont
GRAND-GUIGNOL, 20bis Rue Chaptal
GYMNASE, 38 Boul. Bonne Nouvelle
HÉBERTOT, 78bis Boul. des Batignolles
HUCHETTE, 23 Rue de la Huchette
LA BRUYÈRE, 5 Rue La Bruyère
MADELEINE, 19 Rue de Surène
MARIGNY, Av. de Marigny
MATHURINS, 36 Rue des Mathurins
MICHEL, 38 Rue des Mathurins
MICHODIÈRE, 4bis Rue de la Michodière
MOGADOR, 25 Rue de Mogador
MONCEAU, 16 Rue de Monceau
MONTPARNASSE, 31 Rue de la Gaîté
NOUVEAUTÉS, 24 Boul. Poissonnière
ŒUVRE, 55 Rue de Clichy
PALAIS-ROYAL, 38 Rue Montpensier
DE PARIS, 15 Rue Blanche
PIGALLE, 10 Rue Pigalle
DE POCHE, 75 Boul. Montparnasse
PORTE-ST-MARTIN, 16 Boul. St-Martin
POTINIÈRE, 7 Rue Louis-le-Grand
RÉCAMIER, Rue Récamier (Sèvres-Babylone)
RENAISSANCE, 20 Boul. St-Martin
ST-GEORGES, 51 Rue St-Georges
SARAH-BERNHARDT, Place du Châtelet
STUDIO DES CHAMPS-ÉLYSÉES, 13 Av. Montaigne
TERTRE, 81 Rue Lepic
THÉÂTRE EN ROND, 2 Rue Frochot (Pl. Pigalle)
VARIÉTÉS, 7 Boul. Montmartre
VIEUX-COLOMBIER, 21 Rue du Vieux-Colombier

Music Halls and **Chansonniers** are numerous and vary in character. Clever variety turns may be seen at the former, but many of them are devoted to revues of no very refined nature. The latter have an amusing enough atmosphere, but the visitor should have a very sound knowledge of French in order to appreciate them fully. Smoking is permitted.

BOBINO, 20 Rue de la Gaîté; CASINO DE PARIS, 16 Rue de Clichy; FOLIES-BERGERE, 32 Rue Richer; LIDO (diner-dansant), 78 Champs-Élysées; MAYOL, 10 Rue de l'Echiquier; OLYMPIA, 28 Boul. des Capucines.

Chansonniers. CAVEAU DE LA RÉPUBLIQUE, COUCOU, 1 and 33 Boul. St-Martin; DEUX ANES, 100 Boul. de Clichy; DIX HEURES, 36 Boul. de Clichy; the last two specializing in political satire.

Cabarets and Night-Clubs. The charge for refreshments at these is apt to increase with the price of the seat. The announcement of 'free admission' (entrée libre) at some simply means that the price of admission is added to the charge for 'consommations' which the visitor is expected to order.

Cabarets of all kinds, presenting more or less artistic performances, with refreshments at high prices and usually with facilities for dancing, exist in large numbers in and around the Place Pigalle, and near the Champs-Élysées. The 'Cabarets Artistiques' and 'Caveaux', many of which are highly topical in their shows, are to be found in Montmartre and more frequently in the region of St-Germain-des-Prés; in the latter district the 'Caves Existentialistes' are less frequented than formerly. Full lists of the best of these entertainments can be found in the 'Semaine de Paris', 'Allo Paris', etc.

Cinemas are numerous in all parts of Paris, and performances (often in English) run continuously from about 2 p.m. Smoking is not allowed, and visitors should tip the usherette who shows them to their seats. Full particulars (with convenient Métro stations) of the various shows are given in the 'Semaine de Paris', etc.

Other Entertainments. The following varied places of entertainment are generally open to visitors to Paris.

The MUSÉE GRÉVIN, 10 Boul. Montmartre, the Paris Madame Tussaud's, has admirable waxwork groups and portraits (open 2–6, Sat and Sun 2–10).—The PALAIS DE GLACE, Champs-Élysées (winter only) has a skating rink, buffet bar, etc.—The CIRQUE DE MONTMARTRE (62 Boul. Rochechouart) and the CIRQUE D'HIVER (Place Pasdeloup, Boul. du Temple) both give excellent circus performances.

Art Exhibitions. The chief annual art exhibitions in Paris are the *Salon de la Société Nationale des Beaux Arts et des Artistes Français* (the 'Salon' par excellence) and the *Salon d'Automne*, held in the Grand Palais (Champs-Élysées) in June and October respectively; the *Salon des Indépendants*, held in the Grand Palais in April; and the *Salon des Humoristes*, at 11 Rue Royale, in April. Other exhibitions are held at the Palais de New York (Musée d'Art Moderne), the Petit-Palais, the Musée des Arts Decoratifs, etc.

Smaller art shows are held at various galleries and picture-dealers' shops, mostly in and near the Faubourg St-Honoré, and on the left bank near the Rue Bonaparte and Rue de Seine.

Foreign artists in Paris should take full advantage of the *Maison des Artistes*, 11 Rue Berryer, which is run by a group of French artists willing to help and co-operate with newcomers to Parisian artistic circles.

Music. Particulars of concerts, etc., will be found in the weekly publications of 'Opéra' and 'Le Guide du Concert', as well as in the 'Semaine de Paris'. The following societies give regular weekly concerts of classical music on Sat and Sun, all starting at 5.45 p.m.

Société des Concerts du Conservatoire, at the Théâtre des Champs-Élysées. Sun.

Concerts Colonne, at the Théâtre du Châtelet. Sun.

Concerts Pasdeloup, at various concert halls (Salle Pleyel, 22 Rue Rochechouart; Palais de Chaillot, etc.). Sun.

Concerts Lamoureux, at the Salle Pleyel and the Salle Gaveau, 45 Rue La Boétie.

Performances are arranged at intervals by *Les Amis de la Musique de Chambre* at the Comédie des Champs-Élysées.

Occasional concerts are also given at the Salle Cortot, 78 Rue Cardinet; at the Salle Schola Cantorum, 269 Rue St-Jacques; and at the Salles Chopin and Debussy at 8 Rue Daru.

Excellent CHURCH MUSIC can be heard at the Madeleine, St-Eustache, St-François-Xavier, St-Merry, St-Roch, St-Séverin, St-Sulpice, and Notre-Dame.

Sports and Games. The visitor to Paris at the proper season has many opportunities of seeing interesting sporting events and competitions, a few particulars of which are given below. All the various sporting clubs in France are grouped under one *Comité National des Sports* (headquarters, 4 Rue d'Argenson, 8e).

Athletics are governed by the *Fédération Française d'Athlétisme*, 32 Boul. Haussmann, 9e. The *Paris University Club* ('Puc'), 11 Rue Soufflot, 5e, the *Racing Club de Paris*, 81 Rue Ampère, 17e, the *Racing Club de France*, 5 Rue Eblé, 7e, and the *Club Athlétique des Sports Généraux*, Stade Jean-Bouin, Av. du Général-Sarrail, Pte d'Auteuil, all have their own football and 'rugger' grounds, tennis courts, etc.

Billiards. Good tables are to be found at the *Académie de Billard*, 47 Av. de Wagram, 17e, the *Académie de Billard de la Place Clichy*, 84 Rue de Clichy, 9e, and the *Billard Palace*, 3 Boul. des Capucines, 2e.

Boxing. Information from the *Fédération Française de Boxe*, 62 Rue Nollet, 17e; matches take place at the *Palais de Glace* in the Champs-Élysées, and also at the *Salle Wagram*, 39 Av. de Wagram.

Cycling is governed by the *Fédération Française de Cyclisme*, 1 Rue Ambroise-Thomas, 9e, and the *Fédération Française de Cyclo-Tourisme*, 66 Rue René Boulanger, 10e. The chief cycling tracks in Paris are: *Vélodrome Municipal* (Bois de Vincennes), *Vélodrome du Parc des Princes* (between Pte de St-Cloud and Pte d'Auteuil), and *Palais des Sports* (near Porte de Versailles).

Fencing. Public exhibitions are organized by the *Fédération Française d'Escrime*, 13 Rue de Londres, 9e, and the *Cercle Hoche*, 22 Rue Daru, 8e.

Football. Rugby and Association matches are played in winter in the *Parc des Princes* in the Bois de Boulogne, at *Colombes* (Rue François Faber), at the *Faisanderie* in the Park of St-Cloud, etc. Students at the Sorbonne who wish to play Rugby should apply to the office of the *Paris University Club*, 11 Rue Soufflot (3rd floor, right-hand door).

Golf. An introduction is necessary in order to play on any of the courses mentioned below; information from the *Fédération Française du Golf*, 9 Rue de Miromesnil, 8e. The *Racing Club de France* has an excellent course (18 holes) at La Boulie, near Versailles. There are also courses at St-Cloud, Chantilly (two), Fontainebleau, St-Germain-en-Laye, Marly, Morfontaine, Ozoir-la-Ferrière (beyond Vincennes), and Compiègne.

Horse-Racing in France is governed by the *Fédération Française des Sports Equestres* (6 Rue Lauriston, 16e). The racing season lasts from February to December. The chief meetings are held in the spring at Longchamp and Auteuil, and attract large numbers of fashionable spectators. Bookmaking in France is prohibited by law, and betting can be conducted only through P.M.U. offices of the official 'Pari-Mutuel' or totalizator, which deducts a percentage of its gross receipts for the Société d'Encouragement (see below) and for the poor. The following are the recognized societies, with the race-meetings they control. *Société d'Encouragement pour l'Amélioration des Races*, 11 Rue du Cirque, 8e (Longchamp, Chantilly); *Soc. d'Encouragement à l'Elevage*, 7 Rue d'Astorg, 8e (Vincennes); *Soc. des Steeple-Chases*, 137 Fg St-Honoré, 8e (Auteuil); *Soc. Sportive d'Encouragement*, 133 Fg St-Honoré, 8e (Enghien, Maisons-Laffite, St-Cloud); *Soc. du Sport de France*, 7 Rue Louis-Murat, 8e (Le Tremblay).

The following is a list of the principal racecourses with the chief meetings.

LONGCHAMP (flat-races). Meetings in spring, from the 1st Sun in April; in June, with the Grand Prix de Paris on the last Sunday; in October, with the Prix de l'Arc de Triomphe and the Prix du Conseil Municipal.

AUTEUIL (steeplechases). Meetings in spring, including (April) the Prix du Président de la République (2nd Sun); in summer, including the Grand Steeple-Chase d'Auteuil, on the Sun before the Grand Prix; and in Oct–Dec.

CHANTILLY (flat-races). Meetings on the first two Sun in June, with the Prix de Diane and the Prix du Jockey-Club (the French 'Derby'); and in September.

Other race-meetings are held at *St-Cloud, Vincennes* (Prix du Président de la République in mid-June), *Maisons-Laffitte, Enghien*, and *Le Tremblay* (near Joinville-le-Pont, beyond Vincennes).

Lawn Tennis. The organizing society of tennis clubs is the *Fédération Française du Lawn-Tennis*, 3 Rue Volney, 2e. The *Racing Club de France*, 154 Rue de Saussure, 17e, runs a tennis club with its own courts, etc. For the numerous public courts, apply to the Syndicat d'Initiative.—Davis Cup and other important matches are played at the *Stade Roland-Garros*, just beyond the Porte d'Auteuil, or at the *Stade Pierre-de-Coubertin* (Pte de St-Cloud).

Motor Racing. The principal motor-racing track is at Linas near Montlhéry (Paris office, 26 Rue de la Pépinière).

Polo. The *Société de Polo* (84 Rue Lauriston) has a ground at Bagatelle in the Bois de Boulogne. The season opens in the first week of May.

Riding. Horses may be hired from the following riding schools: *Ecole d'Equitation Manège Pellier*, Jardin d'Acclimatation, Bois de Boulogne; *Manège Macaire, Manège Dabbadie*, 72 and 78 Rue de Longchamp (Neuilly); *Manège Dassonville*, 5 Rue Leroux; *Manège Howlett*, 37 Rue de la Ferme (Neuilly); *Manège du Tattersall Français*, 26 Rue Jacques-Dulud (Neuilly).—Horse show in May at the *Cercle de l'Étrier*, Bois de Boulogne; later in the same month and in Oct at Fontainebleau.

Rowing and Sailing. Rowing boats may be hired at most of the riverside resorts near Paris on the Seine and the Marne, the principal centres being Asnières, Argenteuil, Chatou (on the Seine below Paris), Joinville-le-Pont, and Nogent (on the Marne); for sailing the centres are Dammarie (on the Seine, near Melun), L'Isle-Adam (on the Oise), and Vaires (on the Marne). The leading rowing and yachting societies are the *Yacht Club de France* and *Fédération Française du Yachting* (both at 82 Boul. Haussmann); *Fédération Française des Sociétés d'Aviron* (93 Rue St-Lazare).

Swimming. The *Fédération Française de Natation* (20 Rue de la Chaussée d'Antin) is the controlling body of this sport. Among the covered public baths are the following: *La Jonquière*, 79 Rue de la Jonquière, 17e; *Pontoise-St-Germain*, 19 Rue de Pontoise, 5e; *Amiraux*, 6 Rue Hermann-la-Chapelle, 18e; *La Butte-aux-Cailles*, 5 Place Paul-Verlaine, 13e; *Ledru-Rollin*, 8 Av. Ledru-Rollin, 11e; *Orléans*, Av. du Gen. Leclerc, 14e. *Auteuil-Molitor* has both an open-air and a covered pool at Pte d'Auteuil. Other open-air pools by the Seine are: *Royal*, Quai des Tuileries, 1er; and *Deligny*, 25 Quai Anatole-France, 7e. Championships are decided at the *Stade Nautique Georges-Vallerey*, near the Porte des Lilas (Métro 3 or 11).

VII USEFUL ADDRESSES

Directories. Any required address may be turned up in the *Annuaire du Commerce Didot-Bottin* ('*Le Bottin*'), a large work in five volumes of which the first two deal with Paris. This may be consulted at post offices, hotels, restaurants, cafés, shops, etc. (notices are usually displayed: 'Ici on consulte le Bottin'). Residential and official addresses may be found also in the *Bottin Mondain*, which gives in addition particulars about theatres (plans and prices), and other amusements, etc.

Embassies and Consulates

GREAT BRITAIN. Embassy and Consulate, 35 and 37 Rue du Faubourg St-Honoré, 8e.

UNITED STATES. Embassy and Consulate, 2 Av. Gabriel, 8e.

AUSTRALIA. Embassy and Consulate, 14 Rue Las-Cases, 7e.

CANADA. Embassy, 35 Av. Montaigne, 8e.—Visa Office, 38 Av. de l'Opéra, 1er.

INDIA. Embassy and Consulate, 15 Rue Alfred-Dehodencq, 16e.

PAKISTAN. Embassy and Consulate, 18 Rue Lord-Byron, 8e.

SOUTH AFRICA. Embassy and Consulate, 51 Av. Hoche, 8e.

IRELAND, Republic of. Embassy, 12 Av. Foch, 16e.

English Churches. EPISCOPAL. *British Embassy Church*, 5 Rue d'Aguesseau. —*St George's*, 7 Rue Aug.-Vacquerie.—*Holy Trinity* (American Pro-Cathedral), 23 Av. George-V.—*American Church*, 65 Quai d'Orsay.—*Church of Scotland*, 17 Rue Bayard.—*Congregational Chapel*, 48 Rue de Lille.—*Methodist Chapel*, 4 Rue Roquépine.—*Society of Friends*, 114 Rue de Vaugirard, 5e.—*First Church of Christ Scientist*, 10 Av. d'Iéna.—*Second Church of Christ Scientist*, 58 Boul. Flandrin.—*Third Church of Christ Scientist*, 45 Rue La Boétie.— *Salvation Army* (Armée du Salut), 76 Rue de Rome.—*St Joseph's* (R.C.) *Church*, 50 Av. Hoche.

Banks. Most of the French banks have numerous branches throughout the city. All banks are open 9–12 and 2–4 from Mon to Fri; most banks close on Sat morning but many central branches of the principal banks (including the British banks, see below) have a 'bureau de change' open from 9 to 12. At the main-line stations 'bureaux de change' are open daily 6 or 6.30 a.m. to 10 p.m. (Austerlitz 7.30 a.m.–11.30 p.m.) and at the Aérogare from 6 a.m. to midnight.

BRITISH BANKS. *Barclay's*, 33 Rue du Quatre-Septembre; *Lloyds*, 43 Boul. des Capucines; *Westminster*, 18 Place Vendôme; *Royal Bank of Canada*, Rue Scribe; *Martin's*, 17bis Boul. Haussmann.

AMERICAN BANKS. *Chase Manhattan*, 41 Rue Cambon; *Guaranty Trust*, 4 Place de la Concorde; *Morgan's*, 14 Place Vendôme; *First National City Bank of New York*, 60 Av. des Champs-Élysées.

CHAMBERS OF COMMERCE. *British*, 6 Rue Halévy.—*American*, 21 Av. George-V.

Clubs. Admission to the social clubs of Paris is, as might be expected, obtained only on the introduction of a member. The following are the addresses of some larger French institutions of which foreigners may become members without undue formality.

Automobile Club de France, 6 Place de la Concorde; *Club Alpin Français*, 7 Rue La Boétie; *Touring Club de France*, 65 Av. de la Grande-Armée.

The BRITISH COLONY COMMITTEE (Hon. Sec., 6 Rue Halévy) organizes periodical social events. Among other British institutions are the *British Institute in Paris*, 6 Rue de la Sorbonne; *British Legion*, 8 Rue Boudreau, 9e; *Standard Athletic Club*, at Meudon.

AMERICAN CLUBS. *American Club of Paris* and *University Club*, both at 49 Rue Pierre-Charron, 8e; *American Students' and Artists' Social Center*, 261 Boul. Raspail; *American Library*, 10 Rue Camou, 7e.

The *Y.M.C.A.* has a club-house at 14 Rue de Trévise (9e; Métro station Cadet). The *Y.W.C.A.* has houses at 38 Rue de Laborde (8e), 26 Rue d'Anjou (8e), both near the Gare St-Lazare, and at 90 Rue Alexandre-Dumas (20e; Métro Bagnolet); also in summer at 22 Rue de Naples (8e), near St-Lazare, at 1 Rue Denis-Poisson (17e; Métro Pte Maillot), at 40 Rue Boulard (14e; Métro Denfert), and at 65 Rue Orfila (20e; Métro Martin-Nadaud). The Girl Guide Assoc. Hostel (open to non-members) is at 10 Rue Richelieu (1er; Métro Palais-Royal); Maison des Étudiantes, at 214 Boul. Raspail (14e; Métro Vavin).

The BRITISH COUNCIL has premises at No. 36 Rue des Écoles (5e), with reading rooms, a library of c. 25,000 vols. (all English), and an intake of c. 180 periodicals. Books may be borrowed from the library on payment of an annual subscription of 10 fr. For teachers of English wishing to borrow material for class use there are special facilities free of charge. The library is open to the public daily (except Sun), 1.30–6; also Thurs and Sat, 10–12.

Courses for Foreign Students. The 'Livret de l'Étudiant', published at the beginning of each academic year, gives a complete list of lectures, courses, etc., at the Sorbonne and every other centre of learning in Paris. Students anxious to acclimatize themselves to student life in Paris are advised to take their problems to the Service d'Accueil of the Copar Centre Régional des Oeuvres Universitaires, 6 Rue Jean-Calvin (5e).

Accommodation for foreign students is available in University residences from 1 July to 15 Sept; apply to Office de Tourisme Universitaire et Scolaire, 137 Boul. St-Michel, 5e.

Police. The chief Préfecture de Police is situated in the Boul. du Palais (No. 7). In cases of disputes with cabmen, or when in need of information,

visitors should apply to the nearest policeman (agent de police) to whom no gratuity should ever be offered.

LOST PROPERTY. Articles lost in the streets, in the Métro or in motor-buses, or in theatres and cinemas, should be enquired for at the Préfecture de Police at 36 Rue des Morillons (Métro station: Convention, line 12; motor-bus 39, 49. Open weekdays 9–5.30; 9–12 only on Sat). Note, however, that articles lost in buses or the Métro are held for claiming for the first 48 hrs at the terminus of the route concerned.

Hospitals. *Hertford* (*British*), 48 Rue de Villiers, Levallois (tel. PER 94.10); *American*, 63 Boul. Victor-Hugo, Neuilly (tel. MAI 68.00).

VIII   GENERAL HINTS

Season. The fashionable season in Paris extends from Nov to the 'Grand-Prix' in June. Summer (June–August), sometimes very warm, is the tourist season, though in Aug the city is almost deserted by its regular inhabitants and many of the theatres and libraries, etc., are closed. In spring and autumn, though the days are shorter, the weather is better adapted for the active sight-seer.

TIME. England and France, having both now adopted permanent 'Summer Time', in effect use Central European Time (1 hr ahead of G.M.T.).

Expenses in France, despite popular belief to the contrary, are no higher than those in any of the neighbouring countries to the E.; nor, for the English visitor accustomed to eating good food, higher than he is used to at home. The lowest standards of food encountered in England under the pretext of economy hardly exist in Paris. The average *minimum* cost of luncheon or dinner is about 12 fr., including service and vin ordinaire. The standard of a meal at 25–45 fr. (40–70s.) per head (wine inclusive) will, however, in general, be considerably higher than its equivalent in England. Afternoon tea in a pâtisserie is expensive by English standards; soft drinks are also dear. Rail and motor-bus travel is not costly and good wine is extremely reasonable. The charge for bed and breakfast is inexpensive; small and comfortable hotels may be found where a night's lodging costs 25–30s. Patronage of the leading hotels will naturally increase expenses materially.

Language. The traveller who knows no language but English can get along quite comfortably in Paris, though he will probably pay in cash for his ignorance. Even a slight knowledge of French makes the visit not only cheaper, but also much more interesting and more intellectually profitable.

Some French Usages. Forms of politeness are more ceremonious in France than in Great Britain or America, with much handshaking at meeting and parting. The use of christian names is less widespread than in England and it is polite and usual even after long acquaintance to use 'Monsieur', 'Madame', and 'Mademoiselle' as forms of address without the surname. Business begins earlier in Paris than in London. The usual lunch hour is about 12.30, the dinner hour about 7.45.

House Numbering. In streets parallel with the Seine the houses are numbered from E. to W.; in those at right angles with the Seine, from the end nearest to the river.

Minuterie. The notice 'minuterie' in apartment houses, etc., indicates a push-botton, pressure on which will illuminate the staircase for about a minute.

Public Holidays. The chief public holidays in France are New Year's Day, Good Friday (aft. only), Easter Monday, Ascension Day, 1 May, 8 May (V-E Day), Whit Monday, 14 July (Fête Nationale), Assumption Day (15 Aug), All Saints' Day (1 Nov), Armistice Day (11 Nov), and Christmas Day. Business is generally suspended on these days and banks are closed. Buses do not run on 1 May.

Shops. The best-known shopping streets are the Rue du Faubourg St-Honoré, Rue de la Paix, the Grands Boulevards, Boulevard Haussmann, Rue de Rivoli, and Avenue de l'Opéra, the first two of which may, perhaps, claim to be par excellence the street of the fashionable shop proper. Other very good shops are found in all the streets between the Opéra, the Tuileries, and the Palais-Royal; while several of the excellent large departmental stores lie outside these limits.

Among the best known of the departmental stores, where every ordinary want of the traveller may be met on the premises, are the *Bazar de l'Hôtel de Ville,* 52/64 Rue de Rivoli; *Belle Jardinière,* 2 Rue du Pont-Neuf; *Bon Marché,* 131–137 Rue du Bac; *Galeries La Fayette,* 38/46 Boul. Haussmann; *Magasins Réunis,* 30 Av. des Ternes, 136 Rue de Rennes, and Place de la République; *Au Printemps,* 64 Boul. Haussmann; *Samaritaine,* 67/81 Rue de Rivoli; *Samaritaine de Luxe,* 27 Boul. des Capucines; *Trois-Quartiers,* 17/25 Boul. de la Madeleine.—*British–American Pharmacy,* 1 Rue Scribe; *Drugstores,* 79 and 133 Av. des Champs-Élysées, 149 Boul. St-Germain.

Most shops are closed all day Monday. All food shops are open on Sunday morning until 12 or 1.

Tobacconists usually have postage stamps, post-cards, and carte-lettres on sale.

Markets. Antiques may be sought at the **Village Suisse,** 56 Avenue de la Motte-Picquet, daily (exc. Tues and Wed) 9–7; also, together with bric-à-brac of all kinds, on the stalls of the **Marché aux Puces,** extending for c. 4 m. between Pte de Clignancourt and St-Ouen (all day Sat, Sun, and Mon). The open-air **Stamp Market,** in Av. Gabriel and Av. Marigny (off the Champs Élysées), is open Thurs, Sat, Sun, and holidays, 8–7.

IX   THE SIGHTS OF PARIS

Paris, a city of great diversity, will offer different aspects to each visitor according to personal preference. The experienced traveller should have no difficulty, using the index and the town plans, in choosing and following his own itinerary. The arrangement of Routes 1–19 has been designed to allow the inexperienced traveller to explore the city systematically, whether at the possible but superficial level of two routes per day together with brief visits to museums, or more slowly and thoroughly. A good deal of Paris may be seen in a week by the tireless traveller who makes a free use of taxicabs and is satisfied with the most superficial glance at the treasures of the galleries and museums. For this view of Paris the most important routes are, perhaps, 1–12, 14B, and 17, to which should be added part of the Louvre, the Palais de Chaillot, the Jeu de Paume, and the Musée Nissim de Camondo. But not less than three weeks should be devoted to Paris, and even in that case a careful plan should be made beforehand so as to utilize every hour of every day.

The **Table of the Principal Sights** below, with the information given overleaf, will enable the visitor to arrange his plan of campaign. When alternative hours of closing are indicated, the earlier hours refer to winter (usually Oct–April), the later to summer. Most collections are closed on Tuesdays. Some collections are free on Sundays and others half-price. Special note should be taken of the days and hours at which particular collections are open; and applications for special permits should be made in good time.

Hours and Charges of Admission to the Chief Sights

* closed all day on Tuesday

■   **N.B.** Charges increased 1 Oct 1967; comp. p. vi.   ■

*Archives	2–5	1 fr., Sun 0,50 fr
*Balzac's House	1–5 or 6	0,50 fr., Sun free
Bibliothèque Nationale	9–6	free, closed Sun
Musée des Médailles	10–12, 2–4	closed Sun
*Chantilly, Château de	1.30–5.30 or 6; Sun also 10–12	2 fr., closed Fri, and Nov–Feb
*Conciergerie	10–12, 1.30–4, 5 or 6	1 fr., Sun 0,50 fr.
Eiffel Tower	10 or 10.30–6 or 12	1½–5 fr.
Fontainebleau, Palais de	10–12, 1.15–4 or 5	1 fr., Sun 0,50 fr. Private suites, 1 fr. (not Sun)
*Gobelins	Wed–Fri 2–4	0,50 fr.
Invalides:		
Tomb of Napoleon	9.30–5 or 5.30	1 fr.
*Musée de l'Armée	10–12.15, 1.30–5 or 5.30	1 fr.; closed Sun
Jardin des Plantes:		
Menagerie	9–5 or 6	0,70 fr.
*Galleries	1–5	0,30 fr.
*Louvre	10–5	1 fr., Sun free
*Maison-Laffite, Château	10–12, 2–5	1 fr., Sun 0,50 fr., closed Fri morning
*Malmaison, La	10 or 11–12, 1.30–4 or 5.30	0,50 fr., Sun 0,25 fr.
Mint (workshops)	Tues, Thurs 2–3.30	free
*Musée d'Antiquités Nationales (St-Germain)	10–12, 1.30–5	1 fr., Sun 0,50 fr.
*Musée des Arts Décoratifs	10–12, 2–5	1 fr., Sun 0,50 fr.
Musée des Arts et Métiers	1.30–5.30, Sun 10–5	1 fr., Sun free; closed Mon
*Musée Carnavalet	10–12, 2–5 or 5.30	1 fr., Sun free
*Musée Cernuschi	10–12, 2–4 or 5	1 fr., Sun free
*Musée Cognacq-Jay	10–12, 2–4	1 fr., Sun free
*Musée de Cluny	10–12.45, 2–5	1 fr., Sun 0,50 fr.
*Musée du Costume	10–12, 2–5	1 fr.
*Musée Guimet	10–5	1 fr., Sun 0,50 fr.
*Musée Jacquemart-André	1–4 or 5	1 fr., Sun 0,50 fr. closed Fri
*Musée du Jeu-de-Paume	10–5	1 fr., Sun 0,50 fr.
*Musée Marmottan	Sat and Sun 2–5	1 fr., closed 14 July–15 Sept
Musée Monétaire (Mint)	11–5	free, closed Sat and Sun
Musée Municipal d'Art Moderne	10–12, 2–6	Temp. exhibns, fee varies
*Musée National d'Art Moderne	10–5	1 fr., Sun free
*Musée Nissim de Camondo	2–5, Sun 10–12, 2–5	1 fr., closed July
Musée de l'Opéra	10–5	0,50 fr., closed Sun
*Musée de l'Orangerie	10–5	3 fr.
*Musée Postal	2–6	˙1 fr., Sun 0,50 fr.
*Musée Rodin	1–5 or 6	1 fr., Sun 0,50 fr.

*Musée Victor-Hugo	10–12, 2–5 or 6	1 fr.
*Notre-Dame, Towers	10–4 or 5	5 fr.
Palais de Chaillot:		
*Musée de l'Homme	10–5 or 6	1,40 fr.
*Musée de la Marine	10–5 or 6	1 fr.
*Musée des Monuments	10–5	1 fr., Sun 0,50 fr.
Français		
Palais de Justice	11–4	free, closed Sun
*Panthéon	10–4 or 5	0,50 fr., Sun 0,25 fr.
*St-Denis, Tombs	10–12, 2–4 or 5	0,50 fr., closed Sun morning
*Sainte Chapelle	10–12, 1.30–4, 5 or 6	1 fr., Sun 0,50 fr.
*Sèvres Museum	10–12, 1–5	1 fr., Sun 0,50 fr.
*Trianons, The	2–5 or 6	1 fr.
*Versailles, Palais de	10–5.30	1 fr.
(Royal Apartments daily)		
*Vincennes, Château	10–12, 1.30–5.30	1 fr., Sun 0,50 fr.
Parc Zoölogique	9–5.30 or 7	2 fr.

Although this table includes some of the principal attractions of Paris and its environs, it by no means exhausts the lists of things to see. The traveller is reminded, therefore, of the following additional points of interest, details of which will be found in the text.

PUBLIC AND OTHER INSTITUTIONS. *Arc de Triomphe – Arènes de Lutèce – Banque de France – Beaux-Arts – Chapelle Expiatoire – Chapelle St-Ferdinand – Collège de France – Halles Centrales – July Column – Opera House – Opéra-Comique – Palais Royal – Scots College – Théâtre Français.*

CHURCHES.—Besides *Notre-Dame* perhaps the most interesting churches are the *Sacré-Cœur – St-Eustache – St-Étienne-du-Mont – St-Germain-l'Auxerrois – St-Germain-des-Prés – St-Roch – St-Séverin – St-Sulpice – Sorbonne.*

PARKS AND GARDENS. The *Bois de Boulogne*, the *Tuileries Gardens*, the *Champs-Élysées*, the *Luxembourg Gardens*, etc., are not likely to be overlooked by the visitor to Paris; but some of the less central parks, such as the *Parc Monceau*, the *Parc de Montsouris*, and the *Parc des Buttes-Chaumont*, likewise repay a visit.—CEMETERIES are open 7.30–6 in summer, 8–4.30 in winter. The chief are *Père-Lachaise* and the cemeteries of *Montmartre* and *Montparnasse*; and many will be interested in the little *Cimetière de Picpus*.

Personal Guides may be hired at the Bureau Officiel de Placement des Guides et Interprètes, 83 Rue Taitbout (mid-Mar–Sept).

Conducted Tours and Lectures are organized by several organizations (Monuments Historiques, Musées de France, A travers Paris, Paris et son Histoire, the Touring Club de France, etc.), giving visitors an opportunity of seeing historic buildings and mansions to which the public is not normally admitted. A list of such visits for the day will be found in a number of newspapers.

The 'Monuments Historiques' is a branch of the Department of Fine Arts. It organizes lectures on the spot and visits every day of the year, up to four or five lectures a day. These are delivered by scholars and archaeologists. No advance application is necessary; the visitor merely goes to the place indicated at the time stated and pays a small fee (usually 2 fr.). Leaflets giving the full programme of coming visits may be obtained free of charge by application to the Ministère des Affaires Culturelles et des Beaux Arts, Service des Monuments Historiques, 3 Rue de Valois, Paris 1er.

Illuminations. Every night from 9 to 11 during the season (June–Sept) and on Saturday and Sunday nights off season the principal sights are illuminated. The most impressive are the Place de la Concorde and the flood-lit fountains of the Palais de Chaillot. The following itinerary, easily completed in two hours by car or taxi, passes the main points of interest. We start from the Place de l'Étoile – Champs Élysées – Place de la Concorde (leaving the car and walking around is quite rewarding): the Quays of the Seine (North Bank); just before the Pont du Carrousel turn left, through the Carrousel, to the Place du Théâtre Français; from there look towards the Opera. Drive back to the Quay and go along as far as the Place du Louvre where stand the fine old church St-Germain l'Auxerrois and the famous Colonnade du Louvre. Go along the Quay again. Passing the Île de la Cité we have the Conciergerie on our right. When (on the right) the second bridge of the Île St-Louis is reached, turn left into the Rue des Nonnains d'Hyères. Leave the car and walk around the charming Hôtel de Sens. Take the car again, cross the old Pont Marie, the Île St-Louis, the Pont de la Tournelle which affords the best view of the apse of Notre-Dame Cathedral. Turn right and follow the South Bank of the Seine. We pass the Pont St Michel, the Mint, the Institut de France, the Hôtel de la Légion d'Honneur, the Palais Bourbon. The Invalides are on our left. If not pressed for time, turn left into the Esplanade des Invalides; go round by the left of the Hôtel des Invalides in order to see the dome of the Chapel from the Avenue de Breteuil; then make for the Pont d'Iéna, but first follow the Avenue de la Motte-Picquet and have a look at the École Militaire. The most beautiful fountains lie between the Seine and the Palais de Chaillot.

In the Quartier du Marais some of the old mansions are also illuminated on certain days. Placards throughout the town announce which houses are illuminated and when (it varies from year to year), and information can be obtained at any Bureau de Tourisme.

'Son et Lumière' is given every night (during the season) in the Cour d'Honneur des Invalides—and at the Château de Vincennes. A very elaborate 'Son et Lumière' is given at Versailles on certain days.

X   CALENDAR OF EVENTS

The following is a list of some annual events of interest taking place in and near Paris on fixed or approximately fixed dates.

1 JAN	Jour de l'An; the chief day for exchanging gifts (étrennes).
3 JAN	Pilgrimage to the tomb of St Geneviève at St-Étienne-du-Mont.
6 JAN	Journée des Rois (Epiphany); a day of family parties for which bakers provide a special cake (galette).
2 FEB	La Chandeleur (Candlemas); tossing the pancake in French households.
SHROVE TUESDAY	Mardi Gras; less and less celebrated in Paris.
PALM SUNDAY	Sprigs of box ('buis bénit') carried by the faithful.— Beginning of the following fairs: Foire aux Jambons and Foire à la Ferraille.
APRIL (first half)	Concours Lépine, for inventions of the past year, Quai de New York.
GOOD FRIDAY	Holy Sepulchres decorated in the churches. Butchers' shops closed.
EASTER WEEK	Foire aux Pains d'Épice (Gingerbread Fair) in the Place de la Nation.
APRIL	Opening of Salon des Indépendants, Grand Palais; Salon des Humoristes, 11 Rue Royale.
APRIL (last week)	Azalea show at the Jardin Fleuriste, Porte d'Auteuil.
APRIL (last Sun)	Grand Prix de Paris (motor race at Montlhéry).
1 MAY	Lily of the valley sold in the streets. 'Labour Day'.
MAY (2nd Sun)	Feast of St Joan of Arc; decorations of her statues. Victory celebrations commemorating the liberation of 1945. French football cup final at Colombes.
MAY	Foire de Paris at the Porte de Versailles (usually fortnight ending Whit Monday).
28 MAY	Decoration of the Mur des Fédérés.
30 MAY	American Memorial Day; services at Holy Trinity Av. George-V, and Mont-Valérien Cemetery.
MAY	Concours Hippique (Horse Show) at the Cercle de l'Étrier, Bois de Boulogne.
MAY (late, or early June)	Air Show at Le Bourget.
CORPUS CHRISTI (Fête Dieu)	Processions of 'First Communion' children.
1 JUNE (about)	Salon opens.
JUNE (1st Sun)	Prix de Diane at Chantilly.
JUNE (2nd Sun)	Prix du Jockey-Club (the 'French Derby') at Chantilly.
JUNE (2nd Mon)	Prix du Président at Vincennes.
MID-JUNE	Roses in bloom at Bagatelle.
JUNE (first half)	Special display in shops in the Faubourg St-Honoré.
JUNE (3rd Sun)	Grand Steeplechase at Auteuil.
JUNE (4th Fri)	Journée des Drags at Auteuil.
JUNE (4th Sun)	Grand Prix at Longchamp.
JUNE–JULY	Regattas at Asnières and Courbevoie.
14 JULY	Fête Nationale; review of soldiers in the Champs-Élysées; firework display at the Pont Neuf and elsewhere; popular balls in the streets; free matinée at National theatres.
AUG (end)	'Coupe de Paris' (rowing championship of France) decided at Bry-sur-Marne.
SEPT (1st Sun)	Bicycling championship at Longchamp.
OCT (beginning)	Salon de l'Automobile in the Palais de la Défense.
26 AUG	Celebration of liberation (1944); fireworks, balls, etc.
OCT (2nd Sun)	Prix de l'Arc de Triomphe at Longchamp. Harvest festival in Montmartre.
9 OCT	Feast of St Denis. Pilgrimage to the Basilica.

OCT (second half)	Chrysanthemum show at the Jardin Fleuriste, Porte d'Auteuil.
OCT (4th Sun)	Prix du Conseil Municipal at Longchamp.
25 OCT	Annual General Meeting of the Academies of the Institut.
OCT–NOV	Salon d'Automne at the Grand Palais.
1 NOV	Toussaint ⎫ Decoration of graves in the principal
2 NOV	Jour des Morts ⎭ cemeteries.
11 NOV	Armistice Day.
22 NOV	Sainte-Cécile; choral mass in St-Eustache.
25 NOV	Sainte-Catherine; procession in the Boulevards of un-married working girls who have reached the age of 25; Mass at N.D. de Bonne-Nouvelle; decoration of the Saint's statue, Rue de Cléry.
DEC	Salon d'Hiver opens in the Musée d'Art Moderne.
24 DEC	Midnight masses. Children put their shoes out for presents.
25 DEC	Noël. Crèches decorated in the churches.

Temporary **Exhibitions** of a commercial and industrial nature take place at the *Parc des Expositions*, Pte de Versailles, and at C.N.I.T., Rond-point de la Défense.

XI BOOKS ABOUT PARIS

In the following brief list the books mentioned, most of which are in English, touch upon a variety of aspects and serve as an introduction to the study of Paris.

The standard work on Paris in English may be taken to be *Okey* (*Thomas*): 'The Story of Paris' (1906; reprinted 1919).

Bazin (*Germain*): 'The Louvre' (1957), 'Impressionist Paintings' (1958). *Benoît* (*L.*): 'La Sculpture Française' (Paris, 1963). *Boinet* (*Amédée*): 'Les Églises Parisiennes' (Vol. I; 1958). *Brogan* (*D. W.*): 'The French Nation 1814–1940' (1957). *Bury* (*J. P. T.*): 'Napoleon III and the Second Empire' (1964). *Christ* (*Yvan*): 'Églises de Paris (1957). *Cobban* (*A.*): 'History of Modern France' (3 vols.; 1963). *Cronin* (*Vincent*): 'Louis XIV' (1964). *Dunlop* (*Ian*): 'Versailles' (1956). *George* (*André*): 'Paris', (trans. *J. H.* and *J. M. Denis*; 1957). *Harrison* (*Wilmot*): 'Memorable Paris Houses' (1893). *Herold* (*J. C.*): 'Age of Napoleon' (1964). *Hillairet* (*Jacques*): 'Dictionnaire Historique des Rues de Paris' (Paris, 1963–65). *Hürlimann* (*Martin*): 'Paris' (100 photographs; 1954). *Kemp* (*G. van der*) and *Levron* (*Jacques*): 'Versailles and the Trianons' (trans. *E. Whitehorn*; 1958). *Kunstler* (*Charles*): 'Paris Souterrain' (1953). *Laffont* (*Robert*; *ed.*): 'Paris and its People' (1958). *Lonergan* (*Walter F.*): 'Historic Churches of Paris' (1896). *Mitford* (*Nancy*): 'Madame de Pompadour' (1954). *Pillement* (*G.*): 'Unknown France: Archaeological Itineraries (3 vols.; 1963). *Robiquet* (*J.*): 'Daily Life in the French Revolution' (1964). *Rowe* (*Vivian*): 'Royal Châteaux of Paris' (1956). *Temko* (*Allan*): 'Notre-Dame of Paris' (1956).

Shops specializing in English books: *Galignani*, 224 Rue de Rivoli; W. H. Smith & Sons, 248 Rue de Rivoli; *Brentano*, 37 Av. de l'Opéra.

Three indispensable **Maps** for the serious visitor to Paris are the Taride 'Plan-Guide de Paris par Arrondissements'; the handy general plan of Paris published by the French Government (available from Govt. Tourist Offices); and, for the Banlieue, the Michelin 'Sorties de Paris' at 1:50,000 (3/6).

I PARIS

PARIS, the capital of France, is situated on the Seine, near the middle of the so-called Paris basin, at a height above sea-level varying from 85 ft to 419 ft, and at a distance from the sea of 92 m., or over 200 m. by the windings of the river. Until 1919, Paris, unlike London or New York, was bounded by a definite line of ramparts, which have since been demolished and the sites built upon. The city, c. 38 sq. m. in area, is 8 m. long from W. to E. and 6 m. broad from N. to S. Its population, denser than any other city in Europe, was 2,811,000 in 1963; including the suburbs beyond the line of the old walls it exceeded five millions. The chief magistrate of Paris is the *Préfet de la Seine*, appointed by Government, who is assisted by an elected *Conseil Municipal*. For administrative purposes the city is divided into twenty *Arrondissements*, or municipal boroughs, each with its *Maire* and *Mairie*, or town-hall.

Through the city flows the Seine, describing a curved course from S.E. to S.W. and forming two islands, the *Île St-Louis* and the *Île de la Cité*, near the centre. The division of Paris into N. bank (Rive Droite) and S. Bank is now more psychological than topographical since the banks are joined by no less than thirty-two bridges and are much more nearly of equal importance than the N. and S. banks of the Thames. The RIGHT BANK is lined by the Louvre and the Tuileries; not far away are St-Germain-l'Auxerrois, the Hôtel de Ville, the Palais-Royal, and the Bibliothèque Nationale; farther W. are the collections of the Palais de Chaillot. As well as the great public collections, the leading hotels, restaurants, theatres, and shops are also here. Above on its hill is Montmartre. Paris on the LEFT BANK, the smaller area, has long been famed as the intellectual centre. The numerous learned and scientific institutions in the Latin Quarter make it, now as in the past, the literary, artistic and academic quarter. Farther W. the formerly aristocratic Faubourg St-Germain is now the centre of government offices and embassies and has a number of large military establishments. The Panthéon, the Cluny Museum, the Jardin des Plantes, the Invalides, and the Eiffel Tower are the other chief points of interest on the left bank.

Much of the delight of Paris stems from the way the Seine has been used to unite rather than to divide, vistas from one bank being deliberately extended and perspectives felicitously closed on the other bank by artistic town-planning. If anything tends to divide the city in two, it is the central road axis, with its heavy traffic, a straight line drawn roughly N.W. to S.E., just N. of the river, following the Avenue des Champs-Élysées, Rue de Rivoli, and Rue St-Antoine, cutting Paris into two approximately equal parts. To the N. of this line the Grands Boulevards form an irregular semi-circle, from the Place de la Concorde to the Place de la Bastille, while to the S. a smaller arc is described by the Boul. Henri-IV (crossing the river) and the Boul. St-Germain. The heart of Paris lies within the oval thus defined, becoming more obviously beautiful as one by one its important buildings are being cleaned and restored. Outside lies a ring of old suburbs (faubourgs), bounded by the Outer Boulevards, or Boulevards Extérieurs, the official city limits until 1860, and still farther out are the Boulevards d'Enceinte, skirting the circle of the 19C fortifications. The main N. to S. artery of traffic is formed by the Boulevards de Strasbourg, de Sébastopol, du Palais, and St-Michel.

As in London, various quarters of the city are often more familiarly known

by unofficial titles. Within the curve of the Grands Boulevards, to the W. of the Boul. de Sébastopol, is the chief region of business and pleasure, centring in the Avenue de l'Opéra, the Rue de la Paix, the Rue St-Honoré, and the Rue de Rivoli. Eastward lies the commercial but attractive quarter of the *Marais*, and beyond the Bastille is the *Faubourg St-Antoine*, the centre of Revolutionary Paris. To the N. of the Marais are the *Temple* and *St-Martin*, also primarily commercial. The demolition of old mansions in these areas has now been halted. Between the Place de la Concorde and the Bois de Boulogne are the *Faubourg St-Honoré* and the *Champs-Élysées*, while beyond these lie the elegant residential quarters of *Étoile* and *Chaillot*. In the extreme W., pleasantly situated between the Seine and the Bois, are the districts of *Passy* and *Auteuil*, with *Neuilly* farther N., comfortable rather than fashionable. The wealthy quarters of *Courcelles* and *Monceau*, N.E. of the Arc de Triomphe, are continued by the less fashionable *Batignolles*, which is adjoined on the E. by *Montmartre*, with its famous hill. Thence a series of industrial suburbs (*La Villette, Belleville, Ménilmontant, Charonne*) curves round the N.E. of Paris to join the Faubourg St-Antoine.

On an island in the Seine is the *Cité*, the ancient heart of Paris; and S. of the river the Boul. St-Germain traverses part of the *Latin Quarter*, which is continued on the W. by the aristocratic *Faubourg St-Germain*, with the hotels of the 'vieille noblesse' and many government offices, and that again by the quarter of the *Gros-Caillou*, with its broad avenues. The more southerly district of *Montparnasse* still has large colonies of artists and foreigners and, with the construction of the *Cité Universitaire* to the S., has become an extension of the Latin Quarter.

The open spaces within the walls of Paris are inadequate, some of the largest being cemeteries; but the absence of grass is visually somewhat compensated by the tree-lined avenues and quais. The formal beauties of the *Luxembourg* and *Tuileries Gardens* and the *Champs-Élysées* are balanced by the less stereotyped parks of *Montsouris* (in the S.) and the *Buttes-Chaumont* (in the E.), and supplemented by the natural attractions of the *Bois de Boulogne*, to the W., and the *Bois de Vincennes*, to the S.E., outside the old fortifications.

1   FROM THE PLACE DE LA CONCORDE TO THE LOUVRE AND ST-GERMAIN-L'AUXERROIS

MÉTRO stations: *Concorde* (lines 1, 8, 12); *Palais Royal* (lines 1 and 7).

The ***Place de la Concorde,**** occupying a central position by the Seine, midway between the Étoile and the Île de la Cité, is one of the largest and most beautiful squares in the world. Its beauty is enhanced at night by floodlighting. The present appearance of the square dates from 1852, when the surrounding ditch was filled in, though its perspectives were evidently a design of the First Empire.

The site, then a vacant space outside the city, was chosen in 1757 to receive a bronze statue of Louis XV commissioned by the 'échevins' (comp. Rte 11) in 1748 and unveiled in 1763. The square, completed in 1772, was named after the king, but already in 1770 panic during a firework display for the marriage of the dauphin had provided its first holocaust (133 dead). In 1792 the statue of Louis XV was replaced by a huge figure of Liberty (the object of Mme Roland's famous apostrophe), and the name of the square was changed to Place de la Révolution. The guillotine was erected here for the first time in 1792 for the appropriate execution of the robbers of the crown jewels (comp. below). Louis XVI was guillotined here (on the spot now occupied by the fountain nearest the river) on 21 Jan 1793, and between May 1793 and May 1795 the knife claimed among its victims Charlotte Corday (17 July 1793), Marie-Antoinette (16 Oct), the Girondins (31 Oct), Philippe-Égalité (6 Nov), Mme Roland (10 Nov), Hébert (24 Mar 1794), Danton (5 Apr), Mme Élisabeth (9 May), and Robespierre (28 July). The square first received its present name in 1795 at the end of the Reign of Terror.

On the N. side of the square are two handsome mansions designed by Gabriel in 1763–72 (with pediment sculptures by M. A. Slodtz and G. Coustou the younger) and originally intended as official residences. That to the right, from which the crown jewels were stolen in 1792, has been since 1789 the *Ministère de la Marine* (Admiralty; entrance 2 Rue Royale), that to the left is divided between the *Automobile Club*, with a swimming bath, and the *Hôtel de Crillon*. In this building was signed the treaty of 1778, by which France was the first country to recognize the independence of the United States. Between these buildings passes the Rue Royale, at the end of which appears the Madeleine. To the right of the Admiralty is the 18C *Hôtel de la Vrillière*, built to designs by Chalgrin, where Talleyrand died in 1838 and where the Princesse de Lieven held her salon in 1846–57. To the left of the Hôtel de Crillon is the *American Embassy* (1931–33), carefully designed to complete the symmetry of Gabriel's plans.

To the W. of the Concorde the Champs-Élysées rise towards the Arc de Triomphe. The vista is given its frame by the *MARLY HORSES, two splendid groups by G. Coustou—"ces marbres hennissants" as Victor Hugo calls them—which were brought from the Château de Marly in 1794 and now form pendants to the winged horses at the W. entrance to the Tuileries. In this direction the view extends to the Louvre. On the S. side of the Place runs the Seine, here spanned by the *Pont de la Concorde* (*View; comp. Rte 2) leading to the Palais Bourbon, whose assertive classical façade designedly completes the southern perspective, as that of the Madeleine does the northern.

At the centre of the two axes rises the *Obelisk of Luxor, a monolith of pink syenite, 75 ft high and 250 tons in weight. It originally stood before a temple at Thebes in Upper Egypt and commemorates in its hieroglyphics the deeds of Rameses II (13C B.C.). The obelisk was presented to Louis-Philippe in 1831 by Mohammed Ali (the donor also of Cleopatra's Needle in London). The pedestal, of Breton granite, bears representations of the apparatus used in its erection. The two *Fountains, by Hittorf, copies of those in the piazza of St Peter's at Rome, are adorned with figures emblematic of Inland (N.) and Marine (S.) Navigation.

The eight stone pavilions round the square, built by Gabriel in the 18C, support statues personifying the great provincial cities of France. Strasbourg (as capital of the lost Alsace) was, from 1871, hung with crape and wreaths, and on a shield appeared the date of its capitulation (27 Sept 1870) and the question 'When?' The question was resolved on 22 Nov 1918. Pradier's model for Strasbourg was Juliette Drouet.

Near the statue of Lille is the entrance to the **Sewers** (*Égouts*) of Paris. Visits (0,50 fr.) are arranged (at 2, 3, 4 and 5 p.m.) on the 2nd and 4th Thurs in May and June; every Thurs, 1 July–15 Oct; also the last Sat of each month in May–Sept. The interesting visit (very different from the trying experience of Jean Valjean in 'Les Misérables') is carried out in boats.

The *Jardin des Tuileries, a formal garden of 63 acres adorned with a wealth of statues, extends from the Place de la Concorde to the Place du Carrousel, and is divided into two by the Avenue du Général Lemonnier. The part W. of this avenue was the private garden of the Tuileries palace and has been little altered since it was laid out anew by Le Nôtre in 1664. The earlier work of his grandfather had been the first example in Paris of a public garden in the Italian

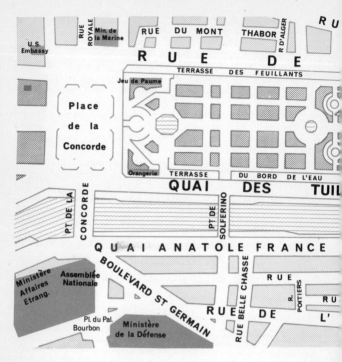

style. The garden became the favourite promenade of the fashionable nobility of
Paris until superseded by the Palais-Royal just before the Revolution.

The gateway opening from the Place de la Concorde has pillars crowned by *Equestrian
figures of Fame and Mercury, by Coysevox (brought from Marly in 1719). A tablet in a
recess on the right commemorates the first gas-balloon ascent from Paris (Dec 1783). The
large octagonal pond is surrounded by statuary of the 17–18C by N. and G. Coustou and
by Van Cleve; while by the steps to the S. is 'Hommage à Cézanne' by Maillol. On the steps
to the N. is a copy of Coysevox's bust of Le Nôtre (comp. St-Roch).

Terraces extend along both sides of the gardens. On the S., overlooking the
Quai des Tuileries, is the TERRASSE DU BORD-DE-L'EAU or *Terrasse de
l'Orangerie*. A passage beneath this from the palace cellars to the Place de
la Concorde provided Louis-Philippe with an escape route in 1848. At the W.
end of the terrace (*View across Place de la Concorde) is the *Orangerie* (1853),
containing paintings by Monet (see Rte 30). The TERRASSE DES FEUILLANTS,
skirting the Rue de Rivoli (Rte 9) on the N. side of the gardens, is named after
a Benedictine monastery which in 1791 was the meeting-place of the 'Club des
Feuillants' (moderate republicans, among whom were Lavoisier and André
Chénier). Here Louis XVI and his family slept in August 1792 before their
removal to the Temple.

At the W. end of the terrace is the **Jeu de Paume** (Rte 30), a real tennis-court
built in 1861, now devoted to paintings of the Impressionist School of the
Musée du Louvre. On the terrace on its S. side is a monument to Charles
Perrault (1628–1703), the writer of fairy tales, at whose suggestion the gardens

were thrown open to the public by Colbert; while below the E. side of this terrace are fragments of the Palais des Tuileries, not in situ.

The *Manège*, the riding-school of the palace, where the National Assembly met from 1789 to 1793 and where Louis XVI was condemned to death in 1793, stood on a site (plaque) farther E., nearly opposite the Rue de Castiglione.

The central avenue of chestnut and plane trees is flanked by trees in regular formation, among which are cafés and open-air shows. Beyond is the *Round Pond*, where children sail model yachts. The grass enclosures contain two semi-circular marble benches set up under the Convention for the old men to watch the floral games. Among the flower-beds are arranged groups of decorative sculpture, notably 18C works by Guillaume and Nicolas Coustou, Coysevox, and Le Pautre. Between the Round Pond and the Avenue du Général Lemonnier survive the railings put up by Louis-Philippe to isolate the 'private garden'.

The PALAIS DES TUILERIES, once the centre and soul of Paris, which stood on the E. side of the Avenue du Général Lemonnier, no longer exists, except for the *Pavillon de Flore* on the S. side and the *Pavillon de Marsan* on the N., both of which have been restored or rebuilt and now form the ends of the W. wings of the Louvre.

The palace was begun by *Philibert Delorme* in 1564 for Catherine de Médicis, who forsook the Hôtel des Tournelles after Henri II's lingering death. The site beyond the city walls was known as the 'Sablonnière' and occupied by tile-kilns (tuileries). Delorme was succeeded by *Jean Bullant* and then, in 1595, by *Jacques du Cerceau*, who built the

Pavillon de Flore. The Pavillon de Marsan was built under Louis XIV in 1660–65 by *Louis Le Vau* and his son-in-law *François d'Orbay*. Louis XVI was brought from Versailles to the Tuileries by the Paris mob in 1789, and confined there (except during his ineffectual attempt to escape in 1791) until the riot of 10 Aug 1792, when the Swiss Guards were massacred. In 1793–96 it was the headquarters of the Convention. Pius VII was lodged in the Pavillon de Flore for four months in 1804–05. The Tuileries became the permanent residence of Napoleon I, Louis XVIII (who died here), Charles X, Louis-Philippe, and Napoleon III. In May 1871, the Communards set fire to the building, which, like the Hôtel de Ville, was completely gutted. The walls stood until 1884, and the site of the ruins was converted into a garden in 1889.

The ARC DE TRIOMPHE DU CARROUSEL, a reduced copy of the Arch of Septimius Severus at Rome (48 ft high instead of 75 ft), was begun in 1806 from the designs of *Fontaine* and *Percier* to commemorate the victories of Napoleon I in 1805. It constituted the main entrance to the courtyard of the Tuileries from the Cour du Carrousel.

On the top are figures of Soldiers of the Empire and a bronze chariot-group by *Bosio* (1828) representing the Restoration of the Bourbons. The original group incorporated the antique horses looted from St Mark's, Venice, and replaced there in 1815. The four sides are decorated with marble bas-reliefs: the Battle of Austerlitz; the Capitulation of Ulm; the Meeting between Napoleon and Alexander at Tilsit; the Entry into Munich; the Entry into Vienna; and the Peace of Pressburg.

The PLACE DU CARROUSEL, lying between the westernmost wings of the Louvre, was down to the middle of the 19C a small square amidst a labyrinth of narrow streets. It derives its name from a kind of equestrian fête given by Louis XIV in 1662. The guillotine set up here in 1792 was later transferred to the Place de la Concorde. The archways on the N. side lead to the Rue de Rivoli; those on the S. side give on the Quai des Tuileries, opposite the Pont du Carrousel, while on its E. side lies the *Square du Carrousel*. Westward the square commands the *View to the Étoile, one of the most beautiful perspectives in any city.

In the centre of the square is a bronze group, The Sons of Cain, by *Landowski*, and in the next small garden is an equestrian statue of La Fayette (1757–1834), by *Paul Wayland Bartlett*, presented to France in 1900 by the school-children of the United States.

The **Palais du Louvre, situated between the Rue de Rivoli on the N. and the Seine on the S. and enclosing the Place du Carrousel, is the most important public building in Paris and one of the largest (40 acres) and most magnificent palaces in the world. The construction of the building, which extended over three centuries, is of great architectural and historical interest.

History. The name of the Louvre is derived either from an early wolf-hunters' rendezvous known as 'Lupara' or 'Louverie', or from a 'Louver', a blockhouse, and the building first appears in history as one of Philip Augustus's fortresses (1190–1202), fragments of which survive in the basement store-rooms. Charles V made it an official royal residence. The W. and S. sides were rebuilt under Francis I (1515–47) and extended by his successor Henri II. Catherine de Médicis, Henri II's widow, began the Long Gallery, facing the river, to connect the Louvre with her new palace at the Tuileries. The building was considerably extended during the reigns of Henri IV and Louis XIII, and the quadrangle was completed, at Colbert's orders, during the minority of Louis XIV. However, the king soon lost interest in the new buildings, and they were left in a state of complete disrepair and occupied by squatters until Louis XV commissioned his architect Gabriel to renovate and repair the palace in 1754. Under Napoleon I the W. part of the gallery on the N. side of the Place du Carrousel was erected, and under Napoleon III the main wings which enclose the Square du Carrousel on the N. and S. were built. The Pavillon de Marsan and Pavillon de Flore (at the extreme W. end) have been rebuilt since their destruction by fire under the Commune.

Catherine de Médicis was resident in the palace after the death of her husband. Here, five days after the marriage of Henry of Navarre (later Henri IV) and Marguerite de Valois, sister of Charles IX, Catherine de Médicis extorted from Charles IX the order for the Massacre of St Bartholomew (25 Aug 1572). In 1591, during the Wars of the League,

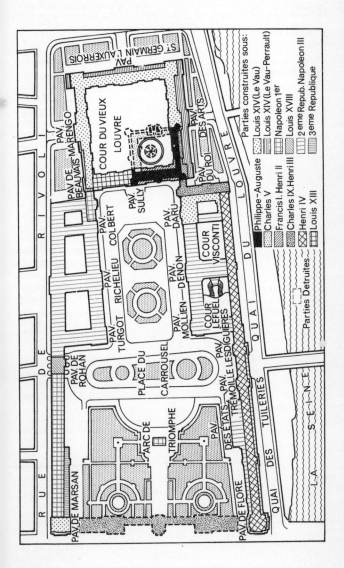

the Duc de Mayenne hanged three members of the 'Council of Sixteen' in the Salle des Gardes (now the Salle des Cariatides). Henrietta Maria, the widowed queen of Charles I of England, found refuge in the Louvre. In 1658 Corneille's tragedy 'Nicomède' was performed in the Salle des Gardes by command of Louis XIV. In 1793 the Musée de la République was opened in the Louvre, and the palace has remained a national art gallery and museum ever since. During the Revolution of 1830 the Louvre was stormed by the mob, and it was set on fire by the Communards, when serious damage was limited to the library.

The Louvre consists of two main divisions: the OLD LOUVRE, comprising the buildings round the Cour du Louvre or Cour Carrée, and the NEW LOUVRE, the 19C buildings N. and S. of the Square du Carrousel, together with the wings stretching W. to the pavillions of the Tuileries. On the W. side of the Cour du Louvre, to the S. of the Pavillon Sully, is the oldest visible part of the Palace (early 16C), by *Lescot*, with sculptural decorations by *Jean Goujon* and *Paul Ponce*. The N. half of the W. façade, and part of the N. façade, were designed by *Lemercier* in imitation of Lescot; the caryatids on the Pavillon Sully are after *Sarazin*. The remainder of the court was built after 1660 by *Le Vau*. The uppermost stories on the N., E., and S. sides, quite out of keeping with Lescot's charming attic, were added in the 17–18C, to bring them to the height of the great colonnade of 52 Corinthian columns and pilasters that now forms the exterior E. façade of the Old Louvre (comp. below). The work of *Claude Perrault* (1667–70), it was designed without due regard to dimensions, and a new outer façade was added on the S. side of the Old Louvre, to meet the projecting S. end. The exterior N. façade was left untouched.

The Galerie du Bord de l'Eau, the long S. façade of the Louvre, along the Seine, was the work of *Pierre Chambiges*, architect to Catherine de Médicis, and *Thibaut Métezeau*, as far as the Pavillon de Lesdiguières. Henri IV had the gallery prolonged farther W. to the Pavillon de Flore, by his architect *Jacques du Cerceau*; but this portion was largely rebuilt in 1863–68. The buildings of the New Louvre, flanking the Square du Carrousel, were begun by *Visconti* in 1852 and completed by *Lefuel* in 1875. The building on the N. side has been occupied since 1871 by the Ministère des Finances.

The principal entrance to the **Louvre Galleries** (see Rte 20) is in the Pavillon Denon, on the S. side of the Square du Carrousel. Points of interest in the interior of the palace are described with its contents.

Either the Quai du Louvre (in 1967 almost inaccessible owing to works for a new urban motorway) or the Rue de Rivoli will take us to the PLACE DU LOUVRE. The square claims to be the point where Cæsar's legions established themselves in 52 B.C. In 1966–67 the E. façade of the Louvre was for the first time given the moat and terreplein intended by Charles Perrault, thus restoring the correct proportions of the colonnade. During the works the base was discovered of an earlier façade, begun by Le Vau and abandoned when Colbert became superintendent of buildings. Opposite stands the *Mairie of the 1st Arrondissement* (1859), which, according to Viollet-le-Duc, seems to have been intended as a caricature of the adjoining church.

*St-Germain-l'Auxerrois is a Gothic church of the 13–16C, drastically restored in the 18–19C. The most striking feature is the porch by Jean Gaussel (1435–39), with a rose window and a graceful balustrade above, which encircles the whole church. The transeptal doorways (15C) are noteworthy, likewise the small Renaissance doorway (1570), N. of the choir.

In 885 the Norman invaders turned the church dedicated to the 5C St Germanus, bishop of Auxerre, into a fortress. A second church was built on the site in the 11C. From the 12C the church was the parish church of the Louvre palace and gradually became too small, so that a third church was built in the 13C. In 1572 it was unwittingly involved in the massacre of St Bartholomew, for the ringing of the bells for matins on St Bartholomew's day was to be the signal for the massacre. Molière was married and his first son was baptized here, and Danton was married here also. Under the Revolution St-Germain, having first served as a granary and then as a printing works, became the 'Temple of Gratitude'. During the July Monarchy the church was sacked by the mob in 1831, and was poorly restored after 1838, the conspicuous N. tower being added in 1860.

Among those buried in St-Germain are Malherbe (d. 1628), the architect of Louis XIII, Jacques Le Mercier (d. 1660), the architect of Louis XIV, Louis Le Vau (d. 1670), the painter Nöel Coypel (d. 1707), and the sculptor Antoine Coysevox (d. 1720).

The INTERIOR (256 by 128 ft) is double-aisled. The 'restoration' of 1745, mingling the classicism of the 18C with 14–15C architecture, mangled the choir-arches, converted the piers into fluted columns, and heightened their capitals. Of the magnificent rood-screen destroyed at the same time, a few fragments are preserved in the Louvre. The pulpit and churchwardens' or royal pew are fine examples of late 17C woodwork by *Fr. Mercier* (designed by *Le Brun*). Behind the latter is a sculptured triptych with painted wings (16C; Flemish), and in the aisle-chapel opposite is another altarpiece (1519), from Antwerp, in sculptured wood. The splendid wrought-iron choir-railings date from 1767. On the left, at the choir-entrance, is a seated wooden statue of St Germanus, on the right a stone figure of St Vincent (both 15C). The entire outer S. aisle is occupied by the CHAPELLE DE LA VIERGE (late 13C; usually locked) in which is preserved a 13C statue of St Germanus of Auxerre, one of the few extant of the Paris School, discovered in 1950 in a vault beneath (it is to be restored to the porch where it belongs); here also are a 15C statue of St Mary of Egypt and, inserted in the 19C reredos, an early 14C Virgin of the Champagne School. The TRANSEPTS alone have retained their *Stained Glass of the 15–16C AMBULATORY (beginning on the S.). Above a small door, 'Vierge à l'oiseau', a charming polychrome Virgin in wood (late 15C). The first inner bay is the base of the 12C belfry. In the 4th chapel are marble statues of Étienne d'Aligre and his son, both Chancellors of France (d. 1635, 1677); 5th chapel, Crucifixion in wood (13C); 6th chapel, beneath the altar, Dead Christ, the sole relic of a Pietà by *Jean Soulas* (1505); and, in the 7th chapel, effigies from the tomb of the Rostaing family (1582 and 1645). In the 8th chapel is the pew built for Queen Marie-Émilie.

The *Muniment Room* (closed) over the porch preserves its original pavement and carved ceiling.

2   THE SEINE

"The Seine," said Napoleon, "is the high road between Paris, Rouen, and Havre", and Paris owes much of its prosperity to its river. It enters the capital at a point over 300 m. from its source (1426 ft) in Burgundy, and the low-water mark at the Pont Royal is only 80 ft above sea-level. The river, flanked within the city by broad quays, is subject to periodic rises, which flood the lower parts of Paris. In its course of 7 m. through Paris the Seine is spanned by thirty-two bridges and footbridges, as compared with the twenty bridges over the Thames in London; but here railway bridges are found only on the outskirts of the city.

The **Port of Paris**, accessible to small sea-going vessels, has its centre in the wharves and quays between the Pont d'Arcole and Pont d'Austerlitz, and is the most important commercial harbour in France, clearing some 12,000,000 tons of merchandise annually.

A RIVER TRIP is interesting and attractive. Beautiful views (especially at sunset) unfold as the launch emerges from beneath the bridges. The best idea of Paris is gained by walking along the Quais, for from them are obtained some of the most beautiful townscapes, while the importance of the Seine in the planning of Paris and its growth is constantly apparent.

RIVER STEAMERS. The 'Bateaux Mouches' run a regular service for visitors. Information about times of embarkation, etc., can be obtained from the office on the Port de la Conférence (by the Pont des Invalides; Tel. BAL 96.10). Smaller launches ('Vedettes') run half-hourly round trips in summer from the Pont d'Iéna (left bank; Tel. INV 33.08) and the Hôtel de Ville (TRE 44.10).

MÉTRO stations near the Seine (going downstream): *Quai de la Gare* (line 6); *Quai de la Rapée* (line 5); *Gare d'Orléans-Austerlitz* (lines 5 and 10); *Châtelet* (lines 1, 4, 7, 11); *Cité* (line 4); *St-Michel* (line 4); *Sully Morland, Pont Marie, Pont Neuf* (line 7); *Concorde* (lines 1, 8, 12); *Chambre des Députés* (line 12); *Invalides* (lines 8 and 14); *Alma-Marceau* (line 9); *Passy* and *Bir-Hakeim* (line 6); *Javel* and *Mirabeau* (line 10).

A   From the Louvre to the Pont National

This route is described in the upstream direction; 'r.b.' and 'l.b.' refer to the right and left bank as seen when proceeding downstream.—Distances from the Louvre are given at each bridge.

In midstream, nearly level with the E. front of the Louvre, the extreme tip of the ÎLE DE LA CITÉ divides the Seine into two branches, the smaller arm flowing past the S. side of the Cité. On the QUAI DE CONTI (l.b.) are the *Institut* and the *Monnaie*. The ***Pont Neuf** ($\frac{1}{5}$ m.), in spite of its name the oldest bridge in Paris, and the most picturesque, was begun by Baptiste du Cerceau in 1578, in the reign of Henri III, finished under Henri IV, and several times repaired since then. It was the first bridge to be built without houses but with pavements. It crosses the 'Pointe de la Cité', on which stands the famous statue of Henri IV.

CHANNEL TO THE S. OF THE CITÉ. The QUAI DES ORFÈVRES, on the bank of the Cité, has a number of jewellers' shops in the old houses backing on the Place Dauphine. Then comes the *Palais de Justice*. Opposite (l.b.) is the QUAI DES GRANDS-AUGUSTINS, with many bookshops, ending at the Place St-Michel.—The **Pont St-Michel** has been rebuilt several times since the 14C (last in 1857). It affords a magnificent view of the façade of Notre-Dame. Opposite the short QUAI ST-MICHEL (l.b.) is the QUAI DU MARCHÉ-NEUF, with the *Préfecture de Police*.—The **Petit Pont** (1853) occupies the site of one of the two Roman bridges of Paris. Down to 1782 it was defended at the S. end by the *Petit Châtelet*, the successor of the Tour de Bois, which, in 886, was defended against the Normans by a handful of citizens.—On the Cité is the *Place du Parvis-Notre-Dame*, with the *Hôtel-Dieu* in the background and the statue of Charlemagne on the river-bank. Behind the QUAI DE MONTEBELLO (l.b.) is seen the little church of *St-Julien-le-Pauvre*.—The **Pont au Double** (1881) takes the place of a 17C bridge for crossing which the toll of a 'double' ($\frac{1}{12}d$.) was charged. The QUAI DE L'ARCHEVÊCHÉ, skirting the S. side of Notre-Dame and the gardens beyond, is named after the archbishop's palace pulled down in 1831; at the far end of the quay is the **Pont de l'Archevêché** (1827) with the best view of the apse of Notre-Dame.

Beyond the Pont Neuf is the QUAI DE LA MÉGISSERIE (r.b.), once known as Quai de la Ferraille from its sword-makers and scrap-iron merchants. The characteristic shops now are those of the corn-chandlers, bird-fanciers, and dealers in fishing-tackle and sporting goods. Here, too, are the *Belle-Jardinière* stores and the *Théâtre du Châtelet*. This quay ends at the *Place du Châtelet* and faces the QUAI DE L'HORLOGE, skirting the N. side of the *Palais de Justice* as far as the clock-tower whence it derives its name.

The **Pont au Change** ($\frac{2}{5}$ m.) was built in 1858–59 to replace a stone bridge (slightly lower down) which dated from 1639 and was lined with moneylenders' shops. At the beginning of the QUAI DE GESVRES (r.b.) is the *Théâtre Sarah-Bernhardt*. Opposite, on the QUAI DE LA CORSE, are the *Tribunal de Commerce* and the *Marché aux Fleurs*.—The **Pont Notre-Dame** ($\frac{1}{2}$ m.), rebuilt in 1913, occupies the site of the chief Roman bridge. The QUAI AUX FLEURS, with the

N. front of the *Hôtel-Dieu*, is connected with the *Place de l'Hôtel-de-Ville* (r.b.) by the **Pont d'Arcole** (⅖ m.), built under the Restoration and named after a young man killed in 1830 while leading a band of insurgents against the Hôtel de Ville. Behind the QUAI DE L'HÔTEL-DE-VILLE is the statue of Étienne Marcel, on the S. side of the Hôtel de Ville. At this point, the junction of the two channels encircling the ÎLE ST-LOUIS, a miniature 'Pool of London' is formed, a busy centre of barge traffic.

The two islands are connected by the **Pont St-Louis** (⅘ m.; 1877), damaged by a lighter in 1939 and at present replaced by a footbridge. On the Île St-Louis are the QUAI D'ORLÉANS and QUAI DE BÉTHUNE. The QUAI DE LA TOURNELLE (l.b.) has at its W. end the Hôtel de Miramion, now the *Musée des Hôpitaux de Paris* (see Rte 4). The old **Pont de la Tournelle** (1 m.), originally (1369) built of wood, was rebuilt in 1634, again under Louis-Philippe, and finally, in reinforced concrete, in 1925–28. The imposing statue of St Geneviève (the patron saint of Paris) at the S. end is by Paul Landowski. The **Pont Sully** (1½ m.), built in 1874–76 to unite the Boul. Henri-IV with the Boul. St-Germain, crosses obliquely both arms of the Seine and the E. end of the island.

CHANNEL TO THE N. OF THE ÎLE ST-LOUIS. The **Pont Louis-Philippe** was rebuilt in 1862. On the Île St-Louis is the QUAI DE BOURBON. Beyond the **Pont Marie** (1614–28), which is named after its builder, are the QUAI DES CÉLESTINS (r.b.), with the striking *Hôtel Fieubet* and lovely views of the Île St-Louis, and, on the Île St-Louis, the QUAI D'ANJOU. Beyond is the Pont Sully (see above).

On the QUAI HENRI-IV (r.b.), occupying with its port what was till c. 1840 the *Île Louviers*, are the *Magasins de la Ville* and the *Archives de la Seine*. At the farther end of the quay is the entrance to the dock, *Gare d'Eau de l'Arsenal*, crossed by the *Pont Morland*. Behind the QUAI ST-BERNARD (l.b.), with its busy wharves, are the Port aux Vins, and the new buildings of the Faculty of Sciences.

The **Pont d'Austerlitz** (1¼ m.), inscribed with the names of the chief officers who fell at Austerlitz (1805), was built in 1802–07, rebuilt in stone in 1855, and widened in 1884–86. On the QUAI D'AUSTERLITZ (l.b.) are the *Gare d'Austerlitz* and a number of yards and factories. A remarkable railway viaduct (Métro) here crosses the river in a single span of 450 ft. The busy QUAI DE LA RAPÉE (r.b.) is lined with wine-merchants' offices, workshops, forage stores, etc. At No. 12 is the *Institut Médico-Légal* (no adm.) which takes the place of the old Morgue that stood at the S. end of the Île de la Cité.

Beyond the **Pont de Bercy** (2¼ m.; 1864) is the QUAI DE BERCY (r.b.), lined with the vast *Entrepôts de Bercy*, warehouses for wine, spirits, vinegar, and oil, which extend beyond the **Pont de Tolbiac** (2¾ m.; 1879–84) to the Pont National. Opposite is the QUAI DE LA GARE (for tankers), with a large goods station. Just within the old fortifications is the **Pont National** (3¼ m.; 1852, enlarged in 1939–42), used by the Ceinture railway as well as by road traffic.

B   From the Louvre to Auteuil

Immediately below the Rue du Louvre is the **Pont des Arts** (foot-passengers only), built in 1802–04, which derives its name from the 'Palais des Arts', as the Louvre was called at that time. It commands a superb *View of the W. end of the Île de la Cité, the *Institut*, and the *Monnaie*.—The chief feature of the QUAI DU LOUVRE (r.b.) is the beautiful S. front of the *Louvre*. On the QUAI MALAQUAIS (l.b.) are some mansions of the 17–18C and part of the *École des Beaux-Arts*.—The **Pont du Carrousel**, originally built in 1834, was entirely

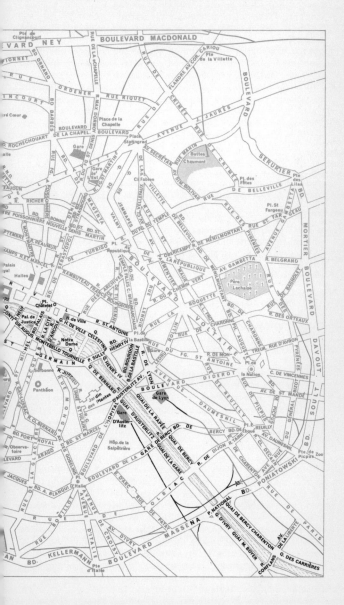

rebuilt in 1935–39. At the ends of the bridge are four seated stone figures by Petitot and Pradier, from the original bridge. Behind the QUAI DES TUILERIES (r.b.) is the long S. façade of the Louvre, the Galerie du Bord de l'Eau with the Pavillon de Flore. Opposite is the QUAI VOLTAIRE.—The **Pont Royal** (⅔ m.) is a five-arched bridge built by Père F. Romain and Gabriel in 1685–89 and commands a splendid view. The last pillar on either bank has a hydrographic scale indicating the low-water mark (zero), besides various flood-marks.

Below the Pont Royal is the QUAI ANATOLE-FRANCE (l.b.) with the *Caisse des Dépôts et Consignations*, the imposing *Gare d'Orsay*, and the *Palais de la Légion d'Honneur*. Behind the QUAI DES TUILERIES (r.b.) lie the *Tuileries Gardens.*—The **Pont de la Concorde** (1 m.; *Views and the wonderful perspective of the Place de la Concorde, Rue Royale and the Madeleine) unites the *Place de la Concorde* with the *Palais Bourbon*. It was built by Perronet in 1788–90, and stone from the Bastille was used in the construction of the upper part. One of the reasons for this is said to be that the Parisians would be able to tread underfoot the symbol of royal despotism. The bridge was widened in 1931–32. The river now flows between the QUAI DE LA CONFÉRENCE and the QUAI D'ORSAY (l.b.), with the *Ministère des Affaires Étrangères* and the *Esplanade des Invalides*, at the S. end of which towers the golden dome of the Invalides. Beyond the Esplanade is the *American Church.*—The beauty of the **Pont Alexandre-III** (1½ m.; 1896–1900) lies in the single steel arch, 350 ft in span and 150 ft wide. Tsar Nicolas II laid the first stone.

The pillars at either end are surmounted by gilded figures of Fame and Pegasus, and other statues adorn the bridge.

The **Pont des Invalides** (1⅔ m.), constructed in 1827–29, rebuilt in 1879–80, and enlarged in 1956, joins the Quai de la Conférence and the Quai d'Orsay. The **Pont de l'Alma** (1⅘ m.), built in 1854–57, with the Place de l'Alma at its N. end, is adorned with stone figures, including a Zouave, the Parisians' gauge for estimating the height of the Seine in flood. The bridge is to be rebuilt.

Between the Pont de l'Alma and the Pont de Bir-Hakeim (see below) is the AVENUE DE NEW-YORK (r.b.); opposite is the QUAI ÉDOUARD-BRANLY. A little above the *Passerelle Debilly* are the two huge buildings of the *Palais d'Art Moderne* (r.b.) and the *Ministry of Economic Affairs* farther on (l.b.). Below the Passerelle, a plaque commemorates Robert Fulton's pioneer work on steam navigation in 1803. We now pass between the gardens of the *Palais de Chaillot* (r.b.) and the *Champ-de-Mars* (l.b.) with the *Eiffel Tower*. The **Pont d'Iéna** (2½ m.), which spans the river here, was built in 1806–13 and widened in 1914, and again in 1936. The **Pont de Bir-Hakeim** (formerly the Pont de Passy, 2⅔ m.; 1903–06) is a double bridge, the upper story being used by the Métro. The centre of the bridge rests on the E. side of the long and narrow *Allée* or *Île des Cygnes* ('Isle of Swans'). On the right bank is the AV. DU PRÉSIDENT-KENNEDY; on the left, the QUAI DE GRENELLE. The river and island are crossed also by an oblique railway-viaduct (1900) and by the **Pont de Grenelle** (3¼ m.), rebuilt in 1875, between which (r.b.) is the huge circular *Maison de la Radio*, designed by Henri Bernard (1960), striking because of its tower and the use of aluminium. On the extremity of the island, facing downstream, is a reduced bronze copy of Bartholdi's famous statue, *Liberty enlightening the World*, presented by the French Republic to the United States, where it stands at the entrance to New York Harbour.

Beyond the Pont de Grenelle are the QUAI LOUIS BLÉRIOT (r.b.) and the QUAI ANDRÉ-CITROËN (formerly Quai de Javel; l.b.) with the Citroën works.

The **Pont Mirabeau** (3½ m.), built in 1895–97, is striking. On the right is the *Institution de Ste-Périne*. The **Pont-Viaduc d'Auteuil** (4 m.) is a fine work by Bassompierre (1866), deprived of its upper railway-viaduct in 1961.

3   THE CITÉ AND THE ÎLE ST-LOUIS

MÉTRO stations: *Cité* (line 4); *Châtelet* (lines 1, 4, 7, 11); *St-Michel* (line 4); *Sully-Morland, Pont-Marie* (line 7).

The **Île de la Cité,** the oldest and earliest inhabited part of Paris, lies in the river like a ship, moored to the banks by numerous bridges, with Notre-Dame as its poop and the 'Pointe', pointing downstream, as its prow. The ship that has always figured in the arms of Paris is therefore most appropriate. The CITÉ was the site of the original Gallic settlement of Lutèce or Lutetia Parisiorum and, after the destruction of the later Roman city on the left bank, became the site of Frankish Paris. It remained the royal, legal, and ecclesiastical centre long after the town had extended to the river-banks. It retains important relics of its pristine glory, notably the two gems of medieval religious art, Notre-Dame and the Sainte Chapelle, and the Palais de Justice. For the visitor with little time a visit to the Cité will give the best idea of the historical development of Paris as well as its beauty.

The Cité derives its importance from its situation at the crossroads of the two natural routes across France. The Capetian kings were the great builders of the Cité, and it remained little changed from 1300 to the Second Empire when Haussmann, after massive demolition, gave it its present appearance.

The Pont Neuf leads from the Quai du Louvre to the W. extremity of the Cité, occupied by the *Square du Vert-Galant*, with its charming garden. Here, close to the bridge, stands the fine equestrian *Statue of Henri IV*, by Lemot, set up in 1818 in place of a statue by Giambologna and Tacca which stood here from 1635 to 1792. The foundryman, an ardent Bonapartist, placed within the right arm a statuette of Napoleon, because he was constrained to use for it the melted-down statue of Napoleon which had surmounted the Vendôme column.

To the E. of the bridge, in front of the Palais de Justice, is the *Place Dauphine*, with two rows of houses dating from Louis XIII's reign, but mostly altered. The square was only saved from further damage by the retirement of Haussmann. No. 26, one of the best houses, was the last home of Ludovic Halévy (1834–1908).

During the 17C and 18C the Place du Pont-Neuf and the bridge were frequented by pedlars and mountebanks. Tabarin, the most famous mountebank, set up his 'theatre' in the Place Dauphine. Here, too, was the original site of the Samaritaine, one of the earliest hydraulic pumps, constructed by a Fleming for Henri IV to supply water for the royal palaces of the Louvre and the Tuileries. It derived its name from a figure of the Good Samaritan on the fountain. The 'bouquinistes' have their second-hand book-stalls on the parapets of the quays.

The ***PALAIS DE JUSTICE,** a huge block of buildings occupying the whole width of the island, includes within its precincts the Sainte Chapelle, the Conciergerie, the Dépôt des Prévenus (remand prison), and the Cour de Cassation (supreme court of appeal). Its oldest surviving portion includes the four towers on the N. side and the Sainte Chapelle (13–14C). The main buildings, of the 18C, were greatly enlarged in 1857–68 and 1911–14.

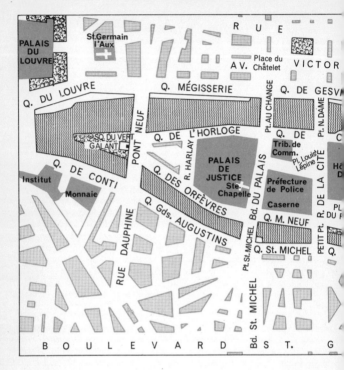

ADMISSION. The *Palais* is open daily (free) from 10–5, except Sun and holidays. The *Sainte Chapelle* and the *Conciergerie* are open daily (except Tues and holidays) 10–12, 1.30–5 or 6. Adm. 1 fr. (0,50 fr. on Sun).

HISTORY. The site of the Palais de Justice was occupied as early as the Roman period by a palace, which was a favourite residence of Julian the Apostate, proclaimed Emperor here in 360. The Merovingian kings divided their time between the Thermes, in the country, and this Palais de la Cité, which was inside the walls. Louis VI died in the palace in 1137, Louis VII in 1180; and in 1200 or 1201 Philip Augustus was married there to Ingeborg, daughter of Valdemar the Great of Denmark. St Louis, the 'father of the Cité', altered the palace and built the Sainte Chapelle. As Dauphin in 1357 the future Charles V witnessed in the Palais de la Cité the murder of two of his marshals by Étienne Marcel's men, which turned him against it. From the reign of Charles VII (in 1431) onwards the whole palace was occupied by the Parlement, which had shared it with the reigning sovereign since the time of St Louis. It acquired its present function at the Revolution. Since then the palace, which has suffered from frequent fires, has been repeatedly rebuilt, enlarged, and restored.

EXTERIOR. The imposing COUR DU MAI, named after the maypole set up here annually by the 'Basoche', or society of law-clerks, is separated from the Boul. du Palais by handsome iron railings, erected in 1785 and reconstructed in 1877. A flight of steps ascends to the Galerie Marchande, above which rises a dome with sculptures by *Pajou*.—The buildings in the Boul. du Palais, between the Cour du Mai and the clock-tower, are in the 14C style and serve in part as the façade of the Salle des Pas-Perdus, which may be entered directly from the boulevard.

The 14C TOUR DE L'HORLOGE or clock-tower, at the N.E. corner, completely renewed in 1852, has an enormous clock copied from the original dial designed c. 1585 by *Germain Pilon*. Fronting the Quai de l'Horloge is a block of buildings of 14C origin (upper stories rebuilt in the original style). These were the additions made for Philip the Fair by Enguerrand de Marigny. Between the TOUR DE CESAR and TOUR D'ARGENT,

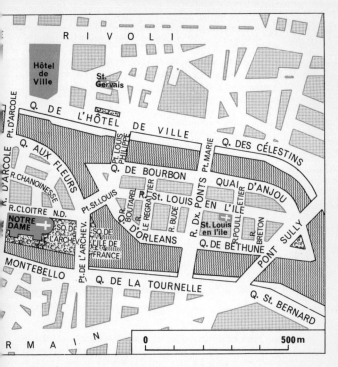

a pair of projecting round towers, is the entrance to the Conciergerie, and farther on is another round tower, the TOUR DE BONBEC (repaired 1935), with the 19C wing of the Cour de Cassation beyond.

The handsome façade in the Place Dauphine (1857–68) is adorned with lions and statues, while to the S., on the Quai des Orfèvres, are the courts of the Tribunal Correctionel (Criminal Court), added in 1914.

At No. 36 Quai des Orfèvres is the *Museum of Police History* (Collections Historiques de la Préfecture de Police; open Thurs 2–5), comprising not only historic police documents and uniforms, etc., but also a room devoted to the Resistance and the Liberation of Paris (1941–44), in which the police played an important part.

A vaulted gateway in the Boulevard du Palais leads to the great COUR DE LA SAINTE-CHAPELLE.

The **Sainte Chapelle**, a gem of Gothic architecture, was built in 1243–48 by St Louis as a shrine for the Crown of Thorns and a fragment of the True Cross. Its design is ascribed to *Pierre de Montreuil* and is remarkable for the impression of lightness. Royal marriages were often celebrated at the Sainte Chapelle, and Richard II of England was betrothed here in 1396 to Isabella of France. In 1837–57 it was restored by *Duban, Lassus* (who built the successful leaden flèche in the 15C style, 108 ft above the roof), and *Viollet-le-Duc*.

EXTERIOR. The chapel, 118 ft long, 56 ft wide, and 138 ft high, gives an impression of great height in proportion to its length and breadth. It consists of two chapels, one above the other, the lower chapel being used by the retainers and servants was dedicated to Our Lady, while the elaborately decorated upper chapel was reserved for the royal family and the court and dedicated to the Crown of Thorns and True Cross. The lofty windows of the upper chapel, an innovation, are surmounted by delicately sculptured gables and a graceful balustrade. The modern lead roof is picked out with gilding. By the fourth window on the right is a little recess constructed (perhaps) by Louis XI so that he could hear mass without being seen. Below this is the Oratory of St Louis. The portal consists of two porches, one above the other; the statues are 19C restorations.

CHAPELLE BASSE. The interior is very low (21 ft), with forty columns and admirable bosses of carved oak. The painted decoration is all by *Bœswillwald*, except for an Annunciation (13C) in the first N. bay of the ambulatory. In the pavement are many 14–15C tombstones.

CHAPELLE HAUTE. A staircase leads from the lower chapel to the porch of the upper chapel, which communicates on the N. side with the palace. The whole of the interior (67 ft high) has been repainted and regilded, but its outstanding decoration is the *Stained Glass (restored in 1845) which glows with the radiance of jewels. The 1st window on the right represents the Legend of the Cross and the removal of the relics. The other windows in the nave and apse depict scenes from the Old and New Testaments; the large rose window of painted glass, with eighty-six panels from the Apocalypse, was a gift of Charles VIII. Beneath the windows on either side run a blind arcade and a bench, with painted quatrefoils (scenes of martyrdom); against the pillars are figures of the *Apostles with consecration crosses (the 4th, 5th, and 6th on the left and the 3rd, 4th, and 5th on the right are original). The two deep recesses under the windows of the 3rd bay were the seats reserved for the royal family. In the 4th bay on the right is Louis XI's recess. In the centre of the (restored) arcade across the apse is a wooden canopy beneath which the sacred relics used to be exhibited on Good Friday. The remaining relics saved at the Revolution are in Notre-Dame.

A celebrated quarrel over the placing of a lectern gave Boileau the theme of his best-known work ('Le Lutrin').

A vaulted passage leads from behind the chapel into the Cour du Mai, the main entrance-courtyard. We ascend the steps to the GALERIE MARCHANDE, at the right end of which is the SALLE DES PAS-PERDUS, which replaces the great hall of the medieval palace, where, in 1431, the coronation banquet of Henry VI of England was celebrated.

It is reached direct from the boulevard by the *Escalier Louis-XVI* (in the right wing of the Cour du Mai), an 18C staircase revealed by alterations in 1932.

This magnificent hall, divided by a row of arches, was rebuilt by *Salomon de Brosse* in 1622, burned by the Communards in 1871, and restored in 1878. It is adorned with monuments to distinguished lawyers, and a memorial to advocates who fell in the First World War, by *Bartholomé* (1922). At the far end on the right is the entrance to the Première Chambre Civile, formerly the GRAND' CHAMBRE or CHAMBRE DORÉE (restored in the style of Louis XII), perhaps originally the bedroom of St Louis. Later it was used by the Parlement, and it was here that Louis XIV coined his famous epigram "L'État, c'est moi". The Revolutionary Tribunal, with Fouquier-Tinville as public prosecutor, sat here in 1793 and condemned to death many famous people, including Charlotte Corday, Marie-Antoinette, the Girondins, and Mme Roland.

The GALERIE DES PRISONNIERS and GALERIE LAMOIGNON traverse the whole length of the building, on the left of the great hall, from the Galerie Marchande to the Vestibule de Harlay. To the right diverges the GALERIE ST-LOUIS, with a painted statue of St Louis, by *Guillaume* (1877), and two wall-paintings from the life of St Louis, by *L. O. Merson*. At the end (l.) the GALERIE DES BUSTES leads to the CHAMBRE CIVILE DE LA COUR DE CASSATION (when the court is not sitting, apply to the usher), elaborately decorated with a ceiling-painting, the Glorification of Law, by *Paul Baudry*. When the court is sitting the entrance is to the right at the end of the Galerie Lamoignon. To the left extends the VESTIBULE DE HARLAY, at the end of which are statues of St Louis, Philip Augustus, Napoleon I, Charlemagne, and a bust of Duc, its architect, by *Chapu*. The grand staircase leads (l.) to the Assize Court and (r.) to the Court of Criminal Appeal; while from the S. end of the Vestibule the GALERIE DE LA PREMIÈRE PRÉSIDENCE, with the Première Chambre de la Cour d'Appel on the right, leads back to the Galerie Marchande.

The **Conciergerie* (entered between the twin towers on the Quai de l'Horloge), one of the famous prisons of the world, originally the residence of the 'Concierge' or chief executive of the Parlement, occupies the lower floor of the right (N.) wing of the Palais. Part of it is still used for prisoners awaiting trial.

The historical associations of the Conciergerie are innumerable. In 1418 the Comte d'Armagnac was massacred with many of his partisans by the hired assassins of the Duke of Burgundy. During the Revolution, first Marie-Antoinette, then Bailly, Malesherbes, Mme Élisabeth, Mme Roland, Mme du Barry, Camille Desmoulins, Danton, André Chénier, and Robespierre passed their last days in the Conciergerie. In the massacres of Sept. 1792 288 prisoners perished here. Later prisoners were Georges Cadoudal (d. 1804), the Chouan leader, Marshal Ney, and the Duc d'Orléans (1890).

On the right side of the courtyard is a door leading to the SALLE DES GARDES, a handsome 14C vaulted room restored in 1877, where visitors await the guide. On the window side are two small staircases (no adm.), that on the right leading to the Tour de César, where Ravaillac, the murderer of Henri IV (1610), was imprisoned. The other stair leads to the Tour d'Argent, which served as a prison for Damiens, who attempted the life of Louis XV (1757). The little staircase on the left of the room in the right-hand corner was ascended by Marie-Antoinette and over 2200 other prisoners on the way from their cells to the Tribunal. The splendid Gothic **SALLE DES GENS-D'ARMES (or de St-Louis) was restored in 1868–80 and is considered the rival of the halls of Mont St-Michel and the Palace of the Popes at Avignon. It now contains sculptured fragments from the old palace.

This is the original 'Salle des Pas-Perdus', said to be so called because the victims of the Revolution walked through it on their way to the Cour du Mai and execution; the name has since been transferred to the hall above and to the waiting-halls of other public buildings.

The CUISINES DE ST-LOUIS (so called), another vaulted 14C hall, has four large fireplaces. At the W. end of the Salle des Gens-d'Armes, the wide gallery known as the RUE DE PARIS served as a prison during the Revolution for the 'pailleux' (prisoners who slept on straw, being unable to bribe their gaolers). It ends at the GALERIE DES PRISONNIERS, the windows of which look out on to the COUR DES FEMMES, where the women prisoners were allowed to take exercise, the scene of the massacres of Sept 1792. The corner exactly opposite the windows of the Galerie des Prisonniers was divided off for the men by a railing that still exists. To the left in the Galerie des Prisonniers is a little room where condemned prisoners had their hair shorn and awaited their departure for the guillotine, and at the end is the iron wicket which was the sole entrance to the prison in Revolutionary times. In front of this was the registrar's office (now a restaurant). At the opposite end of the Galerie des Prisonniers is (l.) the original door (but in a different position) of MARIE-ANTOINETTE'S CELL, which was converted into a chapel of atonement in 1816. Next to the queen's cell, and now communicating with it, is ROBESPIERRE'S CELL. Next comes the

SALLE DES GIRONDINS, where the Girondins spent their last night before execution. Once the chapel of the Conciergerie and used again as a chapel during the Restoration, it has preserved its original appearance, with its gallery for the prisoners. Here are now collected souvenirs of the Revolutionary period including a blade of the guillotine, the lock of Robespierre's cell, a facsimile of a letter written by Marie-Antoinette after her trial, and a crucifix found in her cell; also orders for the arrest of later distinguished prisoners.

On the opposite side of the BOULEVARD DU PALAIS are the *Préfecture de Police* (the 'Scotland Yard' of Paris) and the domed *Tribunal de Commerce* (weekdays, 10–4), built by Bailly in 1860–65. In the *Marché aux Fleurs* (Place Louis-Lépine), behind the Tribunal, a flower market is held on Mon, Tues, Thurs, and Fri (bird market on Sun). The Rue de la Cité (r.) leads to the PLACE DU PARVIS-NOTRE-DAME, the area of which Haussmann increased sixfold by his demolitions. The square is bounded on the S. by the Seine, on the W. by the *Caserne de la Cité* (1865), the former barracks of the Garde Républicaine, now occupied by the police; it was the scene of considerable fighting during the liberation of Paris. On the N. is the *Hôtel-Dieu* (a hospital founded on the S. side of the Parvis by St Landry, bishop of Paris, c. 660 and rebuilt on its present site in 1868–78), while on the E. is Notre-Dame. At the S.E. corner of the square is a colossal group of Charlemagne, Roland, and Oliver, by the brothers Rochet (1882).

On the Parvis the archbishops of Paris tried heretics, and here the condemned knelt before execution to acknowledge their sin and beg absolution. In 1314 the Templar grand-master, Jacques de Molay, summoned to repeat his confession publicly and accept sentence of imprisonment, unexpectedly protested the innocence of his Order to the crowd and was hustled off to the stake. Excavations in the Parvis have uncovered relics of all ages back to the 2C, an exhibition of which was mounted in 1967.

The ****CATHEDRAL OF NOTRE-DAME** is archæologically the most interesting of the Gothic cathedrals of France, though for beauty it ranks after Chartres, Reims, Amiens, and Bourges. Taken in hand at the time when Gothic art was beginning to throw off the traditions of the Romanesque style, Notre-Dame was completed during the 13C, so that it is possible to follow, step by step, the progress of the new style until its decadence in the 14C.

History. The idea of replacing by a single building, on a much larger scale, the cathedral of St-Étienne (founded by Childebert in the 6C) and that of Notre-Dame, farther E., was due to Maurice de Sully, bishop of Paris (d. 1196). The old Notre-Dame had replaced a Roman temple of Jupiter more or less on the site of the present cathedral. The foundation stone of the new building was laid by Pope Alexander III in 1163. The choir was finished in 1182 (except for the great roof), the nave in 1208, and the W. front and its towers c. 1225–50. A girdle of chapels was added: side chapels of nave (1235–50); chapels of the apse by Pierre de Chelles and Jean Ravy (1296–1330). The side porches were begun in 1258. The crossings of the transepts were built by Jean de Chelles and Pierre de Montreuil (1250–67).

In 1430, in the choir of Notre-Dame, Henry VI of England was crowned king of France at the age of ten, and here were celebrated the marriages of Francis II to Mary Stuart (1558), Henry of Navarre to Margaret of Valois (1572), and Charles I (by proxy) to Henrietta Maria (1625). In 1687 Bossuet preached the funeral oration for 'Le Grand Condé'. Until the end of the 17C Notre-Dame had preserved intact its appearance of the 14C, but the reigns of Louis XIV and Louis XV brought deplorable alterations (especially the destruction of the tombs and stained glass). The baptistery of St-Jean-le-Rond, adjoining the N. tower, was demolished in 1748. During the Revolution many of the sculptures and treasures of the cathedral were destroyed, and an opera-singer was here enthroned as the Goddess of Reason. Napoleon I and Josephine were crowned by Pius VII in Notre-Dame in 1804, and other grand ceremonies were the baptism of the King of Rome (1811), the marriage of Napoleon III and Eugénie de Montijo (1853) and the baptism of the Prince Imperial (1856). In 1845 a thorough restoration, guided by technical knowledge and good taste, was begun under the direction of Lassus and Viollet-le-Duc. State funerals held here have included those of Foch (1929), Joffre (1931), and Leclerc (1947). In August 1944 the service of thanksgiving, following Gen. de Gaulle's triumphant entry into Paris, was marred by sniping from the galleries, both inside and outside the cathedral.

EXTERIOR. The *WEST FRONT, in three distinct stories, forms one harmonious whole. The *Porte du Jugement*, or central portal (23 ft high), ruined by Soufflot in 1771, has a 19C statue of Christ on the pier and the Last Judgment, well restored by Viollet-le-Duc, in the tympanum; only the upper tier of sculptures is ancient. The *Porte de la Vierge* (l.) has the most striking sculptures. On the pier is the Virgin trampling the serpent underfoot (restored). In the lower part of the tympanum are three prophets (l.), three kings (r.), and the Resurrection of the Virgin (centre); above is the Coronation of the Virgin. The sides of the pier and the medallions show the monks and their labours. The sculptures of the *Porte de Ste-Anne* (r.) are mostly of 1165–75, designed for a narrower portal, with additions of c. 1240. On the pier is St Marcellus (19C) trampling on the dragon. Above, scenes from the lives of St Anne and the Virgin, and the *Virgin in Majesty, with Louis VII (r.) and Maurice de Sully (l.). The wrought-iron *Hinges of the two side doors are masterpieces of medieval work. On the buttresses between the doors are four beautiful niches with 19C statues.—Above the portals is the *Gallery of the Kings of Judah*, the 28 statues of which, destroyed in 1793 because the Parisians took them to represent the Kings of France, were reconstructed for Viollet-le-Duc to accord with those ornamenting the *Gallery of the Virgin*, above. The magnificent rose window, 31 ft in diameter, is flanked by double windows within arches. Higher still is a fine open arcade with graceful columns.

The TOWERS, 223 ft high, originally intended to be crowned with spires, are open daily (except Tues) 10–4, 5, or 6. Entrance at the door of the N. tower; adm. 1,50 fr. on Sun. The platforms at the top command a superb *View of Paris. The balustrades are adorned with the famous *Gargoyles ('chimères') designed by Viollet-le-Duc, grotesque figures of devils, birds, and beasts. In the S. tower hangs the great bell ('Emmanuel-Louis-Marie-Thérèse'), recast in 1686 and weighing 13 tons.

The side façades and the apse likewise consist of three distinct and receding stories. The flying buttresses of the apse (by Jean Ravy) are especially admired for their boldness and elegance. The *South Porch* (usually seen only in conducted tours of the Service des Monuments Historiques), according to the Latin inscription at the base, was begun in 1257 (1258 n.s.) under the direction of Jean de Chelles. The tympanum (Story of St Stephen) is original as are the medallions depicting a student's life in the 13C. The *North Porch* dates from about the same period. On the pier is a fine original statue of the Virgin; in the tympanum, story of Theophilus. Beyond the N. door is the graceful *Porte Rouge*, a masterpiece of 14C carving, probably by *Pierre de Montreuil*. To the left, below the windows of the choir chapels, are seven bas-reliefs of the 14C (life of the Virgin, and story of Theophilus). The *Flèche* (312 ft above the ground) of lead-covered oak was rebuilt by Viollet-le-Duc in 1859–60 (the original was destroyed at the end of the 18C). The ball below the cross contains relics of the True Cross and the Crown of Thorns.

The best view of the dark **Interior** (closed at 6) is obtained from the W. end beneath the great organ (1733, rebuilt 1868; enlarged 1960). The church (427 ft long, 157 ft wide, and 115 ft high) consists of a nave (ten bays), of great purity of style, flanked on either side with double aisles continued round the choir (five bays), and of 37 chapels encircling the whole building. Over the aisles run fine vaulted galleries, the nave windows above which were altered in the 13C. The vaulting is supported by 75 piers, with capitals of bold and graceful design. In 1963–64 new glass with a pleasing abstract effect was placed in the nave. Of the three great *Rose Windows, which alone retain their 13C glass, the N. window is the finest and best preserved, with patriarchs, prophets, and kings of the Old Testament, with the Virgin in the centre. Against the S.E. pillar of the crossing stands 'Notre-Dame de Paris', a 14C figure, perhaps originally in the Chapelle St-Aignan (see below); against the N.E. pillar is a statue of St Denis by *N. Coustou*. On the S. side of the S.W. pier a simple tablet, unveiled in 1924, commemorates the million subjects of the British Empire who gave their lives in the First World War, the greater part of whom rest in French soil. In the transepts are fresco paintings dating from 1869–70. Seven paintings (by *Ch. Le Brun, Seb. Bourdon*, and others), presented to Notre-Dame by the Goldsmiths' Guild of Paris in 1634–51, hang in the side-chapels of the nave; in the 7th N. chapel is the grisly tomb of Canon Yver (d. 1468).

The CHOIR, modified in 1708–25 by Louis XIV in fulfilment of his father's vow of 1638, attracted Viollet-le-Duc's restoring hand. There remain 78 superb *Stalls (originally 114), adorned with bas-reliefs from the designs of *Jules Degoullons* (1711–15). At the end of the stalls on either side is a canopied archiepiscopal stall, with bas-reliefs of the martyrdom of St Denis (r.) and the healing of Childebert by St Germain of Paris (l.). The bronze angels (1712–13) against the apse-pillars somehow escaped the melting-pot of the Revolution.— In front of the high altar was buried Geoffrey Plantagenet, son of Henry II of England, in 1186. Behind Viollet-le-Duc's altar is a Pietà by *N. Coustou* with a base sculptured by *Girardon*, part of the 'Vœu de Louis XIII'. The *Statue of Louis XIII (S.) is one of the masterpieces of *G. Coustou*; that of Louis XIV (N.) is by *Coysevox*.—In the first four bays of the choir may be seen the remains of the *Screen which, until the 18C, extended round the whole apse; the charming and expressive bas-reliefs on the exterior, finished in 1351, were restored and repainted by *Viollet-le-Duc*. In the blind arches below are the names of the chief persons buried in the church.

The AMBULATORY, decorated with mid-19C frescoes, contains the tombs of Abp Affre, Abp Sibour, and other 18–19C prelates. Behind the high-altar is the tomb-statue of Bp Matiffas de Bucy (d. 1304). In the 2nd chap. S. of the central chapel is the theatrical tomb, by Pigalle, of the Comte d'Harcourt (d. 1769); here are also the (restored) tomb-statues of Jean Jouvenel des Ursins and his wife (d. 1431, 1451).

On the right in the ambulatory is the entrance to the SACRISTY, which contains the *Treasury* of the cathedral (open daily except Sun and feast days; adm. 10–12, 2–5.30; 1,50 fr.).

The visits organized by the Monuments Historiques include a tour of the galleries which provides splendid views of the rose windows as well as a remarkable view of the interior as a whole.

Road mileages in France are calculated from the W. door of Notre-Dame.

At No. 19 Rue des Ursins, N. of the cathedral (behind the Quai aux Fleurs), an antique shop preserves the nave of the *Chapelle St-Aignan* (1115–18), where mass was said in secret in 1789–91. The house in which Boileau died (1711) was in the neighbourhood.

Behind Notre-Dame lies the *Square de l'Archevêché* in which is a bust of Goldoni, the Italian dramatist, who died in Paris in 1793. The name of the square recalls the archbishops' palace, which stood on the quay until 1831. There is a splendid view of the forest of flying buttresses surrounding the apse of Notre-Dame.

In the *Square Île-de-France*, at the extreme E. end of the Cité, is the **Memorial** to 200,000 French victims of concentration camps, inaugurated in 1962 (architect, G. H. Pingusson) in the form of a sunken prison yard and a crypt with the tomb of an unknown camp prisoner.

The **Île St-Louis,** known familiarly as 'L'Île', one of the most peaceful parts of the city, is connected with the right bank of the Seine by three bridges and with the left bank by two. Formerly two islets, it was not built over till the 17C under Richelieu, when as an annexe of the Marais it was given many splendid mansions. It has been little changed since. From the Cité it is reached by the Pont St-Louis (temporary footbridge; comp. Rte 2).

In the Rue St-Louis-en-l'Île No. 51, with a balcony, is the *Hôtel Chenizot* (1730), in 1840–48 the house of Abp Affre. The sumptuous church of *St-Louis-*

en-l'Île was begun by Le Vau in 1664 and finished by Jacques Doucet in 1726. Le Vau had been married in its predecessor. The tower and curious openwork spire, 98 ft high, were added in 1765. The ornamental stone carving in the interior was executed under the direction of J. B. de Champaigne (d. 1681; buried in the church). It contains six Nottingham alabasters from the same

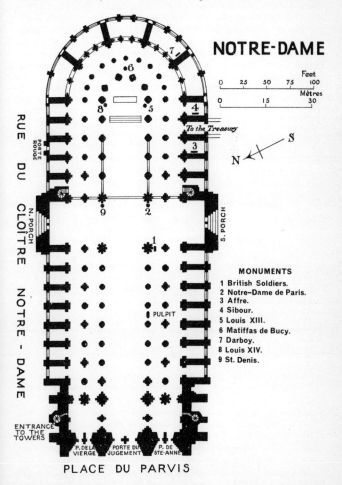

NOTRE-DAME

Feet
0   25   50   75   100

Mètres
0   15   30

To the Treasury

RUE DU CLOÎTRE NOTRE - DAME

PORTE ROUGE

N. PORCH

S. PORCH

PULPIT

ENTRANCE TO THE TOWERS

MONUMENTS

1 British Soldiers.
2 Notre-Dame de Paris.
3 Affre.
4 Sibour.
5 Louis XIII.
6 Matiffas de Bucy.
7 Darboy.
8 Louis XIV.
9 St. Denis.

P. DE LA VIERGE   PORTE DU JUGEMENT   P. DE STE-ANNE

PLACE DU PARVIS

series as those in St-Leu-St-Gilles. The fine 14–15C embroideries from the Abbey of Longchamp are shown by the sacristan.—At No. 12 in this street Philippe Lebon first introduced the principle of lighting by gas in France (1799; tablet). Between Nos. 7 and 9 is an arch of the *Hôtel de Bretonvilliers*, finished by Jean I du Cerceau in 1640; here opens the Rue de Bretonvilliers in which lived Taine in 1856–68 (No. 3). Fénelon lived at No. 3 Rue St-Louis.

No. 2 is the *Hôtel Lambert* (no adm.), by Le Vau (c. 1650), later the residence of Voltaire and Mme du Châtelet. For over 100 years it was the home of the Czartoryski family and a centre of Polish life in Paris.

In the Quai d'Anjou (N. side of the island) is the ***Hôtel Lauzun** or **de Pimodan** (No. 17; 1657), by Le Vau. It was in 1682–84 the residence of the Duc de Lauzun, commander of the French troops at the Battle of the Boyne, who lived here during his secret short-lived marriage with 'la Grande Mademoiselle'. In 1845 Baudelaire lived on the third floor and Gautier had apartments here in 1848; he has described the meetings of the Club des Haschichins, which took place here. It became the property of the city of Paris in 1928. Princess Elizabeth and the Duke of Edinburgh were received here during their visit to Paris in 1948.

For admission, apply to the Directeur-Adjoint, Les Beaux-Arts de la Ville de Paris, 14 Rue François-Miron (4e). The richness of the decoration, the blending of sculpture and painting are remarkable. The artists responsible are Lebrun, Le Sueur, Patel, and Sébastien Bourdon.

Nos. 13 and 15 in the QUAI DE BOURBON (N. side) were the *Hôtel Le Charron* (17C) with a delightful courtyard, while Philippe de Champaigne owned No. 11. No. 1 was the *Franc-Pinot*, an inn kept during the Revolution by the father of Cécile Renault, who tried to murder Robespierre. In the QUAI D'ORLEANS (S. side, with superb views of Notre-Dame) are the *Polish Library* and the *Musée Adam Mickiewicz* (open 3–5 Thurs; No. 6) with souvenirs of the Polish patriot and poet, and also of Chopin. No. 12 (with medallion) was the birthplace of Félix Arvers, the poet (1806–50), who died in the QUAI DE BETHUNE. In the latter (S. side of the island) is the mansion of the Duc de Richelieu, the famous nephew of the cardinal (No. 18); the poet Francis Carco died here in 1958. No. 20 was built by Le Vau. At the E. end of the island is the little *Square Henri IV* with a monument to Barye (1793–1875), the sculptor of animals, who had a studio on the Quai d'Anjou. No. 9 on the Quai d'Anjou was the home of Daumier from 1846 to 1879. No. 3 belonged to Le Vau.

4   THE LATIN QUARTER

MÉTRO stations: *St-Michel* (line 4); *Odéon* (lines 4 and 10).

The **Latin Quarter,** or *Quartier Latin*, is the district to the S. of the Île de la Cité on either side of the Boul. St-Germain and Boul. St-Michel. It grew up with Abelard's removal c. 1200 to the Montagne Ste-Geneviève from the school attached to Notre-Dame. Originally known as the *Université*, this has remained the learned quarter of Paris, deriving its present name (conferred by Rabelais) from the language spoken by the early students. Though most of the old streets and buildings have been swept away, and though increasing numbers have necessitated the creation of the Cité Universitaire, the Latin Quarter still contains the chief educational and scientific institutions of Paris, and it is still famous for its student life. Bookshops and galleries abound. Not the least interest of the quarter is that it occupies the site of Roman *Lutetia*.

The Pont St-Michel links the Boul. du Palais in the Cité with the **Place St-Michel** at the beginning of the Boul. St-Michel. No. 25 Quai St-Michel (at the corner of the Place) was the home of George Sand in 1831–37. The *Fontaine St-Michel*, 85 ft high on the S. side of the Place, was erected by Davioud in 1860, and incorporates a memorial of the Resistance of 1944.

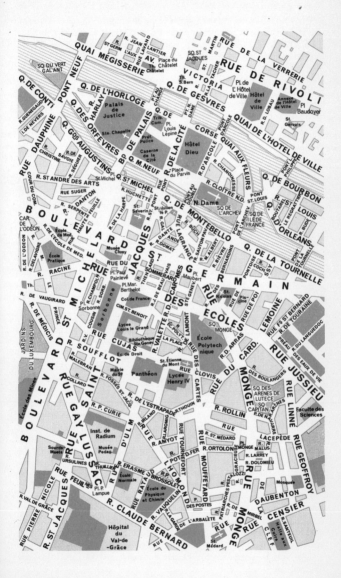

Adjoining the Place St-Michel on the S.W. is the *Place St-André-des-Arts*, where Gounod was born in 1818 (at No. 11).

The BOULEVARD ST-MICHEL (popularly the 'Boul Mich'), the chief thorough-fare in the Quartier Latin, begins at the Place St-Michel and leads S. to ($\frac{4}{5}$ m.) the Carrefour de l'Observatoire, passing the Cluny Museum, the Sorbonne, and the Luxembourg Gardens. Laid out by Haussmann as a direct continuation of the Boul. de Strasbourg and Boul. de Sébastopol, it is a very busy street, especially in its lower part, which swarms with students' cafés.—At a cross-roads, 300 yds S. of the Place St-Michel, the Boul. St-Michel crosses the BOULEVARD ST-GERMAIN, an important thoroughfare roughly parallel with the Seine. Almost the only interest of the main streets, however, springs from their animation; the architectural and historical character of the Quarter is found in the side streets.

To the E. of the Place, behind the Quai St-Michel, lies an interesting but decrepit corner of Old Paris, of which the quaintest streets are the Rue Xavier-Privas, the Rue de la Huchette, and the passage-like Rue du Chat-qui-Pêche, named after an old shop-sign. In the Rue de la Huchette Théophile de Viau composed his Parnasse Satirique (at No. 1) and Bonaparte lodged at No. 8 (or 10) in 1795; the *Théâtre de la Huchette* is the smallest in Paris.

At the end of the Rue St-Séverin is ***St-Séverin,** one of the architectural gems of Paris, rebuilt in the 13–16C on the site of an oratory of the time of Childebert I where in the 12C Foulque of Neuilly-sur-Marne preached the Fourth Crusade. The lower part of the W. front and the W. bays of the nave date from the early 13C; the outer S. aisle was added c. 1350, the outer N. aisle and the E. parts of the church were in construction in 1450–96, the chapels in 1500–20. The main W. portal, of the early 13C, was brought piecemeal in 1837 from St-Pierre-aux-Bœufs in the Cité. The two upper stories date from the 15C. On the left is a tower of the 13C, completed in 1487, with a door which was long the main entrance; the tympanum dates from 1853, but on the frame is a 15C inscription: "Bonnes gens qui par cy passés, Priez Dieu pour les tres-passés." To the left of the tower a niche holds a fine statue of St Séverin.

The INTERIOR impresses immediately by the great breadth of its double ambulatory. The most striking details are the ribs of the vaulting and the choir triforium, which approaches English Perpendicular in style. The apse was classicized in the 17C at the expense of Mlle de Montpensier. In the nave the first three bays contain late-14C glass, much restored (from St-Germain-des-Prés); from the fourth bay onwards the glass is mid-15C; in the choir it is a little later. One of the subjects is the murder of St Thomas Becket (S. side of nave). The W. rose window contains a Tree of Jesse (c. 1500), obscured by the organ of 1745.

To the S. of the choir are the 15C galleries of the graveyard, beneath which the first operation for the stone was carried out successfully in 1474.

Beyond the Rue St-Jacques (see below) is **St-Julien-le-Pauvre,** a tiny church rebuilt c. 1170–1230 and used in the 13–16C as a university church and in 1655–1877 by the old Hôtel-Dieu for various secular purposes. Since 1889 it has been used by the Melchites, Greek Catholics subject to papal authority. The present W. front was built in 1651. Within, the foliated capitals are charming; in the S. aisle is the curious tomb of Henri Rousseau (d. 1445); the iconostasis obscures the E. end.

To the S. of the church lies the RUE GALANDE, probably the oldest existing street in Paris (14C), where (on No. 42) is a carved representation of the life of St Julian. To the N. is the little SQUARE RENÉ-VIVIANI, which commands a magnificent *View of Notre-Dame. The locust tree is one of the oldest trees in Paris.

Off the Rue Lagrange, to the E., the Rue de la Bûcherie runs E.; at No. 13 is the *École d'Administration*, occupied by the École de Médecine from 1483 to 1775, with a rotunda of 1745 built by the Danish doctor, Winslow. The Rue du Fouarre (perhaps named from the 'straw' on which the students sat), which links Rue Lagrange with Rue Galande, was the centre of the four 14C schools of the University and is referred to by Dante (who was once supposed to have attended lectures here). We reach the BOULEVARD ST-GERMAIN at Place Maubert ('la Maub').

Étienne Dolet (1509–46), printer and man of letters, was burned here as a heretic. On the remains of his monument (the statue was melted down in 1942) the inscription is a punning pentameter: "Non dolet ipse Dolet, sed pia turba dolet" (it is not Dolet, but his faithful followers that mourn).—No. 17 Rue des Carmes (S. of the square) is the *Syrian Catholic Church*, which was formerly the chapel (1760) of a community of Irish priests, who established themselves in the 17C in the buildings of the *Collège des Lombards*.

On the left of the boulevard is the ancient and decrepit Rue de Bièvre (l.), where Dante is said to have written part of the 'Divina Commedia'. On the right is the apse of **St-Nicolas-du-Chardonnet** ('of the thistle-field'), a Renaissance church mostly built in 1656–1709, and not completed till 1936. Some of the statues and stucco work are by Nic. Legendre. The clumsy tower (1625) is a relic of an earlier edifice.

Corot's study for the Baptism of Christ is in the 1st chapel of the S. aisle. The 2nd chapel on the right of the choir, beyond the transept, contains the monument of Bignon, the jurist (d. 1656), by *Girardon*. In the 8th chapel (around the apse) is the striking tomb of Le Brun's mother, by *Tuby* and *Collignon*, designed by *Le Brun* in the theatrical style of Bernini; against the window is a monument of Le Brun (d. 1690) and his widow, by *Coysevox*. The wall and ceiling paintings are likewise by *Le Brun*. The 11th chapel contains a 17C wood relief of St Peter repentant. The fine 18C organ-case should be noted. In the sacristy is a Crucifixion by P. Brueghel the Younger.

To the E. of the church is the huge mass of the *Maison de la Mutualité*, built in 1931 on the site of the former seminary of St-Nicolas, where Renan studied theology. The Boul. St-Germain now crosses the Rue de Pontoise, in which (r.) a swimming bath occupies part of the site of the ancient *Collège des Bernadins*; the 14C refectory forms part of the firemen's barracks at No. 24 Rue de Poissy, behind.

To the left the Rue de Pontoise leads to the Quai de la Tournelle, where No. 55, at the corner, is the *Hôtel de Nesmond* (17C). At No. 47 on the quai is the *Musée des Hôpitaux de Paris* (open daily exc. Tues 10–12, 2–5; fee, free Sun) with collections illustrating the work of Paris hospitals throughout the centuries. The collection of pharmacy jars is particularly interesting. The building, which also houses the *Pharmacie Centrale des Hôpitaux*, was originally the convent of the 'Miramiones' or Filles Ste-Geneviève, founded by Mme de Miramion (d. 1696). The Boul. St-Germain and the quai meet at the Pont de Sully.

The dreary RUE MONGE, $\frac{3}{4}$ m. long, runs S.E. from the Place Maubert across the old Faubourg St-Marceau to the Av. des Gobelins. In the triangular *Square Monge*, below the École Polytechnique, is a statue of François Villon, the 15C poet, by Collamarini (1947); also a Louis-XV fountain (1719) from the abbey of St-Germain-des-Prés. We turn right into the Rue du Cardinal-Lemoine (comp. below).

The Rue Monge continues in a long curve. In the Rue de Navarre, diverging to the left, are the ruins of the **Arènes de Lutèce** (2–3C), the amphitheatre of Roman Paris, discovered in 1870 and fully excavated since 1883. It is 62 yds long and 51 yds wide. To the E. of the arena, the gardens of the Square Capitan look on to the Rue des Arènes.

In the Rue du Puits-de-l'Hermite (left of the Rue Monge farther on) was the *Prison de*

Ste-Pélagie, where Josephine, the future empress, and Mme du Barry were confined under the Revolution, and where Mme Roland wrote her memoirs.

St-Médard, farther on (r.), dedicated to the 'St Swithin' of France, is one of the most picturesque churches in Paris. The nave and W. front are of the late 15C; the choir, in construction from 1550 to 1632, was 'classicized' in 1784, when the circular Lady Chapel was added. The church was sacked by Huguenots in 1561 and not much of the 16C glass survives. The charming painting of St Geneviève in the E. choir chapel is by *Charles Eisen* (not Watteau); the organ-gallery is by *Pillon* (1644–46); the pulpit dates from 1718. The churchyard, now a garden, was once notorious for the fanatical orgies of the Jansenist pilgrims ('convulsionnaires') at the tomb of the Abbé Pâris (d. 1727).

The shabby and populous RUE MOUFFETARD leads N. from the front of the church through a picturesque if squalid district. Taking the Rue de l'Arbalète (l.) in which No. 3 was the birthplace of Auguste Rodin (1840–1917) and Nos. 9–16 the buildings of the *Institut National Agronomique*, we reach the RUE LHOMOND (r.) which leads to the Panthéon. Beyond the Place Lucien-Herr (r.) is the old Rue Tournefort with the *Sanctuaire du Christ-Roi* (1935–40). To the left is the Rue Pierre-Brossolette, over-shadowed by the huge brick building of the *École de Physique et de Chimie Industrielles*, where the Curies did their experimental work in 1883–1905. Nos. 12–24 in the Rue Lhomond are taken up by the new laboratories of the *École Normale* and the *Hôpital Curie*. No. 29 has an 18C façade in the courtyard (seen from Rue Amyot) and here Mme du Barry and Juliette Drouet were educated in the Convent de Ste-Aure. At the corner of the Rue des Irlandais (r.) is the *Collège des Irlandais*, founded in 1578, and established here as a seminary in 1769. At No. 17 Rue d'Ulm, on the left, is the Maronite church of *Notre-Dame du Liban*. No. 29 is the *Institut Pédagogique* with a useful library. No. 31 is the *École Nationale Supérieure des Arts Décoratifs*, and No. 45 is the *École Normale Supérieure* (see Rte 17).

The RUE DU CARDINAL-LEMOINE crosses the Rue Monge on its way S.W. from the Pont de la Tournelle. At No. 32 in its N. section (l.) was the *Collège des Bons-Enfants*, where St Vincent de Paul founded his congregation of mission-priests. No. 49 is a fine 17C mansion, the *Hôtel Le Brun*, built by Boffrand for the artist and occupied by Watteau and Buffon. The École Ste-Geneviève, opposite the Rue Clovis, is the old **Scots College** (*Collège des Écossais*; apply to the concierge), founded in 1325 by David, Bp of Moray. The building was erected in 1665 by Robert Barclay. The chapel, on the first floor, contains the tomb of the Duchess of Tyrconnel (d. 1731); a memorial erected to James II (who bequeathed his brain to the college) by the Duke of Perth, with a long Latin epitaph; the tomb of Sir Patrick Menteith, who died in 1675 in the service of Louis XIV, etc. Blaise Pascal died in 1662 on the site of No. 67. In the Rue Rollin (l.) Descartes lived at No. 14 and Rollin died at No. 8 in 1741.

The Rue du Cardinal-Lemoine, going uphill, ends at the *Place de la Contrescarpe*. No. 1 in this square has a tablet commemorating the Cabaret de la Pomme-de-Pin, immortalized by Rabelais and the 'Pléiade'.

The RUE CLOVIS, leading out of the Rue du Cardinal-Lemoine, is crossed by the Rue Descartes, at No. 39 in which Paul Verlaine (1844–96) died. At Nos. 5 and 21 are the entrances to the *École Polytechnique*, founded by Monge in 1794 for the training of artillery and engineer officers and transferred hither in 1805 to the buildings of the *Collège de Navarre*, which were considerably enlarged in 1929–35.

The Collège de Navarre had numbered among its pupils Gerson, Ramus, Henri III, Henri IV, and Henri de Guise, Richelieu, Bossuet, Condorcet, and André Chénier. The *Collège de Boncourt* (No. 21), taken over by the Collège de Navarre in the 17C, had earlier boasted perhaps the first theatre in Paris. In 1792 G. B. Piranesi established his engraving works in the college.

At No. 23 Rue Clovis is the entrance to the *Lycée Henri-IV*, the tower of which (restored) has a Romanesque base and two Gothic upper stories (14–15C) and is a relic of the church (demolished 1802) of the *Abbaye Ste-Geneviève*. Practically the whole of the conventual buildings were rebuilt in the 18C, but the former refectory (now the chapel), adjoining the Place Ste-Geneviève, is a pleasant but over-restored 13C building and the kitchens are likewise medieval. The fact that the abbey came under papal jurisdiction, not that of the Bishop of Paris, influenced Abelard's choice of this area (comp. above).

The Rue Clovis ends at the *Place Ste-Geneviève*, on the E. side of which is the remarkable and interesting church of *St-Étienne-du-Mont, showing the transition from the Gothic to the Renaissance style. It was almost continuously in construction from 1492 to 1586. Margaret of Valois laid the foundation stone of the portal in 1610 and even this preserves certain Gothic motives. The tower, begun in 1492, was completed in 1628. The N. side, with its picturesque porch of 1630–32, is especially attractive.

The church replaced an earlier parish church dependent upon and entered through the abbey church of Ste-Geneviève (comp. above). Under the Revolution it became the 'Temple of Filial Piety'.

The INTERIOR has lofty columns, a wide ambulatory and ribbed vaulting with pendent keystones. Its originality lies in the balustrade which runs along the supporting pillars of the nave and choir. On the floor near the entrance a marble slab marks the spot where Abp Sibour was assassinated in 1857 by an inhibited priest named Verger. The beautiful *ROOD SCREEN, built in 1525–35, is a masterpiece of design and carving; the date 1605 on the side refers only to the doors admitting to the spiral staircases by which it is ascended. The organ-case by *Jean Buron* dates from 1631–32; the pulpit of 1651 is the work of *Germain Pillon*, with sculptures designed by *Laurent de la Hire*. The *STAINED GLASS ranges in date from c. 1550 to c. 1600; the oldest windows are those in the apse. In the S. aisle the 2nd chapel contains the Birth of the Virgin, a masterpiece of *Louis Le Nain*; between the 6th and 7th a tablet commemorates the Jacobins, an order of preaching friars established in the Rue St-Jacques in 1218. Above the 1st S. chapel in the choir, Ex-voto to St Geneviève, with the provost of the merchants and the aldermen of Paris in 1726, by *F. de Troy* (a similar painting of 1696, by *Largillière*, surmounts the next doorway). On either side of the chapel are the epitaphs of Pascal and Racine (by Boileau), whose graves are at the entrance to the Lady Chapel. Also buried in the church are Rollin, and the painter Le Sueur. The next chapel S. of the choir, that of St Geneviève, much visited by the faithful, especially during the 'neuvaine' of St Geneviève (3–10 Jan), contains the copper-gilt shrine of the saint (1853). Within is a fragment of the saint's tomb; her bones were burned by the mob in the Place de Grève in 1801. In the next bay are an exit to the Rue Clovis and (l.) a corridor, at the end of which (r.) is the *Presbytery*, built in 1742 for Louis d'Orléans (son of the Regent), who died here in 1752. On the left is the *Charnier*, or gallery of the graveyard, with twelve superb *Windows of 1605–09; note especially the one depicting the Mystic Wine-press.

To the W. of the Place Ste-Geneviève rises the *Panthéon situated on the 'Mont de Paris', the highest point on the left bank (200 ft) and the burial-place of St Geneviève, patron saint of Paris (422–509 or 512).

In 1744, lying ill at Metz, Louis XV vowed that if he recovered he would replace the former church of Ste-Geneviève (see above). The present building was begun in 1764. The architect *Soufflot* died, of anxiety it is said, owing to criticism that subsidence of the walls would occur because the foundations had been laid on clay pits dug by Roman potters. In 1791, after the death of Mirabeau, the Constituent Assembly decided that the church should be used as a Pantheon, or burial-place for distinguished citizens, and on the pediment were inscribed the words "Aux Grands Hommes la Patrie reconnaissante". The building was again a church from the Restoration to 1830 and from 1851 to 1885, but on the occasion of Victor Hugo's interment it reverted to the name and purpose decreed in 1791.

The Panthéon is an imposing building in the shape of a Greek cross, 360 ft long, 270 ft wide, and 270 ft high to the top of the majestic dome. The pediment above the portico of 22 Corinthian columns is a masterpiece of *David d'Angers*, representing France between Liberty and History distributing laurels to famous men. Flanking the central entrance are marble groups by *Maindron*: the Baptism of Clovis, and St Geneviève and Attila.

ADMISSION. The Panthéon is open daily (except Tues) 10–4, 5, or 6; adm. 0,50 fr.; to the dome (10–12, 1.30–4), 1 fr. Visits to the crypt (gratuity) every 15 minutes.

The INTERIOR, coldly Baroque, is adorned with paintings on a gold ground, of saints and notabilities of France, together with monuments to those who have deserved the gratitude of their country. Among the paintings the Scenes from the Life of St Geneviève, by *Puvis de Chavannes* (S. aisle of nave, and N. aisle of choir), are outstanding, though pallid in colouring. In the S. transept is a monument to unknown and unrecognized heroes, by *Landowski*. By the same artist is the monument to unknown artists, in the N. transept. The colossal group of the Convention, at the E. end, is by *Sicard*.

The DOME is supported by four piers united by great arches. There are three distinct cupolas, of which the first is open in the centre to reveal the second, which has a fresco by *Gros*, the Apotheosis of St Geneviève, including the chief kings of France. By the first pillar (r.) is the monument of Jean-Jacques Rousseau, by *Bartholomé*, with figures of Music, Truth, Philosophy, Nature, and Fame. By the first pillar (l.) is a monument to Diderot and the Encyclopædists by *Terroir*.

Within the dome, in 1852, Léon Foucault, the physicist, gave the first public demonstration of his pendulum experiment proving the rotation of the Earth.

CRYPT (entrance in the apse to the left of the choir). Before the entrance, shrine containing the heart of Gambetta (d. 1882), brought hither in 1920. On the right is the tomb of *Jean-Jacques Rousseau* (d. 1778; transferred hither in 1794); on the left, *Voltaire* (d. 1778; transferred in 1791), with a statue attr. to Houdon; opposite, *Soufflot* (d. 1780), the architect. Between the four central pillars a curious echo may be awakened. Of the well-known men whose remains have been re-interred in the vaults, the most famous are probably *Victor Hugo* (d. 1885) and *Émile Zola* (d. 1902), whose removal hither from Montmartre Cemetery in 1908 created something of a riot; *Berthelot*, the chemist (d. 1907); *Jean Jaurès* (assassinated in 1914), socialist politician; and *Louis Braille* (d. 1852), benefactor of the blind.

Mirabeau (d. 1791) and *Marat* (d. 1793) were interred here with great state but their remains were soon cast out with ignominy; the former now rests in the cemetery of Ste-Catherine, the latter in the graveyard of St-Étienne-du-Mont.

In the N.W. corner of the PLACE DU PANTHÉON is the *École de Droit*, begun by Soufflot in 1771 and subsequently enlarged. The *Mairie of the 5th Arrondissement*, opposite, was built in 1844–50 in the same style. Their curved façades provide an admirable setting for the Panthéon. The **Bibliothèque Ste-Geneviève,** on the N. side of the Place, originated in the library of the famous Abbey of Ste-Geneviève. The present building, by Labrouste (1844–50), is on the site of the 14C *Collège de Montaigu*, where St Ignatius Loyola, Erasmus, and Calvin were students.

The library contains c. 700,000 vols. (nearly 4000 MSS.) and over 30,000 prints and engravings (10,000 portraits). The large reading-room is open daily 10–10 (except Sun and holidays). The reserve reading-room is open 10–12 and 1–4, but prospective students must make written application to M. le Conservateur. The library is closed annually from 15 to 31 Aug inclusive.—The rooms devoted to Scandinavian literature (c. 90,000 vols.; entrance, 8 Place du Panthéon) are open daily (except Sun and holidays) 2–5. The *Bibliothèque Littéraire Jacques Doucet*, bequeathed to the University of Paris in 1929, has been installed in the reserve of the library (open 2–5 on Tues and Fri on application). The collection comprises c. 8000 vols. of late 19 and 20C French authors, and includes MSS. of Rimbaud, Verlaine, Baudelaire, Gide, Paul Valéry, and others.

Among the most valuable illuminated MSS. in the library, which are exhibited from time to time, are an English Bible, copied by Manerius in the 12C; the Chronicles of St-Denis (end of the 13C); several MSS. of the Carolingian period; the 'De Proprietatibus Rerum' of Barthélemy l'Anglais (Catalan translation of the 15C); and 'La Cité de Dieu' of St Augustine (late 15C).

In the Rue Valette, on the right of the library, are the interesting remains of the *Collège Fortet* (No. 21), dating from 1397, where Calvin was a student in 1531.—To the left of the library, at the beginning of the Rue Cujas, is the *Collège Ste-Barbe*, founded in 1460, the oldest existing public educational establishment in France, at which St Francis Xavier was a scholar. The new Law Faculty Library (1958) has been built on part of the grounds of the college (entrance at 2 Rue Cujas).

In the Rue Montagne Ste-Geneviève to the left of the Rue Valette at No. 34 are remains of the *Collège des Trente-Trois*, founded in 1633 by Claude Bernard, friend and follower of St Vincent de Paul, and named after its thirty-three scholarships (one for each year of Christ's life on earth).

The broad RUE SOUFFLOT leads W. from the Panthéon to the Boul. St-Michel, opposite the Luxembourg Gardens. A tablet on No. 14 commemorates the Dominican or Jacobin convent (1217–1790), where Albertus Magnus and St Thomas Aquinas taught.

The Rue Soufflot is crossed by the RUE ST-JACQUES, which is nearly 1 m. long. In medieval times it formed the main thoroughfare of the left bank, keeping the course of the Roman road from Lutetia to Orléans. It formed part of the pilgrim route to St James of Compostella (whence its name) and so attracted many convents. The S. section is described in Rte 17. Near the corner (l.) is No. 151bis, a charming Louis XV mansion. Turning to the N., we pass the *Lycée Louis-le-Grand* (r.), formerly the Jesuit *Collège de Clermont*, founded in 1560 and rebuilt in 1887–96. Molière, Voltaire, Robespierre, Desmoulins, Delacroix, and Victor Hugo studied here. On the left is the Sorbonne.

In the Place Marcelin-Berthelot (r.) is the **Collège de France** (apply to the concierge; gratuity), founded by Francis I in 1530 under Budé's influence to spread humanism and counteract the narrow scholasticism of the Sorbonne. It was independent of the University and its teaching was free and public. The present building was begun in 1610, finished by *Chalgrin* c. 1778, and enlarged in more recent years; during work in 1894 traces were found of Gallo–Roman baths. Above the gateway of the Cour d'Honneur are the words "Docet Omnia", an enterprise provided for by forty professorships. In the courtyard, with its graceful portico, are a marble statue of Guillaume Budé (Budæus; 1468–1540) and tablets with the names of all the professors since the foundation.

Claude Bernard (1813–78), the physiologist, died at No. 40 Rue des Écoles, opposite. In the garden on the N.E. side of the college is a monument to the Pléiade, the 16C poetical coterie (notably Joachim du Bellay and Ronsard) which originated in a vanished college near this site (tablet on No. 11 Impasse Chartière).

The **SORBONNE**, the seat of the University of Paris, was founded as a modest theological college in 1253 by Robert de Sorbon, chaplain to St-Louis. It was rebuilt at Richelieu's expense by *Jacques Lemercier* in 1629, but, with the exception of the church, the present buildings, designed by *Nénot* on an imposing scale, date from 1885–1901.

The University of Paris, which disputes with Bologna the title of the oldest university in Europe, arose in the first decade of the 12C out of the schools of dialectic attached to Notre-Dame. Transferred by Abélard to the Montagne Ste-Geneviève, it obtained its first statutes in 1208, and these served as a model for Oxford and Cambridge and other universities of Northern Europe. By the 16C it comprised no fewer than forty separate colleges. Before the end of the 13C the Sorbonne had become synonymous with the faculty of theology, overshadowing the rest of the University and possessing the power of conferring degrees. Though it has the honour of having introduced printing into France, by allowing Ulrich Gering and his companions to set up their presses within its precincts in 1469, the Sorbonne was distinguished for its religious rancour, supporting the condemnation of Joan of Arc (Pierre Cauchon came from the Sorbonne), justifying the massacre of St Bartholomew, and refusing its recognition to Henri IV. In the 18C it attacked the 'philosophes'. The University was suppressed at the Revolution but was refounded by Napoleon.

The Sorbonne is now the chief seat of the *Faculté des Lettres* and the *Faculté des Sciences*. It houses the University Library (700,000 vols.), the *Académie de Paris*, whose rector is the head of the whole educational system of France, and other minor learned institutions. The University, the largest in Europe, with 17,000 students, confers degrees of 'bachelier', 'licencié', and 'agrégé'.

Visitors are admitted to the great lecture-hall (Grand Amphithéâtre) on application to the Secrétariat, Rue des Écoles. The other lecture-halls are open during lecture hours (consult the notice-boards). The library is open to students and those with special permission from the conservateur 9–12.30, 1.30–6.

The massive block of buildings, between the Rue de la Sorbonne (W.), the Rue des Écoles (N.), and the Rue St-Jacques (E.), is ponderous; the successful *Cour d'Honneur*, entered from the Rue de la Sorbonne, follows the lines of the courtyard of the old college. The chief rooms of the INTERIOR, entered from the Rue des Écoles, are lavishly decorated in the style of 1900. From the *Vestibule*, with statues of Homer and Archimedes, the *Grand Staircase*, with paintings illustrating the history of the University, ascends to the *Banqueting Hall* and the *Grand Amphithéâtre*, or great lecture-hall, with 2700 seats. Here are seated statues of the founder, and of benefactors and teachers of the University; and at the end of the hall is the Sacred Grove, a huge and popular painting by Puvis de Chavannes. In the Place de la Sorbonne is a monument to Auguste Comte (see below).

The **Church of the Sorbonne** (for adm. apply to concierge, 17 Rue de la Sorbonne), on the E. side of the Place, was founded as the college chapel in the 13C and rebuilt by *Lemercier* in 1635–59 at the expense of Card. Richelieu, whose family still has the right of being married and buried here. The *DOME was the first example of a true dome in Paris, those of the Carmes and St-Paul-St-Louis being but half-hearted attempts.

INTERIOR. The spandrel-paintings in the cupola, by *Philippe de Champaigne*, represent Four Fathers of the Church, with angels. On the right is the tomb, by *Ramey*, of the Duc de Richelieu (d. 1822). The marble group by *Sinding*, in the chapel on the left, was presented by Norway to the University. In the S. transept is the dramatic *TOMB OF CARDINAL RICHELIEU (d. 1642), designed by *Le Brun* and sculptured by *Girardon* (1694); the cardinal is represented in an attitude of grief, supported by Religion and Science. In the crypt are the bodies of twelve students of the University killed during the Resistance of 1940–45.

At the N. end of the Rue de la Sorbonne is the *Square Paul-Painlevé*, with a monument to Puvis de Chavannes, by Desbois, a memorial fountain, and a marble statue of Montaigne, by Landowski (1933). Thence a few steps along the Rue Du Sommerard, past the entrance of the **Musée de Cluny** (Rte 25), bring us to the Boulevard St-Michel, just S. of its intersection with the Boul. St-Germain.

In the Boul. St-Germain just to the W. of this point is the imposing façade (1878) of the **École de Médecine,** a huge block erected for the royal Académie de Chirurgie by Gondouin in 1769–76 on the site of the *Collège de Bourgogne* (especially devoted to natural philosophy) and the *Collège des Prémontrés* and greatly enlarged in recent years. The older part, considered the most classical work of the 18C, faces the Rue de l'École-de-Médecine.

In the handsome courtyard are a bronze statue of Bichat, the anatomist (1771–1802), by David d'Angers, and (l.) a marble monument to Dr Brouardel (1837–1906) by Denys Puech.

INTERIOR (apply to the concierge at the door on the right of the railings in the Rue de l'École-de-Médecine; gratuity). The great *Lecture Hall* (800 seats) has a fresco by Urbain Bourgeois depicting the chief masters of the medical art, ancient and modern. The *Library* (open to doctors and students daily 1.30–7, except Aug) contains c. 600,000 vols. and the interesting commentaries of the heads of the faculty from 1395 onwards. The *Musée d'Histoire de la Médecine* (adm. on Tues and Fri 3–5 for parties on application to M. le Doyen de la Faculté) contains pictures, documents, etc. The *Salle du Conseil* is hung with four magnificent *Gobelins of the Louis XIV period, after Le Brun.

Opposite the École de Médecine at Nos. 17–21 Rue de l'École-de-Médecine is the *École Pratique* or laboratories. On the left of the entrance is the former refectory of the *Couvent des Cordeliers*, a 15C Franciscan convent; during the Revolution this was the meeting-place of the extremist Club des Cordeliers, the leaders of which were Marat, Camille Desmoulins, and Danton.

No. 5 Rue de l'École-de-Médecine is the *Institut des Langues Modernes*, occupying the old Amphithéâtre de St-Côme (1691–94), with a beautiful portal. This was originally the lecture-hall of a college of surgery. A plaque here commemorates the birth of Sarah Bernhardt in 1844. At No. 20 (demolished) Marat was stabbed in his bath by Charlotte Corday in 1793.

Farther W. in the Boul. St-Germain, beyond the École de Médecine, is a bronze statue by A. Pâris, of the revolutionary Danton (1759–94), on the site of his house, where he was arrested. A few yards farther on we reach the Carrefour de l'Odéon (Rte 5A).

The ancient COUR DU COMMERCE-SAINT-ANDRÉ leads N. into an area of narrow streets between the Boulevard and the Seine. Here is the house (No. 9) where Dr Guillotin perfected his 'philanthropic beheading machine'; opposite (No. 8) is the printing-office where Marat's journal 'L'Ami du Peuple' was printed; and at No. 4 is the basement of one of Philip Augustus's towers. An alley leads hence (l.) to the 16–17C *Cour de Rohan*, originally part of the palace of the Archbishop of Rouen. Saint-Saëns was born in 1835 in the adjoining Rue du Jardinet. The RUE ST-ANDRÉ-DES-ARTS has several notable mansions (Nos. 52 and 47) of the 17–18C; in the RUE DES GRANDS-AUGUSTINS (l.) Nos. 3–7 are the *Hôtel d'Hercule*, dating from the 17C; No. 21 was the birthplace of Littré (1801–81), and Heine lived at No. 25 in 1841, as had La Bruyère in 1676–91. In the RUE HAUTE-FEUILLE, leading S. again from the Place St-André, is the *Hôtel des Abbés de Fécamp* (No. 5), with a pretty turret. Among its occupiers was the Marquise de Brinvilliers, accomplice of the Marquise de Brinvilliers. Baudelaire (1821–67) was born at No. 15 (demolished). Courbet had his studio (at No. 32) in the former chapel of the Collège des Prémontrés, at the corner of the Rue de l'École de Médecine.

Following the BOULEVARD ST-MICHEL, to the S., we have on the right the Rue de l'École-de-Médecine and the Rue Racine (see below), where George Sand lived at No. 3, on the fourth floor. Farther on (r.) is the *Lycée St-Louis*, built by Bailly on the site of the *Collège d'Harcourt*, the greatest of the

University colleges (1280), facing the Place de la Sorbonne. Racine and Boileau studied here. Next on the right begins the Rue de Vaugirard, leading W. past the Palais du Luxembourg. Beyond that is the Rue Monsieur-le-Prince, at No. 10 in which Auguste Comte (1798–1857), the positivist, lived from 1841. The composer Saint-Saëns lived at No. 14 in 1877–89, and Longfellow had lodgings at No. 49 in 1826, and, in a subsequent winter, at No. 5 Rue Racine. At No. 54 (altered) Pascal lived in 1654–62 and wrote his 'Pensées'. Farther on, opposite the Rue Soufflot, is the *Place Edmond-Rostand*, on the edge of the Luxembourg Gardens, with a fountain and a bronze group by Crauk. In the Rue de Médicis (r.) André Gide (1869–1951) was born at No. 19.

We next pass (r.) the École Supérieure des Mines, occupying the Hôtel de Vendôme, an 18C building enlarged after 1840 and having its principal façade towards the Luxembourg Gardens. The *Museum of Mineralogy and Geology* is open except Tues and Thurs 2.30–4 (closed Aug–mid-Sept). César Franck died at No. 95, nearly opposite, in 1890. The Rue Auguste-Comte (r.) leads to the Avenue de l'Observatoire, opposite the S. side of the Luxembourg Gardens, of which it once formed part. It was laid out under the First Empire by Chalgrin on the site of a Carthusian monastery demolished at the Revolution, and has fine trees and lawns adorned with ornamental sculpture. On the W. side of the avenue are the Moorish-looking *École Coloniale* (1896), the *École de Pharmacie* (1876–85), and, beyond the Rue Michelet, the *Institut d'Art et d'Archéologie* (1927), another mock-oriental edifice (entrance 3 Rue Michelet; library open with permission from Director daily 2–6, except Sun and in vacation). Farther S. is the **Fontaine de l'Observatoire*, a charming fountain by Davioud (1875), with bronze sea-horses and turtles by Frémiet and, in the centre, the four Quarters of the Globe supporting an armillary sphere, a masterpiece by Carpeaux.

The Av. de l'Observatoire and the Boul. St-Michel converge, and end together in the Carrefour de l'Observatoire (Rte 17).

5   THE FAUBOURG ST-GERMAIN

The district still known as the **Faubourg St-Germain** stretches S. from the river opposite the Louvre and the Tuileries, between the Pont des Arts on the E., and the Pont de la Concorde on the W. Until the end of the 16C, this area, the property of the Abbaye St-Germain-des-Prés, was open country. In the following century, with the religious revival, came several convents and in 1670 the Hôtel des Invalides. The construction of the Pont Royal in 1685 provided easy access to the Château des Tuileries, which became the home of the court during the Regency, and this, together with the creation of the École Militaire, are the chief reasons for the building of this aristocratic quarter, which gradually took the place of the Marais. About half of the houses were built between 1690 and 1725, a quarter between 1725 and 1750, and a quarter between 1750 and 1790. In style they are very similar, the most handsome façade is towards the garden, and the gateway on the street leads to the 'Cour d'Honneur'. Today the chief thoroughfares are the wide and modern Boul. St-Germain and Boul. Raspail, which have done much to alter the character of the quarter. The most characteristic streets of the once 'noble faubourg' are the Rue de Lille, Rue de l'Université, Rue St-Dominique, and Rue de Grenelle. About a hundred mansions remain, many of them now belonging to embassies or government departments.

A   The Luxembourg and St-Germain-des-Prés

MÉTRO stations: *St-Germain-des-Prés* and *St-Sulpice* (line 4); *Odéon* (lines 4 and 10); *Mabillon* (line 10).

At the S. end of the Pont des Arts, facing the Louvre, is the Place de l'Institut, at the meeting of the Quai de Conti and the Quai Malaquais (Rte 5B). The ***Palais de l'Institut,** or *Institut de France*, is surmounted by a dome which is one of the outstanding features of this part of the quays, especially since its cleaning and restoration (1961–62).

The courtyards are open daily from sunrise to sunset (except Sun and holidays), and the assembly rooms and dome may be visited on Sat 10–12, 1.30–4.30, on written application to the Secretary, 23 Quai de Conti.

The left wing of the Institut and the Hôtel de la Monnaie cover the site of the *Hôtel de Nesle* (13C) in which was incorporated the 12C *Tour de Nesle* (tablet on the left wing of the Institut), or *Tour Hamelin*, the river bastion of Philip Augustus's wall. The tower is notorious in legend as the scene of the amours of Margaret and Joan of Burgundy, wives of Louis X and Philip the Tall, who used to have their lovers thrown into the river. Later occupants were Isabeau de Bavière, Charles the Bold, and Henry V of England. The W. part, with the tower, known as *Petit-Nesle*, was the workshop of Benvenuto Cellini in 1540 and was demolished in 1663. The E. part, or *Grande-Nesle*, rebuilt in 1648 by Fr. Mansart, became the *Hôtel de Conti* (1670) and in 1770 the Mint.

The present building was erected in accordance with the will of Card. Mazarin, who bequeathed 2,000,000 fr. in silver and 45,000 fr. a year for the establishment of a college for sixty gentlemen of the four provinces acquired by the Treaties of Münster and the Pyrenees, viz.: Flanders, Alsace, Roussillon, and Piedmont (Pinerolo). The building, designed by Louis Le Vau, was erected in 1662–74. The official name of the new college was the *Collège Mazarin*, but its popular name was the *Collège des Quatre-Nations*, perhaps not only in allusion to Mazarin's foundation, but also to the 14C division of the old University into the Écoles des Quatre-Nations (France, Normandy, Picardy, and England). The Institut, founded in 1795 and installed at first in the Louvre, acquired the former Collège Mazarin in 1806.

The Institut de France comprises five academies: the ACADÉMIE FRANÇAISE, founded by Richelieu in 1635 and restricted to forty members, whose special task is the editing of the dictionary of the French language; the ACADÉMIE DES BEAUX-ARTS (1816), founded by Mazarin in 1648 as the Académie Royale de Peinture et de Sculpture; the ACADÉMIE DES INSCRIPTIONS ET BELLES-LETTRES, founded by Colbert in 1664; the ACADÉMIE DES SCIENCES, founded by Colbert in 1666; and the ACADÉMIE DES SCIENCES MORALES ET POLITIQUES, founded in 1832. The Académie Française holds special receptions for newly elected members, tickets of admission to which (apply to the secretary) are much sought after. The five academies meet together at an annual general meeting on 25 Oct (adm. by ticket only).

We pass through the door on the left of the dome into an octagonal courtyard. The portico on the right is the main entrance to the Salle des Séances Solennelles beneath the dome, while that on the left leads to the Bibliothèque Mazarine (see below). There are two further courtyards, of which the third is the attractive little *Kitchen Court* of the old Collège Mazarin. From the second court we enter (l.) and ascend to the upper Vestibule. On the right is the Library (adm. on personal introduction only); on the left the *Salle des Pas-Perdus* leads to the *Salle des Séances Ordinaires des Trois Académies* (Science, Beaux-Arts, Inscriptions) and the *Salle des Séances Ordinaires de l'Académie Française* (used also by the Académie des Sciences Morales). All these rooms are decorated with statues and busts of academicians and other distinguished men; among many of no outstanding merit that of Voltaire by Pigalle is striking.

We return to the first courtyard, and pass through the portico on the right. The SALLE DES SÉANCES SOLENNELLES is the former college chapel. The restoration of 1962 has undone the damage done by Vaudoyer, and Mazarin's *Tomb has been returned from the Louvre. Mazarin's niece, the Duchesse de Mazarin (d. 1699), the famous beauty of the court of Charles II, was also buried here. Here are held the receptions of the members of the Académie Française and the annual general meetings of the five academies and the Institut. It contains about 400 seats (green for members of the Académie Française, red for the other academies).

The Palais de l'Institut contains also the BIBLIOTHÈQUE MAZARINE (open daily 10–5, Sat 10–12; closed Sun and holidays, and from 15 Sept to 1 Oct), a library of c. 350,000 vols., 5800 MSS., and 1900 incunabula. This was the cardinal's own library; opened to scholars in 1643, it became the first public library in France.

The QUAI DE CONTI, named after the Hôtel de Conti, runs E. from the Place de l'Institut to the Pont Neuf and is lined with bookstalls. No. 13 is the *Hôtel de Sillery-Genlis*, often visited by Bonaparte when on leave from the École Militaire. At No. 5, on the corner of the Rue Guénégaud, Col. de Marguerittes of the Resistance set up his headquarters while he was conducting operations for the liberation of Paris, 19–28 Aug 1944.

The *Hôtel des Monnaies, or '*La Monnaie*', the French mint, is a simple but dignified building, adjoining the Institut on the E. It was built by *J. D. Antoine* in 1771–75. The handsome doorway is ornamented with Louis XVI's monogram and elegant bronze knockers; above is the fleur-de-lys escutcheon with Mercury and Ceres as supporters.—The **Musée Monétaire,** or *Museum of the Mint*, is entered from the second landing of the double staircase, on the right of the vestibule, a notable example of 18C architecture. It is open free daily (except Sat and Sun) 1–5. Visits to the workshops take place on Tues and Thurs, 2–3.30.

In the ANTECHAMBER are show-cases containing plaster models of modern medals. On the right is the 'mouton', a special stamping press; on the left is a press used for coining 50-centime pieces from Russian bronze cannon taken at Austerlitz. On either side are two rooms containing punches and modern medals.—The SALLE GUILLAUME DUPRÉ, in the centre of the building, is in the best Louis-XVI style (save its ceiling). Above the doors are four medallions with the initials of four of the civil servants who first organized the mint. The room is devoted to French medals from the Renaissance to the present day, as well as a selection of foreign ones. SALLE SAGE: New acquisitions.—SALLE JEAN WARIN: Portraits of directors of the mint; also, of Jean Warin (1604–72), the Walloon medallist.—SALLE DENON: Medals of the Consulate and Empire periods.—SALLE DUVIVIER: Examples of coins illustrating the evolution of French currency from Merovingian times to the present day.

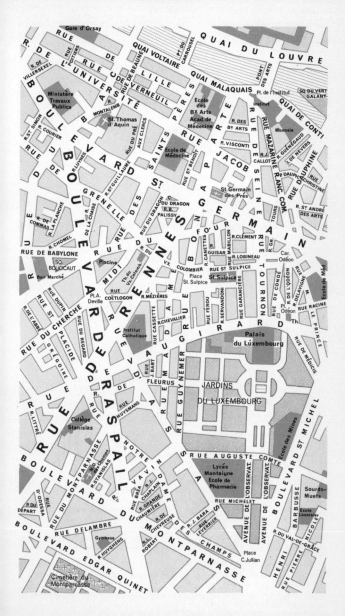

On the right of the second courtyard is the door of the 'Ateliers' or WORKSHOPS, in which the interesting processes in the production of coins and medals are seen. Visitors are escorted through by a guide (no gratuity). The presses in the large *Atelier du Monnayage* are capable of producing about 850,000 coins in a day. Medals may be bought at No. 10 Rue du Quatre-Septembre (closed Mon).

The RUE DE SEINE, which leads S. from the Palais de l'Institut towards the Jardin du Luxembourg, contains several noteworthy houses; No. 31 was George Sand's first Paris home (1831). The RUE MAZARINE, roughly parallel on the E., is noted for its curiosity shops. No. 12 is on the site of the former tennis-court, where the *Illustre Théâtre* was opened in Dec 1643 by Molière's company. No. 42 marks the site of the *Théâtre de Guénégaud*, occupied by the Opéra in 1671–72, by Molière's company in 1673–80, and by the Comédie-Française in 1680–89.—The RUE DE L'ANCIENNE COMÉDIE, straight on, takes its name from the Comédie Française of 1689–1770, which occupied No. 14. The *Café Procope*, opposite, was a favourite haunt of Voltaire and the Encyclopædists, Musset, George Sand, and Gambetta. Just beyond is the CARREFOUR DE L'ODÉON, a busy cross-roads just S. of the Boul. St-Germain. Thence the Rue de l'Odéon runs S. to the PLACE DE L'ODÉON, bordered by 18C houses and the chief façade of the Théâtre de l'Odéon. The *Café Voltaire* (No. 1), the resort of Mallarmé, Verlaine, and their circle, has been replaced by the Benjamin Franklin Library (open 10–9 p.m., Sun from 5). At No. 2 Camille Desmoulins was arrested in 1794.

The **Théâtre de l'Odéon** (otherwise 'Théâtre de France'), built in the form of a classical temple by Wailly and Peyre, on the gardens of the Hôtel de Condé (see below), was opened in 1782 with the title of Théâtre-Français, and rebuilt by Chalgrin after a fire in 1807. From 1946 to 1959 the theatre, known as the Salle du Luxembourg, was part of the Comédie Française. The colonnades round the building are filled with bookshops.

The vestibule and foyer on the first floor contain busts and portraits of contemporary actors and playwrights, and eight panels depicting famous scenes from French Drama. The auditorium (1264 seats) is one of the finest in Paris.

The S. side of the theatre looks on the RUE DE VAUGIRARD, the longest street in Paris, stretching from the Boul. St-Michel to the Porte de Versailles (2¾ m.). Following it to the right (W.), we pass the Rue de Condé and the Rue de Tournon opposite the entrance to the Palais du Luxembourg.

The RUE DE CONDÉ, like the Rue Monsieur-le-Prince, finds the source of its name in the vanished *Hôtel de Condé* (site Nos. 5–9), the home of the princely family of Condé in 1612–1764, demolished by Louis XV to provide a site for the theatre. Lucile Duplessis lived at No. 22 before her marriage to Desmoulins; No. 26 was the home of Beaumarchais in 1763–76, the period of 'Le Barbier de Séville'.

At No. 2 in the RUE DE TOURNON Balzac lived in 1827–30. Marie Lenormand, the fortune-teller consulted by so many Revolutionary celebrities, lived at No. 5 for over fifty years and died there in 1843. Hébert (Père Duchesne), the journalist, lived here in 1793, and Charles Cros, one of the pioneers of the phonograph, died here in 1888. No. 6, the *Hôtel de Brancas*, reconstructed by Bullet during the Regency, now contains the *Institut Tessin*, with a museum and library of Swedish art (open 2–6, Mon, Wed and Fri). Gambetta lived on the top story of the *Hôtel du Sénat* (No. 7). Alphonse Daudet also lived at No. 7 when he first came to Paris. No. 10, a fine 18C mansion, is now used as the barracks of the Garde Républicaine. Paul Jones died in 1792 on the first floor of No. 19.

The **Palais du Luxembourg**, once a royal residence and since 1946 the seat of the Conseil de la République, is noted especially for its beautiful gardens.

The Luxembourg was built by *Salomon de Brosse* in 1615–27 for Marie de Médicis, widow of Henri IV, who, it is said, wished to have a palace to remind her of the Pitti Palace in Florence, her birthplace. She bought a mansion of the Duc de Tingry-Luxembourg (the Petit-Luxembourg) here, hence its name. The building was altered in 1804 and enlarged in 1831–44. The palace after Louis XIII's death came to her second son Gaston, duc d'Orléans, and the 'Palais Médicis' became the 'Palais d'Orléans'. Subsequently the palace belonged in succession to Mlle de Montpensier, the Duchesse de Guise (1672), Louis XIV (1694), and the Orléans family. Among the famous prisoners confined here during the Revolution were Marshal de Noailles, executed at the age of 79 with his wife, daughter, and granddaughter; Hébert, Danton, Desmoulins, Fabre d'Eglantine, and David, who here drew the first sketch for the painting of the Sabine Women. Tom Paine was imprisoned here in 1793 for voting in the Assembly against the king's execution and escaped the guillotine only by an accident. In 1794 the Directory transferred the seat of government from the Tuileries to the Luxembourg, and here Gen. Bonaparte presented the treaty of Campo Formio. In 1800 the 'Palais Directorial' became the 'Palais du Consulat'; under the Empire it was the 'Palais du Sénat' and, later, the 'Palais de la Pairie'. Marshal Ney was confined and tried here in 1815. The ministers of Charles X were tried here under Louis-Philippe in 1830, and Louis Napoléon Bonaparte after his landing at Boulogne in 1840. From 1852 to 1940 the Palais was the meeting-place of the Senate, the upper chamber of the French Republic, except in 1871–79, when it was the seat of the Préfecture de la Seine. In 1940–44 it was occupied by Marshal Sperrle, commander-in-chief of the Luftwaffe on the Western Front. In 1946 the Conseil de la République replaced the Senate as the second chamber of the French parliament.

The N. façade of the Palais du Luxembourg is the original, and the main entrance from the Rue de Vaugirard is surmounted by an eight-sided dome; the two wings, terminating in steep-roofed pavilions, with three orders of columns superimposed, are connected by a single-storied gallery. The S. façade overlooking the gardens is a 19C copy, by *Gisors*. The entrance-doorway is at the back of the great court, to the left.

ADMISSION. Conducted parties are shown the Palais, on application to the Questure (Secrétariat Général), on Sun when the Conseil is in session; at other times, daily. Visitors wishing to attend a session should apply through their diplomatic representative.

The interior, remodelled by *Chalgrin* under Napoleon I, is decorated in the sumptuous 19C manner, with statues and historical and allegorical paintings, mostly of no great merit. The principal rooms on the first floor may be visited. Especially conspicuous are the Apotheosis of Napoleon I, by *Alaux*, on the ceiling of the SALLE DES CONFÉRENCES (the former throne-room), and the statues of statesmen behind the president's chair facing the hemicycle in the SALLE DES SÉANCES, where the Conseil meets, and which is notable for its fine woodwork. The LIBRARY contains the best *Paintings in the palace, by *Eugène Delacroix*: in the central cupola, the Limbo of Dante's Inferno; above the window, Alexander placing Homer's poems in the golden casket of Darius after the Battle of Arbela.—The GALERIE DE JORDAENS has a ceiling decorated with twelve paintings by Jordaens.—The CABINET DORÉ was formerly Marie de Médicis's audience chamber; the BUVETTE, or BUREAU DE TABAC, was her bedchamber.

The adjoining **Petit-Luxembourg** (no adm.), the mansion of the Prince de Tingry-Luxembourg in 1570–1612, was presented to Richelieu by Marie de Médicis in 1626 and is now the residence of the president of the Conseil de la République. Sadi Carnot was born here in 1796 when his father, Lazare Carnot, was a member of the Directory. It includes the cloisters and chapel of the Filles du Calvaire, for whom Marie de Médicis built a convent adjoining her palace. The cloisters now form a winter-garden; the chapel, at the end of the courtyard in the Rue de Vaugirard, is a charming example of the Renaissance style. Farther W. is the orangery, until 1945 occupied by the Musée du Luxembourg.

The ***Jardin du Luxembourg** (c. 57 acres), with its lovely trees, is one of the most beautiful gardens in Paris. Delightfully laid out in the 17C, it was deplorably mutilated in 1782 and 1867 so perhaps little remains of the original garden as known by Marie de Médicis. Its numerous statues are mostly well above the average standard of public monuments. The painters and poets who used to frequent the garden have given place to students and children.

Entering by the gate in the Rue de Vaugirard on the E. side of the palace, we have on the right flower-beds, normally full of colour, and on the left monuments to Théodore de

Banville by *Roulleau* and *Courtois-Suffit* and to Henri Murger by *Bouillon*. Then comes an oblong pool, bordered by planes, at the end of which is the *****Fontaine Médicis**, attr. to *Salomon de Brosse* (c. 1627), removed hither in 1861. In the central niche is Polyphemus about to crush Acis and Galatea; on either side are Pan and Diana; and at the back is a bas-relief, the Fontaine de Léda, brought from the Rue du Regard in 1855.

We now ascend to the EASTERN TERRACE, with its statues of famous women, including Mary, Queen of Scots, Jeanne d'Albret, Mlle de Montpensier, and Margaret of Anjou. Amongst the clumps of trees in this part of the gardens are monuments to Leconte de Lisle, by *Denys Puech*, Flaubert, and *****George Sand, by *Sicard*, etc.

On the lawn between the two terraces, to the S. of the octagonal pond with its fountain, is a monument to Scheurer-Kestner, the Alsatian patriot, by *Becker*, with figures by *Dalou* and *Formigé*. To the E. of the fountain are Marius on the ruins of Carthage; and David, a graceful statue on a column.

On the WESTERN TERRACE is continued the series of famous women, comprising statues of eight royal ladies of France and Petrarch's Laura. Among the clumps of trees on this side are a marionette theatre, tennis courts, and a café. Amid the fine plane trees at the N. end, near the private garden of the Petit-Luxembourg, is a monument to Eugène Delacroix, by *Dalou* and *Menuel*. To the W. of the Petit-Luxembourg is a fine copy of the Venus of Medici, placed on fragments of the ruins of the Tuileries. In the Jardin Anglais, bordering the Rue Guynemer and the Rue Auguste Comte, are numerous statues including Paul Verlaine, by *Rodo de Niederhausern*, Watteau, by *Gauquié* and *Guillaume*, and Sainte-Beuve, by *Denys Puech*; also, in the S.W. corner, the School of Arboriculture.

Farther on in the Rue de Vaugirard, opposite the Petit-Luxembourg, is the Rue Garancière, with the *Hôtel de Sourdéac* (No. 8; 1640). Jules Massenet lived and died (1912) at 48 Rue de Vaugirard (first floor). Opposite the orangery of the Luxembourg diverges the picturesque Rue Férou, leading to the Place St-Sulpice (see below); in this street Mme de la Fayette died in 1692, fifteen years after writing 'La Princesse de Clèves'; No. 50, at the corner, her birthplace in 1634, later became the *Hôtel de la Trémoille*. At No. 15 Rue Férou, Fantin-Latour's house, Whistler painted his famous portrait. The next street on the right is the Rue Bonaparte.

The Rue de Vaugirard continues W. crossing the Rue Madame; No. 25, at the corner, was the home in 1832 of Mlle George, Napoleon's mistress. At the corner of the Rue de Vaugirard and the Rue d'Assas are the buildings of the *Institut Catholique de Paris* (enlarged in 1930; entrance 21 Rue d'Assas); here in 1890 radio waves were discovered by Branly. No. 70, next door, is the *Séminaire des Carmes* with the church of *St-Joseph-des-Carmes*, once the chapel of a Carmelite convent dating from 1613–20. The dome is noteworthy. The crypt contains the bones of some 120 priests massacred in the convent garden in Sept 1792 (apply to the concierge; adm. 1 fr., open daily 2–5 or 6, except Tues; in Aug open only Tues, Wed, and Thurs). Prisoners held here and later released included Gen. Hoche, Josephine de Beauharnais, and Mme Tallien. The Rue d'Assas has a number of interesting associations: David d'Angers died in a house replaced by No. 20; August Strindberg lived at No. 62 in 1895–96; Auguste Bartholdi, sculptor of the Statue of Liberty in New York, died at No. 82; the new Economics and Law Faculty buildings are at No. 92. The Rue de Vaugirard then crosses the Boul. Raspail.

The RUE BONAPARTE runs N. to the Seine. This street, narrow and busy, with its numerous antique shops and picture galleries, is one of the most pleasant and characteristic in the 'business' part of the Faubourg. Its S. section, bordered by the garden of the Allée du Séminaire, leads to the *Place St-Sulpice*. In the centre is the Fontaine des Quatre-Evêques, by *Visconti*, decorated with the statues of four famous preaching bishops: Bossuet, Fénelon, Massillon, and Fléchier. At the former *Séminaire de St-Sulpice*, on the S. side of the square, Renan was a scholar in 1843–44, while on the N. side (No. 6) is a dignified mansion (1754) by Servandoni (the first of a range which never materialized).

St-Sulpice is the wealthiest and most important church on the Left Bank. This rather ponderously classical building, imposing mainly for its size, was described by Gibbon as "one of the noblest structures in Paris" but its chief merit is the mural decoration by Delacroix. The W. front consists of an Ionic colonnade over a Doric. The N. tower, 240 ft high, has seated figures of the Evangelists; the S. tower is 16 ft lower. Victor Hugo compared the towers to clarionets.

It was begun in 1646 by *Gamard* on the site of an older church and continued on a larger scale by *Le Vau* in 1655 and *Gittard* in 1670. After an interval from 1675 to 1719 the work was resumed by *Oppenordt*. The building of the W. front was entrusted to *Servandoni*, who, however, failed to give satisfaction and was replaced in 1745 by *Maclaurin*. His successor, *Chalgrin*, rebuilt the N. tower in 1777, since Maclaurin's design had also failed to please, but the S. tower was left incomplete. Camille Desmoulins was married here to Lucile Duplessis in 1790. Under the Convention St-Sulpice became the Temple de la Victoire and in 1799 a public banquet was given here to Gen. Bonaparte.—St-Sulpice is noted for its music.

The stately **Interior,** a noted example of the 'Jesuit' style, is 360 ft long, 184 ft wide, and 108 ft high.—NAVE. The famous organ, one of the largest in existence (6588 pipes; to be heard on Sun at 11 and 3.30, except in Lent and Advent), was built in 1781 and remodelled in 1860–62 by Cavaillé-Coll; the case was designed by *Chalgrin* and is adorned with charming statues by *Clodion* and decorations by *Duret*. At the beginning of the nave are two huge shells (Tridacna gigas) used as holy-water stoups, presented to Francis I by the Venetian Republic; the marble rocks on which they rest were sculptured by *Pigalle*. The late-18C pulpit, by *Wailly*, bears gilded figures of Faith and Hope, by *Guesdon*, and Charity, by *Dumont*. In the paving of the S. transept is a bronze tablet connected by a meridian line with a marble obelisk in the N. transept; at noon the sun's rays, passing through a small opening in a blind window in the S. transept, strike the meridian at different points according to the time of year.

The CHAPELS encircling the church are decorated with frescoes. In the first chapel (r.) are *Paintings by *E. Delacroix* which are among his last and greatest works (1853–63): on the ceiling St Michael and the Devil; l., Jacob wrestling with the angel; r., Expulsion of Heliodorus from the Temple (best view from the aisle, near the pulpit); and four angels, in grisaille. Fifth chapel, Tomb of the curé Languet de Gergy (1674–1750), founder of the Enfants Malades and responsible for the completion of the church, by *M. A. Slodtz*, a disciple of Bernini.—CHOIR. Scourging of Christ, Mater Dolorosa, and eight Apostles, by *Bouchardon*.

The LADY CHAPEL is well designed by Servandoni. In a niche behind the altar is a marble Madonna, by *Pigalle*, with little angels, by *Mouchy*, floating among the clouds. The paintings on the walls are by *Carle Vanloo*, and in the dome is the Assumption, by *Lemoyne*.

Under the church is a large crypt, with considerable remains of the 16C church (apply to the 'Vicaire de garde').

The Rue Bonaparte continues to the *Place St-Germain-des-Prés*, where it meets the Rue de Rennes and crosses the Boulevard St-Germain at a busy junction.

*St-Germain-des-Prés, on the E. side of the square, is the oldest church in Paris and the only one with any considerable remains of Romanesque architecture.

This church, the chief relic of a great Benedictine abbey founded by Childebert I in the 6C in thanksgiving for his victories in Spain, and the burial-place of St Germanus, Bp of Paris (d. 576), was built at the beginning of the 11C (body of the W. tower), in the late 11C (nave) and in the mid-12C (choir), and was consecrated by Pope Alexander III in 1163. The massive flying buttresses of the choir are among the earliest in France. The W. porch dates from 1607, but preserves the jambs of a 12C door and a battered lintel depicting the Last

Supper. The transepts were remodelled c. 1644. The bell-chamber of the tower was added in the 17C, the spire in the 19C. Flanking the choir are the bases of two towers pulled down in 1822, when the church was drastically restored, after its use as a saltpetre factory in 1794–95.

The *Interior (213 ft by 69 ft, and 62 ft high) is especially interesting for the combination of the Romanesque style in the nave with the first attempts at the Gothic style in the choir. The vault of the nave and aisles dates from 1644–46. The pillars are each flanked by four columns, the sculptured capitals of which in 1848–53 were either recut or removed to the Cluny Museum and replaced by copies. One original remains in the N.W. corner. Both nave and choir are adorned with large mural paintings by *Hippolyte Flandrin* (1842–61), superbly academic but badly lighted.

NAVE. Above each arch are two paintings by *Flandrin*, one a subject from the Old or New Testament, the other representing the corresponding dogma or mystery. The intervals between the windows above are filled with the figures of Prophets and Judges of Israel.

SOUTH AISLE. Large marble statue of Notre-Dame de Consolation, presented to the Abbey of St Denis by Queen Jeanne d'Evreux in 1340. The W. chapel of the S. transept was consecrated by St Francis of Sales in 1619 and contains a cupola-painting by *Restout* (Apotheosis of St Maur, 1756). In the transept itself are a statue of St Margaret (1705) and the tomb of Olivier and Louis de Castellan, killed in the king's service in 1644 and 1669, by *Girardon*. On the left, against the choir wall, is a coloured relief by *Charlier* presented by French Canadians, commemorating the consecration in this church (1658) of François de Montmorency-Laval (1628–1703), first bishop of French Canada. In the first ambulatory-chapel is the tomb of Lord James Douglas (d. 1645; son of the first Marquess of Douglas), a Scottish gentleman in the service of Louis XIII. Second chapel: Tombstones of Descartes, removed from Ste-Geneviève (1819), and of Mabillon (see below). Third: Two marble medallions of the 17C, with profiles of Christ and the Virgin. Fourth: Fragments of stained glass of 1245–55.

CHOIR. The little marble columns in the triforium are re-used material from the 6C abbey of St Vincent; their bases and capitals are of the 12C.—The LADY CHAPEL was rebuilt at the beginning of the 19C, Pope Pius VII laying the first stone of the altar.

NORTH AISLE (as we return). Third chapel: Tombstone of Boileau, removed from the Sainte Chapelle. Fourth: Tomb of William Douglas, 10th earl of Angus (d. 1611), who died in the service of Henri IV. In the N. transept are a statue of St Francis Xavier, by *Guillaume Coustou*; and the theatrical tomb, by *G.* and *B. Marsy*, of John Casimir, king of Poland, who became abbot of St-Germain in 1669 and died in 1672. In the second bay of the nave is a marble monument to Hippolyte Flandrin.

In the little garden to the N. of the church are fragments of sculptures from the great lady-chapel built in 1212–55 by Pierre de Montreuil within the precincts of the abbey. In the Rue de l'Abbaye, to the N. of the garden, is the former *Abbot's Palace*, erected c. 1586 by Cardinal de Bourbon; it is now occupied by a dispensary. At No. 16 a window (13C) is all that remains of the refectory. Behind the palace was the *Prison de l'Abbaye*, where Brissot wrote his memoirs and Charlotte Corday spent her last days. Delacroix died in 1863 at 6 Rue Furstemberg (on the left in one of the quietest and most delightful corners of Paris); in 1857 he built the adjoining studio, which later was shared by Monet and Bazille. A little museum has been arranged here, and an annual exhibition devoted to some aspect of Delacroix's work is held. No. 1 Rue Bourbon-le-Château, a few yards E., was Whistler's first home in Paris (1855–56). To the N. of the Abbey lay the *Pré-aux-Clercs*, a favourite promenade and scene of brawls of medieval students.—In the Place, S.W. of

the church, is a bust of the scholar monk Mabillon (1632–1707).—In a garden adjoining the
boulevard, S. of the church, is a statue of Bernard Palissy (1510–89), whose workshop is
said to have been in the Rue du Dragon. This street runs parallel to the busy RUE DE
RENNES, a modern thoroughfare leading S.W. to Montparnasse. At No. 30 Rue du Dragon
Victor Hugo lived in 1821; at No. 3 is the *American Cultural Centre* (open weekdays 10–9,
Sun 4–9).

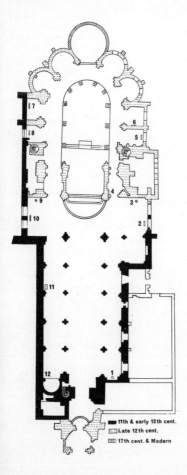

TOMBS AND WORKS OF ART

1. N.D. de Consolation.
2. Castellan.
3. St Margaret.
4. Montmorency-Laval.
5. James Douglas.
6. Descartes.
7. Boileau.
8. Wm. Douglas.
9. St Francis Xavier.
10. John Casimir of Poland.
11. Flandrin.
12. Original capital.

■ 11th & early 12th cent.
▦ Late 12th cent.
▨ 17th cent. & Modern

On the left in Rue Bonaparte at No. 18 the Czech government was formed
in 1916. At No. 16 is the *Académie de Médecine*, founded in 1920, which has
no connection with the Academies of the Institut, and at No. 14 is the main
entrance to the *École des Beaux-Arts*. The *Hôtel du Marquis de Persan* (Nos.
7–9 on the right) was the home of Monge in 1803 and the birthplace of Manet
(1832–83). Off the right side run three streets with interesting associations.

Prosper Mérimée (1842–46) and Corot (1849–55) lived at No. 10 in the RUE DES BEAUX-ARTS, Fantin-Latour at No. 8; at No. 13 Oscar Wilde died in utter destitution in 1900.—In the narrow RUE VISCONTI (then Rue des Marais) Racine lived from 1693 till his death in 1699 (house demolished); at No. 16 Adrienne Lecouvreur died in 1730, in the arms of Marshal Saxe; at No. 17 Balzac had a printing business, liquidated in 1828, and on the 2nd floor is a studio once occupied by Paul Delaroche (1827–34) and Delacroix (1838–43).—Laurence Sterne put up in the RUE JACOB on his arrival in Paris in 1762, and later was a guest of Mme de Rambouillet at No. 46. Wagner lodged at No. 14 in 1841–42, as did Prud'hon, and Mérimée at No. 18 (rebuilt) in 1848. No. 32 belonged to du Cerceau, architect of the Pont-Neuf.

The **École des Beaux-Arts,** begun in 1820 and finished in 1862, replaces the convent of the Petits-Augustins, founded in 1608, of which the only important relics are the convent-chapel and the small chapel of Margaret of Valois. In 1885 the school was enlarged by the acquisition of the Hôtel de Chimay (see above).

The courtyards and principal rooms are open to visitors (accompanied by a guide; gratuity) on Thurs 2–4 (closed 1 July–15 Oct); to parties organized by the Monuments Historiques on Sat 2–4. The library may be used on written application to the Director.

In the centre of the COUR D'HONNEUR is a Corinthian column, with a bronze statue of Abundance (in the style of Pilon); on the farther side are 15–16C sculptures from the demolished Hôtel de La Trémoille. To the right stands the former CONVENT CHAPEL (c. 1600), against the S. wall of which is the central part of the *Façade of the 16C Château d'Anet, by *Philibert Delorme*; the figure of Cupid bending his bow, after the antique, is a later addition. Within, casts of medieval and Renaissance sculpture are displayed, including some from the Hôtel de Ville destroyed in 1871; in the adjoining (E. side) CHAPEL OF MARGARET OF VALOIS, a small domed hexagon, are casts of the chief works of Michelangelo. This has claims to be the first dome built in Paris.—Part of a Renaissance façade from the Château de Gaillon (1500–10) in Normandy separates the first from the SECOND COURTYARD, which leads up to the Palais des Études, a successful work by *Duban* (1858–62). In and about the court are sculptured fragments including carved capitals and friezes from the church of Ste-Geneviève (12C); large stone basin, with masks of pagan gods, from the refectory of the Abbey of St-Denis (13C). Beyond a portico brought from Gaillon (r.), in the garden, is a charming arcade of the Hôtel de Torpane (c. 1570), from the Rue des Bernardins, and the façade of the Hôtel de Chimay (see below).

Within the Palais, a VESTIBULE, with fragments of antique sculpture, admits to the INNER COURT, in the bays of which is a valuable collection of original antique marbles. Two staircases ascend to the HÉMICYCLE, decorated by a huge wax-painting by *Paul Delaroche*, representing the chief masters of every school of art of every period. At the back of the platform is a painting by *Ingres* of Romulus bringing back the spolia opima.

The LIBRARY (comp. above) on the first floor contains about 80,000 vols. and about one million engravings, drawings by famous artists, etc.

Adjoining the Chapel is the pleasant little COUR DU MURIER (Mulberry Tree Court), with Renaissance porticoes on three sides and sculptures by Rome Prize winners, also memorials to students (including one to Henri Regnault) who fell in the wars of the last hundred years. A staircase ascends to the SALLE DE MELPOMÈNE (by *Duban*, 1860–62), which is used for the display of students' works at the time of the competition for the Grands Prix de Rome (annually for painting, sculpture, and architecture; less frequently for engraving, etching, medal design, and gem engraving).

On the QUAI MALAQUAIS are some charming 17–18C mansions: No. 3, a 17C house, was occupied by Marshal Saxe in 1744–47 and by Alex. Humboldt during the Restoration. No. 9 (at the corner of the Rue Bonaparte), *Hôtel de Transylvanie*, is a good example of Louis-XIII architecture. No. 15, part of the *Hôtel de Chimay*, was built by Mansart c. 1640 and altered in the 18C for the Duchesse de Bouillon (d. 1714), the friend of La Fontaine; a tablet records the residence here in 1844–53 of Anatole Thibault (1844–1924), better known as Anatole France (born at No. 19 on the quay). No. 19 was the home of George Sand in 1832–36.

B   West Part of the Faubourg St-Germain

MÉTRO stations: *St-Germain-des-Prés* (line 4); *Sèvres-Babylone* (lines 10 and 12); *Bac, Solférino, Chambre des Députés* (line 12); *St-François-Xavier* (line 14).

The Pont du Carrousel connects the Louvre with the QUAI VOLTAIRE, which continues the Quai Malaquais to the W. and was formerly the Quai des Théatins. Voltaire died in 1778 at the house of the Marquis de Villette (No. 27; tablet); St-Sulpice refused to accept his corpse, which was rushed to an abbey near Troyes to save it from a common grave. Louise de Kéroualle, duchess of Portsmouth, occupied Nos. 3–5 in 1695–1701. Ingres died at No. 11 in 1867. At No. 13 was installed the 'Moniteur Universel', one of the chief newspapers during the Revolution. Here as tenant Delacroix in 1829–36 was preceded by Horace Vernet and followed by Corot. At No. 19 Baudelaire lived in 1856–58, working on 'Les Fleurs du Mal', while Wagner finished the book of 'Die Meistersinger' there in 1861–62. Oscar Wilde was a later tenant in 1883. Alfred de Musset lived at No. 25 in 1841–49. The quay is lined with bookstalls and old curiosity shops, at one of which Balzac's hero bought the 'peau de chagrin'.

The RUE DES SAINTS-PÈRES, running S. from the E. end of the Quai Voltaire, near the Beaux-Arts, across the Boul. St-Germain to the Rue de Sèvres, is also noted for its antique shops. From the *Hôtel de Tessé*, on the corner, in 1742 the Marquis de Becqueville attempted to glide with wings across the Seine. At the corner of the Rue de Lille is the *École des Langues Orientales*, founded by the Convention in 1795. Manet died at No. 5, and the organist Widor (1844–1937) lived at No. 7 in 1910. The S. end of the street is described below.

The QUAI ANATOLE-FRANCE, and, farther to the W., the QUAI D'ORSAY, are the centre of the foreign and diplomatic affairs of the Republic. Beyond the Rue du Bac, and between the Pont Royal and the Pont de Solférino, lies the *Gare d'Orsay*, built in 1898–1900 for the Paris–Orléans railway, on the site of the old Cour des Comptes; part of the building is the Hôtel du Palais d'Orsay.

To the W., beyond the Rue de Bellechasse, is the charming **Palais de la Légion d'Honneur,** the entrance to which (in the Rue de Lille) is flanked by a colonnade with bas-reliefs by *Roland* on the attic story. The Corinthian portico in the courtyard is adorned with a frieze of arabesques with the device 'Honneur et Patrie'. Facing the quay is a rotunda with Corinthian columns and symbolical busts; on the parapet are six mythological statues.

Built by *Rousseau* in 1782–86 for the Prince de Salm-Kyrburg, at the Revolution this elegant 18C mansion was raffled and won by a former wigmaker's apprentice who had made a fortune. After the owner was imprisoned for forgery, the house became the Swedish Embassy. Mme de Staël, the ambassador's wife, gave her famous receptions here under the Directory, and in 1804 it was bought by the government for the grand chancellery of the Legion of Honour.

No. 2 Rue de Bellechasse is the entrance to the Musée de la Légion d'Honneur (open Thurs and Sat 2–5; adm. 1 fr.), which is devoted to medals, decorations, documents, paintings, etc., relating to the history of the Order of the Legion of Honour.

Opposite the Pont de la Concorde, at the beginning of the Quai d'Orsay, is the Palais-Bourbon, the seat of the Assemblée Nationale. This is the lower house of the French parliament, which took the place of the Chambre des Députés in 1946, and corresponds approximately to the House of Commons.

In 1722 a mansion was erected on this site for the Dowager Duchess of Bourbon (legitimized daughter of Louis XIV and the Duchesse de Montpensier), of which only the inner courtyard and main entrance at 128 Rue de l'Université have survived. The Prince de Condé, forced to leave his mansion because of the construction of the Théâtre de l'Odéon, bought the palace from Louis XV and enlarged it from 1784 until the Revolution. He incorporated the Hôtel de Lassay, in which he lived after the Revolution. In 1795 the Palais became national property under the name of Maison de la Révolution, the meeting place of the Council of Five Hundred, and later was occupied by the Archives (1799–1808). It has been used as the House of Parliament since 1815.

In 1940–44 the Palais-Bourbon was the headquarters of the German military administration of the Paris region, and at the time of the liberation considerable fighting took place here, causing some damage to the building and the destruction by fire of over 30,000 vols. from the library.

ADMISSION. Intending visitors should apply in writing to the Questure. Permission to attend a session of the Assembly must be obtained in writing from the Questure or a Deputy. The entrance is in the Place du Palais-Bourbon, on the S. side.

The façade consists of a portico, by *Poyet* (1804–07), with twelve Corinthian columns, and statues of statesmen on either side. The bas-relief on the pediment, by *Cortot*, represents France, standing between Liberty and Order, beckoning to Commerce, Agriculture, Peace, War, and Eloquence.

This neo-Hellenistic piece of imperial bombast is entirely decorative, designed principally to balance the Madeleine when seen from the Concorde.

The decorations in the interior are, with certain exceptions, of no great artistic merit. Many of the rooms have historical paintings by *Horace Vernet* and *Ary Scheffer*. The most notable adornment of the SALLE DES SÉANCES (1828–32), where the Assembly meets, is the bas-relief of Fame and History, by *Lemot*, on the speakers' tribune, which dates from the Council of Five Hundred. The great gallery of the LIBRARY (300,000 vols., including many rarities) displays a magnificent set of twenty religious or historical *Paintings (1838–47) by *Eugène Delacroix*, showing the progress of the civilized arts, with illustrations from classical mythology and ancient history; also noteworthy are the works by *Delacroix* (1833) in the Salon du Roi.

Joined to the Palais-Bourbon by the handsome *Galerie des Fêtes* (1848) is the **Hôtel de Lassay** (1724), the official residence of the President of the Assembly. Farther along the quay towards the Esplanade des Invalides stands the *Ministère des Affaires Étrangères* (Foreign Office), built by Lacornée in 1845. King George VI and Queen Elizabeth were received here during their official visit to Paris in 1938, and the area was a scene of heavy fighting during the liberation of Paris (Aug 1944). By the railings of the garden is a monument to Aristide Briand (d. 1931), by Bouchard and Landowski.

In the **Place du Palais-Bourbon,** to the S. of the Palais, an elegant ensemble of Louis-XVI mansions all built to the same pattern after 1776, is a statue of Law, by Feuchères.——The RUE DE L'UNIVERSITÉ, coming from the Invalides, crosses the Place and then the Boul. St-Germain. No. 51 is a fine 18C mansion by Lassurance. Alphonse Daudet died at No. 41 in 1897 (tablet). Chateaubriand lived at No. 25 in 1816–17. In the courtyard of No. 24 is a notable façade of 1700 by Servandoni. Berthe Albrecht, a young heroine of the Resistance, lived at No. 16 (tablet). Franklin's first lodging on his arrival in Paris in 1776 was at the Hôtel de Hambourg in this street.

We now follow the BOULEVARD ST-GERMAIN, 1 m. long, which extends in a shallow curve from the Pont de la Concorde to the Pont de Sully. No. 288, at the corner of the Quai d'Orsay, is the *Nouveau Cercle*. At the extreme W. end of the building the bullet holes are a reminder of the fighting during the liberation of Paris.

The quiet RUE DE LILLE (parallel with the quays) retains several 18C mansions: the splendid *Hôtel Beauharnais* (No. 78), built by Boffrand in 1714 for himself, once the residence of Queen Hortense, later the German Embassy, then part of the Ministère des Affaires Étrangères, is again since 1961 the German Embassy. No. 121, where Turgot, the minister of finance, died in 1781, is occupied by the *Institut Néerlandais*; and La Fayette lived at No. 123 in 1799.

The *Ministère de la Défense Nationale* (No. 231), built by Bouchot in 1867–77, has a clock-tower at the corner of the Rue de Solférino. Looking down this street to the left, we can see the Sacré-Cœur at Montmartre.

The RUE DE BELLECHASSE, which the Boul. St-Germain next crosses, runs from the Quai Anatole-France to the Rue de Varenne. Monge died at No. 31 in 1818 and Villemin, who discovered that tuberculosis can be transmitted by inoculation, in 1892. Daudet lived here from 1885–97. At No. 41 the Conseil National de la Résistance and the Comité Parisien de la Libération organized operations for the rising of 19 Aug 1944.—No. 5 Rue Las Cases (r.) is the **Musée Social** (open daily 9–12, 2–6, except Sun and holidays), founded by the Comte de Chambrun in 1894 to provide facilities for the study of social legislation. It comprises a special library of 50,000 vols. and the *Institut Léonard de Vinci*, which is intended as a national academy of Industrial Art. Farther on is **Ste-Clotilde**, an uninspired Gothic-revival church (1846–56), by *Gau* and *Ballu*. César Franck was organist here (from 1858) for over thirty years; the composer is commemorated by a monument, by Lenoir, in the square, opposite.

The RUE ST-DOMINIQUE runs W. from the boulevard to the Esplanade des Invalides. Nos. 1, 3, and 5 (E. end) date from c. 1710; No. 3 was occupied by J.-B. Dumas, the chemist (d. 1884). No. 5 was the home of Gustave Doré from 1849 till his death in 1883. Nos. 10–12, now part of the Ministry of Defence, occupy the former *Couvent des Filles de St-Joseph* (1641), established for orphaned girls; it was generously supported by Mme de Montespan, who retired here in 1687 after her fall from royal favour. In 1755 Mme du Deffand did the same and held here a brilliant literary salon. Nos. 14–16, the **Hôtel de Brienne** (1714 and 1730), are also part of the Ministry of Defence. Lucien Bonaparte and later Laetitia Bonaparte lived here. The *Maison de la Chimie* occupies the *Hôtel de La Rochefoucauld-d'Estissac* (1710; enlarged in 1934), at No. 28; and No. 57, the *Hôtel de Sagan*, was built by Brongniart in 1784 for the Princess of Monaco.

Nos. 244–248 in the Boul. St-Germain are the *Ministère des Travaux Publics* (Ministry of Public Works), occupying a modern and two early 18C houses. No. 246, the *Hôtel de Roquelaure* (1722), by Lassurance and Leroux, has a fine courtyard. Cambacérès lived here in 1808. From the junction of the Boul. St-Germain and the Rue du Bac the wide Boulevard Raspail diverges S.E. in a straight line to the Place Denfert-Rochereau (Rte 17), crossing several interesting streets described below.

The RUE DU BAC is one of the oldest streets in the quarter, extending from the Pont Royal to (¾ m.) the Rue de Sèvres. It is named after the ferry by which the Seine was crossed before the construction of the Pont Royal. No. 46, the former *Hôtel de Boulogne*, N. of the boulevard, has a fine courtyard; built in 1744 by Boffrand for Jacques Bernard, who died after a scandalous bankruptcy in 1753, it was the lodging of Chateaubriand in 1815–18. No. 98, with gilt angels above the door, and good iron balconies, was the *Café des Deux-Anges*, the secret rendezvous of the Chouans (c. 1800), and Cadoudal here hatched the conspiracy of 1804. At No. 108bis Laplace, astronomer and mathematician, died in 1827. At No. 110 Whistler (from 1892) was visited by Beardsley and Mallarmé, and got into trouble with his landlord for letting his child-models run about naked in the garden. Nos. 118 and 120, with doors designed by Toro, are the *Hôtel de Clermont-Tonnerre*, where Chateaubriand lived from 1838 till his death in 1848; on the third and fourth floors Mrs Clarke and her daughter Mary (later Mme Mohl) had their famous salon, and here they were visited by Dean Stanley, Mrs Gaskell, and Florence Nightingale. No. 128 is the *Séminaire des Missions Étrangères*, founded in 1663, with relics of martyred missionaries in its 'Chambre des Martyrs' (daily 2–4 except Wed). Nos. 136–40 are the *Hôtel de La Vallière*, with two handsome portals, now occupied by the Sœurs de Charité. At the S. end of the street is the 'Bon Marché'.

A short distance to the N. of the Boul. St-Germain is **St-Thomas-d'Aquin**, begun in 1682 by *Pierre Bullet*, in the Jesuit style, and completed, with the construction of the façade, in 1787. The ceiling-painting in the Lady Chapel

(Transfiguration) is a characteristic 18C work by Lemoyne. Guillaume Apollinaire lived and died (1918) at No. 202 Boul. St-Germain. Farther on the Rue Saint-Guillaume runs S. from the Boulevard, and at No. 27, in the 16C *Hôtel de Mesmes* (enlarged in 1933), is the *Institut National des Sciences Politiques*; the *Hôtel de Créqui* (No. 16), built in 1660–64 and enlarged in 1772, was for a time the home of Lamartine and later of Renan. At the corner of the Rue des Saints-Pères (l.) are the enormous buildings of the *École Pratique de la Faculté de Médecine* (1937–53; the main doorway adorned by Landowski's Æsculapius), and bordering them on the S. side is the little *Chapelle St-Pierre*, rebuilt in 1611, the sole relic of the Hôpital de la Charité, which stood on this site from 1605 to 1937. It is now the church of the Ukrainian Catholic community in Paris (High Mass on Sun 10.30). In the small Square de la Charité is a bust of René Laënnec (1781–1826) who taught in the hospital during the Revolution.

Opposite, in the 18C *Hôtel de Fleury* (by Antoine), is the *École des Ponts et Chaussées*, a civil engineering school, founded in 1747.

No. 184 Boul. St-Germain is the *Hôtel de la Société de Géographie*, founded in 1821, and beyond that (l.) are two cafés noted for the artistic and literary set that frequents them: the *Café de Flore* and the *Deux Magots*. The 'Action Française' was founded in the former in 1898. A few yards farther on is St-Germain des Prés (comp. Rte 5A).

The S. end of the Rue des Saints Pères crosses the RUE DE GRENELLE near its beginning at the Rue de Sèvres. This street describes a curve over a mile long to the Av. de la Bourdonnais on the W. No. 36 has a wrought-iron grille of 1681 (A la Petite Chaise). Jean Ampère lived at No. 52 in 1840–46. We cross the Boul. Raspail. On Nos. 57 and 59 is the fine **Fontaine des Quatre-Saisons*, designed by Bouchardon in 1739, with sculptures of the City of Paris with the Seine and Marne at her feet and bas-reliefs of the Seasons. Alfred de Musset lived at No. 59 from 1824 to 1840 before his departure for Venice with George Sand. Beyond the Rue du Bac No. 79, the *Hôtel d'Estrées*, the Russian Embassy, was built by Robert de Cotte in 1713. No. 85, the *Hôtel d'Avaray* (1718 by Leroux), is the Netherlands Embassy. No. 87 is the fine *Hôtel de Bauffremont*, built in 1721–36. No. 102, the *Hôtel de Maillebois*, built early in the 18C, was altered by Antoine; the Duc de Saint-Simon worked on his 'Mémoires' and died here in 1755. No. 106, dating from 1755, is the *Temple de Panthemont* (by Constant d'Ivry; 1747–56), once the chapel of a convent where Joséphine de Beauharnais lived for several years. Its main building (37–39 Rue de Bellechasse, now belonging to the Ministry of Pensions) housed an aristocratic school for girls, where Jefferson's daughter was a pupil during her father's embassy.

No. 110, the *Ministère de l'Éducation Nationale*, was the Hôtel de Courteilles (1778); No. 116, the old Hôtel de Brissac, rebuilt for Marshal de Villars by Boffrand and Leroux (1731), is now the *Mairie of the 7th Arrondissement*. No. 101, the former Hôtel Rothelin, built by Lassurance in 1700, is now the *Ministère du Commerce*. Nos. 138 and 140 were built by Jean Courtonne in 1724 and decorated by Lassurance in 1734 for Mlle de Sens. Marshal Foch died at No. 138 in 1929; No. 140 is occupied by the *Institut National Géographique*. No. 127, the *Ministère du Travail*, was the **Hôtel du Châtelet*, one of the finest examples of the Louis XV style; it was at one time used as the Archbishop's Palace. No. 142, the *Hôtel de Chanac* (1750), is the Swiss Embassy.

We turn left along the Boulevard des Invalides, then back E. into the RUE DE VARENNE. No. 77, at the corner, is the 18C *Hôtel Biron*, in which is installed the **Musée Rodin** (Rte 32). No. 72 is the *Hôtel de Castries* sacked by the mob in 1790 after the duel between the reactionary Duc de Castries and the radical Comte Charles de Lameth. No. 69, the *Hôtel de Clermont* (1714–75), is now the seat of the Haut Commissariat à l'Énergie Atomique. At No. 1bis Rue Vaneau, to the right, André Gide died in 1951. Just beyond is the ***Hôtel de Matignon** (No. 57), built by Courtonne about 1721 and altered in the 19C; having served as the Austro-Hungarian Embassy in 1888–1914, since 1935 it has been the *Hôtel de la Présidence du Conseil*. One of the most beautiful mansions in the faubourg, it has an unusually large and well-planned garden. Talleyrand lived here in 1808–11. No. 50, the handsome *Hôtel de Gallifet*, with an Ionic peristyle built by Legrand in 1775–96, is now the Italian consulate-general. No. 47 is the *Italian Embassy*.

The Rue du Bac leads S. to the *Grands Magasins du Bon Marché*, a little to the E. of which, between the Rue Babylone and the Rue de Sèvres and opening on the Boul. Raspail, is the large *Square Potain* or *Boucicaut*, with a monument to Mme Boucicaut (foundress of the Bon Marché) and Baroness Hirsch, benefactresses of the city of Paris.

The RUE DE SÈVRES begins at the *Carrefour de la Croix-Rouge*, and leads S.W. to the junction of the Boul. Pasteur and Boul. Garibaldi. At No. 11 Huysmans lived from 1872 to 1898. Just E. of the crossing with Boul. Raspail the Rue Récamier recalls the Abbaye aux Bois, the home of Mme Récamier in 1819–49, where the most frequent visitor at her famous salon was Chateaubriand. At No. 42 Rue de Sèvres, to the W. of the boulevard, is the *Hôpital Laënnec*, formerly a home for incurable women, founded by Cardinal de La Rochefoucauld about 1635, with an interesting courtyard and chapel. Farther on is the *Église des Lazaristes*, with a silver shrine containing the body of St Vincent de Paul. In the Rue St-Roman (l.), in the 18C *Hôtel Choiseul-Praslin*, is the *Postal Museum* (daily except Tues 2–6; 1 fr., Sun 0,50 fr.).—The RUE DU CHERCHE-MIDI, which we next cross, derives its name from an 18C sign on No. 19 (E. part), representing an astronomer tracing a sundial. To No. 37 Victor Hugo came to woo his cousin, Adèle Foucher, and here their marriage was celebrated in 1823. No. 38 is the *Prison Militaire du Cherche-Midi*, where many French patriots were imprisoned during the war. No. 40 belonged to Rochambeau (1725–1807) who fought for the Americans in the War of Independence, notably at Yorktown.—David d'Angers and the historian Michelet lived in the Rue St-Placide where J-K. Huysmans died at No. 31; Parmentier lived in the Rue de l'Abbé-Grégoire; and at No. 3bis Rue de Bagneux was the studio of Augustus Saint-Gaudens, the American sculptor (1897–1900).—All these are side-streets on the S.

6   THE INVALIDES, CHAMP-DE-MARS, AND EIFFEL TOWER

MÉTRO stations: *Invalides* (lines 8 and 14); *Tour-Maubourg, École Militaire, Champ-de-Mars* (line 8); *La Motte-Picquet* (lines 6, 8, 10).

The districts to the W. of the Faubourg St-Germain are overshadowed by the dome of the Invalides and the Eiffel Tower. From the right bank the best approach is from the Champs-Élysées by the Pont Alexandre-III, which affords a wonderful vista of the Invalides at the end of the Esplanade. This walk can conveniently be combined with a return via the Palais de Chaillot (Rte 7), a promenade affording some of the longest and most beautiful vistas of any inland city in the world.

The ESPLANADE DES INVALIDES is a large open space, 490 by 270 yds, laid out and planted with trees along the sides by Robert de Cotte in 1704–20. In its N.E. corner is the **Aérogare,** one of the two city terminals for air passengers. It occupies the former concourse of the *Gare des Invalides*, terminus for the electric railway to Versailles, whose platforms lie below.

The ***HOTEL DES INVALIDES** was founded by Louis XIV in 1671 as a home for disabled soldiers, the first enduring institution of its kind, and at one time housed as many as 7000 pensioners. At present about 150 war-wounded live in the buildings, which form a majestic ensemble. Built from the designs of *Libéral Bruant*, and continued by *J. Hardouin-Mansart*, the Invalides was restored under Napoleon I and Napoleon III and now covers an area of about 31 acres. The chief things to see are the **Musée de l'Armée** (Rte 21) and Napoleon's tomb. The Invalides is the headquarters of the military governor of Paris.

The courtyards of the Invalides are open daily 7–7; the *Dôme*, with *Napoleon's Tomb* (main entrance in the Place Vauban), is open daily 9.30–5 or 5.30; adm. 1 fr.

Passing through the iron entrance-gates, we enter the FORECOURT, in which are two German Panther tanks, captured by the Leclerc Division in Alsace during the liberation. Facing the Esplanade is a row of eighteen pieces of captured artillery, of which the eight on gun-carriages form the *Batterie Triomphale* (removed by the Germans in 1940). Arranged on either side of each half-battery are twenty unmounted pieces. To the left of the main drive is a statue of Prince Eugène de Beauharnais (1781–1824), by *Dumont*.

The dignified FAÇADE is 230 yds long and has no less than 133 windows in its four stories. The dormer windows take the form of trophies each different. Flanking the entrance are statues of Mars and Minerva, by *Guillaume Coustou* (1735), who was responsible also for the equestrian bas-relief above the central door of Louis XIV accompanied by Justice and Prudence.

The COUR D'HONNEUR, 111 by 68 yds, is bordered by galleries adorned with un-finished frescoes (the Military Annals of France), begun in 1867. Opposite the entrance is the door of the church of St-Louis, above which are *Seurre's* original bronze statue of Napoleon, formerly on the Vendôme Column, and an astronomical clock (1781). On either side of the courtyard are the entrances to the **Musée de l'Armée** (weapons and armour on the W., historical collection on the E.; see Rte 21). In the S.W. corner is one of the Renault cars (the Marne taxis), which, commandeered by Gen. Gallieni, carried troops to the Front in Sept 1914.

The **Church of St-Louis,** or chapel of the Invalides, was built by *Bruant*. The INTERIOR (closed on Tues) is decorated with captured ensigns. On the night of 30 May 1814, at the moment of the Allies' entry into Paris, Marshal Sérurier, governor of the Invalides, ordered 1400 enemy flags to be burned in the courtyard. Those remaining were brought from other buildings or are trophies of later wars. The chapel resounded in 1837 to the first performance of Berlioz' Requiem, the score of the 'Grande Messe des Morts' being rein-forced by a battery of artillery on the esplanade.

On the right is a monument to the generals killed in the First World War; the small stone post in front of it contains earth from a battlefield of the Second World War. On the left is the *Chapelle du Soldat de la Grande Armée* in which are deposited the tablets, palms, and other offerings brought from the Tomb of the Unknown Warrior. Here also is a stone containing earth from an American cemetery of the Second World War. A series of these posts ('bornes') crosses France from Cherbourg to Metz, and recalls the campaign of Gen. Patton and his troops in June–Nov 1944. Farther on is the hearse used to transport Napoleon's remains at St Helena, and, near the end of the aisle, the monument to French airmen who lost their lives in the First World War. On the pillars are monuments to marshals of France and governors of the Invalides. The *Chapelle Napoléon*, at the end of the right aisle, contains three stone slabs from the tomb at St Helena, the copper coffin and the velvet pall used for the removal of the remains in 1840, and a plaster mask of Napoleon made by Antommarchi. The plain glass behind the high-altar separates the church from the Dôme des Invalides.

In the *Vaults* (no adm.) are the graves of marshals and generals of France, including Turenne (d. 1675), Jourdan (d. 1833), Bertrand (b. 1844), Grouchy and Oudinot (d. 1847),

Exelmans (d. 1852), President MacMahon (d. 1893), and Franchet d'Espérey (d. 1942). Here too are buried the hearts of Vauban (d. 1707) and Kléber (d. 1800); also that of Mlle de Sombreuil whose courage saved her father, the governor, during the massacres of Sept 1792; and the remains of Gen. Guillaumat (d. 1940), Gen. Giraud (d. 1949), and Marshal Leclerc (de Hautecloque; d. 1947), commander of the famous Division Leclerc, which fought with the Allies in the invasion of Europe, and liberated Paris and Strasbourg.

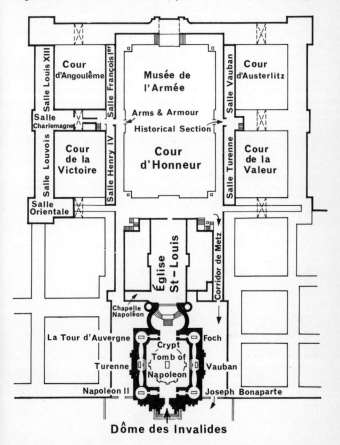

Dôme des Invalides

From the Cour d'Honneur we pass through the Corridor de Metz (on the right as we leave the church) to reach the entrance to the Dome and Napoleon's tomb.

The *Dôme des Invalides, begun by *J. Hardouin-Mansart* in 1675 and finished in 1706, was added to the church of St-Louis as a chapel royal. It is separated from the Place Vauban by a large courtyard enclosed by handsome iron railings. In the niches on either side of the entrance are statues of Charlemagne and St Louis, by *Coysevox* and *Cousteau*. The ribbed dome is roofed with lead, adorned with gilded trophies, and crowned with a flèche 345 ft above the ground.

The ***Interior,** 184 ft square, is in the form of a Greek cross. The most striking features are its admirable proportions, its sculptures, and its mosaic pavements. In the centre is a large circular opening above the tomb of Napoleon. The pendentives are painted with the four Evangelists, and in the cupola is St Louis presenting his sword to Christ, by *Charles de Lafosse*. On the entablature below the windows are sculptured medallions of kings of France, and above the windows are paintings of the apostles.

The first chapel on the right of the entrance is the CHAPELLE ST-AUGUSTIN, with the tomb of Joseph Bonaparte, king of Naples (d. 1844).—Tomb of Vauban (d. 1707), with statues of Science and War, by *Etex*; above the arches are bas-reliefs of St Louis founding the Quinze-Vingts and the Fall of Damietta.—CHAPELLE ST-AMBROISE, with the bronze tomb of Marshal Foch (d. 1929), by *Landowski*.—CHAPELLE ST-GRÉGOIRE, with the tomb of Marshal Lyautey (d. 1934), whose ashes were brought back from Rabat and placed here in 1963, and the heart of La Tour d'Auvergne (d. 1800; "the first grenadier of the Republic").—Tomb of Turenne (d. 1675).—CHAPELLE ST-JÉRÔME. In the centre is the sarcophagus of the Roi de Rome (1811-32), or Napoleon II, the great Napoleon's only son. Originally buried in Vienna, his remains were brought hither by the Germans in 1940, on the hundredth anniversary of the burial of his father in the crypt.

On either side of the altar a staircase descends to the CRYPT (conducted parties only; gratuity). The bronze door is flanked by colossal statues of Civil and Military Power, by *Duret*. The inscription on the impost may be translated: "I desire that my ashes rest on the banks of the Seine, in the midst of the French people whom I have loved so dearly." The **Tomb of Napoleon,** 13 by 6½ ft, and 15 ft high, is of red porphyry from Finland and was presented by Tsar Nicholas I. It rests on a pedestal of green Vosges granite and is surrounded by a gallery with ten bas-reliefs after *Simart*, typifying the benefits conferred on France by the Emperor. Facing the sarcophagus are twelve colossal figures representing the chief victories of the Emperor, *Pradier's* last work, between which are six trophies of fifty-four flags taken at the battle of Austerlitz. The statue of Napoleon in his coronation robes, 8½ ft high, is by *Simart*. In front is a reliquary containing the hat worn by the Emperor at Eylau, the sword he carried at Austerlitz, his grand chain of Legion of Honour, and other relics.

The district to the W., between the Invalides and Champ-de-Mars, is intersected by the Boul. de la Tour-Maubourg and by the wide Av. de La Motte-Picquet, Av. Bosquet, and Av. Rapp. At the corner of the Rue Jean-Nicot and the Quai d'Orsay (No. 63) is the *American Church* (1927-31). Jean Giraudoux (1882-1944), the playwright, died at No. 89 Quai d'Orsay. At No. 1 QUAI BRANLY are the *Ministry of Civil Aviation* and *Meteorological Office*; most of the quay as far as the Champ-de-Mars (see below) is bordered by the *Ministry of Economic Affairs* (1949).

The E. side of the Invalides, the charming domestic architecture of which contrasts with the formal façade on the Esplanade, is skirted by the BOULEVARD DES INVALIDES. On the left diverge the Rue de Grenelle and the Rue de Varenne. Near the beginning of the latter is the Musée Rodin (Rte 32). Farther on in the boulevard is the church of *St-François-Xavier* (1875). In the Rue Duroc (r.) is the *Blind Asylum* or *Maison des Aveugles* (Nos. 5–9), built in 1907, with a sale-room, workshops, museum, and library. The *Institut National des Jeunes Aveugles*, on the right side of the boulevard, was founded by Valentin Haüy in 1793 and transferred to this building in 1843.—The Boul. des Invalides ends at the Rue de Sèvres and is continued by the Boul. du Montparnasse.

The AVENUE DE TOURVILLE, leading W. from the Boul. des Invalides to the Champ-de-Mars, passes between the Dôme des Invalides and the semicircular *Place Vauban*, from the S. side of which radiate the Av. de Villars, the wide Av. de Breteuil, and the Av. de Ségur.

In the Place are statues of Marshals Gallieni (1849–1916) and Fayolle (1852–1928), both by *Jean Boucher.*

The AVENUE DE BRETEUIL (an avenue of trees) crosses the *Place de Breteuil*, in which rises a lofty monument to *Pasteur* (1822–95), by Falguière and Girault, erected in 1904 by public subscription. At the end of the Av. de Breteuil (which provides one of the best views of the Invalides) begin the Boul. Garibaldi and the BOULEVARD PASTEUR, with the buildings of the *Institut d'Optique* (1924–27) on the left.

In the part of the RUE DE SÈVRES between the Av. de Breteuil and the Boul. des Invalides are (l.) the *Hôpital des Enfants-Malades*, founded in 1724, and the *Hôpital Necker*, once a Benedictine nunnery, founded in 1779 by Louis XVI, directed at one time by Mme Necker, and rebuilt in 1840.

From the Place de Breteuil the Avenue de Saxe leads N.W. to the **Place de Fontenoy,** in front of the huge courtyard behind the École Militaire. On the right of the Place are the large buildings (1932) of the *Ministry of the Merchant Marine* and the *Ministry of Labour*, while on the left is the headquarters (1958) of **UNESCO, designed by *M. Breuer, B. Zehrfuss,* and *P. L. Nervi,* consisting of three buildings. The highest (seven floors) is the *Secretariat*: Y-shaped and supported on seventy-two pylons, it completes the semi-circle of the Place de Fontenoy behind the École Militaire designed by *Gabriel.* It is connected to the *Conference Building,* with its accordeon-pleated concrete roof covered in copper, by the Salle des Pas-perdus. In the Conference building are murals by Picasso and Rufino Tamayo. The third building, for the permanent delegations, borders the Av. de Ségur. In the *Piazza* are works by Henry Moore,

Alexander Calder, Jean Arp, and Miro, and a *Japanese Garden* has been designed by Isamu Noguchi. The magnificence of the concrete which gives the conference rooms such majesty is acknowledged, but the buildings still arouse controversy.

Guided Tours take place daily 10–12 and 2.30–6; 3 fr.

The ***École Militaire,** a handsome structure covering 29 acres of the former 'ferme' and 'château' of Grenelle, was built for Louis XV by J. A. Gabriel and enlarged in 1856.

The school was founded in 1751 for the training of noblemen as army officers, opened in 1756 and completed in 1770. In 1777 its rigid rules for entry were modified so that it could take in the élite of provincial military academies, thus in 1784 Bonaparte was chosen from the Collège de Brienne. Closed in 1787 it was used as a store house and a barracks. It is now occupied by the *École Supérieure de Guerre*, or staff college.

A fine 18C railing separates the Cour d'Honneur from the Place de Fontenoy. The entrance façade closes the perspective of the Champ-de-Mars. In the entablature the figure representing victory is in fact Louis XV and this is probably the only likeness that escaped the Revolution. Permission is sometimes granted on written application to the Général Commandant d'Armes to visit some of the rooms of the college. The most striking is the *Salon des Maréchaux* with fine woodwork. A small museum commemorates Marshal Foch, who used to hold his receptions here, when commandant of the college before 1914.

On the N.W. side of the École Militaire, in the *Place Joffre*, is a monument to Marshal Joffre (d. 1931), by Réal del Sarte.

Between the École Militaire and the Seine lies the **Champ-de-Mars,** about 1000 yds long and from 200 to 500 yds wide. It was laid out about 1765 as a parade-ground and made into a park after 1913, and is now the centre of a select but architecturally dull residential quarter.

The ground was the scene of several early aeronautical experiments by the Montgolfier, by Charles and Robert, and by Blanchard (1783–84). Here were held numerous revolutionary festivals, the most famous of which was the Fête de la Fédération on 14 July 1790, when the king, the Assembly, and the delegates from the provinces and the army took the oath at the Autel de la Patrie to observe the new Constitution; the 'Champ de Mai', held by Napoleon on his return from Elba; and many International Exhibitions. Bailly, president of the Constituent Assembly, was brutally executed here in 1793, and Capt. Dreyfus was publicly degraded here in 1894.

At the river end of the Champ-de-Mars, facing the Palais de Chaillot, rises the ***Eiffel Tower** or *Tour Eiffel* (984 ft high; just over 1040 ft with the television installation). This, the third tallest building in the world, dominates the W. end of Paris. Built for the Exhibition of 1889, the tower was granted a life of only 20 years, but its use in radio-telegraphy established in 1904 saved it from demolition in 1909.

The tower was constructed by the engineer Alexandre Eiffel in 1887–89. It weighs 7000 tons and is composed of 12,000 pieces of metal, fastened by 2,500,000 rivets. The base of the tower is/supported by/four huge masonry piers, sunk 30–45 ft in the ground, the surface of each measuring 31 sq. yds. The ascent, which is not recommended in misty, windy, or cold weather, is made in lifts (the first two platforms may be reached also, very tediously, by staircases). The tower is open 10 a.m.–midnight in summer, 10.30–6 in winter (15 Oct–15 Apr); the third platform in summer only (10–6); to the first platform 1½ fr.; second platform 3 fr.; third platform 5 fr. On the first platform (187 ft high) is the restaurant 'En Plein Ciel', on the second (377 ft) another restaurant and café, while the third one (902 ft) sports a bar. The *View, extending over a radius of 50 m. from Paris, is usually clearest about 1 hr before sunset. Underneath the N. leg of the tower is a bust of Eiffel, by Bourdelle.

The Champ-de-Mars is bounded on the S.W. by the AVENUE DE SUFFREN, with the *Hilton Hotel*. Farther S.W., opposite the Pont de Bir-Hakeim, where the Quai Branly

becomes the Quai de Grenelle, is the BOULEVARD DE GRENELLE, which is continued
E. by the BOULEVARD GARIBALDI. In the former boulevard is the huge *Palais des Sports*
(1910), usually known as 'Vél d'Hiv', from its older title of Vélodrome d'Hiver. At the
junction of these boulevards is the PLACE CAMBRONNE, with a statue of Garibaldi (1807–
1882). From the Place Cambronne the Rue de la Croix-Nivert leads S.W. to the Square
St-Lambert, a garden laid out on the site of the old gasworks.

The chief point of interest in the district to the S.W. of the École Militaire
is the **Imprimerie Nationale**, or government printing-works, moved in 1925
from the Hôtel de Rohan to the Rue de la Convention. In front is a statue of
Gutenberg, by *David d'Angers*. Visitors are admitted to the workshops on the
last Thurs of each month at 2.30 on previous application.

Facing the Imprimerie is **St-Christophe-de-Javel**, a modern church (1926–34) by *C. H.
Besnard*, decorated outside with frescoes in cement, by *H. M. Magne*, of St Christopher
as the averter of accidents. The mural decorations in the interior, by *J. M. Ferrières*, are
also noteworthy. A short distance to the N.W. the *Pont Mirabeau* crosses the Seine to
Auteuil.

The Rue Gutenberg leads S.W. from the Imprimerie to the Rue Balard, link-
ing the Pont Mirabeau with the Place Balard. Beyond the Place is the Boul.
Victor, in which are various buildings of the *Ministère de l'Air* and other
Service departments.

7   QUARTIER CHAILLOT AND PASSY

This route comprises the triangle of the 8th arrondissement lying between the Champs-
Élysées and the Seine together with the 16th arrondissement between the Seine and the
Bois de Boulogne.

A   From the Place de la Concorde to the Palais de Chaillot

MÉTRO stations: *Alma-Marceau*, *Iéna* (line 9); *Trocadéro* (lines 6, 9).

The broad COURS-LA-REINE, laid out under Marie de Médicis in 1616 and
leading due W. from the Place de la Concorde to the Place de l'Alma, is called
in its W. part the COURS ALBERT-PREMIER. This was the road from Paris to
the villages of Chaillot and St-Cloud, and to Versailles; it followed the Roman
canal which brought water from Chaillot. At the beginning of the Cours-la-
Reine, in the Place de la Concorde, is an equestrian statue (1938) of Albert I,
king of the Belgians, by Armand Martial. The parallel QUAI DE LA CONFÉRENCE,
on the Seine, takes its name from the Porte de la Conférence (demolished in
1730), through which the Spanish ambassadors entered Paris in 1660 to discuss
with Mazarin the projected marriage between Louis XIV and Maria Theresa.
On the right are the *Petit Palais* and the *Grand Palais*; on the left is the
Pont Alexandre III.

In the Place du Canada, whence the AV. FRANKLIN D. ROOSEVELT leads to
the Rond-Point des Champs-Élysées, are a monument to Alfred de Musset
(1810–57), and a bust of Jacques Cartier (1491–1557), discoverer of the St
Lawrence river. Opposite is the *Pont des Invalides.*

The RUE FRANÇOIS-PREMIER, which diverges here (r.), is crossed at the *Place
François-Premier* by the Rue Jean-Goujon and the Rue Bayard. In the Rue Jean-Goujon
(l.) are the *Armenian Church*, built by A. Guilbert in 1903–05, and **Notre-Dame de
Consolation** (open daily 2–5 Apr–Oct), a sumptuous chapel in the Louis-XVI style,
designed likewise by Guilbert and dedicated to the memory of the 130 victims of the fire
at the Charity Bazaar (4 May 1897) on the spot. Gustave Doré had a studio at No. 1 Rue
Bayard, and in the flat above lived Jules Ferry. No. 2, the so-called 'House of Francis I',
was built c. 1527 at Moret and brought here in 1823; the sculpture has been attributed to

Jean Goujon. The new **Scottish Church** (1959; No. 19), the foundation stone of which was laid by Queen Elizabeth II in 1957, contains the pulpit used by Spurgeon at Menton.

At the end of the Cours Albert Premier is the **Place de l'Alma,** whence the *Pont de l'Alma* crosses the Seine to the Quai d'Orsay, while several handsome streets radiate on the N. bank. Here is the Monument of Belgium's Gratitude for French aid during the First World War.

At the beginning of the AVENUE MONTAIGNE, which leads N.E. to the Rond-Point des Champs-Élysées, is the *Théâtre des Champs-Élysées*, a reinforced concrete building (1911–13) by A. and G. Perret, with bas-reliefs and frescoes by Bourdelle.

In the AVENUE GEORGE-V, leading N., is the American Episcopal Church of **Holy Trinity,** with a graceful tower, built in the early-English Gothic style by G. S. Street (1885–88), with fine glass illustrating the Te Deum. On the left is the *Memorial Battle Cloister*, designed by Bertram Goodhue (1923), in honour of the U.S. army units who suffered casualities in France in 1917–18.

The QUAI DE LA CONFÉRENCE and its continuation the AVENUE DE NEW-YORK are linked by a tunnel beneath the Place, near the entrance to which is a statue of Adam Mickiewicz, the Polish poet, by *Bourdelle*. The Av. de New-York goes on towards Passy, passing between the *Pont d'Iéna* and the Palais de Chaillot (see below).—The AVENUE MARCEAU leads N.W. from the Place de l'Alma to the Étoile, passing the Rue Georges-Bizet (l.), in which is the Greek Orthodox church of *Ayios Stefanos*, with a handsome interior and marble iconostasis. In the wealthy *Quartier Chaillot*, the church of *St-Pierre-de-Chaillot* (1937), in a Byzantine Romanesque style, takes its surname from the vanished village.

From the Av. Marceau the AVENUE DU PRÉSIDENT-WILSON diverges almost immediately on the left. No. 5 was the home of Alphonse Bertillon (1853–1914), inventor of fingerprinting. On the right is the main façade of the *Musée Galliéra* (now given up exclusively to temporary exhibitions; entrance at No. 10 Av. Pierre Ier de Serbie).

On the left is the **Palais d'Art Moderne** (adm. daily except Tues 10–5, 1 fr.; Sun free). This enormous building, extending to the Av. de New-York, was constructed for the Exhibition of 1937 by Aubert, Dondel, Viard, and Dastugue, on the site of the Savonnerie.

The ornamental lake facing the Seine is decorated by four bronze figures, and the wall of the terrace has a fine bas-relief by *Janniot*, depicting the legends of antiquity. On the terrace is a statue by *Bourdelle* of 'La France', in honour of French patriots who fell in the Second World War. Under the peristyle are figures of Strength and Victory, also by *Bourdelle*.

The **Musée National d'Art Moderne,** in the W. wing, entered from the Rue de la Manutention, is devoted to an extensive collection of recent and contemporary schools of French painting and sculpture. The exhibits are mostly arranged under the schools or coteries of their creators. The rooms devoted to painting are indicated by numbers; those containing sculptures by letters. Only a few of the best-known artists are mentioned in the list which follows; the rooms are subject to rearrangement.

GROUND FLOOR. The large hall on the right is reserved for temporary exhibitions.—ROOM A. Sculptures by *Aristide Maillol* (1861–1944).—Paintings: R. 1. Neo-Impressionists: *Paul Signac*.—R. 2. School of Pont-Aven: *Louis Anquetin, Paul Bernard*.—RR. 3, 4. Les Nabis: *Pierre Bonnard, Maurice Denis*.—R. 5. *Maurice Utrillo, Suzanne Valadon*.—R. 6. *Félix Vallotton*.—R. 7. Les Fauves: *André Derain, Othon Friesz, Georges Rouault, Maurice de Vlaminck*.—R. 9. *Albert Marquet*.—R. 10. *Henri Matisse*.—RR. 11, 11bis. *Kees van Dongen, Raoul Dufy*.—R. 12. 20th Century 'Primitives'.—R. 13. *Juan Gris, Louis Marcoussis*.—R. 14. Cubists: *Fernand Léger*.—R. 15. *Albert Gleize*.—R. 16. *Roger de la Fresnaye*.—R. 17. *Robert Delaunay* ('Orphisme').—R. 18. *Pablo Picasso*.—R. 19. *Georges Braque*.—R. 20. *A. Dunoyer de Segonzac, J. L. Boussingault*.—R. 21. Surrealists.

FIRST FLOOR. R. 23bis. Expressionism and the 'École de Paris': *Marc Chagall*.—R. 24. The Abstracts.—R. 25 shows the modern artist at his most attractive, in decorative art, with tapestries by *Raoul Dufy* and *Jean Lurçat*; ceramics, jewellery, goldsmiths' work, enamels, ivories, furniture, and decorative sculpture.—RR. 26–30. Contemporary painters.—R. 31. Temporary exhibitions.—On the grand staircase, tapestry, 'The Woodmen of the Forest of Mormal', by *Marcel Gromaire*.

LOWER GROUND FLOOR. Sculpture. The *Brancusi* bequest (1962) is displayed in a reconstruction of the sculptor's studio (2, Impasse Ronsin) containing also tools and personal furniture. The *Julio Gonsalez* bequest, donated by his wife (1966), includes, in addition to his sculptural work, numerous drawings. Other sculptors whose works are on view include: *Charles Despiau* (1874–1946); *Antoine Bourdelle* (1861–1929); *Paul Landowski* (1875–1961); *François Sicard* (1862–1934).—R. 32. Paintings of 1900–14: *Aman-Jean, Giovanni Boldini*; glassware and ceramics.—R. 33. Salon des Artistes Français.—R. 34. Salon de la Nationale: *Jacques-Émile Blanche, Charles Cottet, René Ménard.*—R. 35. Salon des Indépendants.—RR. 36–38. Salon d'Automne.

The **Musée du Costume de la Ville de Paris** (adm. 1 fr., 12–7; closed Tues), an annexe of the Musée Carnavalet, is entered under the peristyle. A selection of the splendid collection of costumes dating from 1725 is shown in rotation every three months.

The E. wing of the museum building is occupied by the *Musée d'Art Moderne de la Ville de Paris*, with the collection of 20C paintings formerly in the Petit Palais.

Farther on the Avenue du Président-Wilson crosses the PLACE D'IÉNA, in the centre of which is an equestrian statue of *George Washington*, by Daniel French, presented to France by the women of America. On the N. side of the square is the **Musée Guimet** (Rte 28), and on the S.W. side is the *Palais du Conseil Économique et Social*, built by Auguste Perret (1937–38) for the Musée des Travaux Publics. One of the most successful buildings of its period, it was occupied in 1956 by the Third Assembly of the Fourth Republic. An additional wing (1962) bordering the Av. du Président-Wilson houses the *Western European Union* building.

At No. 24 Rue Boissière, to the N.W., the poet Henri de Régnier died in 1936; and at No. 44 Rue Hamelin (to the right of Rue Boissière) Proust died in 1922. The Avenue d'Iéna, where No. 2 is the residence of the U.S. ambassador, leads direct to the Étoile, passing (l.) the agreeable PLACE DES ÉTATS-UNIS. Here are several American monuments, including *Bartholdi's* group of Washington and La Fayette (1895); a monument to American Volunteers of the First World War, by *Victor Boucher*; and busts of Dr Horace Wells, the first dentist to use gas as an anæsthetic (1844), and of Myron T. Herrick, the distinguished ambassador, by *Bertrand Bouthée*. On the right, farther on, is the Anglican church of *St George*, built in 1887–88 at the expense of Sir Richard Wallace. In 1860 Wagner lived in the Rue Newton (on the right) at No. 16 (house gone).

The Av. du Président-Wilson ends at the Place du Trocadéro, 550 yds across and nearly circular in shape, whence six avenues radiate fanwise from the Palais de Chaillot. The Place is situated on the 'Colline du Trocadéro', a little eminence named after a fort at Cadiz, taken by the French in 1823.

Catherine de Médicis built a country house here, on the S.E.; later embellished by Anne of Austria, it was sold to Maréchal de Bassompierre, and in 1651 Henrietta Maria bought it from his heirs and established the Convent of the Visitation of St Mary. Here Bossuet delivered her funeral oration. The convent was destroyed during the Revolution and Napoleon wanted to use the site for a palace for his son which would be more magnificent than the Kremlin, but the disasters of 1812 intervened. For the Exhibition of 1878 the Palais du Trocadéro was built and its successor the huge Palais de Chaillot was built for the Exhibition of 1937.

B   From the Eiffel Tower to the Bois

MÉTRO stations: *Trocadéro* (lines 6, 9); *Georges-Mandel, Muette, Ranelagh* (line 9); *Passy* (line 6); *Michelange-Auteuil* (lines 9, 10).

The best *Approach to the **Palais de Chaillot** is from the Eiffel Tower (Rte 6) by the Pont d'Iéna, crossing the Avenue de New-York. To right and left of the Colline du Trocadéro splendid gardens flank the *Fountains which include a battery of 20 jets 'firing' almost horizontally towards the Eiffel Tower. At the foot of the terrace is the entrance to the Theatre (see below) and to the

Aquarium du Trocadéro (daily 10–6 or 6.30; adm. 0,50 fr.). The *Terrace* affords a magnificent *View from the right bank to the left. Particularly striking is the perspective of the École Militaire seen through the Eiffel Tower and across the Champ-de-Mars. It is the most grandiose and successful modern contribution to the townscape of Paris. The central square, between the two wings of the palais, is adorned with gilded bronze statues by Bouchard and Pommier. Underneath the square is the *Théâtre de Chaillot*, a vast hall seating over 2000, and now the home of the Théâtre National Populaire. Among the painters who have contributed to the decoration are Dufy, Vuillard, Othon Friesz, and Bonnard. It was here that the third General Assembly of the United Nations was held in Sept–Dec 1948. The Palais de Chaillot is described, with its interesting museums, in Rte 26.

The AVENUE KLÉBER (where Aristide Briand, the statesman, died at No. 52 in 1932) leads N.E. from the Place du Trocadéro to the Place de l'Étoile. It passes on the left the Rue Paul-Valéry (formerly Rue de Villejust), No. 40 in which was the home of Paul Valéry (1871–1945) from 1902; this house had been, from 1883, the studio of Berthe Morisot, Valéry's aunt by marriage, and a favourite rendezvous of the literary and artistic society of the day. The AVENUE RAYMOND-POINCARÉ leads N., crosses the *Place Victor-Hugo* and the Avenue Foch, and is continued to the Porte Maillot by the AVENUE MALAKOFF. The church of *St-Honoré d'Eylau* in the Place Victor-Hugo contains an Adoration of the Shepherds by Tintoretto. No. 124 AVENUE VICTOR-HUGO (which leads S.W. from the Étoile to La Muette) marks the site of the house where Hugo died in 1885.

At the beginning of the RUE FRANKLIN, which leads S.W. from the Place du Trocadéro towards Passy, is a statue of Benjamin Franklin (minister plenipotentiary to France 1776–85), by John Boyle, presented to Paris in 1906 by an American banker. Georges Clemenceau lived at No. 8 in 1896–1929, and the house has been preserved in its original state as a memorial (open Thurs, Sat and Sun, 2–5; adm. 1 fr.).—From the AVENUE PAUL-DOUMER (at its Trocadéro end) steps ascend to the small **Cimetière de Passy** (entrance at 2 Rue des Réservoirs), which contains a number of interesting monuments, including those of Debussy (d. 1918), Manet (d. 1883), Marie Bashkirtseff (d. 1884), Las Cases (d. 1842), and Gabriel Fauré (d. 1924).

The shady AVENUE GEORGES-MANDEL leads W. to the *Rue de la Pompe*, and is continued W. to the Porte de la Muette by the AVENUE HENRI-MARTIN, in which, near the Square Lamartine, the poet Lamartine died in 1869 (house demolished). The *Porte de la Muette*, one of the chief entrances to the Bois de Boulogne, is dominated on the S. side by a huge block of flats, while on the N. side is a bronze group of Peter I of Serbia and Alexander I of Yugoslavia, by Réal del Sarte (1936). To the E. of the Av. Suchet are the remains of the ancient royal park of **La Muette,** where the first balloon ascent in France was made in 1783 by Pilâtre de Rozier and the Marquis d'Arlandes.

The royal *Château de la Muette*, originally a hunting-lodge, improved by the Regent Orleans, and restored by Louis XV for Mme de Pompadour, has completely disappeared. It is especially associated with Marie-Antoinette, who was welcomed here by Louis XVI on her arrival in Paris on the eve of her wedding in 1770. Twelve years later she set forth hence for Notre-Dame and Ste-Geneviève on the occasion of the thanksgiving for the birth of the Dauphin. Later the château was occupied by Philippe-Égalité, who stood on the terrace to watch the mob bringing Louis XVI from Versailles to the Tuileries in 1789. From 1820 to 1920 it belonged to the family Erard, the piano builders. The present mansion, built by Baron Henri de Rothschild, is now the property of the European Council of Economic Co-operation.

From the Place de la Muette the BOUL. SUCHET runs S. to the *Porte d'Auteuil*. On the left the Avenue Raphaël leads into the *Jardin du Ranelagh*, which, just before the Revolution, was a fashionable resort designed to emulate its namesake in London. At No. 2 in the Rue Louis-Boilly (l.) is the **Musée Marmottan** (adm. 1 fr.; Sun and Sat 2–5, closed 15 July–15 Sept), which is mainly devoted to furniture and objets d'art of the First Empire. Among the paintings are a fine collection of the work of Boilly. There are also examples of Renaissance tapestry, woodwork and painting, especially French and Flemish. The museum was founded by Jules Marmottan, and left to the Institut de France by his son, Paul (d. 1932).

The residential district of **Passy,** which stretches from the Bois de Boulogne to the Seine and includes some of the area described to the W. of the Place du Trocadéro (see above), is remarkably peaceful and rural. In the middle of the last century it was a favourite residence of artists and literary men, but modern blocks of flats have largely replaced their villas and gardens. No. 47 Rue Raynouard is *Balzac's House* (open daily except Tues, 1.30–5, or 6; adm. 1 fr.), containing a museum of souvenirs of the novelist, who lived here in 1841–47. Here he wrote, among other novels, 'Le Cousin Pons' and 'La Cousine Bette'. This house is one of the most charming in Passy (good view of it from 24 Rue Berton); earlier occupants of the Rue Raynouard include the architect Robert de Cotte and the Abbé Prévost. Benjamin Franklin, who lived at Passy in 1777–85, erected on his house, the *Hôtel de Valentinois* (plaque at the corner of the Rue Singer), the first lightning conductor seen in France. Farther on (l.) is the delightfully rural Rue Berton. In the Rue d'Ankara (its continuation; r.) is the mansion (l.; Turkish Embassy), once the residence of the Princesse de Lamballe and later the private asylum of Dr Blanche where Maupassant died in 1893.

Other distinguished residents of Passy include Fanny Burney (in 1802–06), who, with her husband, bought No. 54 Rue Basse, Béranger (in 1833–35), Rossini (who died here in 1868), Maeterlinck, René Boylesve, Gabriel Fauré who died at No. 32 Rue des Vignes in 1925, and James Joyce who lived at 34 Rue des Vignes during the latter part of his stay in Paris.

From the Chaussée de la Muette the Avenue Mozart runs S. to **Auteuil,** another residential district with traces of 18C elegance. There are several large hospitals here. The 12C parish church of *Notre Dame d'Auteuil* was rebuilt (1877–88) in the Romanesque-Byzantine style. In front of it is the tomb of the chancellor D'Aguesseau (d. 1751) and his wife, a pyramid of red marble, crowned with a globe and cross of gilded copper.

Among residents of Auteuil were Boileau and probably Molière, Dr Émile Blanche and his son the painter J.-E. Blanche (19 Rue Docteur-Blanche), Henri Bergson (47 Boul. Beauséjour), the brothers Goncourt who lived and died at No. 67 Boulevard Montmorency, where they entertained Huysmans, Zola, Daudet and Maupassant, and André Gide who lived in the Avenue des Sycomores.

The Rue d'Auteuil leads W. from the parish church to the *Porte d'Auteuil*, the S.E. entrance to the Bois de Boulogne. Beyond, the Avenue de la Porte d'Auteuil is bordered on its S. side by the **Jardin Fleuriste** (open daily 10–5 or 6; 0,50 fr.). Farther W. is the *Stade Roland-Garros*, famous for the many Davis Cup matches that have been played there (entrance in the Av. Gordon-Bennett). From the Porte d'Auteuil the Av. du Général-Sarrail in which is the *Lycée Fontaine* (l.) leads S., passing on the right the *Piscine Molitor*, to the huge *Vélodrome du Parc des Princes*, built in 1936.

8   FROM THE PLACE DE LA CONCORDE TO THE ARC DE TRIOMPHE

MÉTRO stations: *Concorde* (lines 1, 8, 12); *Champs-Élysées-Clemenceau, Franklin D. Roosevelt, George V* (line 1); *Étoile* (lines 1, 2, 6).

To the W. of the Place de la Concorde extend the *Champs-Élysées, through which the wide Avenue des Champs-Élysées ascends to the Arc de Triomphe, c. 1¼ m. distant. At the beginning of the avenue are the *Marly Horses* (comp. Rte 1). The area, drained and planted in 1670 according to Le Nôtre's designs, was rearranged by the Marquis de Marigny, brother of Mme de Pompadour, in 1770. He extended the avenue to the Pont de Neuilly in 1774. Under the Second Empire it was the fashionable promenade of Paris.

The Champs-Élysées consist of two parts. The first, forming a park nearly ½ m. long and ¼ m. wide, extends to the Rond-Point des Champs-Élysées; the second, the continuation of the Avenue des Champs-Élysées thence to the Arc de Triomphe, is flanked by cafés, large shops, cinemas, and hotels, and is

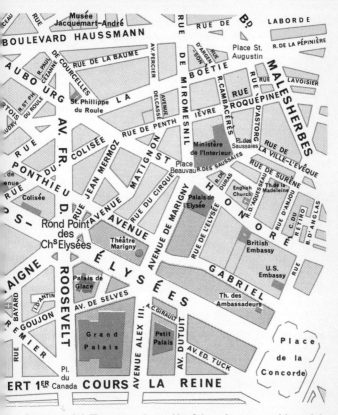

always crowded. The part on the N. side of the main avenue and beyond the Place Clemenceau is a favourite children's playground, with puppet-shows, etc. The drinking-fountains here and elsewhere in Paris were presented by Sir Richard Wallace (d. 1890).

Skirting the N. (r.) side of the Champs-Élysées is the AVENUE GABRIEL, at the E. end of which is the *American Embassy*, at the corner of the Rue Boissy-d'Anglas. On the left among the trees is the *Théâtre des Ambassadeurs*. Farther on are (r.) the gardens of the British Embassy and (l.) the *Pavillon de l'Élysée* and the monument to Alphonse Daudet (1840–97). Next come the gardens of the *Palais de l'Élysée* (Rte 18), the official residence of the President of the Republic.

From the Place Georges-Clemenceau, the Avenue de Marigny leads N.; on the left among the trees is the *Théâtre Marigny* with the Stamp Market (Thurs, Sun, and holidays) to the N. of it. The Avenue Alexandre-III runs S., between the Grand Palais (r.) and the Petit Palais (l.), both of which were built for the Exhibition of 1900. This avenue ends opposite the Pont Alexandre-III, beyond which the vista is closed by the dome of the Invalides. By the S.E. corner of the Place is a statue of Clemenceau, by Cogné (1932).

The **Petit Palais,** or *Palais des Beaux-Arts de la Ville de Paris,* is an imposing building by *Charles Girault.* The tympanum group, by *Injalbert,* represents the Triumph of Paris. The Palais is often occupied by art exhibitions but normally contains the art-collections of the city of Paris. Donated to the city by private collectors, these collections are catholic in taste, ranging from the antique to the 19C; the collection of 20C painting and sculpture is now in the Museum of Modern Art (Rte 7). There is a notable collection of works by *Courbet* and *Carpeaux.* Except during special exhibitions it is open daily (except Tues) 10–12, 2–6; adm. 0,50 fr. (free on Sun). The nearest Métro station is Champs-Élysées-Clemenceau (line 1).

The **Grand Palais,** the work of *Deglane, Louvet,* and *Thomas,* has a classical façade, 260 yds long, with Ionic columns and a lofty portico. On the great pillars flanking the portico are statues of (l.) Art by *Verlet* and (r.) Peace by *Lombard.* The building is used for the annual exhibitions of various societies. Since the Exhibition of 1937 the W. part of the building has housed the *Palais de la Découverte* (entrance in the Av. Franklin Roosevelt), a centre of scientific studies attached to the University, with a museum designed for the layman (and his child).

It is open daily 10–12, 2–6 (except Fri); adm. 1 fr. including cinema. Lectures on scientific subjects are held here, as well as cinema shows (programme available). At the *Planetarium* (adm. 1,50 fr.) commentaries are given daily (exc. Fri) at 3 and 4.30.

To the N. of the Grand Palais, between it and the Rond-Point, is the *Palais de Glace,* an ice-skating rink.

At the ROND-POINT DES CHAMPS-ÉLYSÉES, with its six fountains and its flower-beds, six avenues converge. Heine (1799–1856) died on the fifth story of No. 3 in the Avenue Matignon (r.), after years spent on his 'mattress-grave'. The office of *Le Figaro* is on the right also, at the corner of the Av. Franklin Roosevelt. Farther on, to the left, lies the wealthy *Quartier Marbeuf.* On the corner of the Rue de Berri (r.) a plaque marks the site of the mansion in which Thomas Jefferson lived in 1785–89, as American minister. No. 15 Av. des Champs-Élysées was built by the Duc de Morny for one of his mistresses, and No. 25 belonged to the Marquise de Païva, who here held the political salon which advanced her career of adventuress and spy.

The PLACE DE L'ÉTOILE derives its name from its twelve avenues radiating starwise. In the centre stands the **Arc de Triomphe,* the largest triumphal arch in the world (162 ft high and 147 ft wide). Beneath the arch is the **TOMB OF AN UNKNOWN WARRIOR,* representing the heroic French dead of 1914–18. The remains, after resting in the chamber above the arch from 11 Nov 1920, were interred here in Jan 1921, and now lie beneath a constantly burning flame which is revived every evening by a party of ex-service men. At the foot of the tomb is a bronze plaque, presented by Allied Supreme Headquarters, bearing a symbolic representation of the 'Shaef' shoulder-flash, and dated 25 Aug 1944, the day of the liberation of Paris from the German invader.

Designed by *Chalgrin* and begun by Napoleon I in 1806, the Arc de Triomphe was not completed till the reign of Louis-Philippe (1836). The main façades are adorned with colossal groups in high-relief: facing the Champs-Élysées are (r.) the *Departure of the Army in 1792 or 'The Marseillaise', by *Rude,* and (l.) the Triumph of Napoleon in 1810, by *Cortot;* facing the Av. de la Grand-Armée are (r.) the Resistance of the French in 1814 and (l.) the Peace of 1815, both by *Etex.* The four spandrels of the main archway contain figures of Fame by *Pradier,* and those of the smaller archway have sculptures by *Vallois* (S. side) and *Bra* (N. side). Above the groups are panels in relief of incidents in the campaigns of 1792–1805. On the row of shields in the attic story are inscribed the names of the 172 battles of the Republic and the Empire, and below the side-arches are the names of the generals who took part in the campaigns, the names of those who fell in action being underlined.

Commanding a splendid panoramic *View of Paris, the platform on the top of the arch is open daily, except Tues, 10–4, 5 or 6, and closed on 1 Jan, 1 May, 1, 2 and 11 Nov, and 25 Dec (adm. 1 fr.; 1,50 fr. on Sun, incl. lift). A small *Museum* showing the history of the monument can also be visited.

The route from the Arc de Triomphe along the Champs-Élysées has been used for all great state occasions since the cortège bearing Napoleon's ashes followed it in 1840, watched, despite the intense cold, by 100,000 people. This honour was also bestowed on Victor Hugo, Lazare and Sadi Carnot, Foch, Joffre, Leclerc, and Lyautey. On 14 July 1919, 26 Aug 1944 and 14 July 1945 processions along this route symbolized French rejoicing at their victory and liberation.

9   THE PALAIS-ROYAL AND THE BOURSE

MÉTRO stations: *Concorde* (lines 1, 8, 12); *Palais-Royal* (lines 1, 7); *Pyramides* (line 7); *Quatre-Septembre, Bourse* (line 3).

The *RUE DE RIVOLI, a fine thoroughfare, nearly 2 m. in length, running E. from the Place de la Concorde, was constructed in 1811–56 and named in honour of Bonaparte's victory over the Austrians in 1797. The W. portion skirts the Tuileries Gardens and the Louvre (see Rte 1). The N. side of the street, W. of the Rue du Louvre, is uniform in design, with covered arcades and balconies, and is lined with hotels and shops. Save for the inveterate window-shopper it makes a tiring promenade, and we shortly turn left into Rue Cambon, where (at No. 22) Hubert Robert died in 1808.

Beyond the Rue du Mont-Thabor, where Alfred de Musset died in 1857 at No. 6, and Washington Irving lodged in 1821 at No. 4, we reach the long RUE ST-HONORÉ, the fashionable street of the 17–18C, before the opening of the Rue de Rivoli. To the W. is the church of the *Assumption*, built in 1670 as the chapel of the convent of the Haudriettes and now used by the Polish community. At No. 398 (opposite) once stood the house where Robespierre lodged with the cabinet-maker Duplay from July 1791 to the day of his arrest.

Chateaubriand's first Paris lodging (1801–03) was at No. 203 (then 84), nearly opposite St-Roch (comp. below).

The octagonal *PLACE VENDÔME, a superb example of Louis-XIV style, is surrounded with houses of uniform design by Hardouin-Mansart (d. 1708); in fact he built only the façades. Originally called Place de Conquêtes, it owes its present name to a mansion built here in 1603 by César, duc de Vendôme, son of Henri IV and Gabrielle d'Estrées. No. 4 was the residence of Louis-Napoleon as deputy in 1848. At Nos. 11 and 13 is the *Ministère de la Justice*. No. 15 is the *Hôtel Ritz*, where Theodore Herzl, promoter of the state of Israel, wrote 'The Jewish State' (1898; tablet). Chopin died in 1849 at No. 12; and Law lived at No. 23 as controller general of finance. The **Vendôme Column,** in the style of Trajan's Column at Rome, was constructed by *Denon, Gondouin*, and *Lepère* in 1806–10.

Encircling the column, which is 143 ft high and c. 12 ft in diameter, is a spiral band of bronze bas-reliefs, designed by *Bergeret* and made of the metal of Russian and Austrian cannon, in which the principal feats of arms in the campaigns of 1805–07 are glorified. The statue of Napoleon on the top is a copy (1863) of the original statue by Chaudet torn down by the royalists in 1814 and replaced by a fleur-de-lys. In 1833 Louis-Philippe put up the statue of Napoleon now at the Invalides. In 1863 the present statue was erected and narrowly escaped destruction in 1871 when a group of Communards led by the painter Courbet brought the whole column crashing to the ground. This led to Courbet's exile and ruin, since he had to pay for the repairs.

The RUE DE LA PAIX, which leads from the Place Vendôme to the S.W. corner of the Place de l'Opéra, is the 'Bond Street' of Paris, famous for its luxurious shops. Near the S. end of the street the Rue Danielle-Casanova (named for a heroine of the Résistance), with 17–18C houses, leads to the right to the Av. de l'Opéra. Stendhal died in 1842 at the Hôtel de Nantes (No. 22). We may return to the Rue St-Honoré by the Place du Marché St-Honoré; a large public garage now stands on the site of the Dominican convent where the Jacobin Club met in 1789–94.

Farther E. is the Baroque church of **St-Roch**, containing many interesting works of art of the 17–18C. Begun under Louis XIV by *J. Lemercier* in 1653, the work on the church was abandoned in 1660, but a donation by John Law on his conversion to Rome in 1719 enabled the nave to be completed; *Robert de Cotte* was responsible for the façade (1735).

INTERIOR (413 ft long; oriented N. and S.). To the left of the main entrance is a medallion of the dramatist Pierre Corneille, who died in 1684 in the neighbouring Rue d'Argenteuil (plaque on No. 6) and is buried in the church. To the right of the entrance a plaque commemorates Alessandro Manzoni's 'reconversion' to Rome (1810).—In the 1st bay (r.) are a bust of François de Créquy (d. 1687), by *Coysevox*, and the tomb of the Comte d'Harcourt (d. 1666), by *Renard*; 2nd bay, statue of the diplomatist Card. Dubois (d. 1723), by *G. Coustou*, and monument to Maupertuis (d. 1759), by *Huez*. In the transept, the 'Mal des Ardents' by *Doyen*; against the choir pillar (l.) a statue of St Roch. In the LADY CHAPEL, by Hardouin-Mansart, is a marble *Group of the Nativity, by *Fr.* and *Michel Anguier*, from Val-de-Grâce.—The CHAPELLE DES CATÉCHISMES or *Chapelle du Calvaire* (apply to the sacristan) has a marble Crucifixion by *Michel Anguier*.—We return by the W. AISLE. On the last pillar of the ambulatory (r.) is a bust of Le Nôtre (d. 1707), by *Coysevox*; opposite, Christ in the Garden, by *Falconet*. In the transept, St Denis preaching, by *Vien*, and a statue of St Andrew, by *Pradier*. In the 1st chapel is a monument to the Abbé de l'Épée (d. 1789), creator of a language for the deaf and dumb. The 2nd chapel (beyond the transept) is a memorial to those who died in concentration camps in 1942–45. The 3rd chapel contains a mourning figure, by *J. B. Le Moyne the Elder*, of Catherine, comtesse de Feuquières (c. 1700), incorporated in a monument, the central feature of which is the bust of her father, Pierre Mignard (d. 1695), by *Girardon*; 4th chapel, Baptism of Christ, by *Le Moyne*, and medallion of Mme Lalive de Jully, by *Falconet*.

The neighbouring streets were the scene of Bonaparte's suppression of the royalist rising of 5 Oct 1795; some marks of his 'whiff of grape-shot' may still be detected on the front of the church.

The Rue St-Roch, where Vauban (1633–1707) died (plaque on the corner), rejoins the Rue de Rivoli just W. of the small *Place des Pyramides*, with a spirited bronze-gilt statue by Frémiet of Joan of Arc.

The PLACE DU THÉÂTRE-FRANÇAIS, at the S. end of the Av. de l'Opéra, contains two fountains by Davioud and is linked with the Rue de Rivoli by the busy Rue de Rohan.

The Théâtre-Français, adjoining the S.W. corner of the Palais-Royal, built in 1786–90 by *Victor Louis*, was wholly restored by Guadet after a fire in 1900. It is often referred to as 'la Maison de Molière', although Molière never knew this theatre.

As an institution the Théâtre-Français or Comédie-Française dates from the amalgamation in 1680 of the Hôtel de Bourgogne actors with Molière's old company, which had already absorbed the Théâtre du Marais. In 1812 Napoleon signed a decree at Moscow reorganizing the Comédie-Française, which is still a private company but is controlled by a director nominated by the government and enjoys an annual state subsidy.

The medallions of Corneille, Molière, Racine, and Victor Hugo under the portico in the Rue de Richelieu are by *Denys Puech*; on the Palais-Royal side is a bust of Larroumet by *Roussel*.

The vestibule contains a statue of Talma, the tragedian, by *David d'Angers*; statues of Tragedy (Rachel as 'Phèdre') by *Duret* and of Comedy (Mlle Mars as Célimène in 'Le Misanthrope') by *Thomas*. The staircase and foyer are adorned with busts of eminent dramatists, including Dumas fils by *Carpeaux* and Mirabeau by *Rodin*, and a statue of George Sand by *Clésinger*, her son-in-law. In the foyer is the seated *Statue of Voltaire, by *Houdon* and the chair in which Molière, acting 'le Malade Imaginaire', was struck down by his fatal illness. The ceiling of the auditorium was painted by *Albert Besnard*; on the side nearest the stage are Molière, Racine, Corneille, and Victor Hugo.

The PLACE DU PALAIS-ROYAL, immediately S.E. of the Place du Théâtre-Français, is now a busy crossroads. It has the *Palais-Royal* (see below) on its N. side, the *Grands Magasins du Louvre* on the E., the *Grand Hôtel du Louvre* on the W., and the *Ministère des Finances*, a part of the Palais du Louvre, on the S.

An inscription at the corner of the Rue de Valois marks the site of the *Salle de Spectacle du Palais Cardinal*, occupied by Molière's company from 1661 to 1673 and by the Académie Royale de Musique from 1673 till the fire in 1763.

The *Palais Royal constitutes one of the most attractive and interesting parts of Paris. The name is now applied not only to the original palace but also to the buildings and galleries surrounding the gardens beyond. The latter, freely open to the public and approached from the neighbouring streets by several passages, played an important rôle in the Revolutionary period, and in the more frivolous society of the early 19C. Now, however, it is a quiet and delightful backwater surrounded by busy streets.

History. The Palais-Royal proper was originally known as the 'Palais-Cardinal', having been built by *J. Lemercier* in 1634–39 for Richelieu who, as chief minister, wished to be near the Louvre. He died there in 1642. Bequeathed to Louis XIII, it was first called 'Palais-Royal' during the residence of Anne of Austria (d. 1666), then regent, and her sons Louis XIV and Philippe d'Orléans. Richelieu's apartments were then occupied by Card. Mazarin. During the Fronde they all had to escape to St-Germain-en-Laye; Louis thus disliked the palace and it was Philippe d'Orléans and his wife, Henriette d'Angleterre, who lived here. Her mother, Queen Henrietta Maria, found a refuge here in 1652. Louis acquired the W. wing from Richelieu's heirs and housed the Royal Academy of painting and sculpture (1661–92) as well as his mistress Mlle de la Vallière. This was the period of Mansart's alterations. In 1692 the palace was given by Louis to his brother and his heirs. The palace acquired a dissolute reputation from the 'petits soupers' of Duc Philippe II, the regent (1674–1723). More changes were made for the regent's son Louis-Philippe ('le Gros') by Contant d'Ivry and Cartaud. In 1763 a fire destroyed the E. wing and the theatre (comp. above). The houses and galleries around the gardens were built as a speculation by Philippe-Égalité, the Regent's great-grandson, in 1781–86, under pressure of debt, and let out as shops and cafés. He built the present Théâtre-Français, and the *Théâtre du Palais-Royal*, in the N.W. corner, dates from the same period. The cafés became a meeting-place for malcontents since the police were excluded from entry, and on 13 July 1789 Camille Desmoulins delivered in the gardens the fiery harangue which brought about the fall of the Bastille on the following day. Under the Revolution the palace was renamed 'Palais-Égalité' and used as government offices. In 1814, however, it was handed back to the Orléans family, resuming the name of Palais-Royal, and Louis-Philippe lived there till 1832. After being plundered by the mob in 1848, it was occupied for a time by the 'Rights of Man' club. During the Second Empire the palace was the residence of ex-king Jerome Bonaparte, and Taine, Flaubert, Sainte-Beuve, and the brothers Goncourt were often entertained here. After some damage during the Commune, the Palais was rebuilt by *Chabrol* in 1872–76 and is now occupied by the Conseil d'État, the Ministry for Fine Arts, and various government offices.

The buildings in the *Cour de l'Horloge*, the courtyard adjoining the Place du Palais-Royal, were erected by Contant d'Ivry (1763–70), with sculptures by Pajou (l. wing) and Franceschi (r.; 1875). The façade on the N. side, over-looking the Cour d'Honneur, was begun by Contant d'Ivry, continued by Louis, and finished by Fontaine, with statues by Pajou (l.) and Gérard (r.; 1830). The E. and W. wings were restored by Fontaine also. The so-called 'Galerie des Proues', on the E. side of the court, is the sole relic of Lemercier's 17C building. To the N., the Cour d'Honneur is separated from the gardens by the *Galerie d'Orléans*, a double Doric colonnade by Fontaine (1829–31), which was restored and cleared of its shops in 1935; on the W. side of this court, beyond the Galerie de Chartres, a pillared portico serving as carriage-way leads to the Place du Théâtre-Français.—The GARDENS of the Palais-Royal are surrounded on three sides by galleries and buildings (by Louis, 1781–86), designed in imitation of the Piazza San Marco in Venice and still occupied by shops. On the W. side is the *Galerie de Montpensier*; on the E., the *Galerie de Valois*; and on the N., the *Galerie Beaujolais*. Seen from the gardens they make a charming and harmonious ensemble.

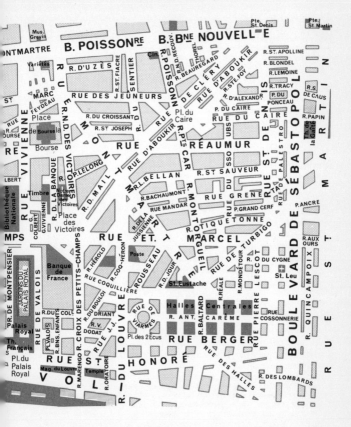

Charlotte Corday bought the fatal knife at No. 177 Galerie de Valois. No. 17 Galerie de Montpensier was in 1785 a museum of waxworks founded by Curtius, uncle of Mme Tussaud. The Grand Véfour (Galerie Beaujolais) was the fashionable meeting place of the writers of the Second Empire. Earlier, in the same house, Mlle de Montansier entertained the leaders of the Revolution of 1789. Among modern residents were Jean Cocteau and Colette (inscription, Rue de Beaujolais).

The Rue de Valois contains the *Pavilion du Palais-Royal* (Nos. 1–3), built in 1766 by Contant d'Ivry and Moreau. As the Hôtel Melusine, Nos. 6–8 saw the first meetings of the French Academy (1638–43); the ox sculptured above the door recalls its period as the restaurant 'Bœuf à la Mode' from 1792 to 1936.

The **Banque de France** (N.E. of the Palais-Royal), founded in 1800, and in its present site since 1811, is one of the great banking institutions of the world. With its main entrance in the Rue Croix-des-Petits-Champs, it occupies huge buildings, incorporating the former *Hôtel de la Vrillière* (in the Rue de la Vrillière), which was built by Mansart in 1635–38 and restored by Robert de Cotte in 1719. Later known as the *Hôtel de Toulouse* from its occupancy by the Comte de Toulouse, son of Louis XIV and Mme de Montespan, it became the residence of the Princesse de Lamballe, murdered in La Force in 1792.

Mansart's projecting angle in the old Rue Radziwill (now a private roadway), supported by a bracket, is admired as a masterpiece of stonework, and within is the *Galerie Dorée*, which can be visited with the Monuments Historiques. The late 17C *Hôtel Portalis* is on the corner of the Rue de la Vrillière and the Rue Croix-des-Petits-Champs, No. 13 of which was occupied by Malherbe in 1606. St Vincent de Paul lived in this street in 1613–16 and Bossuet in 1699–1702 at No. 52. Mme de Pompadour was a resident also in 1725–45, before her departure for Versailles. No. 33 Rue Radziwill has an unusual double staircase. Richelieu is believed to have been born in the Rue du Bouloi.

To the N.E. of the Bank lies the circular **Place des Victoires,** laid out by *J. Hardouin-Mansart* in 1685; the surrounding houses were designed by *Pradot*. The equestrian statue of Louis XIV by *Bosio* (1822) replaces the original, destroyed in 1792; the bas-reliefs on the pedestal depict the Passage of the Rhine and Louis XIV distributing decorations.

On the E. side of the Place des Victoires is the RUE ÉTIENNE-MARCEL leading to the Boul. de Sébastopol. In the RUE HÉROLD, formerly des Vieux-Augustins (on its right), Thackeray lived after his marriage in 1856 and Charlotte Corday lodged before her awful mission. No. 20 is a fine 17C house. On the N.E. is the RUE DU MAIL, in which lived Colbert (at the richly decorated No. 7) and Mme Récamier (at No. 12); Liszt was a frequent visitor to No. 13. Mme de Pompadour (1721–64) was born in its continuation, the Rue de Cléry.

The Place des Petits-Pères, immediately N.W. of the Place des Victoires, has a surprisingly provincial aspect. Here stands **Notre-Dame-des-Victoires,** or the church of the *Petits-Pères*, dedicated in 1629 by Louis XIII in memory of the capture of La Rochelle from the Huguenots but not finished until 1740. In the second chapel on the left is the tomb of Lulli (d. 1687), by *Michel Cotton,* with a bust by *Gaspard Collignon,* and in the choir are elaborately carved stalls and seven paintings by *C. Vanloo.* A striking feature is the large number of ex-votos.

The **Bourse** or *Stock Exchange* (open daily, except Sat and holidays, 12–4; closed for business at 3), resembling the Temple of Vespasian at Rome, with a Corinthian peristyle, was built in 1808–27 by *Brongniart* and *Labarre.* The N. and S. wings were added in 1903.

At the end of the great hall is the 'Parquet', a railed-off space reserved for the 'agents de change' (stockbrokers), with a circular railing in the centre known as the 'Corbeille'. On the right is the 'Marché au Comptant', where the prices are announced; on the left, the 'Coulisse de la Rente', where government bonds are bought and sold. The best view of the scenes of bustle and excitement is from the upper gallery.

Near the Bourse the Rue des Colonnes and Rue des Panoramas have interesting houses and the Rue Feydeau was built on Louis XIII's fortifications.—From the Place de la Bourse, the RUE DU QUATRE-SEPTEMBRE (named from the date of the foundation of the Third Republic) runs N.W., crossing the Rue de Richelieu (see below), to the Place de l'Opéra. Both it and its E. continuation, the Rue Réaumur, are modern thoroughfares, driven through an old quarter.

The RUE VIVIENNE, from the Boul. Montmartre and passing the Place de la Bourse and the Bibliothèque Nationale (see below), contains several fine houses of the 17–18C. At No. 2bis Simon Bolivar lived in 1804.

The RUE DE RICHELIEU, over ½ m. long, laid out by the great cardinal, runs S. from the Grands Boulevards to the Place du Théâtre-Français. Berlioz lived at No. 96 in 1830 and Meyerbeer at No. 91 in 1851. No. 101, with decorative masks in the courtyard, was the home of Abbé Barthélemy, the antiquary (1716–95) who had charge of the royal collection of medals, then housed in the Hôtel de Nevers (comp. below). Brillat-Savarin (1755–1826) died in the house at the corner of the Rue des Filles-St-Thomas (No. 66; tablet). No. 62 is the French News Agency, *Agence Havas,* founded in 1835. On the left, at the corner of the Rue Colbert, stands part of the *Hôtel de Nevers* built by

Mazarin in 1649 to house his great library. As the home of Mme de Lambert it was a famous literary salon in 1710–33 where Montesquieu and Marivaux met. Farther on is a fountain of 1708, and beyond is (r.) the *Square Louvois*, with the *Fontaine Louvois* or Fontaine Richelieu, by the younger Visconti (1844), one of the most attractive fountains in Paris.

The square was laid out in 1839 on the site of a theatre built in 1792 which housed the Opéra from 1794 to 1820. On 13 Feb 1820 the Archbishop of Paris was called here to administer the last sacraments to the Duc de Berry (son of the future Charles X), mortally wounded by a revolutionary. This he consented to do on such unholy ground only on condition that the theatre was afterwards pulled down.—Donizetti lived at No. 5 Rue Louvois in 1840.

On the E. (l.) side of the Rue de Richelieu rises the W. façade of the **Bibliothèque Nationale** (see Rte 24), on the site of a mansion of Cardinal Mazarin.

Just beyond is the crossing of the RUE DES PETITS-CHAMPS (the "New Street of the Little Fields" of Thackeray's 'Ballad of Bouillabaisse'), which runs E. to the Place des Victoires (see below) and W. to the Av. de l'Opéra; No. 45 was the residence of Lulli till 1683, built by him with financial help from Molière. The garret of No. 57 was the home of Rousseau and Thérèse Levasseur c. 1754, and Mme Récamier died of cholera at No. 8 in 1849. Its continuation to the Rue de la Paix, now called the Rue Danielle-Casanova, has been described above.

No. 50 Rue de Richelieu was the early home of Jeanne Poisson (Mme de Pompadour). At the corner of the Rue Molière (at No. 37 in which lived Voltaire and his 'Emilie', Mme du Châtelet) is the *Fontaine Molière*, another fountain by Visconti (1844), with a seated figure of the poet by Seurre and standing figures of Comedy by Pradier. No. 40 Rue de Richelieu stands on the site of the house in which Molière died in 1673; Diderot died in 1784 at No. 39, and Mignard in 1695 at No. 23. No. 21, formerly the Hôtel Dodun, preserves a little of its 18C grandeur.

We have now returned to the Place du Palais-Royal, whence we may continue along the Rue St-Honoré (Rte 10).

10   ST-EUSTACHE AND THE HALLES CENTRALES

MÉTRO stations: *Louvre* (line 1); *Châtelet* (lines 1, 4, 7, 11); *Halles* and *Étienne-Marcel* (line 4); *Réaumur-Sébastopol* (lines 3 and 4); *Sentier* (line 3).

Through the Place du Louvre (Rte 1) the RUE DU LOUVRE runs N. from the Seine to Rue Montmartre, crossing the Rue de Rivoli and the Rue St-Honoré. In the Rue St-Honoré, to the W., is the Protestant Reformed church of the **Oratoire**, designed by Clément Métezeau the younger and Jacques Lemercier, and built in 1621–30 for Card. Bérulle as the mother church in France of his Congregation of the Oratory, but assigned to the Calvinists by Napoleon in 1811. Against the apse of the church, under the arches in the Rue de Rivoli, is a monument to Adm. Coligny (1517–72), the chief victim of the massacre of St Bartholomew, who was murdered in a house now replaced by No. 144 Rue de Rivoli. Here also stood the *Hôtel de Ponthieu* where Sophie Arnould was born in 1744 (inscription).

J. H. Riesener (1734–1806), the cabinet-maker, died at No. 2 Rue St-Honoré. Gallows stood at the point where the Rue de l'Arbre-Sec and Rue St-Honoré cross, and near by Cardinal de Retz was attacked during the Fronde (1648). The present fountain is a reconstruction by Soufflot of a work of 1529. Gabrielle d'Estrées died at No. 21 Rue de l'Arbre-Sec in 1599, a few days before she was to have married Henri IV. Well-preserved houses of the 17C can be seen at Nos. 33–45 Rue St-Honoré; Lavoisier owned No. 47 (18C).

At No. 11 Rue du Louvre, at the corner of the Place des Deux-Écus, are some remains of the fortifications of Philip Augustus. Farther on, a little to the E., is the *Bourse du Commerce* (shown Mon–Fri, 9–6), formerly the Corn Exchange, a circular 18C building remodelled in 1888.

The fluted Doric column (98 ft high) adjoining the building is the sole relic of the *Hôtel de la Reine* (later Hôtel de Soissons), built for Catherine de Médicis in 1572 on the site of the Hôtel d'Orléans which had belonged to Blanche of Castille. The column was perhaps used as an astrologer's tower.—The Rue Sauval leads back S. to the Rue St-Honoré, at the corner of which (No. 96) stood the house in which Molière was born in 1622.

The Rue du Louvre continues past the *Head Telephone Office*; opposite is the *Savings Bank* (Caisse d'Épargne), in the elegant *Hôtel d'Ollone*, built in 1639 and altered in 1730. Farther on, at the corner of the Rue Étienne-Marcel, stands the huge *General Post & Telegraph Office* (Hôtel des Postes et Télégraphes; 1880–84).

The University of Paris was responsible for the postal service for private citizens from the 13C to the 18C, while from 1461 the royal mail was carried by relays of post riders. In 1719 the University lost its privilege and all mail was dealt with by the royal service. In 1757 the postal headquarters was in the Hôtel d'Hervart. On the façade of the Post Office towards the Rue Jean-Jacques Rousseau (where Rousseau lived with Thérèse in 1776) is an inscription marking the site of the Hôtel which had been occupied by La Fontaine at the time of his death (1695). The houses at No. 64 and 68 are worth noting.

The RUE MONTMARTRE, already so named in 1200 because it led to the abbey of Montmartre, runs from St-Eustache (see below) to the Grands Boulevards (Rte 13) and crosses the Rue Réaumur. Émile Zola (1840–1902) was born at No. 10 Rue St-Joseph, off its N. section, and Jean Jaurès, the advocate of peace, was assassinated in 1914 on the eve of war at the corner of the Rue de Croissant, just beyond. In the Rue du Sentier (opposite the end of the Rue du Croissant) his mother lodged in the Rue du Sentier (opposite the end of the Rue du Croissant). In the same year she was buried in the vanished *Cimetière St-Joseph* near by, the original burial-place of Molière also.

We descend Rue Montmartre to the Halles, on the N. side of which, at its intersection with five other streets, rises ***St-Eustache**, sometimes known as 'Notre-Dame des Halles', one of the largest churches in Paris. In detail and decoration it is a Renaissance building, but in plan and in its general lay-out it is of medieval design.

Begun in 1532, perhaps by Pierre Lemercier, it was consecrated in 1637. The main W. doorway was rebuilt in 1754–88 in a completely inharmonious classical style. Both transepts have handsome round-headed doorways (c. 1638–40). The N. transept is approached by a passage from the Rue Montmartre. The open-work bell-tower ('Plomb de St-Eustache') above the crossing has lost its spire. Above the Lady Chapel in the apse is a small tower built in 1640 and restored in 1875.—St-Eustache was the scene of the riotous Festival of Reason in 1793, and in 1795 it became the 'Temple of Agriculture'. Molière was baptized in this church in 1622, Jeanne Poisson (Mme de Pompadour) in 1721; and Lulli in 1662 was married here. In 1791 the body of Mirabeau lay in state here before its removal to the Panthéon; and among the notabilities buried here are Colbert, Louis XIV's minister of finance (d. 1683); Adm. de Tourville (d. 1701); and the composer Rameau (d. 1764).— St-Eustache has always been noted for its music. Berlioz here conducted the first performance of his 'Te Deum' and Liszt his 'Messe Solenelle'. Especially impressive is the music at the midnight mass on Christmas Eve and the services on Good Friday and St Cecilia's Day (22 Nov).

The INTERIOR is strikingly original in its combination of classical forms with a Gothic plan. The double aisles and chapels of the nave are continued round the choir. The square piers are flanked by three stories of columns in Renaissance variants of the classical orders; the pendent bosses of the lierne vaults are finely sculptured. The chapels are decorated with paintings, some dating from the time of Louis XIII, but restored. The eleven lofty windows of the apse, representing the twelve Apostles, the four Latin Fathers, and St Eustace, were executed by *Soulignac* (1631) possibly from the cartoons of

Philippe de Champaigne. The churchwardens' pew by *Pierre Le Pautre* dates from c. 1720. The stalls came from the convent of Picpus.

SOUTH AISLE. The 2nd chapel commemorates Rameau. The 3rd chapel contains the Marriage of the Virgin, a group by *Triqueti*; in the 4th chapel, Christ at the Column by *Etex.* By the S. Transept doorway is a 15C statue of St John the Evangelist. The 2nd choir-chapel (r.) has a Pietà, by *Luca Giordano* (?). In the LADY CHAPEL, on the altar, is a *Virgin by *Pigalle*; the mural-paintings are by *Thos. Couture.*—NORTH AISLE. In the 1st choir-chapel as we return is the tomb of Colbert, designed by *Le Brun*, with statues of Colbert and Fidelity by *Coysevox* and of Abundance by *Tuby.* Above the altar of the 2nd chapel, the Disciples at Emmaus, a painting of the *Rubens* school; in the 3rd, St Mary Magdalen in ecstasy, by *Rutilio Manetti* (Siena; early 17C). Above the W. door is the Martyrdom of St Eustace, by *Simon Vouet.*

At St-Eustache begins the RUE DE TURBIGO, on its way to the Place de la République. This soon crosses the Rue Étienne-Marcel, in which, to the left, at No. 20, rises the *Tour de Jean-sans-Peur*, a graceful embattled tower (c. 1400), once incorporated in the *Hôtel de Bourgogne.* Part of this mansion (tablet on No. 29) was used in the 16–18C as a theatre, where 'Le Cid', 'Andromaque', and 'Phedre' were performed. Farther on the Rue de Turbigo crosses the Rue St-Denis (see below) and, parallel with it, the broad and ugly Boulevard de Sébastopol, which connects the Place du Châtelet (Rte 11) with the Boul. St-Denis (Rte 13).

The **Halles Centrales,** or *Central Markets,* called by Zola "le ventre de Paris", consist of twelve pavilions, designed by Baltard and begun in 1881. They are a splendid example of the use of iron. The W. side was completed only in 1936 when two pavilions were added. The markets spill into the neighbouring streets and the rumbustious atmosphere resounds to the argot of vendors and porters.

Markets have stood here since the early 12C, and Philip Augustus provided the first permanent buildings in 1183. Of the modern pavilions, the six on the E. side are used for fruit, vegetables, butter, fish, cheese, poultry, and game; those on the W. side for meat, poultry, and eggs. The best time to visit the Halles is between 5.30 and 8 a.m. There are plans to move the meat market to Villette and the fruit and vegetables to Rurgis.

To the S. the Rue du Pont-Neuf descends to the Seine, passing between the departmental stores of *La Samaritaine* (*View from roof) and *La Belle-Jardinière.* An alternative is through the more attractive Rue des Bourdonnais, to the E.

To the S.E. of the Halles is the small *Square des Innocents*, on the site of the medieval Cimetière des Innocents, the chief burial ground of Paris until 1785, when the remains were transferred to the Catacombs. Those of La Fontaine (d. 1695) were probably among them. Traces of the arches of the cemetery galleries are still to be seen on the odd-number side of the Rue des Innocents. In the centre of the square is the charming Renaissance *FONTAINE DES INNOCENTS. Erected in 1548 in the neighbouring Rue St-Denis by *Pierre Lescot* with bas-reliefs by *Jean Goujon*, it was remodelled and set up here by *Payet* c. 1788, the additional S. side being decorated by *Pajou.* Three of the bas-reliefs are now in the Louvre. At the N.W. corner of the square is the reconstructed doorway from the office of the *Marchandes Lingères* (1716).

To the S. is the Rue de la Ferronnerie, where Henri IV was assassinated by Ravaillac in 1610, in front of No. 11.

The Square opens on the RUE ST-DENIS, one of the oldest and most entertaining streets in Paris, running from the Place du Châtelet to the Porte St-Denis (¾ m.), parallel with the Boul. de Sébastopol.

No. 32, near the S. end, where the dramatist Eugène Scribe was born in 1791, is marked by his bust. No. 33 has an 18C sign, 'Au Mortier d'Argent'. No. 92 (N. of the Square des Innocents) is the church of St-Leu-St-Gilles (see below). On No. 133 (corner of Rue Étienne-Marcel) are some old statues from the medieval hospital of St-Jacques (on this

site). No. 135 has an inscription showing the former position of the *Porte St-Denis* or *Porte aux Peintres*, a gateway in the walls of Philip Augustus. At the corner of the Rue Tiquetonne (then Rue du Petit-Lion), stood the old shop bearing the sign of the 'Cat and Racket', celebrated in Balzac's story, 'La Maison du Chat qui Pelote'. On No. 142 is the little *Fontaine de la Reine* (1730); on No. 224, at the corner of Rue de Tracy, is a cartouche with the head of Jules Michelet, the historian, who was born in 1798 in a house on this site.

The little church of **St-Leu-St-Gilles** was built in 1235, and first rebuilt after 1319. The nave is of this date, the aisles were added in the 16C, the choir (still partly Gothic) in 1611, the last having been altered in 1858–61 to make way for the boulevard. The façade and windows were remodelled in 1727 and a crypt was constructed in 1780. The church contains three 15C Nottingham alabaster reliefs (in the sacristy entry) and a sculptured group of St Anne and the Virgin, perhaps from Écouen, by *Jean Bullant* (2nd S. chapel). The organ gallery is by *Nic. Raimbert* (1659).

The municipal *Musée d'Hygiène*, housed in the former presbytery, 57 Boul. de Sébastopol, contains maps, plans, diagrams, and models of hygienic installations.

11   FROM THE PLACE DU CHÂTELET TO THE BASTILLE

MÉTRO stations: *Châtelet* (lines 1, 4, 7, 11); *Hôtel de Ville* and *St-Paul* (line 1); *Bastille* (lines 1, 5, 8).

The section of the RUE DE RIVOLI that lies to the E. of the Louvre was constructed by Napoleon III to open up a rapid access for troops to the Hôtel de Ville in case of emergency. Beyond the Rue du Pont-Neuf and the Rue des Halles it crosses the Boul. de Sébastopol (see above). To the right, at their intersection, is the *Square St-Jacques*, in the centre of which rises the **Tour St-Jacques,** the only relic of the church of St-Jacques-la-Boucherie, dating from 1508–22. This graceful flamboyant Gothic tower now serves as a meteorological station.

On the ground level is a poor statue (1854) of Blaise Pascal, who verified on this tower (or on that of St-Jacques-du-Haut-Pas) the barometric experiments he had caused to be made on the Puy de Dôme. The niches are filled with nineteen other 19C statues. At the corners of the roof are St James the Apostle and the symbols of three of the Evangelists, by *Chenillon*. In the square a tablet commemorates the poet Gérard de Nerval, found hanged near by in 1855.

The adjoining **Place du Châtelet** is bounded on the S. by the Seine, which is here crossed by the Pont au Change. The square is named after the vanished *Grand Châtelet*, a fortress-gateway leading to the Cité, once the headquarters of the Provost of Paris and the Guild of Notaries. A plan of this fort may be seen on the front of the *Chambre des Notaires*, on the N. side of the square. On the E. side is the *Théâtre Sarah-Bernhardt*; on the W., the *Théâtre du Châtelet*, in which many Communards were court-martialled in 1871. A tablet on the S. side of the latter marks the site of the house in which the painter Louis David was born in 1748. In the centre of the square is the *Fontaine du Châtelet*, known also as the *Fontaine de la Victoire* or *Fontaine du Palmier*, dating from 1806 and 1858. An inscription indicates the position of the 'Parloir aux Bourgeois', the seat of the municipality of Paris from the 13C till 1357 (comp. below).

The wide AVENUE VICTORIA, so named in honour of Queen Victoria's visit to Paris in 1855, leads from the Place du Châtelet across the Rue St-Martin and past the *Assistance Publique* to the **Place de l'Hôtel-de-Ville**, which is bounded on the N. by the Rue de Rivoli, on the E. by the Hôtel de Ville, and on the S. by the Seine, crossed here by the *Pont d'Arcole*. On the S. side of the Hôtel de Ville is an equestrian statue of Étienne Marcel (d. 1358), the famous 'Prévôt des Marchands'.

In the 11C a port was built here on the strand (grève) and the square was known until the Revolution of 1830 as the *Place de Grève*. This square was the usual site for public executions. Among the more famous (many of them incredibly barbarous) which took place here were those of the Comte de St-Pol (1475), constable of France, on the orders of Louis XI; a long series of Protestants, including Briquemont and Cavagnes, the Huguenot leaders (1572), and the Comte de Montgomery (1574), captured at the siege of Domfront and formerly captain in the Scottish Guard; François Ravaillac, the assassin of Henri IV (1610); Eléonore Galigaï, the favourite of Marie de Médicis, executed for sorcery (1617); the Marquise de Brinvilliers (1676), poisoner; Cartouche, the famous highwayman (1721); and Damiens (1757) who attempted to murder Louis XV. Foullon, the controller-general of finance, and his son-in-law Bertier were hanged here by the mob in 1789. In April 1795 Fouquier-Tinville suffered the same fate as his countless victims. Louvel, murderer of the Duc de Berri, was executed here (1820).

The **Hôtel de Ville**, a splendid building in the style of the French Renaissance, adorned with statues of eminent Frenchmen, was built in 1874–84 from the plans of *Ballu* and *Deperthes*. It is an enlarged and enriched replica of its famous predecessor, begun c. 1532 on the same site, which was burned down by the Communards in 1871.

In 1246 St Louis created the first municipal authority of Paris by allowing the merchants to elect magistrates ('échevins'), chief of whom was the 'prévôt des marchands', who was also head of the 'Hanse des marchands de l'eau' (merchant-guild). This guild, which had a monopoly of the traffic on the Seine, Marne, Oise, and Yonne, took as their emblem a ship, a device that still graces the arms of the city. The first meeting-place of this body known simply as the 'Parlouer aux Bourgeois' was situated near the Grand-Châtelet; later the merchants met at the Grand-Châtelet itself; until finally, in 1357, the Provost Étienne Marcel bought the 'Maison aux Piliers' or 'Maison du Dauphin', a large house in the Place de Grève. In 1532 plans for a new building were adopted, but the work was stopped at the second floor, and the new designs approved by Henri II in 1549 were not completed till 1628.

The historical importance of the building dates more especially from 1789, when it became the meeting-place of the 300 electors nominated by the districts of Paris. On 17 July 1789, Louis XVI received the tricoloured cockade from the hands of Bailly, mayor of Paris. In 1792 the 172 commissaries elected by the sections of Paris gave from here the signal for the insurrection of 10 Aug. In 1794 Robespierre took refuge at the Hôtel de Ville with his friends, but was arrested on 27 July (the 9 Thermidor, An II) and was dragged thence, his jaw shattered by a bullet, to the guillotine. After it had become the seat of the Préfet de la Seine and his council in 1805, a number of brilliant fêtes were given to celebrate Napoleon's marriage with Marie-Louise (1810), the birth of the King of Rome (1811), and numerous other great occasions. During the days of 1830 the Swiss Guards put up a stout defence in the Hôtel de Ville. It became the seat of the provisional government of 1848 under Louis Blanc, and on 15 May it witnessed the arrest of the leaders Barbès and Blanqui. During the dark days of June the building was saved by the courage of a handful of men. On 4 Sept 1870, the Republic was proclaimed at the Hôtel de Ville, and in the following year, on 26 March, the Commune was proclaimed here by the Committee of Public Safety; on 24 May the beautiful building was set on fire by its defenders, many of whom perished in the flames.

In 1938 George VI and his queen were given a civic reception here and in 1957 Elizabeth II, accompanied by her husband, was likewise entertained.

In 1944 the area around the Hôtel de Ville was the centre of the Resistance movement's attack against the German forces of occupation. On 19 Aug the headquarters of the movement was established in the building itself, and managed to repel the attacks of the enemy until the arrival of Gen. Leclerc's division on 24 August. Plaques commemorating the peace of 1919 and the cessation of hostilities in 1945 are affixed to the balustrade outside the main entrance.

Intending visitors (parties only) should apply to the office of the Accueil de Paris, 14 Rue François-Miron (4e).

The magnificent INTERIOR is interesting for its mural paintings, sculptures, carvings, etc., lavishly illustrating the official taste in art of the third quarter of the 19C. The panels of the Seasons, by *Puvis de Chavannes*, in the room at the head of the S. staircase are noteworthy.

The area to the E. of the Hôtel de Ville between the Rue de Rivoli and the Rue St-Antoine to the N., the Boulevard Henri-IV to the E., and the Seine to the S., forms the southern section of the MARAIS (comp. Rte 12). On the E. side of the Hôtel de Ville, beyond the Rue de Lobau, are two large barracks built by Napoleon III (now occupied as annexes of the Hôtel de Ville). Between them lies the *Place St-Gervais* with its elm tree—a reminder of the famous elm of St-Gervais, beneath which justice used to be administered. This was one of the first inhabited areas of the right bank and the Rue François-Miron and Rue St-Antoine follow the course of a Roman road from Lutetia to Senlis.

The church of *St-Gervais-St-Protais, founded in the 6C, dates in its present form from the rebuilding of 1494–1578 (choir and transepts) and 1600–57 (nave, chapels, and tower). The original plans are attributed to *Martin Chambiges*, whose work was continued by his son *Pierre*. The lower stages of the tower are an early-15C survival. The façade (1616–21), by *Clément Métezeau* and (probably) *Salomon de Brosse*, is the earliest example in France of the superposition of the three classic orders—Doric, Ionic, and Corinthian. In 1795 the church was converted into a Temple of Youth. Bossuet preached here; Mme de Sévigné was married here; and here are buried Philippe de Champaigne, Scarron, and Crébillon the elder.

The INTERIOR, impressive from its loftiness and its unity of style, is remarkably rich in works of art. The high windows of both nave and choir contain much stained glass (c. 1610–20) by *Louis Pinaigrier* and *Nic. Chaumet*. The nave was completed in flamboyant Gothic at a time when Renaissance influence was strongest. S. AISLE. The 2nd chapel has an altar commemorating the victims of the bombardment of Good Friday, 1918, when a German shell struck the church and killed fifty of the congregation. In the 3rd chapel, Life of Christ, 17C paintings on wood; 5th and 6th chapels, Stained glass of 1531 (Judgment of Solomon; SS. Gervasius and Protasius). In the 8th chapel, tomb of Chancellor Michel Le Tellier (d. 1685), by *Mazeline* and *Hurtrelle*. The bearded heads supporting the sarcophagus are from the tomb of Jacques de Souvré (d. 1670), by *François Anguier*, the rest of which is in the Louvre; here also is the Beheading of St. John the Baptist, by *Claude Vignon*. The Lady Chapel, a remarkable example of flamboyant Gothic (1517), has a fine pendent keystone, and glass of 1517. The sacristy, in the N. choir aisle, has a good iron grille and woodwork of 1741, and in the N. transept is a painting of the Passion

(Flemish; mid-16C). From the next chapel we enter (apply to the sacristan) the Chapelle Dorée (1628), with Louis-XIII decoration, well restored; while in the following chapel are a 13C relief of the Dormition of the Virgin and a portrait-medallion by *Pajou* (1782) of Mme Palerme de Savy. In the CHOIR the stalls are of the 17C (W. end) and mid 16C, the latter with curious misericords. Against the N. entry-pillar is a 14C figure of the Virgin, called N. D. de Bonne-Délivrance; and on either side of the altar are wooden statues of the patron saints, by *Michel Bourdin* (1625). The 18C gilt-bronze candelabra are by *Soufflot*.

The famous Chanteurs de St-Gervais sing in this church on certain festivals during the year (unaccompanied plain-song). François Couperin (1688–1733), and seven members of his family, served as organist here, and their organ, restored, still survives; Couperin himself was born in a house on the site of No. 4 Rue François-Miron (see below).

Much of the region to the S. between St-Gervais and the Seine has been rebuilt and the S. façade of the church can now be well seen. In the Rue des Barres the restored façades of many of the houses are attractive and at No. 13 is the entrance to the charnel-house of St-Gervais.

The RUE FRANÇOIS-MIRON, leading N.E. from St-Gervais, is one of the finest streets of the district. Nos. 2–14, the Maisons de l'Orme or du Pourtour St-Gervais, built c. 1735, are adorned with wrought-iron work displaying the famous elm (see above). No. 14 provides offices for the Department of Fine Arts of the city of Paris and the Acceuil de Paris. No. 10 was the birthplace of Ledru-Rollin, the radical politician (1804–74). Nos. 30, 36, and 42 all have good features.

In the neighbouring RUE GEOFFROY-L'ASNIER (r.), No. 26 is the early 17C *Hôtel de Chalons-Luxembourg* with a magnificent doorway (1659) and an attractive Louis-XIII pavilion at the end of the courtyard.—No. 22 has a handsome façade (17C) while at No. 17 is the *Memorial to the Unknown Jewish Martyr* (1956) with a study centre for contemporary Judaism.

The Rue de Jouy (see below) diverges right. Farther on in the Rue François-Miron the **Hôtel de Beauvais* (No. 68; 1655) has a fine courtyard, an ornate circular vestibule, and a carved staircase by Desjardins. Anne of Austria and Card. Mazarin watched the entry of Louis XIV and Marie Thérèse into Paris in 1660 from its balcony. Christina of Sweden was a later tenant; and here in 1763 Mozart was the guest of the Bavarian ambassador. The mansion was bought by the city in 1942. No. 82, the *Hôtel du Président Hénault*, has a beautiful balcony.

In the Rue de Jouy No. 7, the **Hôtel d'Aumont*, by Le Vau (1648) and Fr. Mansart (1656), bought by the city in 1936 and occupied by the Pharmacie Centrale, is undergoing restoration. It is to house the Administrative Tribunal of the department of the Seine. Of the interior decoration, Le Brun's work in the Salon survives and in 1947 a fine ceiling was uncovered. At the corner of the Rue du Figuier and the Rue de l'Hôtel-de-Ville is the **Hôtel de Sens**, built c. 1474–1519 for the archbishops of Sens, at a time when the bishopric of Paris was suffragan to the metropolitan see of Sens (before 1623); it is older than the Hôtel de Cluny, the only other example in Paris of the domestic architecture of the 15C. Unfortunately it suffered a long period of neglect and has been poorly restored. Here the ageing Marguerite de Valois led a scandalous life in 1605, seeing one of her young lovers slain on the threshold by another she had cast off and enjoying the murderer's execution. In 1962 it became the home of the *Bibliothèque Forney* (adm. daily exc. Sun and Mon, 1.30–8.30, Sat open at 10), which contains a reference library for the artisans of Paris.

The area between the Rue de Jouy, the Rue de l'Hôtel-de-Ville, the Rue Geoffroy-l'Asnier and the Rue des Nonnains-d'Hyères is destined as an international centre for artists on the pattern of the Cité Universitaire.—The QUAI DES CÉLESTINS continues the Quai de l'Hôtel-de-Ville to the E. opposite the Île St-Louis. No. 32 is the site of the Tour Barbeau which completed the walls of Philip Augustus on the right bank (a section of which survives behind the Rue de l'Ave Maria), and of the tennis-court of the Croix-

Noire (tablet), where Molière performed in 1645 until his arrest for debt. Another tablet, on No. 28, at the corner of the Rue des Jardins-St-Paul, records that Rabelais died in that street in 1553. The quay continues to the Square H. Galli (see below).

The RUE ST-ANTOINE, an ancient and busy thoroughfare with many elegant façades, continues the Rue de Rivoli to the E., beyond the Rue François-Miron and Rue Pavée (Rte 12A). At No. 101 is the entrance to the *Lycée Charlemagne*, which occupies a house of the Jesuits (17C).

The adjoining church of **St-Paul-St-Louis,** or the *Grands-Jésuites,* was built for the Society of Jesus by Louis XIII in 1627–41 to replace a chapel of 1582. It was originally dedicated to St Louis only, the name of St Paul being added in 1796 to commemorate the demolished church of St-Paul-des-Champs. It was designed by *Père Fr. Derrand,* and its florid style, founded on that of the Italian churches of the 16C, is the earliest example of the Jesuit school of architecture in France. Richelieu said the first mass here. The handsome Baroque portal is by *Père Martellange.* The interior is over-decorated but imposing. The shell-shaped holy-water basins were presented by Victor Hugo at the christening of his first-born son. In the left transept is a fine painting of Christ in the Garden of Olives, by *Delacroix* (1827); in the right transept is a painting of Louis XIII offering a model of the church to St Louis, by *Simon Vouet;* and on the left of the high altar is a Mater Dolorosa, of the School of Germain Pilon.

Inscriptions on the nave-pillars commemorate the burial-place of Louis Bourdaloue (d. 1704), and of Bp Huet (d. 1721), the original editor of the Delphin classics. It was in this church that Bourdaloue made most of his famous orations; "he preached like an angel," commented Mme de Sévigné, who was a regular worshipper here.

For the continuation of the Rue St-Antoine, see below. We diverge (r.) into Rue St-Paul, which acquired its present name before 1350 from the church of *St-Paul-des-Champs* (demolished 1799); here were buried Rabelais, the Mansarts, and the 'Man in the Iron Mask'. Part of its belfry survives at No. 32.

To the left opens the RUE CHARLES-V, in which No. 12 was the *Hôtel d'Aubray,* the imposing residence of the infamous Marquise de Brinvilliers, the poisoner. No. 10, the *Hôtel de Maillé,* has a Louis-XIII façade, and No. 15, opposite, dates from 1642.

In the RUE BEAUTREILLIS, which crosses it, No. 7 is one of the finest bourgeois houses of its period in Paris (late 16C): notable features are the wooden staircase and the wrought-iron balcony. No. 6 with its curious clock in the courtyard is probably to be demolished. No. 10 was the *Hôtel des Princes de Monaco,* built c. 1650 but altered in the 18 and 19C. No. 16, the *Petit Hôtel de Charny* (17C), is the birthplace of Victorien Sardou the dramatist (1831–1908); and beneath the carriage-entrance of No. 22, the *Grand Hôtel de Charny,* are some wood-carvings in the purest Louis-XIII style. Baudelaire stayed here in 1858–59.

The RUE DES LIONS has 17–18C mansions on either side, one of the best (No. 10) being the least obvious (passage in modern façade leads to court of 1642). Mme de Sévigné lived at No. 11 in 1645–50.

The Rue St-Paul emerges on the QUAI DES CÉLESTINS (comp. above), where two important mansions overlook the Square H. Galli. At No. 4, the *Hôtel de Nicolaï* (late 17C), the sculptor Barye died in 1875. No. 2, the stately *Hôtel Fieubet,* with an interesting courtyard, was built for Gaspard de Fieubet, chancellor to Anne of Austria, by J. H. Mansart (1676–81); unfortunately badly altered in 1857, it now houses the École Massillon.

At the end of the Quai des Célestins is the BOULEVARD HENRI-IV, which leads on the left to the Bastille and on the right is carried by the *Pont de Sully* across the river and the E. end of the Île St-Louis to join the Boul. St-Germain (the dome of the Panthéon is seen in the distance). At its junction with the Rue de Sully stands the *Caserne des Célestins,* the barracks of the Gendarmerie Mobile, built on part of the site of a famous Celestine monastery founded in 1362.

Retracing our steps to the Rue St-Antoine we continue towards the Bastille.

No. 62 is the **Hôtel de Sully*, built by Jean du Cerceau in 1624–30 and purchased in 1634 by Sully, the minister of Henri IV; acquired by the State in 1945, the mansion will eventually be occupied by the Monuments Historiques. The Rue de Birague, on the left, leads to the Place des Vosges (Rte 12); Nos. 14 and 16 have elegant features. No. 21 in the Rue St-Antoine, the *Hôtel de Mayenne* or *Hôtel d'Ormesson* (the École des Francs-Bourgeois), with its turret and charming staircase, is by the youthful Jean du Cerceau (1613–17). The *Temple de Ste-Marie*, now a Protestant church, was originally the chapel of the convent of the Visitation, a circular building of graceful outline, erected by Fr. Mansart in 1632–34. Fouquet (d. 1680) and Henri de Sévigné (killed in a duel in 1651) were buried here. St Vincent de Paul was almoner of the convent for twenty-eight years. Balzac's first Paris lodging was a garret (at three sous a day) at No. 9 Rue Lesdiguières, on the right. The Rue St-Antoine ends at the Place de la Bastille (Rte 13).

A tablet on No. 5 Rue St-Antoine marks the position of the court of the Bastille, by which the mob gained access to the fortress. Near the junction of this street with the Place is the site of the great barricade of 1848, where Abp Affre was shot while exhorting the people to peace. This spot was also one of the last strongholds of the Communards in 1871.

The **Quartier de l'Arsenal**, named after the arsenal established here by Henri IV, extends from the Seine to the Bastille. At Nos. 1–3 Rue de Sully is the **Bibliothèque de l'Arsenal** (open 10–5, except on Sun, holidays and the first fortnight in Sept), founded in 1757 by Marc René d'Argenson, Minister of War, and partly installed in the former residence of the Grand Master of Artillery, built in 1594 for Sully. The façade on the Boul. Morland is by *Boffrand* (c. 1723).

The library possesses 15,000 MSS., 1,000,000 printed vols., and 120,000 engravings; it is noted especially for its incomparable series of illuminated MSS. and its almost complete collection of French dramatic works. Among the interesting documents are the papers of the Bastille, souvenirs of the 'Man in the Iron Mask', the documents of the 'Affair of the Diamond Necklace', and the letters of Henri IV to the Marquise de Verneuil. St Louis's Book of Hours and Charles V's Bible are shown also. The Gordon Craig Collection was acquired in 1957.—Nodier, Hérédia, Mérimée, and Anatole France were librarians here.

Noteworthy among the rooms shown to the public (Thurs 2–4) are the Salon de Musique, by *Boffrand*, with superb Louis-XV woodwork, and the apartment of the Duchess de La Meilleraie (ceiling by *Simon Vouet*).

12 THE MARAIS

MÉTRO stations: *Bastille* (lines 1, 5, 8); *St-Paul* and *Hôtel de Ville* (line 1); *République* (lines 3, 5, 8, 9, 11); *Temple* (line 3); *Arts et Métiers* (lines 3 and 11); *Réaumur-Sébastopol* (lines 3 and 4).

The ****Marais**, one of the most interesting parts of old Paris, forms a triangle, bounded by the Boulevard de Sébastopol, the Grands Boulevards, and the Seine, which includes the greater part of the 3rd and 4th arrondissements. In spite of past neglect and demolition, it remains substantially as developed in the 17C, and contains many scores of buildings of outstanding architectural interest, affording a fascinating and unique reminder of the elegance of this period. An excellent inventory map, *Le Marais et ses Abords* (1965), is published by the Association pour le Sauvegarde et la Mise en Valeur du Paris Historique, 44–46 Rue François-Miron, Paris 4e, the pioneers in the work of restoration, which will now receive government aid.

So called from the marshy land ('marais', marsh) the Marais only became habitable with the arrival of the Knights Templar and other religious houses who settled here in the 13C and converted the marshes into arable land. Royal patronage began with Charles V who, anxious to forget the associations of the Palais de la Cité with the rebellion of Étienne Marcel in 1358, built the Hôtel Saint-Paul here. In the 16C the Hôtel de Lamoignon and the Hôtel Carnavalet were built, but the seal of royal approval came with the building of the Place Royale (1605). Courtiers unable to find room here began to build themselves houses as near to the Place as possible. The Marais remained the most fashionable residential area of Paris until the creation of the Faubourg St-Germain in the early 18C. However, it was the Revolution of 1789 which ended its reign of splendour. The nobles had to flee; the State confiscated their property and sold it to the growing number of craftsmen and industrialists, and the Marais still remains a commercial area. It is now becoming popular with artists and antique dealers.

In summer the chief buildings are illuminated until 11 or 12 p.m.—The S. section of the Marais has already been described for convenience in Rte 11.

A   From the Bastille to the Square du Temple

From the Place de la Bastille the Rue de la Bastille leads shortly to the Rue des Tournelles, No. 28 in which is the *Hôtel de Mansart-Sagonne*, built for himself by Jules Hardouin-Mansart (1646–1708) and decorated by Le Brun and Mignard. No. 50 has a splendid façade. The cultured and fascinating courtesan Ninon de l'Enclos (1620–1705) lived here from 1644 and died at No. 56. The Rue du Pas-de-la-Mule, before these two houses, leads (r.) to the Boulevard Beaumarchais and (l.) to the Place des Vosges.

The *Place des Vosges, the heart of the Marais, a large square surrounded by houses in red brick with stone facings, was built on a uniform plan with arcaded ground floors (1606–11) and is one of the loveliest squares in Paris. Trees were planted in the central gardens for the first time in 1783, and though they obscure the effect of harmonious symmetry, they provide a welcome shade for children at play. Restoration is in progress (1967). The square is approached direct from the Rue St-Antoine via the Rue de Biragua (Rte 11) and through the *Pavillon du Roi* (see below).

The square occupies the site of the royal *Palais des Tournelles*, the residence of the Duke of Bedford, regent of France after the death of Henry V; in 1559 this was the scene of the fatal tournament when Henri II was accidentally killed by Montgomery; and it was abandoned in consequence by his widow Catherine de Médicis. The square was laid out in its present form probably by Baptiste du Cerceau for Henri IV as the *Place Royale* and opened in 1605; the king's pavilion was above the gateway in the centre of the S. side, while the queen's was the corresponding building opposite (No. 28). In the reign of Louis XIV this was one of the most fashionable addresses in Paris and the centre of the 'Nouvelles Précieuses' satirized by Molière. It acquired its present name in 1799, the department of the Vosges having been the first to discharge its liabilities for the Revolutionary Wars.

At the corners of the square are fountains (1816) and in the centre is a poor equestrian statue of Louis XIII (1825) set up to replace one destroyed in 1792. The *Hôtel de Coulanges* (No. 1bis; 1606), next to the Pavillon du Roi, saw Mme de Sévigné's birth in 1626. No. 3 is the *Hôtel d'Estrades*. No. 6 (see below) was built in 1610 for the Maréchal de Lavardin (d. 1614). No. 7, the *Petit-Hôtel de Sully*, was built by Jean Androuet du Cerceau. No. 9, the *Hôtel de Chaulnes*, was the residence of Rachel (d. 1858), the tragedienne. No. 11 was occupied by Marion Delorme, the courtesan. No. 21 was the mansion of Card. de Richelieu (1615), in front of which was fought in 1627, on the very day after the cardinal's edict against duelling, the famous duel of François de Montmorency and Des Chapelles against Bussy and Beuvron. No. 14, the Hôtel Ribault or de Langres, is now a synagogue. No. 12 occupies part of the *Hôtel Dangeau*, the home of the Marquis de Dangeau (1638–1720), the historian. Théophile Gautier and Alphonse Daudet lived for a while at No. 8.

No. 6 in the Place des Vosges is the *Musée Victor-Hugo (adm. 10–12, 2–5 or 6 exc. Tues and holidays; 1 fr., free on Sun), installed in 1902 in the house of which Victor Hugo occupied the second floor in 1832–48.

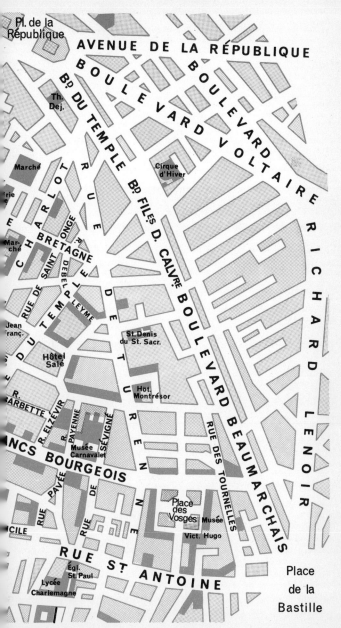

Pl. de la République

AVENUE DE LA RÉPUBLIQUE

BOULEVARD

B^D DU TEMPLE

Th. Dej.

BOULEVARD VOLTAIRE

Marché

Cirque d'Hiver

CHARLOT

RUE

B^D FIL^S D. CALV^{RE}

RICHARD

rie

Mar-ché

BRETAGNE

RUE DE SAINT

RUE DE SAINT-ONGE

DEBEL LEYME

BOULEVARD BEAUMARCHAIS

Jean franç.

RUE DU TEMPLE

St.Denis du St. Sacr.

Hôtel Salé

TURENNE

LENOIR

R. ARBETTE

Hôt. Montrésor

R. ELZÉVIR

R. PAYENNE

RUE DE SÉVIGNÉ

NCS BOURGEOIS

RUE DES TOURNELLES

Musée Carnavalet

RUE PAVÉE

RUE DE

Place des Vosges

Musée Vict. Hugo

ICILE

RUE ST ANTOINE

Égl. St.Paul

Lycée Charlemagne

Place de la Bastille

On the staircase and landings are drawings and water-colours to illustrate Hugo's works.

FIRST FLOOR. Ante-Room. Paintings by *Willette, Carrière, Rioult*, and others. The bust of Hugo is by *Schœnewerk* (1879). R. 1 contains a series of the most interesting of Hugo's drawings. Bust of Hugo by *Rodin*.—R. 2. Drawings by Hugo, and MSS. and first editions of his works.—R. 3 Portraits and souvenirs of Juliette Drouet. Paintings by *Fantin-Latour, Henner*, and others.

SECOND FLOOR. Ante-Room. Bust of Paul Meurice, who commissioned most of the paintings in the museum: bust of Hugo by *David d'Angers* (1838). *Raffaelli*, Fête on Hugo's 80th birthday; *Jeanniot*, Hauteville, Hugo's home in Guernsey.—The Dining Room contains furniture designed by Hugo and a table with inkstands belonging to Hugo, George Sand, Dumas père, and Lamartine, with their autographs.—R. 3 (the former drawing-room) contains the furniture from the dining-room in Juliette Drouet's house at Guernsey. Woodwork and fireplace by Hugo.—RR. 4–6. Decorations, and portraits and souvenirs of the Hugo family; in R. 6, portraits of Hugo's children, including his daughter Léopoldine, who was drowned on her honeymoon.—R. 7. Sketches, portraits, and photographs of Hugo. Head of the author by *Dalou*, modelled the day after his death.—R. 8 is a reconstruction of the room where Hugo died.

From the N.W. corner of the Place des Vosges we cross the Rue de Turenne (r., see below; to the left, in the court of No. 23 is the *Hôtel de Villacerf*, built c. 1660, with a fountain) and enter the Rue des Francs-Bourgeois.

The RUE DES FRANCS-BOURGEOIS, with several interesting side-streets, takes its name from the citizens who, being vassals to a feudal lord, were exempt from municipal taxes. At the corner of this street and the Rue de Sévigné is the **Musée Carnavalet** (Rte 25), in a house once occupied by Mme de Sévigné.

In the RUE DE SÉVIGNÉ, to the right, No. 29, formerly the *Hôtel Le Peletier de St-Fargeau*, built by P. Bullet in 1687, is now the **Bibliothèque Historique de la Ville de Paris** (open daily except hols. 9.30–12, 1.30–5). The library contains over 400,000 vols. and 100,000 MSS. relating to the history of Paris and the Revolution. It is also the seat of the Service des Travaux Historiques de la Ville de Paris. Opposite, at No. 48, the Hôtel de Jonquières, is a relief (1810) from an old fountain; No. 52, built c. 1680 by Pierre Delisle-Mansart for himself, has been much altered.

In the RUE PAYENNE, the next turning to the right (N.), from the Rue des Francs-Bourgeois, is the 18C house (No. 5) in which died Clotilde de Vaux (1846), the friend of Auguste Comte. Since 1905 it has been used as a *Positivist Chapel* on the lines laid down by Comte (adm. 10–4, except Mon and Fri). No. 11, the Hôtel de Polastron-Polignac, and No. 13, the Hôtel de Lude, are good examples of early-18C mansions. Opposite is the Square Georges-Cain with a little lapidary museum behind the Hôtel le Peletier.

The corner house on the left (No. 24 Rue Pavée) is the **Hôtel Lamoignon*, built in 1584 for Diane de France, the legitimized daughter of Henri II, but named after Lamoignon, president of the Parlement de Paris (1658), a later occupant. It was enlarged in the 17C. Alphonse Daudet set up house here on his marriage in 1867. Adjacent are traces of the notorious prison of *La Force* (demolished 1851), where many victims of the Revolution were massacred.

No. 16 Rue Elzévir, the next turning on the right, was the home of Ninon de l'Enclos in 1642. No. 8 has a good façade.

On the S. side of the Rue des Francs-Bourgeois is the *Hôtel d'Albret* (No. 31), built c. 1640 by Fr. Mansart, with the street façade in the 18C. At the end of the courtyard of No. 33 is a fragment of the walls of Philip Augustus; and the *Hôtel de Guillaume Barbès* (No. 35) was built in the second half of the 17C. On the N. side the following houses are noteworthy: No. 26, the *Hôtel de Sandreville* (late 16–18C), No. 30, *Hôtel d'Alméras*, a handsome red-brick mansion of the Henri-IV period. At No. 38 the Allée des Arbalétriers was one of the entrances to the Hôtel Barbette (see below) and led to the field alongside the walls of Philip Augustus which was used as a practice ground by cross-bowmen ('arbalétrier'). Beyond, the Rue Vieille-du-Temple (comp. below) diverges on the right and left.

Farther on in the Rue des Francs-Bourgeois, No. 55 is the head office of the *Crédit Municipal*, formerly the *Mont-de-Piété*, the chief government pawn-broking establishment, founded by Louis XVI in 1777 and reorganized by Napoleon III. In its courtyard are lines marking the course of the city walls of Philip Augustus; and it occupies part of the buildings (1685) of a monastery to which belonged the adjacent church of *Notre-Dame des Blancs-Manteaux*. The name, however, derives from the white habits of an earlier order of mendicant-monks established here in 1258 by St Louis. The church contains a striking rococo pulpit in the Flemish style (1749). The doorway (18C) in the Rue des Francs-Bourgeois comes from the church of St-Barthélemy in the Île de la Cité, demolished in 1863. Among other striking houses in this street are No. 54, the Hôtel de Camus, No. 56, the Hôtel de Fontenay, early 18C, No. 58, which belonged to Louis Le Tonnelier, baron de Breteuil, minister of Louis XVI, and 58bis, the Hôtel d'Assy (early 17C).

The Rue des Francs-Bourgeois ends at the Rue des Archives, at the corner of which stands the splendid *Hôtel de Soubise, the greater part of which was built by Delamair in 1706–12, on the site of the mansion of the Ducs de Guise. Here since 1808 have been housed the **Archives Nationales**, or *Record Office*, the presence of which has ensured the survival of the interior decoration by Natoire, Boucher, Van Loo, Restout, Lemoyne, etc. (1712–45). The gateway with a figure of History, after Delacroix, in the tympanum leads to the *Cour d'Honneur*, which is surrounded by a splendid colonnade and has copies of the 'Four Seasons', by Robert Le Lorrain, on the façade.

The turreted Gothic gateway (1380) at No. 58 Rue des Archives was the entrance to the *Hôtel de Clisson*, built in 1372–75 by the Constable Olivier de Clisson, a loyal supporter of Charles V against the English. Bolingbroke gave a farewell banquet there in 1399 before setting forth to win the crown of England. During the English occupation of Paris (1420–35) the Duke of Clarence and later the Duke of Bedford lived here. With its purchase in 1553 by Anne d'Est, wife of François de Lorraine, duc de Guise, it became the *Hôtel de Guise* remaining in the family until 1696, when Anne de Soubise bought it. The most brilliant occupant during this period was Henri II de Lorraine, who killed in a duel in the Place des Vosges in 1643 the last of the Colignys (his grandfather had instigated the murder of Admiral Coligny in the massacre of St Bartholomew). He entertained lavishly and gave hospitality to Corneille.

The MUSÉE DE L'HISTOIRE DE FRANCE, in which some of the outstanding documents, MSS., etc., belonging to the Archives are exhibited, is open daily 2–5 (exc. Tues), adm. 0,50 fr. The display is arranged to show the development of French institutions as well as to illustrate French history.

Usually on view are letters and wills of French royal personages from Philip Augustus onwards. The earliest document shown is a will of 627 and there are items concerning Clovis III and Charlemagne. There are many letters from foreign potentates (including the Emperor Charles V, Christina of Sweden, and Tamerlane) and statesmen (Benjamin Franklin and Washington); also one from Joan of Arc. Among the state documents are the Treaties of Bretigny, Westphalia, and the Pyrenees; the Report of the Council of the Parlement of Paris, with a contemporary sketch of Joan of Arc; the Edict of Nantes (with the signature of Henri IV) and its Revocation. Among the rich collection of Revolutionary relics may be mentioned the Oath of the Jeu de Paume; Marie-Antoinette's last letter and Louis XVI's will, also his diary with 'rien' written against the date 14 July 1789; the official report on the execution of Louis XVI; a letter of Charlotte Corday; and the keys of the Bastille.

Room E, with decoration by Boucher, etc., is considered a masterpiece of the style of the transition from Louis-XIV to Louis-XV. Room III was decorated by Boffrand, c. 1732–37. The chapel bears traces of the chapelle de Clisson of 1375 transformed in 1533 for the Guise by Primaticcio.

From the Rue des Archives (r.), which we shall traverse later, we enter the RUE DES QUATRE-FILS, in which No. 22 was the residence of the celebrated

Marquise du Deffand (1697–1780). Her salon was frequented by Voltaire, Montesquieu, D'Alembert, and Horace Walpole. No. 20, with a fine doorway, was the residence after 1800 of de Sèze, Louis XVI's lawyer.—In the Rue Charlot, to the left, is the church of **St-Jean-St-François**, built as a Capuchin chapel on the site of a tennis court and completed in 1715. It was enlarged in 1830 and 1855. In the church are statues of St Francis of Assisi by Germain Pilon and of St Denis by Jacques Sarrazin. In the sacristy are preserved the sacred vessels used at the celebration of mass at the Temple on the morning of Louis XVI's execution.

Among the houses in Rue Charlot No. 7, the *Hôtel de Brévannes* (17C), No. 28, the *Hôtel de Bérancourt* (early 18C), and No. 62, the *Hôtel de Bragelone*, are particularly fine.—In the parallel RUE DE SAINTONGE, Robespierre lived at No. 64 in 1789–91; Nos. 2 to 28 form an attractive ensemble.

We again cross the Rue Vieux-du-Temple, this time by the Rue des Coutures-St-Gervais, lined with many 17C houses and the garden façade of the **Hôtel Salé**, the magnificent mansion that stands in RUE DE THORIGNY (No. 5). Built in 1656 by Jean Boullier de Bourges for Aubert de Fontenay, the financier, the *Hôtel de Juigné* was popularly known as the 'Hôtel Salé' on account of the profits its owner had made out of the salt tax. The grand staircase is especially fine. The mansion, owned by the City, houses the *École des Métiers d'Art*. Marion Delorme probably died (1650) in a house on the site of No. 2 in this street; Nos. 6, 8, and 10 were built together as the Hôtel de Percey. No. 8 belonged to Mme de Sévigné in 1669–72.

Any of the short roads on the E. lead to the N. part of the RUE DE TURENNE, where Nos. 52–54 are the *Hôtel de Montrésor* (17C). No. 56 was for a time the home of Scarron (1610–60), who died here, and his wife Françoise d'Aubigné (1635–1719), afterwards Mme de Maintenon. No. 60 is the *Hôtel du Grand-Veneur*, with a boar's head on the façade. No. 66 has traces of the Hôtel de Turenne, built for the great marshal's father. The church of ST-DENIS-DU-ST-SACREMENT, built by Godde in the Grecian style of 1835, occupies the site of a chapel attached to a convent installed in the Hôtel de Turenne. Within, Pietà by Delacroix (floodlit on application to the sacristan). No. 80 belonged to the Marquis de Launay, last governor of the Bastille.

The Rue Debelleyme returns us to the RUE VIEILLE-DU-TEMPLE, which runs S.W. through the heart of the Marais, connecting the Boul. du Temple with the Rue de Rivoli. The *Hôtel d'Espinay* (No. 110), which belonged to a favourite of Henri III, has a magnificent staircase. Nos. 106–100 all preserve features of the early 17C when they were built. At the corner of the Rue des Quatre-Fils, No. 87, the **Hôtel de Rohan,** known also as the *Hôtel de Strasbourg*, was begun in 1704 by Delamair. It was successively occupied by four cardinals of the Rohan family, all of whom were bishops of Strasbourg; the most famous was the Cardinal de Rohan implicated in the 'affair of the diamond necklace' (1784–85). From 1808 to 1925 the mansion was occupied by the Imprimerie Nationale, and it now contains certain departments of the Archives Nationales. In 1928–38 the building was thoroughly restored. In the second court, the *Cour des Écuries* is a relief, the *Horses of Apollo, by Robert Le Lorrain, a vigorous work considered by many to be the masterpiece of French 18C sculpture; and the 'Cabinet des Singes' contains paintings of apes by Chr. Huet (1745–50).

Entry to the courtyards is usually through the Hôtel de Soubise, joined to the Hôtel de Rohan by a garden.—In the RUE BARBETTE, opposite the Hôtel de Rohan, No. 17, the *Hôtel de Brégis*, has a door with two medallions. The street name recalls the *Hôtel*

Barbette, the favourite residence of Isabeau de Bavière, which stood on this site. Several existing houses are of the 17C.

At No. 54, on the corner of the Rue des Francs-Bourgeois, survives the pretty Gothic turret (built c. 1510; restored) of the *Hôtel Hérouët*. The ***Hôtel des Ambassadeurs de Hollande** (No. 47), one of the most splendid of the mansions of the Marais, stands on the site of the house of the Maréchal de Rieux, in front of which the Duke of Orléans, returning from Isabeau de Bavière's house (comp. above), was assassinated in 1407 by the hired bravos of the Duke of Burgundy. The mansion, built by Cottard in 1657–60, has a finely carved oaken door, on the inner side of which is a bas-relief of Romulus and Remus. It was never in fact the property of the Dutch ambassador, but in 1720–27 belonged to the chaplain of the Dutch embassy and its chapel was used several times for Protestant ceremonies. Mlle Necker, the future Mme de Staël, was baptized here in 1766, and a daughter of Benjamin Franklin was married here. It was the home of Beaumarchais, who wrote his 'Mariage de Figaro' here and in 1788 turned the house into a provident institution for poor nursing mothers.

Farther on in the Rue Vieille-du-Temple are more attractive houses, notably Nos. 44, 43, 36 (built at the end of the 17C for Jean Godard, sieur du Petit-Marais; charming door); No. 23 (picturesque courts); and No. 15 (the *Hôtel de Vibraye*, 17C).

To the W. in the RUE DES ARCHIVES (No. 22) is the *Temple des Billettes*, built in 1756 for the Carmelites, but used since 1812 as a Lutheran church. A charming cloister (at No. 24), the only medieval example in Paris, is a relic of an older convent (1427; now part of a boys' school). Hence we may easily reach the Hôtel de Ville (Rte 11); alternatively we may follow the Rue des Archives N. to the Square du Temple (comp. below).

In the Rue de Braque (l.; opposite the Archives), Nos. 4–6, the *Hôtel Le Lièvre de la Grange*, is a fine late-17C mansion. No. 7 belonged to Vergennes, foreign minister to Louis XVI and supporter of American Independence.

At the corner of the Rue des Haudriettes is a pretty fountain, with a naiad by Mignot (1765). The *Hôtel de Guénégaud* (No. 60), by Fr. Mansart (c. 1650), and the *Hôtel de Montgelas* (1709) are handsome houses. Lamennais (1782–1854), the independent religious writer, died in No. 70 (18C). No. 78, built by Bullet (c. 1660) with a beautiful staircase (by Le Muet), was the residence of Marshal Tallard (1712). The street ends at the Square du Temple (see below). At No. 90 are traces of the *Hôpital des Enfants-Rouges* founded by Francis I and his sister Margaret in 1534, so called because the children wore a red uniform.

B   The Quartier du Temple

The densely populated **Quartier du Temple,** which derives its name from the house of the Knights Templar (see below), lies to the S. of the E. part of the Rue de Turbigo. Its chief streets are the Rue du Temple and Rue St-Martin.

The RUE DU TEMPLE, parallel with the Rue des Archives, unites the Place de l'Hôtel de Ville with the Place de la République and contains several interesting buildings. An inscription on No. 17 indicates the site of the house of Du Guesclin (1372–80). The square turret on No. 24 dates from 1610. No. 41, the *Auberge de l'Aigle d'Or* (17C) is the last remaining example in Paris of a coaching inn of the period. At No. 62 (house demolished) Anne de

Montmorency, constable of France, died in 1567. Nos. 67–87 present a charming ensemble of 17C houses. Nos. 71, 73, 75 form the *Hôtel de St-Aignan*, built by Le Muet in 1640–50; the courtyards and gate are particularly elegant. No. 79, the *Hôtel de Montmor*, dates from c. 1620 and has a great gateway and a charming pediment in the courtyard. The mansion was altered after 1751.

The RUE MICHEL-LE-COMTE, a turning on the left, has been little altered since the first half of the 17C. The *Hôtel Le Tellier* (No. 16) has a fine courtyard. No. 21 was the home of Verniquet, architect to Louis XVI. No. 28, the *Hôtel d'Hallwyll*, built by C. Ledoux (18C) is particularly fine; it is the probable birthplace of Mme de Staël (1766).

The entrance to the *Hôtel de Montmorency* (Nos. 101–103) is at No. 5 Rue de Montmorency. No. 51 in the latter street, the *Maison du Grand-Pignon*, was built in the early 15C and restored in 1900. Nos. 106–108 Rue du Temple, belonging to the Central Archives, provide one of the earliest examples of the use of concrete for building (architect, F. Le Cœur, 1920). No. 115 marks the probable site of a residence of Jean Bart (1650–1702), the famous privateer, who was created Admiral of the Fleet by Louis XIV; and Balzac lived at No. 122 after 1814. No. 13 Rue Chapon (l.), with an interesting court, was the house of the archbishops of Reims. After passing the Rue Réaumur and its continuation to the right, the Rue de Bretagne (both with handsome houses), we reach the large **Square du Temple,** on the site of the old stronghold of the Knights Templar, the headquarters of the order in Europe, occupied after 1313 by the Knights of St John. On the E. side is the *Mairie of the 3rd Arrondissement.*

The area owned by the Templars formed roughly the area between the Rue du Temple, Rue de Bretagne, Rue de Picardie and Rue Béranger. Before the Revolution it was occupied by wealthy noble families, artisans who did not belong to the corporations and therefore were free from many restrictions, and debtors who were free here from action for debt. The palace of the Grand Prior of the Knights of St John was renowned for luxurious living. During the Revolution the TOUR DU TEMPLE (1265) was used as a prison for Louis XVI and the royal family brought here in Aug 1792. The king went hence to the guillotine on 21 Jan 1793; on 2 Aug Marie-Antoinette was removed to the Conciergerie; on 9 May 1794, Mme Elisabeth was carried off to execution; the Dauphin (Louis XVII) is believed to have died here on 9 June 1795; and the sole survivor, Mme Royale, was released on 19 Dec 1795. The tower was demolished by Napoleon I, and the last vestiges were removed under Napoleon III.

Farther on in the Rue du Temple, beyond the square, is **Ste-Elisabeth,** a church founded by Marie de Médicis in 1630. The façade is a copy of Santa Maria Novella at Florence. The chief feature is the woodwork, including, in the ambulatory, 16C *Carvings of scriptural scenes from the abbey of St-Vaast at Arras.—Beyond the junction of the Rue de Turbigo with the Rue du Temple, just before the Place de la République, we pass (l.) the Rue Notre-Dame de Nazareth, at No. 38 in which was born Rudolf Diesel (1858–1913), inventor of the engine that carries his name. The façades of Nos. 41–49 are the most interesting in this street which leads W. to the N. end of the Rue St-Martin.

The straight RUE ST-MARTIN, leading from the Pont Notre-Dame to ($\frac{4}{5}$ m.) the Porte St-Martin, was the original Roman road from Lutetia to the north. On the E. side Nos. 270–304, the former *Priory of St-Martin-des-Champs*, rebuilt by Antoine but retaining the beautiful 13C refectory, form the Conservatoire des Arts-et-Métiers (Rte 23). Opposite lies the *Square Emile-Chautemps*, in the centre of which is a column, with fountains, commemorating the Crimean War (1854–55). On the S. side of the square is the *Théâtre de la Gaîté-Lyrique* and on the W. side the Boul. de Sébastopol.

The former 12C church of the priory is well seen from the Rue Réaumur. At the N.W.

corner of the Conservatoire is the *Fontaine du Vertbois*, erected in 1712 and restored in 1886, at the same time as the adjoining tower.

At the corner of the Rue Réaumur is the large church of **St-Nicolas-des-Champs,** with a square tower, built in 1420 but enlarged in 1541–87, when the choir was rebuilt and the outer nave aisles added, with further extensions in 1613. At the Revolution it served as the 'Temple of Hymen'. The original W. doors have survived, and the beautiful S. portal (c. 1576), after *Philibert Delorme*, likewise retains its contemporary doors. There is good woodwork in the nave vestibule. In the baptistery is the Baptism of Christ, by *Gaudenzio Ferrari*, and in the 4th N. chapel a Madonna and saints, by *Amico Aspertini*, two good Italian works of c. 1500. The ambulatory chapels have 17C wall-paintings; also (1st S. chap.) Our Lady of Victories, a fine example of French Renaissance painting of c. 1610–20; and (6th chap.) a notable Italian altar-piece (14C), with Passion scenes. The Apostles at the tomb of the Virgin, with the Assumption (on the 17C high altar), is by *Simon Vouet*.

Budæus (d. 1540), the Renaissance scholar, Gassendi (d. 1655), the astronomer, and Mlle de Scudéry (d. 1701), the 'précieuse', are buried in this church.

The Rue St-Martin crosses the Rue de Turbigo and farther on the Rue du Grenier St-Lazare. Gérard de Nerval was born in 1808 at No. 168 (then 96). More interesting at this point is the narrow street parallel to the W., the RUE QUINCAMPOIX, one of the oldest in Paris, though most of the houses date from the 17 and 18C. At No. 43 John Law (1671–1729), the celebrated Scottish financier, established his Mississippi bank which ended (1720) in a bankruptcy even more catastrophic than the 'South Sea Bubble'. No. 54 (demolished 1958) was the Cabaret de L'Épée de Bois, where the Royal Academy of the Dance had its origins in 1658. After the creation of Law's bank the wealthy 'Missis-sipiens' made it their club, when it was frequented by Louis Racine and Marivaux. Nos. 10, 12, and 14 (farther S.) have rococo façades. No. 89 Rue St-Martin has a 17C bas-relief of the Annunciation.

Near the S. end, half-hidden by houses, is **St-Merri,** built in flamboyant Gothic style (1515–52) on the site of at least two older churches, which covered the grave of St Mederic of Autun (d. 700). In 1796–1801 it was called the 'Temple of Commerce'. The W. front is notable for its rich decoration; the statues are mostly poor replacements of 1842. The N.W. turret contains the oldest bell in Paris (1331); the S.W. tower lost its top story in a fire. The nave has a double aisle on the right, a single aisle on the left; the organ dates from 1567, with an 18C gallery by *P. A. Slodtz*; the pulpit was designed by *M. A. Slodtz* (1753), who at the same time altered the choir. The carved keystone and the vault at the crossing, and the remaining stained-glass windows, contemporary with the church, are specially worthy of note.

In the right aisle, the 1st outer chapel has some remains of an earlier church (13C), while farther on is a large chapel by *Boffrand* (1743–44), with decorations by *P. A. Slodtz*. In the left aisle, the 1st chapel contains a 15C tabernacle, the 3rd a Pietà, attr. to *Nicolas Legendre* (c. 1670), the 4th a painting by *Coypel* (1661). From the 5th a staircase descends to the crypt (1515), which has grotesque corbels and the notable tombstone of Guillaume le Sueur (d. 1530); while in the N. transept is St Merri delivering prisoners, a good example of the work of *Simon Vouet*. Among the many other paintings the most attractive is a late-16C work of the Fontainebleau School (chapel S. of Lady Chapel): St Geneviève guarding her flocks, with Paris in the background.

The old quarter around St-Merri, between the Rue St-Martin and the Rue du Temple, with its narrow and picturesque streets, is one of the poorest parts of Paris; it retains a number of interesting houses, which, however, are in danger of demolition since part of the area is included in the redevelopment scheme for Les Halles.

13   THE OPÉRA AND THE GRANDS BOULEVARDS

The **Grands Boulevards,** a succession of wide thoroughfares extending in a curve from the Place de la Concorde to the Bastille (2¾ m.) were laid out in 1670–85 on the site of the inner fortifications demolished in the reign of Louis XIV. These had comprised the E. part of the 'enceinte de Charles V' erected after 1370 and the new fortifications to the W. built by Louis XIII in 1633–37. Though the Western Boulevards are no longer the centre of fashion they once were, they still have attractive cafés and shops. Their line marks the boundary between the inner 2nd, 3rd, and 4th arrondissements and the outer 9th, 10th, and 11th.

A   The Western Boulevards: from the Rue Royale to the Porte St-Martin

MÉTRO stations: Line 8 follows the route; also *Madeleine* (line 12); *Opéra* (lines 3, 7).

The short and broad RUE ROYALE, though not strictly one of the Boulevards, forms a convenient approach to them from the Place de la Concorde. As far as the Rue St-Honoré it is lined with uniform 18C houses and with fine shops. *Maxim's*, in the 1890's a famous haunt of international high society (including Edward, prince of Wales), is at No. 3; and the Café Weber, celebrated earlier in the century as a literary forum, was at No. 21. Mme de Staël lived for a short time after 1816 at No. 6.

The **Madeleine,** or church of *St Mary Magdalen*, the most fashionable church in Paris, is built in the style of a Roman temple, surrounded by a majestic Corinthian colonnade. Two earlier churches having been demolished unfinished in 1777 and 1798, the Madeleine was built by *P. Vignon* after 1806 at the order of Napoleon, who intended it as a Temple of Glory for the 'Grande Armée'. This was before he had thought of the Arc de Triomphe. A royal decree of 1816 restored it to divine worship, and the church was finished by *Huvé* in 1842. In the pediment is a relief of the Last Judgement (restored) by *Lemaire*. The enormous bronze doors are adorned with bas-reliefs from the Decalogue, by *Triqueti* (1838). The statue of St Luke at the back of the church was decapitated in 1918 by a shell from 'Bertha', the long-range gun with which the Germans bombarded Paris in the First World War.

The INTERIOR, entered also by the little side-doors near the choir, consists of a domed cella, gorgeously decorated but somewhat inadequately lighted, so that the overall impression is of a cold grandeur. The sculptured figures of the Apostles in the spandrels of the domes are by *Rude, Foyatier*, and *Pradier*. In the dark chapels on either side of the organ are the Marriage of the Virgin, by *Pradier*, and the Baptism of Christ, by *Rude*. Beyond the first chapel (r.) is a tablet to the Abbé Deguerry, a former curé, murdered in 1871 at La Roquette. The graceful but somewhat affected group of the Ascension of the Magdalen, on the high-altar, is by *Marochetti*. In the third chapel on the right as we return is a fine St Vincent de Paul group, by *Raggi*.

The church stands in the centre of the **Place de la Madeleine**, on the E. side of which a flower market is held (not Sun and Mon). At No. 2 (now Thos. Cook's agency) stood the Café Durand which played a determinant role in the 1848 Revolution, and where Émile Zola wrote 'J'Accuse', a courageous plea in favour of Dreyfus.

Marcel Proust (1871–1922) spent a great part of his youth at No. 9 in the Boulevard Malesherbes, near the Madeleine.

The BOULEVARD DE LA MADELEINE, the westernmost of the Grands Boulevards, runs E. from the Madeleine. Marie Duplessis, the 'Dame aux Camélias', died at No. 15 (formerly 11) in 1847; and Nos. 17–25 house the huge luxury shop, 'Aux Trois Quartiers'. The *Crédit Foncier* occupies an elegant 18C mansion at No. 19 Rue des Capucines, to the right of the Boulevard.

The BOULEVARD DES CAPUCINES, the most fashionable of the Boulevards, crosses the Place de l'Opéra, with the Opera House on the left (comp. below). Offenbach (1819–80), the composer, died at No. 8 in the boulevard.

On the left of the boulevard the Rue Edouard-VII leads to the Place Edouard-VII in which are the *Théâtre Edouard-VII* and an equestrian statue (by Landowski) of Edward VII (1841–1910), who as Prince of Wales was a frequent and popular visitor to Paris, and as king was the chief promoter of the 'Entente Cordiale'. An arcade leads thence to the Square de l'Opéra-Louis-Jouvet, with the *Théâtre Athénée-Louis-Jouvet*, in which the actor-manager died in 1951.

On No. 14 in the boulevard a tablet records the first exhibition of a cinema film (in the Salon Indien of the Grand Café) given by the brothers Louis and Auguste Lumière on 28 Dec 1895. A few days later in the same room took place the first demonstration with X-rays, a discovery of Dr Roentgen.

The **Musée Cognacq-Jay** (adm. 1 fr., free on Sun; 10–12, 2–5, exc. Tues and holidays), a small and elegant collection of 18C furniture and works of art, occupies rooms at No. 25 adorned with panelling from the château of Eu, in Normandy. Among the paintings are works by Lawrence, Reynolds, Gainsborough, Rembrandt, Guardi, Canaletto, Tiepolo, as well as Boucher, Fragonard, Greuze, Pater, Nattier (Marie Leczinska), Hubert Robert, and others; also drawings by Watteau and pastels by Q. de la Tour. The museum was founded by Ernest Cognacq (d. 1928), who also founded the 'Magasins de la Samaritaine'.—At No. 35 in 1874 an exhibition of paintings by Renoir, Manet, Monet, and Pissarro, including Monet's 'Impression—Soleil levant', gave the group their name.

The **Place de l'Opéra,** with the imposing façade of the opera house as its architectural background on the N., is one of the busiest centres of traffic in Paris. Seven important streets meet here. The Boul. des Capucines crosses it from W. to E. The Rue Auber and the Rue Halévy, to the left and right of the opera house, carry one-way traffic, the latter's leading to the Boul. Haussmann. In the angle between the Boul. des Capucines and the Rue Auber are the Grand-Hôtel and the Café de la Paix. On the S. side of the square radiate the Rue du Quatre-Septembre; the wide AVENUE DE L'OPÉRA, containing good shops and the *French Tourist Office* at No. 8 and leading to (nearly ½ m.) the Place du Théâtre-Français; and the Rue de la Paix.

Mme de Montespan and the painter Rigaud had houses in the Rue Louis-le-Grand, which crosses the Av. de l'Opéra; while Napoleon and Josephine Beauharnais were married in 1796 at No. 3 Rue d'Antin, then the Mairie of the 2nd Arrondissement. The *Fontaine Gaillon* (1828), in the Rue St-Augustin, is by Visconti and Jacquot.

The magnificent **Opéra** or *Opera House* was built in 1861–75 from the designs of *Charles Garnier*, successful entrant of 171 competitors. In superficial area (3 acres) it is the largest theatre in the world, but it contains only 2158 seats as compared with the 3000 of the Châtelet and the 2800 of the Scala at Milan.

It is an appropriate monument to the most brilliant period of the Second Empire. The director (or directors) is appointed by the government.

The first opera house in Paris was established in 1669 by Perrin, Cambert, and the Marquis de Sourdéac on the left bank, between the Rue de Seine and the Rue Mazarine. The first director was the celebrated Lulli, under whom it acquired its secondary title of *Académie Royale de Musique*.

The façade, approached by a broad flight of steps, is lavishly decorated with coloured marble and sculptures. The outermost arches on each side of the arcade opening into the vestibule are flanked with allegorical groups, including (r.) Dance, by *Carpeaux* (now replaced by a copy; original in the Louvre); above these are medallions of composers. Between the monolithic Corinthian columns of the loggia on the first story are bronze-gilt busts of other composers and librettists, and on the attic story is a row of bronze-gilt masks, with figures of Harmony and Poetry at the ends. Behind the low dome of the auditorium is a huge triangular pediment (indicating the front of the stage), crowned with a statue of Apollo of the Golden Lyre.

The side façades of the opera house are adorned with busts of musicians and the coats-of-arms of their native towns. The E. pavilion in the Rue Halévy is the subscribers' entrance, and here and in the Rue Gluck are fine bronze candelabra by *Carrier-Belleuse*. The 'Pavillon d'Honneur' on the W., in the Rue Auber, is the entrance to the Library and Museum, and here stands the monument to Charles Garnier, by *Pascal*, with a bust by *Carpeaux*. This entrance, originally known as the 'Pavillon de l'Empereur', was designed so that the sovereigns' coaches could be driven up to the dress circle—a safety precaution welcomed since Orsini's attempt on the life of Napoleon III on his way to the old opera house in 1858. It was rumoured that this device won Garnier the competition.

Visitors entering by the subscribers' entrance pass through a large circular vestibule, on the ceiling of which is a 'Mauresque' inscription in which Garnier, the architect, has signed and dated his work, and reach the second vestibule through a corridor with a bronze fountain-figure of the Pythoness by *Marcello*.

In the first vestibule are statues of composers; the second vestibule contains the box office (open 11–6.30). the *GRAND STAIRCASE, with its white marble steps 33 ft wide and its balustrade of onyx and rosso and verde antico, is one of the most striking features of the building. On the first floor, where it divides into two, is the entrance to the stalls and the amphitheatre, flanked with caryatids representing Tragedy and Comedy. There are arcades of monolithic marble columns on each floor, those on the third floor supporting a vaulted ceiling. The Avant-Foyer leads into the spacious and elaborate GRAND FOYER, with allegorical paintings by *Paul Baudry* and others. Seven glass doors communicate with the LOGGIA overlooking the Place de l'Opéra; by the middle door is a bust of Garnier by *Carpeaux*. The *AUDITORIUM, decorated in red and gold, has five tiers of boxes. The dome, resting on eight great pillars of scagliola, was redecorated in 1964, some would say inappropriately, by *Chagall*. The STAGE (118 ft high, 174 ft wide, 85 ft deep) is said to be the loftiest and widest in existence. Behind the scenes is the Foyer de la Danse, the scene of many paintings by Degas, with a mirror measuring 23 by 33 ft.

The **Musée de l'Opéra** (open daily 10–5, except Sun and holidays, and the fortnight following the Sun after Easter; adm. 0,50 fr.), on the first floor of the Pavillon d'Honneur in the Rue Auber (l.), is an admirably arranged little theatrical museum. The library consists of a complete collection of operas and ballets performed at the Paris Opéra since its foundation.

The BOULEVARD DES ITALIENS, whose cafés have gradually been replaced by office buildings, derives its name from the Théâtre des Italiens (1783) now superseded by the Opéra-Comique. Donizetti's 'Don Pasquale' was first performed here in 1843. At the corner of Rue Louis-le-Grand (r.; entrance No. 32) are the *Palais de Paris*, a collection of waxworks illustrating the history of Paris, and the *Musée Jules Verne* devoted to exploration (adm. daily 2–9, 2,50 fr.). This occupies the basement of the hideous Palais Berlitz on the site of the Pavillon de Hanovre (transferred to the Parc de Sceaux). Jefferson, in 1784–85, had a lodging in the Impasse Taitbout (now Rue du Helder; l.), and Wagner occupied No. 25 Rue Taitbout in 1840–41. No. 5 Rue Taitbout was the house of Sir Richard Wallace, where Lord Hertford accumulated the art treasures now in the Wallace Collection in London. On the right of the Boulevard is the *Crédit Lyonnais*, a huge block extending to the Rue du Quatre-Septembre. At the corner of Rue Laffitte, on the left, stood the house of Mme Tallien (1775–1835), wife of the revolutionary and afterwards Princesse de Chimay; part of the building (No. 20) later became the Café Hardy, rival of the Café Riche at No. 16 ("Il faut être bien ríche pour dîner chez Hardy, et bien hardi pour dîner chez Riche").

In the RUE LAFFITTE, named after Jacques Laffitte (1767–1844), the patriotic financier, stands the vast building of the *Banque Nationale pour le Commerce et l'Industrie*; right at the end is seen Notre-Dame-de-Lorette, with the hill of Montmartre and the Sacré-Cœur in the background. No. 17 was the residence of Queen Hortense of Holland and here Napoleon III was born in 1808. From No. 27, then Laffitte's residence, was issued the manifesto of Thiers proposing the coronation of Louis-Philippe. Lola Montès (1839–61) occupied No. 40 between her flight from Munich and her emigration to America.—It was in the Rue le Peletier, to the E., that the 'Carbonaro' Orsini, in 1858, flung a bomb at the carriage conveying Napoleon III to the opera here, killing and injuring many people, but doing no harm to the imperial couple.

The narrow Rue Marivaux (r.) leads to the entrance of the **Opéra-Comique** (box-office in the Rue Marivaux), in a somewhat confined position facing the tiny Place Boïeldieu. After a fire in 1887 the theatre was rebuilt by *Louis Bernier* and reopened in 1899. The ornate façade has statues of Music and Poetry by *Puech* and *Guilbert*.

The Opéra-Comique, now a subsidized theatre, originated in a company which produced pieces during local fairs, and in 1715 purchased from the Opéra the right of playing vaudevilles interspersed with ariettas. Discord between the two theatres continued until in 1757 Charles Favart (1710–92) finally established the rights of the Opéra-Comique (still familiarly known as the 'Salle Favart').

At the junction of the Boulevards des Italiens and Montmartre with the Boulevard Haussmann (extended to this point only in 1927) is the busy Carrefour Richelieu-Drouot. To the N. is the Rue Drouot, with the *Mairie of the 9th Arrondissement* in a fine mansion of 1746–48 (No. 6) on the right. No. 9 (l.) is the *Hôtel des Ventes Mobilières* or *Hôtel Drouot*, the main auction-rooms of Paris, where important sales are held from Feb to June. To the S. is the Rue de Richelieu, leading to the Palais-Royal.

The short BOULEVARD MONTMARTRE, in spite of its name, is a long way from Montmartre. At No. 10 (l.) is the *Musée Grévin*, the Parisian Madame Tussaud's. On the right are the Rue Vivienne, leading to the Bourse, and the *Passage des Panoramas*, which once linked two towers displaying views of cities, an entertainment introduced to Paris by Robert Fulton, the American who tested his first steamboat on the Seine in 1803. Here also is the *Théâtre des Variétés*, the scene of several successes of Offenbach. The busy Rue Montmartre (p. 72), at the end of the boulevard (r.), leads to the Halles, while the Rue du Faubourg-Montmartre (l.), ascending towards the 'suburb' of Montmartre, recalls the time when the boulevard formed the city boundary.

At No. 9 Rue du Faubourg-Montmartre is the *Musée de la Mer* (adm. daily 10–8; 1 fr. before 2, 2 fr. after 2), a seawater aquarium with c. 1000 marine creatures.

The Rue Geoffroy-Marie, on the right of the Faubourg-Montmartre, commemorates a saddler and his wife, who in 1260 presented to the Hôtel-Dieu a little farm which in 1840 fetched more than three million francs.

The BOULEVARD POISSONNIÈRE ends at the Rue Poissonnière and Rue du Faubourg-Poissonnière, named after the fishmongers who used to pass through on their way to the Halles. No. 27 in the Boulevard was Chopin's first lodging in Paris (1831–32). The Rue Rougemont (l.) is continued by the Rue du Conservatoire, in which (at No. 2) is the *Conservatoire National d'Art Dramatique*. In its fine small theatre of 1802, reputed for excellent acoustics, concerts are occasionally given by the Société des Concerts du Conservatoire.

In the BOULEVARD DE BONNE-NOUVELLE are the *Théâtre du Gymnase* (façade 1887), where Rachel made her first appearance in 1837, and (l.) the Rue d'Hauteville, at the end of which is seen St-Vincent-de-Paul. In the Rue de la Lune, to the S., is *Notre-Dame de Bonne-Nouvelle*, a church rebuilt in 1824. André Chénier (1762–94) lived in 1793 at 97 Rue de Cléry, close by, the street in which was Corneille's home in 1665–81. The boulevard ends at the Rue St-Denis (r.) or 'Voie Royale', once the processional route of entry into Paris, and Rue du Faubourg-St-Denis (l.; leading to the Boul. de Magenta and Gare du Nord). Here is the **Porte St-Denis,** a triumphal arch 72 ft high, designed by *Blondel* and erected in 1672 to commemorate the victories of Louis XIV in Germany and Holland. The bas-reliefs were designed by *Girardon* and executed by the brothers *Anguier* to commemorate "some of the wonderful feats of arms of Ludovicus Magnus", as Thackeray put it. It was last used for a royal entry into Paris by Queen Victoria in 1855.

The short BOULEVARD ST-DENIS stretches from the Porte St-Denis to the Porte St-Martin and is crossed by the busy thoroughfare formed by the Boul. de Strasbourg and Boul. de Sébastopol, the former leading to the Gare de l'Est, the latter to the Châtelet. The *Pathé Journal* (No. 6 Boulevard St-Denis), opened as the 'Cinéma Saint-Denis' by the brothers Lumière, claims to be the first cinema (1896). The **Porte St-Martin,** facing the Rue St-Martin and the Rue du Faubourg-St-Martin, is a second triumphal arch in honour of Louis XIV, 60 ft high, built in 1674 by *Bullet* and decorated with bas-reliefs of contemporary campaigns by *Desjardins* and *Marsy* (S. side) and by *Le Hongre* and the elder *Legros* (N.).

B   The Eastern Boulevards: from the Porte St-Martin to the Bastille

MÉTRO stations: *Strasbourg-St-Denis* (lines 4, 8, 9); *République* (lines 3, 5, 8, 9, 11); *Filles du Calvaire, St-Sébastien-Froissart* and *Chemin Vert* (line 8); *Bastille* (lines 1, 5, 8).

The BOULEVARD ST-MARTIN, over ¼ m. long, continues the series of the Grands Boulevards. On the left are the *Théâtre de la Renaissance*, the *Théâtre de la Porte-St-Martin*, and the *Ambigu*, three famous theatres. The first two were rebuilt in 1872 and 1873 after being burnt down during the Commune. The Renaissance was managed by Sarah Bernhardt in 1893–99. The Porte-St-Martin, in its original form a foundation of Marie Antoinette, who had it built in seventy-five days in 1781 to house the opera, is noted as the theatre of Frédérick Lemaître (1800–76), and here Coquelin aîné was seized by a mortal illness during a rehearsal of 'Chantecler' in 1909. Paul de Kock (1794–1871), the 'Smollett of France', died in the house No. 8. The Ambigu is in danger of demolition. In front is a monument to Baron Taylor (1789–1879), the author, by Tony Noël (1907).

The **Place de la République,** on the site of the Porte du Temple, is a busy centre of traffic, at the junction of seven important thoroughfares. It was laid out in 1856–65 by Haussmann for strategic reasons, but has maintained a political rôle as the scene of radical or opposition manifestations. The *Monument de la République* (82 ft high) is a striking work by the brothers Morice (1883), the pedestal of which is adorned with bronze bas-reliefs by Dalou.

The *Caserne Vérines,* the barracks (1854), on the N.E. side, was re-named after a lieutenant-colonel in the Resistance, who was shot by the Germans at Cologne in 1943. There was considerable fighting in this area during the Liberation. At the corner of the Rue de la Douane was Daguerre's workshop (1822–35; tablet). Gounod's 'Faust' was first performed in 1859 in the Théâtre Lyrique, where the Métro station now stands. This theatre, inaugurated by Alex. Dumas with 'La Reine Margot' in 1846, stood on the section of the Boulevard du Temple (demolished by Haussmann) known early in the 19C from the melodramas enacted in its many theatres as the 'BOULEVARD DU CRIME', and immortalized by Carné in 'Les Enfants du Paradis'.

Beyond the Place de la République the boulevards are less interesting, and the cafés and shops change their character.

The BOULEVARD DU TEMPLE, $\frac{1}{4}$ m. long, owes its name, like the 'Quartier du Temple' (Rte 12), to the Order of the Knights Templar, who owned most of the property in this region of Paris.

Gustave Flaubert lived at No. 42 in this boulevard in 1867–71. A little to the N. is the site of the house whence Fieschi discharged his infernal machine at Louis-Philippe, in 1835. Marshal Mortier and fourteen others were killed, but the king was uninjured.—Béranger (1780–1857), the great ballad-writer, died at No. 5 in the street now called after him (parallel with the boulevard on the W.).

The short BOULEVARD DES FILLES-DU-CALVAIRE recalls the site of a former convent (1633–1790).—The BOULEVARD BEAUMARCHAIS, nearly $\frac{1}{2}$ m. long, is named after the famous dramatist Caron de Beaumarchais (1732–99), the site of whose luxurious mansion and garden is occupied by Nos. 2 (tablet) to 20. On the right the Rue du Pas-de-la-Mule, leading to the Place des Vosges (Rte 12), crosses the Rue des Tournelles in which is the *Hôtel de Mansart-Sagonne,* well seen from the boulevard (Nos. 21–23).

The **Place de la Bastille** embraces the site of the Bastille, the ground plan of which is marked by a line of white stones between the Boul. Henri-IV and the Rue St-Antoine. Beneath the pavement are large cellars once belonging to the famous prison.

The **Bastille,** or more correctly the *Bastille St-Antoine,* originated as a bastion-tower defending the E. entrance to Paris. It was developed under Charles V into a fortress with eight massive towers, immensely thick walls, and a wide moat. By the reign of Louis XIII the Bastille had become almost exclusively a state prison for political offenders, among whom were the mysterious 'Man in the Iron Mask' (1698–1703) and Voltaire. The arbitrary arrest by 'lettre de cachet' of persons obnoxious to the Court, and their protracted imprisonment without trial, made the Bastille a popular synonym for oppression. Dr Manette, in 'A Tale of Two Cities', was a victim of this practice, as (in real life) was Mirabeau the Younger, albeit at his father's instigation. In 1789, at the outbreak of the Revolution, the mob, aided by a few troops, attacked and overwhelmed the defenders (there were in fact only a handful of prisoners). The prison was razed to the ground in the same year, and the key, presented by La Fayette to George Washington, is now at Mount Vernon. The anniversary of the fall of the Bastille (14 July) is kept by the French as the Fête Nationale.

The **July Column** (*Colonne de Juillet*), 169 ft high, in the centre of the square, is a bronze pillar, crowned by a figure of Liberty, erected by Louis-Philippe to commemorate the victims of the three days' street-fighting of July 1830, who are buried in vaults within the circular base of the column. The victims of the revolution of February 1848 were subsequently interred here, and their names added to the inscription.

Among the allegorical sculptures in bronze adorning the plinth, the most notable is a Lion, by *Barye*, symbolizing the July revolution. The gallery at the top (adm. 0,50 fr., open daily, except Tues, 10–4, 5 or 6; 238 steps) commands a splendid view of Paris.

On the S.E. side of the Place is the *Gare de la Bastille*; on the S. side is the *Gare d'Eau de l'Arsenal*, a dock at the end of the Canal St-Martin, which runs beneath the square. The Rue de la Roquette leads N.E. from the Bastille to Père-Lachaise. At 51bis is the little church of *Notre-Dame d'Espérance* (1930).—The Rue de Lyon leads S. to the Gare de Lyon.

14   THE DISTRICTS TO THE NORTH OF THE GRANDS BOULEVARDS

A   Faubourg St-Martin and Faubourg St-Denis

MÉTRO stations: *République* (lines 3, 5, 8, 9, 11); *Jacques Bonsergent* (line 5); *Gare de l'Est* (lines 4, 5, 7); *Poissonnière, Cadet, Le Peletier* (line 7); *Chaussée-d'Antin* (lines 7 and 9); *Trinité, N.-D. de Lorette*, and *St-Georges* (line 12).

From the Place de la République the long BOULEVARD DE MAGENTA, intersecting various important streets, leads N.W. to the line of the outer boulevards. In the RUE DU FAUBOURG-ST-MARTIN, which crosses it diagonally, is (l.) the handsome *Mairie of the 10th Arrondissement*, with a relief of *International Brotherhood, by Dalou*, in the Salle des Fêtes. Behind at No. 6 Rue Pierre-Bullet is the Hôtel Gouthière of 1722. Beyond the little *Square St-Laurent* (r.), in which is a group (Brother and Sister) by A. Lefeuvre, the Boul. de Strasbourg (see below) crosses the Boul. de Magenta. At the corner is **St-Laurent,** one of the oldest foundations in Paris. Gregory of Tours mentions that a church existed here near the Roman road in 583. The present church, begun before 1429 (with a N. tower surviving from an older building), was continued in the 16–17C, the nave having been vaulted in 1655–59 and the choir remodelled at the same time, with a high altar by *Ant. Le Pautre*. The Lady Chapel dates from 1712. The 17C façade was demolished in 1862–65, when the present flamboyant W. front was built and the spire erected. Mme du Barry (Jeanne Bécu; 1746–93) was married here in 1764. The roof has elaborately carved pendentives.

Just beyond the church the Boulevard de Strasbourg diverges on the right for the **Gare de l'Est,** the terminus of the line to Strasbourg, etc. The courtyard of the station occupies the site of the medieval St Lawrence fair.

The BOULEVARD DE STRASBOURG, uniting the Gare de l'Est with the Boul. St-Denis, forms with its S. extensions, the Boul. de Sébastopol, the Boul. du Palais, and the Boul. St-Michel, one of the chief arteries of N. to S. traffic in Paris.

In the Boul. de Magenta, on the left, beyond the Rue du Faubourg St-Martin, stood the *Prison de St-Lazare*; among its prisoners were Chénier and Hubert Robert. This was the headquarters from 1632 of the Lazarists or Priests of the Mission, founded in 1625 by St Vincent de Paul (1576–1660), but since 1935 it has been partly demolished and rebuilt as a clinic.—The boulevard next crosses the Rue de La Fayette (see below) at the point whence the short Boul. Denain leads (r.) to the **Gare du Nord,** the terminus of the line from Calais, Boulogne, etc., in the Rue de Dunkerque. To the N.W. of the station is the *Hôpital Lariboisière* (1846–53), the largest hospital in Paris (1350 beds).

The BOULEVARD DE LA CHAPELLE, continuing the Boul. de Rochechouart, one of the outer boulevards, to the E., is the S. boundary of the thickly populated QUARTIER DE LA CHAPELLE, which contains numerous workshops and foundries. The Rue Marx Dormoy (l.) leads N. to the quaint old parish church of *St-Denis-de-la-Chapelle* (13C, but much restored). At the side of the entrance is Charpentier's statue of Joan of Arc, who received Communion in this church in Nov 1429 before besieging the walls of Paris. The ugly monumental basilica of *Ste-Jeanne-d'Arc* adjoining on the N., begun in 1932, is as yet unfinished.

The RUE DE LA FAYETTE, one of the longest streets in Paris, stretches from the Rue de la Chaussée-d'Antin on the S.W. to the Place Stalingrad on the N.E. A little to the W. of the intersection of the Boul. de Magenta is the small *Place de La Fayette*, dominated on the N. by **St-Vincent-de-Paul**, a church with two square towers, by *Lepère* and *Hittorf* in 1824–44. It is preceded by a pédimented portico of twelve Ionic columns, approached by a monumental flight of steps. In the nave is a huge processional frieze (558 ft in length and 10 ft high), painted, in imitation of the mosaics of Ravenna, by *Hippolyte Flandrin*. The choir-stalls show portraits of the Orleans princes in the costumes of their patron-saints. In the Rue d'Hauteville, which leads S. to the Grands Boulevards, No. 58 is the charming *Hôtel de Bourrienne* (1787), decorated in the style of the First Empire by Napoleon's friend and secretary.

Following the Rue de La Fayette towards the S.W., we cross the Rue du Faubourg-Poissonnière, where Corot died in 1875 (at No. 56) and which, like the neighbouring Rue de Paradis, still preserves some 18C houses. Farther on, at the Square Montholon, we cross the Rue Montholon, at No. 5 in which was born the chemist Henri Moissan (1852–1907), the first to isolate fluorine; No. 9 was the residence of Franz Liszt in 1831. The Rue de La Fayette beyond the Rue de Châteaudun is noted for its art-dealers, and the side streets on the S. leading to the Grands Boulevards are a centre of trade in diamonds and precious stones. The street then crosses the Rue du Faubourg-Montmartre, the Rue Laffitte (Rte 13A), and the Rue de Provence; it ends at the junction of the Rue de la Chaussée-d'Antin with the Boul. Haussmann.

The important RUE DE LA CHAUSSÉE-D'ANTIN leads N. through the Faubourg-Montmartre from the Boulevard des Italiens to the church of La Trinité.

In the S. section Rossini lived at No. 2 from 1857. No. 5 (rebuilt) sheltered Mozart in 1778 after the death of his mother, and was the residence of Chopin in 1833–36. No. 7 (also demolished) was the residence of the Neckers, who entertained Gibbon here; in 1798 it was bought by Jules Récamier, the banker, whose wife here presided over the most distinguished salon of the Directory. Mirabeau died at No. 42 in 1791. In the Rue Taitbout, the next street to the E., Rossini lodged at No. 28, while musical director of the Théâtre des Italiens in 1824–25. George Sand (at No. 5) and Chopin (at No. 9) lived in 1842–47 in the Square d'Orléans off its E. side.

The conspicuous and ugly church of **La Trinité** was built in 1863–67 by *Ballu*, in a hybrid Renaissance style. The porch is surmounted by a tower 206 ft in height.

The three old streets behind La Trinité (E. to W. the Rue Pigalle, Rue Blanche, Rue de Clichy) are all convenient approaches to Montmartre; each with a theatre, but not now very interesting. Victor Hugo lived at No. 21 Rue de Clichy in 1880, and Daniele Manin (1804–57), the hero of the Risorgimento in Venice, died in exile at No. 70 Rue Blanche.

At No. 14 Rue de La Rochefoucauld, a short distance to the E. of La Trinité, is the **Musée Gustave-Moreau** (adm. 1 fr.; 10–5, closed Sun and Tues, also August), a collection of works (1000 paintings, over 7000 drawings, etc.) by the painter Gustave Moreau (1826–98), bequeathed by him, together with his residence, to the State.

The dull RUE DE CHÂTEAUDUN, running E. from the Place de la Trinité to the Rue de La Fayette, crosses the Rue St-Georges, where Auber lived for thirty years and died in 1871 (at No. 22), and Henri Murger, author of 'Scènes de la Vie de Bohème', was born the son of a concierge in 1822 (at No. 19). **Notre-Dame-de-Lorette,** another of the drearily magnificent basilican churches of the early 19C, in which Bizet was christened, was built in 1823–36 by *Hippolyte Lebas*, with a portico of four Corinthian columns. Attractive musical services are held here in the evenings during May, the month of Mary. Behind the church is (r.) the Rue des Martyrs, an ancient approach to Montmartre, already famous in the 18C for its 'cabarets'; here in 1824 Géricault died at No. 49 (later occupied by Béranger). In the Rue de la Tour-d'Auvergne, a turning (r.) off the Rue des Martyrs, Bizet was born in 1838 at No. 26; while in 1844–57 Delacroix lived at No. 58 (then 54) Rue Notre-Dame-de-Lorette, which leads N.W. to Montmartre viâ the PLACE ST-GEORGES. The 'Lorettes' of this quarter, a favourite subject of the caricaturist Gavarni (1801–66), are represented, with other types of his, on his monument here. No. 27 in this square is the *Hôtel Thiers*, the residence of President Thiers (1797–1877). Burned down by the Communards, the building was reconstructed and bequeathed in 1905 to the Institut de France.

It now contains the BIBLIOTHÈQUE THIERS (80,000 vols. dealing with the history of France from the Revolution to the present day) and the Napoleonic collection of Frédéric Masson (30,000 vols., drawings by *David*, bust of Josephine by *Houdon*, etc.). The former is open on Wed and Thurs, 1.30–5.30, closed mid-July–mid-Sept; adm. on the recommendation of two members of the Institut. The Masson collection is open on request.

At the end of the Rue Notre-Dame-de-Lorette is the Rue Chaptal (l.), at No. 16 in which Charles Dickens sat for his portrait to Ary Scheffer in 1856. The Rue Fontaine goes on thence to the Place Blanche, crossing the Rue de Douai, which leads (l.) to the Place de Clichy, viâ the *Place Adolphe-Max*, with a statue of the composer Berlioz (1803–69), who died at 4 Rue de Calais, close by; Vuillard (d. 1940) had a studio in this Place. Zola died in 1902 at 21bis Rue de Bruxelles (which crosses the Place); while at 30 Rue de Douai (the house of Turgenev and Mme Viardot, the singer) Dickens met George Sand in 1856.

B   Montmartre

MÉTRO stations: *Clichy* (lines 2 and 13); *Blanche* (line 2); *Pigalle* (lines 2 and 12); *Barbès-Rochechouart* (lines 2 and 4); *Abbesses, Lamarck-Caulaincourt,* and *Joffrin* (line 12); *Château-Rouge* (line 4).

The **Place de Clichy** is one of the busiest centres of traffic in the N. of Paris. Here stood the 'Barrière de Clichy', heroically defended against the Russians by pupils from the École Polytechnique and the Garde Nationale under Marshal Moncey on 30 March 1814. In the centre is the monument to Moncey, a bronze group ('The Defence of Paris') 20 ft high (1869). On the E. side of the Place begins the wide BOULEVARD DE CLICHY, one of the outer line of boulevards, forming, together with its E. continuation the Boul. de Rochechouart, the S. boundary of Montmartre. This lively thoroughfare is the centre of the night life of Montmartre with most of the cabarets and night-cafés. Seurat and Signac in 1886 had adjoining studios at No. 128bis. On the left, beside the *Gaumont Palace*, the largest cinema in France (5000 seats), diverges the RUE CAULAINCOURT, which is carried over the cemetery by a viaduct and is the most convenient approach for motorists to the Butte Montmartre.

Towards the middle of the 19C the construction of large new thoroughfares through the N. slums rendered access to **Montmartre** more convenient, and the poorer artists, migrating there because it was both picturesque and cheap, made it for about thirty years a real centre of artistic endeavour. About 1881 the famous 'cabaret artistique' 'Le Chat Noir' (closed in 1897) was opened, and the advertisement thus given to the artistic attractions of the district invited a tide of pseudo-bohemians, foreign tourists, and less desirable hangers-on, before which the serious workers retired. The motley crowds to be seen in the cafés and 'cabarets artistiques' of the Place Pigalle, etc., have now but a shadowy connection with art or letters, and consist mainly of tourist pleasure-seekers and those who cater for their tastes in shady clubs, strip-tease theatres, and bars. The personalities of Montmartre in its great days were vividly depicted by Henri de Toulouse-Lautrec (1864–1901), whose studio was at 5 Av. Frochot, near the Place Pigalle. Its old-fashioned streets have been made familiar to thousands by Maurice Utrillo (1883–1956).

The Av. Rachel, on the left of the Boul. de Clichy, is the direct approach to the **Cimetière de Montmartre**, or *Cimetière du Nord*, on the W. slopes of the Butte. Though less important than Père-Lachaise it contains the graves of many famous people of the 19–20C, notably authors, artists, actors, and musicians.

The cemetery is divided into numbered sections, to which our figures refer. Notable burials include: Jean Giraudoux (1), Théophile Gautier (3), Degas (4), Ad. Adam, the composer, and Vestris, the great 18C ballet dancer (5), Berlioz (7), Delibes and Offenbach (9), the brothers Goncourt and Alfred de Vigny (13), Alex. Dumas, fils (21), Ernest Renan (22), Greuze and Heine (27), Amb. Thomas and Fr. Lemaître (28), Stendhal and Ampère (30). The family tomb of the Cavaignac has a statue by Rude.

The boulevard goes on to the Place Blanche. On the left is the *Moulin Rouge*, converted into a cinema, while the Rue Lepic ascends the Butte, passing the rebuilt *Moulin de la Galette*. Van Gogh (in 1886) and Guillaumin lived at No. 54 Rue Lepic.

The **Place Pigalle** is surrounded by night-cafés and restaurants. The Passage de l'Elysée-des-Beaux-Arts, on the N., leads to the church of *St-Jean-l'Evangéliste*, built of reinforced concrete by A. de Baudot in 1894–1904.

The BOULEVARD ROCHECHOUART continues the Boul. de Clichy beyond the Rue des Martyrs. On the left rises the Butte Montmartre, while on the right are the *Cirque Médrano* and the little *Place d'Anvers*. In the centre of the gardens is a column with a figure of Armed Peace, by Coutan.

From the Place d'Anvers the Rue Steinkerque leads N. to the *Place St-Pierre*, with the little *Fontaine des Innocents*, by Derré. The steep slope of the Butte, known as the Square Willette, with its series of terraces and flights of steps, may be ascended on foot, or by a funicular railway (W. side of the square), to reach the Sacré Cœur.

The ***Butte Montmartre**, the 'butte sacrée', rises 423 ft above sea-level and 335 ft above the level of the Seine.

The name of Montmartre has been variously derived from Mons Mercurii, Mons Martis, and Mons Martyrum. Of these the two first presuppose the existence of a Roman Temple on the hill; the last is based on the probability that St Denis and his companions, SS. Rusticus and Eleutherius, were beheaded at the foot of the hill, St Denis afterwards (it is said) walking to the site of the Basilica of St-Denis with his head in his hands. The *Chapelle du Martyre* (in the convent at 9 Rue Antoinette; adm. 1 fr.) occupies the probable position of a chapel erected on the site of the martyrdom. It was in the crypt beneath this that St Ignatius de Loyola and his six companions, including St Francis Xavier, took the first Jesuit vows, in 1534, thus founding the Society of Jesus.—The Butte Montmartre, commanding as it does the entire city, was the military key to Paris, and its history is one long series of sieges and battles. It was occupied by Henri of Navarre in 1589; here in 1814 took place the final struggle between the French and the Allies; and in 1871 it was held for two months by the Communards.

The **Basilique du Sacré-Cœur**, crowning the Butte Montmartre and only too visible from almost every part of Paris, is a conspicuous oriental-looking church of white stone in a Romanesque-Byzantine style of the 12C derived

from St-Front at Périgueux. Its ugliness does not deter a constant press of pilgrims and visitors. The building of the church was decreed by the National Assembly in 1873 as a national votive offering of humiliation and repentance after the war of 1870–71 and was begun in 1876 from the plans of *Abadie*. Though used for service since 1891 the church was not consecrated as a basilica until 16 Oct 1919. The church is 328 ft long, 164 ft wide (246 ft across the ambulatory), and is surmounted by a dome 197 ft high and by a square bell-tower (308 ft high), the latter being the work of *Magne* (1913).

The façade is richly decorated with sculpture and bas-reliefs. On the angles of the W. portico are two huge equestrian statues in bronze, of St Louis and St Joan of Arc, by *Lefebvre*.

The imposing **Interior** is elaborately decorated. On the right, facing the aisle, is the *Chapelle de l'Armée*, with mosaics of St Joan of Arc and St Louis and a statue of Joan of Arc by Fagel. The *Chapelle de St-Benoît-Labre*, the first in the ambulatory on the right, contains a monument by Fagel to Louis Veuillot (1813–83), the Ultramontane journalist (the nun is a portrait of Veuillot's

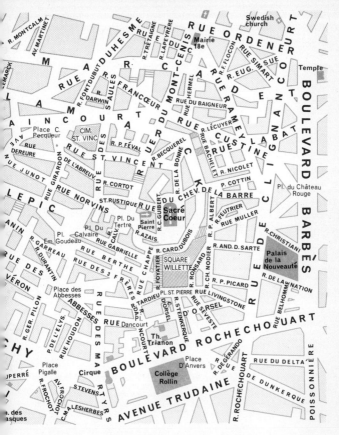

daughter). The first chapel in the left aisle (nearest the entrance) is the *Chapelle de la Marine*.

The fine CRYPT extending under the aisles, transepts, and choir is open 9–12 and 2–6 (adm. 0,50 fr.). The central CHAPELLE DES MORTS contains statues of Card. Guilbert (d. 1886), and of Card. Richard (d. 1908), archbishops of Paris, both buried here.—In the BELL-TOWER hangs the *Savoyarde*, or *Françoise-Marguerite*, a great bell presented by the four dioceses of Savoy and remarkable for its sonorous timbre; it was cast at Annecy in 1895 and weighs nearly 17¾ tons.—The DOME is open 10–1 and 2–5 or 6 (adm. 1 fr.). We first ascend a platform overlooking the church of St-Pierre. From the second gallery, or Galerie des Vitraux, we view the whole of the interior of the Sacré-Cœur. From either the exterior Galerie des Colonnes or the lantern at the top of the dome we obtain a magnificent *View of Paris and its environs, extending over a radius of 30 m.

To the W. of the Sacré-Cœur is a massive building belonging to a reservoir. In the Rue du Mont-Cenis, the street of pilgrimage from Paris to Montmartre (many steps), is the old church of **St-Pierre-de-Montmartre,** the successor of the earliest Christian church in Paris, erected to commemorate the martyrdom of St Denis. The present church, a relic of a Benedictine nunnery founded in

1134 by Adélaïde de Savoie (d. 1154), was consecrated in the presence of Louis VI, her husband, by Pope Eugenius III in 1147. It served as the 'Temple of Reason' in 1794. The façade dates from Louis XIV. Inside, against the W. wall, are two ancient columns with capitals of the 7C, the date also of two other capitals at the apse entrance and one in the N. aisle. The nave has 15C vaulting, but the aisles were vaulted only in the restoration of 1900–05. The choir provides possibly the earliest example of an ogee arch in Paris (1147). Behind the altar is the foundress's tomb. The apse has been almost entirely rebuilt.

In the old graveyard behind the church, on the left (open only on 1 Nov), is the tomb of Bougainville (1729–1811), the famous navigator. Foundations of a Roman temple have been found N. of the church. The *Jardin du Calvaire*, to the right of the church, has stations of the Cross executed for Richelieu and paid for by ladies of the court.

Not much remains of Old Montmartre, with its cottages and little gardens; but the PLACE DU TERTRE, with the former Mairie (No. 3), is still attractive, as are also some of its neighbouring streets, notably the Rue St-Rustique. In the Rue des Saules is the last surviving vineyard in Paris, while at No. 4 is 'Au Lapin Agile', called after a sign painted by A. Gill, and made famous by its artist clientèle. At No. 12 is the *Musée d'Art Populaire Juif* (open Tues, Thurs, and Sun, 2–5).

Berlioz and his actress wife lived in 1834–37 at No. 24 Rue du Mont-Cenis, at the corner of Rue St-Vincent (house rebuilt). No. 17 Rue St-Vincent is the entrance to the *Musée du Vieux-Montmartre* (adm. daily exc. Tues, 10–12, 2–5; 1 fr.), installed in 1960 in the 17C house of Roze de Rosimond, a member of Molière's 'Illustre Théâtre'. It has interesting collections of Montmartre (or Clignancourt) porcelain, made in 1767–99 in a pottery at the junction of Rues Mont-Cenis and Marcadet. The house was occupied in 1875 by Renoir and later by Utrillo, Dufy, and others. In the *Cimetière St-Vincent* are buried Honegger (1892–1955) and Maurice Utrillo (1883–1956). The Rue Ravignan (S.W. of the Place du Tertre) was a favourite 'artistic' residence c. 1910; occupants include Modigliani, Henri Rousseau, and (in 1903) Picasso at No. 13 (the 'Bateau Lavoir'), and Max Jacob, the poet, at No. 7.

C   Quartier de l'Opéra, Quartier de l'Europe, and Batignolles

MÉTRO stations: *Opéra* (lines 3, 7, 8); *Havre-Caumartin* (lines 3 and 9); *St-Lazare* (lines 3, 12, 13); *St-Augustin* (line 9); *Europe* (line 3); *Villiers* (lines 2 and 3); *Malesherbes* (line 3); *Rome* (line 2); *Clichy* (lines 2 and 13).

This district is bounded on the S. by the Boul. de la Madeleine and Boul. des Capucines, on the W. by the Boul. Malesherbes and Av. de Villiers, and on the E. by the Rue de la Chaussée-d'Antin and the Rue and Av. de Clichy. Between the Grands Boulevards and the Gare St-Lazare lies a district of high-class shops and stores, important business offices, and hotels of every grade; to the N.W. of the station is a favourite middle-class and even fashionable residential district; and beyond the Boul. des Batignolles the railway forms a sharp division between the middle-class streets on the W. and a poorer neighbourhood on the E.

The RUE AUBER, a rendezvous for many excursions, leads from the Place de l'Opéra to the Boul. Haussmann and is continued thence to the Gare St-Lazare by the Rue du Havre. On the right of the Rue Auber is the Opera House (see Rte 13). In the Rue Caumartin (r.) is the church of *St-Louis d'Antin* (1782), by Brongniart, the former chapel of a Capuchin convent. The Rue Auber ends at the junction of the Rue Tronchet with the Boul. Haussmann. The *Lycée Condorcet*, No. 8 Rue du Havre, one of the leading boys' schools in Paris, occupies former conventual buildings (with a Doric cloister court) of St-Louis d'Antin.

The BOULEVARD HAUSSMANN (c. 1½ m. long), one of the main streets of Paris, was begun by Baron Haussmann in 1857 as part of a scheme to construct an unbroken thoroughfare from the Boul. Montmartre (Rue Drouot) to the Place de l'Étoile, a distance of 1¾ m. The E. portion of this design, from the Rue Drouot to the Rue Taitbout, was not completed until 1926.

Near its E. end, at the corner of the Chaussée-d'Antin, are the *Galeries La Fayette*, and at the busy junction with the Rue Auber and Rue Tronchet are the large *Magasins du Printemps*. Chopin lived at No. 5 Rue Tronchet in 1839–42.—Following the Boul. Haussmann towards the W., we pass, in the gardens (l.), the **Chapelle Expiatoire** (open daily, except Tues, 10–4, 5 or 6; adm. 0,50 fr., Sun 0,25; entrance in the Rue Pasquier), erected in 1815–26 from the plans of *Percier* and *Fontaine*, in the style of a classical funeral temenos. It was restored in 1966. The chapel was built by order of Louis XVIII and dedicated to the memory of Louis XVI and Marie Antoinette, whose remains, interred in the graveyard of the Madeleine on this site, were removed to St-Denis in 1815. In the interior are two marble groups: Louis XVI and his confessor the Abbé Edgeworth, by *Bosio* ("Fils de St Louis, montez au ciel"; below is inscribed the king's will, dated 25 Dec 1792); and Marie-Antoinette supported by Religion, by *Cortot* (the latter figure bearing the features of Mme Elisabeth; below is inscribed the letter said to have been written by the queen in the Conciergerie to her sister-in-law on 16 Oct 1793). The bas-relief by *Gérard* above the doorway represents the removal of the royal remains to St-Denis.

In the former *Cimetière de la Madeleine*, now Square Louis-XVI, in front of the chapel rest the bodies of the victims of the panic of 1770 in the Place de la Concorde, the Swiss guards massacred on 10 Aug 1792, and all those guillotined between 26 Aug 1792 and 24 March 1794. Among them are Charlotte Corday and Philippe-Égalité.

At No. 8 Rue d'Anjou La Fayette died in 1834 (tablet); Benjamin Constant died at No. 29 in 1830.

At the *Place St-Augustin* the Boul. Haussmann crosses the Boul. Malesherbes. On the N. side is the fashionable church of **St-Augustin,** an early and tasteless example of the use of iron in church-construction (1860–71), by *Baltard*. Above the triple archway of the façade are statues of Christ and the Apostles by *Jouffroy*. Within, the wall-paintings in the transept-chapels are by *Bouguereau*.

The statue of Joan of Arc in front of the church is a replica of the statue at Reims by Paul Dubois.—In the *Square Henri-Bergson* (r.) are a statue of Paul Déroulède (1846–1914), the statesman, by *Landowski*, and 'Quand Même', a marble group by *Mercié*, a copy of the group at Belfort commemorating the defence of that city in 1870–71. It formerly stood in the Tuileries Gardens.

At the corner of the Rue de la Pépinière, on the E. side of the Place, is the *Cercle Militaire*. This street is continued E. by the RUE ST-LAZARE to the **Gare St-Lazare,** the terminus of the western region of S.N.C.F. Georges Feydeau, the writer of farces, intending to stay a week while his family moved house, stayed from 1909 to 1919 at the *Hôtel Terminus*.

Mme Vigée-Lebrun died at No. 29 Rue St-Lazare in 1842. No. 89 in the RUE DE ROME was the home of Stéphane Mallarmé from 1875. In the RUE D'AMSTERDAM lived Edouard Manet (in 1879–83; at No. 77), Jules Favre (in 1868–75; at No. 91), and Alexandre Dumas (from 1854; at No. 97).

The continuation of the Rue St-Lazare, between the station and La Trinité, is the S. boundary of the QUARTIER DE L'EUROPE, the streets of which are named after the chief cities of Europe. The Rue de Londres leads from La Trinité across the Rue d'Amsterdam to the *Place de l'Europe*, formed by a huge iron bridge over the railway lines. Beyond this, at No. 14 Rue de Madrid, formerly a Jesuit college, is the **Conservatoire National de Musique et de Déclamation,** founded in 1765 as the Académie Royale de Chant, amalgamated with the École de Déclamation Dramatique in 1786 and refounded in 1795 by Bernard Sarette, and removed to this site in 1911 from the Faubourg Poissonnière.

The COLLECTION OF MUSICAL INSTRUMENTS (open Thurs and Sat, 2–4, closed 13 July–30 Sept) at the end of the courtyard, on the first floor, originated in the fine Clapisson Collection. It includes the violins of Lulli, Kreutzer, and Sarasate, Beethoven's clavichord, Marie-Antoinette's harp, and many other instruments of great historical and artistic value. The library, on the second floor (open weekdays, 10–5), possesses the most complete series in existence of musical scores, books on music, and valuable MSS. (including Mozart's 'Don Giovanni').

The Rue de Lisbonne continues the Rue de Madrid W. to the BOULEVARD MALESHERBES, a fine modern thoroughfare leading from the Madeleine past St-Augustin to the Porte d'Asnières (1½ m.). We follow the boulevard (r.) past the Av. Vélasquez, which leads to the Musée Cernuschi and Parc Monceau, and cross the Boul. de Courcelles. At the junction of the Boul. Malesherbes with the busy Av. de Villiers is the *Place Malesherbes.*

On the N.W. side is the bronze statue of Dumas père (1802–70), by Gustave Doré, with figures of D'Artagnan and three readers on the pedestal; on the S.E. is the statue of Dumas fils (1824–95), by St-Marceaux, with the 'Dame aux Camélias' among the figures on the pedestal. Here also is a monument to Sarah Bernhardt as Phèdre, by F. Sicard (1926).

Shortly before it reaches the Porte d'Asnières, the Boul. Malesherbes crosses the *Place de Wagram.* Sarah Bernhardt (1844–1923) died at 56 Boul. Péreire, a little to the right.

Farther off to the right is the **Quartier des Batignolles,** which gave its name to a school of impressionist painters under the leadership of Manet.

The AVENUE DE VILLIERS, which bears to the left at the Place Malesherbes, leads to the *Place Pereire* and the Porte Champerret. At No. 43 (l.) is the **Musée Henner** (adm. 1 fr.; open daily except Mon, 2–5), an admirably arranged gallery illustrating the work of *Jean-Jacques Henner* (1829–1905), the Alsatian painter. The house and paintings, mainly studies in the nude, were bequeathed to the nation by M. and Mme Jules Henner, nephew and niece of the artist, in 1924.—The painter Puvis de Chavannes (1824–98) died at 89 Av. de Villiers. The striking church of *Ste-Odile* (1938–46), to the r. (N.) of the Porte Champerret, designed by J. Barge, is built of concrete and brick and has fine stained glass by F. Décorchemont.

15   THE EASTERN DISTRICTS

A   Belleville and the Buttes-Chaumont

MÉTRO stations: Line 11 from *République* to *Porte des Lilas*; *Stalingrad, Jaurès* (lines 2, 5, 7); and line 7 thence to *Place des Fêtes.*

From the Place de la République (Rte 13B) the Rue du Faubourg du Temple leads N.E. towards Belleville. We soon reach the line of the **Canal Saint-Martin,** an early 19C work linking the Bassin de la Villette with the Seine. The S. section as far as the Place de la Bastille was covered in 1860 by Haussmann to make the broad Boulevard Richard Lenoir. We follow the Quai de Jemmapes northwards passing several locks.

Beyond the first lock the Avenue Richerand leads right to the large ***Hôpital St-Louis** (1450 beds), a hospital for skin diseases founded by Henri IV and built by Claude Vellefaux (1607–12); it is an excellent and now rare example of the style of Louis XIII. The splendid courtyards and chapel may be viewed on Thurs and Sun, 1–3.

At the corner of the Rue des Écluses St-Martin and the Rue de la Grange aux Belles was a small graveyard for foreign Protestants (now built over). Paul Jones was buried here in 1792, but his body was subsequently exhumed and is now in the Naval Academy at Annapolis. In the block of houses to the N. was the site of the *Gibet de Montfaucon*, the 'Tyburn' of Paris, set up in the 13C, and finally removed in 1790. It proved fatal to three 'surintendants de finances': Enguerrand de Marigny, who erected it, and Jean de Montaigu, who repaired it; Semblançay, who was careful not to touch it, fared no better. Here Olivier le Daim, confidential barber of Louis XI (1484'; comp. Quentin Durward), was hanged, and Coligny's body was exposed.

We join the Boulevard de la Villette which bears left over the canal to the PLACE DE STALINGRAD, or *Rond Point de la Villette*. The *Rotonde* here is one of the toll-houses built by Ledoux in 1789.

To the N.E. extends the dreary QUARTIER DE LA VILLETTE. Between its two main thoroughfares lies the **Bassin de la Villette,** a large dock, serving as the terminus of the *Canal de l'Ourcq* and *Canal de St-Denis*, and connected also with the Seine (Bassin de l'Arsenal) by the *Canal St-Martin*.—At the end of the Rue de Flandre, beyond the Canal de St-Denis, are the **Abattoirs de la Villette,** the largest slaughter-houses in Paris, built by Baltard (visitors apply to the porter; gratuity). Foot-bridges over the Canal de l'Ourcq connect the abattoirs with the *Cattle Market* (*Marché aux Bestiaux*), which is busiest on Mon and Thurs mornings. The meat and poultry markets from the Halles are to be transferred here.

From the Av. Jean-Jaurès the Av. Laumière leads S. to the Place Armand-Carrel in which are the main entrance to the Buttes-Chaumont and the *Mairie of the 19th Arrondissement*. The ***Parc des Buttes-Chaumont,** the most picturesque of the Paris parks (59½ acres), is situated in the midst of the industrial district of BELLEVILLE. It was laid out under Haussmann's régime in 1866–67 by Alphand and Barillet on the bare hills ('monts chauves'; 275–330 ft) of Belleville, which had till then been used as the rubbish-dump of Paris. The great quarries of gypsum ('plaster of Paris') were ingeniously transformed into rock-scenery.

These heights were the scene of the Battle of Paris in 1814 and were held in 1871 by the Communards, who were, however, dislodged by bombardment from Montmartre (of which the park commands a notable *View). In the park are a lake with an island, a waterfall, a grotto, three cafés-restaurants, a marionette theatre, etc.

The Rue Fessart leads S.E. from the park crossing the Rue de la Villette, where at No. 51 the painter Rouault (1871–1958) was born, and continuing to the Gothic-revival church of *St-Jean-Baptiste*, in the RUE DE BELLEVILLE, erected by Lassus in 1854–59. Beyond the church a cul-de-sac at No. 213 leads to the *Regard de la Lanterne*, an inspection house (1583) of the Belleville aqueduct, which was already bringing water to Paris in the time of Philip Augustus. To the E. the Rue de Belleville passes the *Cimetière de Belleville*, the highest point in Paris (419 ft). An inscription to the right of the entrance in the Rue du Télégraphe records that Claude Chappe here experimented with the aerial telegraph that was to announce the victories of the French Revolutionary Wars. The Rue de Belleville crosses the Rue Haxo, No. 79 in which, to the right, is the **Chapelle des Otages,** built in 1936–38 on the site of the *Villa des Otages*. We walk through the little passage to the right of the chapel and turn left. Here, on 26 May 1871, fifty-two hostages held by the Commune, including Jesuit priests, National Guards, and police, were shot in front of the wall at the end of the garden. In front is the ditch into which their bodies were flung. In a little courtyard (r.) are a statue of Père Olivaint, the Jesuit superior, and the Pavillon de la Tourelle in a room of which the fate of the victims was decided; also a small building where five cells of the Jesuit priests in the Prison de la Roquette have been reconstituted (comp. below).

The Rue de Belleville ends at the Porte des Lilas, where the *Stade Nautique Georges Vallerey* is used for international swimming events.—The Avenue Gambetta (followed by line 3 of the Métro) leads S.W. from Porte des Lilas to Père Lachaise (comp. below), while Métro line 11 follows the Rue de Belleville directly to République.

B   Père-Lachaise

MÉTRO stations: *Père Lachaise* (lines 2, 3) and line 3 from *République* to *Gambetta*.

From the Place de la République the AVENUE DE LA RÉPUBLIQUE leads E.S.E. to (1 m.) the N.W. corner of Père-Lachaise, crossing (l.) the BOULEVARD JULES-FERRY and (r.) the BOULEVARD RICHARD-LENOIR, which runs above the Canal St-Martin to the Bastille. The 'Foire aux Jambons' and 'Foire à la Ferraille' (noted for spurious antiques) are held here during Holy Week and in October. The Avenue de la République ends at the Place Auguste-Métivier, crossed by the BOUL. DE MÉNILMONTANT.

In the latter, opposite the main entrance of Père-Lachaise, is (r.) the Rue de la Roquette, on the N. side of which is the *Prison de la Petite-Roquette* (for women), built in 1899 on the site of the **Prison de la Grande-Roquette**. Outside, the five stones on which the guillotine used to be set up are still to be seen. It was in La Roquette, used in 1853–99 for condemned prisoners awaiting execution, that Abp Darboy, M. Deguerry, curé of the Madeleine, and other hostages of the Commune were shot in 1871.

*Père-Lachaise, or the *Cimetière de l'Est*, is the largest (116 acres) and most fashionable cemetery in Paris; its tombs form an open-air sculpture-gallery in a splendid garden with examples of most of the French sculptors of the 19C. Father La Chaise, from whom it derives its name, was the confessor of Louis XIV and lived in the Jesuit house rebuilt in 1682 on the site of the chapel. The property, situated on the side of a hill, from which Louis XIV, during the Fronde, watched the troops under Condé fight those under Turenne, was bought by the city in 1804 and laid out by Brongniart. The cemetery has since been considerably extended on the E. On All Saints' and All Souls' Days ('Jour de la Toussaint' and 'Jour des Morts'; 1 and 2 Nov) Père-Lachaise is visited by over 100,000 persons. The first interments were those of *La Fontaine* and *Molière*, whose remains were transferred hither in 1804 (Section 25). The popular monument of the 12C lovers *Abélard and Héloïse* (Section 7) was set up in 1779 at their abbey of the Paraclete and removed hither in 1817; the canopy is composed of sculptured fragments collected by Lenoir from the abbey of Nogent-sur-Seine. In the E. corner of the cemetery (Section 97) is the *Mur des Fédérés*, against which the last of the Communards were shot in 1871 and to which the Socialists of Paris bring tributes every year on the anniversary (28 May). Here also is a monument to many thousand Frenchmen who died in German concentration camps or during the Resistance of 1941–45. Most visitors will be impressed by Bartholomé's sublime *Monument aux Morts* (Section 4).

The names of the illustrious dead interred here are too numerous to list in detail; in addition to those already noted, however, many of the following monuments are outstanding: to the authors *Alfred de Musset* (d. 1857), *Alphonse Daudet* (d. 1897), *Beaumarchais* (d. 1799), *Béranger* (d. 1857), *Balzac* (d. 1850; bust by David d'Angers), *Henri de Régnier* (d. 1936), *Oscar Wilde* (d. 1900; monument by Epstein); *Proust* (d. 1922), *Guillaume Apollinaire* (d. 1918), and *Colette* (1873–1954); to the composers *Rossini* (d. 1868), *Chopin* (d. 1849), *Bizet* (d. 1875); to the painters *Géricault* (d. 1824), *J. L. David* (d. 1825), *Ingres* (d. 1867), *Daubigny* (d. 1878), *Daumier* (d. 1879), *Delacroix* (d. 1864), *Corot* (d. 1875), *Modigliani* (d. 1920); also *Sarah Bernhardt* (d. 1923) and *Rachel* (d. 1858); *Thiers* (d. 1887); *Michelet* (d. 1874); *Marshal Ney* (d. 1815); and *Sir Sidney Smith* (d. 1840). For further details a guide-plan of the cemetery may be obtained for a nominal sum from the keeper's lodge at the main entrance.

In the Rue de Bagnolet, to the E. of the cemetery, is *St-Germain-de-Charonne*, a small rustic church of the 13–15C, restored in the 19C, and the only church apart from St-Pierre-de-Montmartre which has kept its cemetery, the centre of the former village of Charonne. To the S.W. of the cemetery lies the Rue Planchat with the impressive concrete church of *St-Jean-Bosco* (1937), by Rotter. The lofty tower contains a remarkable carillon of twenty-eight bells.—The Rue de Charonne, still preserving a few 17–18C houses, prolongs the Rue de Bagnolet westwards towards the Bastille.

The AVENUE GAMBETTA (1⅓ m. long), beginning at the Place Auguste-Métivier, skirts the N. side of the cemetery, leaving on the left the hilly quarter of *Ménilmontant*. In the Square Gambetta (r.) are a number of sculptures, including 'Le Mur', a bas-relief by Moreau-Vauthier (1909), dedicated to the victims of the Revolutions. The avenue crosses first the Place Martin-Nadaud, and then the Place Gambetta, with the *Mairie of the 20th Arrondissement*. The Av. Gambetta goes on N.E. to the *Porte des Lilas*.

C   The Faubourg St-Antoine and Bercy

MÉTRO stations: *Bastille, Nation* (lines 1, 8) and the stations on both lines between; also *Bercy* to *Nation* (line 6).

Almost due E. from the Place de la Bastille issues the RUE DU FAUBOURG-ST-ANTOINE, leading to (c. 1 m.) the Place de la Nation and forming the main artery of the FAUBOURG-ST-ANTOINE, a quarter memorable in the history of the Revolutions of 1789 and 1848. It was the scene of a skirmish during the Fronde (1652), when Turenne defeated Condé. Since the late 13C it has been noted for the manufacture of furniture. The Rue du Faubourg-St-Antoine preserves many 18C houses and courtyards. At No. 1 Fieschi hatched the plot against Louis-Philippe. At No. 61, to the left, at the corner of the Rue de Charonne, is the *Fontaine Trogneux* (1710). To the right, at the junction of the Av. Ledru-Rollin, is the statue, by Boverie, of Baudin, representative of the people for the department of the Ain, killed in 1851 on a barricade in front of No. 151 (tablet), while inciting the Parisians to protest against the coup d'état of Napoleon III.

Farther on (r.) the *Square Trousseau* occupies the site of the *Hospice des Enfants-Trouvés* in the graveyard of which the Princesse de Lamballe was buried, after her corpse had been paraded through the streets. On the same side is the *Hôpital St-Antoine*, rebuilt in 1905 but retaining an important part of Lenoir's 18C building for the former Abbaye de St-Antoine des Champs.

The Rue St-Bernard, nearly opposite, leads N. to the church of **Ste-Marguerite**, built in 1634 but many times altered and enlarged. It is believed that Louis XVII, who in all probability died at the Temple, aged 10, was buried in the graveyard with other victims of the Revolution.

The approach to the Place de la Nation from the Place de la République is made by the BOULEVARD VOLTAIRE (1¼ m.). Beyond the church of *St-Ambroise*, in the early Gothic style by Ballu (1863–69), the boulevard crosses the Place Léon-Blum (formerly Place Voltaire), with the *Mairie of the 11th Arrondissement* on the N. The Rue de la Roquette leads hence E. to Père-Lachaise and W. to the Place de la Bastille.

The spacious circular **Place de la Nation,** formerly the *Place du Trône* (named after the throne erected for Louis XIV's triumphal entry with Maria Theresa), is the meeting-place of the chief thoroughfares of the E. districts of Paris. No fewer than 1300 victims of the Terror were guillotined on this spot in 1794. In the centre rises the *Triumph of the Republic*, a colossal bronze group by Dalou. On the E. side of this 'circus' are two pavilions, built as toll-houses by Ledoux in 1788, each surmounted by a Doric column 100 ft high. On the columns are statues of Philip Augustus (by Dumont) and of St Louis (by Etex), with allegorical sculptures below.

On the S.W. of the Place is the *Collège Moderne Arago*, beside which the Av. Dorian leads to the Rue de Picpus. Ninon de l'Enclos had a villa in the latter (No. 12). At the end of the garden of No. 35, a convent of Augustinian nuns, is the little *Cimetière de

Picpus (gratuity; open 1–4.30 or 7), a private burial-ground for 'émigrés' and descendants of victims of the Revolution; the tombstones display the names of the most illustrious families of France. In the first section lie *Gen. La Fayette* (d. 1834; American soil was specially sent to cover his coffin, and the United States flag surmounts his grave), Montalembert (d. 1870), and members of the families of Chateaubriand, Crillon, Gontaut-Biron, Tascher de la Pagerie, Choiseul, La Rochefoucauld, Du Plessis, Montmorency, Talleyrand-Périgord, Rohan-Rochefort, Noailles, Quélen, etc., as well as sixteen Carmelites of Compiègne martyred in 1794. In the second section are buried members of the house of Salm-Kyrburg and those guillotined on the Place du Trône, among them André Chénier.

The COURS DE VINCENNES, a wide avenue leading E. from the Place de la Nation, is the scene every year in Easter week of the Foire aux Pains d'épice, a festival dating back to the 10C when the last disciples of St Anthony distributed bread made with honey and aniseed. The avenue is prolonged by the Av. Gallieni and the Av. de Paris beyond the line of the old fortifications to the *Château de Vincennes* (see Rte 34).

From the Place de la Bastille the RUE DE LYON, on the right of the Gare de la Bastille, leads S. to the handsome **Gare de Lyon,** the terminus of the railways to Geneva, Lyons, Marseilles, etc. The BOULEVARD DIDEROT, which passes the front of the station, leads from the Pont d'Austerlitz to the Place de la Nation.

The AVENUE DAUMESNIL, diverging from the Rue de Lyon (l.), leads to the Porte Dorée and (1¾ m.) the Bois de Vincennes. It crosses the Boul. de Reuilly at the Place Félix-Eboué, with a fountain adorned with lions by Davioud. Just beyond (r.) is the striking modern church of *St-Esprit* (1928–35), by Paul Tournon, with flat domes recalling St Sophia at Constantinople. The interior is adorned with mural paintings by Maurice Denis and others.

In the BERCY quarter, between the Av. Daumesnil and the Seine, is the huge *Entrepôt des Vins*, bonded warehouses with 115 wine-cellars, facing the quay. The roads of the quarter are named after great French wines.

In the RUE DE CHARENTON, which runs S.E. from the Place de la Bastille, is the *Hospice des Quinze-Vingts*, an asylum for 300 blind persons founded by St Louis in 1260. The building was before 1775 the Caserne des Mousquetaires-Noirs. The houses at Nos. 20–25 are worth noting. Nos. 40–60 occupy the site of the Couvent des Filles-Anglaises de la Conception, which from 1635 to 1655 accepted only daughters of English parents. Farther on we intersect the Av. Ledru-Rollin, leading (r.) to the Pont d'Austerlitz.

16   THE JARDIN DES PLANTES AND FAUBOURG ST-MARCEL

MÉTRO stations: *Jussieu* (lines 7 and 10); *Gare d'Orléans-Austerlitz* (lines 5 and 10; these two stations for the Jardin des Plantes); *St-Marcel, Campo-Formio* (line 5); *Place d'Italie* (lines 5, 6, 7); *Quai de la Gare, Chevaleret, Nationale* (line 6).

From the Pont de Sully and the E. end of the Boul. St-Germain the QUAI ST-BERNARD leads S.E. past the *Halle aux Vins*, a huge bonded warehouse for wine, on the site of the Abbaye de St-Victor (where Thomas Becket and Abélard stayed). This is to be transferred to Bercy and replaced by new buildings for the Faculty of Science of the University, work on which has already started. The quay then skirts the Jardin des Plantes to the semi-circular PLACE VALHUBERT, in which is its main entrance and, on the farther side, the **Gare d'Austerlitz,** the terminus of the railway to Toulouse, etc.

The **JARDIN DES PLANTES,** officially the *Muséum National d'Histoire Naturelle*, 60 acres in area, combining the attractions of a menagerie, botanical gardens, and natural history galleries, is one of the most popular of Paris

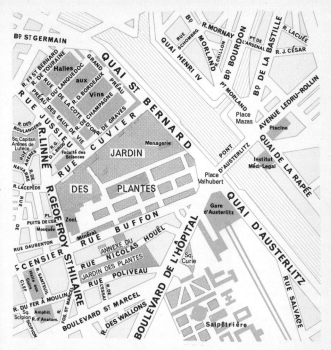

resorts, in spite of its out-of-the-way situation. Its collection of wild and herbaceous plants is unrivalled; in May and June the peonies make a magnificent show.

ADMISSION. The *Gardens* are open free daily from sunrise to sunset; besides the main entrance (see above) there are other entrances in the Rue Cuvier (N.W. side) and Rue Geoffroy-St-Hilaire (W. side). *Menagerie, Reptile House,* and *Aquarium,* daily 9–5 or 7; 1,40 fr. *Zoological Galleries,* daily exc. Tues, 1–5, 0,50 fr. *Alpine Garden* (summer only), Mon–Fri 9–12, 2–5, Sun 9–12, 1 fr.; conducted tours only on Sat 2–5.

Founded in 1626 under Louis XIII as a 'physic garden' for medicinal herbs by the royal physician Guy de la Brosse, the garden was first opened to the public in 1650. Its present importance is due mainly to the great naturalist Buffon, who was superintendent in 1739–88 and greatly enlarged the grounds. In 1793 it was reorganized by the Convention under its present official title, and provided with twelve professorships. The animals from the royal collection at Versailles were brought to form the nucleus of a menagerie. Many distinguished French naturalists have taught and studied here, and are commemorated by monuments in the garden or near by.

Facing the main entrance is a statue of Lamarck (1744–1829), beyond which three main walks traverse the botanic garden.

To the left, along the Allée Buffon, are the *Anatomical Gallery* and the *Botanical Gallery.* At the far end of the last is the trunk of one of the first locust-trees (Robinia pseudoacacia) in Europe, introduced from N. America by Jean Robin in 1601. To the left a special exit in the Rue Buffon leads to the *Musée du Duc d'Orléans* (No. 45, opposite), the principal attraction of which is the hunting collection of the Duke of Orleans (d. 1928), bequeathed by him to the nation. On the left of the Allée Haüy, which prolongs the Allée Buffon, are the *Mineralogical and Geological Galleries,* with the *Library* (c. 500,000 vols. and 2500 MSS.) at the far end, and *Buffon's House,* occupied by him from 1773 to his death, beyond. To the right are the *Zoological Galleries,* in the N. vestibule of which is the tomb of Guy de la Brosse (d. 1641).

On the right, at the end of the central alley, is the *Jardin d'Hiver* (adm. 1 fr.), with houses for tropical plants and cacti. Opposite the tropical house is the **Alpine Garden*, while behind the cactus house is the *Butte*, a hillock with a maze, the first cedar of Lebanon to be planted in France (by Jussieu, 1734), and, on the summit, a bronze belvedere.

Farther back, near the N. wall of the gardens, are *Chevreul's House* and *Cuvier's House*. To the right are the *Administrative Building*, in a mansion of 1785, and the *Amphithéâtre*, or Lecture Hall, of 1788 (restored).

The *Menagerie*, recently much improved, occupies most of the N. side of the gardens. It is entered from the Allée Cuvier, which leads from the Jardin d'Hiver to the main entrance. The monkey house and the elephants are of special interest; and the reptile house is well arranged.

Opposite the exit at the N.W. corner (near Chevreul's House) is the *Fontaine Cuvier* (1840), with groups of animals, including an anatomically impossible crocodile. Thence the Rue Geoffroy-St-Hilaire leads S. to the *Institut Musulman* (entr. in the Place du Puits de l'Ermite, behind), opened in 1925, with a **Mosque**, the first to be erected in France, in the 14C Moorish style (open daily 2–5 or 6.30, except Fri and Muslim holidays; adm. 1,50 fr.). Here are also to be found a restaurant and bazaar and the *Institut Franco-Musulman*.

The Rue Geoffroy-St-Hilaire ends at the Boul. St-Marcel (see below). Near their junction was the *Cimetière Ste-Catherine*, where the bodies of Mirabeau and other revolutionaries were reburied after being ejected from the Panthéon.

The straight BOULEVARD DE L'HÔPITAL extends from the Place Valhubert to (c. 1 m.) the Place d'Italie, intersecting the busy artisan quarter of the FAUBOURG ST-MARCEL and passing the Square Marie-Curie, in which is a statue (1880) of Philippe Pinel (1745–1826), the alienist. On the S. side is the huge **Hôpital de la Salpêtrière**, founded in 1656 as a home for aged or insane women, on the site of a gunpowder factory. In 1684 a criminal wing was added, in which Manon Lescaut and Mme de la Motte were gaoled. Aged couples were later admitted and in 1790 there were said to be 8000 people living here. The main building, by Le Vau and Le Muet, dates from 1657–63; the domed church, built in 1670–77 by Libéral Bruant, has statues by Etex (after 1832) on the front; the whole is a notable example of the austere magnificence of the architecture of the period and to be compared with the Invalides.

Dr Charcot (1825–93), the hypnotist, is commemorated by a monument to the left of the gateway; his consulting-room, laboratory, and library have been preserved intact.

Farther on in the boulevard, on the same side, is the *Hôpital de la Pitié*, transferred in 1911 from the Rue Lacépède, where it had been founded by Marie de Médicis in 1612.

To the right (W.) of the Boul. de l'Hôpital, opposite the Salpêtrière, diverges the BOULEVARD ST-MARCEL, leading to (½ m.) the Av. des Gobelins and continued by the Boul. Arago.

From the E. end of the Boul. de Port-Royal the AVENUE DES GOBELINS leads S. On the right is the **Gobelins* (adm. 0,50 fr., 2–4, Wed, Thurs, Fri; guided tours are arranged by the Service des Monuments Historiques), the famous tapestry factory which has been a state institution for over three hundred years. Most of the buildings have retained their 17C aspect. The museum building (1914), facing the avenue, contains a good collection of ancient and modern tapestries, but has not yet been reopened to the public.

The original royal tapestry factory at Fontainebleau was removed to Paris by Henri II. Suspended during the 16C Religious Wars, the industry was revived by Henri IV and installed in 1601 in the buildings of the Gobelins (two brothers Gobelin, who had set up dye-works here on the banks of the Bièvre, comp. below, at the end of the 15C). In 1662, under Colbert, the royal carpet factory of the *Savonnerie*, started in 1604 in the galleries of the Louvre and subsequently moved to a 'savonnerie' (soap-factory) at Chaillot, was placed under the same management (it transferred its workshops to the Gobelins' factory in 1826). In 1667 Louis XIV added the royal furniture factory, and Charles Le Brun and then Pierre Mignard were appointed as directors. The workshops of the Beauvais tapestry, destroyed by bombardment in 1940, have likewise been transferred here.

In the Cour d'Antin is a marble statue of Le Brun, by *Cordier* (1907). On the left are the two WORKSHOPS, separated by a staircase. The tapestry is woven on high-warp looms, several of which date from the time of Louis XIV. The weaver works on the reverse side of the tapestry, having the painting which he is copying behind him and reflected in mirrors. The average amount of tapestry that a weaver can produce in a day is 2¼ sq. inches.—A passage beyond the second workroom leads to a staircase descending to the workshops for Savonnerie carpets. A covered passage leads hence to the Cour Colbert, with a bronze statue of Colbert, and the former chapel, the treasure of which is exhibited in the sacristy.

The Rue Berbier-du-Mets, behind the factory, covers the Bièvre which used to flow here between the dye-works and workshops. The hunting lodge of M. de Julienne, the patron of Watteau, at No. 7 is now in the Square René Le Gall or JARDIN DES GOBELINS. This garden has been laid out on the former allotments of the tapestry workers, the N. end of which is occupied by the huge, but not unpleasing, building of the *Mobilier National* (by Perret; 1935). The entrance is decorated by two fine mastiffs, by Abbal. The charming garden, bordering the Rue Croulebarbe and Rue Corvisart, is strictly formal in its adherence to the 16C style.

The Av. des Gobelins ends on the S. at the **Place d'Italie,** the meeting place of seven great thoroughfares. On the N. side is the *Mairie of the 13th Arrondissement* (1867–77).

17   OBSERVATOIRE, MONTPARNASSE, AND THE CITÉ UNIVERSITAIRE

MÉTRO stations: *Montparnasse* (lines 4, 6, 12, 14); *Vavin* (line 4); *Raspail* (lines 4 and 6); *Denfert-Rochereau* (lines 4, 6, S.); *Mouton-Duvernet, Alésia, Porte d'Orléans* (line 4); *Edgar-Quinet, St-Jacques, Glacière* (line 6); *Port-Royal, Cité Universitaire* (S.).

This excursion forms a natural pendant to the exploration of the Latin Quarter (Rte 4), the area described forming the S. extension of the learned and student quarter dependent upon the Sorbonne.

The quarter lying E. of the S. part of the Boul. St-Michel and S. of the Quartier Latin contains a notable number of scientific institutions. At the E. corner of the Luxembourg Gardens diverges the RUE GAY-LUSSAC, in which, at the corner of the Rue St-Jacques, is the *Institut Océanographique*, founded by Prince Albert I of Monaco in 1910.

Adjacent are the *Institut de Géographie*, and, in the Rue Pierre-Curie, the *Institut de Biologie Physico-Chimique* (Fondation S. de Rothschild), the *Institut Henri-Poincaré*, the *Institut du Radium*, the *Laboratoire de Chimie-Physique*, and the *Institut de Chimie Appliquée*.

George Sand's last Paris home, in the 1870's, was in the Rue Gay-Lussac (No. 5); in 1864 she was living at 97 Rue des Feuillantines (now Rue Claude-Bernard).

The Rue Gay-Lussac ends at the Rue Claude-Bernard and Rue d'Ulm. At the corner (45 Rue d'Ulm) is the *École Normale Supérieure*, established in 1794 for the training of teachers. On the wall of the building is a medallion of Pasteur commemorating the site of the laboratory where he worked from 1864 to 1888. Among pupils here have been Taine, Bergson, Lavisse, Péguy, Romain Rolland, Giraudoux, Jules Romains, Jean Jaurès, and Ed. Herriot.

To the S.W. runs the historic RUE ST-JACQUES, the N. section of which has been described in Rte 4. No. 218 occupies the site of the house of Jean de Meung, part-author of the 'Roman de la Rose' (c. 1300). *St-Jacques-du-Haut-Pas*, a plain classical building (1630–88), the favourite church of the Jansenists, was completed only because of the help of the Duchesse de Longueville. No. 354, at the corner of the Rue de l'Abbé-de-l'Épée, is the *Deaf and Dumb Asylum* (*Institution des Sourds-Muets*), founded by the Abbé de l'Epée about 1770 and taken over by the State in 1790; the building, once the Oratorian seminary of St Magloire, was reconstructed in 1823. In the courtyard is a statue of the Abbé, by Félix Martin, a deaf-and-dumb sculptor (1789).

A little farther on (Nos. 269 and 269bis; l.) is the **Schola Cantorum** (visitors admitted; gratuity), a free conservatoire of singing and music, established in 1894 by three pupils of César Franck, including Vincent d'Indy. The buildings (1674) are those of the English Benedictine monastery of St Edmund, founded in France in 1615, and established on this site from 1640 to 1818; they still belong to the English Roman Catholic authorities. The salon and the staircase are good examples of the Louis-XIV style; the lower part of the chapel is now the concert hall; and the 'chapelle ardente', where James II's body lay in state, is now a bedroom.

James II (d. 1701), his daughter Louisa (d. 1712), and the Duke of Berwick (d. 1734), his son by Arabella Churchill, are buried here; the bodies, hidden at the Revolution, are probably in the catacombs, which were once accessible from the house. The last burial here was that of Berwick's second son Charles (d. 1787). Dr Johnson (1775) and Benjamin Franklin were guests of the English monks here.

The door between columns, at the end of the courtyard of No. 284, was once an entrance to the distinguished Carmelite convent to which Louise de La Vallière, mistress of Louis XIV, retired in 1674. Another relic of the convent is a crypt beneath No. 25 Rue Henri-Barbusse, at the back.

At Nos. 277–279 Rue St-Jacques (l.) the handsome ***Val-de-Grâce**, since 1790 a military hospital, was from 1624 the house of the Benedictine nuns of Val-Profond, whose patroness was Notre-Dame du Val-de-Grâce. The present much more extensive buildings, however, were erected by Anne of Austria in thanksgiving for the birth of Louis XIV (1638), and the first stone of the new work was laid by the young king in 1645. In the courtyard is a bronze statue of Baron Larrey (1766–1842), Napoleon's surgeon, by *David d'Angers*.

François Mansart was succeeded as architect before 1649 by *Jacques Lemercier*, and after 1654 the buildings were finished by *Le Muet* and *Le Duc*, the church being completed in 1667. The remains of royal personages interred here, including Anne of Austria and Henrietta Maria, were dispersed at the Revolution. The Army Medical School was added in 1850.

The façade of the church (by Mansart) is a fine example of the Jesuit style and the ***Dome** (by Le Duc) is one of the best in France. The sculptures within are by *François* and *Michel Anguier*, *Pierre Sarazin*, and others. The high altar, with its six huge twisted marble columns, is inspired by Bernini's in St Peter's at Rome; but the sculptured Nativity on it is a copy of M. Anguier's original (now at St Roch). The huge painting in the dome is by *Pierre Mignard*; in the chapel on the right of the choir is a portrait of Anne of Austria, borne by an angel; and in the Chapel of the Sacrament, behind (shown by the sacristan), is the Communion of the Angels, by *J. B. de Champaigne*.

The imposing cloister may be visited on Tues, Thurs, Sat, and Sun (12.30–5); the *Musée du Service de Santé*, in the former refectory, illustrates the history and practice of military hygiene, and may be seen (Mon–Fri 9–11, 2–5).

Val-de-Grâce was only one of the religious houses with which this district abounded until the Revolution. Just to the N. are the Rue des Ursulines and Rue des Feuillantines,

whose names recall vanished convents; almost opposite were the Carmelites; to the S. stood Port-Royal (see below); and, in the Boul. d'Arago beyond, the *Hôpital Broca* stands on the site of a 13C Franciscan nunnery. In the buildings of the Feuillantines Victor Hugo spent part of his boyhood (1808–13; inscription).

The Rue St-Jacques ends on the S. at the BOULEVARD DE PORT-ROYAL, which continues the line of the Boul. du Montparnasse S.E. from the Carrefour de l'Observatoire to the Av. des Gobelins, opposite the Boul. St-Marcel (comp. Rte 16). At the W. end, on the S. side, is the *Hôpital de la Maternité* (no adm.), which has occupied since 1814 the buildings of *Port-Royal*, a branch of the Jansenist abbey of Port-Royal-des-Champs. In the chapel (service on Sun at 10.30), built by Le Pautre in 1647, is the tomb of Angélique Arnaud (d. 1661), the famous reforming abbess. Conducted lecture-tours are organized by the Service des Monuments Historiques.

At the S. end of the Boul. St-Michel, and crossed by the Av. de l'Observatoire, is the **Carrefour de l'Observatoire,** with a monument to the explorer François Garnier (1839–73), by Puech. On the E. was the *Bal Bullier*, once the most famous of the public dance-halls of the Left Bank. Here now stands the CENTRE SPORTIF UNIVERSITAIRE JEAN-SARRAILH (1958–62), with rooms for students and sport and medical facilities. On the W. is Rude's *Statue of Marshal Ney (1769–1815; "le brave des braves"), near the spot where the marshal was shot for espousing Napoleon's cause on his return from Elba. Balzac lived in 1830–36 at 3 Rue Cassini, which crosses the Av. de l'Observatoire beyond the Boul. du Montparnasse, and wrote 'La Peau de Chagrin' there. Alain Fournier lived at No. 2. In the garden at the end of the avenue is a statue of the astronomer Le Verrier (1811–77), by Chapu, situated exactly on the meridian of Paris and facing due N. To the E., at No. 38 Rue du Faub. St-Jacques, the Société des Gens de Lettres occupies the *Hôtel de Massa* (1784), removed from the Champs-Élysées in 1927.—The **Observatoire** was founded by Louis XIV and built by Claude Perrault in 1667–72.

The four sides of the Observatoire face the cardinal points of the compass, and the latitude of the S. side is the recognized latitude of Paris (48° 50' 11″ N.). A line bisecting the building from N. to S. is the meridian of Paris (2° 20' 14″ E. of Greenwich), which was till 1912 the basis for the calculation of longitude on French maps. The Observatoire is the headquarters of the *Bureau International de l'Heure*, which sends out the correct time by wireless.—Visitors who have obtained permission from the director are shown round on the 1st Sat of the month, at 2.30.

On the first floor of the main building is a *Museum* of instruments, and the contents of the *Rotunda* in the W. tower illustrate the history of astronomy. The room on the second floor, on the pavement of which is traced the Paris meridian, contains old physical and astronomical instruments.—A shaft descending from the roof of the main building into the catacombs has been used for the study of falling bodies. In the E. cupola is the great equatorial telescope of 14 in aperture.

From the Carrefour de l'Observatoire the BOULEVARD DU MONTPARNASSE, 1 m. long, leads N.W. to the Rue de Vaugirard and Rue de Sèvres, crossing the Boul. Raspail at the busy *Carrefour Raspail*. Here stands the famous *Statue of Balzac, by Rodin, erected here in 1939. The statue was commissioned in 1898 by the Société des Gens de Lettres, but rejected by them as unsuitable.

The cross-roads may be regarded as the centre of the quarter of **Montparnasse.** Its well-known cafés, *Le Dôme* and *La Rotonde* (partly submerged in a cinema), succeeded those of Montmartre in 1910–40 as the principal artistic and bohemian rendezvous of Paris, but, like Montmartre, the district was invaded by a horde of pseudo-bohemians and would-be artists. The cafés and 'boîtes' of the neighbourhood, however, still attract a variegated and polyglot crowd.

Although large and tall new buildings are springing up, the neighbouring streets are full of associations with the artists of the late 19 and early 20C, from Whistler and Rodin to Picasso and Braque. Trotsky and his fellow-revolutionists frequented the Rotonde in the

years before 1917. No. 3 RUE CAMPAGNE-PREMIÈRE was one of Whistler's earliest
homes in Paris; he and Rodin had studios in the same building (demolished) at 132 Boul.
de Montparnasse. Rilke and Modigliani also lived in Rue Campagne-Première. In 1892–
1900 Whistler's studio was at No. 86 RUE NOTRE-DAME DES CHAMPS, and his
academy of painting was in the Passage Stanislas (now Rue Jules-Chaplain). An earlier
dweller in the Rue Notre-Dame-des-Champs was Victor Hugo (at No. 11 in 1827).
Sainte-Beuve, the critic, lived at No. 19 in this street, and died at No. 11 RUE DU
MONTPARNASSE in 1869.

Beyond the church of *Notre-Dame des Champs* (1867–76), the boulevard
crosses the *Place du 18 juin 1940*, on the S. side of which was the old Gare
Montparnasse. In the Rue l'Arrivée is the *Musée du Montparnasse* (adm.
daily exc. Sun and Mon, 3.30–6.30), which with photographs, letters, and
paintings evokes the history of Montparnasse in its heyday.

The hideously obtrusive new *Gare de Montparnasse* in the Av. de Maine, terminus of
the western region of French Railways, is the first of a series of skyscrapers in the
Maine–Montparnasse redevelopment plan.

From the PLACE BIENVENUE the Boul. de Vaugirard leads W. to the Boul.
Pasteur. In the Rue du Docteur-Roux, to the left of the latter, is the **Institut
Pasteur,** founded by Louis Pasteur in 1887–89, and built by private subscription.
It is devoted not only to scientific research (carried on also in the *Institut de
Chimie Biologique*, opposite) but also runs a hospital (Hôpital Pasteur, 213 Rue
de Vaugirard) for the free treatment of infectious diseases. The Institut also
carries out research work on tuberculosis in special laboratories at No. 96 Rue
Falguière. In front of the Institut is a bronze sculpture by Truffot, the shepherd
Jupille wrestling with a mad wolf. Jupille, who later became concierge of the
institute, was one of the first to be inoculated by the Pasteur method. In the
Crypt (adm. on application to the Director of the Institut) is the *Tomb of
Pasteur* (1822–95). In the gardens is the tomb of Dr Emile Roux (1853–1933),
inventor of the treatment of diphtheria by serum-injection.

On the left of the Av. du Maine, just N. of the Place Bienvenue, is the Rue Antoine-
Bourdelle. Here the *Musée Antoine-Bourdelle* (daily except Tues 10–12, 2–5) occupies
the house (No. 16) of the famous sculptor (1861–1929) and contains his furniture, many
works of art, and personal souvenirs, bequeathed by Mme Bourdelle.
In the Rue de Vaugirard to the left is the round church of *Notre-Dame de Salette*
(1965) built to replace St-Lambert de Vaugirard.

In the BOULEVARD EDGAR-QUINET, which runs E. from the Place Bienvenue
to the Boul. Raspail, is the main entrance of the **Cimetière Montparnasse,** laid
out in 1824 and ranking third in size (45 acres) and interest among the Paris
cemeteries. Like that of Montmartre, this cemetery contains the graves of many
artists and writers, including Baudelaire and Maupassant, also Dalou, Rude
and Houdon, sculptors, and César Franck, d'Indy and Saint-Saëns, musicians.

From the Av. de l'Observatoire the Av. Denfert-Rochereau leads S.W. to
the **Place Denfert-Rochereau,** a busy centre of traffic. Known as the Place
d'Enfer until 1879, it received its present name in honour of the brave defender
of Belfort, Col. Denfert-Rochereau (1823–78). In the centre is the *Lion of
Belfort*, a reduced copy of Bartholdi's splendid sculpture at Belfort, and the
gardens are adorned with statues.

In the Av. Denfert-Rochereau (formérly Rue d'Enfer; originally Rue Inférieure,
because lower than Rue St-Jacques) No. 72 is the *Hôpital St-Vincent-de-Paul*, for
children, with a chapel of 1650–55; while two other hospitals (Nos. 88–92) occupy the
site of the *Infirmerie Marie-Thérèse*, where Chateaubriand lived in 1826–38 in the grounds
of this institute (for aged priests) directed by his wife.

The BOULEVARD ST-JACQUES runs E. from the Place Denfert-Rochereau to be continued by the Boul. Auguste-Blanqui. In the Rue de la Tombe-Issoire (r.) is the church of *St-Dominique* (1913–21), by Gaudibert.

The name is derived from the epic of Guillaume d'Orange, who killed in this street Isoré, king of the Saracens, hence Tombe d'Isoré and the present corrupted name. At No. 101 the artists Gromaire and Lurçat lived.

On the S.W. side of the Place Denfert-Rochereau, in one of the octroi pavilions of the old Barrière d'Enfer (1784), is the main entrance to the **Catacombs.** These are a vast series of underground quarries, dating from the time of the Romans and extending from the Jardin des Plantes to the Porte de Versailles and into the suburbs of Montrouge, Montsouris, and Gentilly. In the 18C they were converted into a charnel-house for bones removed from disused Paris graveyards, and in 1944 they became the main command post of the Resistance movement. Among the remains transferred hither were those of Mme de Pompadour (d. 1764) and of victims of the massacres under the Terror.

Visitors are escorted round the catacombs at 2 p.m. on the 1st and 3rd Sat of each month, from 16 Oct to 30 June; every Sat from 1 July to 15 Oct; adm. 0,50 fr. (torches should be carried). The tour lasts over an hour and is apt to be a trifle monotonous.

We descend a spiral staircase and follow a narrow passage for about ten minutes, leading to the huge charnel-house (ossuaire), which is said to contain the remains of nearly three million persons and consists of a labyrinth of galleries lined with bones and rows of skulls. The exit is in No. 36 Rue Remy-Dumoncel, E. of the Av. du Général-Leclerc.

The AVENUE DU GÉNÉRAL-LECLERC, which runs S. from the Place Denfert-Rochereau, was the route of Leclerc's entry into Paris on 25 Aug 1944. On the left of the avenue is the *Hospice La Rochefoucauld*, a 'maison de retraite' founded by the Frères de la Charité under the title of Maison Royale de Santé. At the Place Victor-Basch, farther on in the Av. Leclerc, is *St-Pierre de-Montrouge*, built in the style of the early Italian basilicas (by Vaudremer; 1863), with a tower 165 ft high.

In the Rue Hippolyte-Maindron (W. of the Av. du Maine) the sculptor Alberto Giacometti lived and worked from 1927 to his death in 1965.

The renamed Avenue René-Coty leads S. from the Place Denfert-Rochereau to the **Parc de Montsouris,** some 40 acres in area. The *Bardo* (100 yds N. of the Boul. Jourdan) is a reproduction of the Bey's Palace at Tunis, which was made for the exhibition of 1867 and is now used as a meteorological observatory. In the N.E. corner of the park is a lake with a pleasant summer-restaurant (Pavillon du Lac).

Among the artists who lived in this tranquil quarter was Georges Braque (1882–1963), in the Rue du Douanier.

Facing the park, on the opposite side of the Boul. Jourdan, is the **Cité Universitaire** (founded 1922), a group of large hostels for students, extending some three-quarters of the length of the boulevard towards the Porte d'Orléans, with a station on the railway to Sceaux. The twenty-six different foundations, each built in the characteristic architecture of its own country, as well as four or five specialized university buildings, present a wide diversity of styles. The enormous *Maison Internationale* (1936), a students' club, with swimming-baths, theatre, and restaurants, and the Swiss foundation (by Le Corbusier; 1933) are especially noteworthy. Opposite the United States foundation (1928) is a bronze statue of Tom Paine (1737–1809). The British hostel was opened in 1937. To the S. of the Maison Internationale, in the Av. Vaillant-Couturier, is the church of the *Sacré Cœur* (1936).

18   FAUBOURG ST-HONORÉ AND NEUILLY

MÉTRO stations: *Villiers* (lines 2 and 3); *Monceau, Courcelles,* and *Ternes* (line 2); *Étoile* (lines 1, 2, 6); *Argentine, Porte Maillot, Sablons, Pont de Neuilly* (line 1).— ELECTRIC TRAINS every 10 min. from the Gare St-Lazare to *Neuilly-Porte Maillot* (change at Pont Cardinet).

The RUE DU FAUBOURG-ST-HONORÉ, the N.W. continuation of the Rue St-Honoré, stretches from the Rue Royale to the Place des Ternes (1¼ m.), following the course of the medieval road from Paris to the village of Roule. It became fashionable at the end of Louis XIV's reign and in the 18C its splendid mansions made it the rival of the Faubourg St-Germain. It intersects an aristocratic quarter and contains several fashionable dress shops, as well as jewellery, print, and curiosity shops. Near its S.E. end is the *Hôtel de Charost* (1723), now the **British Embassy.** The mansion was bought in 1803 by Pauline Bonaparte, Princesse Borghese (much of whose furniture remains), and was sold by her to Wellington in 1814 for £32,000. The *Embassy Church* is in the Rue d'Aguesseau, opposite.

Sydney Smith preached an eloquent sermon in the dining-room (then serving as a chapel), and here were married Berlioz and Harriet Smithson (with Liszt as best man) in 1833 and Thackeray in 1836. Lytton died in the embassy in 1891 and Somerset Maugham was born there in 1874.

No. 41 in the Faubourg is the *Hôtel Pontalba,* built by Visconti and restored by E. de Rothschild; No. 45 was the residence of Thiers at the end of his term as President, in 1874. Farther on is the **Palais de l'Élysée** (no adm.), at the corner of the Av. de Marigny. This mansion (since greatly altered and enlarged) was built as the *Hôtel d'Evreux* in 1718. It was occupied later by Mme de Pompadour, Murat, Napoleon I (who signed his abdication here in 1815), Wellington, and Napoleon III, who lived here as President from 1848 until he went to the Tuileries as Emperor (1852) when the Élysée again became the residence of visiting heads of state. Since 1873 it has been the official residence of the President of the Republic. Here Queen Elizabeth II stayed on a state visit in 1957. On the right, at the Place Beauvau, is the *Ministère de l'Intérieur* (Home Office), built c. 1770.

The Rue des Saussaies leads from Place Beauvau to the Place des Saussaies and the **Hôtel du Maréchal Suchet* (No. 16 Rue de la Ville-l'Évêque), built by Boullée c. 1750.

No. 100 Rue du Faubourg St-Honoré was Fanny Burney's residence in 1806–12. Beyond the Av. Matignon is the Rue de Penthièvre (r.), in which No. 26 may occupy the site of Benjamin Franklin's city office. In the Rue Jean-Mermoz (l.), formerly Rue Montaigne, Gambetta lived in 1871–78 and Meyerbeer died in 1864. At the busy crossing of the Rue La Boétie, where the Av. Franklin-Roosevelt comes in on the left, is the classical church of ST-PHILIPPE-DU-ROULE, built in 1769–84 by Chalgrin on the site of the parish church of Roule, and later enlarged.

The *Salle Gaveau,* at 45 Rue La Boétie, is one of the most important concert halls in Paris.

The very long RUE DE COURCELLES runs N.W. from St-Philippe-du-Roule (see above), viâ the Place Péreire, to the Porte de Courcelles. No. 38 in this street (then No. 48) was Dickens's lodging in 1846; at No. 45 Proust lived in 1901–05; and Saint-Saëns occupied No. 83bis.

Just beyond the crossing with the Boul. Haussmann (comp. below) is the *École Pratique des Gardiens de la Paix* (police school); in the garden is a monument to members of the force who fell in the Liberation of Paris in 1944. The buildings are those of the old *Hôpital Beaujon* (1784), removed in 1935 to new premises at Clichy, where Eleutherios Venizelos (1864–1936), the Greek statesman, died. Just opposite, at No. 11 Rue Berryer, is the *Maison des Artistes* (the former Hôtel Salomon-de-Rothschild), where Pres. Doumer was assassinated in 1932.

No. 252 (r.), beyond the Av. Hoche, is the *Salle Pleyel* (1927), the largest concert hall in Paris. A little farther is the Place des Ternes, whence the Av. de Wagram leads left to the Étoile.—Alfred de Vigny died at No. 6 Rue d'Artois (l.) in 1863.

The Rue de Monceau runs N.E. Théodore Herzl, proselyte of Zionism, lived at No. 8 in 1891–95. No. 28, belonging to Prince Murat, was the residence of President Wilson during the Peace Conference of 1919; No. 32 was the birthplace of Oscar I of Sweden (1799–1859), son of Bernadotte. To the left the Avenue Ruysdaël leads to the S. entrance of the Parc Monceau.

The *Parc Monceau, a charming little park of 217 acres, derives its name from a vanished village and is a remnant of the private park laid out by Carmontelle in 1778 for Philippe-Égalité d'Orléans, duc de Chartres, the father of Louis-Philippe. It was then known as the 'Folie de Chartres'. It is surrounded by the handsome private houses of this quarter, which has retained its elegance and is now one of the most aristocratic in Paris.

Various 'picturesque' details in the taste of the 18C have survived from the Orléans park, such as the brook, the tomb in the woods, and the *Naumachie*, a large oval basin in the N.E. part of the park. The Corinthian colonnade on this lake is supposed to have come either from the Château du Raincy or from the great rotunda begun to the N. of the cathedral of St-Denis by Catherine de Médicis as a mausoleum for Henri II and herself. At the main entrance in the Boul. de Courcelles is the round *Pavillon de Chartres*, a toll-house of the 18C city wall erected by the Farmers-General, now used as the keeper's lodge. Near the Naumachie is a large Renaissance arcade from the old Hôtel de Ville. The park is adorned with sculpture, and there are monuments to Maupassant; to the composer Ambroise Thomas; to Gounod; to the poet and dramatist Edouard Pailleron (1834–99), by Bernstamm; and to Chopin (1809–49).

No. 7 in the Av. Vélasquez, leading E. from the park to the Boul. Malesherbes, is the **Musée Cernuschi** (adm. 0,50 fr., free on Sun; daily exc. Tues 10–12, 2–5 or 6), the nucleus of which is an interesting collection of Chinese and Japanese art formed by M. Cernuschi, who, in 1895, bequeathed it, together with his house, to the city of Paris. The bronzes are specially valuable and there is a remarkable painting of the T'ang period (Horses and grooms), but the whole collection is surpassed by the Musée Guimet. Good temporary exhibitions are frequently held. At No. 63 Rue de Monceau, behind it, is the **Musée Nissim de Camondo** (Rte 31).

To the N. of the Parc Monceau is a quarter favoured by the wealthier literary and artistic set, with specially fine houses in the Rue de Prony and Rue Jacques de Bingen. Edmond Rostand wrote 'Cyrano de Bergerac' at No. 2 Rue Fortuny, where he lived in 1891–97. In the Rue de Chazelles were formerly the foundries where the Statue of Liberty was cast (inscription No. 25). National styles of architecture have been used for the *Swedish Church* (1913) in the Rue Médéric, and for the *Russian Church* (1859–61) in the Rue Daru (W. of the park).

By the Avenue de Messine, in which No. 26 was the birthplace and home of André Tardieu (1876–1945), we may descend to the W. section of the Boulevard Haussmann (comp. Rte 14c). No. 102 was Proust's home in 1905–1919, with his notorious 'sound-proof' room lined with cork. To the W. of the Av. de Messine the Boul. Haussmann passes (No. 158; r.) the **Musée Jacquemart-André** (Rte 27), and crosses successively the Rue de Courcelles and the Rue du Faubourg-St-Honoré.

Beyond the Rue du Faubourg-St-Honoré the line of the Boul. Haussmann is continued by the AVENUE DE FRIEDLAND to the Place de l'Étoile (Rte 7). Balzac died in 1850 in the cross-street that bears his name (then Rue Fortunée; No. 22, demolished, replaced by No. 12, tablet); No. 7 is the *Syndicat d'Initiative de Paris.*—Beyond the Étoile we follow the wide AVENUE DE LA GRANDE-ARMÉE. This is the continuation of the Champs-Élysées towards Neuilly and contains numerous motor and cycle shops. No. 65 (l.) is the headquarters of the *Touring-Club de France.*

Neuilly (66,000 inhab.) is the most fashionable suburb of Paris. Its N. half, formerly the park of Louis-Philippe's château, built in 1740 and burned down by the mob in 1848, was developed as a colony of elegant villas, but latterly the construction of large blocks of flats has practically overwhelmed the distinctive character of the neighbourhood.

We leave Paris by the *Porte de Neuilly.* On the left is the *Porte Maillot,* the N.E. entrance to the Bois de Boulogne, and on our right is the semicircular PLACE DE VERDUN, with the Boulevard Pershing leading N. to the PLACE DES TERNES. On the right in the Boul. Pershing is the **Chapelle St-Ferdinand,** a mausoleum in the Byzantine style, erected in 1843 on the site of the inn in which Ferdinand, duc d'Orléans, son of Louis-Philippe, died as the result of a carriage accident on 13 July 1842. Within (apply at No. 13; gratuity), on the right, is the cenotaph of the duke, who is buried at Dreux. It was designed by Ary Scheffer and sculptured by Trequeti.

From the Place des Ternes the AVENUE DU ROULE runs W. to the Place Winston-Churchill. At the Collège Ste-Croix de Neuilly, in the avenue, Sacha Guitry and Henri de Montherlant were pupils. The church of *St-Pierre* (1898) has a central porch and two side doors redecorated in 1946–48 with sculptures by students of the Atelier Saupique of the Beaux Arts. On the N. side of the Place is the BOULEVARD d'INKERMANN, with the huge red buildings of the *Lycée Pasteur* on the left. Beyond the church, to the W., is the *Hôtel de Ville,* with a bust of Mermoz (1901–36), the aviator, and a statue of Parmentier (1737–1813), who made his first experiments in potato growing at Neuilly.

The wide AVENUE DE NEUILLY continues the Av. de la Grande-Armée N.W. to the handsome *Pont de Neuilly,* the stone bridge of Perronet (1768–72), almost entirely rebuilt in 1935–39. A bridge was first built here in 1606 after Henri IV and Marie de Médicis were almost drowned here. There is a charming view downstream to the Temple of Love. Théophile Gautier died in 1872 at a house on the site of No. 33 Rue de Longchamp, on the left a little short of the bridge; and in the old cemetery, a little nearer Paris, is the grave of Anatole France (1844–1924). The *Île du Pont,* by the bridge, has been laid out in decorative gardens.

Beyond the bridge, the *Av. du Général de Gaulle,* between *Puteaux* (l.) and *Courbevoie* (r.), ascends to the ROND-POINT DE LA DÉFENSE. Here stands the *Palais de la Défense* (by Zehrfuss; 1959), a domed edifice covering 18 acres, specially built to house exhibitions and shows, notably those hitherto accommodated in the Grand Palais. It is the first of a new group of monumental buildings projected in the district between the Pont de Neuilly and the Rond-Point, to which Métro line 1 is to be extended.

At *Courbevoie,* where Carpeaux died in 1875, is a museum (adm. Thurs, Sat, and Sun 2–6), largely devoted to his life and work. It occupies the grounds of the Château de Bécon (destroyed in 1943–44), where Richelieu and Thiers lived.

19   THE BOIS DE BOULOGNE

MÉTRO stations: *Porte Maillot* (line 1): *Sablons* (line 1); *Porte Dauphine* (line 2); *Ranelagh* (line 9); *Porte d'Auteuil* (line 10).—ELECTRIC TRAINS from the Gare St-Lazare to *Neuilly-Porte Maillot, Av. Foch, Av. Henri-Martin, Passy, Auteuil-Boulogne* (change at Pont-Cardinet).

There are five entrances to the Bois from Paris, namely the *Porte Maillot* and *Porte Dauphine* (the two main entrances), and the *Porte de la Muette, Porte de Passy,* and *Porte d'Auteuil.*

The usual approach to the Bois is the handsome AVENUE FOCH, opened in 1855 as the Av. de l'Imperatrice, leading from the Étoile to (⅔ m.) the Porte Dauphine. Not far from the Étoile is (r.) a monument to Adolphe Alphand (1817–91), who laid out the Bois and most of the other parks of Paris in their present form. On the left (No. 59) is the **Musée Dennery** (open Sun, 1–4 or 5, free; closed Aug), a collection of oriental art formed by the dramatist Dennery (1811–99) and bequeathed by him to the State together with his house. The ground floor houses the *Museum of Armenian Art.* Anatole France was buried in 1924 from his home at No. 5 Villa Saïd (r.), and Raymond Poincaré died ten years later at 26 Rue Marbeau, just to the N. No. 80 Avenue Foch was the residence of Claude Debussy (1862–1918). At the end of the Av. Foch, above the Bois, Mont-Valérien and the hills of St-Cloud, Bellevue, and Meudon come into sight. At the Porte Dauphine is the huge *NATO Building,* by Carlu (1955–59), in plan like the letter A and incorporating gifts of materials from the member-nations.

The ***Bois de Boulogne,** familiarly known as the 'Bois', lies just outside Paris on the W., and is bounded by the former fortifications on the E., the Seine on the W., Neuilly on the N., and Boulogne on the S. Though the châteaux of La Muette, Madrid, and Bagatelle and the abbey of Longchamp were erected on its borders, until 1852 the Bois was utterly neglected. In that year it was handed over by the State to the city of Paris and was transformed into the present splendid park of 2155 acres, the favourite promenade of the Parisians. The model was Hyde Park, which had so impressed Napoleon III.

Between the Porte Maillot and the Porte d'Auteuil the former fortifications skirting the E. side of the Bois have been replaced since 1930 by handsome streets adorned with memorial and other sculpture.

From the Porte Dauphine we follow the Route de Suresnes, straight in front of the gate, past the Pavillon Dauphine (café-restaurant) to (½ m.) the ROND ROYAL or CARREFOUR DU BOUT-DES LACS (Pavillon Royal Restaurant, expensive), whence two roads follow respectively the right and left (W. and E.) banks of the Lac Inférieur to (¾ m.) the Carrefour des Cascades at the other end. The road on the W. bank skirts the sports-grounds of the *Racing Club;* that on the E. bank passes the starting-point of the ferry to the island in the lake.

The Route de Suresnes, which diverges at the Rond Royal, leads S.W. to the Carrefour de Longchamp, crossing the *Carrefour de la Croix-Catelan* (18C pyramid of stones), and skirts the enclosure of the **Pré-Catelan,** in which is a fashionable café-restaurant (dancing, etc.) and an open-air theatre in the 'Jardin Shakespeare'. The garden contains all plants and trees mentioned in Shakespeare's plays. Arnaud Catelan was a troubadour murdered here c. 1300.

The LAC INFÉRIEUR, or *Grand Lac,* has two islands, linked together by a bridge, on the larger of which is the Chalet des Îles, a café-restaurant (reached by boat from the E. shore). The *Carrefour des Cascades*, with a waterfall under which one may walk, divides it from the LAC SUPÉRIEUR. The *Butte Mortemart*, beyond the S. end of the latter, overlooks the *Champ de Courses d'Auteuil*, a racecourse devoted to steeplechasing (second half of June).

From the Carrefour des Cascades the Route de la Vierge aux Berceaux, passing a monument to thirty-five young men who were shot by the Germans in August 1944, leads W. to the CARREFOUR DE LONGCHAMP, at the S.W. end of the long Allée de Longchamp. Here the *Grande Cascade*, an artificial waterfall c. 30 ft high, descends from the Mare de Longchamp. Just beyond is the famous Longchamp racecourse.

The **Hippodrome de Longchamp**, opened in 1857, is one of the premier racecourses of the world, and has stands accommodating 10,000 spectators. It is seen at its gayest on the day of the 'Grand Prix' in June. The Route des Tribunes, which skirts the N. and W. sides of the racecourse, passes the windmill (restored) which is practically the only relic of the *Abbey of Longchamp*, founded in 1256 by St Isabella of France, sister of St Louis.— The Route de Suresnes, going on from the Carrefour to the Pont de Suresnes, passes the Polo Ground.

From the Carrefour de Longchamp the Rue de Longchamp runs N., passing (l.) the *Champ d'Entraînement*, dating from 1856, now used for football, tennis, etc., beyond which appears the Seine with the large *Île de Puteaux*, with more sports grounds. On the right is the beautiful park (59½ acres) of **Bagatelle** (adm. 0,50 fr.; restaurant), famous for its rose-garden. Once the residence of Lord Hertford (d. 1870) and Sir Richard Wallace (d. 1890), it was purchased by the city in 1904 and is open to the public till dusk (cars not admitted). Art exhibitions are sometimes held in the little palace, which was built for a wager within sixty-four days by Bélanger for the Comte d'Artois (1779), afterwards Charles X.

The broad ALLÉE DE LONGCHAMP or *Allée des Acacias*, nearly 2 m. long, which leads from the Carrefour de Longchamp to the Porte Maillot, is a favourite resort of riders in the Bois. About ½ m. from the Carrefour it is crossed by the *Allée de la Reine-Marguerite*, another wide drive. These were the only existing roads kept by Haussmann.

This leads from the Porte de Boulogne (1¼ m.; r.) to the Porte de Madrid (⅔ m.). Beside the latter once stood the *Château de Madrid*, built in 1528 by Francis I, who is said to have named it in memory of his captivity in Spain. It was gradually demolished between 1793 and 1847, but has given its name to the S.W. quarter of Neuilly.

Farther on the Allée de Longchamp passes (l.) the enclosure of *Les Acacias*, with pigeon-shooting and skating clubs, between which and the Jardin d'Acclimatation lies the *Mare de St-James*, a pond surrounded by charming woods. Beyond is the *Pavillon d'Armenonville*, a fashionable café-restaurant.

At the N. end of the Bois, between the Porte des Sablons and the Porte de Neuilly (entrances at both gates), is the **Jardin d'Acclimatation** (open daily 9–7 or dusk; adm. 0,50 fr.; a miniature railway runs from the Porte Maillot to the entrance). The gardens, founded in 1854 with the idea of introducing and acclimatizing exotic animals and plants, have since 1919 developed into a high-class playground for children, with a small-scale zoo.

Outside the Bois to the S. is the former village of **Boulogne** (originally Menus-lès-St-Cloud), which was given its name by Philip IV, who was a devotee of N. D. de Boulogne-sur-Mer. The church, *Notre-Dame-des-Menus*, preserves its 14C nave but has been frequently restored, notably by Viollet-le-Duc. The town hall is the masterpiece of Tony Garnier (1931–32). Notable are the *Jardins Albert Kahn*, Quai du Quatre-Septembre (adm. daily 2–6, 16 Mar–15 Nov; 0,80 fr.).

Le Corbusier (1887–1965), the architect, lived here.

II THE LOUVRE AND OTHER GREAT COLLECTIONS

With the exception of the Musée de l'Armée, the Musée de Cluny, and the Musée Rodin, the Great Public Collections of Paris are situated on the N. side of the river. All are closed on Tuesday except the Conservatoire des Arts-et-Métiers. But all (with the exception of the Bibliothèque Nationale) are open on Sunday. A table of hours of admission appears in the Practical Information section.

20 THE COLLECTIONS IN THE LOUVRE

The Palais du Louvre as a building is described in Rte 1.

Entrances. The principal entrance is in the Pavillon Denon, the central pavilion on the S. side of the Square du Carrousel. Other entrances are by the Porte Barbet-de-Jouy, on the Quai du Louvre (200 yds W. of the Pont des Arts), in the Pavillon de La Trémoille, on the Quai des Tuileries, and in the Pavillon St-Germain-l'Auxerrois, on the E. side of the Cour du Louvre. Umbrellas must be left at the entrances.

Admission. The galleries of the Louvre are closed every Tuesday, and on New Year's Day; Ascension Day; 1 May; the second Wed after Easter and Whitsun; 14 July; 1 and 11 Nov; and Christmas Day. Also on 15 Aug, provided that this date does not fall on a Sunday. Otherwise, they are open daily 10–5; weekdays 1 fr. (0,50 fr. for those holding a student's card); Sun free (also on Thurs aft. for students). Some rooms are closed at midday (see notice board). No cameras admitted unless a special ticket has been obtained. All tickets, etc., are acquired in the Galerie de Vente (see below), where umbrellas must be given up (gratuity) at the cloakrooms; lavatories are at the far end of the Galerie de Vente.—Refreshments in the Pavillon Mollien.

Guide-Lectures (in English, etc.) on weekdays at 10.30 and 3; details are obtained in the Galerie de Vente.

History of the Collections. The nucleus of a royal art collection was formed by Francis I (d. 1547). At his request Leonardo da Vinci spent the last few years of his life in France, dying there in 1519. Henri II and his queen, Catherine de Médicis, carried on the tradition of their predecessor. Louis XIV made some notable additions to his collection of Old Masters, and Louis XVI acquired some important paintings of the Spanish and Dutch Schools. In 1793 the Musée de la République was opened to the public, and a large number of the most famous paintings in Europe, captured by the victorious Republican and Napoleonic armies, were exhibited here; though after 1815 the French Government was obliged by the Allies to return them to their former owners. Under Louis XVIII, the Vénus de Milo and over a hundred pictures were acquired. In 1848 the Museum became the property of the State, and an annual grant was made for the purchase of works of art; and these have been generously supplemented by private bequests. During the war years, 1939–45, the collections were dispersed, for the sake of security, throughout the country; since then practically all the collections have been restored to their permanent place.

GROUND FLOOR

We enter by the Pavillon Denon, on the S. side of the Square du Carrousel, and cross the Vestibule Denon to the Galerie de Vente and the cloakrooms beyond.

Greek and Roman Sculpture. GALERIE MOLLIEN (to the left as we return). On the floor and end walls are Byzantine mosaics from Kabr-Hiram (Phœnicia); at the end are fine Græco-Phœnician sarcophagi from Carthage. This gallery is used for temporary exhibitions.

The adjacent staircase (Escalier Mollien) and lift ascend to the galleries of paintings. On the first landing is a bronze copy of the Victory of Brescia.

From the GALERIE DENON (on the other side of the Vestibule), with more sarcophagi and bronzes from the antique cast for Francis I by Primaticcio from moulds brought from Italy, we reach the Escalier Daru, which ascends to the Picture Galleries (p. 132). On the top landing is the **Nike of Samothrace, or 'Winged Victory'.

This magnificent statue of Parian marble, the centrepiece of a fountain, was found in the Sanctuary of the Great Gods, on the island of Samothrace, in 1863. Further excavation in 1950 led to the discovery of the mutilated right hand (in a case on the right), and established the probable date of the statue as c. 200 B.C.; The breast and left wing are of plaster.

We pass to the left of the staircase, through the *Rotonde d'Anne d'Autriche* (p. 143) to the SALLE ARCHAÏQUE (Pl. 1). Greek sculpture of the 7–5C B.C.: 3098. Statuette of 'La Dame d'Auxerre'; 3101. Apollo of Paros; 2792. Torso of Apollo (Miletus); 3600. Draped kouros (6C), very unusual; 3104. The 'Rampin' head with a plaster cast of the equestrian figure (Acropolis Mus., Athens) to which it belongs (6C); *701. 'Exaltation of the Flower' (bas-relief); **686. Hera of Samos, one of the oldest and best authenticated works of island sculpture (c. 520 B.C.). The name Cheramues is inscribed on the mantle. 687, 688. Kouroi from Actium.

The SALLE DU PARTHENON (Pl. 2) is devoted to sculpture of the 5C B.C., the apogee of Greek art. Among the outstanding exhibits are: *738. Fragment of the East Frieze of the Parthenon at Athens (the greater part of the frieze, which represents the Panathenaic procession, is in the British Museum); 696. Frieze with Apollo and Hermes and nymphs and graces (early 5C), archaic in feeling, from Thasos; 736. Metope from the Parthenon, Centaur carrying off a Lapith woman; 737. Lapith head from another; 716–718. Metopes from the temple of Zeus at Olympia, with Hercules overcoming the Cretan bull, and presenting to Athene one of the Stymphalian birds. In the passage leading to the following room, *740. The 'Laborde Head', a fine head of a goddess from one of the pediments on the Parthenon. The SALLES DE PHIDIAS and DE POLYCLÈTE (Pl. 3, 4) contain replicas of 5 and 4C sculpture, including works by Pheidias and Polycleitus and their respective schools. *3070. Torso of Athene, known as the 'Medici Torso', a Roman replica of an original work of the Pheidian school. The statue was found in Rome by Ingres. 525. Venus Genetrix, 'Great Mother of Æneas' race'. The apple is an idea of the restorer; the original is attributed to Callimachus.—SALLES DE PRAXITÉLÈS (Pl. 5, 6). Replicas of works by Praxiteles and his school (4C B.C.), including 439. Venus of Arles, altered by Girardon; *441. Apollo Sauroktonos; *2184. Aphrodite of Cnidos, the most celebrated of Praxiteles's works.

SALLE DE LA VÉNUS DE MILO (Pl. 7). In the centre, **399. Vénus de Milo, one of the most beautiful and one of the most celebrated antiques that have come down to us. This famous statue, unrecorded by any ancient writer, was found in 1820 by a peasant in the island of Melos (Milo) in the Greek Archipelago. Purchased for 6000 francs by the French Ambassador in Turkey, it was presented to Louis XVIII, and restored in the Louvre. It was found in five fragments and is 6 ft 8½ in. in height. The goddess is nude to the waist; the drapery at the back is rough-hewn. The statue was once held to date from the 4C B.C., and much controversy revolved round the base and the disputed inscription to 'Agesandros, son of Menides, of Antioch on the Mæander'. It is now generally regarded as a copy by an unknown master of the 2 or 1C B.C., after a 4C original.

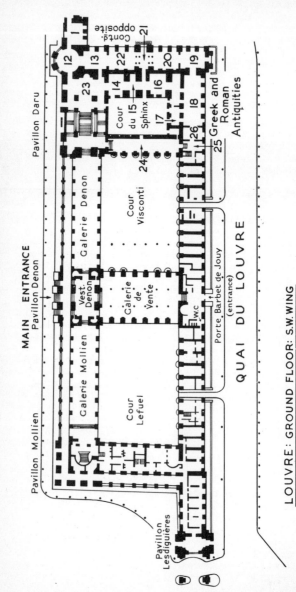

LOUVRE: GROUND FLOOR: S.W.WING

SALLE DE LYSIPPE (Pl. 8). Works after Lysippus, the great master of the Alexandrine period (4C B.C.). Note especially 83. Hermes fastening his sandal, antique copy of the original; and 448. Eros stringing his bow.—SALLE DES POÈTES GRECS (Pl. 9). *440. Bust or term of Homer, Hellenistic period (4–1C B.C.).—SALLE D'ALEXANDRE (Pl. 10). 436, 855. Two busts of Alexander the Great (336–323 B.C.), the latter after Lysippus; *1204. Head of Antiochus the Great (ruler of Syria, 223–183 B.C.); 79, 80. Seated figures of the philosophers

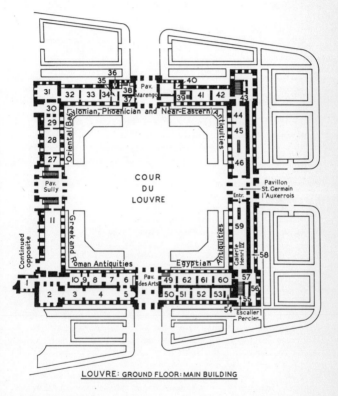

LOUVRE: GROUND FLOOR: MAIN BUILDING

Chrysippus and Thales; 3169. Young Egyptian (?) prince, delicately modelled (1C B.C.).

We pass through the CORRIDOR DE PAN (in the three cases on the right wall are female heads, fragment of a funerary stele, etc., of the 5–4C B.C.). On the right is the SALLE DES CARIATIDES (Pl. 11), so called from the Caryatids by *Jean Goujon*, which support the gallery at the far end. The other decorations and the chimneypiece at the nearer end are by *Percier* and *Fontaine* (c. 1806).— The gallery contains sculpture of the Hellenistic period. In the centre, opposite the first window, *527. Fighting Gladiator, or 'Borghese Warrior', signed on the tree-trunk by Agasias, an otherwise unknown sculptor of the late Hellenistic period (found at Anzio in the 17C). On the right, by the first window, 324. Wounded Gaul. In a recess (l.), Sleeping Hermaphrodite (the mattress added by Bernini). In the centre, *589. Huntress Artemis, known as 'Diana of Versailles' (c. A.D. 100), acquired by Francis I from Rome. Opposite the second window, 2240. Crouching Venus, known as the 'Vénus de Vienne'. On her back are traces of the left hand of a Cupid. On the left, between the second and third window, *542. Marsyas suspended by the wrists to the trunk of a pine tree. On the right, by the fifth window, *40. Boy with a goose, marble replica of a bronze attributed to Boethus (found at Rome in 1789).

We turn right through the Salle Archaïque into the ROTONDE D'ANNE D'AUTRICHE (Pl. 12) with ceiling-paintings by *Mauzaisse* and decorations in stucco by *Michel Anguier* (1653). To the right, *86. Borghese Vase, an antique replica of an original of the 1C B.C., decorated in relief with a Bacchic orgy. Busts or terms of philosophers.—To the left of the Rotonde is the SALLE DES BAS-RELIEFS HELLÉNISTIQUES (Pl. 13), with a ceiling by *Meynier*. In the centre, 666. Astrological altar, from Gabii, with heads of the twelve gods and the signs of the zodiac; on the walls, copies and originals of Greek bas-reliefs. The SALLES DES RELIEFS FUNÉRAIRES ET VOTIFS (Pl. 14, 15) are devoted to Greek stelæ, mostly of the 5–4 B.C.

COUR DU SPHINX. Antique monumental sculpture. N. Wall, *2825–29. Metopes and bas-reliefs from the architrave of the Temple of Assos (near Troy) in Asia Minor. The scenes represent Hercules battling against Triton, a banquet, processions of animals and centaurs, etc. W. Wall, 2881. Frieze from the Temple of Artemis at Magnesia on the Maeander, illustrating a battle between Greeks and Amazons (2C B.C.); below, fragments of the Temple of Didymaean Apollo at Miletus; *593. God of the Tiber, a colossal group, found, along with the Nile (now in the Vatican), in the 16C. In the centre, 3444. The Four Seasons, a huge mosaic from near Antioch (4C).—SALLE DES RELIEFS ROMAINS (Pl. 16). 975. Sacrifice to Mars, from the Temple of Neptune in the Campus Martius at Rome. 978, 1089. Augur consulting the entrails of a bull before the Temple of Jupiter in the Forum of Trajan, Rome (2C A.D.); 1096. Sacrifice of a pig, a goat and a bull (Rome, 1C A.D.); 1088 Fragment of the frieze of the Ara Pacis.—SALLE DES MUSES (Pl. 17). Roman busts of the Republican and Augustan periods. By entrance to Cour du Sphinx, *3445. Head of an unknown Roman woman (1C B.C.).—SALLE D'AUGUSTE (Pl. 18), with ceiling-paintings by *Matout*. Roman busts of the 1C B.C. to the 1C A.D. At the far end, between 1210. Nero as a youth wearing the golden 'bulla', and 682. Young girl, *1212. Statue of Augustus. On the left, *1207. Roman orator ás Mercury, a portrait of Octavius (later Augustus Cæsar), an almost intact statue of Parian marble, found at Rome, and signed 'Cleomenes of Athens, son of Cleomenes', on the tortoise at the foot. 1233. Head (in black basalt) of Octavia, sister of Augustus; 1208. Agrippa; 3498. Gaius, grandson of Augustus. Busts of Claudius, Caligula, and others.—SALLE DES ANTONINS (Pl. 19). This, and the three following rooms, with ceiling-paintings by *Romanelli*, contain busts and effigies of Emperors and others (1–3C), including (l.) 1205. Antinous as Osiris, the eyes of which were represented by semi-precious stones. Portraits painted on wood or canvas (2C A.D.).—SALLE DES SÉVÈRES (Pl. 20). On the right, 3440. Young Gaul.—SALLE DE LA PAIX (Pl. 21). In the centre, 1075. Julia Mammæa, mother of Alexander Severus, as Ceres.—SALLE DES SAISONS (Pl. 22). 3441. Bas-reliefs with the sacrifice of a bull to the Persian sun-god Mithras, found in the Mithraic grotto of the Capitol at Rome.—

VESTIBULE DES PRISONNIERS BARBARES (Pl. 23). Roman sculptures in coloured marbles: *1354. Old fisherman, a greatly restored statue in black marble with drapery in alabaster; *82 and *90. Pair of large shallow alabaster vases, remarkable for the acoustic properties by virtue of which a whisper uttered in one is distinctly heard at the other.

We turn left, past the Escalier Daru, into the SALLE DU PHÉNIX (Pl. 24), which is devoted to frescoes from Rome, Pompeii, etc. (1C B.C.–1C A.D.), and mosaics from N. Africa and Syria (1C B.C.–4C A.D.). The motifs are, for the most part, mythological. Paintings: on the left, P 23. Winged Genius (1C B.C.); P 1. Woman playing with a goat (Pompeii, 1C A.D.). Mosaics: *3443. Judgement of Paris (Antioch, 2C A.D.); 3442 The Phœnix (Antioch, 5C A.D.); on the right, 1880. Triumph of Neptune and Amphitrite (Constantine, 3C A.D.).—Down the steps at the end of the room are the two SALLES D'ART CHRÉTIEN (Pl. 25, 26), with fragments of mosaics, sarcophagi, and inscriptions from Italy, Gaul, and N. Africa (4–5C).

The department of the **Egyptian Antiquities** (Monumental Statuary) is entered either by the Pavillon St-Germain-l'Auxerrois (E. side of the Cour du Louvre), or by the staircase leading to the crypt from the second Salle de Praxitélès (Pl. 6, Greek and Roman Antiquities).

CRYPT. On the staircase (l.), C 26. Stele of Antef, first herald in the service of King Thothmes III (1504–1450 B.C.) and other steles of the 12th Dynasty. In the crypt, on the left, D 38. Stele dedicated by the Queen Hatshepsut to her father Thothmes (1530–1520 B.C.). On the ceiling, circular sandstone zodiac from the Temple of Hathor at Dendera. To the right, A 23. Colossal sphinx in pink granite, from Tanis (Lower Egypt, 22nd Dyn.). On the staircase, six canopic jars that contained the entrails of Apis bulls (18th Dyn.).—ROOM 1 (Pl. 49). A 24. Colossal statue of Seti II (19th Dyn.) in red sandstone.—On the wall (r.), Fragment of Coptic material from Antinoë (4 or 5C; comp. p. 129).

ROOM 2. (Pl. 50). SALLE DU MASTABA. To the right, *Sacrificial chamber of the 'mastaba' or tomb of Akhouthotep, a high Egyptian dignitary (c. 2500 B.C., 5th Dyn.), found at Sakkara and built of limestone; inscribed on the architrave above the door are the occupant's names and titles. Within, the walls are covered with vivid scenes in bas-relief of contemporary life in the Old Kingdom, as well as those depicting the funeral of the deceased; some of them among the finest extant examples of the art. The offerings of food and drink were placed on the table of pink granite, now by the window.

ROOM 3 (Pl. 51). A 39. Diorite statue of an official of the 3rd Dyn. (c. 2750 B.C.). C 287. *Stele of King Zet, known as the Serpent King, as his name is represented here by a serpent; the falcon, above, symbolizes Horus, the god of kingship. The sculpture was found in the king's tomb at Abydos (c. 3000 B.C.). In the recesses, bas-reliefs, and, against the N. wall, statues of the 4th and 3rd Dynasties.

ROOM 4 (Pl. 52). OLD KINGDOM (2650–2100 B.C.). Wall case in the passage Stele of Nefertiabet, in painted stone (4th Dyn.); she is seated before a table of offerings, dressed in a leopard's skin. *Three fine columns in pink granite with palm-leaf capitals; the column on the left is marked with the name of King Uni (5th Dyn.); the other two, which were taken by Rameses II, are undoubtedly of the same period. In the centre, Sarcophagus in the 'palace façade' style, found at Abu Roash (5th Dyn.). Statues, stelæ, etc., of the 4–6th

Dynasties. ROOM 5 (Pl. 53). In the centre, small limestone **Figure of a scribe seated cross-legged, known as the 'Scribe Accroupi'.

This statue, one of the masterpieces of the Old Kingdom, is remarkable for its lifelike appearance. The eyes are of white quartz, rock crystal, and ebony.

In the wall-cases, alabaster and stone vessels dating from pre-dynastic times to the 6th Dyn. (c. 3400–2300 B.C.). In the passage, limestone group of the official Raherka, and his wife Merseankh (5th Dyn.); altar-stele of Senpu (12th Dyn.).—ROOM 6 (Pl. 54). MIDDLE KINGDOM (2100–1750 B.C.). On the left (W. wall), fine limestone lintel of Sesostris III (1887–1850 B.C.); the king is shown making an offering of bread. In the recess (N. wall), Colossal royal statue in diorite. In a recess (W. wall), A 123. Sandstone statue of the scribe Mentuhotep. The relics on the E. wall should also be noted.—ROOM 7 (Pl. 55). On the right, in the cases: Statuette of Sesostris III, in green schist, and part of the head of the same king in grey granite; statue of a functionary of the 12–13th Dyn.; statue in black granite of Sesostris III, as an old man; wooden statue of the Chancellor Nakhti, from Assiut, one of the largest wooden funerary effigies known of this period (c. 2100 B.C.); Sesostris III, as a young man. In the left-hand case of the third recess, **Statue of stucco and painted wood known as the 'Porteuse d'Auge'.

A young girl, clothed in a tunic of netted pearls, carries on her head a little trough containing a joint of an ox—an essential of the funeral offering.

A 47. Red sandstone group of two high priests of Ptah, from Memphis (12th Dyn.). Wall-cases: on the right, Statuette of a royal concubine, the thumbs of which have been intentionally cut off; on the left, five amusing little wooden figures of girls carrying offerings. Huge statue of Sebekhotep IV (13th Dyn.).—ROOM 8 (Pl. 56). On the left, the inner case of the coffin of Chancellor Nakhti; note the two mystical eyes painted on the outside. In a case (l.), silver and lapis lazuli treasure discovered in four bronze caskets, marked Amenemhat II (1938–1904 B.C.), in the foundations of the temple at Tod. On the right, models of funerary boats for transporting the dead down the Nile. A portico with papyrus-like columns (13th Dyn.).—ROOM 9 (Pl. 57). To the left, limestone statue of the bull of Apis (comp. R. 12) of the 30th Dyn. (378–341 B.C.). A 70. Statue of the scribe Sethi, kneeling, and holding a naos containing a figure 'of Osiris (19th Dyn.). N. wall, huge basalt statue of Isis (Roman period). Around the room, canopic jars, stelæ, statues, etc.—The Galerie Épigraphique (ROOM 10) is temporarily closed.

The *Escalier Percier* ascends to the Egyptian rooms on the first floor (note the limestone Dog half-way up).

ROOM 11 (Salle Henri IV; Pl. 59). NEW KINGDOM. The end walls are divided into bays, containing sculpture, sarcophagi, naos, paintings, etc. Outstanding among these are: E. wall (r.), 3rd Bay, D 1. Sarcophagus of Rameses III, 'the last of the heroes' (20th Dyn.), the lid of which is at Cambridge; 5th Bay, *Painted bas-relief of Seti I and the goddess Hathor, from the tomb of the former (19th Dyn.); 7th Bay, Red granite fragment from the base of the obelisk of Luxor (Rte 1, with four cynocephali adoring the rising sun and cartouches of Rameses II.—W. wall, 2nd Bay, A 18. Base and feet of a huge pink granite statue of Amenophis III (18th Dyn.); a list of the peoples he subdued is inscribed on the base; 3rd Bay, A 19. Colossal head of Amenophis III, the right half of the face considerably eroded by sand and wind; also several statues of Sekhmet, the lion-headed goddess; Hathor capital of pink granite, from

Bubastis, where Sekhmet was especially worshipped; Dog's head in limestone; and, by the crypt-stairway, Statue of Nekht-Hor-Heb (late Saïte).

The crypt which leads to the Department of Asiatic Antiquities contains two Sarcophagi, the farther one being that of the Priest T'aho, with a frieze of jackals round the top, outside, and figures of Nephthys and Isis at the head and foot, within (26th Dyn.). On the left in the recess, *Wooden statue of Osiris with the diadem of Alef; in all probability this striking statue was actually worshipped as an idol.

We retrace our steps to R. 9 and turn right into ROOM 12 (Pl. 60), which contains mainly objects discovered by Mariette in 1850–53, in the Serapeum at Memphis. In the centre six of the limestone sphinxes which bordered the approach to the Serapeum for more than 250 yards. The big sphinx at the far end (post-Ptolemaic period) comes from Medamoud (found in 1931). Around the room, stelæ of Apis bulls, supposedly the incarnation of Ptah, the great god of Memphis; also sculptures, including the limestone statue of the grotesque god Bes (r.), from the temple of Nectanebo. The four canopic jars contained the entrails of two Apis bulls of the 18th Dynasty.

ROOMS 13, 14 (Pl. 61, 62) are devoted to objects of the Græco-Roman and Copto-Byzantine periods, following the last indigenous dynasty. Noteworthy (in R 13) are the funeral masks and a painting on wood of Christ and St Mennas; Coptic fabrics, including a dalmatic of the 3C; and bronze lamps and candlesticks. In R. 14 are sculptured fragments from a church at Bawît (5–6C); note the relief of St Sisinius spearing the serpent and (opposite; under window) of Horus spearing Set (the pre-Christian version of the subject); also Jonah emerging from the whale.

Oriental Antiquities. The visitor may enter either through the Salle des Caryatides (Pl. 11) or by the Pavillon St-Germain-l'Auxerrois (Egyptian Antiquities) to reach the Crypte Sully, which is situated underneath the Pavillon de l'Horloge or de Sully.

CRYPTE SULLY. Sculptural and architectural fragments from the Near East. 2nd Bay. In the centre, Jar in which were preserved the Dead Sea Scrolls (2C B.C. and 1C A.D.) found by Bedouin in 1947. **Moabite Stone, or stele of Mesha, king of Moab (896 B.C.), found in 1868 in a remote village E. of the Dead Sea.

The 34-line inscription, recording victories over the Israelites, in the reigns of Omri, Ahab, and Ahaziah, is one of the most important, if not the earliest example of the alphabetic writing which has come down to us from the Phœnicians through Greek and Latin.—In cases are small exhibits including jewellery, glass and metalwork, etc., and the Mount Carmel ewer (2–3C A.D.). By the Syrian Bay, Jupiter Dolichenus (Roman).

ROOM 1 (Pl. 27) Sumerian antiquities from Lagash (Mesopotamia), and Semitic reliefs and sculptures of the Akkadian dynasty (3000 B.C.) from Susa. Wall-case 1 (4th–3rd millennium). Bas-reliefs of a 'plumed figure' from Tello (Chaldæa) and of Ur-Nanshe, prince of Lagash, carrying a basket of bricks on his head, with his sons; bronze bull's head, etc. Opposite, *Stele of the Vultures, commemorating the victory of Eannadu, king of Lagash, over a rival city, Umma. In the centre, Silver *Vase of Entemena with a frieze of incised animals and the Lagash 'crest', a lion-headed eagle. Woman's head in alabaster and a vase decorated with palm leaves (Case 2). By exit, *Stele of the victorious Naram-Sin, king of Akkad.—R. 2 (Pl. 28). Sumerian antiquities of c. 2400 B.C., diorite *Statues of Gudea, ruler of Lagash. Case 13. Two large clay cylinders recording, in cuneiform, Gudea's skill as an architect. Case 10. 'Head with a turban' (Gudea), Goblet belonging to Gudea decorated with serpents and winged dragons with scorpions' tails. Small case, *Alabaster statuette of Ur-Ningirsu, son of Gudea. Case 9. Woman with a scarf, from Tello. Case 12. Terracotta figurines (one strangling a bird). Latest known (3–2 B.C.) Cuneiform documents (Case 6); seals and cylinders (Case 15).

ROOM 3 (Pl. 29). Mari and Larsa. Objects from the Temple of the goddess Ishtar (c. 3000 B.C.) at Mari, including an alabaster *Statue of the intendant of Mari, Ebih-Il (centre case); head of Ishtar (Case 7); on the wall, two mural *Paintings from the Palace, depicting Ishtar investing King Zimrili with the regal powers, and a sacrificial scene. Small case, Two bronzes, one of a man on bended knee, his face and hands covered in gold leaf, the other a group of three rampant ibex, with horns interlaced, from Larsa. Ceremonial Vase from Larsa, with Ishtar and figures of animals (Case 5). Note the relief of a goddess smelling a flower (Case 3) and a panel of the king of Mari with naked prisoners (Case 1); also statuette of Idi Ilum, prince of Mari. By the exit, Bronze lion from the temple of Dagon.

ROOM 4 (Pl. 30). Babylon. In the centre, **Code of Hammurabi, a cone of black basalt, covered with the closely written text of the 282 laws embracing practically every aspect of Babylonian life of c. 2000 B.C., at the top of which the god Shamash dictates the law to the king. 'Kudurrus', or boundary-stones, with inscriptions. Along the E. wall, Statues of the princes of Ashnunnak, a rival state. The statues were captured by Shutruk-Nakhuntè, a Babylonian prince, who erased the original inscriptions and substituted his own (c. 1100 B.C.). In cases, Alabaster statuettes, lively terracottas in relief, bronze horned dragon (6C B.C.), symbol of Marduk.

ROOMS 5–13 contain mainly the result of excavations made at Susa (Mesopotamia). R. 5 (Pl. 31). Iran. Bronzes and ceramics of 4th–2nd millennia (centre); *Ceramics from Susa, known as 'Style I', of the 4th millennium (wall-cases). Case 5. Jewellery, goldsmiths' work, silverware, etc., from all periods and regions of the Near East. The ornamental *Vase-handle of silver inlaid with gold, representing a little ibex, is particularly beautiful. Cases 8, 9. Vases (animal and bird-like shapes) and statuettes (end of the 4th millennium); on the walls, in brick relief, two lions, winged bulls and griffins (5–4C).—R. 6 (Pl. 32). Susa. In the centre, headless *Statue of Queen Napir-Asu (bronze; 1500 B.C.); *Ritual scene in bronze, known as the Sit Shamshi, a ceremony celebrating the rising of the Sun. Opposite, *Vase 'à la cachette'; the objects displayed in the case were hidden inside it. Vessels in bitumen, terracottas (Case 5), votive offerings and toys (Case 6), of the 3rd–2nd millennium; a seated statue of the goddess Inanna; on the wall, deities beside a palm (brickwork).—R. 7 (Pl. 33). Monumental *Capital in grey marble from the palace of Artaxerxes II at Susa (405–362 B.C.). In the centre (Case 1), Lion in enamelled terracotta (1100 B.C.); on the walls, reliefs of a winged bull and a lion, also two warriors, in enamelled brick. Case 6. Two rhytons (silver and bronze), gold fibula, bronze cup decorated with an ostrich hunt; etc.—R. 8 (Pl. 34). Frieze of enamelled brick with royal **Archers in relief, also, in relief, lions, griffins, and winged sphinxes, from the palace of Darius I (6–4C). Case 2. Charter of Darius (521–486 B.C.), telling how the king had the rare materials needed for building his palace brought from distant lands.—RR. 9–10 (Pl. 35–36). Enamelled bricks with reliefs of griffins and lions; also man's head in stone and a bronze lamp (note the monkey on the lid); bronze utensils and ceramics from Luristan.—R. 11 (Pl. 37). Another frieze of the famous **Archers.— In R. 12 (Pl. 38), Sassanid and Mussulman antiquities (3–9C A.D.). Cast of mural niche from the palace of Shapur (3–4C A.D.).—We descend to the Crypte Marengo, passing (r.) four large earthenware pots from Susa (3–2C B.C.).

CRYPTE MARENGO. Phœnician sarcophagi, including (l.) the *Sarcophagus of Eshmunazar, king of Sidon (5C B.C.). Although Egyptian in style, th: inscription, a long malediction against any eventual violator of the tomb, is in Phœnician.—ROOM 14. Busts and funerary reliefs from tombs found at Palmyra in Syria, also three divinities in military costume (2–3C A.D.).—On the right of the staircase are Phœnician sculptures from Sidon and elsewhere.— We reach the collections from the great Phœnician cities of Baalbek (Heliopolis), Sidon, Tyre, Byblos and Ras-Shamra (Ugarit). R. 16 (Pl. 39). Bust of the Pharaoh Osorkon (924–895 B.C.); the 'Lady of Byblos' stele (5–4C) and an unusual three-sided stele in relief; woman's head in marble (3C B.C.). In cases, Statuette of Jupiter of Heliopolis, flanked by bulls (3–2C), votive hand and other examples of the same cult; head of a sphinx, from a throne of a divinity (Roman; Baalbek); lively terracotta figurines; plaquettes in gold; Syrian glass; etc. In a small room (R. 17) adjoining, Small headless statue of Aphrodite from Dura-Europos, also a wall-painting of a wild-ass hunt (194 B.C.).—R. 18 (Pl. 41). Fragment of the architrave of the temple of Eshmun (Sidon); Canaanite, Cypriot, Mycenæan ceramics from Ras-Shamra (Cases 1, 6, 10; 19–13C B.C.). Case 16. Sphinx dedicated by Itar, daughter of the Pharaoh Amenemhat II (1938–1904 B.C.), two Mycenæan amphoræ (14–13C). Swords and lances, etc., an offering to the High Priest of Ugarit (Case 2); a small showcase containing a painted Cretan cup, a rare example of 'Minoan' ceramics; Ivory boxes, pyxes and combs, statuettes of Baal and of the goddess of fertility (Cases 9, 14).—R. 19 (Pl. 42), Cyprus. In the centre, the famous 'Vase of Amathus', a huge monolithic ritual cistern (5C B.C.). Among the statues, 'King of Cyprus' (5C B.C.); also sculptured heads in the Greek style. Gold jewellery and repoussé work from Enkomi (Case 7); Bronze Age ceramics, Mycenæan kraters, terracotta and painted stone figurines, etc.—R. 20 (Pl. 43), Hittite and Cappadocian antiquities. Near the door (l.), three little bas-reliefs from Tell Halaf: winged genius, hunter drawing his bow, and a lion rampant. Stelæ of the gods Hada (l.) and Ishtar standing on a bull and on a lion; on the right, head of a divinity from Djabboul; etc. Wall-cases with ceramics, bronze animals, small stele of the god Teshub (Tell Ahmar); terracotta head of a bull from Boghaz-Keui, and votive shoe (Case 4); rein-guides in bronze, ram's-head rhyton (Case 3); gold covering of a column from Khorsabad, jewellery, etc. (Case 1).—RR. 21–23 (Pl. 44–46) are mainly devoted to reliefs (9–7C B.C.) from the great Assyrian palaces at Nimrud (Nos. 1–11), Khorsabad (Nos. 12–58), and Nineveh (Nos. 59–74). In the cases (l.) in R. 21, carved *Ivories from Arslan-Tash. In the four corners of R. 22, Winged *Bulls (7C B.C.) from Khorsabad, each with an extra leg, for the sake of symmetry. Note especially the reliefs of King Assurnasirpal (No. 7), of King Tiglathpileser III (No. 9), and of King Sargon with his ministers (Nos. 28–30); also a fine bronze lion from Khorsabad. The desk cases (r.) contain fragments of wall-paintings from Tell Ahmar.

The staircase in the centre of the room leads to the department of Egyptian Antiquities. The first half of the Crypt (which contains the famous 'idol' of Osiris, see p. 129) is decorated with reliefs depicting the kingly state and the miseries of war, from the Palace of Assurbanipal at Nineveh. The two bulls at the foot of the stairs come from the temple at Arslan-Tash (8C B.C.).

FIRST FLOOR

Several of the major Picture Galleries are at present closed for repairs, and the most important works are temporarily housed in other rooms. Printed below is the previous arrangement of the paintings, since there is no indication what the future order is to be. We suggest, however, that during this period the visit begin with the Salle des Sept Mètres (Pl. p. 134), followed by the Salon Carré, Salles Percier and des Fresques (Italian School, 14–15C), Galerie Daru (French, early 19C), Salle des États (Italian, 16C), Galerie Mollien (French, mid 19C), the Bestegui Collection and French Portraits (19C). A special passage leads from here to the W. end of the Grande Galerie (French, Italian and Spanish, 17C), Salle Van Dyck (Dutch, 17C), Galerie Médici, the Petites Cabinets (Primitives) and the Galerie Rembrandt. See also p. vi.

To reach the **Picture Galleries** we pass through the Galerie Denon and ascend the Escalier Daru at the far end. On the top landing is the magnificent 'Winged Victory' (p. 123).

From the landing below a double staircase leads to the Salle des Sept Mètres (see below) and to the French School of the 19C.

We turn right from the upper landing into the SALLE PERCIER (ceiling by Meynier): Frescoes by *Botticelli*, from the Villa Lemmi, near Florence.— SALLE DES FRESQUES: on the right, *Luini*, Christ blessing; on the left, *Luini*, *Nativity, *Adoration of the Magi, all from an oratory near Milan; between these two, *Fra Angelico*, Christ on the Cross, from the Dominican monastery at Fiesole. At the far end, *Ant. Rizzo* (d. 1499), *Two pages, statues from a tomb in Venice.—The SALON CARRÉ, in which the wedding feast of Napoleon and Marie-Louise was celebrated in 1810, is devoted to Italian, French and Flemish paintings of the 16–17C, among which are examples of the School of Fontainebleau; here also are four large cartoons by *Giulio Romano*, from Mantua, given to Louis XVI by Richard Cosway. *Fra Bartolomeo*, Marriage of St Catherine; *Pontormo*, Holy Family; *Giulio Romano*, Circumcision, Nativity, from Mantua; *G. B. Rosso*, Descent from the Cross; *Nic. dell' Abate*, Continence of Scipio, Moses in the bulrushes; *Raphael*, St Michael overcoming Satan, an academic and unconvincing canvas, in part the work of Giulio Romano, despite the signature and date (1518); *Martin Noblet*, Ceres; *Jean Cousin*, Last Judgement; *Ant. Caron*, Massacre of the Triumvirs, Sibyl of Tibur; works by *Ann. Carracci* and *Fed. Barocci*, also *Jan Matsys, J. van Hemessen, Fred. Sustris, J. Beuckelaer*.

We pass through the W. door into the Grande Galerie, where we turn at once to the right.

The **Salle des Sept Mètres** contains mainly Italian Primitives (late 13–late 15C) of the SIENESE AND FLORENTINE SCHOOLS, arranged in five bays. The fine *Madonna and angels by *Cimabue* (fl. 1272–1302), on the landing of the Escalier Daru, is opposite the other entrance to the gallery.

Beginning at the Escalier Daru entrance: *Taddeo di Bartolo* (long unattributed), Crucifixion; *Bernardo Daddi*, Anunciation, Crucifixion; *Lorenzo Monaco*, Jesus on the Mount of Olives, and the Holy Women at the Tomb, a diptych; *Bartolo di Maestro Fredi*, Presentation in the Temple; *Simone Martini*, *Bearing of the Cross; *Lorenzo Veneziano*, Madonna; *Lippo Memmi*, St Peter.—*Giotto*, *St Francis of Assisi; *Fra Angelico*, **Coronation of the Virgin.

This early work, idealized, overcrowded, and fascinating, includes numerous saints with their emblems and, in the predella, the Legend of St Dominic.

Domenico Ghirlandaio, Old man ('the Bottlenosed Man') and his grandson, an appealing panel which transmutes ugliness into beauty; *Master of the Nativity of Castello* (? *Fra Diamante*), Virgin and Child; *Benozzo Gozzoli*, Triumph of St Thomas Aquinas; *A. Baldovinetti*, Madonna; *Fra Angelico*, Martyrdom of SS Cosmas and Damian; *Lor. Monaco*, Madonna; *Sano di Pietro*, Life of St Jerome; *Botticini*, Madonna and Child with St John; *Gentile da Fabriano*, Presentation in the Temple, part of the predella in the Uffizi; *Francesco di Giorgio*, Rape of Europa; *Pisanello*, *Ginevra d'Este (?).— Sassetta*, Madonna with angels, and St Anthony and St John, a triptych; *Dom. Ghirlandaio*, Visitation, in many ways not characteristic but wholly the work of this Florentine realist.—*Iac. Bellini*, *Madonna with donor (probably Sigismondo Malatesta and not Pandolfo or Leonello d'Este); *Mantegna*, *Calvary; *Antonello da Messina*, *Condottiere, a late work of 1474; *Vinc. Catena*, Giulio Mellini; *Lotto*, St Jerome, an early signed panel of 1500; *Giov. Bellini*, Portrait of a man; *Cosimo Tura*, St Anthony of Padua; *Botticelli*, Madonna of the Guidi (an early work); *Leonardo da Vinci* (? formerly attr. to Lor. di Credi), *Annunciation; *Perugino*, Apollo and Marsyas; *Raphael*, *St George, *St Michael, painted on the back of a chess board for Guidobaldo, duke of Urbino; *Signorelli*, Birth of St John the Baptist; *Botticelli* (?), Madonna with five angels; *Iac. del Sellaio*, St Jerome.

The **Grande Galerie** contains a magnificent selection of paintings. The length of the gallery as far as the Tribune, in which hangs 'La Gioconda', is devoted to the FLORENTINE, UMBRIAN, AND LOMBARD SCHOOLS on the S. wall (l.) and to the VENETIAN and other N. ITALIAN SCHOOLS on the N. wall (r.). Beyond the Tribune are 16–17C masterpieces of the FRENCH, ITALIAN, AND SPANISH SCHOOLS.

On the S. wall (l.), 1st panel: *Bartolomeo di Giovanni* (?), Triumph of Thetis; *Master of the Nativity of Castello* (? *Fra Diamante*), Virgin of the goldfinch; *Mainardi*, Virgin and Child with St John the Baptist; *Filippo Lippi*, Virgin between two saints; *Botticelli* (?), Madonna with St John; *Botticelli*, Portrait of a young man; *Bart. di Giovanni* (?), Marriage of Thetis and Peleus.— 2nd panel: *School of Filippo Lippi*, Nativity; *Paolo Uccello*, Battle of San Romano in 1432 (companion pieces are in the National Gallery and the Uffizi); *Botticini*, Virgin in Glory.—3rd panel: *Lorenzo Costa*, Triumph of Peace, or Kingdom of the Muses, represented by the court of Isabella d'Este; *Albertinelli* (attr.), Christ appearing to Mary Magdalen, perhaps an early picture by *Fra Bartolomeo*, his partner; *Lor. di Credi*, Christ appearing to Mary Magdalen; *Perugino*, *St Sebastian, Combat of Love and Chastity.

On the N. wall (r.), 1st panel: *Piero di Cosimo*, Virgin with the dove; *Lorenzo di Credi*, Madonna with St Julian and St Nicholas; *School of Verrocchio*, Virgin.—2nd panel: *Mantegna*, *Virgin of Victory (commemorating the battle of Fornovo, 1495), painted for Fr. Gonzaga, marquis of Mantua, who kneels before the Madonna; *Bartolomeo Vivarini*. St John Capistran; *Bart. Veneziano*, Circumcision; *Cosimo Tura*, Pietà; *Crivelli*, St James of the Marches; *Mantegna*, *St Sebastian.—3rd panel: *Mantegna*, *Parnassus, with Mars and Venus and the Muses (see below); *School of Giov. Bellini*, Virgin between two saints; *Giov. Bellini*, Madonna and saints, *Christ blessing, an early work; *Lor. Costa*, Janus and Mercury chasing the Vices from Olympus; *Mantegna*, *Wisdom triumphant over the Vices, formerly in the 'studiolo' of Isabella d'Este at Mantua, and seized, together with the 'Parnassus' (see above), at the sack of that city in 1630.

On the S. wall (l.), 4th panel: *Perugino*, Virgin between saints and angels; *Andrea Solario*, Charles d'Amboise; *Bergognone*, St Augustine and donor,

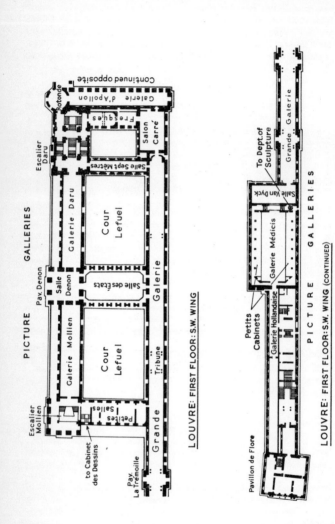

LOUVRE: FIRST FLOOR: S.W. WING

LOUVRE: FIRST FLOOR: S.W. WING (CONTINUED)

Presentation at the Temple, St Peter Martyr and donor; *Césare da Sesto*,
Virgin of the scales; *Boltraffio*, *Madonna of the Casio family, perhaps his
best picture.—5th panel: *Leonardo da Vinci*, *Madonna and Child with St
Anne; *Sodoma*, Love and Chastity; *Leonardo da Vinci*, St John the Baptist,
apparently painted from a female model or worked on later by another hand
(given by Louis XIII to Charles I and bought by Louis XIV in 1661), *Virgin
of the Rocks, probably earlier (1482) than the similar composition in London;

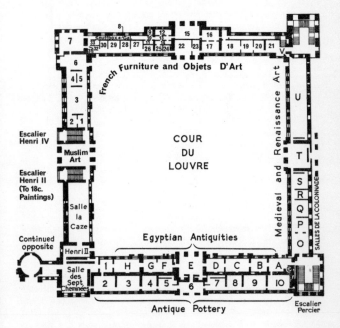

LOUVRE: FIRST FLOOR: MAIN BUILDING

Luini, Salome; *School of Leonardo da Vinci*, The so-called 'Belle Ferronnière'
(long believed to be a portrait of Lucrezia Crivelli), Bacchus.

On the N. wall (r.), 4th panel: *School of Gentile Bellini*, Reception of Dom.
Trevisano, the Venetian ambassador, in Cairo; *Bart. Veneto* (officially attr. to
the 16C Venetian School), Portrait of a lady; *Iac. de Barbari* (d. before 1516),
Virgin; *Cima*, *Madonna with St John and Mary Magdalen, a large and finely
coloured signed work; *Bart. Montagna*, Ecce Homo; *Cariani* (attr.), Portrait
of two men; *Carpaccio*, *St Stephen preaching in Jerusalem.—5th panel:
Titian, Madonna and saints, Portrait of a man; *Giorgione*, **Pastoral concert,
an idyllic group, one of the masterpieces of this short-lived Venetian; *Titian*,
**'Man with a glove', a noble and finely coloured and signed portrait (c. 1520),
*Allegory (c. 1533), representing Alfonso d'Avalos entrusting his wife to
Chastity and Cupid.—For the continuation of the Grande Galerie, see below.

The **Salle des États,** on the right, contains large paintings of the VENETIAN SCHOOL; a diversion into this room is recommended before continuing down the Grande Galerie. On the right, in the Salle des États: *Tintoretto,* *Paradise, a cartoon for the colossal painting in the Doge's Palace in Venice; *Paolo Veronese,* St Mark crowning the theological Virtues (ceiling of the antechamber of the Council of Ten in the Doge's Palace); *Titian,* *Venus of El Pardo (from the collection of Philip II); *P. Veronese,* Susanna and the Elders (comp. below the same subject by Tintoretto); *Bonifacio Veronese* (?), Raising of Lazarus (from St Luigi de' Francesi in Rome); *Titian,* **Entombment (1523), one of the world's great pictures (formerly in the collection of Charles I, it was sold by Cromwell for £125); *Marco d'Oggiono,* Contemporary copy of Leonardo da Vinci's 'Last Supper' at Milan and related to the copy at Burlington House (London); *Paolo Veronese,* 'La Belle Nani'; *Palma Giovane,* Adm. Cappello; *Tintoretto,* *Susanna and the Elders; *Bonifacio Veronese,* Holy Family; *P. Veronese,* Supper at Emmaus, *Marriage at Cana (at the far end), painted for the refectory of S. Giorgio Maggiore, Venice; *Titian,* Christ crowned with thorns, signed (1542); *Francesco Bassano,* Descent from the Cross; *Bonifacio Veronese,* Christ and the adulteress; *P. Veronese,* Christ in the house of Simon; *Titian,* *Supper at Emmaus, a magnificent work of the master's middle period; *Lotto,* Holy Family; *P. Veronese,* Swoon of Esther, Jupiter hurling thunderbolts against the Crimes (for the ceiling of the Hall of the Council of Ten in the Doge's Palace).

GRANDE GALERIE (continued), on the N. wall (r.), 6th panel: *Moretto,* Saints; *Lotto,* Christ and the adulteress; *Palma Vecchio,* Adoration of the shepherds; *Titian,* Virgin with the rabbit (c. 1518); *Veronese* (attr.), Bearing the Cross; *Savoldo,* Man in armour; *P. Veronese,* Madonna with saints and a monk.—7th panel: *Titian,* St Jerome (c. 1533); *Bordone,* Jerome Crafft; *P. Veronese,* Madonna with saints; *Tintoretto,* Self-portrait (1590); *Girol. Bassano* (d. 1621), Animals entering the ark; *P. Veronese,* *Calvary; *Giov. Calcar* (pupil of Titian), Portrait of Melchior von Brauweiler; *P. Veronese,* Flight from Sodom.

On the S. wall (l.), 6th panel: *Correggio,* Allegory of Vice; *Andrea del Sarto,* *Charity, painted in France 1518; *Raphael* (?), Virgin with the blue diadem, one of many paintings from the hand of *Giulio Romano,* Raphael's assistant; *Raphael,* **Madonna, known as 'La Belle Jardinière', an early work (1507) of delicate and poetic charm, *The Holy Family of Francis I, a late work (1518), original in composition but executed by *Giulio Romano,* notwithstanding the signature; *And. Solario,* Madonna of the green cushion (c. 1500), acquired by Card. Georges d'Amboise for his château at Gaillon; *Correggio,* Allegory of Virtue.—7th panel: *Seb. del Piombo,* *Visitation, signed and dated "in Rome 1521"; *Giulio Romano,* Portrait of a man; *Correggio,* **Jupiter and Antiope, remarkably fine in its sensuous rhythm and mythological significance (at one time in the collection of Charles I); *Pontormo,* Portrait; *And. del Sarto,* Holy Family; *Paolo Zacchia,* Viol player.

TRIBUNE, on the S. wall (l.): *Leonardo da Vinci,* **Monna Lisa, known as 'La Gioconda' ('La Joconde'), traditionally assumed to be a portrait of Monna Lisa Gherardini, third wife of Francesco del Giocondo.

Leonardo worked intermittently on this portrait for four years from 1500. In spite of drastic restoration at different periods, this remains one of the outstanding achievements of the Italian Renaissance. In August 1911 it was stolen from the Salon Carré by a thief disguised as a workman, but was recovered in Florence in December 1913. It has recently been claimed that the sitter was Costanza d'Avalos, mistress of Giuliano de' Medici, and that another somewhat similar portrait in a private collection represents Monna Lisa.

Titian, Lady at her toilet, called 'Alfonso da Ferrara and Laura de' Dianti'; *Raphael*, **Baldassare Castiglione, a superb late work formerly in the collection of Charles I. Opposite, on the N. wall: *Correggio*, **Marriage of St Catherine, remarkable for its chiaroscuro and gradation of tone; Portrait of Joan of Aragon, by *Giulio Romano* with the exception of the face (by *Raphael*); *Titian*, *Francis I, painted from a medal of the king whom the artist never saw.

On the S. wall (l.), Eclectic and other late Italian Schools. 8th panel: *Girol. Bassano*, The Vintage; *Mor*, Dwarf of Card. Granvella; *Nic. dell' Abate* (a mannerist), Rape of Proserpine; *Bronzino*, Portrait of a sculptor; *Leandro Bassano*, Moses striking the rock.—9th panel: *Dom. Feti*, Melancholy, the work of a mannerist; *17C Neapolitan School*, Concert; *Caravaggio*, Death of the Virgin; *J. de Boullongne* (Le Valentin), Fortune-teller; *Caravaggio*, Alof de Wignacourt (1608); *Domenichino*, St Cecilia; *Ann. Carracci*, Fishing, Hunting, characteristic, in both technique and subject, of the decadent period; *Guido Reni*, David with the head of Goliath, St Sebastian, painted with false and fitful idealism.—10th panel: *Guercino*, Raising of Lazarus, Saints; *Orazio Gentileschi*, Holy Family.

On the N. wall (r.), *17C Spanish School*. 8th panel: *El Greco*, St Louis, king of France; *Velazquez* (perhaps by *J. B. del Mazo*, his son-in-law and assistant), *Infanta Margarita (c. 1655); *El Greco*, *Christ on the Cross, with donors (signed in Greek characters), Antonio Covarrubias; *Velazquez*, *Queen Mariana of Austria (c. 1652).—9th panel: *Ribera*, *Club-foot, a strongly outlined figure silhouetted against a cloudy sky, Adoration of the shepherds; *Murillo*, *Beggar boy, an unattractive subject rendered with great artistic skill; *Caravaggio*, Fortune-teller; *Zurbaran*, St Bonaventure, *Funeral of St Bonaventure; *Murillo*, Legend of San Diego, known as 'Angels' Kitchen'.—10th panel: *Castiglione*, Melchizedek and Abraham, The money-lenders driven from the Temple; *Salvator Rosa*, A battle.

1st Rotunda: *Zurbaran*, St Apollonia; *Louis Le Nain*, Return from haymaking, Forge.

On the S. wall (l.), 11th panel: *Nic. Tournier*, Concert, Crucifixion; *Georges de la Tour*, Mary Magdalen, *Christ in the carpenter's shop; *J. de Boullongne*, Concert.—11th panel: *Le Sueur*, Clio, Euterpe, and Thalia; *N. Poussin*, *Self-portrait (1650); *Chas. Le Brun*, Chancellor Séguier (acquired in 1942); *Ph. de Champaigne*, Arnauld d'Andilly; *Le Sueur*, Melpomene, Erato, and Polyhymnia.

On the N. wall (r.), 11th panel: *Le Sueur*, Death of St Bruno, Death of Raymond Diocrés (two pictures from a series); *Louis Le Nain*, Peasant family; *Ph. de Champaigne*, The artist's daughter with Mère Catherine-Agnès Arnauld; *G. de la Tour*, Adoration of the shepherds.—12th panel: *Ph. de Champaigne*, *Card. Richelieu, Provost of the merchants, Louis XIII crowned by Victory; *Louis Le Nain*, Peasants' repast; *Mathieu Le Nain*, Party of connoisseurs.

Beyond the 2nd Rotunda (*Baugin, Jac. Linard*, Still Life) are fine examples of Poussin and Claude, both of whom lived in Rome; Poussin was considerably influenced by Raphael and Titian. On the N. wall (r.): *Poussin*, Orpheus and Eurydice, Philistines stricken with the plague, *Triumph of Flora (c. 1630), Rape of the Sabines, Summer (Ruth and Boaz); *Claude*, Campo Vaccino in Rome, Harbour at sunset.—On the S. wall (l.): *Claude*, Cleopatra at Tarsus, Ulysses and Chryseis, Village Fête; *Poussin*, Echo and Narcissus, Poet's Inspiration, Shepherds in Arcadia ('Et in Arcadia ego'), Bacchanal.— At the far end, *Rigaud*, *Louis XIV (1701).

We enter next the **Salle Van Dyck,** devoted to masterpieces of the FLEMISH
SCHOOL of the 17C. *Rubens*, *Henri de Vicq, an admirable portrait of the
ambassador who obtained for the artist the commission to paint the Medici
canvases; Landscape; Suzanne Fourment; Virgin surrounded by Holy
Innocents, an early and rather coarse production; Study for the face of St
George (1620); Joust by the castle moat, romantic in its realism; Philopœmen
recognized; **Flight of Lot from Sodom, signed and dated 1625; *Helena
Fourment, the artist's second wife, with two of her children, only in part
finished; Kermesse, an exuberant achievement of his late period; Elevation
of the Cross, *Sacrifice of Abraham, Abraham meeting Melchizedek, three
sketches for the ceiling of the Jesuit church at Antwerp (1629).—*Van Dyck*,
Francisco de Moncada, Governor-General of the Spanish Netherlands; Rinaldo
and Armida; **Charles I, one of the greatest pictures in the collection, painted
for £100 in 1635; Madonna with donors, painted shortly after the artist's visit
to Italy; Charles Louis, Elector Palatine, and Rupert of the Rhine, of the
artist's late English period; Marchioness Doria; Man with a ruff.—*Jordaens*,
Four Evangelists, Childhood of Jupiter, Portrait of a man. Works by *Jan
Brueghel the Elder, D. Teniers the Younger, Snyders,* and *Jan Fyt*; *Bern.
Strozzi*, Holy Family, showing Flemish influence.

The **Medici Gallery** (Galerie Médicis) contains large *Allegorical Paintings
depicting the life of Marie de Médicis, which were designed in 1622–25 by
Rubens for the decoration of the Luxembourg Palace. In the execution of these
works Rubens was largely aided by his pupils.

To follow the chronological sequence we begin with the painting to the left of the
entrance, I. The Fates spin the destiny of Marie. On the left, II, III. Birth, and Education,
of Marie.—IV. Henri IV receives the portrait of Marie.—V. Marriage at Florence in Oct
1600; the Grand Duke Ferdinand stands proxy for Henri IV.—VI. Marie lands at
Marseilles (1600).—VII. Marriage at Lyons of Marie as Juno and Henri IV as Jupiter
(Dec 1600).

VIII. Birth of Louis XIII at Fontainebleau in 1601, with Fortuna and the Genius of
Health.—IX. Henri IV starts for the war with Germany and entrusts the regency to the
queen.—X. *Coronation of the queen at St Denis (1610), with the king (already crowned)
in the gallery at the back.—XI. Apotheosis of Henri IV (assassinated in 1610), with Marie
as regent.—XII. Government of Marie.—XIII. The queen's journey to Ponts-de-Cé to
quell rebellion.—XIV. Exchange of the two princesses (1615), by treaty between France
and Spain; Elizabeth of France is betrothed to Philip IV of Spain, and Anne of Austria to
Louis XIII of France.

XV. Prosperity of the Regency; the queen enthroned, with Minerva, Fortuna, and
Abundance.—XVI. Majority of Louis XIII, to whom the Regent mother entrusts the
ship of state.—XVII. Marie's nocturnal flight from the Château of Blois (Feb 1619).—
XVIII. The queen receives overtures of peace from her son.—XIX. Conclusion of Peace
(April 1619).—XX. Reconciliation of the queen and her son, with the dragon of rebellion
overcome. To the left as we leave, XXI. Triumph of Truth.

For the **Petits Cabinets** (FRENCH AND FLEMISH PRIMITIVES) flanking the
Medici Gallery, we descend the stairs on the Seine side (S.) and pass a few
Spanish Primitives including *Pedro Diaz of Oviedo*, Robing of St Ildefonso
by the Virgin (a staircase here descends to the Medieval Sculpture gallery).—
1st Cabinet: *French School*, Portrait of John II (le Bon), c. 1360; *School of
Avignon*, Two fragments of a reredos; *Parisian School* (1373–78), *Altar frontal
painted on silk, from Narbonne; *Malouel* and *Bellechose*, *Last Communion
and Martyrdom of St Denis, from the Chartreuse de Champmol (Dijon);
Rhenish School (c. 1340), Four small panels. In the case: *Malouel* (?), Pietà;
School of Dijon, Pietà, Entombment; *School of Avignon*, Bearing of the
Cross.—2nd Cabinet: *Petrus Christus*, Pietà; *Jan van Eyck*, **Madonna with
Chancellor Nicolas Rolin, the earliest (before 1430) and perhaps the most

important primitive Flemish picture in the Louvre, taken by Napoleon I from Autun cathedral; *Rogier van der Weyden*, **Salvator Mundi between the Virgin and St John, with SS John the Baptist and Mary Magdalen on the wings, a remarkably fine triptych; *Dirk Bouts*, Descent from the Cross, and other examples.—3rd Cabinet: *School of Avignon*, *Pietà (c. 1460), from the Chartreuse at Villeneuve-lès-Avignon.—4th Cabinet: *Simon Marmion* (?), Invention of the Cross; *School of Paris*, Christ on the Cross (from the Palais de Justice) with a view of Paris in the background, Pietà (from St Germain-des-Prés.—5th Cabinet: *Burgundian School* (c. 1475), Margaret of York, wife of Charles the Bold and sister of Edward IV; *Froment* (?), King René and Jeanne de Laval, a diptych, also the 'pochette' that formerly contained it; *Fouquet*, *Charles VII (c. 1444), Juvénal des Ursins, Chancellor of France; *French School* (?), Madonna (c. 1500), Man with a glass of wine (c. 1455); *Master of Moulins*, *Mary Magdalen and donor, Child praying, Portraits of Pierre, duc de Bourbon, and of Anne, his wife; *Master of the Aix Annunciation*, Fragment of a triptych, a remarkably early example of 'Still Life' in the manner of Van Eyck.—6th Cabinet: *Hans Memling*, *Portrait of an old lady; *Mystic marriage of St Catherine, Jean du Cellier presented by St John, a charming little diptych painted c. 1475; Triptych; Virgin and donor; Study of a head; *Juan de Flandes*, Christ and the Samaritan, part of a polyptych painted for Isabel the Catholic; *Cologne School*, Panel of an altarpiece.—7th Cabinet (from r. to l.): *Hieronymus Bosch*, *Ship of Fools; *Geertgen tot Sint Jans* (a rare Haarlem primitive), Raising of Lazarus; *Gerard David*, Marriage at Cana, probably begun by the master and completed by his pupil Ysenbrandt; *Quinten Massys*, *Banker and his wife, the original of many versions and heralding a new era, Dead Christ, Madonna. In the demi-Rotunda, Ideal portraits of philosophers (1430–76) from the 'studiolo' in the ducal Palace at Urbino.

To continue the chronological order of the paintings, we should go through the Medici Gallery and turn left for the **Petits Cabinets** on the N. side; 16C GERMAN, DUTCH, AND FRENCH SCHOOLS, also small works of the 17C DUTCH SCHOOL. By the entrance, *Master of the St Bartholomew Altarpiece*, Descent from the Cross; *Master of the Death of Mary*, Descent from the Cross, with predella and lunette.—1st Cabinet (from r. to l.): *Hans Holbein the Younger*, *Erasmus, an outstanding and veracious portrait painted for Sir Thomas More (once in Charles I's collection); *Nicholas Kratzer, Henry VIII's astronomer (1528); *Anne of Cleves, a fine portrait of an unattractive sitter (1539); Wm. Warham, Archbp of Canterbury, an inferior work in spite of the inscription. *Dürer*, Self-portrait (1493). *L. Cranach the Elder*, Portrait of a girl.—2nd Cabinet: *Mabuse*, *Jean Carondelet, Chancellor of Flanders, painted in 1517 in the primitive tradition, *Madonna, companion panel, duly signed; *Jacob Cornelisz. van Oostzanen*, Portrait of a man; *B. van Orley*, Portrait of an old man; *Patinir*, St Jerome; *Lucas van Leyden*, Lot and his daughters; *P. Brueghel the Elder*, The beggars (1568).—3rd Cabinet: *French School*, Portrait of a musician (1556); *J. Clouet* (?), François I; *F. Clouet*, *Pierre Quthe (1562), one of the few authenticated works by this artist; *French School* (c. 1594), Gabrielle d'Estrées.—4th Cabinet: *16C French School*, Small portraits in original frames, including Elizabeth of Austria and Henri II.—5th Cabinet: *Adam Elsheimer*, Good Samaritan; *Pieter Lastman*, Sacrifice of Abraham. *Rembrandt*, **Christ at Emmaus, poignant in its grief and masterly in its technique and contemplative mood (1648); *Holy Family in the carpenter's shop, a representative work of a period when the painter was undergoing much domestic anxiety (1640); *Carcase of an ox (1655; repellent but masterly); Meditating philosopher; Archangel leaving Tobias and Tobit (1637); Château at twilight.—6th Cabinet: *Vermeer*, *Lacemaker; *P. de Hooch*, The card players; *Terboch*, *The military gallant, dexterous in composition and delicate in technique. Examples of *Metsu, Willem Duyster, Willem Heda, Jan van der Heyden*, and *Hendrik Pot*.—7th Cabinet: *Terborch*, *Concert; *Jan Steen*, *Bad company, excellently composed and handled but far from refined; *N. Maes*, *Grace before meat, an early work; *A. van Ostade*, Family group, perhaps the artist's family, of his best period (signed and dated 1654); *Bart. van der Helst*, Officers of the Guild of St Sebastian, a smaller version of the painting in Amsterdam; *Paul Potter*, White Horse, almost his last picture (1653); *P. de Hooch*, Interior; works by *Claes Berchem, Van der Hagen*, and *Thomas de Keyser*.—8th Cabinet: *Paul Potter*, Wood at the Hague; *A. van Ostade*, Schoolmaster, full of observation; *David Teniers the Younger*, Interior of a tavern; *Jan Breughel the Elder*, Earth and Air, part of a series of the Four Elements, taken from Milan in 1796; the other two have been returned. Also examples of *A. Brouwer, Denis van Alsloot, Adr. van de Venne* and *Roelant Savery*.

The **Rembrandt Gallery** (Galerie Hollandaise), divided into six bays, contains 17C DUTCH PAINTINGS. 1st Bay (School of Utrecht and the Mannerists): *Jan Woutersz Stap* (?), Old man; *Hendrik Terbrugghen*, Duet; *Honthorst*, Concert; *Hendrik Pot*, Van Beresteyn family; *Frans Hals*, *Lady in a black dress, characteristically lifelike and masterly in technique; *Terborch*, Reading lesson; works by *Gerard Verspronck, Willem Duyster, Jan Miense Molenaer* and his wife *Judith Leyster*.—2nd Bay: *Frans Hals*, *Gipsy girl, vivacious and deservedly popular; *Rembrandt*, *Hendrikje Stoffels and her child as Venus and Cupid (1662); also works by *Pieter Codde, Judith Duyster*, and *Van Goyen*.—3rd Bay: *Rembrandt*, Self-portrait, bareheaded (1633), Portrait of his son Titus, St Matthew inspired by an angel (1661), The Good Samaritan (*studio of Rembrandt*, 1648); *S. van Ruisdael*, The Landing-stage.—4th Bay: *Rembrandt*, Hendrickje Stoffels (1652), *The Artist at his easel (1660), Bathsheba (1654), Self-portrait, with cap (1637); *G. Metsu*, The Herb-seller; *Van der Heyden*, Town Hall at· Amsterdam.—5th Bay: Good examples of 'Still Life' by *Metsu* (unusual for this artist), *Floris van Schooten, Willem Kalff, Jan de Heem*, and *Pieter Claesz*.—6th Bay: *N. Maes*, Bather; *C. Netscher*, Portrait of a young princess; *F. Bol*, Portrait of a mathematician.

From the landing of the Escalier Daru (below the 'Winged Victory') we turn sharp right or left, leaving the Salle des Sept-Mètres on our left, to enter the **Galerie Daru.** This gallery shows 19C FRENCH PAINTINGS of the Classical School, many of which are large canvases of greater historical than artistic significance. *Gérard*, Mme Visconti. *David*, *Mme Récamier, in a familiar pose; Coronation of Napoleon I by Pius VII in Notre-Dame (2 Dec 1804); *Rape of the Sabines, a typical work of the classicist school, unconvincing as an interpretation of history; The oath of the Horatii; Paris and Helen, exhibited at the Salon of 1789 (a frigid and academic work); Lictors bring his sons' bodies to Brutus; Leonidas at Thermopylæ. *Girodet-Trioson*, Atala (from Chateaubriand's romance), notable for its powerful lighting but rather unmoving incident. *Gros*, Bonaparte visiting the plague-stricken at Jaffa; Christine Boyer; Count Fournier-Sarlovèze. *Prud'hon*, Empress Josephine; Justice and Divine Vengeance pursuing Crime, painted in 1808 for the Palais de Justice.

Ingres, Turkish bath; *Apotheosis of Homer, with figures of Æschylus, Virgil, Dante, Tasso, Molière, and others (for a ceiling; 1827). *Guérin*, Return of Marcus Sextus, signed and dated in the 'year VII' and exhibited in 1799. Busts of David by *Rude*, of Girodet by *J. B. Roman*, of Guérin by *Aug. Dumont*, and of Prud'hon by *Nanteuil*.

SALLE DENON (French School of the early 19C). *Ingres*, Woman bathing (Rome; 1808), Joan of Arc at the Coronation of Charles VII (1854); *Guérin*, Hippolytus accused by Phædra, Æneas at the court of Dido; *Chassériau*, Susanna and the Elders, Trade and Peace (from a mural for the Cour des Comptes); *Girodet*, The Flood; *Couture*, Romans of the Decadence, well known but tiresome; *Courbet* (founder of the realistic school), Roe-deer's haunt, Étretat; good examples of *Troyon*. Mercury fastening his sandal (bronze), by *Rude*. On the left opens the Salle des États (see p. 136).

The GALERIE MOLLIEN is devoted to the French Romantic School. *Delacroix*, Algerian women; Liberty guiding the people ('Les Barricades'), a dramatic and defiant allegorical work; Massacre at Chios, a work that had a stormy reception in the Salon of 1824; Constantinople taken by the Crusaders in 1204; Death of Sardanapalus; Self-portrait. *Gros*, Napoleon at the Battle of Eylau (with portraits of Berthier, Murat, Soult, and Davoust); Alcide de la Rivallière. *Eug. Devéria*, Birth of Henri IV. *Géricault*, *Raft of the 'Medusa', Wounded cuirassier, Officer of the Chasseurs de la Garde. *Courbet*, The artist's studio, *Burial at Ornans, Battle of the stags. *Decamps*, Defeat of the Cimbri. *Chassériau*, The two sisters, J. B. Lacordaire. *Th. Rousseau* (Barbizon School), *Sunset in the forest of Fontainebleau.

On the landing of the Escalier Mollien is *Carpeaux's* bronze group, Ugolino and his sons.—The **Cabinet des Dessins**, reached by the staircase at the entrance to the Petites Salles, contains a superb collection of drawings (over 75,000), a selection of which are on view.

We pass (l.) into the **Petites Salles**. *David*, Self-portrait (1794); Pius VII, signed and dated 'at Paris, 1805'.—Bestegui Collection, bequeathed in 1953: *Franco-Flemish School* (c. 1390), Virgin; *Master of Moulins*, Portrait of the Dauphin Charles Orlando (1494).—*Rubens*, Death of Dido; *Van Dyck*, Portrait of (?) Livio Odescalchi; *Nattier*, Duchesse de Chaulnes as Hebe; *Gérard*, Mme Lecerf (1794); *Fragonard*, Portrait of a young artist, 'Le Feu aux Poudres'; *Lawrence*, Mrs Cuthbert; *Drouais*, Wife of the artist; *Largillière*, Marie-Anne Mancini (?), Duchess of Bouillon.—*David*, Bonaparte (c. 1797), a sketch, Portraits of M. Meyer and of Mme de Verninac, sister of Delacroix; *Ingres*, Lor. Bartolini (1820), Mme Panckoucke; *Goya*, Countess del Carpio, Marchioness of Solana; two works by *Meissonier*.—*Courbet*, Man with a leather belt (self-portrait, 1849); *Corot*, Lady with the pearl; *Ingres*, M. Bertin, Mme Marcotte; *Gros*, Bonaparte at Arcole (1796); *Delacroix*, Chopin, Self-portrait (c. 1838).—*David*, *Portraits of M. and Mme Sériziat, fresh in colour and finely preserved but somewhat superficial; *Ingres*, Portraits of the Rivière family and others.

Paintings of the 18C are exhibited on the Second Floor, reached by the Escalier Henri II (Pl. p. 135).

The works on display in the following rooms tend to be changed frequently.

ROOM 1. English School. *Lawrence*, Sir Thomas Bell, J. J. Angerstein and his wife; *Gainsborough*, Conversation in a park; *Raeburn*, Capt. Robt. Hay of Spott.—R. 2. *Pannini*, Celebrations in Rome on the birth of the Dauphin to Louis XV; *Gaudi*, a group of eight Venetian festival scenes, and others; *Seb. Ricci*, Allegory; *G. B. Tiepolo*, Last Supper, Apollo and Daphne; *Pittoni*, The continence of Scipio, The sacrifice of Polyxena, Christ giving the keys to St Peter; *Gainsborough*, Lady Gertrude Alston; *Goya*, Woman with a fan, Ferdinand Guillemardet, Still-life; *Louis Meléndez*, Self-portrait, Still-life.—R. 3. French School. The left wall is devoted almost exclusively to *Chardin*, including Boy with a teetotum, Grace before meat, Ape as a painter; the far wall to *Boucher*, including, Odalisque (Madame de Pompadour?), 'Le petit déjeuner', *Diana after the bath (1742). On the next wall, *Fragonard* is represented by *The music lesson, Inspiration, Women bathing (an early work in the style of *Boucher*), 'La chemise enlevée', Sleeping bacchante (sketchy in treatment, but fine in colour); the final wall contains examples of the work of *Greuze*, Dead bird, Milkmaid, Paternal curse (a melodramatic composition), and of *Hubert Robert*, 'Grande galerie du Louvre', The Grande Galerie in ruins, Fountain beneath the grotto.—R. 4. French School. *Watteau*, *l'Embarquement pour Cythère' (the artist's reception picture of 1717, sketchy, imaginative and vaguely melancholy), Gay company in a park, *l'Indifférent', 'La finette', Jupiter and Antiope, *Gilles (a magnificent life-sized portrait of a clown), 'Le faux-pas'. Also works by *Pater, Coypel* and *Rigaud*.—R. 5. New acquisitions.—R. 6. Temporary display.

The 19C paintings (French) are reached from the first Egyptian room (Salle A) by the spiral staircase (see Pl. p. 135).

To the right is the de Croy collection of Dutch paintings. The slippers (artist unknown); *G. Van Honthorst*, The dentist; portraits by *Honthorst, N. Maes, de Vries, Verspronck,* and *Roosendael*. Seascapes by *Ruysdael, Storch,* and *Van Beyeren*. Landscapes by *Van de Meer* (1628–91), *Croos,* and *Peeter Bout. Van de Meer*, The laundresses of Overween; *Dirck Hals*, Man in a brown hat; *Craesbeeck* (1608–c. 1662), Shellfish for lunch; *Nauwinck*, Baptism of the eunuch; etc. The collection includes some French paintings: *Guérin*, Study of a woman.

The 19C rooms begin to the left of the stairs.—R. 1. Neo-Classical portraits, including several by *David*.—R. 2. This room contains many celebrated nudes by *Ingres*, *The great reclining odalisque (1814), The great bather, known as the Valpinçon (1808), *The little bather, Turkish bath.—R. 3. (Gallery and cabinets). Works by painters of little domestic scenes and landscapes, of whom the most important is *Corot*.—RR. 4–9. The Romantic rooms contain works by *Delacroix*, Young tigers playing, (R. 4); *Huet*, 'Brissants à la pointe de Granville'; *Constable*, Storm approaching Weymouth bay (R. 6); *Corot* (later works), *Morning, Dance of the nymphs, Belfry at Douai (1871), Woman in blue; *Millet*, The reapers, Spring (R. 9).—R. 10. The school of Realism is here first represented by *Daumier* (1808–79), The emigrants (bas-relief, plaster), Crispin and Scapin.—R. 11. *Courbet*, The covered brook, 'La roche de dix heures', The spring; *Dégas*, The Bellini family, Study of hands; *Whistler*, Portrait of his mother.

When this room is closed some of the paintings are on display in R. 6 of the 18C rooms. The Personnaz collection of Impressionist paintings (R. 12) can be seen at the Jeu de Paume during repairs to the Gallery. It includes works by *Monet, Sisley, Pissaro, Renoir, Dégas* and *Lautrec*.

For the GALERIE D'APOLLON we mount the steps to the left of the 'Winged Victory' and pass into the Rotonde d'Apollon. We enter the gallery by magnificent wrought-iron gates of c. 1650 brought from the Château de Maisons, near Paris. Built under Henri IV, burned down in 1661, but rebuilt under Louis XIV by Charles Le Brun, this splendid gallery is finely proportioned, and the decorations, including the ceiling-painting (notably the central subject, Apollo's Victory over the Python, by *Delacroix*), are admirable.

The glass cases contain a magnificent collection, of the highest historical and artistic worth, of **Medieval and Renaissance Goldsmiths' Work,** gems, rock crystal vessels, etc. In front of the entrance is a large Florentine mosaic table (from the Château de Richelieu). In the centre, Cases 1, 3, and 5 contain what is left of the remarkable collection belonging to the French royal house. Case 1. Semi-precious vessels of lapis-lazuli, jade, amethyst, amber, and red and green jasper.—Case 2. Bronze statuette of Charlemagne (9C); *Crown of St Louis (c. 1255), presented to St Louis by the Dominicans of Liège; 'Ring of St Louis' (14 or 15C gold ring) from St-Denis; Crown of Louis XV (1722): after his coronation (according to custom) the gems were replaced by coloured stones; Crown of Napoleon I (after Charlemagne's), never placed on his head; Coronation ring of Napoleon I.—Case 3. French rock crystals from the royal collection, including a vase with decorations illustrating Noah at work in his vineyard.—Case 4 contains the Crown Jewels that were retained when the remainder were sold in 1887, including the *'Regent', one of the finest diamonds known (137 carats), bought by the Regent in 1717; 'Côte de Bretagne', a ruby once owned by Marguerite de Foix, Anne of Brittany, Claude de France, and Francis I, and afterwards cut into the shape of a dragon as a decoration of the Order of the Golden Fleece; Sword of Charles X; the 'Hortensia' diamond, acquired in 1691; Reliquary brooch of the Empress Eugénie (1855); Plaque of the Order of the Saint-Esprit.—Case 5. Vessels in agate, sardonyx, and basalt. Beyond the case is a coloured marble table-top dating from the reign of Louis XIV (the base from 1873), and at the far end of the gallery is one of the thirteen Savonnerie carpets (1667; usually rolled) which originally covered the floor.—Wall-case 6 (r.). Ecclesiastical ornaments from the Treasury of the Abbey of St-Denis, presented by Abbot Suger: **Antique (? Egyptian) porphyry vase mounted in silver gilt as an eagle, with a Latin inscription round the neck; *Rock crystal vase, given by Eleanor of Aquitaine to Louis VII, who gave it to Suger; *Antique sardonyx ewer, mounted c. 1150; *Crystal ewer (Muslim) of the 10C; **Serpentine paten inlaid with gold dolphins (5–6C), set in an 8–9C border; *Lapis-lazuli plaque with figures of Christ and the Virgin (Byzantine; 11–12C); Two Byzantine reliquary *Plaques (the Three Maries at the Tomb) from the Treasury of the Sainte Chapelle.—Wall-case 7. **Silver gilt statuette of the Virgin (French; 14C), presented in 1339 to the Abbey of St-Denis by Jeanne d'Evreux, widow of Charles IV; *Gold sceptre of Charles V surmounted by a statuette of Charlemagne; *Coronation gold spurs, set with garnets and fleurs-de-lys (12C, restored in the 19C); *Coronation sword of the kings of France known as the 'Sword of Charlemagne' (? 11C).—Wall-case 8. *Enamelled gold shield and morion of Charles IX; Candlestick and rock crystal mirror presented to Marie de Médicis on her marriage to Henri IV (1600); Sword and dagger of the Grand Master of the Knights of Malta (Augsburg; 16C), given to Napoleon in 1797.—Wall-cases 9 and 10. Reliquaries and church plate from the Chapel of the Order of the Saint-Esprit, founded by Henri III in 1578.

The Rotonde d'Apollon opens out into the SALLE DES BIJOUX. On the left, fragments of Græco-Roman frescoes; in window-cases, Roman cameos, Roman necklaces from Kertch, and ivory plaques (Etruscan; 6–5C B.C.). Near wall: silver *Treasure of Graincourt-les-Havrincourt. In the centre, *Treasure of Boscoreale (near Pompeii), a collection of superbly decorated silver objects discovered in 1895 in a fine state of preservation on the site of a villa overwhelmed by an eruption of Vesuvius (A.D. 79). By the far wall, Gallo-Roman treasure from Notre-Dame d'Allençon (S. of Angers) discovered in 1852, notable among which are two silver masks.

Beyond is the SALLE DES SEPT-CHEMINÉES, with two large canvases by *Charles Le Brun*, Alexander the Great entering Babylon, Atalanta's Hunt; also *Simon Vouet*, Presentation in the Temple; *Jean Jouvenet*, Descent from the Cross. Here is an exhibition (probably permanent) of a small **Collection of early Christian art and (as a contrast) examples of 14–17C work from Russia. Among the treasures are: relief of Jonah and the Whale (late 3C) from the Catacombs of Sta Priscilla, Rome; marble panel from St Denis (transenna?); wing of a diptych with the name of Areobindus (A.D. 506), one of the last Roman consuls (Carolingian work on the reverse); wing of the 'Barberini' diptych (Constantinople; c. 500); diptych of the Muses (6C), and one with Circus Games (Gaul; c. 400); statuette of the Good Shepherd (Rome, 3C); Vase of Emesa, embossed silver (Homs; 6C); Egyptian funeral portrait (Antinoë; late 3C); mosaics (Byzantine; 6 and 11C); fragment of pulpit with symbols of SS. Mark and John (Pomposa; 11–12C); a last Judgement; etc.

Thence we pass on to the SALLE CLARAC (Pl. 1), the first room of the **Antique Pottery** collection, which contains exhibits of the pre-Hellenic civilizations. Pithoi from Cnossos, Crete (1700–1600 B.C.), and from Thera and Rhodes (14C B.C.); in the cases: marble idols from the Cyclades (2500–2000); terracotta and bronze figurines and painted ceramics (Minoan) from Crete (14–12C B.C.), also funerary objects. The ceiling-painting in this room is 'The Apotheosis of Homer', after *Ingres*; those in the following rooms are by mid-19C artists and illustrate the history of French art.

SALLE DU DIPYLON (Pl. 2; r.). Pottery of the Geometric Style (10–7C B.C.). Bœotian figurines, idols, animals, etc.; Attic vases found in the Dipylon cemetery (c. 800 B.C.); note the œnochoe with funeral procession. Pottery from the Greek Islands and vessels in the Orientalizing style. In the standard case, the 'Lévy Œnochoe'. Pithos from Bœotia with Perseus and the Gorgon in relief.—SALLE DE CORINTHE (Pl. 3). Pottery from Corinth (7–6C B.C.), including small vases in the form of human figures, animals, owls, etc.; Tyrrhenian amphoræ, kraters, and other vessels decorated with reliefs of battles and banqueting scenes, etc. In the centre, the Hydriæ of Cerveteri, a series of vases decorated with the story of Hercules, Deianira and Nessus, etc.—SALLE D'AMASIS (Pl. 4). Later *Attic black-figure pottery (c. 550–530 B.C.). Works by *Exekias* and his school, with decorations illustrating scenes from epic subjects, etc.; Attic amphoræ; works by the 'Little Masters' and the 'Affected Painter'—the last so called because of the peculiar style of his decorations. In the centre, works by the potter *Amasis*.—SALLE D'ANDOKIDES (Pl. 5). Attic pottery (c. 530–510 B.C.). *Amphoræ and other vessels, including works signed by *Andokides* and *Nikosthenes* (kylix with galley-race), a fine bowl attributed to *Oltos* and an amphora with both black and red figures.—SALLE D'EUPHRONIOS (Pl. 6). Attic pottery (500–475 B.C.). Central case, Works by *Euphronios*, *Douris*, and *Myson*, including a *Krater with the Combat of Hercules and

Antæus, a kylix with Eos and Memnon, and an amphora with Crœsus on the pyre. In Case 1, *Bowl by *Brygos*, with the Arrival of Helen at Troy.— SALLE DES PLAQUES DE MILO (Pl. 7). Pottery of the pre-Classical period (first half of 5C). To the right, Krater with the Massacre of the Niobids; terracotta figurines and funerary plaques.—SALLE DES LECYTHES BLANCS (Pl. 8). Pottery of the Classical period (second half of 5C).—SALLE DU IV SIÈCLE (Pl. 9). Terracotta figurines, and statuettes from Tanagra.—SALLE DE MYRINA (Pl. 10). *Figurines of the Hellenistic period and (alcove) antique glassware.

The upper Egyptian gallery may be reached either from this room, or from the ground floor, by the Escalier Percier. The spiral staircase in the first Egyptian room ascends to the 19C paintings (see p. 142).

Egyptian Antiquities. In the vestibule at the head of the staircase, stands a black granite *Statue of the god Amon protecting Tutankhamen (18th Dyn.). SALLE A is devoted to the prehistoric and Thinite periods (4000–2800 B.C.). Cases 1–3. Stone vessels and pottery; Cases 6–7. Schist palettes, for grinding and mixing paints; Cases 8–9. Knives in white flint, and other weapons; in the case facing the fireplace, *Knife from Gebel-el-Arak (c. 3400 B.C.).—SALLE B. Old Kingdom (2650–2100 B.C.). Red sandstone head of King Didoufri (c. 2650 B.C.); Case 5. Funerary furniture from Chancellor Nachti's tomb (c. 2159 B.C.); Case 8. Group in wood (4th Dyn.), very damaged, but nevertheless one of the masterpieces in wood of the Old Kingdom; small model houses for the departed souls of the dead; Case 10. *Painted limestone male head (4th Dyn.; the 'Salt head'); Case 11. Alabaster vessels for ceremonial oils and a 9th Dyn. brazier.—SALLE C. Middle Kingdom (2100–1750 B.C.), Second Intermediary Period (1700–1560 B.C.), and New Kingdom (1560–1320 B.C.). In the centre, Prince Ahmosis, seated statue in painted limestone. On the right of the door, Cynocephalous statue (limestone), connected with sun-worship; over the chimneypiece, bas-relief in painted limestone of Amenmes and his wife Depet; Case 2. Alabaster vases of the Middle Kingdom and 18th Dyn.; Case 3. Red sandstone head of Amenophis III(?); Case 11. *Wooden statuettes, including the priestess Toui (1200 B.C.) and Queen Ahmes-Nefertari, beautiful works of the New Kingdom; Case 12. *Royal head in blue glass paste (18th Dyn.), also *Jewellery of the New Kingdom; Cases 13–14. 'Books of the Dead' of the New Kingdom.—SALLE D. New Kingdom (Ramesside Period; 1320–1086 B.C.). Case 1. 'Ushabti' figures of stone, which were placed in tombs to serve the dead in the next world; Case 3. Bas-reliefs of Rameses II; Case 8. Statuette of the priestess Naha, in green enamelled schist; two statuettes of Nebmertuf, the scribe, writing to the dictation of the god Thoth. 'Heart' scarabs, which were placed on the chests of the embalmed bodies of the dead; Case 10. Bronze mirrors; Case 11. 'Kneeling prisoner', bronze statuette inlaid with silver.—SALLE E. Amarna Period. In the centre, *Limestone bust of Amenophis IV (who adopted the name of Akhnaton); Case 9 (facing the second window). *Akhnaton and his queen Nefertiti, a fine bas-relief in painted limestone; gold seal of Horemheb; fragment of a painting depicting birds, butterflies, etc. In two separate cases: *Painted limestone head of a princess of El-Amarna; Cases 3–5. Writing and *Cosmetic articles; Case 6. Musical instruments and games.—SALLE F. Pre-Saïte Period (1085–663 B.C.), and Saïte Period (663–525 B.C.). Case 1. Painted wooden stele (man playing a harp); Case 8. *Bronze tablet cover decorated in silver, gold, and electrum; bronze sistrum; triad of Osorkon II, in gold and lapis lazuli, with the divinities Osiris, Isis, and their son, Horus; Case 9. Objects in a blue enamel known as 'Deir el-Bahara blue', ushabtis from the tombs of various high officials; Case 10. Leather-covered wooden harp; Case 11. Bronze statuettes of Baster, the cat-faced goddess of Bubastis; Case 12. Figures in bronze of kings and of priests. In a case close by, *Statuette (bronze) of Queen Keramana, wife of Takelothis I (22nd Dyn.).—SALLE G. Saïte Period and Later Dynasties (663–333 B.C.). Figures of Bes, god of recreation, and of other deities in the form of animals; Statuettes in granite, notably Head of an old man (Case 2); also Amulets (Case 10).—Between Rooms G and H is a black basalt 'healing statue' covered with magic signs.—SALLE H. Ptolemaic and Coptic Periods. In the centre, *Bronze statue of the falcon-god Horus, offering a libation; Ptolemaic pottery, and terracotta figures; Coptic textiles, liturgical bronzes, pottery, glass, ivories, and ornamental woodwork; Jewellery and other precious objects, including a priest's ceremonial breast-plate decorated with a winged scarab; Two statuettes of Horus as a Roman soldier; Papyri. Case 2. Coffin-lids in the shape of mummies.

Returning through the Salle Clarac again, we turn right into the SALLE HENRI II, or SALLE ETRUSQUE (ceiling by Braque), which contains **Etruscan Pottery.** This splendid collection includes early black ('bucchero') ware and fine black-figured and red-figured vases in the Greek style. The best specimens are in the central case. Also five Etruscan terracotta *Panels from Cerveteri, apparently from a burial chamber (600 B.C.), and representing scenes of death and sepulchral ceremonies; in the centre, terracotta **Sarcophagus (6C B.C.), discovered at Cerveteri in 1850 by Campana.

On a funeral couch recline the life-like figures of a man and his wife represented as if still alive and conversing. The lady wears a cap (tutulus) and a small gorget; the man is draped with his feet bare.

The SALLE LA CAZE contains **Greek, Roman, and Etruscan Bronzes,** jewellery, arms, utensils, etc. On the right, near the window, Roman cockerel, found at Lyons; Case 25. Apollo, the 'messenger'. In the centre, *'Apollo of Piombino', an antique Greek statue retrieved from the sea near Piombino, probably a replica of a work by Kanakhos (c. 500 B.C.); Case 21. Mirrors (Greek; 4C B.C.); Cases 15, 16. Bronze figurines (Roman); Case 1. Archaic Greek statuettes, including the *'Javelin Thrower'; Case 12. Statuettes and busts from Roman Gaul. The central case contains a magnificent collection of *Jewellery and goldsmiths' work, from all the periods and regions covered by the other exhibits. Case 26. *'Triumphant Athlete' (5C B.C.), an example of the best period of Greek art, found at Benevento; Case 19. Silver figurine of Hercules (5C B.C.) and a fine rhyton from S. Russia; Case 11. Hellenistic Egyptian art; Case 3. Hellenistic art, including two statuettes of Aphrodite and 'Napoleon's' cist; Case 27. Dionysos, a flute-playing satyr, and Mænads dancing (Alexandrian style); infant Eros and Psyche; sleeping Eros; Cases 23–24. Engraved Etruscan mirrors (5–3C B.C.). At the far end, *Apollo, a gilt-bronze statue found near the Roman theatre at Lillebonne, in 1823. Case 4. Etruscan statuettes, including a winged Athene; Case 2. Greek statuettes (5C B.C.), notably an Athlete, Hercules resting, Ephebus (School of Polykleitos), and a 6C group, Lycurgus and the Mænads.

The staircase beyond this room leads to the 18C paintings (p. 141).

In the PAVILLON SULLY (closed by 17C gates) is the collection of **Muslim Art,** which comprises exhibits from Syria, Mesopotamia, Persia, Turkey, Egypt, N. Africa, and Spain (6–14C). The wall-cases contain faience and ceramics from Persia, Syria, Egypt, and Asia Minor. S. wall (l.), Fragment of a Persian silk winding-sheet embroidered in silver and gold, called the 'Suaire de St Josse', and said to have served as a covering for a relic of this saint.—By the windows, Weapons from Persia and Afghanistan (6–7C); Case 12. Ivory box made for the Prince of Cordova (A.D. 967); Mesopotamian and Egyptian ivories (12–14C); Case 15. Bronze censers (12–13C; Persian) in the form of a bird and of a lion, also 11–12C vases. In the centre, Case containing enamelled glass mosque lamps from Egypt (14C). N. wall (r.), Magnificent Persian carpet from the Cathedral at Mantes (16C). Below, the 'Barberini' vase (1259), bronze inlaid with silver. In the centre, the *'Baptistery of St Louis', a large copper basin inlaid with silver, which, according to tradition, was brought to the Château de Vincennes by Louis IX from the Crusades, and used for royal christenings.

Beyond the Escalier Henri IV we reach the department of *French Furniture and Objets d'Arts. The first two rooms house the Thiers Collection (*A. Thiers*, 1797–1877).—R. 1. Antiques, bronzes, and china; 'La Déposition' (case opposite entrance), attr. to Michelangelo.—R. 2. On the left, Sèvres and Vincennes porcelain (18C); door with marquetry panels illustrating *Poussin's* 'Seven Sacraments'. Right, 18–19C china from Meissen, Paris, etc.

CAMONDO COLLECTION (comp. Rte 31). Ceiling by *Blondel* (1827); Brussels tapestry after *Teniers*; *Falconet*, clock called The Three Graces; *Schlichtig*, *Commode, bearing Marie-Antoinette's initials; *Delanois*, chaise-longue; Furniture by *Lacroix*, *Brizard* and *Jacob*. The first opening on the left leads into the

SALLE SCHLICHTIG (Pl. 4). Centre, *Roentgen* (attr.), cylinder desk (c. 1780); commode, stamped *Leleu*; *Gay*, child's chair, said to have belonged to the Dauphin; three chairs covered with Beauvais tapestry after *Jacques* and *Casanova* (c. 1780); *Dubuisson*, clock; *Nattier*, portrait of the Duc de Chaulnes.

Also leading off the Salle Camondo is the SALLE ROTHSCHILD (Pl. 5), containing Renaissance religious art. Tapestry, Miracle of the loaves, Flanders (?) 15C; triptych reliquary (1254) from the Abbaye de Floreffe, Flanders; Venetian censer, 15C.

SALLE LOUIS XVIII (Pl. 7). *Molitor*, two lacquer and ebony cabinets (c. 1820); cradle belonging to the King of Rome (son of Napoleon), by *Thomire* after *Prud'hon* and *Percier*; Savonnerie carpet; balustrades by *Jacob-Desmalters*, originally made for the throne-room in the Tuileries; satin-wood Secretaire (c. 1829) in Louis-XVI style.

SALLE EMPIRE. Napoleon I's throne, dominated by the Imperial Eagle in Savonnerie tapestry which hangs behind it; *J.-Desmalters*, pair of jewel caskets of ebony, yew, mother-of-pearl, and bronze (1812); large jewel cabinet in mahogany, amaranth, mother-of-pearl, and bronze (made for Josephine, 1809); *J.-Desmalters*, console-table, marble top; right; commode with biscuit panels and Wedgwood insets (c. 1790).

In the alcove are a gold-plated tea-service by *Biennais* and *Giroux*, ordered by Napoleon for his marriage to Marie-Louise, and a Sèvres coffee-service, made for the wedding and later taken to St Helena.

SNUFF-BOX GALLERY (Pl. 8), a superb collection of *Snuff-boxes and *Watches of the 17–18C with examples by *Moynat* (1746–59), *Noël Hardivilliers* (1752–79), *J. J. Barrière* (1765–76), the *Drais* family (1769–82), and *Menière* (1773–82), as well as representative work from foreign countries, notably Switzerland.

SILVER-WARE ROOM (Pl. 9). 17–18C. On the wall, a fragment of the Gobelins tapestry, Triumph of the gods, after *Coypel*; heavy bracket candelabra; *Leblond*, bowl bearing the arms of Monseigneur, son of Louis XIV; examples of Louis-XV silverware.

Cabinet des Porcelaines (Pl. 10, 11). Wall-panelling from the Hôtel de Villemaré. In the show-cases, china from Vincennes and Sèvres; flat-topped bureau stamped *Séverin*. Alcove: 'grotesque' Beau tapestries designed by *Bérain*; *Carlin*, pedestal table, top of Sèvres china. Rotonde des Saisons (Pl. 12, 13, 14). Four Rouen china busts representing the seasons. Alcove (l.): Rouen pottery (18C). Alcove (r.): pottery from Moustiers, Marseilles, Sceaux, etc.

SALLE RÉGENCE. (Pl. 15), *Coypel*, Tapestry (1620–25) depicting the Story of Psyche, after *Jules Romain*; Savonnerie carpet bearing the arms of France. Left, flat-topped bureau, *Boulle* (attr.), tortoise-shell on brass ground, the counterpart to which is in the next room. Right, *Cressent*, flat-topped bureau (c. 1730); pair of Chinese lacquer cabinets.

SALLE DE L'ÉLECTEUR DE BAVIÈRE (Pl. 16). Gobelins tapestry and Savonnerie silk door-hangings; *Boulle* (attr.), *Pair of large ebony cupboards; centre, *Boulle* (attr.), flat-topped bureau, brass on tortoise-shell. Left, *Boulle*, magnificent bureau with drawers (early 18C), decorated with tortoise-shell, brass and gilt bronze, the drawers surmounted by a clock.

SALLE ANDRÉ-CHARLES BOULLE (Pl. 17). Boulle (1642–1723), the master ébéniste of the 17C. *Two ebony cupboards, one with coloured wood marquetry on tortoise-shell, the other, tortoise-shell and brass inlays, gilt bronze in relief; between the doors, an ebony cabinet inlaid with brass and pewter.

CHAMBRE DU MARÉCHAL D'EFFIAT (Pl. 18). Louis-XIII period. Gobelins tapestry, Life of Scipio (1689); bed and chairs covered in matching fabric. Right, cabinet, doors lined with ivory inlaid with jasper, marble, and amethysts (17C); bureau inlaid with metal and cane-work, said to have belonged to Marie de Médicis; glass cabinet containing faïence from Nevers.

SALLE DES BRONZES. Renaissance. Pre-Gobelins tapestries from designs after *Vouet*; on the consoles are bronze statues of Classical inspiration from the *Jean Bologne* workshops, 'Day', 'Night', and 'Dusk', inspired by *Michelangelo*.
SALLE RENAISSANCE (Pl. 20). Tapestries illustrating the story of Moses by *Lefèbre*, after *Poussin* (1686–89); in the cases, jewellery, plate, watches, etc.
The following room is in the process of being arranged. It will be devoted to glass-ware. Return to the Salle Régence (Pl. 15). Turn left into:

SALLE LOUIS XV (Pl. 22). Gobelins tapestries (1765); furniture (r.) upholstered in Beauvais tapestry after *Boucher*; ebony bureau lacquered black and gold (c. 1750); Savonnerie covered armchair stamped *Gourdin*. Left, *Lemoyne*, console-table, marble top and carved decorations. To the left is the entrance to
SALLE MARIE-LECZINSKA (Pl. 23). *Nécessaire offered to Marie-Leczinska on the occasion of the birth of the Dauphin; *Boulle* (attr.), commode; clock in brass marquetry. Salle Louis XV leads into the
PETITE SALLE LOUIS XV (Pl. 24). Gobelins tapestries (1765) after *Coypel*; *Van Risen Burg*, delicate coffee table (1766); *Lelarge*, four armchairs. SALLE DU BUREAU DU ROI. Woodwork, doors, and fireplace from the Hôtel de Villemaré; Gobelins tapestry, representing June, or the Sheepshearing; flat-topped bureau stamped *Migeon* and *Dubois*; *Germain*, incense-burner. SALLE OEBEN. J. F. Oeben (d. c. 1765). Notice the chequered marquetry design which decorates many of his works. Flat-topped bureau; bureau (r.) 'en capucin'; secretaire and matching chiffonier; table (l.) 'à la Bourgogne'. SALLE CONDÉ. Marquetry commode stamped *Leleu* (1772); *Joubert*, writing-table; *Dubois*, pair of ebony and Japanese lacquer 'bas-armoire'; *Oudry*, armchairs and stool, upholstered in Beauvais after *Boucher*; by the window, case of 18C small-arms. CABINET LOUIS XVI. *Flat-topped bureau by *Hauré* and *G. Beneman* (1787), the top is of green leather and it is decorated with gilt bronze by *Thomire*;

Riesener, *Secretaire in mottled mahogany, travelling chest; *Jacob,* two arm-chairs (1787); columns of yellow marble and porphyry. SALLE LEBAUDY. Panelling from the Hôtel de Chevreuse. In the centre, *Riesener,* flat-topped desk; *Boulard,* three armchairs and ten chairs (1785); against the walls, four marquetry stools in the style of *Boulle.* CABINET CHINOIS. On the walls panels of Chinese wallpaper (18C); armchairs and chairs by *Jacob* and *Rode* (1777); *Carlin,* commode, Japanese lacquer and gilt bronze; to the right of the window, *Levasseur,* secretaire with hinged lid (1785). FIRST PRIVATE ROOM of Marie-Antoinette. In the niche lined with a hanging of shadow-taffeta is a roll-topped desk by *Riesener; Hauré,* pair of semi-cabriolet armchairs; *Riesener,* writing-desk; Gobelins tapestry illustrating the story of Don Quixote, after *Tessier* and *Coypel.* SECOND PRIVATE ROOM. *Daguere* and *Weisweiler,* *Writing-desk in bronze, ebony steel, and mother-of-pearl (1784); 'Don Quixote' tapestry.

THIRD PRIVATE ROOM. Adorned with granite pilasters with white marble capitals; glass-cases (r.), lacquer, porcelain and hard-stone trinkets, resting on table-plates of petrified wood; glass-cases (l.), travelling-case made in Paris for Marie-Antoinette (c. 1787).

Medieval and Renaissance Art. We may enter this department either from the ground floor by the Escalier Percier or through the Department of Egyptian Antiquities on the first floor. We begin the visit by the SALLES DE LA COLONNADE, the VESTIBULE (Pl. O) of which is decorated with fine 17C wood-work from the Château de Vincennes. In the cases are four ceremonial mantles of the Order of the Saint-Esprit (comp. the Galerie d'Apollon). The CHAMBRE À ALCÔVE (Pl. P) has panelling (restored by Louis XIV) from Henri II's apartments in the Louvre; the 17C bed is from the Château d'Effiat in the Puy-de-Dôme. The CHAMBRE DE PARADE (Pl. Q) contains good panel-ling, mostly of the period of Henri II, also a Mortlake tapestry (1630–35) and 17C wall-hangings in silver thread depicting the story of Deborah.

ROOM 1 (Early Middle Ages; Pl. R). Ivories, silver and goldsmiths' work, and enamels. In the centre, *Shrine of St Potentin in copper gilt, from Steinfeld near Treves (13C). The beautiful and extensive collection of ivories includes: the Harbaville **Triptych (Byzantine; 10C), with Christ enthroned between the Virgin and St John the Baptist surrounded by saints; triptych of the Nativity (Byzantine; 11C); caskets with scenes of the Life of Christ (Metz; 10C) and with mythological scenes (Byzantine; 10C); plaques of the 5–6C (Christ and St Peter) and of the 8–11C (Miracle of the Loaves; Ottoman, 10C), also a 3C plaque (the Rout of Silenus; Alexandria); two 6C pyxes; Madonna (English?; 11C); liturgical comb with Samson and the lion (Metz; 10–11C); chessmen of the 12C, etc. Enamels: Reliquary of the Arm of Charlemagne (Mosan; c. 1170), from Aix-la-Chapelle; cross-reliquary given to the abbey of St Vincent at Laon (1174–1205); champlevé work of the 12–13C from Cologne and the Moselle; chalice and paten (Spanish; c. 1200) from the abbey of Pelayos, etc. The two porphyry columns are from the 4C Basilica of St Peter at Rome. On the walls, Three hangings illustrating scenes in the life of St Anatole de Salins (Bruges; early 16C), and a tapestry of the Adoration of the Magi (Flemish; 15C).

To the left, by the exit, Limoges and other enamels of the 12–13C, including a small shrine, a Crucifixion, and a Eucharistic dove for the safe-keeping of the consecrated Hosts (Limoges work).—R. 2 (Pl. S). By the windows, Altar-piece in ivory, with the lives of Christ, St John the Baptist, and St John the Evangelist (by the Embriachi, c. 1400), presented to the abbey of Poissy by Jean, duc de Berri. In the centre, 13–14C *Ivories from the Paris workshops:

Madonna, Coronation of the Virgin, Descent from the Cross, Virgin and Angel of the Annunciation, and a Prophet; also *'Casket of St Louis', a wooden box with enamel and metal decoration (Limoges; late 13C); *Enamelled ciborium (mid-13C), signed 'G. Alpais of Limoges'. Case 3. Limoges enamels with repoussé work (13C); Case 4. Ivories of the Paris School (c. 1320 and c. 1340) with distinctive decoration; Case 5. Limoges champlevé work (12–13C) including reliquary of St Francis of Assisi; Case 6. *Reliquary of the Arm of St Louis of Toulouse (Italian; 1337), *Reliquary of St Martin (14C), reliquary of Jaucourt (Byzantine 11–12C work with French 14C supporters), reliquary of St Henry the Emperor (German; 12C); Case 7. Spanish and Italian ivories and enamel work, notably a 14C communion cup (Spanish); wing of diptych (English; 15C). In other cases, less important metal-work and 'dinanderie' (12–15C), etc. Also noteworthy, Embroidered cross from a chasuble (Bohemia; early 15C). On the walls, Flemish and Brussels tapestries, including St Luke painting the Virgin (Brussels; 16C), and (r.) Madonna in Glory (Flanders; 1485). Between the rooms, fragments of 13C stained glass from Reims, depicting the Martyrdom of SS Nicasius and Eutropia.

SALLES DE LA RENAISSANCE. 1st Room (Pl. T). By the windows, 15–16C Florentine bronzes, including the Flagellation, attributed to *Donatello* (Case 10); Gnome with a snail (Paduan School, 15C); *Eight bronze reliefs in the classical style, by *Andrea Riccio* (1470–1532), from the tomb of Marcantonio della Torre, in San Fermo, Verona. Cases by the 3rd window contain 16C engraved Italian crystals (including works by *Valerio Belli*), twelve small busts of Cæsars (Italy, 16C), etc.; on the left of exit, French and Italian medals, by *Pisanello, Matteo de' Pasti, G. Pilon,* and *G. Dupré*. In the centre, the *'Spinario', a Renaissance cast of the antique original (c. 1541); 16C Florentine table with a fountain in bronze (Spain). In the central cases, *Bronzes of the Florentine and Paduan Schools (15–16C), including works by *Donatello* (Case 1), *Bellano,* and *Sperandio* (Fr. Gonzaga, marquis of Mantua), and by *Riccio* (Case 3). The Renaissance furniture includes (by the E. wall) the throne of the archbishops of Vienne (France, 16C); Brussels tapestry of 1520. Between the rooms are fragments of Swiss stained glass (16–17C; note the little enamel fly on one of the panels). 2nd Room (Pl. U). The vases in the centre contain a superb collection of Italian and Limoges **Enamels, mainly of the 15–16C, but still virile, though more elaborate, in the 17C. Case 1. Medallion with a self-portrait by *Jean Fouquet*. Cases 3, 4, 5. Limoges enamels from the workshops of the 'Master of the Æneid', Poillevé, Jean and Pierre Pénicaud, Nouailher, and others (16C), and by *Léonard Limousin* and his school (16C). Case 5. **Portrait of the Constable Anne de Montmorency, in a frame set with plaques, signed and dated by *Léonard Limousin,* 1556. Cases 6, 7. Enamels by *Pierre Reymond* and his school. Cases 8, 9, 10. Enamels by *Jean* and *Suzanne de Court, Pierre Courteys, J.* and *Martial Reymond, Jacques I* and *Jacques II Laudin, Jean Limousin, Jacques* and *Pierre Nouailher*. The eight wall-cases and one central case (17) contain a magnificent collection of Hispano-Moresque, French, and Italian *Ceramics of the 15–17C, with fine examples by *Bernard Palissy* (c. 1510–89; Cases 18, 19) and from the St-Porchaire workshop (Case 17); note also three intarsia panels attributed to *Fra Vicenzo da Verona* (c. 1500), and four ceramic medallions attributed to *Girolamo della Robbia,* from the Château of St-Germain-en-Laye (16C). Below, in the centre, is a large 16C French chest; and on the two steps are decorated tiles from Isabella d'Este's palace at Mantua and the Petrucci Palace at Siena. At the opposite end is a similar chest flanked by two fine oak cabinets of the 16C, on top of which are a faïence bust of a woman from Urbino, and a Christ attributed to *Giovanni della Robbia* (Florentine, 16C). Around the walls (starting from the N.E. corner) is a series of twelve tapestries of the months, 'Les Chasses de Maximilien', after *B. van Orley* (Brussels, c. 1530).—The small antechamber (Pl. V; l.) contains a suit of armour known as Henri II's, a case of 16C 'dinanderie' and goldsmiths' work, including an ivory Madonna (Flanders, 16C), and a tapestry by *Jean Cousin* (1543).

Sculpture of the Middle Ages, Renaissance, and 17C. We enter this department (ground floor) either through the Porte La Trémoille (Pavillon La Trémoille), or by the staircase descending from the W. end of the Grande Galerie.

SALLE ROMANE (Pl. 63). *Sculpture of the 11–12C. Right to left: Fragment of the cloister at St-Genis-les-Fontaines; Head of Christ, in painted wood, from Lavaudieu; two capitals from Moutiers-St-Jean, one depicting wine-

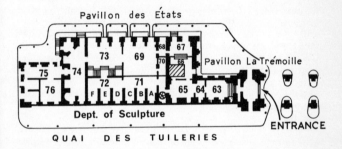

harvesting (rare at this period); Christ Crucified, in painted wood. In a case, Madonna from Forez. In the second window-recess, Merovingian capital (marble), recarved in the 11C, from the former abbey of Ste-Geneviève, Paris. Third window-recess, several heads of men (c. 1140), part of the portal of the Royal Abbey of St-Denis. Doorway from the priory of Estagel (Gard).

FIRST GOTHIC ROOM (Pl. 64). Early French 'Gothic' sculpture. On the right: fragments of a frieze from Notre-Dame-en-Vaux (Chalons-sur-Marne); reredos in painted stone showing the Virgin between the Annunciation and the Baptism of Christ (12C), Carrières-St-Denis; on either side, Solomon and Sheba, column statues from Notre-Dame-de-Corbeil (c. 1180–90). In the window-recess, seated Virgin holding Child (Crespières); under glass, remarkable head of St Peter (1170–89), the eyes lined with lead, by the monk *Martin* (Autun).

SECOND GOTHIC ROOM (Pl. 65). Flanking the entrance, five statues of angels (Poissy, late 12C); 1st window-recess, Woman's head (1220–30) from Reims Cathedral; statue of St Geneviève (Paris); St Matthew writing his gospel at the dictation of an angel (13C); 2nd window-recess, Descent to Limbo, *Pierre de Chelles* (early 14C), Notre-Dame-de-Paris; centre, Virgin holding the Child (traces of colour still visible), Île-de-France (13C). The Calvary of Nivelles (15C), from Belgium, stands out in the bay-frame. Facing the windows is a passage cut into the wall: in a recess in the form of a vault is the marble figure of Guillaume de Chanac (d. 1348); graceful painted wood statue of a Woman praying (early 14C).

THIRD GOTHIC ROOM. Opposite the windows, fragments of the Jubé of Bourges cathedral; above the arcades decorated with apostolic figures are a series of high-reliefs in painted stone with stained-glass motifs; on the lateral walls, two Prophets (Bourges, 13C). The steps lead down to:

PAUL VITRY ROOM. 15C sculpture of the Burgundian school. *Tomb of Philippe Pot, Grand Seneschal of Burgundy; window-recess, *Vluten*, effigy of Anne of Burgundy; carved stone cross (r.) from the cemetery at St-Léger-les-Troyes.

SALLE MICHEL COLOMBE (early 16C). Far end, St George fighting the dragon, marble high-relief by *Michel Colombe*; marble tomb (r.) of Renée d'Orléans (c. 1515–24) from the Célestins church (Paris); busts of Queen Louise de Savoie and Chancellor Duprat (?), in terracotta (Touraine); window-recess, two Virgins with Child; *G. Regnault* and *G. Chaleveau*, *Tomb of Louis de Poncher and his wife, St-Germain-l'Auxerrois (Paris).

SALLE JEAN GOUJON (Pl. 69). The French 'Renaissance'. 1st window-recess, *G. Pilon*, *Group of the three Graces (c. 1536–90), a funeral monument for the heart of Henri II; 2nd window-recess, *Jean Goujon*, *Deposition and the Evangelists (reliefs, c. 1545); 3rd recess. *Pilon*, Mater Dolorosa (painted terracotta). Centre, Diana leaning on a stag, an early garden figure (Château d'Anet). Far end, Consistory door, from Toulouse. Monumental fireplace, studio of *Germain Pilon*, from the Château de Villeroy; *B. Prieur*, Heart monument of the Constable Anne de Montmorency, also effigies of the Constable and his wife, from their tomb; *Bontemps* (attr.), tomb-statue of Admiral Chabot in armour. A passage leads to the High Gallery (Pl. 70). Note the altarpiece from Champagne, and the fine Head of Christ, painted stone (16C).

HIGH GALLERY (Pl. 71). Small sculptures of the French middle ages. Bay A. 16C stone and marble work. Centre, recumbent figure of a princess, daughter of Charles V (?). Bay B. Wooden statues, 13–15C. Statuette of St Étienne (r.), painted and gilded (Burgundy). Opposite this bay, statue of St John (Loche). Bay C. Marble and stone statuettes, 15–16C. Note the gracious Saint holding a book. Second High Gallery (Pl. 72). The Isenheim Virgin from the monastery of Antonites in Isenheim (c. 1470–80). Bay D. Eastern France, Rhineland and Bohemia. Kneeling Christ at the Mount of Olives (Rhineland, 15C). Bay E. German School. Virgin of the Annunciation kneeling, by *Tilman Riemenschneider* (1468–1531), one of the greatest German sculptors of the late Middle Ages (painted and gilded marble); nude St Mary Magdalene, 'the beautiful German girl', *Gregor Erhart* (1470–1571). Bay F. Netherlands Schools. A fine collection of late 15C and early 16C wooden statuettes; large retable, painted and gilded wood, representing the Childhood and Passion of Christ, showing strong influences from the Mystery plays (Antwerp, early 16C). The stairs lead down to:

MICHELANGELO ROOM (Pl. 73). Flanking the door: *Michelangelo Buonarroti* (1475–1564), *Two slaves. Intended for the tomb of Pope Julius II, they symbolize the Arts as prisoners of death without their great papal protector. Four remaining slaves are at the Fine Arts Academy, Florence. Bronze bust (r.) of *Michelangelo*, by one of his pupils; statue of Jason (bronze), attr. to Michelangelo during his youth. Over the door: *Benvenuto Cellini* (1500–72), Nymph of Fontainebleau (bronze bas-relief); enamelled terracottas from the workshop of the *Della Robbias*. On the landing: *Jean Bologne* (1524–1608), *Mercury flying. Stairs lead to:

THE LOWER GALLERY. Italian sculpture, 15–16C. 1st Bay. Pisan School.

Fra Gugliemo (attr.), statue of Faith (c. 1627). 2nd Bay. Four Cardinal Virtues (late 13C). Right of staircase, *Nino Pisano*, Virgin of the Annunciation (1368). The left section of this room is devoted to enamelled earthenware from the Florentine workshop of *Della Robbia*. Note the bust of a young man and the sensitive face of St John as a child. Descend two steps into a further gallery. On the reverse side of the pillar, *Mino da Fiesole* (1418–81), Diotisalvi Nerobi (marble); *Agostino di Duccio*, *Virgin and Child surrounded by angels (marble bas-relief); end wall, between two Sienese Virgins, *Jacopo della Quercia*, Virgin with Child from the Carmelite convent of Ferrara. 1st Bay. *Donatello* (1386–1468), *St John the Baptist as a youth, Virgin and Child. 2nd Bay. In a case, *Bust of a Woman, in painted and gilded wood, attr. to the workshop of *Desiderio da Settignano*; by the same sculptor, Christ and St John as children (medallion). 3rd Bay. Sculpture from Lombardy, late 15C. *Gian Cristoforo Romano* (attr.), bust of Beatrix d'Este. From the Salle Michelangelo, the door (l.) from the Stanga palace, Cremona, leads to: SALLE PUGET (Pl. 75). Sculpture, 17C. Right, *Barthelemey Tremblay* (d. 1629), Henri IV in armour; *P. Francheville*, four slaves seated in chains; *Jean Bologne*, Nude seated. Left wall, *Simon Guillain*, Louis XIII, Anne of Austria, and Louis XVI as a child; *Puget* (1620–94), *Milon de Cretone attacked by a lion (a powerful and moving work in bronze), Hercules at rest, Perseus and Andromeda.

GALLERY GIRARDON. Art of Versailles. Either side of the door, *Girardon* (1628–1715), two vases from the gardens at Versailles; centre, *Coysevox*, Venus crouching; *Nicolas Coustou*, Adonis resting after hunting; *Coysevox*, bust of the Grand Condé.

SALLE COYSEVOX. Centre, *Coysevox* (1640–1720), *Duchess of Burgundy as Diana; right, *Puget*, Diogenes and Alexander (bas-relief); *G. Coustou*, terracotta bust of his brother Nicolas; below the tapestry, *Coysevox*, Nymph with a shell; on either side, Apollo and Daphne, by the *Coustou* brothers, nephews of Coysevox.

The SCULPTURE OF THE 18–19C will be on exhibition in the Pavillon de Flore when this is no longer occupied by the Ministry of Finance. The following is a summary of some of the more important works of art not at present on view. *Bouchardon*, Cupid fashioning his bow from the club of Hercules (1750); *Pigalle*, bust of the surgeon Guérin; *Pajou*, Marie Leczinska, Psyche abandoned. The early 19C is represented by *Bosio, Chaudet, Chinard, David d'Angers*, and others, followed by *Rude, Pradier* and *Maindron*. Later masters include: *Carpeaux* ('Dance', cast for the group at the Opéra); *Chapu* (Joan of Arc); *Frémiet* (Pan and bear-cubs); *Dalou*; and *Barye*, with typical sculptures of animals.

21 THE MUSÉE DE L'ARMÉE

MÉTRO station: *Invalides* (lines 8 and 14).
ADMISSION 1 fr.: open daily (except Sun morning and Tues) 10–12.15, 1.30–5 or 5.30. The *Musée des Plans-Reliefs* (see below) is open daily (except Tues) 10–12, 2–5.30 (0,50 fr., Sun 0,25 fr.).

The **Musée de l'Armée** at the Invalides comprises two departments, one devoted to arms and armour, the other to military souvenirs. Plan, see p. 53.

The **Section des Armes et Armures** (entrance on right of Cour d'Honneur) has a particularly rich collection of offensive and defensive weapons of all periods, the 15–16C exhibits being of great artistic interest.—VESTIBULE. Chinese, Turkish, Spanish, and French cannon.—SALLE FRANÇOIS-PREMIER (to the r.). Frescoes depicting the conquests of Louis XIV in Holland;

Renaissance Arms and Armour (1400–1574); many of the helmets, pieces of armour, etc., are masterpieces of damascening, chasing and ivory carving. A trooper's armour of Charles VII's reign; the 'Lion' suit of armour; *Henri II's armour with the insignia of Diane de Poitiers; *Suit said to have belonged to the Duke of Alba; horse armour of François I and of the Elector Palatine Otto Henry; Sword of the Constable of France.—SALLE HENRI-IV (16–17C) with frescoes by 'Martin des Batailles'. Suits of armour worn by Louis XIII and Henri IV and one of Louis XIV, made in Brescia (1668); armour of the Princes of Condé and of Monaco, also of Turenne; swords and rapiers of the 16–17C.

SALLE CHARLEMAGNE (through passage opposite entrance to Museum). Weapons of the Old and New Stone Ages and coats of mail and shields (15C) of the Greeks, Romans, Franks, Crusaders, etc.—SALLE LOUIS XIII (r.). Arms of the 14–17C including arquebuses, pistols, muskets, swords; Edward III's battle-axe and James II's wheel-lock musket; Richelieu's match-lock; sword with chased hilt by Benvenuto Cellini; sword of Henri II de Condé.—SALLE LOUVOIS. Weapons of the 18–20C; note especially ornamental weapons of the Revolution and Empire; examples of weapons made at the 'Manufacture de Versailles'.—SALLE ORIENTALE. Weapons from Greece, Turkey, Circassia, and the Balkans. Military costumes and armour from Persia, India, and the Far East.

We retrace our steps through the Salle Charlemagne to the corridor, passing between the Cour d'Angoulême (l.) and the Cour des Victoires (r.), and mount the staircase (r.) to the SALLE 1914–1918, containing paintings, sketches, and other souvenirs of the First World War. The SALLE JOFFRE contains uniforms of the Army under the Third Republic.—Second Floor. SALLE DES ALLIÉS. Souvenirs and uniforms of the Allied armies of the First World War. SALLE GRIBEAUVAL. Scale models of artillery pieces dating from the reign of Henri II.

The **Section Historique** is entered from the left side of the Cour d'Honneur.— VESTIBULE. Flag standards taken from the enemy during the Revolutionary and Empire periods.—SALLE TURENNE (r.) Colours of French Regiments from the First Republic to the present day (visitors remove their hats); frescoes by *Van der Meulen*; German regimental colours captured in 1914–18 (far end of room). Personal souvenirs of Napoleon, including his uniform as general of division worn at Marengo (1800), a grey frock-coat, pistols, sabre, etc.— SALLE VAUBAN (l.). Paintings by *Edouard Detaille* (1848–1912), including Napoleon reviewing the troops after Jena (1806), and The Dream. Life-sized models in uniforms, including those of the Second World War. We ascend to the first floor.

SALLE LA FAYETTE, with souvenirs of Gen. La Fayette (1757–1834).— VESTIBULE. Portraits of governors of the hospital; uniforms of the Revolution and Empire.—SALLE LOUIS XIV (l.). 1st Section: Revolutionary, Directory, and Consulate periods; uniforms and presentation weapons awarded for distinguished service during these periods. 2nd Section: Souvenirs of the army under the monarchy; the cannon-ball that killed Turenne; Louis XIV's saddle-cloth; the colours of the Irish Clancarty regiment (1642); portrait of Turenne attributed to *Le Brun*; small cannon presented by the Franche-Comté to Louis XIV after its annexation to France in 1674; uniforms and equipment; English mortar presented to a French regiment by Washington after the fall of Yorktown in 1781. 3rd Section: Souvenirs of the Invalides.—SALLE NAPOLÉON (1804–15). Souvenirs of the First Empire and personal relics of the Emperor and his family; cast of his hand; death mask; Napoleon's bed at St Helena; stuffed skin of his horse, 'Vizir'; portrait by *Ingres* (1806).

Second Floor. VESTIBULE. Uniforms of the Second Empire.—SALLE BUGEAUD. Souvenirs of the Restoration (1815–30), the Spanish Expedition of 1823, the Constitutional Monarchy (1830–48) and its Algerian campaign; the Second Republic of 1848–52; etc.— SALLE PÉLISSIER. Second Empire (1852–70). Souvenirs of the Crimean War and of the Franco-Prussian War.—SALLE NEY. Flag standards of the Revolutionary and Empire periods; four saddles formerly belonging to the Mamelukes, taken during the Egyptian campaign of 1798; opposite, collections of toy soldiers.

The **Musée des Plans-Reliefs**, reached from the second floor of this side of the Musée de l'Armée, contains relief models of fortresses. The collection was founded by Louvois and is of great historical interest.

22   THE MUSÉE DES ARTS DÉCORATIFS

MÉTRO station: *Tuileries* (line 1), or *Palais-Royal* (lines 1, 7).
ADMISSION 1 fr.; open daily (except Tues and holidays) 10–12, 2–5.

The ***Musée des Arts Décoratifs**, at 107 Rue de Rivoli, occupies the *Pavillon de Marsan*, the N.W. wing of the Palais du Louvre. This valuable and interesting museum, especially rich in French works, illustrates decorative and ornamental art from medieval to modern times. The objects on display are fully described in lists hung on the wall of each room.

The Ground Floor is reserved for temporary exhibitions.

First Floor. This is devoted to Gothic and Renaissance art, and the period of Louis XIII to Louis XV.—R. 21. Flemish tapestries of the 15 and 16C.— RR. 22, 23. French sculpture of the 13–16C; tapestries, including The Woodcutters (15C).—R. 24 (Salle Raoul Duseigneur). Stonework and German and Flemish metalwork.—RR. 25–29 (French Renaissance): R. 26. Chest (1546) decorated with scenes from the labours of Hercules, showing the transition of medieval ornamental style to the Renaissance imitation of classical themes; cupboard of the second half of the 16C, with varied decoration incorporating Classical and religious themes and motifs; Limoges enamels of the second period of their greatness.—In the corridor is a fragment of a Fontainebleau tapestry, from the short-lived workshop founded by Francis I, c. 1530; another example (R. 28) represents Adonis.—R. 29. Cupboard in the plain style of the late 16C.—R. 30. Bookbindings, including bindings embossed with the arms of Madame du Barry and Madame de Pompadour; wooden panelling.— On the landing of the *Escalier Marsan* are tapestries, late 17C paintings and faience of the 14–18C (French).—R. 33 (Louis-XIII and early Louis-XIV). Cabinet attributed to *Jean Macé de Blois*, first half of the 17C; chair of c. 1650 showing the early stages of the Louis-XIV period, with a high back and carved acanthus-leaf decoration; tapestries including 'Herminie chez les Paysans', a scene from Tasso's 'Gerusalemme Liberata', c. 1660.—RR. 34–35 (Louis XIV, Regency and Louis XV). R. 34. Cupboard attributed to *Boulle*, c. 1680–90; tapestry after *Lebrun*, Juno or Air; examples of Beauvais tapestry, including Offering to Pan, after *J. B. Monnoyer*, the colleague of Jean Bérain.—R. 35. 'La Sultane', a painting by *C. Van Loo*, from the 'Chambre à la Turque' in Mme de Pompadour's Château de Bellevue.—RR. 36, 37. Painted woodwork from mansions in the Place Vendôme.—R. 39. Designs for interior decoration by *Watteau* and *Lancret*.—R. 41. Cupboard attributed to *Charles Cressent*, c. 1725, decorated with bronze medallions and arabesques.—R. 42. Ceiling, c. 1705–10, by *Claude Audran*.—R. 43. Faience of Aprey.—R. 44. Silverware.—

R. 45. Faience of Sceaux and a marquetry secretaire.—R. 46. Decorative woodwork, Paris, c. 1730–40; secretaire by *J. F. Leleu*, c. 1765, with typical Louis-XV decoration in Chinese lacquer with bronze moulded corners.— R. 47. Swords and carpets.—R. 48. Faience of Rouen showing strong Chinese influence (Chinese works of art arrived at the port of Dieppe, near by); faience of Sinceny (1737–75).—R. 49. The Gohun Family, one of *Boilly's* best paintings, showing his sharp eye for domestic detail and atmosphere; more examples of the Louis-XV style and the love of the 'Chinese' style.—R. 53. Faience of Vincennes and Meissen porcelain.—R. 53 (Salle Penard). Fine panelling.— R. 56. French glass from the 14–18C.—R. 58. Gilt woodwork.—R. 59. Musical instruments of the 17 and 18C; watches.

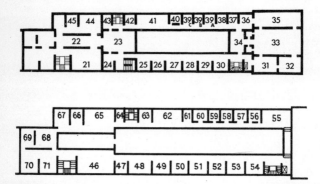

Second Floor. RR. 60–70 are devoted to the end of the reign of Louis XV and to the reign of Louis XVI: Porcelain of Sèvres and Vincennes; chairs of the period; a commode by *Riesener*, a characteristic work with charming decoration, a vase of flowers in marquetry-work and bronze laurel leaves; a typical Louis-XVI salon (both R. 65); printed cloth wall-covering showing Louis XVI opening the port at Cherbourg (R. 66); a bed in steel and bronze gilt attributed to *Boulet*, c. 1780–89 (R. 67); a cylinder-top secretaire by *Riesener* and Lyre-back chairs (R. 68); a Louis-XVI tric-trac table and furniture of the Directory (R. 70).

*RR. 73–79 have been specially decorated and furnished to show typical interiors of the period from the First Empire until the end of the July Monarchy of Louis-Philippe and the beginning of the Second Empire; wall-coverings and borders have been copied from originals and colours carefully chosen, the whole effect is elegant and pleasing.—R. 73 (First Empire). Paintings by *Boilly*, including Houdon's studio; Classical influence is seen in the furniture.— R. 74 (First Empire; the décor reproduces that of the palace of Compiègne). Chairs by the *Jacob* brothers; an early painting by *Ingres*, 'Casino de Raphaël à Rome'.—R. 75. (First Empire). Silverware and bronze 'coiffeuse' used by Josephine at the Tuileries.—R. 76 (Restoration). A sketch by *Delacroix* for a painting of Justinian for the Conseil d'État, destroyed in 1871; cradle offered to the Duc de Bordeaux by the city of Paris (1820).—R. 77 (Restoration; wallpaper painted with scenes showing the Incas). Boat-shaped bed by *F. Beaudry* (1827) remarkable for its oval shape and for the marquetry-work.—R. 78.

Typical furniture of the end of the Restoration and the reign of Louis-Philippe.—R. 79 (Louis-Philippe and the Second Empire). Piano of 1840; iron chairs; furniture incorporating 17C Italian mosaics; chairs showing Gothic influence.

The THIRD FLOOR is occupied mainly by the collections of foreign decorative art (closed 1966).

23   THE CONSERVATOIRE DES ARTS ET MÉTIERS

MÉTRO station: *Arts et Métiers* (lines 3 and 11).

ADMISSION 1 fr. (0,50 fr. for those holding a Student's Card); free on Sun. The *Museum* is open weekdays (except Mon) 1.30–5.30, Sun 10–5, the *Library* 2–7.30, Sun 10–12.30. LECTURES (adm. free) on applied science in the evenings between November and May.

The **Conservatoire des Arts et Métiers,** the Science Museum of Paris, situated on the E. side of the Rue St-Martin (No. 292), occupies the church, cloisters, refectory, etc., of the ancient priory of *St-Martin-des-Champs.*

This wealthy priory, founded by Henri I in 1060 and presented to the abbey of Cluny by Philip I in 1079, stood outside the city until the early 14C. Richelieu was one of its titular priors. During the Revolution the priory was occupied by the Société des Jeunes Français, an educational institution, and later it became a small-arms factory. In 1798 it was assigned to the Conservatoire des Arts et Métiers, which had been founded by a decree of the Convention in 1794, and here were assembled the collections of Vaucanson and other scientists.

On either side of the entrance gateway (1850) are statues of Science and Art, and the portal leading into the Cour d'Administration (left of the Cour d'Honneur) is flanked with statues of (l.) Nicholas Leblanc and (r.) Denis Papin.

On the right of the Cour d'Honneur is the *REFECTORY, a 13C masterpiece, built by Pierre de Montreuil (architect of the Sainte Chapelle). This magnificent hall (138 ft by 39 ft), the columns of which recall those of the Église des Jacobins at Toulouse, now contains the *Library*. Note the 13C reader's pulpit at the E. end, on the left, and the painting of St-Martin by Steinheil, inside the S. doorway; externally this door is a fine example of decorated Gothic and the sole relic of the original cloisters.

On the right of the Cour d'Honneur a passage leads into the Cour des Laboratoires and the courtyard in front of the church. The 13C portal has been restored and the turret on the right is a modern addition. Between the church and the library is the Great Lecture Hall.

Ground Floor. We enter the Museum by the central staircase in the Cour d'Honneur, then descend the central flight of the double staircase (designed by Antoine) to ROOM 2, known as the SALLE DE L'ÉCHO because a whisper in one corner is distinctly audible in the diagonally opposite corner. The room contains a model of Lavoisier's laboratory. We turn left into R. 21, containing models of locomotives and rolling-stock of various periods; among the former is the first one wholly built in France, by Séguin (1829), Stephenson's (1846) for the Nord railway, and an American one with bogie by Norris (1841).—RR. 20–13. *Astronomy, Surveying, Clocks.* Telescopes, field glasses, seismograph, theodolites, set of chronometers by Berthoud, etc. Clocks by Berthoud, Lepaute, Bréguet, Janvier, and other celebrated 18C clock-makers; orreries and astronomical clocks; musical clocks, and a water-clock of 1699 (R. 18); 'Nef de Charles-Quint' (R. 17), an elaborate 16C timepiece; automata including Marie-Antoinette's 'Joueuse de Tympanon' (R. 15; 1785).

Returning to the Salle de l'Écho, we enter the rooms on its S. side.—RR. 4, 5, 8, 9. *Metallurgy.* Note the model of the balloon gondola used by Prof.

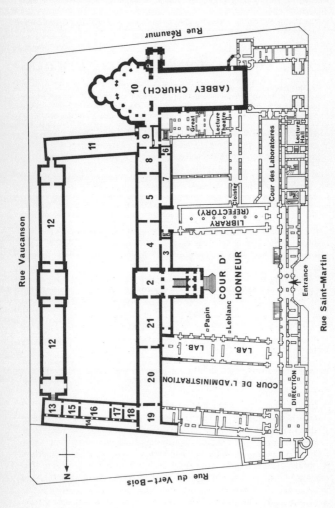

Piccard in his stratospheric attempts (R. 4); models of machinery used for the production of steel, iron, copper, etc. (R. 5); models of rolling-mills and samples of various metals, etc. (R. 8); power hammers, drop-forging presses, etc. (R. 9).—R. 10 is the former *Abbey Church* restored in 1854–80. The aisle-less nave dates from the end of the 13C; the choir, with its 'chevet' of chapels, has perhaps the earliest Gothic vault in Paris (1130–40). In the choir: electrical machines, aeroplane and motor-car engines, Foucault's pendulum for demonstrating the rotation of the earth. In the nave: aeroplanes of Ader (1897) and of Esnault-Pelterie (1906), the plane in which Blériot made the first flight across the Channel (1909), the Bréguet plane that flew from Fez to Casablanca in 2 hrs 50 min. (1911); among the prototypes of the motor-car, Cugnot's steam-carriage (1770), and one by Serpollet (1888); petrol-driven vehicles include a

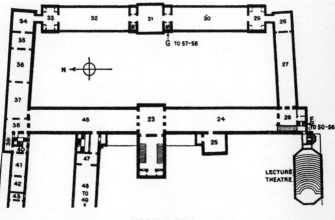

FIRST FLOOR

Peugeot (1893), a Panhard (1896), a Berliet phaeton (1898), a De Dion-Bouton (1899), a Renault (1900), etc. Here are also velocipedes and bicycles.—R. 11. *Agricultural Machinery.*—R. 12. *Prevention of Accidents* and *Industrial Hygiene* (temporarily closed).

First Floor. We return to the Salle de l'Écho and ascend the staircase to R. 23, the Salle d'Honneur, with the microscope belonging to the Duc de Chaulnes (18C), Pascal's multiplying and adding machine, Papin's autoclave (1680), first sewing-machine (1830) by Thimonnier, and Gambey's theodolite.—R. 46 (l.). *Industrial Chemistry, Printing and Engraving.*—RR. 47–49. *Spinning and Weaving.*—RR. 38, 39. *Photography.* Apparatus used by Daguerre and Niepce.—RR. 40–41. *Cinematography.* Apparatus used by Reynaud, de Marey, Lumière, and other pioneers.—R. 42. Aerial and colour photography.

We retrace our steps through R. 38 to RR. 37–35. *Ceramics.* Roman terracottas from Vaison (Vaucluse). Pottery and brick kilns; pottery and porcelain: in the cases are Japanese, Chinese, and English porcelain, Sèvres porcelain and faience, including a head of Balzac in Sèvres 'grès', after Rodin.—RR. 34–32. *Glassware, Enamels,* and *Terracottas.* Raw materials and apparatus; artificial gems, crystal glass by Lalique, Daum, etc., and from Baccarat and Val St-Lambert; enamels.—RR. 32, 31. *Machine-tools, Gears.* Lathe used by

Louis XVI.—R. 30. *Acoustics, Optics,* and *Electricity.* Stringed instruments, including a harpsichord of 1786 by Joachim Swann, a viol of 1730, and double-bass of 1663; piano belonging to Mme de Maintenon; Edison's first gramophone; optical instruments.—RR. 29, 28. *Electricity.* Radio set formerly installed in the Eiffel Tower (1910); valves and electrodes, etc.; periscope (R. 28— in cubicle).—R. 27. *Electricity (Heat).* Static electricity apparatus; note the machines belonging to Van Marum and Nairne (18C); original apparatus used by Coulomb' in his experiments with electrostatics and magnetism; physical apparatus belonging to Charles and the Abbé Nollet.—RR. 26, 25. *Mechanics and Physics.* Apparatus of Gen. Morin.—R. 24. *Machines.* Séguin's tubular boiler; model of Watt's steam engine; diesel engines; turbines, etc. Model of the 'Machine de Marly'.

Second Floor. For RR. 50–60, we ascend staircase E, in R. 26. ROOM 50. *Heating and Lighting.*—R. 51. *Weights and Measures. Instruments for Mechanical Observations. Meteorology.*—RR. 52–56. *Telegraphic and Telephonic Instruments.*—For RR. 57, 58, we ascend Staircase G, in R. 31.—Room 57. *Geometry. Mechanical Drawing.* Gen. Monge's Collection.—R. 58. *Calculating Machines.*

24   THE BIBLIOTHÈQUE NATIONALE

MÉTRO station: *Bourse* (line 3).

ADMISSION. The public are admitted to the *Cabinet des Médailles et des Antiques* every weekday 10–12, 2–4, 0,50 fr.; they are also admitted to exhibitions in the Galleries Mansart and Mazarine (when there is no exhibition, apply to the doorkeepers). The *Reading Room* (Salle de Travail des Imprimés) and *Periodicals Room* (Salle Ovale) are open for readers from 9 to 6, except on Sun, holidays, and during the fortnight following the Sun after Easter. Foreigners wishing to use the Library should apply to the Secretary's office. A letter of recommendation from their ambassador or consul (students should apply to their director of studies) and two identity photographs are necessary before an entry card is issued. The *Print Rooms* and the *Geographical Rooms* are open 10–5; the *Manuscript Rooms,* 9–5.

The **Bibliothèque Nationale** ranks with the British Museum in London as one of the two largest libraries in W. Europe. The catalogue of printed books (over six million), which already fills 185 vols., has been compiled only as far as the letter U. The extensive buildings were erected at various times on the site of the 17C *Hôtel Mazarin,* a portion of which has survived (see below), and occupy an area of 4¼ acres, bounded by the Rue de Richelieu, Rue des Petits-Champs, Rue Vivienne, and the Rue Colbert. It includes the *Hôtel Tubeuf,* whose brick and stone façade, set back in the Rue des Petits-Champs, was built by *Le Muet* in 1635.

The Bibliothèque Nationale, formerly known as the *Bibliothèque Royale* and the *Bibliothèque Impériale,* is in line of direct descent from the private libraries of the French kings. Dispersed, for the most part, at the end of the Hundred Years War, the Library was re-founded by Louis XII and moved to Blois. During the following two centuries the collection was removed to Fontainebleau and then to Paris, and in 1721 found its present home in the Rue de Richelieu. The reigns of Henri IV, Louis XIV, and Louis XV saw the addition, by purchase or gift, of many famous libraries and collections (including Colbert's library). At the Revolution the Library was greatly enlarged by the collections of the suppressed religious establishments, and in 1793 it was enacted that a copy of every book, newspaper, etc., printed in France, should be deposited by the publishers in the Bibliothèque Nationale. The yearly intake of books is now not less than forty thousand.

We enter by the gateway at No. 58 Rue de Richelieu, turn to the right across the Cour d'Honneur and mount the steps leading up to the Vestibule. The cloakroom (obligatory but no charge) is on the left and opposite is the READING

Room (*Salle de Travail des Imprimés*), into which visitors may look through the glass door. This hall, which is roofed by nine faience domes, seats 360 readers who have access to more than 10,000 books of reference. The upper galleries and the *Magasin Central*, which lies beyond the hemicycle accommodating the librarians, contain over 1,000,000 volumes.

At the end of the Vestibule is a staircase leading to the first floor. To the left of the staircase is a passage leading to the Periodicals Room (*Salle Ovale*). To the right is the Prints Department (*Cabinet des Estampes*), with over five million prints, which was re-opened in 1946 after a complete renovation. The Galerie Mansart, used for exhibitions, was formerly Mazarin's sculpture gallery; note his arms above the door and the carved foliage and paintings by Grimaldi. At the end of the gallery is the *Vestibule du Cabinet des Estampes*, from which a staircase and a lift both ascend to the Research Rooms on the second floor.

First Floor. At the top of the staircase (r.) is the entrance to the **Cabinet des Médailles et des Antiques**; the iron gates are automatically opened on pressing the bell (tickets obtained in R. 2). The collection, founded in the 16C, contains a priceless selection of antiques, as well as c. 400,000 coins and medals.—Room 1. In the centre, Torso of Aphrodite, in Parian marble (Hellenistic). In the table-cases, French and foreign coins, medals, engraved gems, jewels, and Italian Renaissance *Medals, etc. The wall-cases contain Egyptian terracottas, small bronzes, and painted limestone statuettes, etc.—R. 2. The central case contains the most precious objects in the museum. Note especially: *Ivory chessman representing a Hindu king on an elephant, reputed to have belonged to Charlemagne; bust of Constantine the Great, once the head of the cantor's wand at the Sainte Chapelle; 'Patère de Rennes', a Roman gold dish found in 1774; Merovingian chalice and oblong paten (6C) found at Gourdon in the Charollais; *'Grand Camée' from the Sainte Chapelle, representing the Apotheosis of Germanicus, with Tiberius and Livia; it is the largest antique cameo known; Agate nef from St-Denis; *Cup of Chosroes II, king of Persia, c. A.D. 600; Cup of Ptolemy, in sardonyx, carved with the mysteries of Ceres and Bacchus; Aquamarine intaglio of Julia, daughter of Titus, one of the best glyptic portraits extant; engraved Chaldæan stone (1100 B.C.) found near Baghdad. In single cases, *Red-figured amphora, signed Amasis (Athene and Poseidon), Cylix of Arcesilaus, king of Cyrene. In a case (r. of entrance), Amphoræ and cylices; on the left, Vase of Berenice (239–227 B.C.) from Benghazi, and other vases. By the window, *Throne of Dagobert, on which the kings of France were crowned, a Roman curule chair of bronze, with arms and back added in the 12C by Abbot Suger; Gold objects from the tomb of Childeric I at Tournai; ivory *Consular diptychs (including those of Anastasius and of Philoxenus, 517 and 525) and Byzantine triptychs, gold bullæ of Charles II of Anjou, king of Naples (1285–1309), and of Baldwin I, emperor of Constantinople in 1204–06. In a table-case, Gold coins found at Chécy (Loiret) in 1952, bracelets (one called 'of Diane de Poitiers'), bulla of Edmund, earl of Lancaster, titular king of Sicily, 1255–63. In case (r. of entrance to R. 3), *Silver hoard from the temple of Mercurius Canetonensis, found near Berthouville (Eure), including silver figurines and vessels of the 2C B.C. and others of the best Greek period.—R. 3. In the wall-case (l.), Sword, late 15C, said to have belonged to Boabdil, last Moorish king of Granada, 11C oliphant, ancient helmets, Sassanid dish (6C A.D.), Roman bronze statuettes, domestic utensils, etc.; on the right, Greek and Etruscan vases; table-case, chronological collection of antique coins; wardrobes, one by *Cressent* and two of Coromandel lacquer, and coin-cabinets by *Slodtz*.

From the Cabinet des Médailles we ascend the stairs to the landing above. On the right is the MANUSCRIPT ROOM (more than 130,000 manuscripts, of which some 10,000 are illuminated), and on the left is the GALERIE MAZARINE. Built in 1645 by Mansart, with a ceiling by Romanelli, this delicately proportioned room is devoted to temporary exhibitions of bookbinding, book-printing, etc. At the far end of the gallery is the staircase (r.) to the Print Room (for researchers); to the left is the *Department of Maps and Plans* (reopened in 1954), with the library of the *Société de Géographie*, occupying most of the Hôtel Tubeuf (see above); in its entrance hall is a collection of globes, astrolabes and astronomical instruments.

25   THE MUSÉE CARNAVALET

MÉTRO station: *St Paul* (line 1).
ADMISSION 0,50 fr. (free on Sun); open daily (except Tues and holidays) 10–12 and 2–5 or 6. Umbrellas and sticks must be given up in the cloak-room (no charge) on the right of the gateway.

The **Musée Carnavalet,** or *Musée Historique de la Ville de Paris*, at the corner of the Rue des Francs-Bourgeois and the Rue de Sévigné, is a highly important collection illustrating the history of Paris from the 16C to the middle of the 19C. The section on the Revolution deserves special notice.

The museum is housed in the HÔTEL CARNAVALET, a fine mansion begun in 1544 for Jacques des Ligneris, President of the Parlement, and adorned with charming sculptures by *Jean Goujon*. It was altered in 1660 by Mansart, who built the present façade, but retained the 16C gateway with its Goujon sculptures (on the keystone, a winged figure of Abundance standing on a globe which was later carved into a carnival mask, in punning allusion to Carnavalet). Further alterations and enlargements were made in 1905–14, and again in 1923–25. The name Carnavalet was derived from the Breton family of Kernevenoy, the second owners of the mansion. Madame de Sévigné lived here from 1677 till her death in 1696; her apartments, which were shared by her daughter, Madame de Grignan, and her uncle, the Abbé de Coulanges, were on the first floor (now RR. 46–51, 58–60, and 42).

The bronze statue of Louis XIV in the centre of the COURTYARD is by *Coysevox*. Of the sculptures in the courtyard, the best are those by *Jean Goujon* on the entrance arch and above the door on the left side. The large reliefs of the Seasons, on the side opposite the entrance, were probably executed under Goujon's direction. On the right side, the relief above the door is a copy (1870) of the one opposite; those on the first story are by *Van Opstal* (1660).

From the entrance hall (RR. 1–3) the steps lead into R. 4 (Salle des Enseignes; see below) but we cross the courtyard to reach the stairs (l.) to the First Floor. Through the doors opposite are RR. 17–20, illustrating the TOPOGRAPHY OF PARIS from the 16C to the beginning of the 18C. On the left wall (R. 19) is an anonymous portrait of Mary Stuart, in a white mourning veil (1561).—R. 21. Drawings, sketches, and gouaches of the 17C.—R. 23 (r.) contains richly painted and gilded woodwork (c. 1656), brought from the Hôtel Colbert de Villacerf at 23 Rue de Turenne.—R. 24 is the 'Grand Cabinet Doré' from a mansion, Le Vau, at 14 Place des Vosges; the ceiling-painting, representing Sunrise, is by *Le Brun*.—R. 25 has decorations from the same hôtel; the ceiling by *Le Brun* (restored) represents Olympus, Mercury presenting Hebe to Jupiter, and the Muses (1651). On the walls are general views of Paris and its environs c. 1665–1740.

Leaving R. 25, we turn right into RR. 61–63, which are devoted to the Revolution. R. 61. Objects and documents relating to the Convention; military equipment, etc.—R. 62 is decorated with Louis-XV panelling from No. 7 Rue de Varenne; prints illustrating the Spirit of each Revolutionary Month; Garden of the Musée des Monuments Français, by *Hubert Robert*; swords and sabres,

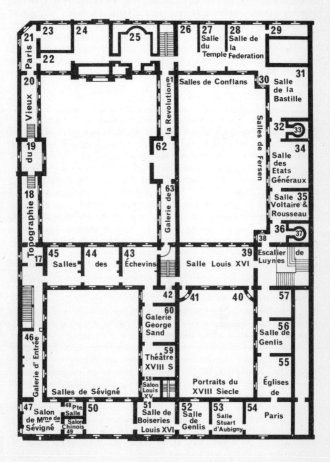

including those of Masséna and Augereau, and portraits of Kléber and Marceau and other generals.—R. 63. Examples of popular art during the Revolution. In the cases are fans, curios, miniatures, medals, faience, etc. Note the 'Iconographie des Martyrs de la Liberté', in the second table case on the left.

We retrace our steps through R. 61 and turn right into further Revolutionary rooms. The SALLE DE LA CONVENTION (R. 26) and the three following rooms are decorated with woodwork from the Château de Conflans-Charenton. Robespierre's half-finished signature and bloodstains, following the attack on him on 9 Thermidor (27 July) 1794, also a lock of his hair; Couthon's mechanical chair; portraits of Marat, Robespierre, and Danton. In the case to the right of the window, works executed by *Hubert Robert* during his imprisonment; caricatures, by *Gabriel*, of notables of the Revolution. Festival of the Supreme Being, 8 June 1794, by *Naudet*. On the mantelpiece is a calendar clock marked with revolutionary months.—The SALLE DU TEMPLE (R. 27) contains personal souvenirs, letters, furniture (Mme Elisabeth's bed), etc., of Louis XVI and his family during their imprisonment in the Temple.—SALLE DE LA FÉDÉRATION (R. 28). Fête de la Fédération, by *Swebach-Desfontaines*; paintings by *Hubert Robert*, *Boze*, and *Le Guay*; furniture with republican emblems; plaster *Bust of Barnave, by *Houdon*, etc.—R. 30. Strong-box from the Bastille.—R. 31. Model of the Bastille cut out of one of its stones under the direction of *Palloy*, the demolition contractor; (above) Taking of the Bastille, by *Singleton*; Demolition of the Bastille, by *Hubert Robert*. In the cases, souvenirs of the Bastille, including 'Lettres de Cachet' signed by Louis XV, etc.—RR. 33–37 are decorated with woodwork from the Hôtel de Breteuil, No. 17 Rue de Matignon, once the home of Axel de Fersen, the Swedish count who aided Louis XVI and his family in their abortive attempt to escape from Paris in 1791. R. 33. Terracotta statuettes (revolutionary allegories), by *Chinard*.—R. 34 contains souvenirs of the States General, including portraits of Fauchet, Guillotin, Bailly, and of Camille Desmoulins (by *Boilly*); busts of Mirabeau and Bailly.—R. 35. Personal souvenirs and portraits of Voltaire and Rousseau; *Portrait of Voltaire aged 24, by *Largillière*; clock of 1791, with decorations illustrating the removal of Voltaire's remains to the Panthéon; death-mask of Voltaire (central case).—R. 36. Portrait of B. Franklin, by *Duplessis*.—R. 37 is the rotunda from the ground floor of the Hôtel de Ferson. —R. 38. Screens with scenes relative to the birth of the Dauphin (22 Oct 1781); paintings by *Demachy*; snuffboxes.—The ESCALIER DE LUYNES, a reconstruction of the stairway from the Hôtel de Luynes, is decorated with wall-paintings of the family, by *Brunetti* (1748).

We turn right into the SALLE LOUIS XVI (R. 39). *Hubert Robert*, Demolition of the houses on the Pont au Change and on the Pont Notre-Dame. In the central case, personal relics of the royal family, in particular of Marie-Antoinette (her fan, scissors, slippers, etc.), also the Dauphin's bonnet, and the Cross of the Order of the Saint-Esprit worn by Louis XVI; drawings by *Duvivier*; 18C porcelain. By the windows, the cases contain fans, buttons, watches, etc. In the recess (R. 40) on the left, views of Paris, etc.; and at the far end on the left (R. 41), faience illustrating the aeronautical efforts of the brothers Montgolfier.

We return to the landing of the Escalier de Luynes, and turn right into R. 57. Paintings by *Hubert Robert*, *Demachy*, and others.—R. 56. Woodwork from the Hôtel de Genlis; views of Paris by *J. B. Lallemand*, *Demachy*, *Génillon*, *A. J. Noël*, etc.—RR. 55, 54 contain woodwork of the Louis-XV period from the Collège des Prémontrés; sketch of La Rochelle by *C. Vanloo* (comp. Notre-Dame-des-Victoires); bust of Abbé Nollet by *Defernex*; paintings and drawings of Paris churches, by *Hubert Robert* and *Demachy*; models of statues in St-Sulpice by *Dumont*; paintings and drawings by *Demachy*, *Delarue*, *J. B. Oudry*, *Jeaurat*, *P. D. Martin*, *Saint-Aubin*, and others.—R. 53. Woodwork from the music room of the Hôtel Stuart-d'Aubigny; terracotta bust of the Abbé Delille, translator of Virgil and Milton; portraits by *Tocqué*, *J. F. Colson*, *S. B. Lenoir*, and *Vestier*, etc.—R. 52. Regency woodwork from the Hôtel de Genlis; paintings by *N. B. Lépicié*, *Lajoue* (Abbé Nollet), and

Pierre Subleyras.—R. 51. Louis-XVI period. Panelling from the Rue de Grenelle. In the cases, *Drawings by *St-Aubin.* On the walls, water-colours and drawings by *Carmontelle,* including Mozart when a child; also drawings by the *Chevalier de Lespinasse.*—R. 58 (r.) has polychrome woodwork from the Rue de Fleurus; Study of a foot by *Boucher,* and 18C fans.—R. 59 is devoted to the 18C French theatre.—The GALERIE GEORGE-SAND (R. 60) contains the collection of souvenirs of George Sand (1804–76) and her family, presented in 1923 by Mme Lauth-Sand, granddaughter of the novelist. Among the portraits is a pastel by *Quentin de La Tour* of Marshal Saxe, the novelist's great-grandfather, and a bust by *Houdon* of Claudine Houdon.

We return to R. 51, and turn right to enter the apartments of Mme de Sévigné (RR. 46–49; R. 50 closed for repairs).—The SALON CHINOIS (R. 49) has lacquered panelling in a Chinese design from the Hôtel Lariboisière, and a large mirror framed in foliage (Louis XV).—The SALON DE MME DE SÉVIGNÉ (R. 47), the drawing-room of the Marquise, retains its original panelling. Above the mantelpiece is a pastel portrait of Mme de Sévigné by *Robert Nanteuil;* opposite is a portrait of her daughter, Mme de Grignan, by *Mignard.* In the central case are personal souvenirs, letters, etc. The adjoining PETITE SALLE (R. 48) contains a couch from Mme de Sévigné's house at Vichy. R. 46 still retains its 17C panelling. On the right is a bust of Henri II de Montmorency, beheaded at Toulouse in 1632; portraits of Louis XIV by *Nanteuil,* of Mme de Grignan (?) and of a canon of Notre-Dame (17C French School); Louis XIII at the siege of La Rochelle, painted on marble; wax bust of Henri IV (attr. to *Michel Bourdin).*—The SALLES DES ÉCHEVINS (RR. 45–43), dedicated to the officers of public works of the city of Paris, include portraits of aldermen by *Largillière, de Troy,* and *Duplessis,* and Allegory of the Peace of Aix-la-Chapelle (1749), by *Dumont le Romain.* In R. 45 is a monumental chimneypiece (Louis-XIII period) and in R. 43 aldermen's purses with the city arms.—R. 42. Paintings of the 18C by *N. Raguenet* (to be transferred to R. 50).

We descend the staircase, pass through RR. 12–7 containing material relating to the history of trades and guilds, and turn left up the steps to enter the SALLE DES ENSEIGNES (R. 4) with a fine wrought-iron grille. This room contains a collection of shop and tavern signs of the 15–19C. In the central cases are weights and measures and models of glass works and locksmiths' works; merchants' tokens; paintings illustrating various trades, etc.—R. 5 is devoted to a further collection of shop signs. The frontage of a First Empire apothecary's shop. In the courtyard is an equestrian statue of Henri IV, by *Lemaire* (1838).

We cross the vestibule of the Escalier de Luynes to R. 64. Bust of Napoleon in 1798, by *Corbet.*—SALLE DU PREMIER EMPIRE (R. 65). *Gérard,* *Madame Récamier; Boilly,* The Conscripts of 1807 leaving the Porte St-Denis; *Prud'hon,* Talleyrand in 1809. In the cases are personal souvenirs of Napoleon and his family, including (r.) Napoleon's field outfit.—SALLE DE LA RESTAURATION (R. 66). Drawings and paintings illustrating historical events of 1815–30, by *Boilly* and *Lecomte;* views of Paris (1820–30) by *Canella;* Duc de Bordeaux as a child (bronze) by *Lemaire.*—R. 67. Souvenirs of the July Revolution (1830) and the insurrections of 1832; bust of Queen Marie-Amélie by *Moine;* souvenirs of Fieschi's attempt at assassination in 1835 (p. 95); and of the return of Napoleon's body (1840); incidents of the Revolution of 1848. In the recess (R. 68) on the left and in R. 69, views of Paris by *G. Michel, Dagnan, Bouhot, Th. Rousseau,* etc.—R. 70 contains souvenirs of the French theatre including some of Rachel; drawings by *Gavarni;* portrait of Liszt by *Lehmann;* also letter appointing Michelet Professor of History at the Collège Ste-Barbe.—

R. 71 is devoted to French painters of the 19C; cartoons for the ceiling-paintings in the Hôtel de Ville (destroyed in 1871) by *Delacroix*. In a case, *Isabey*, The artist and his wife; also palette belonging to Daumier.—R. 72. Portraits of actors by *Boilly*, souvenirs of Rachel and of Talma; *Fragonard*,

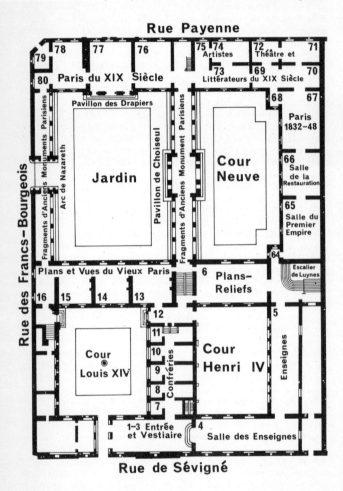

Self-portrait; *Eug. Isabey*, Wife and daughter; *Eug. Lami*, Carnaval (1834).— R. 73. *Corot*, Quai des Orfèvres and the Pont St-Michel, and other views of Paris by *Canella* and *Werhason*.—R. 74. Souvenirs of Balzac, Béranger, and Lamartine; Paul and Alfred de Musset as children, by *Dufau*; portraits of Balzac and Benj. Constant and of Eug. Delacroix, by *Champmartin*; sketch of Victor Hugo by *Fr. J. Heim*.—R. 75. Restoration furniture; collection of satirical statuettes by *Dantan*; *Nanteuil*, 'Descente de la Courtille'.—R. 76

(Second Empire). Cradle of the Prince Imperial and his christening robe; busts by *Carrier-Belleuse* of Napoleon III, the Comtesse de Castiglione, and Marguerite Bellanger, the actress. *Yvon*, Baron Haussmann; *Carrière*, Blanqui; contemporary views of Paris.—R. 77 (The Commune and the Siege). Illustrations include two allegorical sketches of the Siege by *Puvis de Chavannes*, and impressions of the Commune by *Daniel Vierge*; portraits of Jules Vallès by *Courbet* and Rochefort by *Baud-Bovy*; Gambetta's balloon ascent, by *Guiaud* and *Didier*; statuettes of Gambetta, Thiers, and Boulanger.—R. 78 (later 19C). *Forain*, 'La Loge'; scenes of Parisian Life by *Jean Béraud*; *A. Gill*, Boulevard Montmartre; *Grandjean*, Place de Clichy; *Zawiski*, Moulin Rouge; *Lebourg*, Pont St-Michel; *Prins*, Cabaret du Lapin Agile; *Signac*, Montmartre; *Foujita*, Boulevard Edgar-Quinet; *Braquaval*, Place du Delta; drawings and watercolours by *Andrieux, Lepère, Signac* and *Laboureur* and a sketch by *J. E. Blanche*.—R. 79 (19C theatre). Victorien Sardou with his family by *A. de la Brély*; Coquelin cadet (bronze) by *Bourdelle*; also letters from Sarah Bernhardt and Victor Hugo.—R. 80 (Literary world). *Béraud*, Salon de Comtesse Potocka; Prosper Merimée, pastel by *Rochard*; desk, chair, and souvenirs of Alphonse Daudet; bust of Aimée Desclée by *Carrier-Belleuse*.

Returning to R. 76 we regain the entrance by the central colonnade. The rooms (RR. 13–16) on the right and R. 6 on the left are devoted to models and plans of the old quarters of Paris (16–19C). R. 13 has a 16C chimneypiece with the arms of Ligneris.

26   THE PALAIS DE CHAILLOT

MÉTRO station: *Trocadéro* (lines 6 and 9).
ADMISSION. The three museums in the Palais de Chaillot are open daily, except Tues, from 10 a.m. The Musée des Monuments Français (reproductions of works of art) closes at 5 p.m. (adm. 1 fr., Sun 0,50 fr.); the Musée de la Marine closes at 5 (adm. 0,60 fr.); the Musée de l'Homme (adm. 1 fr.) closes at 5 or 6 (in summer). In the Musée de l'Homme the library is open every weekday, 10–12, 2–6, and cinema shows ('Le Tour du Monde') are given on Thurs, Sat and Sun at 4 in the lecture hall.

The **Palais de Chaillot**, in the Place du Trocadéro (Rte 7), erected for the Paris exhibition of 1937, replaces the *Palais du Trocadéro*, which was designed for the Exhibition of 1878. This huge building, by Carlu, Boileau, and Azéma, with curved wings separated by a square, encases the two wings of the original structure. On the central buildings are gold-lettered inscriptions by Paul Valéry; the principal entrances, in the Place du Trocadéro, are adorned with sculptures by Delamarre and Sarrabezolles.

The ***Musée des Monuments Français**, in the E. wing, was founded in 1879 as the Musée de Sculpture Comparée by Viollet-le-Duc.

The arrangement of the exhibits is in perfect taste, and the lighting is exceptionally good, making the collection—admittedly a collection of copies—a real revelation of the scope of French art. The sculpture collection is illustrated and explained by documents and pictures epitomizing the history of each period, while the execution and setting up of the reproductions of ancient mural paintings—many of the originals of which are fast disappearing—is a marvel of ingenuity. Faithful copies of some masterpieces of French stained glass—from the Sainte Chapelle and the cathedrals of Bourges, Chartres, Le Mans, and Rouen—are exhibited in the main entrance hall.

The SCULPTURE DEPARTMENT is on the left of the main entrance hall.—R. 1. Early Romanesque Period. Merovingian and Carolingian works. RR. 2–6 illustrate French Romanesque Art, divided into the schools of Languedoc, Burgundy, Western France, Auvergne, and Provence.—R. 7. 'Art of the Crusades' (12–13C); Frankish masterpieces from the Holy Land.—R. 8. Gothic work of the 12C.—RR. 9–13. Gothio sculpture of the 13C, mainly from the great cathedrals of Northern and Central France.—RR. 14–15. Gothic work of the 14C.—RR. 16–18. 15C and 16C art, including some very fine tomb-statues.—RR. 19–21 oover the period 1500–30.—Staircase. Renaissance bas-reliefs. The room (r.) contains models of buildings of outstanding architectural merit.—R. 22 (*Salle Jean Goujon*) and R. 23 (*Salle Ligier Richier*) are devoted to the sculpture of the first half of the 16C; R. 24 (*Salle Germain Pilon*) to the late 16C and first half of the 17C.—R. 25. 17C works by *Puget, Coysevox, Nicolas* and *Guillaume Coustou, Michel Anguier*, and *Girardon*.—RR. 26, 27. 18C sculpture: works by *Falconet, Bouchardon*, and others; busts by *Houdon, Pajou, Pigalle, Caffieri, Clodion*, and others, including portraits of Molière, Voltaire, Franklin, Mirabeau and Rousseau.—RR. 28 (*Salle Rude*) and 29 (*Salle Carpeaux*) continue the series to the middle of the 19C.

The *WALL-PAINTINGS (Peinture Murale) occupy the rooms on the right of the entrance hall. On the *Ground Floor* (Carolingian period), Story of St Stephen, in the crypt of St-Germain at Auxerre (c. 850); Visitation, Bathing of the Child, Crucifixion, etc., in the choir of St-Pierre-les-Églises (Vienne), among the earliest in France; etc.—*First Floor*. The Romanesque period (11–12C). These splendid copies of mural and ceiling paintings, many of which are still extant, are mainly from churches of Central and Southern France. The principal masterpieces include (facing the garden): Christ in Majesty, in the apse of the Chapelle St-Gilles at Montoire; Nativity, Adoration of the Magi, Christ in glory, etc. (Catalan style), in the chapel of St-Martin-de-Fenouillar (Roussillon); St Maurice and the 'Crowned Knight', in the baptistery of St-Jean, Poitiers; Christ in glory surrounded by saints, in the apse of the church at Berzé-la-Ville, near Cluny; series of Old and New Testament scenes, from the choir of St-Martin at Vicq, near Nohant (Indre); the great figure of St Michael in Le Puy cathedral; Story of St Giles, in the crypt of the church of St-Aignan-sur-Cher; biblical and allegorical paintings in the crypt of Tavant church (Indre-et-Loire) and the chapel at St-Chef (Isère); Annunciation and Visitation, at Rocamadour (Lot); Deposition, Death of the Virgin (deeply religious in feeling), Tree of Jesse and Saints, in the chapel of Le Liget, near Loches; and the majestic array of scenes from Genesis and Exodus which adorn the nave of the church at St-Savin in Poitou, also Passion scenes (tribune) and scenes from the Apocalypse (porch), at either end.—*Second Floor*. Gothic period of the 13–14C. Among the fine examples (l. of staircase, facing the garden): Scenes of Hell, in the church at Asnières-sur-Vègre; paintings in the vault of the Chapelle St-Julien at Le Petit-Quevilly, near Rouen; Life of St Blaise, in the church of St-Jean at Vic-le-Comte (Puy-de-Dôme). In the centre: the dome of Cahors cathedral; Holy Women and St Catherine, in the N. transept of Le Puy cathedral; Life of St Andrew, at Frétigny (Eure-et-Loir); Life of St Martin, at Étigny (Yonne); Coronation of the Virgin, in a disused church at Vernais (Cher). Facing the Place du Trocadéro: Concert of Angels, in the castle-chapel of La Clayette (Saône-et-Loire); Martyrdom of St Catherine, in the Chapelle du Chalard, at St-Geniès (Dordogne); Clement IV investing Charles of Anjou with the Kingdom of Naples, in the Tour Ferrande, at Pernes (Vaucluse); Life of John the Baptist, from the Chartreuse at Villeneuve-lès-Avignon; Christ of the Apocalypse, in the crypt of Auxerre cathedral. Facing the square: Childhood of the Virgin, at Vieux-Pouzauges (Vendée); Entry of Christ into Jerusalem, at Lutz-en-Dunois (Eure-et-Loir); Christ in glory with SS. Peter and James, in the crypt at St-Aignan-sur-Cher; Transfiguration, in Le Puy cathedral.—The *Third Floor* is devoted to the 15 and early 16C. Tree of Jesse, at St-Bris-le-Vineux (Yonne); Scenes from the Life of the Virgin and of Christ, in the choir of Kernascléden (Morbihan); Visitation, Nativity, Flight into Egypt, etc., in the cloister at Abondance (Haute-Savoie); Dance of Death, at La Chaise-Dieu; Last Judgement, at Ennezat, near Riom; Instruments of the Passion, Life of the Virgin, and Saints, from the chapel of the Château du Pimpéan, near Angers; Last Judgement, at Albi cathedral; Hunting scenes (temp. Louis XIII), at the château of Rochechouart.

The **Musée des Arts et Traditions Populaires,** entered from the ground floor, is devoted to French folklore and customs and their social and artistic development. The collections in their present restricted accommodation are shown in rotation. It is proposed to move them to a new building in the Jardin d'Acclimatation in the near future.

The **Musée de l'Homme** is installed in the W. wing of the Palais de Chaillot. Formed by the amalgamation of the Galerie d'Anthropologie and the Musée d'Ethnographie du Trocadéro, the museum presents a comprehensive analytical and comparative study of the Science of Man. As the exhibition is more or less self-explanatory, only a generalized description is given below.

VESTIBULE. Vitrine du Mois, recent acquisitions.—FIRST FLOOR (staircase on l.). The first room (l.) is reserved for temporary exhibitions.—ANTHROPOLOGY ROOM. Maps, diagrams, and show-cases relating to the analysis and comparison of the varied physical and pathological characteristics of mankind, both prehistoric and modern; skeletons of a giant and a dwarf; examples of funerary rites, including a shrunken head and a mummified woman and child from Bolivia (Case 17); artificial deformities (Case 13). PALAEONTOLOGY AND PREHISTORY ROOM. Skeletons, photographs, etc., illustrating human evolution. Neanderthal man (Case 22); a series of cases devoted to physiological racial distinctions. At the far end of the room, examples of prehistoric art (cases 44–47), including the oldest known 'portrait' found near Angles-sur-l'Anglin (nr Poitiers).—PREHISTORIC AFRICAN ROOM. Cases 51–59. Palaeontological finds from African countries; sculptured and engraved menhirs (Case 55A); stone-age implements from N. Africa and the Sahara; prehistoric African art (Cases 61–62); (r.) Cliff-drawings and cave-paintings.—AFRICAN ROOM (Black Races). Fine examples of jewellery, religious and ceremonial costumes, ritual carvings, sculpture, and pottery. Aduno Koro (Case 74), a ritual representation of 'the ark of the world' which descended from heaven with the ancestors of humanity; 'Nimba' (Case 94), straw-covered goddess of fecundity, from French Guinea; throne, royal statues in wood and an iron 'god of war' from Dahomey; masks and musical instruments from the Belgian Congo; exhibits from Madagascar (although the island has come predominantly under Indonesian influence); paintings and manuscripts from the church of Antonius at Gondar, Ethiopia.—AFRICAN AND NEAR EASTERN ROOM (White Races). Religious objects, Islamic (Case 151) and Jewish (Case 161). Costumes, pottery, etc., of the nomadic tribes of N. Africa and the Near East; palanquin (Case 157) used by wealthy Bedouin women; agricultural implements, etc., of the sedentary Levantine peoples; Tuareg costumes and stone idols.— EUROPEAN ROOM. Exhibits of art and industries indigenous to European countries, excluding France.—SECOND FLOOR. ARCTIC ROOM. Domestic utensils of the Eskimo; bone carvings; funerary masks from the Aleutian Islands; kayak from Greenland.—RUSSIAN AND ASIATIC ROOM. Costumes, weapons, religious objects, and exhibits of folklore from Northern, Central, and Southern Asia, China, Indo-China, and Japan; funerary statues from the Ukraine and Kafiristan; silver work from Afghanistan; model of a Chinese actor; costumes from Tonkin; ceremonial masks and headgear from Siam and Malaya; bamboo toys from Japan.—PACIFIC ISLANDS ROOM. Exhibits from Indonesia, Polynesia, Melanesia, and Australia; paintings by Australian aborigines; tomb of a Maori chief; jewellery from Melanesia; jade caskets and tiki from Hawaii; carved prow of a Maori man-o'-war; exhibits from Easter Island.—AMERICAN ROOM. Pottery, jade, sculpture, and weapons from Mexico, Peru, Argentina, Chile, and Brazil (pre-Columbian period); carved necklace to assist the memory in the performance of a three-day ceremonial dance, from the Amazon basin (Case 454); Peruvian funerary rites; carved wooden chair from the time of Columbus (West Indies); Mayan art; stele of Copan (Honduras); Aztec and Zapotec art: a crystal skull; pottery and weapons of the Mound-builders (N. America); American-Indian costumes; zoomorphic masks (Case 502); painted skins; statue of Chaman, the healer (Case 505), etc. Stairs from this room lead to:

SALLE DES ARTS ET TECHNIQUES. General survey of Man's artistic and technical abilities. Domestic industries are displayed on the right; art and crafts—musical instruments, theatrical masks and puppets, etc.—on the left.

The upper floors are occupied by the photographic and phonographic collections (Third Floor; adm. only on application to the director), and the library (Fourth Floor; adm., see p. 167).

The **Musée de la Marine** occupies part of the Aile de Paris (W. wing of the Palais de Chaillot). Devoted to the history and development of the French Navy and Merchant Marine, the museum displays state barges, figureheads, and maritime relics, as well as numerous models and paintings of famous French ships and naval occasions. There is also an interesting collection of hydrographical and navigating instruments, historic diving equipment and a fascinating series of models illustrating the transportation of the obelisk of Luxor and its raising in the Place de la Concorde.

27   THE MUSÉE DE CLUNY

MÉTRO station: *Odéon* (lines 4, 10).
ADMISSION 1 fr.; open daily (except Tues) 10–12.45, 2–5.

The **HÔTEL DE CLUNY, which houses the Musée de Cluny, is at No. 6 Place Paul-Painlevé (reached from the Boul. St-Michel viâ the Rue Du Sommerard). Built at the end of the 15C on the site of a Roman mansion, it is one of the finest extant examples of medieval French domestic architecture. An archway, surmounted by the Amboise arms, gives access to the courtyard. The entrance to the museum is the door in the right-hand corner. The *Musée de Cluny,** with its incomparable collections, is mainly devoted to the arts and crafts of the Middle Ages.

The property was bought in 1340 by Pierre de Chalus, abbot of Cluny in Burgundy, and the mansion was built c. 1490 by Abbot Jacques d'Amboise, as the town house of the abbots, but was rarely occupied by them. In 1515 it became the residence of Mary Tudor, daughter of Henry VII and widow of Louis XII, known as 'La Reine Blanche' from the white mourning worn by her as queen of France. James V of Scotland was lodged here before his wedding with Madeleine, daughter of Francis I, in 1537. Later occupants were

Card. de Lorraine, Claude de Guise, Mazarin, and the papal nuncios (1600–81). In the
18C the tower was used as an observatory by the astronomer Messier, who is said to have
discovered twenty-one comets here. At the Revolution the mansion became national
property, and in 1833 it was bought by Alexandre Du Sommerard (1779–1842) and filled
with the treasures of every age which he spent his life in collecting. These were bought by
the State and supplemented by many new acquisitions; but since the complete reorganiza-
tion of the museum in 1949–56, only a selection of the choicest medieval treasures is now
on view.

GROUND FLOOR. In the windows are fragments of Swiss-German heraldic
glass (16C).—ROOM I. *Accessories of Medieval Costume.* Case 1. Pins, buckles,
clasps, girdles (one with ivory carving used by an abbess), caskets; Case 2.
Footwear including a 15C shoe 'à la poulaine' with pointed toe; Cases 3, 4.
Examples of worked leather; above Case 4, Two fragments of 14C 'broderie

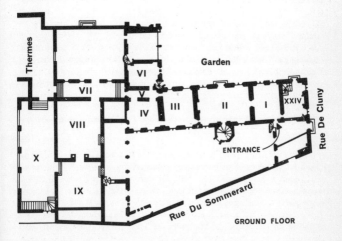

GROUND FLOOR

anglaise' with the Arms of England; statuette in wood of a Peasant (French;
1500); Arras tapestries (15C): Offering of the heart, Resurrection; 15C carved
wooden pillar from St-Pierre-le-Moûtier; leather targes (16C).—R. II. French
Tapestries including Miracle of St Quentin (15C), Deliverance of St Peter (c.
1460), Vintage scene and Concert (c. 1500); painted trestle table (German;
16C); leaden font (German; 14C); a statuette in wood, St George (Flemish;
late 14C).—R. III. *Textiles and Embroidery.* Case 1. Episcopal shoe (Sicily;
12C), bishops' mitres (French; 14–15C), fragments of embroidered chasuble
(Flemish; 15C) and other ecclesiastical vestments; bishop's gloves (French or
Italian; 15C), alms purses (French; 14C), etc.; Case 3. Byzantine fabrics
(6–7C), including some Egyptian examples; Cases 4, 5. Italian and Spanish
fabrics (14–15C), also German textiles; examples of Egyptian cloth (3–6C).
On the walls, 13C Irish embroidery, Story of St Martin, and 14C Rhenish
altarcloth.—R. IV. Medieval interior, including a 15C fireplace and furniture;
*'La Vie Seigneuriale', tapestries illustrating the activities of a nobleman's
household, c. 1500.—RR. V–VI. Woodwork and cabinet-making of the Middle
Ages and more tapestries of 'La Vie Seigneuriale'.

We descend a few steps to enter R. VIII which retains some Gallo-Roman work. *Sculpture and Painted Woodwork of the late Middle Ages*. Statuette of Jeanne de Laval (15C); Pietà, painted c. 1457 for Jeanne's chamber at the Château de Tarascon; painted wooden panels (Amiens; The Coronation of David, 1501); Story of the Santa Casa of Loreto (altarpiece from Ourscamp; 16C), and other early Picard works; Presentation at the Temple (marble; 14C); 14C Burgundian stalls; statues of the Madonna and SS. James and Anthony (Burgundian school; 15C); St John the Baptist (Florentine school; 15C); St Mary Magdalene (Flemish; 15C); statues of the Madonna and of St John the Evangelist (French; 14–15C); altarpiece of gilded wood, 'The Eucharist' (Antwerp; c. 1513); Ecstasy of the Virgin (Burgos; late 15C); The Dead Christ (Spanish; c. 1500); ivories of the 14C, etc.—R. IX. *Sculpture*. Four mutilated *Statues of the Apostles from the Sainte Chapelle (c. 1245); Crucifixion (Burgundian School; late 12C), Virgin and St John (Italian; 13C); five Apostles (14C) from the Hôpital St-Jacques by Robert de Lauroy (Rte 10); Scenes from the Life of the Virgin, painted on wood (English; c. 1300); 14C painted stone retable (Scenes of the Passion) from the Île de France; 12C capitals (French and Catalan) and 13C bosses from the Collège de Cluny.—R. X. Merovingian sarcophagus; Statue of Adam and 11C capitals from St-Germain-des-Prés. Thence we descend to the *Palais des Thermes, or briefly the *Thermes*, adjoining the mansion on the W. This consists of the ruined baths of a Roman building (almost certainly not a 'palace'), probably built during the reign of Caracalla (212–17). The Thermes, or Salle (65 ft long and 38 ft wide), preserving its vault, unique in France, was probably the *Frigidarium*, with the *Bath*, or *Piscina*, on the N. side. Fragments of Gallo-Roman sculpture are displayed here.

FIRST FLOOR. From R. X we ascend to the ROTUNDA (R. XI) in which are displayed the series of six famous and exquisite early-16C French **Tapestries, 'La Dame à la Licorne'.—R. XII. *Enamels*. Gallo-Roman and Byzantine enamels (Case 1); Mosan and Rhenish work of the 12C (Case 2); Limoges work of the 12C including Christ in Majesty with the symbols of the Evangelists (Case 3); also 13C Limoges crosses, plaques, shrines, reliquaries, and pyxes, including an enamel of the Martyrdom of Thos. Becket (Case 4).—R. XIII. *Jewellery*. Central case on the right. Three votive *Crowns (7C), of massive gold and jewelled, found at Guarrazar near Toledo in 1858–60 with six others; the latter, including one owned by King Reccesvinth (649–72), are at Madrid (Museo Arqueológico Nacional) on an exchange arrangement dating from Dec 1940; Cases 1, 2, 4. Merovingian and Gallo-Roman jewellery; Case 5. 13–14C jewellery and coins found at Colmar; Case 6. Golden *Rose given by Pope Clement V (early 14C) to the prince-bishop of Basle; Case 7. Jewellery of the 12–16C; Case 8. Two lion-heads, Roman rock-crystal.—R. XIV. *Goldsmiths' and Silversmiths' Work*. Case 1. Portable altar (English; 11C), golden cross (6–7C), a tiny purse-shaped shrine (8–9C), evangelistary-cover with the Rivers of Paradise (Italian; mid-12C), and other treasures. By the window, seated Madonna (c. 1300), a mutilated statuette in polychrome stone. Case 2. Processional cross (Barcelona; 14C), chalice and paten (French; 15C); Virgin and Child (late 14C); 13C reliquary from the Sainte Chapelle; 14C cross from Bordeaux; incense vessel (Italian; 14C); Case 3. St Anne, by *Hans Greiff* (1472); 14C plate engraved with animals and flower decoration, etc.—We pass along the corridor (R. XV) to R. XVI containing *Stained Glass* of c. 1260 from Rouen and 13C medallions from the Sainte Chapelle.—R. XVII. *Ceramics*. Medieval tiles and pottery; 15C Italian majolica; and a fine collection of

Hispano-Moresque ware (15C). We retrace our steps to R. XVI and, passing through RR. XVIII and XIX, reach the Chapel (R. XX). The ***Chapel,** with a central pillar and a star vault, is a masterpiece of sculptural decoration, with God the Father blessing His dying Son, and angels with the instruments of the Passion in the vault of the oriel window. On the wall, The Mass of St Gregory, a retable from Belgium by Jean de Molder, 1513. In the Chapel (and in the next two rooms) are *Tapestries depicting the Life of St Stephen in twenty-three scenes; the sequence of events begins here (description of each scene is on the wall). These were woven for Jean Baillet, bishop of Auxerre (c. 1490), and for more than three centuries hung in the choir of the cathedral at Auxerre.—*R. XIX. *Medieval Treasures.* Golden altarpiece given to Basle

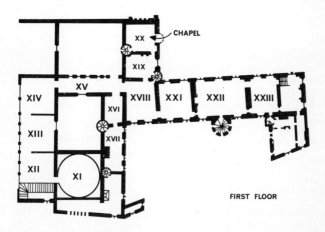

FIRST FLOOR

cathedral by the Emperor Henry II (c. 1019); early 11C tau-cross from St-Germain-des-Prés; Case 1. Byzantine and Muslim caskets, chasubles, vestments, etc.; Case 3. Leaf of diptych of Areobindus (Byzantine; A.D. 506); Case 4. Crystal casket of Muslim work (10–12C); Cases 5, 6. Ivories including leaf of a diptych (Rome; 4C), plaques of St Menas (Alexandria; c. 600), St Paul (? Antioch; 6C), Christ crowning Otho II and Theophano, Christ blessing, Christ in Majesty (Byzantine; 11–12C); also Carolingian work.—*R. XVIII. *Life in the Middle Ages,* a series of cases, arranged according to the ordinary activities of every-day medieval life. Case 1. The table; Case 2. The toilet; Case 3. Court life illustrated by ivories; Case 4. Military life; Case 5. Hunting; Case 6A. Riding; Case 6B. Travel; Case 6C. The Sciences; Case 7. Toys; Case 8. Games; Case 9D. Writing; Case 9E. Books; Case 9F. Seals; Book of Hours (French; 15C); tapestries of St Stephen, see above.—R. XXI. *Brass and Bronze Work.* Lectern, dated 1383, from St-Nicolas at Tournai; 15C bronze ewers in the shape of lions, griffins, etc.; 14C cauldrons (Case 1); candlesticks and thuribles (Case 2); decorative bronzes, including a Crucifix of the 12C, and a crozier, also 12C (Case 3); 16C tapestry, the Prodigal Son.—R. XXII. *Copper and Wrought Iron.* Wrought-iron locks and keys of the 15C (Case 1); knives, helmets, spurs, and armour of the 12–15C (Cases 2, 3, 5); executioner's sword, and the sword of Frederick III (1439–93; Case 4); alms boxes, caskets, etc., of

BGP–H

the 14–15C (Case 6); three medallions worked in copper, with scriptural scenes—the eyes of the figures are in enamel; beaten copperware from Limoges (13C); 13C reliquaries, etc. (Cases 7, 8). The chimneypiece (15C), from Le Mans, is ornamented with a rare iron plate bearing the arms of France; in front is a cage for smoking fish or meat.—R. XXIII. *Pewter and Lead.* Pewter ware, including a chalice of the 13C, and ewers of the 15–16C, from Eastern France or Switzerland (Case 1); objects in lead, toys, buttons, etc. (Case 2); pilgrims' badges (Case 3); Misericords from St-Lucien, Beauvais, depicting crafts of the 15C.—We descend to R. XXIV, or the SALLE DU SOMMERARD, with personal souvenirs of the founder of the museum.

28   THE MUSÉE GUIMET

MÉTRO stations: *Iéna* (line 9); *Trocadéro* (lines 6, 9).
ADMISSION 1 fr. (0,50 fr. on Sun); open daily (except Tues) 10–5. The Library and photographic section is open daily (except Sun and Tues) 2–5; admission by written application to the Conservateur. Lack of staff prevents all the rooms from being open at one time.

The **Musée Guimet** is installed at No. 6 Place d'Iéna. Founded at Lyons in 1879 by Émile Guimet, the museum was presented by him to the State and removed to Paris in 1888. In 1945 it officially became the Département des Arts Asiatiques des Musées Nationaux, the original collection having been considerably augmented. The collections illustrate the religions, history, and arts of India and the Far East.

GROUND FLOOR. VESTIBULE (A). In wall cases, exhibits from all the departments. We pass through the central hall (see below) into ROOM N (r.), which is devoted to *Indian Sculpture* of the Amaravati (2–4C) and Mathura schools (1–2C). The glass case (r.) contains small terracotta figures of the 3C.— ROOM O. *Sculptures from India* include a Buddha and other pieces of the 'classical' period (4–8C). Under the cupola are 12–14C *Bronzes from S. India: Siva, king of the dance; Siva, master of the arts (r.); etc. In the case (l.) are objects illustrating Jainism; images of Tirthankaras and Jain divinities, etc.; statuettes of Krishna and Vishnu, Hindu divinities.—ROOM P. *Javanese Art.* Heads of divinities (7–9C); door lintel decorated in the Prambanan style (9C); Javanese bronzes including *Statuettes of Avalokitesvara, and of Kubera, god of riches—note the seven little pots of treasure at his feet. On the left is a case of leather marionettes for a shadow-theatre and a Javanese calendar on painted fabric.—ROOM I. *India and Ceylon.* Frescoes of the Gupta era (5–7C); gouaches and water-colours of the Mogul School (16–18C).—CENTRAL HALL (l.). *Khmer Sculptures and Antiquities* from Cambodia. Wall-case (r.), Bronzes, including one of the sacred serpent (Naga); *Statue of Hari-Hara (pre-Angkorian style, second half of 6C), uniting the two gods Siva and Vishnu in one person; door lintels (7–8C); sculptures of the 9–10C; *Pediment of the temple of Bantaisrei (A.D. 967); four seated Brahmins; Naga and Garuda (fabulous bird; 12C); balustrade decoration of five serpents.—ROOM M. *Antiquities from Annam.* Note especially the head of Buddha (9C) and the statues of two young elephants and a dancer (10C).—ROOM K (*Salle Delaporte*). Centre: Khmer antiquities. Left: Siamese art and sculpture. Bronze statue of Buddha standing

(15C); bronze head of Buddha (15–16C). On the walls, paintings and worked leather hangings (18C). Right: Tibetan art. Statuettes; religious objects; ornaments in gilded bronze, worked silver, etc. On the walls, paintings illustrating the life of Buddha; Buddhist saints, etc.—ROOM F. *Khmer Sculptures* of the Bayon style (12–13C); each statue wears the enigmatic 'Angkorian smile'; friezes in high-relief; the 'Perforated Stele' of a dancing Apsarus, early 12C (?) from Beng Mealea.

The FIRST FLOOR contains exhibits from China, Central Asia, Afghanistan, and N.W. India. The collections of the Asiatic department of the Louvre are also exhibited here.

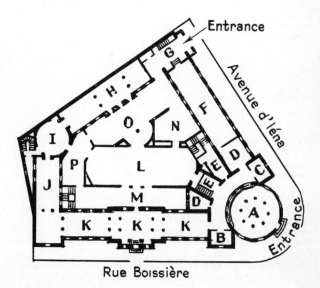

ROOM D. *Chinese Bronzes.* Lacquered *Cabinet decorated in gold (Ming dynasty; 14–17C).—ROOM F. Bronze implements, ritual vases, etc., of the Chang-Yin dynasty (14–12C B.C.) found at Ngan-Yang, the capital city of the dynasty. Ritual vase with a decorated base in the form of a tortoise; bell of the Fighting Kingdoms dynasty, 5–3C B.C.; ritual *Vase (Hou style; 11–9C B.C.); arms, bowls, ritual vases, etc., of the Fighting Kingdoms dynasty, notably a *Sword adorned with jade.—ROOM G. *Chinese *Jades*, of which the earlier ones are in the form of symbols; Pi, the sky; Tsong, the earth; Kwei, the mountain (Chou dynasty; 11–9C B.C.).—ROOM H. *Chinese Sculpture.* Buddha from Yun-Kang (5C A.D.); Buddha in meditation, Wei dynasty (6C A.D.); Dvarapāla, guardian of the Temple (T'ang dynasty; 7–10C A.D.); *Ananda, disciple of Buddha (Suei), marble with traces of polychrome; head of a monster, Suei dynasty (6–7C A.D.); funerary statuettes of the T'ang dynasty (Case 30), including a small *Stele representing Sakyamuni and Prabhutaratna (dated 518).—ROOM I. In the cases, gilded bronze figures of the Wei, Suei, and T'ang dynasties, 5–10C (Case 34); on the walls, textiles from Tuen-Huang (7–10C A.D.); frescoes from Qizl and Quomtoura (Turkestan); statues of Lokapala,

guardian of the four cardinal points.—ROOM J (*Salle Pelliot*). Buddhist paintings, banners, manuscripts, clay figures, etc., discovered by Paul Pelliot in
Chinese Turkestan during his expedition of 1906–08.—ROOM K (*Salle Foucher-
Hackin*) is devoted to objects discovered by the French archæological mission
in Afghanistan since 1922. First Section. Examples of Græco-Buddhist art
from Gandara (N.W. India), 1–8C A.D. Second Section. Exhibits from the
Buddhist monastery of Hadda: *Genie carrying a floral offering (single case
at the end of the section), to the right of which is *Demon in a fur mantle. In
the wall-case, fragments of the original frescoes from the Buddhist monastery
at Kakrak (c. 5C A.D.). Third Section. *Collection of Indian ivories, bronzes,
Græco-Roman stuccoes, Syrian and Alexandrine glassware, and Chinese
lacquer work, discovered in Afghanistan in 1937 and 1939–40.

The *Grandidier Collection of *Chinese and Japanese Ceramics*, on the
second floor, was transferred from the Louvre, and was opened here in May
1950. Especially notable are three statues of Lohans, or chief disciples of
Buddha. Other rooms on this floor contain lacquer-work and Japanese and
Annamite ceramics.

29   THE MUSÉE JACQUEMART ANDRÉ

MÉTRO station: *Miromesnil* (line 9).
ADMISSION 2 fr. (1 fr. on Sun); open daily (except Fri) 1–4 or 5.

The **Musée Jacquemart André**, at No. 158 Boulevard Haussmann, contains
a priceless collection illustrating French art in the 18C (Ground Floor), the
Renaissance and Italian art (First Floor).

The house was built c. 1870 by Edouard André (d. 1894), who in 1881 married Nélie
Jacquemart, a well-known portrait-painter. Mme André, who survived her husband till
1912, bequeathed their collections, home, and fortune to the Institut de France.

ROOM I (Waiting Room), on the left. In this room the exposition alternates
between 18C English portrait-painters from *Reynolds* to *Lawrence*, and French
portraits, including works by *David*, *Fragonard* and *Drouais*.—R. II (Salon
Rotonde). Four panels of Gobelins tapestry (the Seasons; Louis-XV period)
and a Savonnerie carpet (1663); 11. *Ducreux*, Self-portrait; 1263. *Tocqué*,
Portrait of an unknown man; 60. *Nattier*, Marquise d'Antin; 63. *Houdon*,
bust of Caumartin; *65. *Coysevox*, bust of Gabriel, the architect; *Slodtz*, bust
of Nicholas Vleugels, the painter; *Le Moyne*, bust of the Marquis de Marigny.
In the centre is a writing-table presented by Louis XV to the town of Langres.—
R. III (Tapestry Room). 183–185. Beauvais tapestries (Russian Games) after
Le Prince; miniatures by *Van Blarenberghe* and *Savignac*; 195. *Falconet*, The
glory of Catherine II; 1265. *Le Moyne*, Louis XV. Furniture of the Louis-XV
period.—R. IV (Study). 414. *Rubens* (atelier), Portrait of a Flemish couple;
420. *Rubens*, Hercules strangling the lion; 419. *Van Dyck*, Time cutting the
wings of love; *422. *Leyster*, Child laughing; *425. *Van Dyck*, Count Henry
of Peña; 426. *Jan de Bray*, Portrait of a man; *429. *Quentin Massys*, Posthumous portrait of an old man (1513); 431. *Van Dyck*, Magistrate; 662. *Moro*,
Duchess of Parma. In the case, MSS., books and medals: *255. The Boucicaut
Book of Hours or the Visitation, which belonged to Diane de Poitiers.—
R. V. (Salle des Dessins). Ceiling, Peace and Justice, by *Tiepolo*. 9–10

Canaletto, St Marks Square, the Rialto; 235. *Goya*, Second-Lieutenant in the Dragoons (sketch); 236. *Chardin*, Still-life; sketches by *Prud'hon* (Empress Josephine) and *Fragonard*; drawings by *Lancret, Pater, Watteau*, and *Boucher.*—R. VI (Library). 1503. Beauvais tapestry after *Boucher*; 12. *Mme Vigée-Lebrun*, Countess Catherine Skravonska; 244. *Prud'hon*, Cadet de Gassicourt; 322. *Greuze*, Girl in Confusion; 226. *Fragonard*, Head of an old man; 230. 1501. *Perroneau*, Woman in a bonnet, Portrait of the painter Gillequin. On the mantlepiece, Woman's head by *Chinard*.

We return through the Salon Rotonde to R. VII (Great Hall). 430. *Murillo*, Franciscan; 663. *Luini*, Virgin with SS. Margaret and Augustine; 1016. *Bramantino*, Madonna; 1029. *Carpaccio*, Embassy of Hippolyta to Theseus; 1045. *Mantegna*, Mocking of Christ; *409. *Rembrandt*, Pilgrims of Emmaüs; 672. *Bugiardini*, Portrait of a woman; 416. *Ruysdael*, Landscape; *1018. *École de Bruges*, Virgin and child illuminating a book; 432. *Rembrandt*, Dr Arnold Tholinx; 427. *Hals*, Portrait of a man. Case with antique bronzes, goldsmiths' work and glassware (Syro-Egyptian enamelled lamp); *448. *Donatello*, Martyrdom of St Sebastian, a bronze plaquette; 445. attr. to *Leonardo da Vinci*, Horse in gilt bronze (table A). By the windows, small 15–16C bronzes (447. *Riccio*, Moses as Jupiter Ammon); 16C ivories and an enamelled plaque by Jean Pénicaud I (517. Bearing of the cross); 16C enamels.—R. VIII (Winter Garden). 604. Wingless Victory, a Græco-Roman copy of an unknown Greek statue; Eros (2C A.D.).—R. IX (Smoking Room). Late 16C Venetian ceiling. 658, 673. *Di Conti*, Head of a young woman, Head of a man; **1038. *Uccello*, St George killing the dragon; 667. *Venetian School*, St George, slayer of the dragon; 1043. *Signorelli*, Holy family; 657. *Pontormo*, Young lute-player; 946. Stained-glass (Bologna, 15C), Virgin and child; In the cases, books bound for connoisseurs and nobles, medallions and silverware.

STAIRCASE. *Tiepolo*, three frescoes, including: Henri III welcomed by Fed. Contarini to the Villa de Mira.—GALLERY. Brussels and French tapestries, late 16C; 433. *Montemezzano*, 'La présentation au temple'; 745. *Veronese* (?), Portrait of a woman; *737. *Florentine School*, Battle (after *Uccello*).—RR. X–XI are devoted to the Renaissance. 754. Marble doorway (Venice, late 15C); (r. to l.) terracottas from the *Della Robbia* workshops; *778. *Luca della Robbia*, Virgin and child; *849. *Venetian School*, Legend of St Emilian (marble bas-relief in the form of a triptych); 770. *Mino da Fiesole*, St John as a child (marble bust); 893. *Donatello*, two winged torch-bearers (bronze); 834. Marble door (c. 1500), in a sculptured frame attr. to *Bened. da Rovezzano*; 837. Fountain of Istrian stone, from the workshop of *Pietro Lombardo*; *892. *Desiderio da Settignano*, Young hero (marble bas-relief); In the centre, 841. *Sienese School*, Virgin of the Nativity (painted and gilded wood; *842. *Donatello*, bust of Lodovico Gonzaga, Marquis of Mantua; 843. *Ricciarelli*, posthumous bust of Michelangelo (bronze); 908. *Pietro di Giovanni d'Ambrogio*, double-faced Processional banner (1444); 900. *Bellano*, Dead Christ held by his mother (terracotta bas-relief); 846. *Florentine School*, Love and Psyche; etc., etc.— R. XI. Stone and marble doorways of the 16C; Brussels tapestries: The bearing of the cross; 944. *Botticini*, Dead Christ with the Virgin, saints, and others; 1049. *Venetian School*, Portrait of a young man; *997. Choir-stalls with marquetry and arabesques (c. 1505); In the cases, a collection of oriental knives, Italian faience (16C), and games.—R. XII. Sculptured doors and escutcheons; *'Encyclopaedic Ceiling' with twenty-five panels in grisaille, attr. to *Girol. Mocetto* (15C); 1023. *Bartolemeo*, Life of the Virgin (triptych); 739. School of *Botticelli*, Flight into Egypt; 1869. *Fra Angelico* (attr.), God between two angels; 1020. *Mantegna*, Virgin and child between two saints; 1812. *School of Lombardy*, Portrait of a woman; 1868. *School of Ferrari*, Virgin and child.—R. XIII (Dining room). 17–18C ceiling frescoes by *Tiepolo*, transferred to canvas, Fame announcing the visit of Henri III. Five Brussels tapestries of the story of Achilles (1745); Sèvres, Meissen, Vincennes, and Vienna porcelain; Chinese porcelain and stoneware (Case E); 1166. *Warin*, bust of Richelieu; 1165. *Tremblay*, bust of Henri IV; 1159. Large console-table, in the style of *Jacob* (early Louis-XVI); 1160. Two low Closets (late Louis-XV).

30   THE MUSÉE DU JEU DE PAUME

MÉTRO station: *Concorde* (lines 1, 2, 12).
ADMISSION 1 fr. (0,50 fr. on Sun); open daily (except Tues) 10–5.

The ****Musée du Jeu de Paume** (or Musée de l'Impressionisme) occupies the former tennis-court at the W. end of the N. terrace of the Tuileries gardens, overlooking the Rue de Rivoli. It houses the national collection of works of art of the Impressionist School.

This magnificent collection of paintings is admirably exhibited. In 1958 the museum was reopened after a thorough renovation and a complete rearrangement. Particular attention has been devoted to the framing of the pictures; the unorthodox manner in which Monet's 'studies' are displayed is highly successful. This superb collection is largely derived from private bequests and several rooms are named after these benefactors.

VESTIBULE (Salle Fantin-Latour). Works by *Fantin-Latour* (1836–1904) of historical interest only, including: Hommage to Delacroix, Studio in the Batignolles; *Bazille* (1841–70), The artist's studio; *Renoir* (1841–1919), Portraits of Monet and of Bazille; *Camille Pissarro* (1830–1903), Self-portrait (1873).— SALLE BOUDIN (l.). Precursors of the movement and allies: *Boudin* (1824–98; Jetty at Deauville, etc.), *Corot* (1796–1875), *Cals* (1810–80), *Daubigny* (1817–78), *Jongkind* (1819–91), *Lépine* (1836–92), *Rouart* (1833–1912). Also *Monet* (1840– 1926), Normandy farmyard, and 'Bateau de plaisance', part of a triptych with *Pissarro's* Edge of the village and *Sisley's* Île St-Denis.—SALLE MOREAU NÉLATION (r.). Works by *Manet* (1832–83), including 'Déjeuner sur l'herbe' (the scandal resulting from its exhibition in 1863 made *Manet* the head of the group of painters consisting of *Renoir, Sisley, Monet, Bazille, Cézanne* and *Pissarro*); Lady with a fan (Berthe Morisot), 'La Blonde aux seins nus'; *Monet*, chiefly landscapes (Railway bridge at Argenteuil, The Bas-Bréau road, 'Les coquelicots', 'Le repos sous les lilas', etc.); *Pissarro*, The diligence at Louve-ciennes; *Sisley* (1839–99), The canal at Argenteuil, Bougival Lock, Snow at Marly, and other landscapes; *Berthe Morisot* (1841–95), Catching butterflies.— SALLE LAUTREC. Poster for the booth of 'La Goulue' by *Toulouse-Lautrec* (1864–1901); *Manet*, Clemenceau; *Degas* (1834–1917), Self-portrait, Degas and Volernes, etc.; *Renoir*, William Sisley, the painter's father; bronzes by *Degas* of dancers and horses, showing his great interest in movement. Near the stairs, illustrations of the various techniques of Impressionism, with its history and topography, also photographs of the artists.—FIRST SALLE CAMONDO (r.). *Manet*, Lola de Valence, 'Le fifre', 'Femme au chapeau noir', and other works; *Degas*, 'Foyer de la Danse' (first of the series, 1872), 'L'Absinthe (portrait of M. Desboutin)—the outcry caused when this picture was exhibited in London in 1893 induced the Scottish owner to dispose of the offending work.—SECOND

SALLE CAMONDO. *Degas*, 'Danseuse au Bouquets', Dancing class (1874), and some of his most famous studies of dancers, The pedicure, 'Les repasseuses', The tub and other bathing scenes, At the races (two works); *Sisley*, The flood at Port Marly, The flood (perhaps a study for the former), The village of Voisins, Snow at Louveciennes; *Toulouse-Lautrec*, Cha-u-Kao.—SALLE BAZILLE. *Bazille*, The pink dress (1865), Family reunion; *Guigou* (1834–71), La Gineste road, Washerwoman; *Manet*, Mme Manet on a blue couch; *Monet*, 'Déjeuner sur l'herbe' (fragment), Portrait of Mme Monet, and other works.—SALLE MANET. *Manet*, Olympia (exhibited in the Salon of 1865 and met with the accustomed shower of abuse), Portraits of Zola (1868) and of Mallarmé (1876), The Balcony (portrait of Berthe Morisot), 'La Dame aux éventails', and other works; *Eva Gonzalès* (1849–83), Box at the theatre; *Monet*, Portrait of Mme Gaudibert; *Berthe Morisot*, Portrait of Mme Pontillon, her sister.—SALLE DEGAS. *Degas*, Self-portrait and other early portraits including H.-R. de Gas, his grandfather (painted on his visit to Italy in 1857), and the Bellelli family; Study of hands; 'Femme se coiffant'; the famous 'Danseuse sur la Scène'; Orchestra (with portraits of the musicians); among the later portraits, A young woman and Marie Dihau, the pianist; Café in Montmartre (1877); and examples of his treatment of historical themes.

On the stairs, Judgement of Paris (original plaster) by *Renoir*.—First Floor. The SALLE GACHET contains Dr Gachet's collection of works by *Van Gogh* (1853–90), all painted in 1890 when he lived with the doctor at Auvers: Self-portrait, Auvers church, Cottages at Cordeville, Portrait of Dr Gachet, and other works; also *Paul Cézanne* (1839–1906). A modern Olympia, Dr Gachet's house, Still life including Flowers in a Delft vase, etc.; two works by *Paul van Ryssel* (Dr Gachet; 1828–1909); *Monet*, Chrysanthemums (1878); *Guillaumin* (1841–1927), Self-portrait, Sunset at Ivry, Nude, Barges, Snow scene (1869); works by *Pissarro* (three landscapes), *Renoir* (Portrait of a model) and *Fr. Oller* (1833–1917).—SALLE RENOIR (right of the stairs). *Renoir*, Girl reading; At La Grenouillère; Girl seated; Gabrielle with a rose, and other brilliant studies; Portraits of Mme Alphonse Daudet, Mme Georges Charpentier, and the Bernheim family; Moss roses; Seine at Argenteuil, Path through long grass, Barges on the Seine; two Algerian scenes.—SALLE CAILLEBOTTE. *Renoir*, Wagner, Moulin de la Galette (1876), The swing, Girl in a straw hat (1908), Nude in the Sunlight (c. 1875), and other nudes including a late work, The Bathers (1918); *Pissarro*, St-Jacques at Dieppe (1901), 'Les toits rouges', Fruit trees in blossom, The Ennery road, Harvest, Seated peasant girl, etc.; *Sisley*, La route, Molesey regatta (1874), Seine at Suresnes, St-Mammès, Snow scene; *Guillaumin*, Interior; *Monet*, In the garden (c. 1866), 'Le Déjeuner' (c. 1873), Gare St-Lazare (1877), Regatta at Argenteuil (c. 1872), Rocks at Belle-Île, and other landscapes; *Manet*, 'La serveuse de bocks'; *Berthe Morisot*, The cradle, Young girl at the ball, Hydrangeas, Children of Gabriel Thomas; *Caillebotte* (1848–94), Boats at Argenteuil; *Mary Cassatt* (1845–1927), Mother and child.— SALLE MONET. *Monet*, Self-portrait (1917), 'Les Cathédrales' (a series of studies of Rouen Cathedral), Young woman with a parasol (two studies), Houses of Parliament (1904), Hoar frost, Sunset at Vétheuil and other Seine landscapes, Water-lily pool (two studies); also *Sisley*, Loing Canal (1892).

The rooms on the left of the stairs illustrate the Reactions against Impressionism. SALLE CÉZANNE. *Cézanne*, Self-portrait (c. 1880), 'La Madeleine', 'La maison du pendu', Card players, Head of an old man, Poplars, Dahlias (painted at Dr Gachet's in 1875), L'Estaque, Le Pont de Mennecy, 'La femme à la cafétière', Still life, and other works.—SALLE GAUGUIN. *Gauguin* (1848–1903),

'La belle Angèle', 'Les Alyscamps', Still life, two Breton landscapes, Schuffe-necker family, Vaïrumati, The white horse; *Van Gogh*, Restaurant de la Sirène, Portrait of the painter Bock, Head of a peasant, La Guinguette, Still life, Caravans, The artist's bedroom at Arles (1889); *Seurat* (1859–91), Studies of a model for 'Les Poseuses' (one with the frame also painted in pointilliste style); Port-en-Bessin, Circus (1891), Sketch for 'La Grande Jatte'. *Rousseau 'Le Douanier'* (1844–1910), Snake-charmer, La Guerre; *Signac* (1863–1935), River bank; *Toulouse-Lautrec*, Justine Dieuhl, 'Femme tirant son bas' (1894), Lady with the gloves, 'La Toilette', 'La femme au boa noir', Portraits of Paul Leclercq and of Louis Bouglé.—Alcove adjoining, *Gauguin*, Tahitian women (1891), 'Et l'or de leur corps' (1901), Breton village in the snow (1894), also carved lintel from his Tahitian house and other souvenirs; *Odilon Redon* (1840–1916), Portrait of Gauguin.

'Les Nymphéas', a series of mural paintings of water-lilies by *Monet*, are exhibited in the **Orangerie**, 5 min. walk across the Tuileries gardens (adm. daily, except Tues, 10–12.45, 2–5; 1 fr., 0,50 fr. on Sun). Temporary exhibitions are frequently held here. The Orangerie will eventually house the **Guillaume-Walter Collection** of Modern Painting, one of the greatest bequests to the Louvre, with superb examples of Cézanne, Rousseau, Modigliani, Soutine, Matisse, Renoir, Picasso and Derain, collected by the great art dealers Paul Guillaume and Jean Walter and given by their widow.

31   THE MUSÉE NISSIM DE CAMONDO

MÉTRO station: *Villiers* (lines 2 and 3).
ADMISSION 1 fr.; open weekdays (except Tues) 2–5; Sun 10–12, 2–5. Closed on national holidays and 14 July–15 September.

The ***Musée Nissim de Camondo,** at No. 63 Rue de Monceau, was inaugurated as an annexe of the Musée des Arts Décoratifs in 1936. It was bequeathed to the Union Centrale des Arts Décoratifs by Count Moïse de Camondo as a memorial to his airman son, Nissim, killed in 1917. The aim of the collection is to present a tastefully furnished mansion of the late 18C; the collection includes an unusually large number of Savonnerie and Aubusson carpets.

Ground Floor. VESTIBULE. Writing-table by *Riesener.*—GALERIE. Fountain in red marble (1765) from the Château de St-Prix, Montmorency.—GRAND ESCALIER. Two lacquered Chinese corner cupboards (Louis-XV) and a pair of Regency chairs upholstered in Savonnerie tapestry.

First Floor. GRAND BUREAU. Ornamental chimneypiece in white marble (c. 1775); pair of low cabinets by *Leleu*; cylinder-top *Desk and secretaire by *Saunier*, the latter from the Château de Tanlay (Yonne); desk-armchair of 1778; table by *Carlin*, from the Château de Bellevue; pair of low chairs by *Sené*; eight chairs by *N. Q. Foliot* covered in Aubusson tapestry (with scenes from La Fontaine); Aubusson tapestries with six fables from La Fontaine after *Oudry*, and a Beauvais screen with the fable of the Cock on the Dunghill; bronze bust of Mme le Comte by *G. Coustou* (1716–77); *Vigée-Lebrun,*

Bacchante.—GRAND SALON. Panelling from No. 11 Rue Royale; table and *Bureau de dame by *Carlin*; marquetry cabinet and tables by *Riesener*; pair of low cabinets by *Weisweiler*; table attr. to *Rœntgen* and one by *Lacroix*; suite of furniture (which belonged to Sir Richard Wallace), including two sofas and an armchair by *Georges Jacob*; four chairs by *Henri Jacob*; six-leaved Savonnerie screen; 'L'Été' (Hubert Robert's daughter), marble bust by *Houdon*; paintings by *Drouais*; *Vigée-Lebrun*, Mme le Coulteux du Molay (1788); Beauvais tapestry after *Boucher*; among the Savonnerie carpets, one ('L'Air') woven for the Grand Galerie of the Louvre (1678) and one made in 1660.—SALON HUET. 'Scènes pastorales', seven door panels and three lintels painted by *J. B. Huet* (1766); cylinder-top *Desk by *Oeben*, recalling the 'Bureau du Roi'; pairs of small cabinets by *Garnier* and by *Carlin*, the latter once belonging to Admiral de Penthièvre; sofa, two bergères and eight chairs by *Sené*; table with chased bronze, given to Vergennes by Louis XVI; silver-gilt candlesticks by *Germain*, embossed with the arms of Mme de Pompadour (1762).—SALLE À MANGER. Console and a pair of tables in ebony and chased bronze by *Weisweiler*; pair of small cabinets by *Leleu*; silver including two splendid souptureens by *Auguste* and *Roettiers* (the latter's work was ordered by Catherine II of Russia for Orloff).—CABINET DES PORCELAINES. Services in Sèvres, Chantilly and Meissen porcelain, silver-gilt service by *Dehanne* and *Cardeilhac*.—GALERIE. Sofa and chairs by *Pierre Gillier*; Aubusson tapestries after *Boucher* ('La Danse Chinoise', etc.).—PETIT BUREAU. Furniture by *Leleu, Stadler*, and *Topino*; snuffboxes, clocks, Chinese porcelain (c. 1775); medallions in terracotta by *J. B. Nini*; Mme le Comte, marble bust by *Coustou*; *Guardi*, four views of Venice (two of them belonged to Sir Richard Wallace); *Duplessis*, Portrait of Necker; works by *Hubert Robert*; *Oudry*, Eight sketches for a Gobelins tapestry, 'Les Chasses de Louis XV'.—STAIRCASE. 'Scènes Chinoises', Aubusson tapestries after *Boucher*.

Second Floor. GALERIE. Sofa and chairs by *Nogaret*; engravings after *Chardin*; Chinese porcelain (18C).—SALON BLEU. Pair of tables attr. to *Riesener*; bookcase attr. to *Carlin*; red morocco casket embossed with the arms of Marie-Antoinette; views of Paris, by *Bouhot, Canella, Demachy*, and *Raguenet*; water-colours by *Jongkind* and by *T. S. Boys*; Chinese porcelain (1662–1795).—BIBLIOTHÈQUE. Secretaire by *Leleu*; two candelabra in bronze and Sèvres biscuit by *Blondeau* after Boucher; works by *Hubert Robert*; Aubusson tapestry screen (1775).—CHAMBRE À COUCHER. Furniture by *Cramer, Topino*, and the brothers *Jacob*; six-leaved screen by *Falconet* (1743); *Danloux*, Rosalie Duthé, painted in England (1792); *Lancret*, Les Rémois, on copper; *Lavreince*, Singing lesson (gouache); *Drouais*, Alex. de Beauharnais as a child; *Houdon*, Sabine Houdon(?), plaster bust; Savonnerie carpet (1760) for the chapel at Versailles.—DEUXIÈME CHAMBRE. Secretaire attr. to *Riesener*; screen by *Jacob*; 'Scènes de chasse', by *Swebach, Vernet, de Dreux, Wm. Shayer*, etc.; *Caffieri*, La Fidélité (statuette).

32   THE MUSÉE RODIN

MÉTRO stations: *St-François-Xavier* (line 14); *Invalides* (line 8).
ADMISSION 1 fr. (0,50 fr. on Sun), plus 1–2 fr. during temporary exhibitions; open daily (except Tues) 1–6 (1–5 Oct–March).

The ***Musée Rodin**, in the *Hôtel Biron* , at No. 77 Rue de Varenne, contains the works and collections of *Auguste Rodin* (1840–1917), which the famous sculptor left to the State. Among the exhibits are originals of works executed in marble and bronze, and a fine selection of his drawings.

The Hôtel Biron, built in 1728–30 by Aubert and Gabriel, was occupied by the Duc de Biron in 1753 and in 1820 by the aristocratic convent of the Sacré-Cœur. The State bought the house and its immense garden in 1901. In 1910 two ground-floor rooms were used by Rodin as a studio.

Chapel. The former convent-chapel (1875), on the right of the gateway, is arranged as a *Musée Monumental*, and contains plaster groups and figures for monuments.

Hôtel Biron. GRANDE SALON. St John the Baptist; 'l'Homme qui marche'; *The kiss; *The hand of God; Iris; The cathedral and The secret, two studies of hands; In the rooms to the left, early works (1863–76), including Girl with flowers in her hair and *Man with a broken nose; *The Bronze Age (l'Age d'Airain); Eve and the serpent. To the right of the Grande Salon, 'La Source'; Orfeus; The wave; Fugit Amor; Ovid's Metamorphosis; Eve. THE STAIRCASE, Three shades, from the Gate of Hell (see below).

FIRST FLOOR. R. 10. Case of models for the Gate of Hell; Meditation; Resurrection of Adonis; Prodigal son.—R. 11. Temptation of St Anthony; Poet and muse; Balzac (nude); Creation of Woman.—R. 12. Martyr; The good genius; Eternal spring; bust of Lord Howard de Walden.—R. 13. Crouching woman; Three studies of Psyche; Death of Adonis.—R. 14. Earth and Moon; 'Devant la mer'; Shell and pearl; three paintings by *Van Gogh*.—R. 15. The Thinker; The athlete; 'Je suis Belle'.—R. 16. Young mother; Children with a lizard; Triton and Nereid on a dolphin; Water-fairy. On the walls, *Renoir*, Nude; *Monet*, Belle-Isle-en-Mer.

The **Garden** contains many bronzes and marbles, including: The Thinker; Victor Hugo at Guernsey, formerly in the gardens of the Palais Royal; The shadow: The Gate of Hell, a composition Rodin was engaged upon for twenty years; 'Eve au rocher'; Ugolino; Burghers of Calais (near the entrance).

III   EXCURSIONS FROM PARIS

As well as being the capital of France, Paris is the centre of the ancient province of the *Île de France*, one of the most interesting and important regions in the whole country. The number of profitable excursions is, therefore, almost unlimited, and restrictions of space allow the mention here of only a few of the most important. Abundant railway facilities and excellent roads have brought a great number of interesting points within reach of an easy day's excursion, but public road transport is less conveniently developed than in the neighbourhood of London.

In addition to the places mentioned below the traveller with time to spare may be reminded of the following points of interest within comfortable reach of Paris: Enghien and Montmorency; Chevreuse and Les Vaux de Cernay; Sceaux and Robinson; Meudon and Bellevue; Poissy, Pontoise, and Mantes; Rambouillet, with the President's country residence, and a lovely garden and park open to the public; and Meaux and the valley of the Marne. Farther afield, but still within a day's compass, are Chartres, Dreux, Beauvais, Compiègne and Pierrefonds, Provins, and Sens, with their famous cathedrals, churches, or castles.

Walkers will find the wooded country around St-Cloud attractive, especially the Forêt de Marly; the Forêt de St-Germain is less interesting, though also preserving some fine trees, while the Bois de Meudon is still agreeable, but apt to be over-popular at fine week-ends. Best of all, though considerably more distant, is the Forêt de Fontainebleau, the attractions of which are almost limitless.

The early Gothic architecture of the Île de France is particularly fine, and, apart from the great churches and cathedrals of the famous towns mentioned above, the lover of medieval building may be reminded of the village churches of Gonesse, Fontenay-en-Parisis, and Louvres (on the way to Chantilly), with *St-Leu-d'Esserent a little to the W.; Lagny on the Marne; *Morienval, near Pierrefonds; and Longpont, Arpajon, and Dourdan, in the Orge valley S. of Paris.

33   VERSAILLES

RAILWAYS (electric). From the Gare de Montparnasse to *Versailles–Chantiers* (10½ m., 17 km.), frequent trains in 15–25 min. viâ Sèvres (R.G.) and Viroflay (R.G.). From the Gare des Invalides to *Versailles–Rive Gauche* (11 m., 18 km.), every ¼ hr. (½ hr. on Sun) in 32 min. viâ Meudon and Viroflay (R.G.). From the Gare St-Lazare to *Versailles–Rive Droite* (14¼ m., 23 km.), every ½ hr. in 32 min. viâ St-Cloud, Sèvres-Ville d'Avray and Viroflay (R.D.—MOTOR-BUS No. 171 from the Pont de Sèvres (terminus of Métro service 9) viâ Sèvres, Chaville, and Viroflay.

The main road from Paris to Versailles (N. 10) starts at the Porte de St-Cloud, crosses the Seine by the Pont de Sèvres (new bridge projected), and traverses the town of **Sèvres**, with the woods of the Parc de St-Cloud rising on the right and the Bois de Meudon on the left. The famous *Porcelain Factory*, founded in 1738, was transferred hither from Vincennes in 1756 at the instance of Mme de Pompadour, whose taste and enthusiasm for its products brought it international reputation. Since 1760 the factory has been a State concern. The workshops are shown 2–5 on the first and third Thurs of each month; saleroom, Mon–Fri 9–12, 2–6. A fine historical collection of the ware produced here may be seen in the *Musée Céramique* (adm. 10–4 or 5, closed Tues; 0,50 fr., Sun 0,25 fr.).

To the S. of Sèvres lies **Meudon**, another residential suburb, the home at various times of Ronsard, Wagner, and Rodin, whose villa 'des Brillants' is now a museum. Here too is the *Musée de l'Air* (adm. free 9–4.45; Sat, Sun, and holidays 10–12, 2–6), on the edge of the Forêt de Meudon (in the Parc de Chalais), a quite insufficient home for a notable collection of fifty-four heavier-than-air craft, from the 'Vuia' of 1906 to the 'Spitfire' of 1940. Near by is the *Observatoire d'Astronomie Physique* (adm. 2nd Sun in the month, on application to the director). The building, formerly the Château Neuf, was built for the Grand Dauphin, son of Louis XV, by Mansart, but fire in 1870 reduced the building to the single-storied pavilion which it is today.

Another road (N. 185) from the Porte Maillot traverses the Bois de Boulogne by the Allée de Longchamp and crosses the Seine at *Suresnes*, beneath the fort of *Mont Valérien*, where 4500 Frenchmen were murdered during the German occupation of 1941–44. An undying flame is kept burning in memory of them, and a memorial shrine covers the bodies of fifteen French men and women, killed either in battle or in the Resistance. A sharp ascent leads to (5 m.) *Montretout*, the upper part of the pleasant town of **St-Cloud** (*Rest. La Réserve*), with the headquarters (1967) of Interpol, and a racecourse and two golf links near by. The royal castle of St-Cloud, where Henri III was assassinated in 1589 and Napoleon's second marriage was celebrated in 1810, was burned down during the German occupation in 1870; but its lovely park (1000 acres) is open to the public, and the fountains play on the 2nd and 4th Sun of the summer months. About 2 m. S.W., beyond *Garches*, is the park of *Villeneuve-l'Étang*, with the monumental memorial (1928–30) to the La Fayette Squadron of American volunteer airmen who fought for France in the First World War. Pasteur died in the château, which is now a medical research institution.— The Versailles road crosses the park and traverses (7 m.) *Ville d'Avray* (Rest. Cabassud, first-class; Estoril, des Hirondelles, less expensive, all near the Étangs, see below), a pleasant residential suburb of Sèvres, with the *Villa des Jardies* (on the left, near the station), the country retreat of Balzac, where he was visited by Victor Hugo and Théophile Gautier. Later the house belonged to Gambetta, who died here in 1882, and some relics of his sojourn are shown. The 18C church, in the Rue de Sèvres, is decorated with frescoes by Corot.—Farther on the Versailles road passes the two Étangs de Ville d'Avray (a favourite subject of Corot's brush) in the Bois de Fausses Reposes, where a monument to the American army (statues of La Fayette and Pershing) stands at the top of the descent to Versailles.

VERSAILLES (84,445 inhab.), the chief town of the department of Seine-et-Oise and the see of a bishop, lies on a low sandy plain between two lines of wooded hills. With its regular streets and its three imposing avenues converging on the palace, it still retains the cachet of a royal city.

Railway Stations. *Rive Droite* (Pl. 5), Rue du Maréchal-Foch, for St-Lazare; *Rive Gauche* (Pl. 17), Av. Thiers, for the Invalides; *des Chantiers* (Pl. 18), Rue des Chantiers, for Montparnasse.

Hotels. Trianon Palace (a; 10), Boul. de la Reine, first-class, with garden; **Royal** (b; 11), 3 Rue Neuve-Notre-Dame; **Vatel** (c; 10), 38 Rue des Réservoirs; **de France** (d; 11), 5 Rue Colbert; **de la Chasse** (e; 17), 2 Rue de la Chancellerie; **St-Louis**, meublé, 28 Rue St-Louis (Pl. 23).

Restaurants. *De Londres, Au Rocher de Cancale*, 7 and 9 Rue Colbert; *Brasserie Muller*, 23bis Av. de St-Cloud; *Brasserie de l'Île de France*, 45 Rue Carnot; *du Chapeau-Gris*, 7 Rue Hoche; *Brasserie Métropôle*, 6 Place Lyautey; *au Chien qui Fume*, 72 Rue de la Paroisse; small and inexpensive restaurants in the Rue de Satory (Pl. 17).

Post Office (Pl. 17), 8 Av. de Paris.—SYNDICAT D'INITIATIVE, 7 Rue des Réservoirs; kiosk at the Rive Gauche station.

Motor-Buses from the Rive Droite and Rive Gauche stations to the Trianons.

History. Versailles emerged from obscurity in 1624, when Louis XIII built a hunting lodge here, which he subsequently developed into a small château. But the real creator of Versailles was Louis XIV, who in 1661 conceived the idea of building a lasting monument to his power and glory. *Louis Le Vau* was entrusted with the renovation and embellishment of the old château round the Cour de Marbre and at the same time *Le Nôtre* laid out the park. After Le Vau's death in 1670 the work was continued by his pupil *François d'Orbay*, while the interior decoration was superintended by *Charles Le Brun*. In 1682 Louis XIV transferred the court and the seat of government from St-Germain. *Jules Hardouin-Mansart*, appointed chief architect in 1676, remodelled the main body of the palace and built the two great N. and S. wings, giving the immense façade a total length of 634 yds, with 375 windows. The chapel, begun by him, was finished by his brother-in-law *Robert de Cotte* in 1710. More than 30,000 workmen were employed at one time on the building of the palace and in laying out and draining the grounds, and the cost is believed to have amounted to over 60 million livres (£10 million). In 1687 *Mansart* built the Grand Trianon. Under Louis XV a series of royal apartments, decorated in the current style, was incorporated in the palace; and one of the colonnaded pavilions in the entrance court, the interior of the opera-house, and the Petit Trianon were built by *J. A. Gabriel*. Louis XVI redecorated a suite of apartments for Marie-Antoinette and built the 'rustic village' of the Petit Trianon.

At the Treaty of Versailles, signed in 1783 by England, France, and Spain, the independence of the United States was formally recognized. Versailles played an important part during the Revolution. The meeting of the Assembly of the States General was held here in 1789, and on 20 June the deputies of the Third Estate constituted themselves into the National Assembly and took the 'Oath of the Tennis Court' not to separate until they had given a constitution to France. On 6 Oct the Paris mob, led by the women of the Halles, marched to Versailles, massacred the bodyguard, and brought the King and royal family to the Tuileries. In 1814 the palace was occupied by Tsar Alexander and Frederick of Prussia. Under the Restoration the second colonnaded pavilion was completed by *Dufour*, but the palace fell into disrepair. Its restoration as a museum (in somewhat doubtful taste) is due to Louis-Philippe. In the Franco-Prussian War Versailles became the headquarters of the German armies operating against Paris, the palace being used as a hospital and Moltke occupying No. 38 Boulevard de la Reine. On 18 Jan 1871, William I of Prussia was crowned German Emperor in the Galerie des Glaces; and on 26 Jan the peace preliminaries were signed by Thiers, Jules Favre, and Bismarck at the latter's quarters, 20 Rue de Provence. In 1871–75 the National Assembly sat in the opera-house, and here the Republic was proclaimed on 25 Feb 1875.

During the First World War Versailles was the seat of the Allied War Council, and the Peace Treaty with Germany was signed in the Galerie des Glaces, on 28 June 1919. An extensive restoration in 1928–32 was made possible by the munificence of John D. Rockefeller, Jr, and his family's benefactions have continued since the Second World War. During that war Allied G.H.Q. was at Versailles from Sept 1944 to May 1945, and many of the buildings in the town as well as those belonging to the Château were taken over by the military, Mass was said in the Chapelle Royale every Sunday for the soldiers stationed here.

Versailles was the birthplace of Louis XV (1710–74), the Abbé de l'Epée (1712–89), Houdon (1741–1828), the sculptor, Marshal Berthier (1753–1815), Louis XVI (1754–93), Louis XVIII (1755–1824), Charles X (1757–1836), Rodolfe Kreutzer (1766–1831), the violinist to whom Beethoven dedicated his famous sonata, Gen. Hoche (1768–97), and Ferdinand de Lesseps (1805–94; at 18 Rue des Réservoirs). Mme de Pompadour died in the palace in 1764.

The Palace of Versailles

ADMISSION 1 fr. (Sun 0,50 fr.), plus 1½ fr. for guide-lectures where necessary. The Galerie des Glaces, the Chapel, and the State Apartments are shown daily between 10 and 5 p.m. (conducted parties only). The remainder of the Palace is *always closed* on Tuesday. Among the other galleries open are: the Petits-Appartements du Roi and de la Reine and the Appartement de Mme du Barry at certain hours daily; Appartement de Mme de Maintenon, daily on request; the Galerie des Batailles, the Salle de 1792 and the Salle du Sacre, 10–5; the Salle du Premier Empire (Attiques de Chimay et du Midi), 2–5; the Salles du XVIII Siècle, May–Oct, 2–5. The Opéra (Salle de Spectacles) is shown daily (adm 1½ fr.; conducted parties). The Galerie de Pierre and the Salles des Croisades are open by previous arrangement. In any case, the notice-board in the Vestibule (R. 23) should be consulted for the hours of admission, etc., and for details of guide-lectures.— For Son et Lumière, see p. 194. There is a self-service restaurant in the Galerie Napoléon (open 10–5).

The PLACE D'ARMES, where the great Avenues de St-Cloud, de Paris, and de Sceaux converge, is bounded on the E. by the GRANDES-ÉCURIES and the PETITES-ÉCURIES, the royal stables, built by *Mansart* in 1679–85, and now occupied by the École de l'Air. Opposite are the vast buildings of the palace. Flanking the gateway with Mansart's original grille are groups of sculpture: (r.) France victorious over the Empire, by *Marsy*, and over Spain, by *Girardon*; (l.) Peace, by *Tuby*, and Abundance, by *Coysevox*.

The AVANT-COUR (forecourt) or COUR DES MINISTRES is flanked by detached wings once assigned to secretaries of state. Beyond the equestrian statue of Louis XIV (1837) is the COUR ROYALE, between two colonnaded pavilions dating from 1772 (r.) and 1829 (l.). The visitors' entrance to the palace is in the right-hand pavilion.

Before entering the palace, visitors should inspect the charming little COUR DE MARBRE, a deep, marble-paved recess at the end of the Cour Royale; this was the court-yard of Louis XIII's château and the nucleus of the whole palace, but was completely transformed by *Le Vau* and *Mansart*.

We first enter the VESTIBULE GABRIEL (R. 23), with the ticket office and the cloak-room (obligatory for sticks, parcels, etc.) at the far end. On the immediate right are the SALLES DU XVE and DU XVIE SIÈCLES, which contain a valuable collection of 15–16C portraits, for the most part unsigned. Beyond the Vestibule Gabriel is the VESTIBULE DE LA CHAPELLE, which has handsome carved and gilded doors and contains a bas-relief of Louis XIV crossing the Rhine, by *Nicolas* and *Guillaume Coustou*. From the vestibule, we pass through the SALLES DU XVIIE SIÈCLE (RR. 2–12), which contain historical paintings and portraits of the period. On the right of the parallel GALERIE DE PIERRE (R. 16) are the five SALLES DES CROISADES (RR. 17–21).

At the far end of the gallery is the FOYER DE L'OPÉRA, retaining its 18C decorations by *Pajou*. The *OPÉRA (adm. see above), or SALLE DE SPECTACLES, was built for Louis XV by *Gabriel* in 1753–70, and first used on the occasion of the marriage of the Dauphin (Louis XVI) and Marie-Antoinette. Repainted in the poor taste of the period by Louis-Philippe, it was the scene of a banquet to Queen Victoria in 1855, the meeting-place of the National Assembly in 1871–75 and of the Senate in 1875–79. In 1955–57 it was completely and skilfully restored by *Japy*, even the upholstery being copied from the original specifications. Seating 700 spectators and with a stage second in size only to the Paris Opera, it is now reserved for rare gala performances. Modelled on the King of Sardinia's theatre in Turin, it is a perfect example of Louis-XV decoration.

Returning to the Vestibule de la Chapelle, we ascend the little staircase on the left of the chapel door to the first floor. The striking *Upper Vestibule* (R. 83) of the chapel contains figures of Virtues, by various sculptors. Through a door with a wonderfully chased lock by *Desjardins*, we enter the royal gallery, which commands the best view of the *CHAPEL, begun in 1699 by *Mansart* and completed in 1710 by *Robert de Cotte*. The high altar is of marble and gilded bronze, with sculptures by *Van Cleve* and *Guillaume Coustou*. The central ceiling-painting represents God the Father in Glory, by *Antoine Coypel*, and above the royal pew is the Descent of the Holy Ghost, by *Jouvenet*.

On the right of the vestibule is the GALERIE DE PIERRE (R. 96), and running parallel to it are ten rooms (RR. 84–93) containing paintings, and portraits and busts of famous personalities of the late 17C and early 18C: *Coysevox*, Maréchal de Villars; portrait of John Churchill, duke of Marlborough, by an unknown artist (R. 84); *Gérard*, Duc d'Anjou (Philip V of Spain; R. 85); *Saint-André*, Louis XIV; *Ferdinand Elle*, Madame de Maintenon; self-portraits by *Largillière, Rigaud,* and *Coypel* (R. 86); *Mignard*, Madame de Maintenon; *Rigaud*, Louis XIV in armour (R. 87); portraits by *Mignard* (R. 88); *French School*, Battle of Fleurus; *Largillière*, Le Grand Dauphin (R. 89); *Warin*, bust of Louis XIV (R. 90); paintings by *Van der Meulen*; busts by *Nicolas Coustou* (Colbert), *Coysevox* (Le Grand Dauphin), *Houdon* (Molière), *Caffieri* (Boileau), *Bernini* (self-portrait), *Boizot* (Racine), etc. (RR. 92, 93). Beyond R. 93 a staircase ascends to the ATTIQUE DU NORD, with historical paintings ranging from the Restoration to the First World War (RR. 151–162). Of special interest to English visitors are the pictures (RR. 158–59, 161) illustrating the visit of Queen Victoria and Prince Albert to the Château d'Eu and of Louis-Philippe's return visit to Windsor (by *Winterhalter*) and of the youthful Victoria also by *Winterhalter*. Returning to the vestibule viâ the Galerie de Pierre we pass (l.) the SALLES D'AFRIQUE, DE LA RESTAURATION, etc. (RR. 98–104).

From the Chapel Vestibule (R. 83) we enter the SALON D'HERCULE (R. 105), fitted up by Louis XV in the Louis-XIV style. The elaborate decorations were sculptured by *Vassé* (1729–34). In the large frame at the end, Louis XIV crossing the Rhine, by *Pierre Franque*, after *Le Brun* and *Van der Meulen*. The portrait of Louis XIV above the chimneypiece is by *Mignard*. On the ceiling (one of the largest in the world) is the Apotheosis of Hercules, by *Fr. Lemoyne*, who worked for three years (1733–36) on this masterpiece and on its completion committed suicide.

Swiss Guards used to be posted here to prevent the intrusion into the state apartments of "those freshly marked with small-pox, the shabbily dressed, petitioners, begging friars, and dogs".

The SALON DE L'ABONDANCE (R. 106) is the first of the **King's State Apartments,** which, though they have lost their original furniture, have preserved their beautiful decorations of marble inlay, sculptured and gilded bronzes, carved doors, and painted ceilings, executed under the superintendence of *Charles Le Brun*. Gobelins *Tapestries of the famous Histoire du Roi series, by *Le Brun*, are normally displayed in these apartments; their subjects include: Louis XIV entering Dunkirk; Capture of Dôle; Siege of Tournai and of Douai; and Defeat of the Spaniards at Bruges. Others are in the Queen's State Apartments (p. 191). The ceiling-painting of the Salon de l'Abondance, which was used as a refreshment room at royal receptions, is by *Houasse* (freely restored). The battle-scenes on the walls are by *Van der Meulen*.

The SALON DE VÉNUS (R. 107), named after its ceiling-painting, by *Houasse*, is noteworthy for its marble decorations in the early Louis-XIV style. The carved doors are by *Caffieri*; above are the beautiful bronze bas-reliefs. The mural decorations of this salon (and the succeeding one) are original. In the central alcove is a statue of Louis XIV in Roman costume and wig, by *Warin*; and on either side of the room are trompe-l'œil paintings by *Jacques Rousseau*.

The SALON DE DIANE (R. 108), the former billiard room, has a ceiling, by *Blanchard*. The bust of Louis XIV in the centre is by *Bernini* (1665). Over the chimneypiece, with its charming bas-relief attr. to *Sarazin*, Sacrifice of Iphigeneia by *Lafosse*; opposite, Diana and Endymion by *Blanchard*.

The SALON DE MARS (R. 109), once the Salle des Gardes, later a gaming-room and subsequently a ballroom and concert-room, has a ceiling by *Audran*, *Jouvenet*, and *Houasse*. The sopraporte (Prudence, Justice, Fortitude, and Temperance) are by *Simon Vouet*, and the *Portrait of Marie-Antoinette and her children, by *Mme Vigée-Lebrun* (1787). The Gobelins tapestries are the first of a series by Le Brun, illustrating 'The Life of the King'. They are among the earliest works from the Gobelins manufactory (1668–72).

The SALON DE MERCURE (R. 110), a card-room under Louis XIV, where that monarch lay in state for eight days, has a ceiling by *J. B. de Champaigne*, Mercury in a chariot drawn by two cocks and preceded by the morning star. The Savonnerie carpet and the clock, by *Morand*, should be noticed.

The SALON D'APOLLON (R. 111), the former throne-room, is the last of the king's state apartments. On the ceiling, by *Lafosse*, is Louis XIV (the 'Roi Soleil') as Apollo in a chariot escorted by the Seasons.

The three following rooms—the Galerie des Glaces, with its two ante-chambers, the Salon de la Guerre and the Salon de la Paix—together form a magnificent decorative ensemble designed as a grandiose monument to the

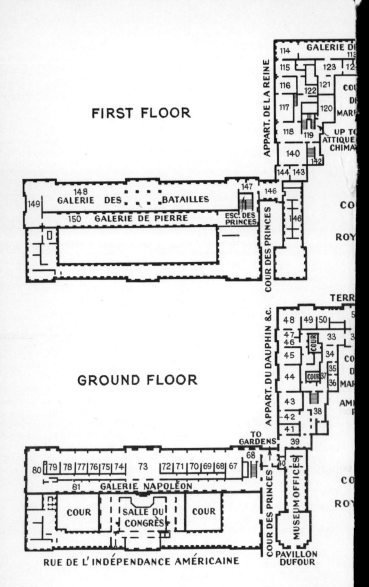

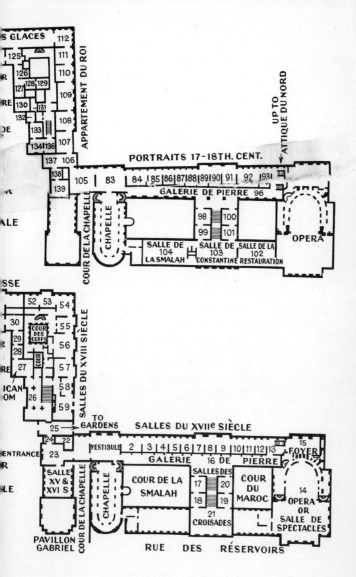

pride and glory of Louis XIV.—The SALON DE LA GUERRE (R. 112), completed in 1678, has preserved its original decoration of coloured marble and bronze and contains six busts of Roman emperors, bequeathed by Mazarin. Over the mantelpiece is a stucco relief of Louis XIV on horseback, by *Coysevox*. The *Ceiling-painting, the first of the series designed by *Charles Le Brun* and executed by himself and his pupils, represents France victorious, with a thunderbolt in one hand and a laurel-wreathed portrait of Louis XIV in the other; in the semi-circles appear Bellona in anger and figures of defeated Germany, Holland, and Spain.

The **GALERIE DES GLACES or GRANDE GALERIE (R. 113), 235 ft long, 30 ft wide, and 43 ft high, is a masterpiece of the Louis-Quatorze style. It was begun by *Mansart* in 1678 and its decoration, designed by *Le Brun*, was completed in 1686. Among the artists employed in the decoration of the gallery were *Caffieri, Coysevox, Le Comte,* and *Tuby,* for the sculptures; *Cucci,* for the frames of the mirrors; and *Ladoiseau,* for the trophies on the walls. The gallery is lighted by seventeen large windows looking on to the park, and facing these are as many bevelled mirrors of equal size. The red marble pilasters have bronze capitals decorated with cocks' heads, fleurs-de-lys, and suns. The cornice of gilded stucco is adorned with crowns and the collars of the Orders of the Holy Ghost and St Michael. The marble statues of Venus, Paris, Mercury, and Minerva in the niches are copies from the antique. The central ceiling-painting represents Louis XIV as supreme sovereign, while the numerous other paintings, large and small, depict the Victories over Holland, Germany, and Spain, the Peace imposed by Louis on his enemies, the Ambassadors sent to all the people of the earth, the Protection of the Arts and the People, and the great Foundations established in his reign. Opposite the windows are two doors adorned with mirrors. For the Salon de la Paix, see below.

We pass through the first door into the CABINET DU CONSEIL (R. 125) which dates in its present form from 1753. It contains the desk used at the Treaty of 1919 (p. 185). The carved *Woodwork is by *Antoine Rousseau*.

Off this room open the **Petits Appartements du Roi** or **Cabinets du Roi** (RR. 126–130), constructed by Louis XV in 1738 to provide a retreat from the tedious etiquette of court life. The CHAMBRE DE LOUIS XV (R. 126) has carved woodwork by *Verberckt* and Gobelins tapestries (Story of Don Quixote). Here Louis XV died of small-pox in 1774.— The CABINET DE LA PENDULE (R. 127) derives its name from *Passemant's Clock* (1749), executed by *Dauthiau*, with chased designs by *Caffieri*, surmounted by a crystal globe marking the phases of the sun, moon, and planets. Five tables of fine workmanship (1730–57) illustrate the evolution of Rococo furniture.—The CABINET DES CHIENS (R. 128), with a frieze of hunting-scenes, was occupied by the lackeys and the king's favourite hounds. On the staircase descending hence Damiens attempted to assassinate Louis XV in 1757.— On a table of the SALLE À MANGER (R. 129) are locksmith's tools used by Louis XVI. This room overlooks the Cour des Cerfs (much altered). We return to R. 127 to enter the CABINET DE TRAVAIL DE LOUIS XV (R. 130). The woodwork (1753) is by *Verberckt*. The superb *Desk, the *Bureau du Roi*, specially ordered by the king in 1760 for this room, was designed by *Oeben* and *Riesener* (1769) with bronzes by *Duplessis, Winant,* and *Hervieux*.—CABINET DE MADAME ADÉLAÏDE (R. 132), with woodwork by *Verberckt*. In 1763 Mozart played here before the princess.—BIBLIOTHÈQUE DE LOUIS XVI (R. 133) is decorated by *Antoine Rousseau*, with a chimneypiece by *Boizot* and *Gouthière* and a candelabrum attributed to *Thomire*.—The SALON DES PORCELAINES (R. 134), with a flat-topped desk by *Leleu*, was so called because of the annual sale of Sèvres ware arranged for the Court, which occupied also the two following rooms. These, the SALLE DE BILLARD and SALLE DES JEUX (RR. 136–37), where Louis XIV's collections of paintings and gems (now in the Louvre and the Bibliothèque Nationale) were housed, later became part of Mme Adélaïde's suite. The adjoining staircase ascends to the **Apartments of Mme du Barry** on the second floor. The beautiful woodwork here has been restored since 1949 and repainted in its original colours.

The CHAMBRE DU ROI (R. 124), Louis XIV's bedchamber (in which he died in 1715), opens on the right of the Cabinet du Conseil and overlooks the Cour de Marbre. Here took place the ceremonious 'lever' and 'coucher' of the king, who used to lunch daily at a little table placed before the middle window. It was from the balcony of this room that Marie-Antoinette and Louis XVI, at La Fayette's desire, showed themselves to the mob on the fateful 6 Oct 1789. The decorations of carved wood and the balustrade separating the bed from the rest of the room are original. The sculpture of gilded stucco above is by *N. Coustou.* The two chimneypieces date from Louis XV (1761) with bronzes by *Caffieri*; on one of them is a fine bust of Louis XIV, on the other a bust of the Duchess of Burgundy, mother of Louis XV, both the work of *Coysevox.*

The Chambre du Roi is followed by the ŒIL-DE-BŒUF (R. 123), named after its small 'bull's eye' window. Here the courtiers used to wait for admission to the king's lever and here arose the scandals of the reign of Louis XV, somewhat monotonously recounted in the 'Chroniques de l'Œil-de-Bœuf'. The decorations are original, including the stucco frieze showing children's games on a gold background, by *Van Cleve, Hurtrelle,* and *Flamen.* A curious picture by *Nocret* represents the royal family in mythological costume.

We now return to the Galerie des Glaces, and at its left end enter the SALON DE LA PAIX (R. 114), which was the queen's card-room. The ceiling completes *Le Brun's* magnificent scheme (see above). It depicts France, bringing the benefits of peace to Europe, with pairs of doves symbolizing dynastic marriages. In the hemicycles are seen Germany, Holland, Spain, and Europe generally enjoying the peace bestowed by Louis XIV. Over the chimneypiece (left unfinished by Le Brun) is a painting by *Lemoyne* (1729), showing Louis XV following his great-grandfather's example as the bringer of peace.

The CHAMBRE DE LA REINE (R. 115), or queen's bedchamber, the first of the **Queen's State Apartments,** was redecorated under Louis XV and Louis XVI. It was restored in 1951–52 to its pre-Revolution appearance, the chimneypiece having been brought back from the Trianon and the silk hangings copied (at Lyons) from portions of the original material. In this room died Marie-Thérèse (1683) and Marie Leczinska (1768), and here the confinements of the queens of France took place. The jewel cabinet of Marie-Antoinette (by *Evalde*; 1770) was brought from the Château of St-Cloud. Above the doors are allegorical paintings of the children of Louis XV by *Natoire* and *De Troy.* The grisaille panels on the ceiling (Charity, Abundance, Fidelity, and Prudence) are by *Boucher,* and the fine portrait of Marie-Antoinette is by *Mme Vigée-Lebrun.* Here is also an unfinished pastel of the queen by *Kucharski* (1792).

From the Chambre de la Reine we may visit the ***Petits Appartements de la Reine** or **Cabinets de la Reine,** the private apartments of Marie-Antoinette (R. 122). This small and cramped suite has preserved its superb decorations of the time of Marie-Antoinette. The BOUDOIR or PETITE MÉRIDIENNE DE LA REINE, with its gilded woodwork and mirror-frames, and the LIBRARY, with imitation bookshelves, were designed by *Mique* (c. 1781).— In the SMALL LIBRARY, used by the ladies-in-waiting, is a marriage-chest of Marie-Antoinette.—The SALON DE LA REINE has elaborate decorations by the brothers *Rousseau* (1783). Here the queen received her intimate friends and her musicians, Gluck and Grétry, and sat to Mme Vigée-Lebrun for her portraits. The last two rooms are the BATH ROOM and the CHAMBRE DE REPOS or SALON JAUNE.

The SALON DE LA REINE (R. 116), or SALON DES NOBLES, was the queen's presence chamber. The Gobelins tapestries represent the Coronation of Louis XIV at Reims, the Marriage of Louis XIV at St-Jean-de-Luz, and the Treaty between Louis XIV and the Swiss. The ceiling, Mercury protecting the

Arts and Sciences, is by *Michel Corneille* (d. 1708). The busts are of Louis XVI, by *Pajou*, and Marie-Antoinette, by *Le Comte*.

In the ANTICHAMBRE DE LA REINE (R. 117), where the queen used to dine in public, the ceiling depicts the Family of Darius at the feet of Alexander, a copy of *Le Brun's* painting in the Louvre. The subjects of the Gobelins tapestries are: Audience of the Spanish ambassador, Surrender of Marsal, Louis XIV visiting the Gobelins, and Audience of the Papal nuncio. Here are three royal busts: *Louis XIV, a masterpiece (1681) by *Coysevox*; Louis XV, by *Gois*; and Louis XVI, by *Houdon*.

The SALLE DES GARDES DE LA REINE (R. 118) has coloured marble decorations of the time of Louis XIV. The ceiling, by the elder *Noël Coypel*, represents Jupiter with Justice and Piety. On 6 Oct 1789, the Paris mob burst into this room, and three of the Swiss Guards perished here in the queen's defence.

To the left of the guard-room is the landing of the ESCALIER DE MARBRE or ESCALIER DE LA REINE, built by *Le Vau* and *Mansart*, with beautiful marble decorations and an interesting perspective painting in the Italian style. Across the landing is a loggia (R. 119) overlooking the Cour de Marbre, in which the door on the right admits to the apartments of Mme de Maintenon (see below), while on the left open the SALLE DES GARDES DU ROI (R. 120) and the ANTICHAMBRE DU ROI (R. 121), where Louis XIV dined in private, on the rare occasions when he did so.

We may descend the Escalier de Marbre to quit the palace by the Cour de Marbre, or we may ascend the Escalier de Stuc, built under Louis-Philippe, to the second floor, on which are the ATTIQUE DE CHIMAY (r.) and the ATTIQUE DU MIDI (l.), which contain historical paintings, sculptures, etc., illustrating the early Napoleonic era, 1796–1804. This is the first section to be re-opened of the National Museum of Versailles, founded 1837 by Louis-Philippe.

The **Apartments of Mme de Maintenon** (RR. 141–143; shown on request), entered from the loggia (R. 119), were furnished by Louis XIV in 1682 for Mme de Maintenon, who became his second wife in 1685. The ANTICHAMBRE (R. 141) contains the *Medallion profile in wax of Louis XIV (at the age of 68), by *Antoine Benoist*, with a wig once perhaps worn by the king himself.—The BEDCHAMBER (R. 142) became, under Mme de Maintenon's domination, the centre of the government of France where all business of state was transacted. Here are drawings by *Le Brun* for the Galerie des Glaces, a sketch by *Lemoyne* for the Salon d'Hercule, and a model of a coach by the crown jeweller *Chobert*.—The GRAND CABINET (R. 143), where Racine's 'Esther' was played before the king and where his 'Athalie' was presented in 1702 by the princes and princesses, contains a sketch of Marie-Antoinette by *Duplessis*; the chest for the infant dauphin's layette, presented by the city of Paris in 1782; and Mme Adélaïde's old Cremona violin.

In the SALLE DU SACRE (R. 140), previously the Grande Salle des Gardes, it was the custom for the king to wash the feet of thirteen poor children on Maundy Thursday. The room was completely spoiled under Louis-Philippe, but was restored in 1948. The ceiling-painting, by *Callet*, is an allegory of the 18 Brumaire (Fall of the Directory, 1799). The sopraporte are by *Gérard*. On the walls are three huge paintings: *J. L. David*, Napoleon presenting eagles in the Champ-de-Mars (1804), Coronation of Napoleon at Notre-Dame (1804); *Gros*, Murat at the Battle of Aboukir (1799).

The SALLE DE 1792 (R. 145) was originally the 'Salon des Marchands', to which vendors of goods were admitted for the convenience of the inmates of the palace. It now contains military pictures.

We cross the landing of the ESCALIER DES PRINCES (R. 147), a notable work by *Mansart*, which gives access to the S. wing of the palace, once reserved for the princes of the blood.

The GALERIE DES BATAILLES (R. 148), nearly 400 ft long and 40 ft wide, was constructed under Louis-Philippe by throwing into one most of the rooms on the first floor of this wing. It contains busts of famous soldiers killed in battle, and the wall-paintings form a pictorial record of French military history from Tolbiac (496) to Wagram (1809). The chronological order begins on the left. Note especially, *Delacroix*, Taillebourg (1242; defeat of Henry III of England by St Louis).

Descending the Escalier des Princes, we may either pass out from the vestibule into the Cour des Princes and thence enter the gardens, or we may visit (l.) the SALLES DE LA RÉPUBLIQUE ET DE L'EMPIRE (RR. 67–80), on the ground floor of the S. wing, re-opened in 1959. The paintings illustrate French history from 1793 to 1815 and include works by *Gros*, *Horace* and *Charles Vernet*, and others; the furnishings, made in the 1950s, reproduce original Napoleonic designs.

A passage on the S. side of the Cour des Princes leads to the SALLE DU CONGRÈS (no adm.), built in 1875 to accommodate the Chamber of Deputies which sat here till 1879. The Congrès, or united sitting of the two French chambers, for the purpose of electing the President of the Republic, took place here until 1940. After 1947 the hall became the meeting-place of the Union Française, a legislative body representing French territories both in Europe and overseas.

Entering the door on the right of the vestibule of the Escalier des Princes, we pass through ROOM 66 and the ARCADE DU MIDI (RR. 40 and 39) to reach the vestibule of the Escalier de Marbre, in which are 17C sculptures from fountains formerly in the gardens.

The **Salles du Dix-huitième Siècle,** which we enter from this vestibule, on the ground floor of the central block, looking out on the gardens, were occupied at various times by the Regent Orléans, and the sons and daughters of Louis XV, and are also known as the *Appartements du Dauphin et de la Dauphine, et de Mesdames.* They have been repeatedly altered, and most of the original decorations were swept away by Louis-Philippe. They now contain an admirable *Collection of 18C portraits. ROOM 42. *Rigaud*, Louis XV; *Santerre*, The Regent Orléans. R. 43. *J. B. Vanloo* and *Parrocel*, *Louis XV on horseback. R. 44. *J. B. Vanloo*, Louis XV. R. 45. Louis XVI, Louis XVIII, and Charles X were born in this room, which was also the bedroom of Marie-Antoinette on her arrival in France; *Nattier*, Mme de Pompadour; *Tocqué*, *Marquis de Marigny, brother of Mme de Pompadour, and Tournehem, her mother's protector, Marigny's predecessor as director of the royal buildings. R. 46. *Nattier*, Marie-Josèphe de Saxe (mother of Louis XVI). R. 47 has retained part of its charming Louis-XV decoration. R. 48 (Grand Cabinet du Dauphin). *Nattier*, Portraits of the daughters of Louis XV. The fine Louis-XIV balcony of wrought and gilded iron commands a splendid view of the gardens. R. 49 was the Regent's study, where he died in 1723, and later the bedroom of the Grand Dauphin, son of Louis XV. It preserves many decorative details, including woodwork by *Verberckt*, and a red marble chimneypiece, with figures of Flóra and Zephyrus by *Caffieri*; also *Nattier*, Infanta Maria Isabella (1759), Marie Leczinska (replica of the painting in R. 53); *N. Coustou*, bust of Marie Leczinska. R. 50 retains traces of its Louis-XIV decorations. The gouache drawings by *Van Blarenberghe* depict the campaign of 1744–48 in Flanders.

The GALERIE BASSE (R. 51), below the Galerie des Glaces, has been completely altered since the reign of Louis XIV, when Molière gave several of his plays in it, including the first performance of 'Tartuffe' (1664). It contains an interesting series of paintings, by *Martin* and *Lenfant*, of the battles of Louis XV, in fine frames. R. 52 is the first of the 'Appartement des Bains', a suite originally fitted up as bath rooms under Louis XIV and later occupied by Mme de Montespan, Mme de Pompadour, and the daughters of Louis XV.

Nattier, *Mme Adélaïde as Diana, *Mme Henriette as Flora. R. 53. *Nattier,* The Duke of Burgundy as an infant, Isabella, daughter of the Infanta Maria Isabella and grand-daughter of Louis XV, and *Marie Leczinska (1748). R. 54. Gobelins tapestry portrait of Louis XV, after *L. M. Vanloo. Roslin,* *Portrait of the Dauphin, son of Louis XV. R. 55. *Noël Hallé,* Allegory in honour of the Peace of 1763; *L. M. Vanloo,* Choiseul (1763); *Rigaud,* Chancellor Maupéou, Comte d'Argenson; *Carle Vanloo,* Soufflot; *Drouais,* Louis XV. R. 56. *Vassé,* Venus. RR. 57–59 contain paintings of personalities and historical scenes of the Louis-XVI period. The king is represented in a standing portrait by *Duplessis,* while two views of Versailles by *Hubert Robert* (R. 58) are especially noteworthy. The 'perspective' decoration of R. 59 was restored in 1943–45.

We turn right (through R. 26) into ROOM 27, the **Room of American Independence.** Portraits of Washington, after *C. W. Peale; Van Blarenberghe,* Capture and Siege of Yorktown (gouache); *G. P. A. Healy,* Series of portraits of American personalities painted for Louis-Philippe. R. 28. *Vigée-Lebrun,* *Marie-Antoinette; *Duplessis,* Louis XVI. R. 29. *Vigée-Lebrun,* The Dauphin and Madame Royale as children. R. 30. Two cartoons for the Oath of the Tennis Court (p. 200), by *David; Duplessis,* portraits of Mme and M. Necker; *Houdon,* bust of La Fayette. We pass through R. 32 into ROOM 33, which is devoted to scenes from the Revolution. Note the little bust of the Dauphin (Louis XVII) as a child, by *Deseine* (1790). ROOMS 34, 35 are devoted to the Convention and the Directory.

The gardens are conveniently entered either through the passage near the entrance to the palace or by the Cour des Princes.

The ***Gardens** of Versailles were designed for Louis XIV by *André Le Nôtre* (1613–1708), the celebrated landscape-gardener, to whom London owes Greenwich Park and Rome the Quirinal and Vatican gardens. The fountains and hydraulic machinery were the work of *J. H. Mansart* and the engineer *François Francini,* while the sculptural decoration was executed under the supervision of *Le Brun* and *Mignard.*

The gardens were first laid out in 1661–68. The preliminary work of levelling and draining the site was prodigious, and thousands of trees were brought hither from all parts. Inspired by Italian originals which were interpreted with an amplitude and harmony hitherto unknown, Versailles is the masterpiece of French gardening. The gardens are essentially formal, with their carefully planned vistas and straight walks lined with trees, their artificial lakes and ponds, arranged with geometrical precision, their groves and clumps of trees, lawns and terraces, all interspersed with innumerable statues and vases of marble and bronze, and enlivened with fountains of infinitely varied form. In their general lines and their sculptural decoration, with the characteristic stressing of the 'classical' note, the gardens remain as they were laid out under Louis XIV; but it was not until the 18C that the planting of the trees was developed to its present extent, so that on the whole we have before us today the gardens of Louis XV and Louis XVI.

ADMISSION. Gardens and park (no picnics) are open free all day to pedestrians except on special occasions; cars are admitted to the park on payment of 1 fr. The *Fountains* play on the first and third Sun of the month, May to Sept inclusive, at 4.45 p.m. (adm. 1 fr.). The *Fêtes de Nuit,* at the Bassin de Neptune, take place c. 3 and 31 July, 14 Aug, and 4 Sept (adm. 4–20 fr.), varying annually; the local press should be consulted for alterations. *Son et Lumière* on every Fri (adm. 10 fr.), Sat and Sun (adm. 3 fr.) from mid-June to the end of Sept except on the occasion of the Fêtes de Nuit.

A complete exploration of the gardens would occupy almost two hours; in the brief itinerary below only the most outstanding features are singled out.

The TERRACE behind the central block of the palace is adorned with bronze statues after the antique and with marble vases typifying War (by *Coysevox*) and Peace (by *Tuby*). Beyond the PARTERRES D'EAU, two large ornamental pools adorned with bronzes (1690), are the MARCHES DE LATONE, a flight of steps commanding the best view of the palace and, in the other direction, one of the famous vistas of the gardens, especially fine at sunset. Flanking the steps are the FONTAINE DE DIANE (r.) and the FONTAINE DU POINT-DU-JOUR. By the former are statues of Air, by *Le Hongre*, and Diana the Huntress, by *Desjardins*. On the right of the Terrace extend the PARTERRES DU NORD, where the original design of Le Nôtre has been largely respected. Just beyond is the charming FONTAINE DE LA PYRAMIDE, in lead, by *Girardon*, and among the sculptures in the cross-walk (l.) is Winter, also by *Girardon*. The ALLÉE D'EAU, designed by *Perrault* and *Le Brun* (1676–88), with its charming groups of children, leads straight on to the BASSIN DE NEPTUNE (1740), the largest fountain-basin in the gardens, and one of the most attractive. We return by the Allée des Trois Fontaines (parallel to the Allée d'Eau) to reach the BAINS D'APOLLON (r.), a grove laid out by *Hubert Robert* under Louis XVI, in a 'romantic' spirit very different from the formal symmetry of Le Nôtre.

The ALLÉE DE L'ÉTÉ leads to the ALLÉE ROYALE or TAPIS VERT, a stretch of grass, 360 yds long and 40 yds wide, lined with marble vases and statues, many of them copies of the antique. Note, on the left, Venus, by *Le Gros*, and Achilles at Scyros, by *Vigier*. Towards the end (r.) is the entrance to the BOSQUET DES DÔMES, with several fine statues, including Acis and Galatea, by *Tuby*, while almost opposite is the BOSQUET DE LA COLONNADE, with its beautiful *Circle of marble arches by *Mansart* (1685–88); in the centre is the *Rape of Proserpine, by *Girardon*. At the end of the Tapis Vert is the large BASSIN D'APOLLON, with a fine group of Apollo's Chariot, by *Tuby*. To the right is the PETITE VENISE, where the Venetian gondoliers of Louis XIV were housed. Beyond the Bassin d'Apollon, and separated from the gardens by railings, is the PETIT PARC, divided by the GRAND CANAL, just over 1 m. long and 60 yds wide, the scene of Louis XIV's boating parties. At its centre it is crossed by a transverse arm, extending from the Grand Trianon to the few remaining buildings of the former royal Menagerie (1200 yds). Boats may be hired at the palace end of the Grand Canal, near the Café La Flottille (luncheons).

To regain the palace we may traverse the SALLE DES MARRONNIERS, a chestnut grove behind the Colonnade, and, passing the BASSIN DE SATURNE and BASSIN DE BACCHUS, with charming sculptures by *Girardon* and *Marsy*, reach the BOSQUET DE LA REINE. This grove became notorious as the principal scene of the court scandal known as the 'Affair of the Necklace' (1784–85), in which Cardinal de Rohan (seeking the favour of Marie-Antoinette by means of a costly gift) was duped by the Comtesse de la Motte. Thence the PARTERRES DU MIDI lead back to the palace. To the right, two flights of steps, known as the CENT MARCHES, descend alongside the Orangery (no adm.), by *Mansart*, to the road to St-Cyr, beyond which is the PIÈCE D'EAU DES SUISSES (800 yds long and 150 yds wide), excavated in 1678–82 by the Swiss Guards, many of whom are said to have died of malaria during the operation.

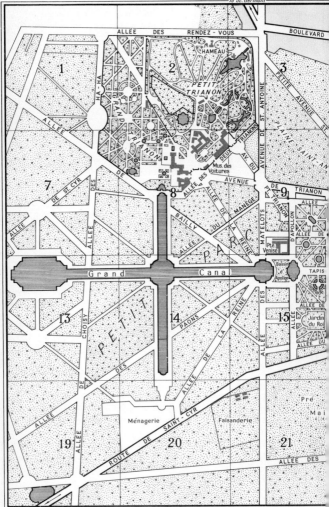

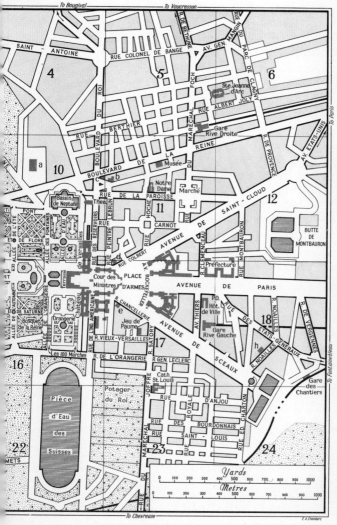

The Trianons

The Trianons are reached from the town by motor-bus viâ the Boulevard de la Reine and Avenue de Trianon. From the palace they are about 20 min. walk across the park.

ADMISSION. Both Grand and Petit Trianon are open daily (conducted parties), except Tues, 2–5 or 6 (1 fr.). The *Théâtre de la Reine* is shown on request (conducted parties). The *Musée des Voitures* is open daily 2–5 or 6. The fountains of the Grand Trianon play on the second Sun of each month from May to Sept at 4 p.m.

The ***Grand Trianon**, a beautiful miniature palace, designed by *J. H. Mansart* and *Robert de Cotte*, with sumptuous marble decorations, was built for Louis XIV in 1687 as a retreat from the ceremonious life at the court of Versailles. It replaced an earlier 'Trianon' in porcelain on the site of the village of Trianon.

The palace was occupied for a time by Mme de Maintenon. It was redecorated for Napoleon, who frequently occupied it, and the Empire furniture which he installed still remains. In 1818 the Duke of Wellington dined here with Louis XVIII. Louis-Philippe did his best to spoil the interior decoration in 1837. In 1873 Marshal Bazaine was tried for his surrender of Metz and sentenced to death in the Péristyle, then a windowed gallery. The Treaty of Trianon (1920), between the Western Allies and Hungary, was signed in the Grande Galerie. A thorough restoration of both Trianons was carried out in 1925–27 and in 1959.

The entrance from the courtyard is on the left, in front of the splendid open colonnade or PÉRISTYLE. In the left wing, the rooms visited are: the SALON DES SEIGNEURS, with decoration of 1691–92; the ANTICHAMBRE (formerly the Chapel) and CHAMBRE DE MONSIEUR (i.e. the Dauphin, son of Louis XIV), with Napoleon's bedstead, later used by Louis-Philippe; and the SALON DES GLACES, with mirrors in the Louis-XIV style.

Beyond the Péristyle, in the right wing, the handsome SALON DES COLONNES or SALON ROND has preserved most of its Louis-XIV decoration. Beyond the SALON DE MUSIQUE and the GRAND SALON of Louis-Philippe is the GRAND SALON of Napoleon (or Cabinet du Couchant) which contains a *Bowl of malachite mosaic given to Napoleon by Alexander I of Russia, after the Treaty of Tilsit, in 1807. Beyond again is the SALON FRAIS. To the left is the GRANDE GALERIE, decorated by *Mansart*.—Beyond the SALON DES JARDINS (in which Queen Elizabeth II, then princess, was entertained in 1948) is the wing known as TRIANON-SOUS-BOIS.

From the Salon Frais we enter the SALON DES SOURCES, which contains paintings by *J. B. Martin*. The five rooms forming the APARTMENTS OF MME DE MAINTENON were subsequently occupied by Stanislas Leczinski, king of Poland (1741), Mme de Pompadour, and Napoleon and Marie-Louise; note the Empire bed from the Château de Meudon. Then follows the ANTI-CHAMBRE DU ROI, with a Louis-XV chimneypiece. The CHAMBRE DU ROI was furnished (in poor taste) for Queen Victoria, who, however, never occupied it.

The charming **Gardens** of the Grand Trianon were laid out by *Mansart* and *Le Nôtre*. The terrace overlooking the Grand Canal commands a fine view. The BUFFET, designed by *Mansart*, with bas-reliefs and figures of Neptune and Amphitrite, is the chief fountain in the gardens. From the JARDIN DU ROI, behind the palace, a bridge leads to the gardens of the Petit Trianon.

Between the Grand and the Petit Trianon, to the left of the exit from the Jardin du Roi, is the **Musée des Voitures,** an interesting little collection of state carriages: State coach used at the coronation of Charles X (1824) and the christening of the Prince Imperial (1856); carriage used at the christening of the Duc de Bordeaux (1820) and the marriage of Napoleon III and the Empress Eugénie (1853); carriage of Napoleon I, used at his marriage with Marie-Louise (1810).

The **Petit Trianon** (1762–68) was built by *Gabriel* for Louis XV as a country retreat for himself and Mme de Pompadour, who did not survive its completion. Mme du Barry then occupied it; but its special interest lies in its association with Marie-Antoinette, who chose it as her favourite residence. The palace was subsequently occupied by Pauline Borghese, Napoleon's sister. The furniture was sold at the Revolution, but has been replaced by pieces belonging to Marie-Antoinette or of her period.

On the left of the courtyard is the CHAPEL (not shown), and at the end is the palace, in the style of a simple but elegant private mansion. We ascend the graceful staircase to the first floor. The ANTECHAMBER has sopraporte by *Natoire* and *Caresme*. The DINING ROOM has a painting of a ballet danced by Marie-Antoinette as a child with her brothers at Schönbrunn. The chimney-piece is by *Guibert*, who designed also that in the Grand Salon, as well as most of the woodwork in the palace. Traces of the trap-door, through which, in Louis XV's reign the tables used to appear ready-laid, are still visible in the floor. The PETIT SALON was Marie-Antoinette's billiard-room. The GRAND SALON, used as a concert-room, has beautiful Louis-XV woodwork and superb furniture designed by *Riesener, Leleu, Demay*, and others; the two vases of petrified wood are supposed to have been given to Marie-Antoinette by Joseph II of Austria (her brother). The queen's BEDROOM has a fine clock adorned with eagles, a table decorated by *Weisweiler*, and a small table by *Levasseur*. The BOUDOIR retains its decoration specially designed for the queen by *Mique*. In the last room are a charming desk by *Beneman* and some interesting portraits, including one, after *Kucharski*, believed to represent Louis XVII.

The *Gardens of the Petit Trianon were originally a menagerie and a botanical garden laid out by Jussieu for Louis XV, but were altered for Marie-Antoinette in the English style (1774–86). To the right is the *Temple d'Amour* with its Corinthian colonnade and Monchy's copy (1780) of Bouchardon's statue of Love. The HAMLET is a sort of theatrical village built by Marie-Antoinette to gratify her taste for 'nature' as popularized by Rousseau. The work of the farm, however, was done by real peasants. It comprises a mill near the lake; the Maison de la Reine (with dining-room, card-room, billiard-room, etc.), with the 'Réchauffoir' (kitchen), behind, and the 'Boudoir', on the right; the Colombier, with pigeon-cote and fowl-run; the Dairy, where the queen used to make butter; the 'Tour de Marlborough', and farm-buildings. Near the smaller lake is an octagonal *Belvedere* (by Mique) with charming interior decoration, to the right of which is the grotto where Marie-Antoinette was resting on 5 Oct 1789, when she was told that the mob had broken into Versailles. Within a few steps we reach the THEATRE, where Marie-Antoinette made her début in court-theatricals (1780; restored 1936; adm. see above). We next visit the JARDIN FRANÇAIS, commanding a view of the main façade of the palace. The PAVILLON FRANÇAIS (r.) was built by *Gabriel* in 1751 for Louis XV and Mme de Pompadour.

The TOWN of Versailles, though naturally overshadowed in interest by the palace, nevertheless contains several buildings of note. In the Rue des Réservoirs (Pl. 10), bordered by the N. wing of the palace, is the *Hôtel des Réservoirs* (at No. 7), built by Lassurance for Mme de Pompadour and now much altered, but still bearing the Marquise's arms. The *Théâtre Montansier* (at No. 13), founded by the actress Mlle Montansier, was built by Heurtier and Boulet in 1777 (restored). In the Rue de l'Indépendance-Américaine (Pl. 16), flanked by the S. wing of the palace, is the *Grand-Commun*, built by Mansart in 1684, with fine bas-reliefs and courtyard. It formerly housed a crowd of minor court officials and is now a military hospital. No. 3 is the former *Hôtel de la Guerre* (1759). No. 5, the old Hôtel de la Marine et des Affaires Étrangères (1761), is the *Bibliothèque de la Ville*, with a small museum and fine Louis-XV decorations; here the Treaty of 1783 was drawn up (adm. on application to the Bibliothécaire en chef). Louvois died in 1691 at No. 6, once the *Hôtel de la Surintendance*.

The Rue du Vieux-Versailles (on the left) brings us to the **Jeu de Paume** (Pl. 17), the royal tennis court, built in 1686. In 1789 the deputies of the Tiers-État, finding themselves locked out of the States General, adjourned hither and, with Bailly as their president, took the famous oath not to separate until they had given to France a proper constitution. Used as a studio by Gros and Horace Vernet, it was in 1889 converted into a *Museum of the Revolution* (adm. on application to M. le Conservateur, Château de Versailles). In the Rue du Maréchal-Joffre (a little to the S.) is the **Cathedral of St-Louis** (Pl. 17, 23), built by *Jacques Mansart de Sagonne* in 1743–54, a rare example of a Louis-XV church. In the interior are the monument, by *Pradier*, to the Duc de Berri, assassinated by Louvel in 1820 (S. aisle), and paintings by *Boucher* and *Jouvenet*.

The Rue Hardy passes the *Potager du Roi* (Pl. 17, 23), formerly the royal kitchen-garden, now a school of horticulture (shown on application to the Directeur de l'École Nationale d'Horticulture). The Rue d'Anjou (Pl. 23, 24) leads from the cathedral to the *Place du Marché-St-Louis*, with its quaint 18C houses. No. 4 in the Rue St-Médéric, to the right farther on, was the *Parc-aux-Cerfs* (a house named after an old quarter of the town), purchased in 1755 by Louis XV for the indulgence of his frivolous amours.

In the Av. de Paris (Pl. 17, 18) the *Chambre de Commerce* (No. 3) occupies the *Hôtel de Mme du Barry* (1750; adm: on written application to the Chambre de Commerce), in which are preserved contemporary woodwork, a bust of Mme du Barry by Pajou, etc. Farther on, at Nos. 57–61, are the charming *Laiterie de Madame* and *Pavillon de Musique*, built by Chalgrin in 1780 in emulation of the 'hameau' at the Petit Trianon for Madame Elisabeth, comtesse de Provence, wife of the future Louis XVIII.

In the N. part of the town is the church of *Notre-Dame* (Pl. 11), built by J. H. Mansart in 1684, the parish church of the palace (interesting registers). The pulpit (1686) is a fine example of its period.—The *Musée Houdon* (Pl. 11), occupying the 18C Hôtel Lambinet in the Boul. de la Reine (No. 54), contains works of sculpture by Houdon, and good examples of 14–18C religious art (free daily except Mon, 2–5).

34   VINCENNES

MÉTRO stations: *Château de Vincennes* (line 1), for the Château itself; *Porte Dorée* and *Porte de Charenton* (line 8) are more convenient for the Zoo and the Colonial Museum.—RAILWAY from *Paris–Bastille* (Gare de Vincennes) to *Vincennes* in c. 10 min. (c. every 20 min. on weekdays, hourly on Sun). The trains go on to Boissy-St-Léger.—MOTOR-BUSES: Route 125 from Porte d'Orléans, 115 from Porte des Lilas, and, for the Zoo, 46 and 86.

Vincennes (*Restaurant du Cygne*, 22 Av. de Paris), a town of 50,450 inhab., c. 5 m. E. of the Louvre, has much of interest to offer the visitor. Apart from the magnificent château, the Jardin Colonial, the Musée de la France d'Outre Mer, and the Zoological Gardens are well worth a visit.

The **Château de Vincennes** is rectangular in plan and is flanked by nine square towers, reduced to the level of the walls in the 19C, with the exception of the entrance tower, the largest and finest of all, which has lost only its statues. This is situated in the middle of the N. front, in the Avenue de Paris, just short of the Cours Marigny and the Cours des Maréchaux.

Admission daily except Tues, 0,50 fr. (Sun 0,25 fr.). Visitors are conducted in parties at 10, 11, 1.30, 2.30, 3.30, 4.30 (and 5.30 in summer). Son et Lumière on Wed and Sat (adm. 2 fr.).

History. The present castle, succeeding an earlier royal hunting-lodge fortified by St Louis, was begun by Philip VI in 1337, and its fortification was completed by his grandson Charles V (1364–73). The chapel, however, begun by Charles, was not finished until 1552.

The foundations of the Pavillons du Roi and de la Reine were laid in the 16C, but these buildings were not completed for nearly a century, when the château, then in Mazarin's possession, was altered and decorated by Le Vau. With the completion of the Palace of Versailles (c. 1680) Vincennes was deserted by the court. The château was occupied in 1745 by a porcelain factory (transferred to Sèvres in 1756), in 1753 by a cadet school, and in 1757 by a small-arms factory. It was offered for sale in 1788, like the other royal palaces, but found no purchaser, and in 1791 La Fayette rescued it from destruction by the mob. Napoleon converted the château into an arsenal in 1808, when the surviving 13C buildings were demolished. In 1840 it was made into a fortress, and much of Le Vau's decoration was destroyed or masked by casemates; but in 1930 the Army was removed and a scheme was set on foot to restore the castle to its earlier appearance. During the Second World War the castle was again militarized, and the German occupying forces had a supply depôt here. In 1944, when they were endeavouring to evacuate the building, the Pavillon de la Reine was partially destroyed by an explosion. Since 1945 the château has been undergoing a thorough restoration.

The historical associations of Vincennes are endless. St Louis used to administer justice beneath an oak tree in the forest. It witnessed the death of Louis X in 1316, of Philip V in 1322, of Charles IV in 1328, of Charles IX in 1574, and of Mazarin in 1661; and Charles V was born here in 1337. In 1422 Henry V of England died at Vincennes, seven weeks before the death of Charles VI, whom he was to succeed as king of France. During the reign of Louis XIII the keep was used as a state prison; and among its famous prisoners were the Grand Condé, Card. de Retz, Fouquet, Diderot, and Mirabeau. A later prisoner was J. H. Latude (1725–1805), who, for a fraudulent attempt to extract money from Mme de Pompadour, was incarcerated here (and elsewhere), untried, for thirty-five years. In 1804 the Duc d'Enghien, son of the Prince de Condé, arrested five days previously by Napoleon's orders, was tried by court-martial and shot the same night. Gen. Daumesnil was governor of the château from 1809 to 1814, during the Hundred Days, and from 1830 till his death in 1832. When summoned to surrender by the Allies in 1814, his answer was "First give me back my leg" (he had lost a leg at Wagram). In 1830, when the Paris mob broke into the fortress in search of some of the former ministers of Charles X, he dispersed them by threatening to blow up the powder-magazine. In 1944, three days before the evacuation, the Germans shot some thirty hostages against the interior of the ramparts.

We enter by the splendid main gateway beneath the 14C *Tour du Village, 155 ft high. In the great courtyard are the chapel with the keep opposite and, at the farther end, the two great 'pavillons', built in 1654–60 by Le Vau, who connected them by a wall (destroyed) across the courtyard as well as converting the S. entrance of the enceinte (the *Tour du Bois*) into a monumental gateway and rebuilding the S. wall.

On the left, before the chapel, a stone commemorates the hostages of 1944 (see above). The oak tree near by, planted in 1952, perpetuates the memory of St Louis (see above).

The CHAPEL, founded by Charles V in 1379, was completed under Henri II in 1552 though retaining the Gothic style. The Flamboyant *Façade has a magnificent rose window surmounted by an ornamental gable filled with tracery. The vaulting is notable for its lightness and grace.

The *Stained Glass of the seven east windows, by Beaurain (16C), was completely restored after an explosion in 1870. The five apse windows represent scenes from the Apocalypse, while the other two represent the Labourers in the Vineyard (r.) and the Last Judgement (l.). On either side of the choir are charming small doorways of the 15C. The Duc d'Enghien (see above) is commemorated by a monument (four marble statues by Deseine; 1816), removed from the choir by Napoleon III to the oratory on the left.

The well-preserved *KEEP, 170 ft in height, a square tower flanked with round turrets, is enclosed in a separate turreted enceinte and is the finest in France since the Château de Coucy was blown up by the Germans (in 1917). It is specially notable for its vaulting and corbels, and contains a small historical museum.

The two doors on the ground floor facing the postern came from the prison of Louis XVI in the Temple. On the first floor the vaulting springs from a beautifully sculptured column and the corbels at each corner of the room symbolize the four Evangelists. The second floor was the favourite residence of Charles V: the Chambre du

Roi has a fine chimneypiece and vaulting with a central pillar; the king's oratory is in the N.W. turret. Henry V (of England) and Charles IX died on this floor. The third floor was used in the 17C for prisoners of state. The E. corridor on the third floor contains the most ancient of their inscriptions (1587 onwards). The roof, reached by a flight of 260 steps, commands a wide view of the forest and of Paris.

Flanking the W. side (r.) of the immense Cour d'Honneur is the *Pavillon du Roi*, built for Louis XIV and his youthful queen and destined for the Army Archives. The *Pavillon de la Reine*, opposite, where Mazarin died, has recently been restored (comp. above) and is once again occupied by the *War Museum* (1914–18) and Library. The explosion which caused the damage here also destroyed the casements enclosing the S. wall of the enceinte, so that Le Vau's design for this is now largely revealed.

The **Bois de Vincennes,** first enclosed in the 12C, was replanted in 1731 by Louis XV and converted into a park for the use of the citizens of Paris. In 1860 the Bois was further enlarged to the S.W. In 1934 the ground between the E. side of the château and the Nouveau Fort (1839) was cleared and relaid to form the pleasant *Cours des Maréchaux*, while on the S. side of the château the manœuvre-ground is gradually being replanted. To the S.W. of the château, bordering the Av. Daumesnil, is the **Parc Zoölogique de Vincennes* (open daily 9–7 or dusk; adm. 1 fr.; café-restaurant), one of the finest zoos in Europe (35 acres), containing some 600 mammals and over 1200 birds. A splendid view of the Bois is obtained from the summit of the Grand Rocher at the N. end of the park. Farther W. along the Av. Daumesnil (r.) is the *Musée de la France d'Outre Mer* (open daily, except Tues, 2–5.30 or 6; adm. 0,50 fr.), housed in a magnificent building constructed for the Colonial Exhibition of 1931. The museum is devoted to the history and development of the French colonies. Below the ground floor (entrance to the left of the vestibule) is a fine aquarium, with a collection of giant tortoises as its most noteworthy feature.

To the E. of the château the Av. des Minimes leads S.E. to the charming *Lac des Minimes* (the prettiest of the three lakes in the Bois). At the N. end of the lake a bridge crosses to the *Île de la Porte-Jaune* (café-restaurant, boats for hire, etc.). In the Av. de la Belle-Gabrielle, to the E. of the lake, is the *Jardin Tropical* (open Thurs, 2–4), with the buildings of the Institut National d'Agronomie Coloniale, and a charming little Indo-Chinese pagoda.

35   MALMAISON

MOTOR-BUS No. 258 from the Pont de Neuilly (terminus of Métro service No. 1), in c. ½ hr viâ Puteaux, Nanterre, and Rueil, going on to St-Germain. No. 158 goes as far as Rueil only.

Rueil (8¼ m.) and *St-Germain* (12½ m. in ½ hr) are reached from Paris (Gare St-Lazare) also by ELECTRIC RAILWAY (frequent trains), following the oldest railway line from Paris (1837). *Maisons-Laffitte* (10½ m.) is served by motor-bus No. 262 from the Pont-de Neuilly (40 min.) and by trains from the Gare St-Lazare (hourly in 25 min.).

In the church of *Rueil* (5½ m.), on the left of the uninteresting road from Paris, is the tomb of the Empress Josephine, erected in 1825 by her children, Eugène and Hortense de Beauharnais. The tomb of Queen Hortense, in the chapel opposite, was erected by her son, Napoleon III, in 1858. The 15C Florentine organ-case, by Baccio d'Agnolo, was a gift from Napoleon III.

The famous château of **Malmaison,** 6¾ m. from Paris, was the home of Josephine Bonaparte after 1798. The rather featureless building of 1622 was extended in 1800 and contains collections of great historical interest (open daily except Tues, 10–12 and 1.30–5.30 in summer, 11–12 and 1.30–4 in winter; adm. 0,50 fr., Sun 0,25 fr., gratuity to guide).

At the height of her power the empress held a literary and artistic salon at Malmaison, and after her divorce in 1809 she retired hither and devoted herself to gardening. She died here in 1814 of a chill caught while doing the honours of the grounds to the allied sovereigns. Napoleon spent five days here in 1815, between Waterloo and his departure for St Helena. Malmaison was bought in 1814 by Maria Cristina, Queen of Spain, and in 1861 by Napoleon III. Though later despoiled of most of its contents, it was bought and furnished in 1896 by M. Osiris, who in 1906 presented it to the State as a Napoleonic museum. Since then, by gift or purchase, further appropriate acquisitions have been made, and, latterly, contemporary colour-schemes have been used in the decoration of the principal rooms.

GROUND FLOOR. From the central VESTIBULE, with busts of members of Napoleon's family, we enter the DINING ROOM, with its original frescoes of Pompeian dancers, by *Laffitte*, restored. Here also is the silver-gilt 'surtout', or set of table-decorations, presented to Napoleon by the city of Paris on the occasion of his coronation; it was used at a state banquet given to George VI of England and his queen at the Quai d'Orsay in 1938. The COUNCIL CHAMBER, shaped like a tent, contains a writing-desk of yew-wood, the gift of the city of Bordeaux, and a clock from the Tuileries. In the LIBRARY, which retains its original decoration by *Percier* and *Fontaine*, are Napoleon's bureau and arm-chair, a statuette of Napoleon and a clock made for Louis XVI by *Janvier* in 1791 but bought by Napoleon. Here, and in the next room, is the notable assemblage of books from Napoleon's own library, which found their way to Germany and were repurchased and given to the collection. The BILLIARD ROOM contains Napoleon's throne from Fontainebleau, his portrait in Gobelins tapestry, and a Savonnerie carpet with Napoleon's insignia. In the SALON DORÉ are Josephine's embroidery frame, etc., a screen embroidered by her, her portrait by *Gérard*. The chimneypiece was given to Napoleon by Pope Pius VII; its valuable decorations were torn off by the Germans who occupied Malmaison in 1871. The MUSIC ROOM, a long pillared gallery, restored in 1950 to what was presumably its original appearance, contains a spinet, a piano, and a harp which possibly belonged to Josephine; her marble bust, by *Chinard*; and *Girodet's* remarkable painting of Ossian welcoming the Glorious Dead into Valhalla.

FIRST FLOOR. On the landing, Tapestry, after *Gérard*, of Josephine at Malmaison. In the corridor are fashion-plates of 1799–1814 and water-colours, by *Redouté*, of flowers cultivated at Malmaison. The FIRST CONSUL'S ROOM is a reconstruction of Napoleon's bedroom at the Tuileries, with the original furniture and hangings. Here also is a drawing by *Isabey*, of Napoleon, as Premier Consul, at Malmaison. The three following rooms contain costumes worn by Napoleon and Josephine; sumptuous services of Sèvres ware; the magnificent 'Table d'Austerlitz' decorated with portraits of Napoleon and his marshals in gold and Sèvres ware; the silver-gilt ewer and basin used at the coronation, etc.—JOSEPHINE'S APARTMENTS. ANTECHAMBER. Water-colours of Malmaison, by *Garnerey*, of great topographical importance; portraits of the Empress; her fans; and many other personal souvenirs. In the EMPRESS'S BEDROOM is the bed, designed by *Jacob*, in which she died in 1814; other contemporary furniture; and a fine Sèvres clock. The SALLE DES ATOURS, hung with silk, contains a work-table (from St-Cloud) and dresses, etc., worn by Josephine. The BOUDOIR is likewise hung with silk, and in the BATHROOM are her dressing-table and dressing-case, both lavishly decorated, by *Rémond*, and still containing the Empress's toilet-articles.—The SALLE DE STE-HÉLÈNE, hung with the brocade that covered the catafalque in which the Emperor's remains were transported to his tomb, contains the camp bed on which Napoleon died in 1821, his death-mask moulded by Antommarchi (his Corsican doctor); clothing; MSS.; and paintings.

The SECOND FLOOR, devoted mainly to souvenirs of Queen Hortense (mother of Napoleon III) and of Eugène Beauharnais, Josephine's children by her first marriage, is at present closed for repairs.

The PARK, of which but 15 acres are left out of 500, contains a rose garden planted with the varieties of rose that were grown by Josephine. The *Coach House*, to the right of the entrance, contains the 'Opal', the state carriage in which Josephine drove to Malmaison after her divorce, and a gala coach (temp. Louis XIV) used by Napoleon. Behind this is the *Pavillon Osiris*, with paintings of Napoleon's exploits. At the other end of the park is the *Summe House* (closed for repairs) used as a study by Napoleon when First Consul.

Travellers with time to spare may go on by motor-bus No. 258 to St-Germain past (8 m.) *Bougival* (Rest. du Coq-Hardi, not cheap), pleasantly situated on a bend of the Seine, and thence along the river viâ (8¾ m.) *Marly-la-Machine* and (9¼ m.) *Port-Marly* (Rest. du Lion d'Or). The original Machine de Marly was constructed for Louis XIV to raise water from the Seine to the Marly aqueduct which carried it to the gardens of Versailles. The present machine, which takes its water from underground sources, dates only from 1855–59. The little town of *Marly-le-Roi* stands at the head of a small valley, 1¼ m. above Port-Marly. Its royal château, built in 1680 by Louis XIV, and, with Louis XV, a favourite retreat from Versailles, was destroyed at the Revolution, but the park has a superb fountain (jet of 30 ft) and fine perspectives across the valley. The Forêt de Marly (5000 acres), behind the town, affords pleasant walks.

10 m. **St-Germain-en-Laye** (*Hot. du Pavillon Henri-IV*, first class, closed Dec–Feb; *Pavillon d'Estrées, Pavillon Franklin, Pavillon Louis-XIV, Villa Dauphine; de l'Aigle d'Or*), splendidly placed on a hill above the Seine, is famous for its ancient royal *Castle*, built in the 12C by Louis VI and completely rebuilt in 1539–48 by Francis I, except for the keep. The so-called *Château-Neuf*, below the original castle, constructed by Henri II and Henri IV, was pulled down in 1776, except for the *Pavillon Henri-IV* and the *Pavillon Sully*, at Le Pecq (Av. de Lattre de Tassigny, near the church) at the foot of the steep slope (open Wed, Sat, Sun 2–6). It was in this 'new' castle that Louis XIV was born in 1638, five years before the death of his father in the same building; and it remained one of the principal seats of the French Court until the completion of Versailles in 1682. Meanwhile the old château afforded refuge to the widowed Queen Henrietta Maria of England, and after 1688 it was the residence of the exiled James II, who died there in 1701. His tomb, erected by George IV in the church, opposite the castle, contains only his heart.— Claude Debussy (1862–1918) was born at St-Germain.

After many vicissitudes the château became a museum under Napoleon III, and it now houses the ***Musée d'Antiquités Nationales** (open daily, except Tues, 10–12, 1.30–5; adm. 0,50 fr.), a magnificent collection of prehistoric and Gallo-Roman antiquities. The Treaty of St-Germain, between the Western Allies and Austria, was signed in the château in Sept 1919.

To the N. of the castle is the *Parterre*, a park originally laid out by Le Nôtre. At its S.E. corner is the *Pavillon Henri-IV* (see above), a famous hotel since 1836, where Dumas wrote 'The Three Musketeers' and 'Monte Cristo', and where Thiers died in 1877. The *Terrace of St-Germain*, extending N. from the Pavillon for 1½ m., commands a magnificent view, compared by James II to that from the Terrace at Richmond. It leads N. to the Grille Royale, at the entrance to the *Forêt de St-Germain*, a former royal hunting-ground over 9000 acres in extent, with many fine drives and walks.

Near the N. end of the forest is **Maisons-Laffitte** (*Hôtel de la Vieille-Fontaine*), a residential town on the Seine, 4 m. from St-Germain viâ Carrières-sous-Bois, 5½ m. through the forest. Jean Cocteau (1889–1963), the writer and artist, was born here. It possesses a well-known racecourse and training stables, and a celebrated *Château*, the masterpiece of François Mansart (1642–51), now containing a collection of church) and 17–19C French furniture but notable especially for its interior decoration (open 10–12, 2–4 or 5; closed all day Tues and on Fri morning; adm. 0,50 fr., Sun 0,25 fr.). The château was bought in 1818 and the park cut up into building-lots by Jacques Laffitte, banker, who had profited by the Napoleonic wars.—From Maisons motor-bus 262 returns to Paris in c. 40 minutes.

36   SAINT–DENIS AND CHANTILLY

RAILWAY from the Gare du Nord to *St-Denis*, frequent service in 7 min.; to *Chantilly*, 25¼ m. (41 km.) in ½–¾ hour.

MOTOR-BUSES to *St-Denis*. Nos. 155 from the Porte de Clignancourt (Métro service 4); 156 from the Porte de la Chapelle (Métro service 12); 142, 153, 154, 168 from Carrefour Pleyel (St-Ouen; Métro service 13).

AUTOCARS of the Renault and Citroën companies to *Chantilly* twice daily in summer from the Porte Maillot (Boul. Gouvion-St-Cyr) in 1½ hrs, going on to *Senlis*.

ROAD ROUTE. The most direct route to (2½ m.) *St-Denis* (N. 1) is from the Porte de la Chapelle, traversing the uninteresting suburb of *La Plaine-St-Denis*, the scene of the celebrated 'Foire du Lendit' from Dagobert's time until 1552. The alternative routes from the Porte de Clignancourt or Porte de St-Ouen, through *St-Ouen*, or from the Porte Maillot or Porte Champerret viâ *Clichy* and *St-Ouen*, are only a little longer.

SAINT-DENIS (*Hôtel du Grand-Cerf*, opposite basilica; *Rest. La Marmite*), now an unattractive industrial suburb of Paris (80,700 inhab.) on the right bank of the Seine, was founded on the probable site of *Catolacus*, almost certainly the burial place of the missionary apostle of Paris (comp. Montmartre). Its basilica, containing the tombs of the royal house of France, was one of the most important churches in France.

The *Basilica of St-Denis*, in the centre of the town, though in itself a fine example of Gothic architecture, is overshadowed in interest by its series of royal tombs, a gallery of French funerary sculpture from the time of St Louis (c. 1250) to the close of the 16C.

History. The abbey of St-Denis was founded c. 475, perhaps at the instance of St Geneviève. It was rebuilt by Dagobert I in 630–38 partly in answer to his own vow to thank the Holy Martyrs for their protection, also because he wished to be buried near them. He also founded a monastery for Benedictines. The first substantial church on the present site was built by Abbot Fulrad in 750–75, under Pepin the Short, and in 754 Pope Stephen II consecrated Pepin and his wife and sons, thus establishing them securely on the throne. This church was replaced by Abbot Suger, minister of Louis VI and Louis VII, and the narthex (W. porch) apse (c. 1136–44), which survive from his building, rank among the most important examples of the earliest Gothic architecture. The crypt, of the same period, retains the Romanesque arch. The rest of the church was built under St Louis in 1231–81 from the design of *Pierre de Montreuil* (d. 1267), and the chapels on the N. side of the nave were added c. 1375.

It was not until the time of Louis IX (St Louis; d. 1270) that St-Denis became recognized as the mausoleum of the royal house. The effigies of earlier kings were mostly made at the order of St Louis, though a few were brought here from other churches after the Revolution. Of all the kings since Hugh Capet only Philip I, Louis XI, Louis-Philippe, and Charles X have tombs elsewhere in France. In 1422 the body of Henry V lay in state in the church on its way from Vincennes to Westminster. Seven years later Joan of Arc dedicated her armour here, but the English captured the town soon after and held it until 1436. When Condé's Huguenots took the place in 1567 he prevented them from despoiling the basilica; in the same year he was defeated in the plain to the S., though the Catholic leader, Anne de Montmorency, was mortally wounded. In 1593 Henri IV solemnly abjured protestantism at the W. doorway.

After some injudicious alterations in the 18C, the abbey was suppressed at the Revolution, when the church was unroofed, the tombs rifled and dispersed, and the royal ashes desecrated. The best of the monuments were saved from complete destruction by Alexandre Lenoir, who preserved them in his Musée des Petits-Augustins (École des Beaux-Arts). Restoration was taken in hand by Debret in 1813, but was so incompetently carried out that the stability of the N. tower was endangered, and it had to be taken down in 1847. A subsequent restoration by Viollet-le-Duc and Darcy went some way to repair the harm; but the explosion of a bomb-dump in 1915 caused further damage. Recent excavations (1938–39 and since 1946) have led to important discoveries concerning the early churches.

EXTERIOR. The W. front, though dating from Suger's time, was disfigured at the Revolution and poorly restored thereafter; but the surviving (S.) tower is of good 12C design, with a low modern steeple. The transeptal portals, each with a rose window above it, are of mid-13C work. The S. portal depicts the seasons and labours of the year, here represented by men whereas at Chartres women are shown. The central portal shows the scenes of the life and passion of Christ; Abbot Suger is shown at the feet of Christ in the scene of the Disciples at Emmaus. In a little garden in front of the basilica is a fragment of a '*Montjoie*', one of the small monuments erected (somewhat like Eleanor Crosses) at the places where Philippe le Hardi paused to rest when carrying the embalmed remains of his father St Louis (d. at Tunis, 1270) from Notre-Dame to their final burial-place.— Outside the N. door is a plan of the Holy Places at Jerusalem, engraved on stone in 1595. Inside, the narthex is particularly fine.

ADMISSION to the W. part of the nave is free: visitors to the royal tombs are conducted (rapidly) in parties every ¾ hr (except Sun morning and Tues), 10–12 and 2–4 or 5, on Sun 2–4 or 5 (1 fr.). The crypt is visited at the same times. For a more leisurely visit apply for a student's ticket to the Administration des Beaux Arts, 3 Rue de Valois, Paris 1, which admits also to the ritual choir.

INTERIOR (Only the more important tombs are listed here). The conducted visit begins in the N. AISLE, in which are the tombs (13–14C) of members of the royal family, including *Louis* (d. 1260), the eldest son of St Louis, with Henry III of England as one of the bearers.—N. TRANSEPT. *Tomb of *Louis XII* (d. 1515) and *Anne of Brittany* (d. 1514), made by Jean Juste (Giov. di Giusto) in 1516–32. The royal pair are depicted naked and recumbent on the tombstone, and kneeling on the canopy (the conventional design for the Renaissance tombs); bas-reliefs illustrate episodes in the king's career. Opposite, *Henry II* (d. 1559) and *Catherine de Médicis* (d. 1589), a splendid tomb designed by Primaticcio in 1560–73, with recumbent and kneeling effigies of the king and queen, and supporters and reliefs by Germain Pilon and other contemporary sculptors. The king and queen were kneeling at a bronze prie-dieu melted down at the Revolution. Here also are the tombs of *Philip V* (d. 1322), *Charles IV* (d. 1328), *Philip VI* (d. 1350), and *John II* (d. 1364, prisoner at the Savoy, London), the last two by André Beauneveu.

CHOIR and AMBULATORY. In the chapel to the left, at the top of the steps, draped statues of *Henri II* and *Catherine de Médicis*, by Germain Pilon (1583). The Lady Chapel and the chapels on either side of it preserve some stained glass of the 12–13C. In the Sanctuary is the *Altar of the Relics* (by Viollet-le-Duc), on which are placed the reliquaries (given by Louis XVIII) of St Denis and his fellow-martyrs.—The TREASURY, off the S. side of the ambulatory, is relatively unimportant, but a 17C silver-gilt altar-frontal is noteworthy. Outside hangs a conjectural reproduction of the *Oriflamme*, the red and gold banner adopted by Louis VI as the royal standard of France. The original, last used at the battle of Agincourt (it disappeared at the Revolution), was thereafter superseded by the fleur-de-lys as the royal emblem.

Near the top of the choir steps is the tomb of *Childebert I* (d. 558), a 12C statue brought from St-Germain-des-Prés; then *Frédégonde* (d. 597), queen of Chilperic I, a remarkable slab in cloisonné mosaic (11C), also from St-Germain. On either side of the sanctuary are interesting 13–14C tombs, from other churches in Paris, including (from Royaumont) *Blanche* and *Jean* (d. 1243), children of St Louis, fine enamelled plaques, and *Léon de Lusignan* (d. 1393).

The S. TRANSEPT contains (among others) the tombs of *Charles V* (d. 1380), by André Beauneveu, and *Charles VI* (d. 1422), with their queens; and of *Bertrand Du Guesclin* (d. 1380), the champion of France against the English (his heart is buried at Dinan, his entrails at Le Puy), one of the few people buried here who is not of royal blood. Beyond is the fine *Tomb of *Francis I* (d. 1547) and *Claude de France* (d. 1524), a masterpiece by Philibert Delorme, Pierre Bontemps, Primaticcio, and others, begun in 1548. Here again the royal pair appear both recumbent and kneeling (with their children), and reliefs depict the king's military exploits.—S. AISLE. Urn (1549–55), by Bontemps, with the heart of Francis I. Tomb of *Louis d'Orléans* (d. 1407) and *Valentine de Milan* (d. 1408), a fine Italian work of 1502–15, commissioned by their grandson, Louis XII. Opposite, against the S.W. pillar of the crossing, is the heart-tomb of *Francis II* (d. 1560), by Germain Pilon and Ponce Jacquiau.

In the RITUAL CHOIR the splendid High Stalls (1501–07) are from the chapel of the Château de Gaillon; the Low Stalls are 15C work from St-Lucien, near Beauvais. Most of the monuments here were erected by St Louis in honour of the early kings of France, and of these the tomb of *Dagobert I* (d. 638) is the most interesting, with reliefs showing the torment and redemption of the king's soul, and the beautiful 13C statue of *Queen Nanthilde. The figures of Dagobert and his son are 19C restorations. At the W. end of the choir are several later tombs, including those of *Louis X* (d. 1316) and *John*, his son (d. 1316), *Philip IV* (le Bel, d. 1314), and *Philip III* (le Hardi, d. 1285). The last, by Pierre de Chelles and Jean d'Arras, is remarkable as being one of the earliest known French portrait-statues, the earliest at St-Denis. The effigy of his queen, *Isabella of Aragon* (d. 1271), is particularly fine.

The CRYPT, entered on either side of the choir, was constructed by Suger round the original Carolingian 'martyrium', the site of the grave of St Denis and his companions. The capitals show interesting 12C work. The central chamber (Caveau Royal; seen through narrow openings) contains the sarcophagi of Louis XVI, Marie-Antoinette, Louis XVIII, and other 18–19C royal personages (these are to be put in a new chamber behind the ossuary); while the ossuary on the N. side contains the bones that were thrown into a pit when the royal tombs were rifled in 1793. In one of the side chapels is the charming 12C *Madonna, originally at the abbey of Longchamp. Work is in hand here to discover traces of the earlier churches.

To the S. of the basilica, the monastic buildings, rebuilt in the 18C by Robert de Cotte and Jacques Gabriel, have been occupied since 1809 by a *Maison d'Education de la Légion d'Honneur*, for daughters of members of the Legion. The splendid wrought-iron grille should be compared with that of the *Museum* (opposite), which occupies the site of the former Hôtel-Dieu (adm. 10–12, 2–6 exc. Tues), a good collection of local interest, including the reconstituted pharmacy of the Hôtel-Dieu, and a fine series of drawings, notably by modern painters, Cézanne, Léger, Dufy, etc., and the study of Paul Eluard, the poet, born at St-Denis.

From St-Denis N. 1 goes on through (8½ m. from Paris) *Pierrefitte*, beyond which we bear right on N. 16 for Chantilly through (10½ m.) *Sarcelles*, where the church displays building of the 12C, 15C, 16C and 17C.—12½ m. **Écouen** is notable for its *Château begun c. 1535 for the Constable Anne de Montmorency. This is now a school for children of members of the Legion of Honour, and may be visited on Thurs and Sun 3–5, by ticket obtained on application to the Grand Chancellerie de la Légion d'Honneur, 1 Rue de Solférino, Paris, 7e. Among the artists employed in its construction were Jean Goujon and Jean Bullant, to the former of whom are ascribed the façade of the right wing, and the chimneypiece of the great hall. The vaulting of the main staircase and of the chapel are specially noteworthy. In the parish church the choir of 1544 contains fine contemporary stained glass.—15 m. Le Mesnil-Aubry has a charming Renaissance church of 1531–82.— Beyond (17½ m.) the fine 18C château of *Champlâtreux* (l.; no adm.) we reach the ancient little town of (19½ m.) **Luzarches**, once famous for the relics of the saintly physicians, Cosmas and Damian. The interesting church dedicated to them bears, within its porch, sculptured medallions relating to their lives. The building, though preserving important 12C remains, dates principally from the mid-16C, and like Le Mesnil, is the work of Nicolas de St-Michel.—The Chantilly road traverses woodland, in a clearing in the midst of which is (18 m.) *Lamorlaye* (Hostellerie du Lys), with several training establishments associated with Chantilly.

25½ m. **CHANTILLY**, a quiet little town (7050 inhab.) noted for its château and superb art-collections, is also the Newmarket of France and important race-meetings have taken place here since 1836. The numerous training stables in and near the town have attracted a large English colony.

Hotels. Du Parc, 24 Av. du Maréchal-Joffre; des Terrasses, 8 Av. Joffre, meublé; d'Angleterre, Place Omer-Vallon (centre of the town); du Château, 22 Rue du Connétable.

Restaurants. *Tipperary,* 2 Av. du Maréchal-Joffre; *du Cygne Royal* (closed in winter), 11 Rue du Connétable; *Jockey-Club,* 17 Av. du Général-Leclerc; *du Connétable,* 67 Rue du Connétable.

Syndicat d'Initiative (15 March–15 Oct), Place de la Gare.—**Post Office,** Rue du Connétable.

Golf Course (18 and 9 holes) at *Vineuil,* ¾ m. N. of the château.

The main road from Paris passes near the station and reaches the château viâ the Av. du Maréchal-Joffre and Rue du Connétable, turning right at the Place Omer-Vallon, at the farther end of which is the *Hospice* founded by the mother of the Grand Condé. A shorter and pleasanter way is viâ the Route de l'Aigle through the forest and past (l.) the grand-stands and (l.) the chapel of *Sainte-Croix* (one of the seven chapels erected in the 16C by Madeleine of Savoy, wife of the Great Constable) to the Carrefour des Lions, where the road on the left leads to the château.

The ***Château de Chantilly,** standing in a lake stocked with carp, consists of two connected buildings, the *Petit Château* or *Capitainerie,* on the S.W., and the *Grand Château,* or château proper, on the N.

History. Chantilly came into the possession of the Montmorency family in 1484 and after the execution of Henri II de Montmorency passed to the Grand Condé (whose mother was a Montmorency) in 1632. The present Petit Château was erected about 1560 (probably by Jean Bullant) for the Constable Anne de Montmorency. The Grand Château, rebuilt by Mansart for the Grand Condé, on the site of the mansion built by Chambiges for Constable Anne in 1528–31, was described by Lord Herbert of Cherbury as "an incomparably fine residence, admired by the greatest princes of Europe". Molière's 'Les Précieuses Ridicules' was given for the first time at Chantilly in 1659. During a visit of Louis XIV in 1671, Vatel, the famous maître d'hôtel, is said to have committed suicide because the fish was late. The Grand Château was destroyed at the Revolution, but after some repairs had been carried out by the last of the Condés (d. 1830), it was entirely rebuilt in 1875–81 by his heir, the Duc d'Aumale (1822–97), son of Louis-Philippe, from the designs of Daumet. After the confiscation of the property of the Orleans family in 1853, the Château was bought by the English banking firm of Coutts, but the property was returned to its rightful owner by a decree of the National Assembly in 1872. In spite of his banishment from France, the Duc d'Aumale bequeathed the whole domain, together with his priceless art-collections, to the Institut de France. Chantilly marks the farthest advance of the German troops in France in Sept 1914; it was later the headquarters of Marshal Joffre.

ADMISSION. From the first Sun in March to 1 Nov the château is open daily 1.30–5.30 (in May–Sept 1.30–6 and on Sun 10–6) except on Tues and Fri and on race days (notably the first two Sun in June). Adm. 1½ fr.; on Sun and Thurs the park is open free 1.30–4.30 (to 6.30 in May–Sept). The tour is guided except on Sunday.

After passing the iron gates, or Grille d'Honneur, we leave on the right the *Château d'Enghien* (1770), built by Leroy for the unfortunate Duc d'Enghien (comp. Vincennes) and now the curators' residence. We cross the *Terrasse du Connétable,* with a statue of the Constable Anne de Montmorency (1492–1567), by P. Dubois, pass between two bronze groups of hounds by Cain, cross the moat, and enter the *Cour d'Honneur* through a colonnade with copies of Michelangelo's Slaves. In the corner on the left of the courtyard is the chapel, with a statue of St Louis by Marqueste.

The ****Musée Condé,** one of the most attractive collections within easy reach of Paris, is charmingly installed on the ground floor of the Grand Château and part of the first floor of the Petit Château. Though its special glory is its unique collection of French paintings and illuminations of the 15–16C, it offers also a comprehensive array of works of art, including a complete collection of Chantilly ware from the factory founded by the Duc de Bourbon in 1730, and a library of rare and valuable books.

GRAND VESTIBULE. On the left is the Grand Staircase. We, however, ascend the steps on the right and enter the GALERIE DES CERFS, on the ceiling of which are the arms of the successive owners of Chantilly. The walls are hung with 17C Gobelins tapestries of hunting scenes. Above the chimneypiece, Vision of St Hubert; above the doors, Venus and Cupid, and Diana, all by *Baudry*.

GALERIE DE PEINTURE. On the right: 278. *French School*, Gabrielle d'Estrées in her bath; 531. *Rosa Bonheur*, Shepherd in the Pyrenees; *515. *Meissonier*, Cuirassiers of 1805; 545. *A. de Neuville*, Fight on a railway line; 475. *Decamps*, Souvenir of Turkey in Asia; 528. *Fromentin*, Hawking; 428. *Baron Gros*, Bonaparte among the plague-stricken at Jaffa (sketch for the picture in the Louvre); 456. *Delacroix*, Doge Francesco Foscari condemning his son to banishment; *448. *Corot*, 'Concert champêtre'; 395. *Drouais*, Marie-Antoinette as Hebe; 145. *Sir J. Reynolds*, Philippe, Duc de Chartres, later Duc d'Orléans; 332. *Largillière*, Portrait of a lady; *De Cort*, 148, 149 (opposite), Views of Chantilly (1781); *383. *Lancret*, 'Déjeuner au jambon'. On the opposite wall: 366. *De Troy*, Oyster lunch; 9. *Italian School* (probably *Giovanni di Paolo*), Angels dancing in the sunlight: *Nic. Poussin*, 305. Massacre of the Innocents. 301. Numa Pompilius and Egeria, 304. Holy Family. On consoles flanking the entrance are two bronzes: Stag hunt by *Barye*, Boar hunt by *Mène*. The chairs are of Beauvais tapestry. In the centre is a marble bust of the Duc d'Aumale, by *Paul Dubois* (1896).

From the end of the Galerie we enter the ROTONDE (Pl. 1; in the Tour Senlis), which has a ceiling-painting by *Baudry*, and a mosaic pavement from Herculaneum. By the window is a statue of Joan of Arc by *Chapu* (1873). On the walls are water-colours and drawings: *Meissonier*, Picture connoisseurs; *458. *Delacroix*, St Louis at the Bridge of Taillebourg; *Portail*, Red chalk drawing of a warrior; *Ferdinand Bol*, Red chalk drawing of a young woman; 139. *J. van Ruisdael*, Landscape.—We return to the Galerie de Peinture and, turning to the left, pass through the VESTIBULE DU MUSÉE (Pl. 2).

The GALERIE DU LOGIS (Pl. 3) contains, on the right, French portrait drawings of the 16C by or attributed to the *Clouets*, including a fine portrait of Mary, Queen of Scots (1561), and portraits of Henri II, Catherine de Médicis, Francis II as a child, Thonin, jester to Henri II, and Triboulet, jester to Francis I. Also *Ph. de Champaigne*, Mère Angélique Arnaud; *Boucher*, Watteau; and works by *Lagneau*, *Dumonstier*, and *Caron*. Opposite are 16–17C *Portraits, the bequest of the Vicomtesse de Poncin, including: *Rubens*, *Jacqueline de Cordes; *Pourbus*, Henri II de Montmorency; *Memling*, Marie, daughter of Charles the Bold of Burgundy; and further examples by the *Clouets*.

PETITE GALERIE DU LOGIS (Pl. 5). *Greuze*, The family (a drawing of 1763); *Carle Vanloo*, Louis XIV. Centre case: Sèvres and Chinese vases; *Toilet Set of the Empress Maria Theresa; distaff of the Princess de Lamballe and workbox of the Duchesse d'Aumale.

The VESTIBULE DU LOGIS (Pl. 4) contains *Drawings by Old Masters, including studies ascribed to *Raphael* and *Perugino*; *Leonardo da Vinci*, La Gioconda (Monna Lisa), in black chalk heightened in white.

If not by Leonardo himself this drawing was at least produced in his immediate circle. The boldness it expresses rather repels, as compared with the mystery of the painting of La Gioconda in the Louvre.

SALLE DE LA SMALAH (Pl. 6). 553. *Bonnät*, Duc d'Aumale; 439. *Perrault* (after Horace Vernet), Louis-Philippe and his sons leaving Versailles; *Bellangé*,

464, 464a. Exploits of the Duc d'Aumale in Algeria (1840); 437. *Vernet*, Louis-Philippe when Duc d'Orléans; 424a. *Isabey*, Marie d'Orléans.

ROTONDE DE LA MINERVE (Pl. 7) in the *Constable's Tower*. In the centre: *55. Minerva, an exquisite Greek statuette of the best period, found at Besançon; vase from Nola; *Pourtalès Amphora, red-figured vase of the time of Pheidias; Tanagra figures; bronze ewers from Herculaneum; Silenus, a terracotta from Myrina. Here also are drawings by *Poussin, Ingres, Prud'hon*, and *Claude*; above, Cupids, by *Baudry*.

CABINET DES ANTIQUES (Pl. 8). On the left: 157. *Lawrence*, Francis I of Austria; 172. *Lear*, Philæ. Wall-case: Vases and bronze utensils, and coins minted within ten years of the eruption of Vesuvius A.D. 79, all found at Pompeii.

CABINET DU GIOTTO (Pl. 9). 299. *Poussin*, Leda and the swan; *111. *Enguerrand Charonton*, Virgin of pity; 14. *C. Rosselli* (or rather Iacopo del Sellaio), Madonna; 1. *School of Giotto*, Death of the Virgin.

SALLE ISABELLE (Pl. 10). 506. *Rousseau*, Landscape; 457. *Delacroix*, Corps de Garde Marocain; 140. *W. van de Velde the Younger*, Calm sea; 441. *Géricault* and *H. Vernet*, Race-horse leaving its stable; 546. *J. P. Laurens*, The Duc d'Enghien; 434. *Ingres*, Paolo and Francesca; *473. *Descamps*, Turkish landscape (and other typical studies); 533. *Gérôme*, Duel after the ball; 424. *Boilly*, Draught-players (1817); 514. *Meissonier*, Dragoon; 138. *J. van Ruisdael*, Coast at Scheveningen.

SALON D'ORLÉANS (Pl. 11). 552. *Bonnat*, Duc d'Aumale (1880); 521. *Jalabert*, Queen Marie-Amélie (1865); 44. *Pierino del Vaga*, Holy Family; 491. *Winterhalter*, Louis-Philippe in 1793, as 'Professor Chabot' in Switzerland. In this room in portfolios is kept the remarkable collection of drawings and water-colours not on exhibition owing to lack of space, including examples of *Primaticcio* (decorations for Fontainebleau); of *Watteau*, the *Clouets*, and *Carmontelle* (18C portraits in water-colour).

SALLE CAROLINE (Pl. 12). 330. *Largillière*, Mlle Duclos as Ariadne; *Greuze*, 393. Tender affection, 391. Girl, Study for the 'Village Marriage Contract' in the Louvre, 394. 'La Surprise' (a very late work); 386. *Duplessis*, Duchesse de Chartres watching her husband's departure for Ushant (1778); *372. *Watteau*, 'L'Amante Inquiète'; 319. *Mignard*, Comtesse de la Suze; 376. *Nattier*, Duchesse d'Orléans as Hebe; 419. *Carle Vernet*, Duc d'Orléans and Duc de Chartres (1788); 334. *Largillière*, Portrait; *371. *Watteau*, 'La Sérénade'; 315. *Mignard*, Henrietta of England, duchess of Orléans; 328. *Nattier*, Duchesse de Nantes, daughter of Mme de Montespan.

CABINET CLOUET (Pl. 13). *F. Clouet*, 267. Charles IX, 275. Diane de Poitiers; 130. *D. Teniers the Younger*, Le Grand Condé (1653); 335. *Rigaud*, Louis XIV (smaller original of the portrait in the Louvre); *Mme Vigée-Lebrun*, 404. Queen of Etruria, 403. Queen of Naples, 402. Marie-Thérèse; 241, *French School* (16C), Francis I as a young man; *F. Clouet*, *258. Elizabeth of Austria, 266. Duc de Nemours.—Returning through the Salle Caroline, we find ourselves again in the—

PETITE GALERIE DU LOGIS (Pl. 5). On the bottom shelf of the wall-case are three little Spanish ivory figures. We once more cross the Vestibule and the Galerie de Peinture, and enter the—

GALERIE DE PSYCHÉ. The forty-four stained-glass windows (forty-two of which are here), representing the Loves of Cupid and Psyche (as related by Apuleius in 'The Golden Ass'), were made about 1541 for the Constable de

Montmorency's château at Écouen and were probably designed by *Michael Coxcie*. At the end is a wax portrait bust of Henri IV (1610) by *Guillaume Dubois*. On the wall are important portrait drawings of which many are ascribed to the *Clouets* and others to *Jean Perréal*: 1. Diane de Poitiers; 5. Marshal Strozzi; 9. Hercule François d'Alençon; 13. Margaret of Valois, queen of Navarre, sister of Francis I; *15. Jeanne d'Albret, mother of Henri IV; 20. Henri II; 21. Henri, duc de Guise; 22. François, duc de Guise; 23. Jeanne, queen of Navarre; 24. Francis II; *25. Margaret of France (La Reine Margot), first wife of Henri IV; 26. Charles IX as a child; 27. Anne

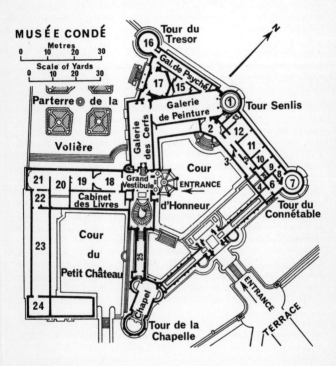

de Montmorency; 30. Admiral Coligny; 35. Henri II as a boy; 41. Marshal Brissac. Above these and near the door of the Santuario are large drawings: Children fighting, attributed to *Raphael*, Cupids dancing by *Van Dyck*, and the Last Judgement after *Michelangelo*.

The SANTUARIO (Pl. 15) contains the chief artistic treasures of the collection. **39. *Raphael*, the Madonna of the House of Orleans, an exquisite little panel painted about 1505. **38. *Raphael*, the Three Graces (or the Three Ages of Womanly Beauty), a rather earlier and smaller panel. Between these, 19. Esther and Ahasuerus, a long panel painted in tempera which, although catalogued here as being by Filippino Lippi, is probably by an unknown pupil of Botticelli ('*Amico di Sandro*').—**200–240. Forty Miniatures executed in 1453–60 for the Book of Hours ordered by Étienne Chevalier (1410–74),

Treasurer of France. They were acquired by the Duc d'Aumale in 1891 for 250,000 fr., and are plausibly ascribed to *Jean Fouquet* (1415–81), though they have not yet been proved to be the work of that early French master. Nos. 201 and 202 (right wall) represent Étienne Chevalier and his patron saint adoring the Madonna and Child.

Returning from the Galerie de Psyché, we turn to the left, to reach the CABINET DES GEMMES (Pl. 16) in the *Tour du Trésor* (fine views). In the table-case near the centre window are an enamel of Apollo guiding the Chariot of the Sun, attributed to *Cellini*, and the *Rose Diamond known as the 'Grand Condé' (recovered after a theft in 1926). The dagger of Abd-el-Kader, captured at the taking of the Smalah (stolen at the same time), is still missing. In the wall-cases: Large Cross from the Treasury of Basle (German, 15C); Blade of the sword used by the Duc d'Aumale in the charge at the Smalah; Snuff boxes, with plans and views of Chantilly (1775); *Collection of old fans, miniatures, and enamels (including Apollo's Chariot, attr. to *Cellini*).—We return to the Galerie de Psyché, turn sharp to the right, and pass through a small room in which is a bas-relief of the Departure of Phaethon, by *Jean Goujon*.

The TRIBUNE (Pl. 17) is a large octagonal room, in the middle of which is a *Vase by *Clodion*. On the panels above the cornice are represented eight houses and châteaux connected with the Duc d'Aumale, each of which gives name to the side ('façade') of the room below it: Collège Henri-IV, Aumale, Palais Royale, Palermo, Écouen, Guise, Villers-Cotterets, and Twickenham. We begin with the 'Façade du Collège Henri-IV': *146. *Sir Joshua Reynolds*, Countess Waldegrave and her daughter (1761); 450. *Delaroche*, Murder of the Duc de Guise; 445. *A. Scheffer*, Prince Talleyrand; *370. *Watteau*, 'Plaisir pastoral'; 125. *Van Dyck*, Gaston, duc d'Orléans; 369. *Watteau*, Love disarmed; *Luini*, 25. Child with grapes, *24. The Saviour; *107, *108. *Memling* (?), Small Diptych with the Madonna appearing to Jeanne de Bourbon, daughter of Charles VII, and Christ on the Cross; *15. *Perugino*, Madonna with SS. Jerome and Peter; *10. *Sassetta*, Mystic Marriage of St Francis (1444); **13. *Piero di Cosimo*, Simonetta Vespucci; *11. *Pesellino* (not Lippi), Madonna with SS. Peter and Anthony; 16. *Botticelli* (?), Autumn (once loosely attributed to Mantegna); 48. *Fr. Clouet*, Cardinal Odet de Coligny; *105. *Flemish School*, Anthony, the 'Grand Bastard' of Burgundy; *313. *Mignard*, Molière; *Ingres*, 433. Venus Anadyomene, 431. Madame Devauçay, painted in Rome in 1807; *247. *Corneille de Lyon*, Gabrielle de Rochechouart; *F. Clouet*, *257. Jacques de Savoie, duc de Nemours, **254. Jeanne d'Albret of Navarre; *245. *Corneille de Lyon*, Marguerite de France; *Clouet*, **255. Marguerite de France as a child, 253. Montaigne. In the small room beyond is the Fall of Phaethon, by *Goujon*, the pendant to the bas-relief in the other vestibule.

We now return through the Galerie des Cerfs to the Grande Vestibule and turn to the right to visit the *Apartments in the Petit-Château, decorated in honour of the Grand Condé, from 1686, by *J. H. Mansart* and furnished with Beauvais tapestry and contemporary clocks, ornaments, and woodwork.

ANTECHAMBER (Pl. 18). Paintings by *Oudry* and *Desportes*. Enamel of Henri IV, by *Claudius Popelin*. Chantilly, Sèvres, Chinese and Rouen porcelain.—SALLE DES GARDES (Pl. 19). *126, *127. *Van Dyck*, Comte Henri de Bergues and Princesse Marie de Brabançon; four *Enamel Portraits by *Léonard Limosin*; 132. *Justus van Egmont*, The Grand Condé (1658). The mosaic above the chimneypiece is from Herculaneum.—BEDROOM (Pl. 20).

Painted panels by *J. B. Huet*. On a *Commode by *Riesener* is the despatch case of the Grand Condé.—CABINET (Pl. 21). Equestrian statuette of the Grand Condé, by *Frémiet*; bureau of the Duc de Choiseul.—The SALON DES SINGES (Pl. 22) is named from the decorative panel paintings of "Singeries ou différentes actions de la vie humaine", by *Christophe Huet*.

GALERIE DES ACTIONS DE M. LE PRINCE (Pl. 23). The panels of this long room were painted in 1686–96 by *Sauveur Lecomte* with scenes from the battles fought by the Grand Condé. Over the fireplace is a *Trophy, formed of his sword and pistols; above is his portrait when twenty-two years of age, at Rocroi, by *J. Stella*; below, a medallion by *Coysevox* of 1686, the year of the Prince's death. The flag taken at Rocroi, 19 May 1643, is claimed to be the oldest captured colour in France. The bust of the Grand Condé in biscuit de Sèvres on the mantelpiece is by *Roland* (1785).—In the CABINET (Pl. 24) at the end are a fine wardrobe by *Boulle* and a table by *Leleu*.—We retrace our steps to the Antechamber, where we turn right to enter the—

*CABINET DES LIVRES, practically unchanged since the death of the Duc d'Aumale. It contains a fine library of some 13,000 volumes of the 13–18C, many of great value and rarity. The superb bindings are worthy of study. Perhaps the greatest treasure here is the **'Très Riches Heures du Duc de Berri' (bought in 1855 for 18,000 francs), which is noted for its magnificently illuminated pages of the Months, executed about 1415 by *Pol de Limbourg* and his brothers, direct from nature and not treated conventionally as had previously been the universal practice.

We return to the Grande Vestibule. On the right is the GRAND ESCALIER (no adm.), with its superb balustrade of steel and copper designed by *Daumet* and executed by the brothers *Moreau*, caryatids by *Chapu*, and Gobelins tapestry after *Boucher* and *De Troy*.—Passing the staircase we enter the GALERIE DE LA CHAPELLE (Pl. 25), with Drawings: Annunciation (1526) by *Dürer*; Flight into Egypt by *Domenichino*; Head of Christ by *Seb. del Piombo*; Madonna by *Raphael*.

The CHAPEL, founded early in the 14C, but many times rebuilt, and virtually destroyed during the Revolution, was restored for the Duc d'Aumale in 1882 by *Honoré Daumet*. The *Altar, by *Jean Bullant* and *Jean Goujon*, the *Woodwork (1548), and the *Stained Glass (1544; portraits of the Great Constable's children) were all brought from the Château d'Écouen. Behind the altar are the mausoleum of Henri II de Condé (d. 1662), with sculptures by *J. Sarazin*; and a cippus to which the hearts of the princes of Condé were transferred from the church (see below) in 1883.

The *Park (adm., see p. 208) was laid out for the most part by *Le Nôtre* for the Great Condé and is adorned with sculpture and ornamental water. The principal points of interest are the Maison de Sylvie, the 'Hameau', and the Jeu de Paume (open Thurs and Sun only). On the way to the MAISON DE SYLVIE we pass the chapel of ST-SÉBASTIEN (1552) and the CABOTIÈRE (Louis-XIII period). 'Sylvie' was the name given to Marie Félice Orsini, duchesse de Montmorency, by the poet Théophile de Viau, who, when he was condemned to death in 1623 for his licentious verses, was hidden by the duchess in this building. Rebuilt by the Great Condé in 1684, the Maison de Sylvie was in 1724 the scene of the romantic love-affair of Mlle de Clermont, sister of the Duc de Bourbon, and M. de Melun, who was killed in a hunting accident. It now contains Chinese curios, paintings, tapestry, woodcarvings, etc. The HAMLET, a group of cottages built in 1776 by the last Condé but one, was the scene of many 'fêtes champêtres' of the period. The JEU DE PAUME (1757) or tennis-court, near an exit from the park, is now a museum and contains Abd-el-Kader's tent, tapestry, two leaden dogs from Twickenham, state carriages, etc.

On quitting the park we turn to the right, and, beyond the Porte St-Denis, enter the Rue du Connétable, the principal street of Chantilly. On the left is *Notre-Dame*, the church (1686–92), built by the son of the Grand Condé. Behind this are the *Grandes-Écuries* (open Thurs and Sun afternoon), built by Jean Aubert in 1719–35, vast stables with room for 240 horses, beside which is a bronze equestrian statue of the Duc d'Aumale, by Gérôme (1899). Thence we may strike across the racecourse to the station.

The **Forest of Chantilly** (5190 acres), stretching to the S.E. of the town, is composed mainly of oaks, limes, birches, and some splendid clumps of Scots pines. It is intersected by numerous roads (signposts), many of which are covered with sand in the interests of the training-stables, while nearly all are forbidden to motors.

Travellers with time to spare should go by road (motor-bus) to (8¼ m. E.) **Senlis** (*Hôtel du Grand-Cerf; du Nord*), a peaceful old town with the beautiful 12C church of *Notre-Dame* (formerly the cathedral), many old houses, and two concentric lines of ramparts, the inner Gallo-Roman, the outer medieval. A *Museum of Hunting* (Musée de Vénerie), opened in 1937, occupies the former hospital-chapel of La Charité, in the Rue de Meaux (adm. 0,50 fr., daily in summer except Wed 10–12, 2–6; Oct–Easter, Sun and Thurs only). The *Musée Régional* (adm. 0,50 fr., daily except Tues 10–12, 2–5 or 6) in the Rue Ste-Geneviève, opposite, occupies a 16C mansion and is notable for its Roman collection, mainly of local origin.

37   FONTAINEBLEAU

RAILWAY from the Gare de Lyon, 37 m. (59 km.) in 1–1½ hr.

AUTOCARS, in summer, of the Renault company (starting from the Place Denfert-Rochereau; Métro services 4 and 6); of the 'Phocéens Cars' (starting from the Porte d'Italie; Métro service 7); and of the C.G.E.A. (Thurs and Sun morning from 127 Champs-Élysées), make the journey in c. 1½ hours.

The main road from Paris to Fontainebleau (N. 7; 35 m., 56 km.) leaves Paris by the Porte d'Italie and, running through the suburb of *Villejuif*, passes *Rurgis*. The Halles Centrales are to be transferred here. At 7 m. is the airport of *Orly* (Air Hôtel; Restaurants: Les Trois Soleils, Le Tournebroche, Le Snack Bar).—8¼ m. *Juvisy* stands near the confluence of the Orge with the Seine; the main road crosses the Orge on a graceful bridge of 1728.—16½ m. *Essonnes*, an industrial town with large paper-mills, is continuous with the old town of *Corbeil*, on the Seine (l.), which is also important industrially, with huge flour-mills, and printing and railway-engineering works. Near the church of St-Spire, with 12C nave and an earlier transept (the Romanesque part of the choir has been detached from the 15C addition in 1962), is the 14C gatehouse of a former abbey.—Beyond (28½ m.) *Chailly-en-Bière* (Auberge de l'Empereur), Millet painted 'The Angelus' here and is buried in the church. The route to Barbizon (1½ m.) bears off to the right, the main road enters the Forest of Fontainebleau, and soon passes the well-known Auberge du Grand-Veneur, a favourite tourist resort.—35 m. *Fontainebleau*.

An alternative route (N. 5; 34 m., 55 km.), leaving Paris by the Av. Daumesnil and the Porte de Picpus, traverses the Forêt de Vincennes and crosses the Marne from Charenton to Maisons-Alfort.—8 m. *Villeneuve-St-Georges*, on the Seine.—Beyond (10 m.) *Montgeron* the road runs for 5 m. through the Forêt de Sénart.—16 m. *Lieusaint*.—24½ m. *Melun* (*Hôtel du Grand-Monarque*; *de France*) is a market town of Gallo-Roman foundations, and capital of the Seine-et-Marne department. It suffered considerable damage in the fighting of 1944. As at Paris, the oldest part of the town stands on an island in the Seine. The bridges connecting this with the mainland were blown up in 1944 but have been rebuilt. On the island is the church of *Notre-Dame*, founded by King Robert, who died at Melun in 1031, while on the N. bank is *St-Aspais*, a 15–16C church damaged in 1944. Abelard founded a school of philosophy here when he was twenty-two (1101), which earned him great renown.—Soon after passing the railway station of Melun, N. 5 enters the forest, leaving on the left the small town of *Bois-le-Roi* (Hôtel de la Gare), a favourite resort on the edge of the forest and near the Seine.—34 m. *Fontainebleau*.

FONTAINEBLEAU, with its famous palace, second in interest to Versailles alone, is finely situated in the middle of its forest and is perhaps the pleasantest and healthiest summer resort in the neighbourhood of Paris. The military headquarters of the Allied Powers in Europe were formerly housed in parts of the palace.

Railway Station, N.E. of the town, c. 1½ m. from the Palace.

Hotels. De l'Aigle Noir, 27 Place Dénecourt; **Legris & du Parc,** 36 Rue du Parc;

Napoléon, 9 Rue Grande; **du Palais,** 25 Place Dénecourt; **de Londres,** Place du Général de Gaulle; **Anciens Courriers,** 48 Rue de France, all near the Palace; **de la Forêt,** 79 Av. Roosevelt, near the station.

Restaurants. *Le Filet de Sole,* 5 Rue du Coq-Gris, near the Palace; *Chez Arrighi,* 53 Rue de France; *Les Choupettes,* facing the Palace; *au Cerf-Noir,* 4 Rue de France; *La Potinière* (tea-room), 11 Rue Dénecourt; *Neuville,* and others, in the Rue Grande.

Syndicat d'Initiative, 38 Rue Grande.—**Post Office,** Place Dénecourt.

Motor-Bus from the station to the Palace.—**Autocars** starting daily from the Place Dénecourt (c. 9.30 a.m.) and the station (in connection with the Paris train arriving c. 10 a.m.) make circuits of the forest in the forenoon (N. circuit viâ Tour Dénecourt and Gorges d'Apremont; S. circuit viâ Montigny, Marlotte, and Gorges de Franchard); afternoon circuit (Gorges de Franchard and d'Apremont, and Barbizon) from the Place Dénecourt c. 2 p.m.

Golf Course (18 holes), 1¼ m. S.W. of the Palace, on the Orléans road.—**Swimming Pool,** Av. Roosevelt, near the station.

History. Fontainebleau is first mentioned as a royal hunting-seat in the reign of Louis VII, 1137, and in 1169 St Thomas Becket, then a refugee in France, consecrated the chapel of St-Saturnin. In 1259 St Louis founded, near by, a monastery for the Trinitarians, who had a hospital here. Philip IV, Louis X, Philip V, and Charles IV were born at Fontainebleau, and Philip IV and V died here. But the real creator of Fontainebleau was Francis I, who here assembled a group of Italian painters and sculptors, including Serlio, Rosso, Primaticcio, Vignola, and Nicolo dell'Abate. Francis found the palace more or less in ruins as Charles VII and his successors had deserted it for the Loire. Henri IV spent vast sums on the palace, where in 1601 his son, Louis XIII, was born. Queen Christina of Sweden retired hither in 1657, and here in 1685 Louis XIV signed the revocation of the Edict of Nantes. Louis XV received many distinguished foreign visitors here, including Peter the Great (1717) and Christian VII of Denmark (1768). Napoleon I spent twelve million francs on the restoration of the palace. Pius VII was received here in 1804 on his arrival in France to crown the emperor; in 1812 he became a prisoner in the palace and in the following year he signed an agreement renouncing temporal power. In 1814 Napoleon here signed the act of abdication, and took a touching farewell of his Old Guard in the Cour du Cheval-Blanc. Less than a year later, however, he had returned from Elba and here reviewed his old grenadiers before leading them to the Tuileries. The palace was again restored by Louis-Philippe, at enormous cost but with his usual questionable taste. In 1941–44, the palace was the headquarters of Gen. von Brauchitsch; the town was liberated by Gen. Patton's Americans in Aug 1944.

The roads from Corbeil (Rue de France) and from Melun (Rue Grande), the latter joined by the approach from the station, meet in the PLACE DÉNECOURT, just N. of the palace. Thence the Rue Dénecourt leads to the Place du Général de Gaulle, with the main public entrance to the palace. On the opposite side of this square is the doorway of the *Hôtel du Cardinal de Ferrare,* the only authentic work by Serlio (see above) surviving. Fragments of other old mansions remain in the Boul. Magenta and the Rue Royale.

The ***Palace** is composed of many distinct buildings, erected at various times and for the most part two-storied, and has been called "un rendez-vous de châteaux". Because the stone used was unsuitable for sculpture the exterior is plain while the interior decoration is sumptuous.

The state apartments are open daily 10–12, 1–5 in summer; 10–12, 1–4 in winter; adm. 1 fr., Sun 0,50 fr. The chief courtyards and gardens are open all day. On Sun and holidays in summer the palace is overcrowded and the smaller rooms closed.—The summer schools of the American Conservatoire of Music and the American School of Fine Arts occupy the S. wing of the Cour des Adieux in June–September.

The COUR DU CHEVAL-BLANC (500 ft by 370 ft), which we enter first, is named after a vanished cast of the horse of the equestrian statue of Marcus Aurelius in Rome. It is known also as the COUR DES ADIEUX, from Napoleon's farewell to his Guards (see above). In front of the central pavilion is the *Escalier en Fer-à-Cheval,* a horseshoe-shaped staircase erected by Jean du Cerceau in 1634. Beneath this is the visitors' entrance, whence we mount the Escalier François-I to the first floor.

The APARTMENTS OF NAPOLEON I, in a wing built by Louis XVI, are furnished partly in the Empire style. The ANTICHAMBRE DES HUISSIERS (Pl. 4) has 18C sopraporte. The clock, which has ten dials, was specially made for Napoleon. Here are kept Napoleon's hat, worn on the return from Elba, and a lock of his hair. In the CABINET DES SECRÉTAIRES (Pl. 6) are a piece of the willow tree from Napoleon's grave at St Helena and a fragment of his coffin. The CABINET DE L'ABDICATION or SALON ROUGE (Pl. 7) still contains the little table on which Napoleon signed his abdication in 1814 (though probably not in this room), and a facsimile of the actual document. In the STUDY (Pl. 8) is Napoleon's camp-bed; in the BEDROOM (Pl. 9), with Louis-XVI decorations, are the emperor's bed and the cradle of the King of Rome.

The next wing, as far as the Galerie de Diane, was built between 1545 and 1565. The magnificent *SALLE DU CONSEIL (so used by Charles IX but the decoration belongs to the reign of Louis XV) is decorated by *Boucher*, *C. Vanloo*, and *J. B. Pierre*, c. 1753; the bay, with a ceiling by *Lagrenée*, was added in 1774. A small adjacent room is the 'BRÛLE-TOUT', where state papers were burned after the council-meetings.—The SALLE DU TRÔNE was first used as a throne-room under Napoleon; it served previously as the king's bedroom. The magnificent ceiling dates from the time of Louis XIII. The fine portrait of Louis XIII is after an original by *Philippe de Champaigne*, which was burned in 1793. The lustre-candelabrum is of rock-crystal; the carpet is from the Savonnerie. The woodwork is Louis-XIV.

APPARTEMENTS DE LA REINE or DE MARIE-ANTOINETTE who chose new decoration). The beautiful little BOUDOIR (Pl. 13) has a ceiling-painting of Aurora by *Barthélemy*, stucco sopraporte (the Muses) by *Beauvais*, window-fastenings said to have been forged by Louis XVI, and a bust of the queen, by *Pajou*, in Sèvres biscuit-ware. The flooring of the room is in mahogany. The BEDROOM (Pl. 14), with its fine ceiling, was occupied successively by Marie de Médicis, Marie-Thérèse, Marie Leczinska, Marie-Antoinette, Joséphine, Marie-Louise, Marie Amélie, and the Empress Eugénie, and is sometimes known as the 'Chamber of the six Maries'. The silken hangings of the bed were given to Marie-Antoinette by the city of Lyons. The MUSIC-ROOM (Pl. 15) was Marie-Antoinette's card-room. The grisaille sopraporte and the table of Sèvres ware (1806) are noteworthy. The harp may have belonged to Joséphine. The next two rooms (Pl. 16, 17) contain Louis-XIV woodwork, and a Louis-XV lantern.

The GALERIE DE DIANE, over 260 ft long, was built by Henri IV and re-modelled under the Restoration, and has ceiling-paintings of that period. It has served as a library since 1859, and includes fine editions (15–16C and modern) of books which belonged to various celebrities.

From R. 17 we enter the APPARTEMENTS ROYAUX, looking on to the Cour Ovale. These were the royal suite of Francis I, but Louis XIV made them into *salles de réception*. In the ANTECHAMBER (Pl. 19) are three Gobelins (the Seasons) of the time of Louis XIV. The SALON DES TAPISSERIES contains Gobelins tapestries of the 17C (Story of Constantine). The SALON FRANÇOIS PREMIER (a dining-room under Napoleon) has an original chimneypiece with a charming medallion of Venus and Adonis, by *Primaticcio*, and several fine Gobelins tapestries depicting hunting-scenes. The *SALON LOUIS-TREIZE, known also as the Grand Cabinet du Roi or Chambre Ovale, one of the most interesting rooms in the palace, was decorated by *Paul Bril* under Henri IV, and restored in 1837. Marie de Médicis gave birth to Louis XIII here in 1601.

Ambroise Dubois painted thirteen pictures (the Loves of Theagenes and Chariclea) for this room, but three were removed under Louis XV when the doors were widened to admit the voluminous dresses of the period. The little Venetian mirror was one of the first to be seen in France. The SALON DE ST-LOUIS, in the original keep of the castle, was the king's bedchamber until the 17C; it was redecorated by Louis-Philippe with paintings of episodes in the life of Henri IV. On the chimneypiece is an equestrian statue of Henri IV by *Jacquet* (1599), from the 'great chimneypiece' (see below). The SALON DES AIDES-DE-CAMP, or Salle du Buffet, contains three pictures removed from the Salon Louis-XIII, other works by *Dubois*, and two fine ebony cabinets of the Louis-XIII period. The SALLE DES GARDES, completed in 1564 by Charles IX, was redecorated in 1834. The ceiling and frieze, however, date from Francis I and Henri II. The magnificent marquetry floor reproduces the design of the ceiling. The chimneypiece, with figures of Strength and Peace, by *Jacquet*, was made up, under Louis-Philippe, of portions of the great chimneypiece of Henri IV removed from the next room (not visited) when it was turned into a theatre under Louis XV.

The ESCALIER DU ROI was built by *Gabriel* in 1749, the upper part having been the *Bedchamber of the Duchesse d'Étampes in Francis I's time. The sculptures are ascribed to *Primaticcio*: the nude figures ('the nymphs of Fontainebleau') were veiled at the request of Marie Leczinska. The frescoes, in which Francis I is depicted as Alexander the Great in eight episodes from the life of the Macedonian hero, were painted by *Nicolo dell' Abate* from Primaticcio's designs and restored by Pujol. The stucco figures are of the period of Jean Goujon.—After a vestibule, with a statue of Mercury, by *Francavilla*, we traverse a narrow corridor.

The *SALLE DE BAL or GALERIE HENRI-II, 100 ft long, was built by Francis I and decorated under Henri II, *Philibert Delorme* being the designer. The windows command the best view of the Cour Ovale. The elaborate ceiling is of walnut-wood, and the design of the parquet floor (made under Louis-Philippe) corresponds with it. Everywhere are seen the interlaced monograms of Henri II and Diane de Poitiers and the emblems of Diana (bows and arrows, and crescents). The mythological paintings were designed by *Primaticcio*, executed by *Nicolo dell' Abate* (1552), and restored under Henri IV and again in 1834. This is the most splendid room in the palace.

Returning, we visit the APARTMENTS OF MME DE MAINTENON, with Boulle furniture, and a fine clock. It is said that the Revocation of the Edict of Nantes was signed in her salon (1685).—Traversing the Salle des Gardes, we enter the *GALERIE FRANÇOIS-PREMIER, 210 ft long, which was built in 1528–44 with beautiful Renaissance decorations. The initial and salamander device of Francis I are conspicuous. The paintings and stucco reliefs, by *Rosso*, were completed after his death by *Primaticcio*. The frescoes represent allegorical and mythological scenes, with more or less reference to the life of Francis I. This is one of the few examples left of Francis I's original palace, where Italian influence is seen at its strongest.

The VESTIBULE D'HONNEUR (Pl. 33) has six massive oaken doors, two of them original (temp. Louis XIII). Thence we enter the royal gallery of the CHAPELLE DE LA SAINTE-TRINITÉ, built by Philibert Delorme for Henri II and decorated by Henri IV. This was the scene of the marriage of Louis XV and Marie Leczinska and of the baptism of Napoleon III. In the centre of the ceiling are five large religious paintings by *Fréminet*, while the woodwork and

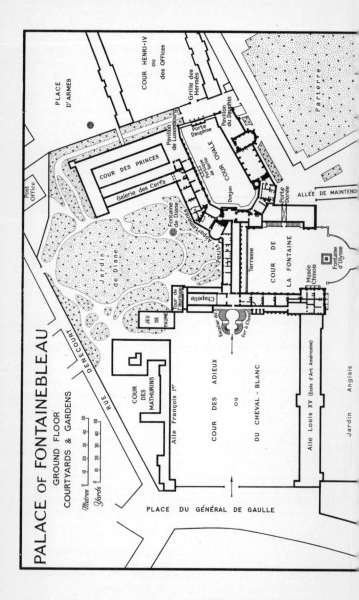

PALACE of FONTAINEBLEAU
GROUND FLOOR
COURTYARDS & GARDENS

Metres 0 10 20 30 40 50
Yards 0 10 20 30 40 50

PLACE D'ARMES

Post Office

COUR HENRI-IV ou des Offices

Grille des Hermès

Parterre

Pavillon du Dauphin
Porte Dauphine
Pavillon de Luxembourg
COUR DES PRINCES
Galerie des Cerfs
Chapelle de la Porte de Selle
COUR OVALE
Donjon
Porte Dorée

ALLÉE DE MAINTENO

Fontaine de Diane
Appartements
Petits
Jardin de Diane

Terrasse
COUR DE LA FONTAINE
Fontaine d'Ulysse
Musée Chinois

DENECOURT
RUE

Tour de l'Horloge
JEU DE PAUME
Chapelle
Escalier du Fer à Cheval

COUR DES MATHURINS
Aile François Ier

COUR DES ADIEUX ou DU CHEVAL-BLANC

Aile Louis XV (École d'Art Américaine)

Jardin Anglais

PLACE DU GÉNÉRAL DE GAULLE

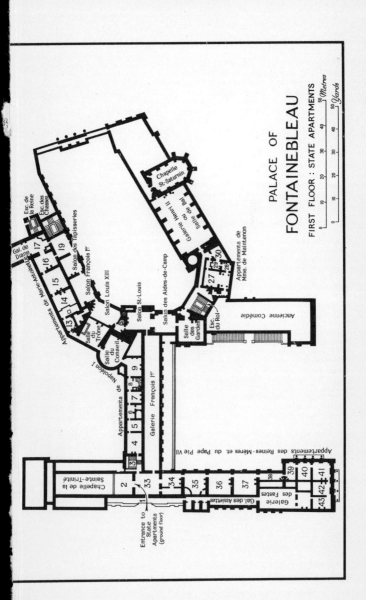

PALACE OF
FONTAINEBLEAU
FIRST FLOOR : STATE APARTMENTS

the elaborate reredos (by *Bordoni*) are of the time of Louis XIII. The great horseshoe staircase leads down to the exit.

The following rooms are open on weekdays: APARTMENTS OF THE QUEENS-MOTHER and of PIUS VII (Pl. 34–43), entered from the Galerie François-Ier. They were occupied by Catherine de Médicis, Anne of Austria, and Marie-Thérèse, and by the Pope both as a guest and as a prisoner. In the ANTECHAMBER are paintings. The SALON DES OFFICIERS and the GRAND SALON DE RÉCEPTION both contain interesting furniture. The first room has a splendid *Commode, by *Riesener*; the second room has a ceiling designed by *Philibert Delorme* and portraits (over the doors) of Charles IX and Catherine de Médicis. The QUEEN-MOTHER's BEDROOM has fine old Gobelins and a ceiling decorated with paintings by *Cotelle de Meaux*. Above the doors are portraits of Anne of Austria and Marie-Thérèse, by *Desève*. The *Furniture is upholstered in Beauvais tapestry, with subjects taken from La Fontaine's fables. The POPE'S STUDY contains a replica of David's portrait of Pius VII.

In the CABINET DE TOILETTE are tapestry portraits of Henri IV and Louis XIII. The POPE'S BEDROOM contains a Louis-XVI bedstead, and another fine *Commode (by *Beneman*). In the SALON D'ANGLE Pius VII used to say mass during his captivity. The SALLE D'ATTENTE has an 18C 'Chinese' lacquered commode. The ANTECHAMBER commands a view of the lake.—The GALERIE DES FASTES has superb carved foliage (Louis-XV period) and three fine tapestries of the Victories of Louis XIV (after *Le Brun*).— The GALERIE DES ASSIETTES is adorned with plates painted with views of French royal palaces. On the ceiling are frescoes by *Ambroise Dubois*.

On the ground floor, between the Cour de la Fontaine and Cour Ovale and the Jardin de Diane, are the PETITS APPARTEMENTS DE NAPOLÉON ET DE JOSÉPHINE (adm. 0,25 fr.; weekdays only), which preserve their Louis-XV and Louis-XVI decorations and contain Empire furniture and Napoleonic relics. Beyond is the GALERIE DES CERFS (so called because of the stag-heads which form part of the decoration) where Christina of Sweden had her favourite, Monaldeschi, murdered in 1657. It is adorned with paintings of royal residences and contains state carriages, etc.

The CHINESE MUSEUM (open on request at the same hours as the rest of the palace) is entered from the Cour de la Fontaine and occupies three rooms once included in the suite of the 'grand maréchal' of the palace. It includes many beautiful examples of Chinese art and industry. The APPARTEMENTS DES CHASSES (beyond the apartments of Marie-Antoinette, on the first floor) are entered from the Escalier de la Reine. At present under rearrangement, they contain paintings illustrating the hunting achievements of Louis XV.

By permission of the Conservateur, visits may be paid to the *Chapelle St-Saturnin*, in the S.E. wing, rebuilt for Francis I; to the *Theatre* and the *Musée Rosa-Bonheur*, on the ground floor of the Cour des Adieux; and with permission of the person on duty to the *Musée de l'Histoire du Château* (1 fr.) on the second floor. The remainder of the palace is private.

EXTERIOR. A pleasant walk may be taken round the outside of the château, starting in the N.E. corner of the *Cour des Adieux*, where a passage between the Francis-I wing (l.) and the Tennis Court (Jeu de Paume) leads to the *Jardin de Diane* (entered also from the Rue Dénecourt), with its bronze fountain-figure of Diana (1684). Turning right we pass the outer façade of the Tour de l'Horloge, with Egyptian caryatids. Opposite is the Galerie des Cerfs. Thence we bear right round the Cour des Princes, and, following the line of the old moat, pass between that courtyard and the *Cour Henri-IV* or *Cour des Offices* (l.; no adm.) dating from 1609, the main entrance of which faces the Place d'Armes. It is quite well seen through the *Grille des Hermès* (l.) adorned with heads of Hermes (Mercury) by Gilles Guérin (1640). On our right is the *Porte Dauphine* (by Primaticcio); it is one of the entrances to the *Cour Ovale*, which is not open to the public. Beyond the *Pavillon du Dauphin* (r.) we reach the *Parterre*, a formal garden with ornamental waters, laid out by Henri IV and again by Le Vau for Louis XIV. On the right is the apse of the Chapelle St-Saturnin, and farther on the *Porte d'Orée*, with decorations by Primaticcio (poorly restored), where Louis XIII was christened, admits to a passage leading to the *Cour de la Fontaine*. To the S. are the *Étang des Carpes* and the *Jardin Anglais*, laid out for Napoleon.

The **Park** (212 acres) extends to the E. of the Parterre. Along the N. wall is the *Treille du Roi*, a vinery yielding a crop of 3–4 tons of excellent white grapes ('chasselas de Fontainebleau'; harvest festival second Sun in Oct). On the S. side beyond a canal dug by order of Henri IV are the buildings of the former *School of Artillery* and the village of *Avon* where the 13–16C church contains the tomb of Monaldeschi. In the cemetery is the tomb of Katherine Mansfield (1888–1923), the author, who died at the Prieuré des Basses-Loges.

The *Forest of Fontainebleau, 42,000 acres in area and 56 m. round, lies in the angle between the Seine (E.) and the Loing (S.). With its groups of ancient trees and its sandy and rocky heaths, it is a great attraction in spring and autumn. Oak, beech, hornbeam, birch and Scots pine are the commonest trees.

The legend of the 'Grand Veneur' tells how Henri IV shortly before his assassination, hearing the sound of a rapidly approaching hunt, suddenly found himself faced by a Black Huntsman of huge and hideous appearance who uttered a warning cry and straightway vanished.

The forest is best explored on foot; but it is traversed by several good roads, and a fair idea of its attractions may be gained from the circular tours made by motor-coaches (see above) on Thursdays and Sundays (Easter–October).

The best general view of the forest and its surroundings is commanded by the *Tour Dénecourt* (3 m. N.E. of the palace), a tower erected in 1851 by C. F. Dénecourt (1788–1875), nicknamed 'Le Sylvain', who devoted his life and fortune to the study of the forest.—The most famous of the picturesque sites in the forest (alluded to in Stevenson's short story 'The Treasure of Franchard') are the *Gorges de Franchard* (3–5 m. W.; good restaurant), a rocky wilderness c. 3 m. in circumference, lying S. of the road to Arbonne and Milly; and the *Gorges d'Apremont* (3½–4½ m. N.W.), another remarkable rock-strewn area a little farther N., not far S. of the main road to Paris. Though skirted by roads, the actual gorges must be explored on foot. They can easily be combined in one excursion, which may be prolonged to **Barbizon** (*Hôtel des Pléiades*; *du Bas-Bréau*; *les Charmettes*; *Bellevue*), a village on the W. edge of the forest, 5½ m. N.W. of Fontainebleau. It was famous in the last century as the headquarters of the Barbizon School of painters, headed by Corot, J. F. Millet, Th. Rousseau, Diaz, and Daubigny. Though more sophisticated than in the early days, Barbizon is still a favourite resort of artists.

Milly, on the W. outskirts of the forest, viâ Arbonne, has an 11–12C church, a ruined castle (also 12C), a fine market hall of 1479, and the *Chapelle St-Blaise* (12C), restored and decorated by Jean Cocteau, with stained glass by Oidtmen de Linnich (1960; open daily Easter–October 10–12, 2–6; in winter Sun only). It is surrounded by a herb-garden.

KEY to Sectional PLANS

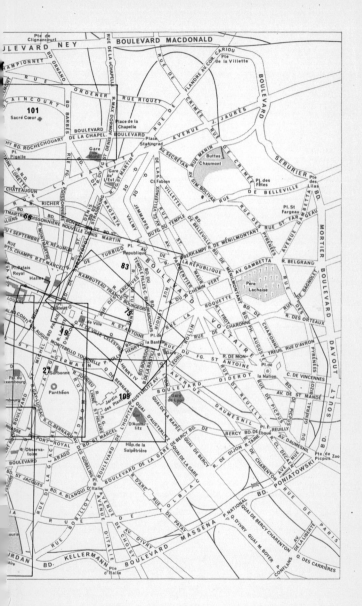

INDEX

Names of buildings, collections, etc., and topographical names are printed in bold type, names of eminent persons in italics, other entries in Roman type. Names beginning with *Saint* (*St*) or *Sainte* (*Ste*) are indexed under 'Saint'. *Avenues, Boulevards, Cafés, Châteaux, Hôpitaux, Hôtels* (mansions), *Musées, Places, Rues, Squares*, etc., are indexed in alphabetical sub-groups under these headings. An alphabetical list of *Theatres* will be found on p. xxxix of the text.

Abattoirs 105
Abbaye Ste-Geneviève 31
Abélard 26, 34, 106, 108, 214
Acacias, Les 121
Académie Française 37
Académie de Médecine 45
  „ de Musique 92, 67
  „ de Paris 34
Academies of the Institut 37
Adélaïde de Savoie 102
Aérogare 51, xxix
Affre, Abp 24, 80
Aguesseau, H. F. d' 61
Air services xxv, xxvi
Air Termini xxix
Albertus Magnus 33
Alembert, Jean d' 86
Alexander III, Pope 22, 43
Alexander I, Tsar 185
Allée de Longchamp 121
Alphand, Ad. 120
American Churches 54, 58, xlii
American Clubs xliii
American Cultural Centre 45
American Embassy 63
American Hospital xlvi
American Independence 5, 194
American Memorial Cloister 58
American Volunteers' Monuments 59, 184
Ampère, Jean 50, 99
Amusements xxxviii
Anne of Austria 78, 112, 220
Apollinaire, Guillaume 50
Apremont, Gorges d' 221
Aquarium 60
Arc de Triomphe du Carrousel 8
  „ „ de l'Étoile 64
Archives de la Seine 13
Archives Nationales 85
Arènes de Lutèce 29
Argenson, A. R. d' 80
Armagnac, Comte d' 21

Armenian Church 57
Arnaud, Angélique 114
Arnould, Sophie 71
Arrondissements xliv
Arsenal 80
Art Exhibitions xl
Arts-et-Métiers, Conservatoire des 157, 88
Arvers, Félix, 26
Assemblée Nationale 47
Assumption, Church of the 65
Athletics xli
Auber, D. F. 97
Auberge de l'Aigle d'Or 87
Aumale, Duc d' 208, 212
Auteuil 61, xli
Automobile Club 5, xliii
Avenue Alexandre-III 63
  „ de Breteuil 55
  „ des Champs-Élysées 62–64
  „ Daumesnil 108
  „ Foch 120
  „ Franklin D. Roosevelt 57
  „ de Friedland 119
  „ Gabriel 63
  „ Gambetta 107
  „ du Général de Gaulle 119
  „ du Général Leclerc 116
  „ George-V 58
  „ Georges-Mandel 60
  „ des Gobelins 110
  „ de la Grande Armée 119
  „ Henri-Martin 60
  „ Kléber 60
  „ Marceau 58
  „ de Marigny 63
  „ de Messine 118
  „ Montaigne 58
  „ de Neuilly 119
  „ de New-York 58
  „ de l'Observatoire 36, 114
  „ de l'Opéra 91
  „ Paul-Doumer 60

Avenue du Président-Wilson 58
  „ Raymond-Poincaré 60
  „ de la République 106
  „ du Roule 119
  „ de Suffren 56
  „ de Tourville 55
  „ Victor-Hugo 60
  „ Victoria 76
  „ de Villiers 104
Avon 220

Bagatelle 121
Bailly, Jean Sylvain 21, 56, 76, 200
Bal Bullier 114
Balzac, Honoré de 40, 46, 61, 74, 80, 88, 106, 114, 119, 184
Banks xliii
Banque de France 69
Barbès, Armand 77
Barbizon 221
Barclay, Robert 30
'Barrière de Clichy' 98
Bart, Jean 88
Barthélemy, Abbé 70
Bartholdi, Auguste 42
Barye, Antoine Louis 26, 79
Basilique de St-Denis 205
Basilique du Sacré-Cœur 99
'Basoche' 18
Bassin de la Villette 105
Bastille 95, 164
Batignolles, Les 104
Baudelaire, Ch. 26, 33, 15, 47, 79, 115
Bazaine, Marshal 198
Bazille, J. F. 44
Beardsley, Aubrey 49
Beauharnais, Eugène de 204, 52
Beaumarchais, Pierre Caron de 40, 87, 95, 106
Becket, Thomas 108, 215
Bedford, Duke of 81, 85
Belgian Monument 58
Belleville 105

Benjamin Franklin
Library 40
Béranger, Pierre Jean de
61, 95, 98, 106
Bercy 108
Bergson, Henri 61, 111
Berlioz, Hector 52, 70,
72, 98, 99, 102, 117
Bernard, Claude 33
Bernhardt, Sarah 35, 94,
104, 106
Berri, Duc de 71
Berthélemy, Abbé 70
Berthelot, Marcelin 32
Berthier, Marshal 185
Bertier, Louis 76
Bertrand, Gen. 52
Berwick, Duke of 112
Bibliography lii
Bibliothèque de l'Arsenal
80
„ Forney 78
„ Historique de
la Ville 84
„ Jacques-
Doucet 33
„ Mazarine 38
„ Nationale
160, 71
„ Ste-Geneviève
32
„ Thiers 98
Bicycles xxvi
Bièvre, The 111
Billiards xli
Bismarck, Prince von 185
Bizet, Georges 98, 106
Blanc, Louis 77
Blanche, Jacques-Émile
61
Blanqui, Auguste 77
Blind Asylum 54
Boileau, Nicolas 20, 24,
36, 44, 61
Bois de Boulogne 120
Bois de Vincennes 202
Bois-le-Roi 214
Bolivar, Simon 70
Bonaparte, Joseph 54
„ Pauline 117,
199
Bonheur, Rosa 220
Books about Paris lii
Bossuet, J. B. 22, 30, 59,
70, 77
Botanical Gardens 109
'Bottin' xli
Boucicaut, Mme 51
Bougainville, L. A. de
102
Bougival 204
Boulevard Beaumarchais
95
„ de Bonne-
Nouvelle 94
„ des Capucines
91

Boulevard de la Chapelle
96
„ de Clichy 98
„ Diderot 108
„ Edgar-Quinet
115
„ des Filles-du-
Calvaire 95
„ Garibaldi 55
„ de Grenelle 57
„ Haussmann
103, 93, 118
„ Henri-IV 79
„ de l'Hôpital
110
„ d'Inkermann
119
„ des Invalides
54
„ des Italiens 92
„ Jules-Ferry
106
„ de la Madeleine
91
„ de Magenta 96
„ Malesherbes
104
„ de Ménil-
montant 106
„ Montmartre 93
„ du Montpar-
nasse 114
„ du Palais 22
„ Pasteur 55
„ Poissonnière
94
„ de Port-Royal
114
„ Raspail 49, 51
„ Richard-Lenoir
106
„ Rochechouart
99
„ St-Denis 94
„ St-Germain 29,
35, 48
„ St-Jacques 115
„ St-Marcel 110
„ St-Martin 94
„ St-Michel 28,
35
„ de Sébastopol
74, 80
„ de Strasbourg
96
„ Suchet 60
„ du Temple 95
„ Voltaire 107
Boulogne 121
Bourdaloue, Ant. 79
Bourdelle, Antoine 115
Bourget, Le xxix
Bourse, La 70
Bourse de Commerce 72
Boxing xli
Boylesve, René 61
Braille, Louis 32

Branly, Ed. 42
Braque, Georges 114, 116
Briand, Aristide 48, 60
Brillat-Savarin, A. 70
Brinvilliers, Marquise de
76, 79
British Council xliii
British Embassy 117, 63
British Hospital xlvi
Brosse, Guy de la 109
Budé, Guillaume 33, 89
Buffon, Comte de 30, 109
Bureau International de
l'Heure 114
Burney, Fanny 61, 117
Butte Montmartre 99
Buttes Chaumont 105

Cabaret du Chat-Noir 99
„ de l'Épée-de-Bois
89
„ de la Pomme-de-
Pin 30
Cabaret Shows xl
Cabinet des Médailles
161
Cadoudal, Georges 21, 49
Caesar 10
Café des Deux-Anges 49
„ des Deux-Magots 50
„ du Dôme 114
„ de Flore 50
„ Procope 40
„ de la Rotonde 114
„ Voltaire 40
Cafés xxxiii
Caisse d'Épargne 72
Calendar of Events li
Calvin, Jean 33
Cambacérès, J. J. de 49
Canals 105
Carco, Francis 26
Car Ferries xxvi
Carnot, Lazare 65
Carnot, Sadi 41, 65
Carpeaux, J. B. 119
Carrefour de la Croix-
Rouge 51
„ de l'Observa-
toire 114
„ de l'Odéon 40
Cartier, Jacques 57
Cartouche, Louis 76
Caserne de la Cité 22
„ des Célestins 79
„ Vérines 95
Catacombs 116
Cathedral of St-Louis 200
Catherine de Médicis 7,
8, 59, 72–83, 206, 220
Cattle Market 105
Cellini, Benvenuto 37
Cemeteries (see also
Cimetières) xlix
Centre Sportif
Universitaire 114
Chailly-en-Bière 214

Chambers of Commerce xliii
Chambre des Notaires 76
Champaigne, Ph. de 26, 77
Champ de Mai 56
Champ-de-Mars 56
Champlâtreux 207
Champs-Élysées 62
Chansonniers xxxiv
Chantilly 207, xli
Chapelle Expiatoire 103
„ **des Otages** 105
„ **St-Aignan** 24
„ **St-Ferdinand** 119
„ **St-Pierre** 50
Charcot, Dr. 110
Charlemagne 12, 85
Charles IV 8, 201, 206, 215
„ *V* 81, 200, 201, 206
„ *VI* 206
„ *IX* 8, 201, 202
„ *X* 8, 121, 185, 193, 198
„ *I of Britain* 22
„ *the Bold* 37
Charonne 106
Château de Chantilly 207
„ **d'Enghien** 208
„ **de Madrid** 121
„ **de Maisons** 204
„ **de la Muette** 60
„ **de St-Germain** 204
„ **de Vincennes** 200
Chateaubriand, Vicomte de 48, 49, 51, 65, 115
Châtelet, Mme du 26, 71
Chénier, André 6, 21, 30, 94, 96, 108
Childebert 22, 28, 43
Chopin 26, 65, 94, 97, 103, 106, 118
Chouans 49
Christian VII 215
Christina, Queen 78, 85, 215, 220
Churches xlii
Cimetière de Belleville 105
„ **des Innocents** 73
„ **de Montmartre** 99
„ **du Montparnasse** 115
„ **de Passy** 60
„ **du Père-Lachaise** 106
„ **de Picpus** 107
„ **Ste-Catherine** 110

Cimetière St-Joseph 72
„ **St-Vincent** 102
Cinemas xl
Circuses xl
Cirque d'Hiver xl
„ **Medrano** 99
Cité, The 17
Cité Universitaire 116
Clemenceau, Georges 60, 63
Clisson, Olivier de 85
Clubs xliii
Cluny Museum 170, 35
Cocteau, Jean 69, 204, 221
Colbert, J. B. 8, 70, 72, 73, 160
Colette 69, 106
Coligny, Adm. de 85, 71, 105
Collège des Bernadins 29
„ **des Bons-Enfants** 30
„ **de Bourgogne** 35
„ **de Clermont** 33
„ **des Écossais** 30
„ **Fortet** 33
„ **de France** 33
„ **d'Harcourt** 35
„ **des Irlandais** 30
„ **des Lombards** 29
„ **Mazarin** 37
„ **de Montaigu** 33
„ **de Navarre** 30
„ **des Prémontrés** 35
„ **des Quatre-Nations** 37
„ **Ste-Barbe** 33
Comédie Française 40, 66, xxxiv
Commune and Communards 8, 10, 20, 65, 67, 76, 77, 80, 94, 98, 99, 105, 106
Comte, Auguste 36, 84
Concerts xl
Conciergerie 21
Condé, Louis II de (le Grand) 22, 106, 201, 208
Conducted Tours xlix
Conseil Économique et Social 59
Conseil d'État 67
Conseil de la République 40
Conservatoire d'Art Dramatique 94
„ **des Arts-et-Métiers** 157, 88
„ **de Musique** 104
Constant, Benj. 103
Consulates xlii
Coquelin aîné, Constant 94

Corbeil 214
Corday, Charlotte 5, 20, 44, 69, 70, 103
Corneille, Pierre 10, 66, 85, 94
Corot, J. B. 46, 47, 97, 106, 184, 221
Coulanges, Abbé de 162
Coulomb, Charles de 160
Couperin, François 78
Cour du Commerce-St-André 35
„ **de Rohan** 35
Courbet, Gustave 35, 65
Courbevoie 119
Cours Albert-Ier 57
„ **des Maréchaux** 57
„ **-la-Reine** 57
„ **de Vincennes** 108
Courses for Foreign Students xliii
Coysevox, Antoine 11
Crébillon, Prosper 77
Crédit Municipal 85
Curie, Marie and *Pierre* 30
Currency xxviii
Custom House xxviii
Cycling xli

Dagobert, King 205, 207
Daguerre, Louis 95
'Dame aux Camélias' 91
Damiens, R. F. 21, 76, 190
Dangeau, Marq. 81
Dante 29
Danton, G. J. 5, 21, 29, 35, 41
Darboy, Abp 106
Daubigny, C. F. 106, 221
Daudet, Alphonse 40, 48, 49, 61, 63, 81, 84, 106
Daumesnil, Gen. 201
Daumier, Honoré 26, 106
David, Louis 41, 76, 106
David d'Angers, P. J. 51
Deaf and Dumb Asylum 112
Debussy, Claude 60, 120, 204
Deffand, Marquise du 49, 86
Delacroix, Eug. 33, 44, 46, 47, 98, 106
Delaroche, Paul 46
Delorme, Marion 81, 86
Dénecourt, C. F. 221
Department Stores xlvii
Déroulède, Paul 103
Descartes, René 30, 44
Desmoulins, Camille 21, 33, 35, 40, 41, 43, 67
Diamond Necklace Affair 80, 86, 198
Diane de France 84

Diaz, Narcisse 221
Dickens, Chas. 98, 117
Diderot, Denis 71, 201
Diesel, Rudolf 88
Directories xlii
Dôme des Invalides 53
Donizetti, Gaetano 71, 93
Dolet, Étienne 29
Doré, Gustave 49, 57
Doumer, Pres. 118
Dreyfus, Capt. 56, 91
Drouet, Juliette 5, 30
Du Barry, Mme 21, 30, 96, 190, 199, 200
Dufy, Raoul 102
Du Guesclin, Bertrand 87, 206
Dumas fils, Alex. 99, 104
Dumas père, Alex. 95, 103, 104, 204
Dumas, J. B. 49
Duplessis, Lucille 40, 43
Duplessis, Marie 91
Du Sommerard, Alex. 171

Échevins 4, 76
École d'Administration 29
„ des Beaux-Arts 46
„ Coloniale 36
„ de Droit 32
„ des Gardiens de la Paix 117
„ des Langues-Orientales 47
„ de Médecine 35
„ des Métiers-d'Art 86
„ Militaire 56
„ Normale Supérieure 111
„ de Pharmacie 36
„ de Physique et de Chimie Indust. 30
„ Polytechnique 30
„ des Ponts-et-Chaussées 50
„ Pratique de Médecine 50
„ Ste-Geneviève 30
„ Supérieure des Arts Décoratifs 30
„ Supérieure de Guerre 56
„ Supérieure des Mines 36
Écouen 207
Edward VII 91
Égouts 5
Eiffel Tower 56
Élisabeth, Mme 5, 21, 88
Elizabeth II 26, 58, 77, 117, 198
Embassies xlii
Enghien, Duc d' 201, 208
English Churches xlii

Entrepôts de Bercy 13
Entrepôt des Vins 108
Épée, Abbé de l' 66, 112, 185
Erasmus 33
Esplanade des Invalides 51
Essones 214
Estrées, Gabrielle d' 71
Eugénie, Empress 22, 216
Expenses xlvi

Fabre d'Eglantine, Ph. 41
Fantin-Latour, Ignace 42, 46
Faubourg St-Antoine 107
„ St-Germain 37
„ St Honoré 117
„ St-Marceau 29
„ St-Marcel 110
„ St-Martin 96
Fauré, Gabriel 60, 61
Favart, Charles 93
Favre, Jules 103, 185
Fencing xli
Fénelon, François de la Mothe 25
Ferries, Car xxvi
Ferry, Jules 57
Fersen, Axel de 164
Fête de la Fédération 56
Feuillants, Club des 6
Feydeau, Georges 103
Fieschi, J. M. 95, 107
'Figaro' Office 64
Flaubert, Gustave 67, 95
Foch, Marshal 22, 50, 54, 56, 65
Foire à la Ferraille 106
„ aux Jambons 106
„ du Lendit 205
Folies-Bergère xxxiv
Fontaine du Châtelet 76
„ Cuvier 110
„ Gaillon 91
„ des Innocents 73
„ Louvois 71
„ Médicis 42
„ Molière 71
„ de l'Observatoire 36
„ des Quatre-Evêques 42
„ des Quatre-Saisons 50
„ de la Reine 74
„ St-Michel 26
„ Trogneux 107
„ du Vertbois 89
Fontainebleau 214
Football xli
Force, La 84
Fôret de Chantilly 214
„ de Fontainebleau 221
„ de Marly 204

Forêt de St-Germain 204
„ de Sénart 214
Foucault, Léon 32
Foullon, Joseph 76
Fouquet, Nicolas 80, 201
Fouquier-Tinville, A. 20, 76
France, Anatole 47, 80, 119, 120
France, Théâtre de 40
Franchard, Gorges de 221
Franchet d'Espérey, Gen. 52
Francis I 8, 33, 121, 122, 204, 206, 215
„ II 22, 207
Franck, César 36, 49, 115
Franklin, Benjamin 48, 56, 61, 112
Frederick William III 185
Fulton, Robert 16, 93

Galerie Dorée 70
Galerie des Glaces 190
Galigaï, Eléonore 76
Gambetta, Léon 40, 32, 117, 184
Games xli
Garches 184
Garden, see Jardin
Gare d'Austerlitz 108, xxix
„ de la Bastille 96, xxix
„ d'Eau de l'Arsenal 13, 96
„ de l'Est 96, xxix
„ des Invalides 51, xxix
„ du Luxembourg xxix
„ de Lyon 108, xxix
„ Montparnasse 115, xxix
„ du Nord 96, xxix
„ d'Orsay 47, xxix
„ St-Lazare 103, xxix
„ de Vincennes 200, xxix
Garibaldi 57
Garnier, Charles 92
Gaskell, Mrs 49
Gassendi, Pierre 89
Gaulle, Gen. de 23
Gautier, Théophile 26, 81, 99, 119, 184
Gavarni 98
Geological Galleries 109
George VI 48, 77, 203
George, Mlle 42
Géricault, Th. 98, 106
Gering, Ulrich 33
Giacometti, Alberto 116
Gibbon, Edward 42, 97
Gibet de Montfaucon 105

Gide, André 33, 36, 51, 61
'Gioconda, La' 136, 209
Giraud, Gen. 52
Giraudoux, Jean 54, 99, 111
Girondins 5, 20, 21
Gluck, C. W. 191
Gobelins 110
Goldoni, Carlo 24
Golf xli
Goncourt, Brothers 61, 67, 99
Gounod, Charles 28, 95, 118
Grand Châtelet 76
Grand Palais 64
Grand Trianon 198
Grands Boulevards 90
Greek Catholics 28
Greek Church 58
Grétry, A. E. M. 191
Grignan, Mme de 162
Gros, Baron 200
Grouchy, Marshal 52
Guénégaud, Th. de 40
Guides xlix
Guillaumat, Gen. 52
Guillaumin, Armand 99
Guillotin, Dr. 35
Guillotine 8, 106
Guise, Claude de 171
Guise, Duchesse de 41

Halévy, Ludovic 17
Halle aux Vins 108
Halles Centrales 73
Hanse des Marchands 76
Haussmann, Baron 17, 22, 28, 95
Haüy, Valentin 54
Hébert, Jacques-René 5, 40, 41
Heine, Heinrich 35, 64, 99
Henner, J, J, 104
Henri II 81, 110, 122, 206
„   *III* 184
„   *IV* 17, 22, 73, 80, 99, 104, 205, 215, 221
Henrietta Maria 10, 22, 59, 112, 204
Henry III 30
„   *IV* 30, 85
„   *V* 37, 201, 202, 205
„   *VI* 20, 22
Hérédia, J. M. de 80
Hertford, Lord 93, 121
Hertford Hospital xlvi
Herzl, Theodore 65, 118
Hippodrome de Long-champ 121
Hirsch, Baroness 51

Hoche, Gen. 42, 185
Holidays xlvii
Holy Trinity Church 58
Honegger, Arthur 102
Hôpital Beaujon 118
„   **Broca** 114
„   **de la Charité** 50
„   **Curie** 30
„   **des Enfants-Malades** 55
„   **Laënnec** 51
„   **Lariboisière** 96
„   **de la Maternité** 114
„   **Necker** 55
„   **Pasteur** 115
„   **de la Pitié** 110
„   **St-Antoine** 107
„   **St-Louis** 104
„   **St-Vincent-de-Paul** 115
„   **de la Salpêtrière** 110
Horse-Racing xli
Hortense, Queen 49, 93, 203, 204, 221
Hospice des Enfants-Trouvés 107
„   **La Rochefoucauld** 116
„   **des Quinze-Vingts** 108
Hotels (for travellers) xxix
Hôtels (mansions and public buildings):
Hôtel des Abbés-de-Fécamp 35
„   **d'Albret** 84
„   **d'Alméras** 84
„   **des Ambassadeurs de Hollande** 87
„   **d'Aubray** 79
„   **d'Aumont** 78
„   **d'Avaray** 50
„   **Barbette** 87, 84
„   **de Bauffremont** 50
„   **Beauharnais** 49
„   **Beauvais** 78
„   **Biron** 50, 182
„   **de Boulogne** 49
„   **de Bourgogne** 73
„   **de Bourrienne** 97
„   **de Bragelonne** 86
„   **de Brancas** 40
„   **de Brégis** 86
„   **de Bretonvillers** 25
„   **de Brévannes** 86
„   **de Brienne** 49
„   **de Brissac** 50
„   **Carnavalet** 162, 84
„   **de Chalons-Luxembourg** 78
„   **de Chanac** 50
„   **de Charny** 79
„   **de Charost** 117
„   **du Châtelet** 50
„   **de Chaulnes** 81

Hôtel Chenizot 24
„   **de Chimay** 46
„   **de Choiseul-Praslin** 51
„   **de Clermont** 51
„   **de Clermont-Tonnerre** 49
„   **de Clisson** 85
„   **de Cluny** 170
„   **de Condé** 40
„   **de Coulanges** 81
„   **de Courteilles** 50
„   **de Crillon** 5
„   **Dangeau** 81
„   **-Dieu** 22, 28
„   **Drouot** 93
„   **d'Estrades** 81
„   **d'Estrées** 50
„   **d'Evreux** 117
„   **Fieubet** 79
„   **de Fleury** 50
„   **du Grand-Veneur** 86
„   **de Guénégaud** 87
„   **Guillaume Barbès** 84
„   **de Guise** 85
„   **d'Hallwyll** 88
„   **d'Hercule** 35
„   **Hérouët** 87
„   **d'Hervart** 72
„   **des Invalides** 52
„   **de Juigné** 86
„   **Lambert** 26
„   **Lamoignon** 84
„   **de La Rochefoucauld** 49
„   **de Lassay** 48
„   **de La Trémoïlle** 42
„   **de Lauzun** 26
„   **de La Vallière** 49
„   **Le Brun** 30
„   **Le Charron** 26
„   **Le Peletier de St-Fargeau** 84
„   **de Mme du Barry** 200
„   **de Maillé** 79
„   **de Mansart-Sagonne** 81, 95
„   **du Maréchal Suchet** 117
„   **du Marquis de Persan** 45
„   **de Massa** 114
„   **de Matignon** 51
„   **de Mayenne** 80
„   **Mazarin** 160
„   **Melusine** 69
„   **de Mesmes** 50
„   **des Monnaies** 38
„   **de Montgelas** 87
„   **de Montmor** 88
„   **de Montmorency** 88
„   **de Montrésor** 86
„   **de Nesle** 37

Hôtel de Nesmond 29
„ de Nevers 70
„ de Nicolaï 79
„ d'Ollone 72
„ d'Ormesson 80
„ Pimodan 26
„ Pontalba 117
„ de Ponthieu 71
„ Portalis 70
„ des Postes 72
„ de la Présidence 51
„ du Président-
    Hénault 78
„ de la Reine 72
„ de Rohan 86
„ de Roquelaure 49
„ de Sagan 49
„ de St-Aignan 88
„ de Sandreville 84
„ du Sénat 40
„ de Sens 78
„ de Sillery-Genlis 38
„ de Soubise 85
„ de Sourdéac 42
„ de Strasbourg 86
„ de Sully 80
„ Thiers 98
„ de Toulouse 69
„ de Transylvanie 46
„ Tubeuf 160
„ de Valentinois 61
„ de Vendôme 36
„ de Vibray 87
„ de Villacerf 84
„ de Ville 76
„ de la Vrillière
    (Banque de
    France) 69
„ de la Vrillière (Rue
    St-Florentin) 5
Houdon, Jean A. 115,
    185, 200
House Numbering xlvi
Huet, Bp 79
Hugo, Victor 5, 32, 33,
    45, 51, 60, 65, 79, 81,
    97, 114, 115, 184
Huguenots 76
Huysmans, J-K 51, 61

Île de la Cité 17
„ des Cygnes 16
„ de France 183
„ de Puteaux 121
„ St-Louis 24
Illuminations xlix
Illustre Théâtre 40
Impressionist School 91,
    104, 178
Imprimerie Nationale 57
Indy, Vincent d' 115
Information Bureaux
    xxxviii
Ingres, J. A. D. 47, 106
Institut Agronomique 30
„ d'Art et d'Arché-
    ologie 36

Institut de Biologie 111
„ Catholique 42
„ de Chimie
    Appliquée 111
„ de Chimie
    Biologique 115
„ de France 37
„ de Géographie 50
„ Géographique 111
„ Henri-Poincaré
    111
„ des Jeunes
    Aveugles 54
„ des Langues
    Modernes 35
„ Léonard de Vinci
    49
„ Médico-Légal 13
„ Musulman 110
„ Néerlandais 49
„ Océanographique
    111
„ d'Optique 55
„ Pasteur 115
„ Pédagogique 30
„ du Radium 111
„ des Sciences
    Politiques 50
„ Tessin 40
Institution des Sourds-
    Muets 112
Interpol 184
Invalides, The 52
Irving, Washington 65
Isabeau de Bavière 37, 87
Isabella of France 19
Italian Embassy 51
Italiens, Th. des 92

Jacob, Max 102
Jacobin Club 66
James II 30, 112, 204
James V of Scotland 170
Jardies 184
Jardin d'Acclimatation
    121
„ Fleuriste 61
„ du Luxembourg 41
„ des Plantes 108
„ du Ranelagh 60
„ Tropical 202
„ des Tuileries 5
Jaurès, Jean 32, 72, 111
Jefferson, Thomas 64, 93
Jeu de Paume (Tuileries)
    6, 178
Jeu de Paume (Versailles)
    200
Joan of Arc 34, 66, 85,
    97, 205
Joan of Burgundy 37
John II 206
Johnson, Dr. 112
Joffre, Marshal 22, 56,
    65, 208
Jones, Paul 40, 105

Josephine, Empress 22,
    30, 50, 91, 202, 216
Joyce, James 61
Julian the Apostate 18
July Column 95
Jussieu, B. de 110, 199
Juvisy 214

Kérouaille, Louise de 46
Kléber, Gen. 53
Knights Templar 81, 88,
    95
Kock, Paul de 94

La Bruyère, Jean de 35
La Fayette, Gen. 8, 49,
    59, 95, 103, 108, 184,
    191, 200
La Fayette, Mme de 42
Laffitte, Jacques 93, 204
La Fontaine, J. de 47, 72,
    73, 106
Lamartine, Alph. de 50,
    60
Lamballe, Princesse de
    61, 69, 107
Lamennais, F. R. de 87
Lamorlaye 207
La Motte, Mme de 110,
    195
Language xlvi
Laplace, Marquis de 49
La Rochefoucauld, Card.
    51
Latin Quarter 26
La Tour d'Auvergne,
    Théophile de 54
Latude, J. H. 201
Launay, Marquis de 86
Lauzun, Duc de 26
La Vallière, Louise de
    112
Lavoisier, Antoine 6, 71,
    157
Law, John 65, 66, 89
Law Courts 17
Lawn Tennis xli
Lazaristes, Église des 51
Lebon, Philippe 25
Le Brun, Charles 29, 111
Leclerc, Gen. 22, 53, 65,
    77, 116
Le Corbusier 121
Lecouvreur, Adrienne 46
Lectures xlix
Le Daim, Olivier 105
Ledru-Rollin, Alex. 78
Lemaître, Frédérick 94,
    99
Lemercier, Jacques 11
L'Enclos, Ninon de 81,
    84, 107
Lenoir, Alex. 205
Lenormand, Marie 40
Le Nôtre, André 5, 66,
    184, 194, 213

Leonardo da Vinci 122, 136
Le Vau, Louis 11, 25, 26
Le Verrier, Urbain 114
'Liberty' Statue 16
Libraries, see **Bibliothèques**
Lieusaint 214
Lion of Belfort 115
Liszt, Franz 70, 97, 117
Littré, Émile 35
Longchamp 121, xli
Longfellow, H. W. 36
Lorraine, Card. de 171
Lost Property xliii
Louis VI 18, 204
  „ *VII* 18
  „ *IX (St. Louis)* 18, 76, 200
  „ *X* 201, 207, 215
  „ *XI* 20
  „ *XII* 206
  „ *XIII* 204, 215, 216, 220
  „ *XIV* 20, 57, 78, 94, 107, 112, 185, 191, 198, 204, 208, 215, 217
  „ *XV* 8, 31, 56, 190, 215
  „ *XVI* 4, 8, 60, 85, 86, 88, 103, 185, 186, 191, 193, 207
  „ *XVII* 88, 107
  „ *XVIII* 8, 103, 185, 193, 207
Louis-Philippe 6, 8, 67, 95, 192
Louvel, Louis 76
Louvois, Marq. de 199
Louvre, The 122, 8
  Bronzes
    Etruscan 146
    Greek and Roman 146
    Renaissance 148, 150
  Egyptian Antiquities
    Horus 146
    Mastaba 127
    Monumental Statuary 127
    Small Statuary 145
  Furniture 147
  Gold and Silver Work
    Crown Jewels 143
    French 142
    Medieval and Renaissance 143, 150
    Roman 144
  Near-Eastern Antiquities 129
  Objets d'Art
    Early Christian 144
    French 147
    Medieval 149

Louvre, The *(contd.)*
  Objets d'Art *(contd.)*
    Renaissance 150
    Thiers Coll. 147
  Oriental Antiquities 129
  Painting
    Bestégui Coll. 141
    Charles I 138
    Dutch, 16–17C 139
    „ 17C 140
    „ Medici Gall. (Rubens) 138
    „ De Croy Coll. 142
    English, 18C 142
    Entombment 136
    Flemish, Primitives 138
    „ 16–17C 132
    „ 17C 138
    French, Primitives 138
    „ 16C 139
    „ 16–17C 133, 137
    „ 18C 142
    „ 19C 140, 142
    Italian, 13–15C 132
    „ 15–16C 133
    „ 18C 142
    Monna Lisa 136
    Ship of Fools 139
  Pottery and Ceramics
    Antique 144
    Etruscan 146
    Porcelain, French 147, 148
    Renaissance 150
  Sculpture
    Fettered Slaves 152
    French, 17C 153
    Greek and Roman 122
    Medieval 151
    Renaissance 152
    Venus de Milo 123
    Winged Victory 123
  Watches 147
Lulli, J. B. 70, 71, 72, 92
Lumière Brothers 91, 94
Lutetia 17
Luxembourg, Palais du 41
Luzarches 207
Lycée Charlemagne 79
  „ Condorcet 102
  „ Fontaine 61
  „ Henri-IV 31
  „ Louis-le-Grand 33
  „ Pasteur 119
  „ St-Louis 35
Lytton, E. Bulwer 117

Mabillon, Jean 44
MacMahon, Pres. 53

Madeleine, La 90
Maeterlinck, Maurice 61
Maintenon, Mme de 86, 192, 198, 217
Maison des Artistes 118, xl
  „ des Aveugles 54
  „ de la Chimie 49
  „ Internationale 116
  „ de la Mutualité 29
  „ de la Radio 16
Maisons-Laffitte 204
Malesherbes, Lamoignon de 21
Malherbe, F. de 11, 70
Mallarmé, Stéphane 40, 49, 103
Malmaison 202
Manège, The 6
Manet, Édouard 45, 47, 60, 103, 104
Manin, Daniele 97
'Man in the Iron Mask' 79, 80, 95
Mansart, François (fl. 1620–66) 204
Mansart, Jules Hardouin (d. 1708) 79, 81
Mansfield, Katherine 220
Marais, The 80
Marat, Jean Paul 32, 35
Marcel, Étienne 18, 76
Marché aux Bestiaux 105
  „ aux Fleurs 22
Margaret of Burgundy 37
Margaret of Valois, 22, 31, 78
Maria Cristina 203
Marie-Antoinette 5, 20, 21, 22, 60, 88, 85, 103, 149, 164, 185, 186, 191, 193, 195, 207, 216
Marie Leczinska 191, 216, 217
Marie-Louise 76, 132, 198, 147, 216
Marie de Médicis 40, 41, 138, 216
Marie-Thérèse 78, 107, 191, 216, 220
Marigny, Marq. de 62, 105
Marivaux, Pierre de 71, 89
Market, see Marché
Marly Horses 5
Marly-la-Machine 204
Marly-le-Roi 204
Maronite Church 30
Mary, Queen of Scots 22, 42
Mary Tudor 170
Massacre of St Bartholomew 8, 11, 34, 85

Massenet, Jules 42
Maugham, Somerset 117
Maupassant, Guy de 61, 115, 118
Mayenne, Duc de 10
Mazarin, Cardinal 37, 38, 57, 67, 71, 78, 161, 171, 201
Mazarin, Duchesse de 38
Melun 214
Ménilmontant 107
Mérimée, Prosper 46, 80
Mesnil-Aubry, Le 207
Messier, Charles 171
Meteorological Office 54
Métro xxxiv, xxxvi
Meudon 184
Meung, Jean de 112
Meyerbeer, Giacomo 70, 117
Michelet, Jules 51, 74, 106
Mickiewicz, Adam 26, 58
Mignard, Pierre 66, 71
Millet, J. F. 214, 221
Milly 221
Ministère des Affaires Economiques 54
„ des Affaires Étrangères 48
„ de l'Air 57
„ de l'Aviation Civile 54
„ du Commerce 50
„ de la Défense 49
„ de l'Education 50
„ des Finances 10, 67
„ de l'Intérieur 117
„ de la Justice 65
„ de la Marine 5
„ de la Marine Marchande 55
„ du Travail 50, 55
„ des Travaux Publics 49
Mint, The 38
Mirabeau, Marquis de 32, 72, 95, 97, 110, 201
'Miramiones' 29
Mobilier National 111
Modigliani, A. 102, 106, 115
Mohl, Mme 49
Moissan, Henri 97
Molay, Jacques de 22
Molière, J.-B. 11, 33, 40, 61, 66, 67, 71, 72, 78, 81, 106, 193, 208
Moltke, Count von 185

Monaldeschi, Marchese di 220
Moncey, Marshal 98
Monet, Claude 44, 180
Monge, Gaspar 49
Money xxviii
'Monna Lisa' 136, 209
Monnaie, La 38
Montès, Lola 93
Montespan, Mme de 49, 91, 193
Montesquieu, Baron de 71, 86
Montfaucon 105
Montgeron 214
Montgomery, Comte de 76, 81
Montmartre 98
Montmorency, Constable Anne de 87, 205, 207, 208
Montmorency-Laval, Bp 44
Montparnasse 114
Montpensier, Mlle de 28, 41, 69
Mont-de-Piété 85
Montretout 184
Mont-Valérien 184
Monuments Historiques xlix
Monument aux Morts 106
Monument de la République 95
Moreau, Gustave 97
Morisot, Berthe 60
Mortier, Marshal 95
Mosque 110
Motor-Buses xxxvi
Motor Coaches xxxvi
Motoring xxvi
Motor Racing xli
Moulin Rouge 99
Mozart, W. A. 72, 78, 97, 104, 190
Muette, La 60
Mur des Fédérés 106
Murat, Joachim 117
Murger, Henri 42, 98
Musée de l'Air 184
„ d'Antiquités Nationales 204
„ de l'Armée 153, 52
„ d'Art Moderne 58
„ d'Art Juif 102
„ des Arts Décoratifs 155
„ des Arts Populaires 169
„ Bourdelle 115
„ Carnavalet 162, 84
„ Cernuschi 118
„ de Cluny 170, 35
„ Cognacq-Jay 91
„ Condé 208
„ du Costume 59

Musée Dennery 120
„ de la France d'Outre Mer 202
„ Galliéra 58
„ Grévin 93
„ Guimet 174, 59
„ Gustave-Moreau 97
„ Henner 104
„ de l'Histoire de France 85
„ d'Histoire de la Médecine 35
„ de l'Homme 169
„ des Hôpitaux de Paris 29
„ d'Hygiène 74
„ Jacquemart-André 176, 118
„ du Jeu de Paume 178
„ Jules Verne 93
„ de la Légion d'Honneur 47
„ de la Marine 170
„ Marmottan 61
„ de la Mer 93
„ de Minéralogie 36
„ Monétaire 38
„ du Montparnasse 115
„ des Monuments Français 167
„ Nissim de Camondo 180, 118
„ de l'Opéra 92
„ Postal 51
„ Rodin 182, 51
„ de Santé 112
„ Social 49
„ de Vénerie 214
„ Victor-Hugo 81
„ de Vieux-Montmartre 102
„ des Voitures 198
Music xl
Music Halls xxxiv
Musset, A. de 40, 47, 5ᶜ, 57, 65, 106

Napoleon I 8, 17, 22, 28, 34, 38, 41, 43, 56, 59, 65, 66, 76, 90, 91, 117, 132, 154, 184, 198, 203, 215, 216
Napoleon I, Tomb of 54
Napoleon II (King of Rome) 22, 54, 76
Napoleon III 8, 41, 65, 92, 93, 117, 198, 217
National Assembly 6, 186
NATO 120
Necker, Jacques 97
Necker, Mme 55
Nerval, Gérard de 75, 89
Netherlands Embassy 50

Neuilly 119
Ney, Marshal 21, 41, 106, 114
Nightingale, Florence 49
'Nike of Samothrace' 123
Noailles, Marshal de 41
Nodier, Charles 80
Notre-Dame 22
„   des Blancs-Manteaux 85
„   de Bonne-Nouvelle 94
„   des Champs 115
„   de Consolation 57
„   d'Espérance 96
„   du Liban 30
„   de Lorette 98
„   de Salette 115
„   des Victoires 70

Obelisk of Luxor 5
Observatoire 114
Odéon 40
Œil-de-Bœuf 191
Offenbach, Jacques 91, 93, 99
Opéra 91, xxxiv
Opéra-Comique 93, xxxiv
Orangerie 6, 180
Oratoire 71
Orleans, Ferdinand, duke of 119
Orleans, Gaston, duke of 40
Orleans, Louis, duke of 87
Orleans, Philippe, duke of (Regent) 67, 193
Orleans, Philippe, duke of (Égalité) 5, 60, 67, 103, 115
Orleans, Philippe, duke of (d. 1926) 21, 109
Orly 214, xxix
Orsini, Félix 93
Oscar I 118
Oudinot, Marshal 52

Paine, Tom 41, 116
Palais des Beaux-Arts 64
„   -Bourbon 47
„   -Cardinal 67, 86
„   de Chaillot 59, 167
„   du Conseil Économique 59
„   de la Découverte 64
„   de la Défense 119
„   de l'Élysée 117, 63

Palais de Fontainebleau 215
„   de Glace 64
„   de l'Institut 37
„   de Justice 17
„   de la Légion d'Honneur 47
„   du Luxembourg 40
„   de Paris 93
„   -Royal 67
„   des Sports 57
„   des Thermes 172
„   des Tournelles 81
„   des Tuileries 7
„   de Versailles 185
Palissy, Bernard 45
Panthéon 31
Parc des Buttes-Chaumont 105
„   -aux-Cerfs 200
„   Monceau 118
„   de Montsouris 116
„   Zoölogique 202
Pâris, Abbé 30
Parlement 18, 20
Parloir aux Bourgeois 76
Parmentier, Antoine 51, 119
Pascal, Blaise 30, 31, 36, 75
Passage des Panoramas 93
„   Stanislas 115
Passports xxvi
Passy 61
Pasteur, Louis 55, 111, 115, 184
Pavillon de Chartres 118
Péguy, Charles 111
Pecq, Le 204
Père-Lachaise 106
Perrault, Charles 6
Peter the Great 215
Petit-Châtelet 12
„   -Hôtel de Sully 83
„   -Luxembourg 41
„   -Montrouge 116
„   -Palais 64
„   -Pont 12
„   Trianon 199
Petrol xxvi
Pharmacie Centrale 29
Philip Augustus 8, 18, 73
„   III 206, 207
„   IV 207, 215
„   V 201, 206, 215
„   VI 200, 206
Philippe-Égalité 5, 60, 67, 103, 118
Picasso, Pablo 102, 114
Picture Galleries xl
Pierrefitte 207
Pilâtre de Rozier, J. F. 60
Piranesi, G. B. 30
Pius VII 22, 215, 220
Place Adolfe-Max 98
„   de l'Alma 58

Place d'Anvers 99
„   de la Bastille 95, 81
„   Bienvenue 115
„   de la Bourse 70
„   de Breteuil 55
„   Cambronne 57
„   du Carrousel 8
„   du Châtelet 76
„   de Clichy 98
„   de la Concorde 4
„   de la Contrescarpe 30
„   Dauphine 17
„   Denfert-Rochereau 115
„   Edmond-Rostand 36
„   des États-Unis 59
„   de l'Étoile 64
„   de l'Europe 104
„   de Fontenoy 55
„   Georges-Clemenceau 63
„   de Grève 76
„   de l'Hôtel de Ville 76
„   d'Iéna 59
„   de l'Institut 37
„   d'Italie 111
„   du Louvre 10
„   de la Madeleine 91
„   Maubert 29
„   de la Nation 107
„   de l'Odéon 40
„   de l'Opéra 91
„   du Palais-Royal 67
„   du Parvis-Notre-Dame 22
„   Pereire 104, xxix
„   des Petits-Pères 70
„   Pigalle 99
„   des Pyramides 66
„   de la République 95
„   Royale 83
„   St-André-des-Arts 28
„   Ste-Geneviève 31
„   St-Georges 98
„   St-Gervais 77
„   St-Michel 26
„   de Stalingrad 105
„   des Ternes 119
„   du Tertre 102
„   du Théâtre-Français 66
„   du Trocadéro 59
„   Valhubert 108
„   Vauban 55
„   Vendôme 65
„   de Verdun 119
„   des Victoires 70
„   Victor-Hugo 60
„   des Vosges 81
Plaine-St-Denis, La 205
Planetarium 64
Plantagenet, Geoffrey 24
Pléiade, The 30, 33

Poincaré, Raymond 120
Police 22, 19, xliii
Police Museum 19
Polish Library 26
Polo xlii
Pompadour, Mme de 60, 70, 71, 72, 116, 117, 183, 185, 193, 198, 199
Pont Alexandre-III 16
  „ de l'Alma 16, 58
  „ de l'Archevêché 12
  „ d'Arcole 13
  „ des Arts 13
  „ d'Austerlitz 13
  „ de Bercy 13
  „ de Bir-Hakeim 16
  „ du Carrousel 13, 47
  „ au Change 12
  „ de la Concorde 16
  „ au Double 12
  „ de Grenelle 16
  „ d'Iéna 16
  „ des Invalides 16
  „ Louis-Philippe 13
  „ Marie 13
  „ Mirabeau 17
  „ Morland 13
  „ National 13
  „ Neuf 12, 17
  „ de Neuilly 119
  „ Notre-Dame 12
  „ Royal 16
  „ St-Louis 13
  „ St-Michel 12
  „ Sully 13, 79
  „ de Tolbiac 13
  „ de la Tournelle 13
  „ -Viaduc d'Auteuil 17
Porte d'Auteuil 60, 61
  „ Champerret 104
  „ Dauphine 120
  „ des Lilas 107
  „ Maillot 119, 120, 121
  „ de la Muette 60
  „ de Neuilly 119, 121
  „ de Passy 120
  „ aux Peintres 74
  „ St-Denis 94, 73
  „ St-Martin 94
  „ St-Martin, Th. de la 94, xxxviii
Port-Marly 204
  „ de Paris 11
  „ -Royal 114
Positivist Chapel 84
Postal Information xxxvii
Postal Museum 51
Post Office, General 72, xxxvii
Pré-aux-Clercs 44
Pré Catelan 120
'Précieuses' 83
Préfecture de Police 22, 12
Prévost, Abbé 61

Prévot des Marchands 76
Prison de l'Abbaye 44
  „ du Cherche-Midi 51
  „ de la Force 84
  „ de la Roquette 106
  „ St-Lazare 96
  „ de Ste-Pélagie 29
  „ du Temple 88
Prix de Rome 46
Proust, Marcel 59, 91, 106, 117, 118
Prud'hon, Pierre 46
Puteaux 119
Puvis de Chavannes, Pierre 104

Quai Anatole-France 47, 16
  „ d'Anjou 26, 13
  „ de l'Archevêche 12
  „ d'Austerlitz 13
  „ de Béthune 26, 13
  „ de Bourbon 26, 13
  „ des Célestins 78, 13
  „ de la Conférence 57, 16
  „ Conti 38, 12
  „ de Corse 12
  „ Ed. Branly 16, 54
  „ aux Fleurs 12
  „ de la Gare 13
  „ de Gesvres 12
  „ des Grands-Augustins 12
  „ de Grenelle 16
  „ Henri-IV 13
  „ de l'Horloge 12
  „ de l'Hôtel-de-Ville 13
  „ du Louvre 13
  „ Malaquais 46, 13
  „ du Marché-Neuf 12
  „ de la Mégisserie 12
  „ de Montebello 12
  „ des Orfèvres 12, 19
  „ d'Orléans 26, 13
  „ d'Orsay 47, 54, 16
  „ de la Rapée 13
  „ St-Bernard 108, 13
  „ St-Michel 12
  „ des Théatins 47
  „ de la Tournelle 29, 13
  „ des Tuileries 16
  „ Voltaire 47, 16
'Quand Même' Memorial 103
Quartier de l'Arsenal 80
  „ des Batignolles 104
  „ de Chaillot 58
  „ de la Chapelle 96
  „ de l'Europe 104
  „ Latin 26

Quartier du Marais 80
  „ Marbeuf 64
  „ du Temple 87
  „ de la Villette 105

Rabelais, François 26, 30, 79
Racecourses xli
Rachel, Mme 81, 94, 106
Racine, Jean 31, 36, 46, 192
Racine, Louis 89
Railways xxv, xxviii
Railway Termini (see also Gare) xxviii
Rambouillet, Mme de 46
Rameau, Jean 72
Ravaillac, François 21, 73, 76
Récamier, Mme 51, 70, 71, 97
Régnier, Henri de 59, 106
Renan, Ernest 29, 42, 50, 99
Renoir, Aug. 102
Resistance, The 19, 26, 35, 38, 48, 49, 77, 95, 106, 116, 184
Restaurants xxx
Retz, Card. de 71, 201
Richard II 19
Richelieu, Cardinal 30, 34, 41, 67, 70, 79, 81, 119, 157
Richelieu, Duc de 26
Riding xlii
Riesener, J. H. 71
Rigaud, Hyacinthe 91
Rilke, Rainer-Maria 115
Rimbaud, Arthur 33
River Steamers 12, xxxvii
Robert, Hubert 65, 96
Robespierre, Max. 5, 21, 33, 65, 76, 86, 163
Rodin, Auguste 30, 114, 115, 182, 184
Rohan, Cardinal de 86, 195
Roland Mme 4, 5, 20, 21, 30
Rond-Point des Champs-Élysées 64
Rond-Point de la Défense 119
Roquette, La 106
Rossini, Gioacchino 61, 97, 106
Rostand, Edmund 118
Rousseau, Henri 28, 102
Rousseau, Jean Jacques 32, 71, 72
Rousseau, Théodore 221
Roux, Dr Émile 115
Rowing xlii
Royale, Mme 88

Rue d'Amsterdam 103
„ de l'Ancienne-
    Comédie 40
„ des Archives 85, 87
„ Auber 102
„ du Bac 49
„ Barbette 86
„ Beautreillis 79
„ des Beaux-Arts 46
„ de Bellechasse 49
„ de Bièvre 29
„ Blanche 97
„ Bonaparte 42
„ du Cardinal-Lemoine
    30
„ Caulaincourt 98
„ de Charenton 108
„ Charles V 79
„ Charlot 86
„ de Châteaudun 97
„ du Chat-qui-Pêche
    28
„ de la Chaussée
    d'Antin 97
„ du Cherche-Midi 51
„ de Cléry 70, 94
„ de Clichy 97
„ Clovis 30
„ Condé 40
„ de Courcelles 117
„ Danielle-Casanova
    66, 71
„ du Dragon 45
„ Drouot 93
„ Étienne-Marcel 70
„ du Faubourg-
    Poissonnière 97
„ du Faubourg-St-
    Antoine 107
„ du Faubourg-St-
    Denis 94
„ du Faubourg-St-
    Honoré 117
„ du Faubourg-St-
    Martin 96
„ du Faubourg-
    Montmartre 93
„ Férou 42
„ de la Ferronnerie 73
„ du Figuier 78
„ de Flandre 105
„ du Fouarre 29
„ François-Miron 78
„ François-Premier 57
„ des Francs-Bourgeois
    84
„ Franklin 60
„ Galande 28
„ Gay-Lussac 111
„ Geoffroy-l'Asnier 78
„ Geoffroy-Marie 93
„ des Grands-Augustins
    35
„ de la Grange-aux-
    Belles 104
„ de Grenelle 50
„ Hautefeuille 35

Rue du Havre 102
„ Hérold 70
„ de l'Hôtel-de-Ville 78
„ de la Huchette 28
„ Jacob 46
„ J. J. Rousseau 72
„ de Jouy 78
„ La Boétie 117
„ de La Fayette 97
„ Laffitte 93
„ Le Peletier 93
„ Lhomond 30
„ de Lille 48
„ des Lions 79
„ de Longchamp 119,
    121
„ du Louvre 71
„ Madame 72
„ du Mail 70
„ des Martyrs 98
„ Mazarine 40
„ Michel-le-Comte 88
„ Monge 29
„ Monsieur-le-Prince
    36
„ du Mont-Cenis 102
„ Montholon 99
„ Montmartre 72, 93
„ Mouffetard 30
„ de la Paix 66
„ Payenne 84
„ des Petits-Champs
    71
„ Pigalle 97
„ de la Pompe 60
„ du Pont-Neuf 73
„ des Quatre-Fils 85
„ du Quatre-Septembre
    70
„ Quincampoix 89
„ Réaumur 70, 89
„ de Rennes 45
„ de Richelieu 70
„ de Rivoli 65, 75
„ de Rome 103
„ de la Roquette 96,
    106
„ Royale 90
„ St-André-des-Arts 35
„ St-Antoine 79
„ St-Denis 73, 94
„ St-Dominique 49
„ St-Honoré 65, 71
„ St-Jacques 33, 112
„ St-Lazare 103
„ St-Louis-en-l'Île 24
„ St-Martin 88
„ des Saints-Pères 47
„ de Seine 40
„ de Sévigné 84
„ de Sèvres 51, 55
„ Soufflot 33
„ Taitbout 97
„ du Temple 87
„ Thorigny 86
„ des Tournelles 81
„ Tronchet 102

Rue de Tournon 40
„ de Turbigo 73
„ de Turenne 86, 84
„ de l'Université 48
„ de Varenne 50
„ de Vaugirard 40, 42,
    36
„ Vieille-du-Temple
    86, 84
„ Visconti 46
„ Vivienne 70
Rueil 202
Russian Church 118
Russian Embassy 50

Sacré-Cœur 99
Sailing xlii
St-Ambroise 107
St-Augustin 103
Ste-Beuve, C. A. de 67,
    115
Sainte Chapelle 19
St-Christophe-de-Javel 57
Ste-Clotilde 49
St-Cloud 184
St-Denis 205
St Denis 99, 205
St-Denis-de-la-Chapelle 97
St-Denis-du-St-Sacrement
    86
St-Dominique 116
Ste-Elisabeth 88
St-Esprit 108
St-Étienne-du-Mont 31
St-Eustache 72
St Francis Xavier 33, 99
St-François-Xavier 54
St-Gaudens, Aug. 51
St Geneviève 13, 31, 205
St George's 59
St-Germain-l'Auxerrois 10
St-Germain-de-Charonne
    106
St-Germain-en-Laye 204
St-Germain-des-Prés 43
St Germanus of Paris 43
St-Gervais-St-Protais 77
St-Honoré-d'Eylau 60
St Ignatius of Loyola 33,
    99
St-Jacques-la-Boucherie
    75
St-Jacques-du-Haut-Pas
    112
St-Jean-Baptiste 105
St-Jean-Bosco 106
St-Jean-l'Évangéliste 99
St-Jean-St-François 86
St-Joseph-des-Carmes 42
St-Julien-le-Pauvre 28
St-Laurent 96
St-Leu-St-Gilles 74, 25
St Louis, see Louis IX
St-Louis (Invalides) 52
St-Louis-d'Antin 102
St-Louis-en-l'Île 24
Ste-Marguerite 107

St-Martin-des-Champs 157
St-Médard 30
St-Merri 89
St-Nicolas-des-Champs 89
St-Nicolas-du-Chardonnet 29
Ste-Odile 104
St-Ouen 205
St-Paul-des-Champs 79
St-Paul-St-Louis 79
St-Philippe-du-Roule 117
St-Pierre (Neuilly) 119
St-Pierre-de-Chaillot 58
St-Pierre-de-Montmartre 101
St-Pierre-de-Montrouge 116
St-Roch 66
St-Simon, Duc de 50
St-Saëns, Camille 35, 36, 115, 117
St-Séverin 28
St-Sulpice 42
St Thomas Aquinas 33
St Thomas Becket 215
St-Thomas-d'Aquin 49
St Vincent de Paul 30, 51, 70, 80, 96
St-Vincent-de-Paul 97
Salle Gaveau 117, xl
  „ des Pas-Perdus 21
  „ Pleyel 118, xl
  „ du Spectacle 67
'Salon' xl
Samaritaine, La 17
Sanctuaire du Christ-Roi 30
Sand, George 26, 35, 40, 42, 47, 97, 98, 111, 165
Sarcelles 207
Sardou, Victorien 79
Savonnerie 110
Saxe, Marshal 46
Scarron, Paul 77, 86
Scheffer, Ary 98
Schola Cantorum 112
School, see École
Scots College 30
Scottish Church 57
Scribe, Eugène 73
Scudéry, Mlle de 89
Season xlvi
Seine, The 11
Séminaire des Carmes 42
  „ des Missions Étrangères 49
  „ de St-Sulpice 42
Senate, The 41, 186
Senlis 214
Seurat, Georges 98
Sévigné, Henri de 80
Sévigné, Mme de 77, 79, 81, 84, 86, 162

Sèvres 183
Sewers 5
Shops xlvii
Sibour, Abp 24, 31
Signac, Paul 98
Smith, Adm. Sir Sidney 106
Smith, Sydney 117
Smithson, Harriet 102, 117
Société des Gens de Lettres 114
Société de Géographie 50
Son et Lumière 1
Sorbonne 34
Soufflot, Jacques 32
Sports xli
Square de l'Archevêche 24
  „ Boucicaut 51
  „ du Carrousel 8
  „ Émile-Chautemps 88
  „ des Innocents 73
  „ Louvois 71
  „ Montholon 87
  „ Paul-Painlevé 35
  „ René-Le Gall 110, 111
  „ René-Viviani 28
  „ St-Lambert 57
  „ du Temple 88
  „ du Vert-Galant 17
  „ Willette 99
Stade Nautique Georges Vallerey 105
Stade Roland-Garros 61
Staël, Mme de 47, 87, 88, 90
Stamp Market 63
Stanley, Dean 49
Steamers, Channel xxvi
Steamers, River xxxvii, 12
Stendhal (H. Beyle) 66, 99
Sterne, Laurence 46
Stevenson, R. L. 221
Stores xlvii
Strindberg, August 42
Students, Courses for xliii
Suger, Abbot 205
Sully, Duc de 80
Sully, Maurice de 22
Suresnes 184
Swedish Church 118
Swimming xlii
Swiss Embassy 50
Swiss Guards 8, 76, 103, 187, 192, 195
Syrian Church 29

Tabarin 17
Taine, Hippolyte 25, 67, 111
Tallard, Marshal 87

Talleyrand-Périgord, Prince 5, 51
Tallien, Mme 93
Tamerlane 85
Tardieu, André 118
Taxis xxxvi
Tea Rooms xxxiii
Telegrams xxxviii
Telephones xxxviii
Temple des Billettes 87
  „ de Panthemont 50
  „ de Ste-Marie 80
'Temple of Agriculture' 72
  „ „ Commerce' 89
  „ „ Filial Piety' 31
  „ „ Gratitude' 11
  „ „ Hymen' 89
  „ „ Reason' 102
  „ „ Victory' 43
Tennis xli
Thackeray, W. M. 70, 71, 117
Théâtre National Populaire xxxiv
Théâtre-Français 66, xxxiv
Theatres xxxviii
Thermes, Palais des 172
Thiers, Adolphe 93, 98, 106, 117, 119, 185, 147, 204
Timetables xxv
Tobacconists xlvii
Toulouse-Lautrec, Henri de 99
Tour Barbeau 78
  „ Eiffel 56
  „ Jean-sans-Peur 73
  „ de Nesle 37
  „ St-Jacques 75
  „ du Temple 88
Touring Club de France 119
Tourist Agents xxv, xxxviii
Tourville, Adm. de 72
Trianons, The 198
Tribunal de Commerce 22
Trinité, La 97
Trotsky, Léon 114
Tuileries, Palais des 7
Turenne, Marshal de 52, 54, 56, 107, 154
Turgenev, Ivan 98
Turgot, Jacques 49

Ukrainian Church 50
Underground Railways xxxiv, xxxvi
UNESCO 55
Union Française 193
University 34, 26
Unknown Camp Prisoner's Memorial 24
Unknown Warrior's Tomb 64, 52

Unknown Jewish Martyr's Memorial 78
Utrillo, Maurice 99, 102

Val-de-Grâce 112
Valéry, Paul 33, 60
Van Gogh, Vincent 99
Vatel 208
Vauban, Marshal de 54, 66, 53
Vaux, Clotilde de 84
Vélodrome d'Hiver 57
Vélodrome du Parc des Princes 61
Vendôme Column 65
Venizelos, Eleutherios 118
Ventes Mobilières 93
'Vénus de Milo' 123
Verlaine, Paul 30, 33, 40
Vernet, Horace 47, 200
Versailles 184
   „   Gardens 194
   „   Palace 185
Viardot, Mme 98

Viau, Théophile de 28, 213
Victoria, Queen 76, 94, 186
Vigée-Lebrun, Mme 103, 191
Vigny, Alfred de 99, 118
Ville-d'Avray 184
Villejuif 214
Villeneuve-l'Étang 184
Villeneuve-St-Georges 214
Villette, La 105, 73
Villon, François 29
Vincennes 200
Viollet-le-Duc, Eug. 10, 167
Viroflay 183
Voltaire, Fr. 26, 32, 33, 40, 47, 67, 71, 86, 95
Vuillard, J. E. 98

Wagner, Richard 46, 47, 59, 93, 184
Wallace, Sir Richard 59, 63, 93, 121

Walpole, Horace 86
Washington, George 59, 95, 154
Watteau, Antoine 30, 111
'Welcome' Services xxx, xxxviii
Wellington, Duke of 117, 198
Wells, Dr Horace 59
Whistler, J. McN. 42, 44, 49, 114, 115
Wilde, Oscar 46, 47, 106
William I of Prussia 185
Wilson, President 118
'Winged Victory' 123

Y.M.C.A. xliii
Y.W.C.A. xliii

Zola, Émile 32, 61, 72, 73, 91, 98
Zoological Gardens 109, 202, 121
Zouave, The 16

FILMSET AND PRINTED IN GREAT BRITAIN
BY BUTLER & TANNER LIMITED, FROME AND LONDON